DICTIONARY
OF
COMPUTERS,
DATA PROCESSING,
AND
TELECOMMUNICATIONS

OTHER BOOKS BY THE AUTHOR

Automation, Manpower, and Education

The Computer Prophets

*The Death of Privacy: Do Industrial and Government Computers
   Threaten our Personal Freedom?*

Dictionary of Business and Management, 2nd edition

Dictionary of Banking and Finance

*Inside The Wall Street Journal: The History and Power of
   Dow Jones & Company and America's Most Influential Newspaper*

DICTIONARY OF COMPUTERS, DATA PROCESSING, AND TELECOMMUNICATIONS

Jerry M. Rosenberg, Ph.D.

Professor, Graduate School of Management
Chairman, Department of Business Administration
Newark College of Arts and Sciences
Rutgers University

JOHN WILEY & SONS

New York • Chichester • Brisbane • Toronto • Singapore

Library of Congress Cataloging in Publication Data:

Rosenberg, Jerry Martin.
   Dictionary of computers, data processing, and
telecommunications.

   Bibliography: p.
   1. Computers—Dictionaries. 2. Electronic data
processing—Dictionaries. 3. Telecommunication—
Dictionaries. I. Title.

QA76.15.R67   1983   001.64′03′21   83-12359
ISBN 0-471-87638-0
ISBN 0-471-88582-7 (pbk.)

Printed in the United States of America

10 9 8 7 6 5 4

This book is affectionately dedicated to

Elizabeth

and to her future

Preface

The 1980s began with a growing relationship between the utilization of computers and its natural partner, telecommunications. As day-to-day activities in transmitting and comprehending all forms of information expand they have produced a tidal wave of terms and phrases.

This work of more than 10,000 entries has been prepared with the hope that awareness of the accepted meanings of terms may enhance the process of sharing ideas. Though it cannot eliminate the need for the user to determine how a writer or speaker treats a word, such a dictionary shows what usages exist. It should reduce arguments about words and assist in stabilizing terminology. Most important, it should aid people in saying and writing just what they intend with greater clarity.

A word can take on different meanings in different contexts. There may be as many meanings as there are areas of specialty. A goal of this dictionary is to be broad and to establish core definitions that represent the variety of individual meanings. My purpose is to enhance parsimony and clearness in the exchange process within the fields of computers, data processing, and telecommunications.

Many terms are used in different ways. I have tried to unite them without the bias of giving one advantage or dominance over another. Whenever possible (without creating a controversy), I have stated the connection among multiple usages.

Commonly used symbols, acronyms, and abbreviations are given. Foreign words and phrases are included only if they have become an integral part of our English vocabulary.

Other dictionaries that deal with a similar subject tend to define their task rather narrowly, whereas this work purports to identify individual specialties and then proceeds to specify the relationships among computers, data processing, and telecommunications.

This work contains terms that relate directly or indirectly to usage of hardware and software including the broad categories of computers, data processing, distributed data processing, home computers, information transmission, microprocessors, minicomputers, personal computers, programming languages, telecommunications, and word processing.

The entries offer the most recent information taken from contemporary practices. The book closes with an appendix of French and Spanish equivalents for terms contained within the dictionary.

ORGANIZATION

This is a defining work rather than a compilation of facts. The line is not easy to draw because in the final analysis meanings are based on facts. Consequently, factual information is used where necessary to make a term more easily understood.

All terms are presented in the language of those who use them. Obviously, the level of complexity needed for a definition will vary with the user; one person's complexity is another's precise and parsimonious statement. Several meanings are sometimes given—the relatively simple for the layman, the more developed and technical for the specialist.

I have organized the dictionary to provide information easily and rapidly. Keeping in mind two categories of user—the experienced person who demands precise information about a particular word, and the newcomer, support member, teacher, or student who seeks general explanations—I have in most cases supplied both general and specialized entries. This combination of "umbrella" entries and

specialized definitions should make this dictionary an unusually useful reference source.

Alphabetization. Words are presented alphabetically. Compound terms are placed where the reader is most likely to look for them. They are entered under their most distinctive component, usually nouns, which tend to be more distinctive than adjectives. Should you fail to locate a word where you initially look for it, turn to a variant spelling, a synonym, or another, different word of the compound term.

Entries containing mutual concepts are usually grouped for comparison. They are then given in inverted order; that is, the expected order of words is reversed to allow the major word of the phrase to appear at the beginning of the term. These entries precede those that are given in the expected order. The terms are alphabetized up to the first comma and then by words following the comma, thus establishing clusters of related terms.

Headings. The currently popular term is usually given as the principal entry, with other terms cross referenced to it. Some terms have been included for historical significance, even though they are not presently in common usage.

Cross Reference. The rule followed for cross references calls for going from the general to the specific. Occasionally, *see* references from the specific to the general are used to inform the user of words related to particular entries. *See* references to presently accepted terminology are made wherever possible. The use of *cf.* suggests words to be compared with the original entry. *Deprecated term* indicates that the term should not be used and that there is a preferred word or phrase.

Synonyms. The word *synonymous* following a definition does not imply that the term is exactly equivalent to the principal entry under which it appears. Usually the term only approximates the primary sense of the original entry.

Disciplines. Many words are given multiple definitions based on their utilization in various fields of activity. The definition with the widest application is then given first, with the remaining definitions listed by area of specialty (identified in boldface italic type). Since the areas may overlap, the reader should examine all multiple definitions of a term.

JERRY M. ROSENBERG

New York, New York
November 1983

Acknowledgments

No dictionary can be the exclusive product of one person's effort. Even when written by one individual, such a work requires the tapping of many sources, which is especially true of this book. By the very nature of the fields included, I have had to rely on the able and extensive efforts of others.

When I have quoted a definition from another source, a letter in brackets appears at the end of the definition. This letter indicates the primary reference used in defining the term. The following sources were used:

(A) *American National Dictionary for Information Processing*, Computer and Business Equipment Manufacturers Association, American National Standards Institute.

(*A*) Same as above for *all* definitions cited within the specified word or term.

(B) *Vocabulary of Data Processing*, International Organization for Standardization, International Standards Organization (ISO).

(C) International Telecommunications Union—CCITT/ITU.

(D) Technical Committee 95 of the ISO—(requiring agreement for adoption)—TC 95.

(E) Technical Committee 97 of the ISO—(having agreement for adoption)—TC 97.

(F) *Engineering and Operations in the Bell System*, Bell Laboratories.

(G) *Telecommunications Glossary*, AT&T.

When no reference source is shown following a term, this suggests that I have not deliberately quoted the definition from any copyrighted source. Any apparent similarity to existing, unreleased definitions in these cases is purely accidental and the result of the limitations of language.

Much assistance has come indirectly from authors of books, journal articles, and reference materials. They are too numerous to be named here. Various organizations have aided me directly by providing informative source materials.

Some government agencies and not-for-profit associations have provided a considerable amount of usable information.

On a more personal level, I thank the various individuals I used as a sounding board to clarify my ideas and approach; they offered valuable suggestions and encouraged me to go on with the project. Stephen Kippur, my editor, of John Wiley & Sons, had the foresight to initiate this book, and with sensitivity and creativity followed it through to publication. And I thank, once again, my wife Ellen and my daughters Elizabeth and Lauren, who showed understanding and offered full support during the preparation of this book.

Credits and Permissions

IBM Vocabulary for Data Processing, Telecommunications, and Office Systems, October 1977.

This material is reproduced with permission from American National Standards Committee X3 Technical Report, *American National Dictionary for Information Processing*, X3/TR-1-77, copyright, 1977 by the Computer and Business Equipment Manufacturers Association (CBEMA), copies of which may be purchased from the American National Standards Institute, 1430 Broadway, New York, NY 10018.

Engineering and Operations in the Bell System, Bell Laboratories, 1981.

Telecommunications Glossary, AT&T, March 1981.

Computer Communications and Telecommunications Terminology, The Computer Communications Group, Ottawa, April 1977.

Federal Telecom Standard 1037 Vocabulary for Telecommunications, May 1978.

Glossary of Digital Switching Terms and Abbreviations, Stromberg-Carlson Corporation, Sanford, Florida, 1978.

Post Office Telecommunications Journal, Autumn 1979.

International Communications Association Glossary, February 1981.

Feedback

The definitions given here have been reviewed by specialists and educators. However, I am solely responsible for choosing the terms to be included. The vast range of material makes it inevitable that definitions may vary based on perspective, background, and connotation. I welcome critical comments bringing errors to my attention, to make it possible to correct them in later editions, thus evolving a greater conformity of meaning for all.

J.M.R.

Contents

A

(1) see *adder*.
(2) see *ampere*.
(3) see *analog*.
(4) see *angstrom*.
(5) see *asynchronous*.
(6) see *attribute*.

A and I: abstracting and indexing.

abbreviated address calling: calling that enables a user to employ an address having fewer characters than the full address when initiating a call.

ABEND: see *abnormal end of task*.

aberration: an error condition, usually in the cathode ray tube of a terminal.

abnormal end of task (ABEND): termination of a task prior to its completion because of an error condition that cannot be resolved by recovery facilities while the task is executing.

abnormal termination: the cessation of processing prior to planned termination.

abort: to terminate, in a controlled manner, a processing activity in a computer system because it is impossible or undesirable for the activity to proceed.

abort timer: a device which stops dial up data transmission if no data are sent within a predetermined time period.

above 890 decision: a 1959 FCC decision which allowed individual firms to build their own private microwave systems utilizing radio frequencies "above 890 megacycles." (G)

ABSLDR: see *absolute loader*.

absolute address

(1) an address in a computer language that identifies a storage location or a device without the use of any intermediate reference. (B)
(2) an address that is permanently assigned by the machine designer to a storage location.
(3) synonymous with *explicit address, machine address, specific address*. (*A*)

absolute addressing: a method of addressing in which the address part of

1

an instruction contains an absolute address. (A) (B)

absolute assembler: an assembly-language program designed to yield binary programs only with absolute addresses and address references.

absolute code: coding designed so that all instructions are described in basic machine language. synonymous with *specific code.*

absolute coding: coding that uses computer instructions with absolute address. synonymous with *specific coding.* (A)

absolute command: in computer graphics, a display command that causes the display device to interpret the data following the command as absolute coordinates, rather than relative coordinates. cf. *relative command.* (E)

absolute coordinate: in computer graphics, one of the coordinates that identifies the location of an addressable point with respect to the origin of the specified coordinate system. cf. *relative coordinate.* (E)

absolute data: in computer graphics, values in a computer program that specify the actual coordinates in a display space or image space. cf. *relative data.*

absolute error

(1) the algebraic result of subtracting a true, specified, or theoretically correct value from the value computed, observed, measured, or achieved. (B)

(2) the amount of error expressed in the same units as the quantity holding the error.

(3) loosely, the absolute value of the error, that is, the magnitude of the error without regard for its algebraic sign. (A)

absolute expression: in assembler language, an assembly-time expression whose value is not affected by program relocation. An absolute expression can represent an absolute address.

absolute instruction: a computer instruction in its final, executable form. (A)

absolute loader (ABSLDR): a routine that reads a computer program into main storage, beginning at the assembled origin. (A)

absolute order: deprecated term for *absolute command.* (E)

absolute term: a term whose value is not affected by relocation.

absolute value: a quantity, the magnitude of which is known by the computer, but the algebraic sign is not relevant.

absolute vector: in computer graphics, a vector whose starting and ending points are specified in absolute coordinates. cf. *relative vector.* (E)

abstract: a shortened representation of the contents of a document.

abstract symbol

(1) a symbol whose meaning and use have not been determined by a general agreement but have to be defined for each application of the symbol. (B)

(2) in optical character recognition, a symbol whose form does not suggest its meaning and use; these should be defined for each specified set of applications. (A)

A-bus: the major internal bus within a microprocessor.

AC

(1) see *acoustic coupler.*

(2) see *alternating current.*

ACC

(1) see *accumulate*.

(2) see *accumulator*.

acceleration period: the period in which a card reader and/or punch actually move(s) the card into position where data can be read.

acceleration time: that part of access time required to bring an auxiliary storage device, typically a tape drive, to the speed at which data can be read or written.

accent: a mark placed above or below a character; frequently to show its pronunciation.

acceptance test: actions made to prove that a system fulfills agreed upon criteria; for example, that the processing of specified input yielded expected results.

access: the manner in which files or data sets are referred to by the computer. see *direct access, direct-access storage, immediate-access storage, remote access, serial access*.

access arm: a part of a disk storage unit that is used to hold one or more reading and writing heads. (A)

access arrangement: used in reference to the interconnection of customer-provided data modems or automatic calling units in which data access arangement (DAA) service includes the provision of a data access arrangement with appropriate loop conditioning (including adjustments for loop loss) to meet data requirements. synonymous for *protective connecting arrangement*. (F)

access authority: an authority that relates to a request for a type of access to data sets. The access authorities are NONE, READ access, UPDATE access, CONTROL access, and ALTER access.

access button: synonymous with *skip key*.

access charge: a charge by the local telephone company, for use of the local company's exchange facilities, and/or interconnection with the telecommunications network. see also *exchange network facilities for interstate access*. (G)

access environment: a description of the current user including current connect group, user attributes, group authorities. An access environment is constructed during user identification and verification.

access level: see *physical-access level*.

access line: a telecommunication line that continuously connects a remote station to a data switching exchange (DSE). A telephone number is associated with the access line.

access mechanism: a group of access arms that move together as a unit.

access method: a technique for moving data between main storage and input/output devices. see also *access method routines, basic access method, basic direct access method, basic indexed sequential access method, basic partitioned access method, basic sequential access method, basic telecommunications access method, queued indexed sequential access method, queued sequential access method, queued telecommunications access method, telecommunications access method, virtual telecommunications access method*.

access method routines: routines

that move data between main storage and input/output devices.

access mode: a technique that is used to obtain a specific logical record from or to place a specific logical record into a file assigned to a mass storage device. (A)

accessory: a basic part, subassembly, or assembly used with another assembly, unit, or set.

access scan: a procedure for receiving data from files by searching every data item until the required one is obtained.

access time
(1) the time interval between the instant at which an instruction control unit initiates a call for data and the instant at which delivery of the data is completed. Access time equals latency plus transfer time. (A) (B)
(2) the time interval between the instant at which data are requested to be stored and the instant at which storage is started.
(3) deprecated term for *cycle time*. (A) (B)
(4) see also *latency, seek time*.

accordion: a printed circuit connector contact.

accounting machine
(1) a keyboard-actuated machine that prepares accounting records.
(2) a machine that reads data from external storage media, such as cards or tapes, and automatically produces accounting records or tabulations, usually on continuous forms.
(3) see *electrical accounting machine*. (A)

ACCUM: see *accumulator*.

accumulate (ACC): to enter the result of an operation in an accumulator.

accumulating reproducer: equipment that reproduces punched cards and possesses limited additional capabilities of adding, subtracting, and summary punching.

accumulator (ACC) (ACCUM)
(1) a device in which the result of an arithmetic or logical operation is determined.
(2) a register that stores a quantity. When a second quantity is entered, it arithmetically combines the quantity and stores the result in the location of the register.

accumulator register: synonymous with *accumulator*.

accumulator shift instruction: a computer instruction causing the contents of a register to be displaced by a specific number of digit positions left or right.

accuracy
(1) a quality held by that which is free of error. (B)
(2) a qualitative assessment of freedom from error, a high assessment corresponding to a small error. (B)
(3) a quantitative measure of the magnitude of error, preferably expressed as a function of the relative error, a high value of this measure corresponding to a small error. (*A*) (B) cf. *precision*.

accuracy control character: a control character used to indicate whether the data with which it is associated are in error, or are to be disregarded, or cannot be represented on a particular device. synonymous with *error control character*. (*A*)

accuracy control system: a system of error detection and control.

ACD: see *automatic call distributor*. (F)

ac/dc ringing: a method of telephone ringing that uses alternating current to operate a ringer and direct current to actuate a relay that stops the ringing when the called party answers.

ac dump: an intentional, accidental, or conditional removal of all alternating current or power from a system or component.

ac erasing: to erase magnetic recording material by a device powered with alternating current.

acetate base: magnetic tapes having a transparent backing of cellulose acetate film.

ACH: see *attempts per circuit per hour*. (F)

ACIA (asynchronous communications interface adapter): provides the data formatting and control to interface serial asynchronous data communications information to bus organized systems.

ACK
(1) affirmative acknowledgment; used in block transmission, indicates that the previous transmission block was accepted by the receiver and that it is ready to accept the next block of the transmission.
(2) see *acknowledge character*. (A)

acknowledge character (ACK)
(1) a transmission control character transmitted by a station as an affirmative response to the station with which the connection has been set up. (B)
(2) a transmission control character transmitted by a receiver as an affirmative response to a sender. An acknowledge character may also be used as an accuracy control character. (*A*)

acknowledgment: the transmission, by a receiver, of acknowledge characters as an affirmative response to a sender.

ACL: audit command language; a high level programming language.

ACM: Association for Computer Machinery; a major professional society devoted to the consistent advancement of the science and art of computer technology.

A-conversion: a FORTRAN instruction to transmit alphanumeric data to and from variables within storage.

acoustic coupler (AC): a type of telecommunication equipment that permits use of a telephone network for data transmission by means of sound transducers.

acoustic coupling: a method of coupling a data terminal equipment or similar device to a telephone line by means of transducers that utilize sound waves to or from a telephone handset or equivalent. (C)

acoustic delay line: a delay line whose operation is based on the time of propagation of sound waves in a given data medium. synonymous with *sonic delay line*. (*A*)

acoustic memory: deprecated term for *acoustic storage*. (A)

acoustic modem: a modulator-demodulator unit that converts electrical signals to telephone tones and back again.

acoustic storage: a storage device consisting of acoustic delay lines. (A)

ACR: see *alternate recovery*.

ACS: see *Advanced Communications Service*.

action: activity or processing activity steps, operations, etc.

action cycle: any total operation performed on data.

action line: the line of the raster that is used when the cathode-ray storage tube is functioning in a serial mode.

action message: a message issued because of a condition that requires an operator response.

action specification: in a PL/1 ON statement, the on unit or the single keyword SYSTEM, either of which specifies the action to be taken whenever an interruption results from raising of the named on condition. The action specification can also include the keyword SNAP.

activate (a block): in PL/1, to initiate the execution of a block. A procedure block is activated when it is invoked at any of its entry points; a begin block is activated when it is encountered in a normal flow of control, including a branch.

activation: in a network, the process by which a component of a node is made ready to perform the functions for which it was designed. cf. *deactivation*.

active

(1) operational.

(2) pertaining to a node or device that is connected or is available for connection to another node or device. cf. *inactive*.

active file: a permanent file or a temporary file, having an expiration date that is later than the job date.

active line: a telecommunication line that is currently available for transmission of data. cf. *inactive line*.

active link: a link that is currently available for transmission of data. cf. *inactive link*.

active master file: a master file holding relatively active items.

active master item: the most active items on a master file measured by usage of the data.

active program: any program that is loaded and ready to be executed.

active satellite: a satellite that transmits a signal, in contrast to a passive satellite that only reflects a signal. The receive signal is usually amplified and shaped before it is retransmitted.

active station: a station that is currently eligible for entering or accepting messages. cf. *inactive station*.

active storage: see *main storage*.

activity: the percentage of records in a file that are processed in a run. see also *volatility*.

activity level: the value taken by a structural variable in an intermediate or final solution to a programming problem.

activity loading: a method of storing records on a file in which the most frequently processed records can be located with the least number of reads.

activity ratio: the ratio of the number of records in a file that are in use to the total number of records in that file.

actual address: synonymous with *absolute address*.

actual code: synonymous with *absolute code*.

actual data transfer rate: the average number of bits, characters, or blocks per unit of time transferred from a data source and received by a data sink.

actual decimal point: in COBOL the physical representation, using either of the decimal point characters (. or ,), of the decimal point position in a data item. When specified, it will appear in a printed report, and it requires an actual space in storage.

actual instruction: deprecated term for *effective instruction*. (A) (B)

actual key: in COBOL, a key that directly expresses the physical location of a logical record on a mass storage medium. (A)

actual time: the performance of computing during the specific time where the related process, event, problem, or communication takes place.

actual work time (AWT): the average time an operator requires to handle a call. This corresponds to the expected value (mean value) of the holding time distribution used in the Erland C model. (F)

actuating signal: an input impulse in the control circuitry of computers.

ACU: see *automatic calling unit*.

A/D: analog-to-digital; indicating a conversion from analog information to digital form.

ADA: a high-level language for real time processing problems. Developed in 1983 by computer scientists at New York University it is the first successful version of a key program for the U.S. Defense Department to develop a standard computer language for the military. It is named after Augusta Ada Byron, Lord Byron's daughter, who is considered the world's first programmer.

ADAPSO: association of the U.S. and Canadian data-processing service organizations including a software developer and marketing units.

adapter: a mechanism for attaching parts, for example, parts having different diameters. see *channel-to-channel adapter, line adapter*.

adaptive channel allocation: a means of multiplexing where the information capacities of channels are not predetermined but are instead assigned on demand.

adaptive transversal equalizer: a transversal filter that automatically adjusts its characteristics to compensate for linear distortion. Adaptive equalizers are particularly important in data modems where their use has permitted voice-band data rates to be increased for approximately 3000 bits per second to approximately 10,000 bits per second. (F)

ADC: see *analog-to-digital converter*.

ADCCP: advanced data communications control procedures.

add: see *false add*. (A)

added entry: in cataloguing, a secondary entry, that is, any entry other than the main entry.

addend: in an addition operation, a number or quantity added to the augend. (A) (B)

adder (A) (ADDR)
(1)   a device whose output data are a representation of the sum of the numbers represented by its input data. (B)
(2)   a device whose output is a representation of the sum of the quantities represented by its inputs.
(3)   see *full adder, serial adder*. (A)

adder subtracter: a device that acts as an adder or subtracter depending upon the control signal received. The adder subtracter may be constructed so as to yield the sum and the difference at the same time. (A) (B)

add file: a file to which records are being added.

addition: in data processing, combining quantities according to various circuitry designs, machine rules regarding changes in values, and types of carryover operations. see *parallel addition, serial addition.*

additional character: synonymous with *special character.*

addition record: a record which results in the creation of a new record in the master file being updated.

addition table: the area of main storage holding a table of numbers used during the table-scan concept of addition.

additive attributes: in PL/1, attributes for which there are no defaults and which, if required, must always be added to the list of specified attributes or be implied.

add mode: on a calculator, the placement of the decimal marker in addition and subtraction operations to a predetermined number of decimal places referenced to the last digit entered. (D)

add-on: circuitry or system that is attached to a computer to increase memory or performance.

add operation
(1) a disk or diskette operation that adds records to an existing file.
(2) an operation caused by an add instruction.

ADDR
(1) see *adder.*
(2) see *address.*
(3) see *addressing.*
(4) see *address register.*

address (ADDR) (ADRS)
(1) a character or group of characters that identifies a register, a particular part of storage, or some other data source or destination. (A) (B)
(2) to refer to a device or an item of data by its address. (A) (B)

(3) the part of the selection signals that indicates the destination of a call. (C)
(4) in word processing, the location, identified by an address code, of a specific section of the recording medium or storage. (D)
(5) a sequence of numbers that identifies the telephone to which a call is directed. The address is usually a seven- or ten-digit number, depending on whether the destination is inside or outside the numbering plan area where the call originated. synonymous with *destination code.* (F)
(6) digital information (a combination of bits) that identifies a location in a storage device or equipment unit. (F)
(7) see also *absolute address, base address, direct address, effective address, four address, four-plus-one address, generated address, immediate address, indexed address, indirect address, instruction address, machine address, multiaddress, multilevel address, n-level address, one-level address, real address, relative address, relocatable address, return address, self-relative address, single address, specific address, symbolic address, two-level address, virtual address, zero-level address.*

addressability
(1) in micrographics, the number of addressable positions within a specified film frame, as follows: number of addressable horizontal positions by number of addressable vertical positions. (A)
(2) in computer graphics, the number of addressable points within a specified display space or image

space. (E)

addressability measure: in computer graphics, the number of addressable points within a specified display space or tablet. (E)

addressable horizontal positions

(1) in micrographics, the number of positions within a specified film frame at which a vertical line can be placed. (A)

(2) in computer graphics, the number of positions within a specified raster, at which a full length vertical line can be placed. synonymous with *display line*.

addressable point: in computer graphics, any point in a display space or tablet that can be addressed. synonymous with *addressable position*. (E)

addressable position: see *addressable point*.

addressable register: a temporary storage location with a fixed location and address number.

addressable vertical positions

(1) in micrographics, the number of positions within a specified film frame at which a horizontal line can be placed. (A)

(2) in computer graphics, the number of positions, within a specified raster, at which a full length horizontal line can be placed. synonymous with *display column*.

address bus: a unidirectional bus over which appears digital data identifying either a particular memory location or a particular input/output device.

address code: in word processing, a program instruction that identifies an address. (D)

address comparator: a unit that veri-

fies that the correct address is being read. The comparison is made between the address read and the specified address.

address computation: computer operations which create or modify the address portion of instructions.

address constant: a value, or an expression representing a value, used in the calculation of storage address.

address conversion: the translation of the symbolic addresses or relative addresses into absolute addresses using the computer and an assembly program or by manual means.

addressed memory: memory units that hold each individual register.

addressee: the intended recipient of a message.

address effective: any modified address; an address actually considered for use in a particular execution of a computer instruction.

addresses: see *decoding*.

addresses of address: programming technique used primarily with subroutines.

address field: that part of a computer word containing either the address of the operand or the information needed to derive that address.

address format

(1) the arrangement of the address parts of an instruction. The expression "plus-one" is frequently used to indicate that one of the addresses specifies the location of the next instruction to be executed, such as one-plus-one, two-plus-one, three-plus-one, four-plus-one.

(2) the arrangement of the parts of a single address, such as those required for identifying a channel, module, or track on magnetic disk. (*A*)

addressing (ADDR)

(1) the assignment of addresses to the instructions of a program.

(2) the means whereby the originator or control station selects the unit to which it is going to send a message.

(3) see *absolute addressing, deferred addressing, implied addressing, indirect addressing, one-ahead addressing, relative addressing, repetitive addressing, self-relative addressing, symbolic addressing.* see also *polling.*

addressing characters: identifying characters sent by the computer over a line that cause a particular station (or component).

addressless instruction format: an instruction format containing no address part, used either when no address is needed, or when the address is in some way implicit.

address mapping: conversion of data showing the physical location of records with assignment of these records to storage locations; for example, the translation of a virtual address to an absolute address.

address mark: a byte of data on a disk or diskette, used to identify the data field and ID field in the record.

address modification: any arithmetic, logic, or syntactic operation performed on an address. (A)

address part: a part of an instruction that usually contains only an address or part of an address. (A) (B)

address reference: synonym for *address* (2).

address register (ADDR): a register in which an address is stored. see also *base address register, instruction address register.* (A)

address signals: signals used to convey call destination information such as telephone station code, central office code, and area code. Some forms of address signals are called *pulse*; for example, dial pulses, multifrequency pulses. (F)

address size: the maximum number of binary digits in an instruction used in directly addressing memory.

address space: the complete range of addresses that is available to a programmer.

address space identifier (ASID): a unique, system-assigned identifier for an address space.

address stop: a capability to specify at the system console an address which when encountered causes a halt in processing. see also *breakpoint, instruction address stop.*

address trace: a service aid by which the contents of selected areas of communication controller storage and selected external registers can be recorded at each successive interrupt.

address track: a track that contains addresses used to locate data on other tracks of the same device. (B)

address translation

(1) the process of changing the address of an item of data or an instruction to the address in main storage at which it is to be loaded or relocated.

(2) in virtual storage systems, the process of changing the address of an item of data or an instruction from its virtual storage address to its real storage address.

address translator (AT): in a virtual storage system, a functional unit that transforms virtual addresses to real addresses. (E)

add-subtract time: time needed to perform one addition or subtraction, exclusive of the read or write time.

add time: the time required for one addition, not including the time required to get the quantities from storage and return them to storage.

add to storage: the process that instantly enters the final sum of the accumulator into the computer memory.

ADI: American Documentation Institute, now, American Society for Information Science (ASIS).

ADIS: abbreviation for *Automatic Data Interchange System.*

adjacency: in character recognition, a condition in which the character spacing reference lines of two consecutively printed characters on the same line are separated by less than a specified distance. (A)

adjacent: in a network, pertaining to devices, programs, or domains that are connected by a data link or that share common control.

adjacent channel: a channel whose frequency band is adjacent to that of the reference channel.

adjacent domains
(1) domains that are connected by a direct data link. (E)
(2) domains sharing a common subarea node (e.g., a communication controller) or two domains connected by a cross-domain subarea link with no intervening domains.

adjacent link storage image: information within a node about an adjacent link station.

adjacent nodes: two nodes that are connected by one or more data links with no intervening nodes. (E)

adjacent subareas: two subareas connected by one or more links, with no intervening subareas.

adjoint (system): computational method based on the reciprocal relations between a system of ordinary linear differential equations and its adjoint.

adjustable extent: in PL/1, a bound (of an array), length (of a string), or size (of an area) that may be different for different generations of the associated variable. Adjustable bounds, lengths, and sizes are specified as expressions or asterisks (or by REFER options for based variables), which are evaluated separately for each generation. They cannot be used for static variables.

adjust (line end): in word processing, a feature that automatically adjusts the line endings of text to comply, within the line-end zone, with the original margin setting or to changed settings, with or without ending. (D)

adjust text mode: in word processing, a mode that reformats text to accommodate specified line lengths and page sizes and to help the operator to adjust line endings using word-processing control functions.

ADMIN: see *administrator.*

administration: in operating companies, dial or network administration is a number of related functions with the objective of ensuring the overall provision of service by a switching system. It includes assignment of lines and trunks to switching system terminals, collection of traffic data, analysis of troubles and customer complaints, and requests for additions and modifications to switching systems. (F) see *telecommunication administration*.

administrative data processing: automatic data processing used in accounting or in management. synonymous with *business data processing*. (A) (B)

administrative operations: store operations other than direct selling; usually performed by managers and supervisors.

administrative operator: see *control operator*.

administrative operator station: see *control operator's terminal*.

Administrative Support System: a word processing system used primarily by business managers.

administrator (ADMIN): see *system administrator*.

ADP: see *automatic data processing*. (A)

ADPE: abbreviation for *automatic data processing equipment*.

ADPS: abbreviation for *Automatic Data Processing System*.

ADP system: synonymous with *computer system*.

ADR: see *address*.

ADRS: see *address*.

ADU: see *automatic dialing unit*.

Advanced Communications Service (ACS): a planned shared switched data communications network service; ACS would provide information movement, communications processing, and network management functions. ACS would include the capability of allowing incompatible terminals and computers to communicate with each other. ACS would have the potential of being as accessible to small data communications users as to large users. (G)

Advanced Information Systems: see *AIS*.

Advanced Mobile Phone Service: formerly known as High Capacity Mobile Telecommunications Service (HCMTS), AMPS is a dial mobile telephone service which Illinois Bell began offering on a developmental basis in Chicago during 1978. The AMPS concept includes a cellular system of low power radio stations and a mobile telephone switching office. The use of low power radio signals, the ability to have numerous cells in an area, and the switching capability of the office combine to significantly increase mobile telephone capacity. (G)

advanced optical character reader (AOCR): optical character reader capable of storing approximately 90 fonts to typewritten addresses.

ADX: an automatic exchange in a data transmission network.

AED: automated engineering design system. An MIT-designed extension of ALGOL affinity-based routing in which a temporary relationship, or routing affinity, is established between a source and a destination; all messages from the source station are routed to the destination for the duration of the relationship.

aerial

(1) a device which receives the signal and feeds it in electrical form to receivers.

(2) in radio communication systems, a device which radiates the transmitted electrical signal into space.

aerial cable: a telecommunication cable connected to poles or similar overhead structures.

AFIPS: American Federation of Information Processing Societies.

AFR: automatic field/format recognition; a computer input facility.

AFT: see *analog facility terminal.* (F)

agenda: set of control-language statements prescribing a solution path or run procedure; an ordered listing of major operations as part of a procedure for a solution or computer run.

aggregate: a transmitted carrier signal that consists of the 12 single sidebands being sent over the transmission circuit. see *data aggregate.*

aggregate expression: in PL/1, an array expression or a structure expression.

AI: see *artificial intelligence.*

AIC: see *automatic intercept center.* (F)

aiming circle: synonymous with *aiming symbol.*

aiming field: synonymous with *aiming symbol.*

aiming symbol: on a display space, a circle or other pattern of light used to guide the positioning of a light pen, or to indicate that area within the presence of a light pen can be detected at a given time. synonymous with *aiming circle, aiming field.* (E)

airline reservation system: an on-line application in which a computing system is used to keep track of seat inventories, flight schedules, and other information required to run an airline. The reservation system is designed to maintain up-to-date files and to respond, within seconds or less, to inquiries from ticket agents at locations remote from the computing system.

AIS
(1) *Advanced Information Systems:* An American Bell subsidiary, set up on June 11, 1982, to market a network product enabling different types and brands of computers and terminals to communicate directly with each other over the telephone network. see also *Net 1.*
(2) see *automatic intercept system.* (F)

AL: see *assembler language.*

ALD: see *automated logic diagram.*

alerting (alerting signal): a signal sent to a customer. PBX, or switching system to indicate an incoming call. A common form is the signal that rings a bell in the telephone set being called. (F)

algebraic expression manipulation statement: a statement that specifies the operands and operations that are to be performed on symbols rather than on numeric values. (E)

algebraic language: an algorithmic language many of whose statements are structured to resemble the structure of algebraic expressions, for example, ALGOL, FORTRAN. (A)

algebraic manipulation: the processing of mathematical expressions without concern for the numeric values of the symbols that represent numbers.

algebraic sign conventions: the rules of algebra that determine whether a result is positive or negative when numbers are added, subtracted, multiplied, or divided.

ALGOL (algorithmic language): a language primarily used to express computer programs by algorithms. (A) see also *AED.*

algorithm: a finite set of well-defined

rules for the solution of a problem in a finite number of steps; for example, a full statement of an arithmetic procedure for evaluating sin x to a stated precision. cf. *heuristic.* (*A*) (B)

algorithmic language: an artificial language established for expressing algorithms.

algorithmic routine: a program or routine that directs a computer specifically toward a solution of a problem in a finite number of distinct and discrete steps as contrasted to trial-and-error methods, that is, heuristic methods or routines.

alias

(1)   an alternate label. For example, a label and one or more aliases may be used to refer to the same data element or point in a computer program. (A)

(2)   an alternate name for a member of a partitioned data set.

(3)   in pulse code modulation, a spurious signal resulting from beats between the signal frequencies and the sampling frequency.

aliasing: removing the jagged line, or 'step edge' effect on graphic displays.

alias name: an alternate name.

alignment: the storing of data in relation to certain machine-dependent boundaries. see *boundary alignment.*

all-number calling (ANC): the system of telephone numbering that uses all numbers and replaces the two-letter plus five-number (2L + 5N) numbering plan. ANC offers more usable combinations of numbers then the 2L + 5N numbering plan and is becoming the nationwide standard. (F)

ALLOC: see *allocation.*

allocate: to assign a resource, such as a disk or a diskette file, to a specific task.

allocated storage: see *storage.*

allocation: see *dynamic storage allocation, resource allocation, storage allocation.*

allowance: the downward adjustment in the selling price of merchandise because of damage, trade-in, or promotion.

all-purpose computer: a computer combining the benefits previously assigned solely to general-purpose or special-purpose computers. synonymous with *general purpose computer.*

alphabet

(1)   an ordered set of all the letters used in a language, including letters with diacritical signs where appropriate, but not including punctuation marks. (B)

(2)   an ordered set of symbols used in a language, for example, the Morse code alphabet, the 128 ASCII characters. (*A*)

alphabetic character: a letter or other symbol, excluding digits, used in a language.

alphabetic character set: a character set that contains letters and may contain control characters, special characters, and the space character, but not digits. (A) (B)

alphabetic character subset: a character subset that contains letters and may contain control characters, special characters, and the space character, but not digits. (A) (B)

alphabetic code: a code according to which data is represented using an alphabetic character set. (A) (B)

alphabetic-coded character set: a coded character set whose character set is an alphabetic character set. (A) (B)

alphabetic shift: a control for selecting the alphabetic character set in an alphanumeric keyboard printer.

alphabetic string

(1) a string consisting solely of letters from the same alphabet. (B)

(2) a character string consisting solely of letters and associated special characters from the same alphabet. (*A*)

alphabetic word

(1) a word consisting solely of letters from the same alphabet. (B)

(2) a word consisting of letters and associated special characters, but not digits. (*A*)

alphageometrics: a means of generating videotex images on a screen. Displays are made from geometric elements.

alphameric: synonymous with *alphanumeric*. (A)

alphamosaic: a means for generating videotex images on a screen. Displays are made using a mosaic of dots.

ALPHANUM: see *alphanumeric.*

alphanumeric (ALPHANUM): pertaining to a character set that contains letters, digits, and usually other characters, such as punctuation marks. synonymous with *alphameric*. (*A*)

alphanumeric character set: a character set that contains both letters and digits and may contain control characters, special characters, and the space character. (A) (B)

alphanumeric character subset: a character subset that contains both letters and digits and may contain control characters, special characters, and the space character. (A) (B)

alphanumeric code: a code according to which data is represented using an alphanumeric character set. (A) (B)

alphanumeric-coded character set: a coded character set whose character set is an alphanumeric character set. (A) (B)

alphanumeric data: data represented by letters and digits, perhaps with special characters and the space character. (A) (B)

alphanumeric display device: synonymous with *character display device.*

alphanumeric edited character: in COBOL, a character within an alphanumeric character string that contains at least one B or O.

alphanumeric field: a field that can contain any alphabetic, numeric, or special character.

alphanumeric instruction: the name given to instruction that can be used equally well with alphabetic or numeric kinds of data.

alphanumeric keyboard: a keyboard used to enter letters, numbers, and special characters into a display station buffer; it is also used to perform special functions such as backspacing and to produce special control signals.

alphanumeric sort: process in which a word processor puts a list into alphabetical or numerical order, or both.

alterable memory: a storage medium that can be written into.

alteration switch: a manual switch on the computer console or a program-simulated switch that can be set on or off to control machine instructions.

altering: any operation for inserting, deleting, or changing information.

alter mode: a program condition that allows changing or updating data in storage.

alternate path retry (APR): a facility that allows an input/output operation that has failed to be retrieved on another channel assigned to the device performing the input/output operation. It also provides the capability to establish other paths to an on-line or off-line device.

alternate recovery (ACR): a facility that attempts system recovery when a processing unit fails by transferring work to another processing unit.

alternate route: a secondary or back-up route that is used if normal routing is not possible.

alternate routing: a means of selectively distributing traffic over a number of routines ultimately leading to the same destination. (F)

alternate track: on a direct access device, a track designated to contain data in place of a defective primary track.

alternating current (AC): an electrical current, the direction of which is periodically reversed. The frequency of reversal is of the order of many cyles each second.

alternation: synonymous with *OR operation*.

alternative attribute: an attribute that may be chosen from a group of two or more alternatives. If none is specified, one of the alternatives is assumed.

alternative denial: synonymous with *NOT-AND operation*.

ALU: see also *arithmetic unit logic unit*.

AM: see *amplitude modulation*.

AMA: see *automatic message ac-counting*.

ambiguity error: an error resulting from an incorrect choice when there are two possible readings of a digitized number.

ambiguous reference: in PL/1, a reference that is not sufficiently qualified to identify one and only one name known at point of reference.

amendment record: synonymous with *change record*.

American Bell: created to comply with a 1982 FCC order, it began offering new communications equipment on January 1, 1983. A fully separate subsidiary of AT&T; in July 1983 U.S. Court demanded AT&T relinquish Bell name; nicknamed *Baby Bell*. see also *A/S*.

American National Standard control characters: control characters defined by American National Standard FORTRAN.

American National Standard Labels (ANL): magnetic tape labels that conform to the conventions established by the American National Standards Institute.

American National Standards Institute (ANSI): an organization for the purpose of establishing voluntary industry standards.

American Standard Code for Information Interchange: see *ASCII*.

amount tendered: cash or cashlike document given to a salesperson by a customer in partial or complete payment for merchandise.

ampere (A.): a unit of measure for electric current that is equivalent to a flow of one coulomb per second, or to the steady current produced by one volt applied across a resistance of one ohm.

amphibolous: relating to an ambiguity; an uncertainty; doubtfulness.

amplifier: a device that, by enabling a received wave to control a local source of power, is capable of delivering an enlarged reproduction of the essential characteristics of the wave. see also *repeater.*

amplitude: the size or magnitude of a voltage or current waveform.

amplitude modulation (AM): a form of modulation where the amplitude of a carrier wave varies by an amount proportional to the amplitude of the modulating signal.

AMPS: see *Advanced Mobile Phone Service.*

AMR: see *automatic message routing.*

analog (A): pertaining to data in the form of continuously variable physical quantities. see *network analog.* cf. *digital.*

analog adder: a device where analog output variable is equal to the sum, or a weighted sum, of two or more analog input variables. synonymous with *summer.* (B)

analog channel: a data communication channel on which the information transmitted can take any value between the limits defined by the channel. Voice-grade channels are analog channels.

analog computer
(1) a computer in which analog representation of data is mainly used.
(2) a computer that operates on analog data by performing physical processes on these data.
(3) see also *digital computer, hybrid computer.*

analog data: data represented by physical quantity that is considered to be continuously variable and whose magnitude is made directly proportional to the data or to a suitable function of the data. (A) (B)

analog divider: a device whose analog output variable is proportional to the quotient of two analog input variables. (B)

analog facility terminal (AFT): a voice-frequency facility terminal that performs signaling and transmission functions and includes analog channel banks. It interfaces between an analog carrier system and a switching system, a metallic facility, a digital facility terminal, or another analog facility terminal. (F)

analog input module: devices that convert analog input signals from process instrumentation into a digit code for transmission to the computer.

analog integration: integration of an analog computer, performed by means of an operational amplifier with a capacitor instead of a resistor in the feedback loop.

analog multiplier: a device whose analog output variable is proportional to the quotient of two analog input variables. (B)

analog representation: a representation of the value of a variable by a physical quantity that is considered to be continuously variable, the magnitude of the physical quantity being made directly proportional to the variable or to a suitable function of the variable. (A) (B)

analog scaling: considering the limited range of values obtainable on the computer.

analog signal: a signal that varies in a continuous manner, such as voice or music. An analog signal may be contrasted with a digital signal which represents only discrete states. The signal put out by a data set has both analog and discrete characteristics. (F)

analog simulation: the use of an electrical system to represent any physical system.

analog switch: a switching equipment designed, designated, or used to connect circuits between users for real-time transmission of analog signals.

analog system: system that simulates major factors by means of an electronic or fluidic flow.

analog-to-digital converter (A/D)
(1) a functional unit that converts analog signals to digital data. (B)
(2) a device that senses an analog signal and converts it to a proportional representation in digital form.
(3) an electromechanical device that senses an electrical signal and converts it to a proportional representation in digital form.

analog-to-digital encoder: a device for placing analog signal samples in a coded format.

analog transmission: transmission of a continuously variable signal as opposed to a discrete signal. Physical quantities such as temperature are described as analog while data characters are coded in discrete pulses and referred to as digital.

analogue: see *analog.*

analysis: the methodical investigation of a problem, and the separation of the problem into smaller related units for further detailed study. see *flow analysis, numerical analysis.* (A)

analysis block: relocatable portion of the computer storage where program testing or statistical data are kept which can later be used to analyze the performance of the system.

analysis mode: a mode of operation where special programs monitor the performance of the system for subsequent analysts.

analyst: a person who defines problems and develops algorithms and procedures for their solution. (A)

analytical engine: one of Charles Babbage's earliest computer machines. Developed in 1833, it was the first general-purpose automatic digital computer.

analytic relationship: the relationship existing between concepts and corresponding terms, by virtue of their definition and inherent scope of meaning.

analyzer: see *differential analyzer, digital differential analyzer, network analyzer.*

ANC: see *all-number calling.* (F)

ancestral task: in PL/1, the attaching task or any of the tasks in a direct line from the given task to, and including, the major task.

ancillary equipment: synonym for *auxiliary equipment.*

AND: logic operator having the property that if P is a statement, Q is a statement, R is a statement, . . . , then the AND of P,Q,R, . . . is true if all statements are true, false if any statement is false. synonymous with *logical multiply.* (A) (B)

AND circuit: synonymous with *AND element.*

AND element: logical element that performs the boolean operation of conjunction. (B) synonymous with *AND gate.*

AND gate: see *AND element* synonymous with *AND circuit* and *AND gate*.

AND-not operation: deprecated term for *exclusion*. (A) (B)

AND operation: see *conjunction*. (A)(B)

angle modulation: see *modulation*.

angstrom (A): one hundred-millionth of a centimeter, a unit used in measuring the length of light waves. synonymous with *angstrom unit*.

ANI: see *automatic number identification*. (F)

anisochronous transmission: a transmission process in which there is always an integral number of unit intervals between any two significant instants in the same group. see also *asynchronous transmission*. (E)

annex memory: a small memory unit used as a go-between for the input and output units and main memory. synonymous with *buffer*.

annotation: an added descriptive comment or explanatory note. (A)

annunciator: a visual or audible signaling device, operated by relays, that indicates conditions of associated circuits.

ANSI: see *American National Standards Institute*.

answerback: the response of a terminal to remote controls signals. see also *handshaking*.

answer delay: the time from the beginning of ringing until the called station answers. (F)

answering: the process of responding to a calling station to complete the establishment of a connection between data stations. (E)

answering time: represents the time which elapses between the appearance of a signal and the response made to it.

answer lamp: a telephone switchboard that lights when a connecting plug is inserted into a calling jack, goes out when the called telephone answers, and lights when the call is completed.

answer list: a list of switched-line station identifiers with any required control information. This list is used to insure that the switched line is connected to an authorized user.

answer only: modems capable of answering calls on dial-up systems but not of initiating calls.

answerphone: a unit for automatically responding to telephone calls, recording messages for playing back later.

antenna: any structure or device used to collect or radiate electromagnetic waves.

anticipation mode: a visual way of representing binary data, represented by a line, or lack of line.

anticipatory buffering: a technique by which data are stored in a buffer before they are needed. (A)

anticipatory paging: the transfer of a page from auxiliary storage to real storage prior to the moment of need. (E)

anticoincidence element: a logical element operating with binary digits providing one output signal from two input signals.

anticoincidence operation: pertaining to a logical operation applied to two operands.

any mode

(1) the form of a RECEIVE request that obtains input from any one (unspecified) session.

(2) the form of an accept request that completes the establishment of a

session by accepting any one (unspecified) queued CINIT request.

any sequence queue: a collection of items in the system that are waiting for the processor's attention; organized so that items can be removed from the collection without regard to the sequence in which they entered it.

AOCR: see *advanced optical character reader.*

AP

(1) see *application program.*

(2) see *attached processor.*

aperiodic antenna: an antenna designed to have an approximately constant input impedance over a wide range of frequencies, for example, terminated rhombic antennas and wave antennas.

aperture

(1) one or more adjacent characters in a mask that cause retention of the corresponding characters. (B)

(2) an opening in a data medium or device such as a card or magnetic core; for example, the aperture card combining a microfilm with a punched card, or in a multiple aperture core.

(3) a part of a mask that permits retention of the corresponding portions of data.

(4) see *multiple aperture core.* (A)

aperture card: a processible card of standard dimensions in which microfilm frames can be inserted. (A)

aperture core: see *multiple aperture core.* (A)

aperture time: time needed to make a measurement or conversion with an A/D converter; is considered to be a time uncertainty or amplitude uncertainty. The aperture and amplitude

uncertainty are related by the time rate of change of the signal.

APF: see *authorized program facility.*

"A" pins: module pins used for interconnecting purposes, with the physical circuit of a single substrate.

APL (a programming language)

(1) a programming language with an unusual syntax and character set, primarily designed for mathematical applications, particularly those involving numeric on literal arrays. (E)

(2) a general-purpose language for diverse applications such as commercial data processing, system design, mathematical and scientific computation, data-base applications, and the teaching of subjects such as mathematics.

append: adding to the end of a structure, as in appending a character to a character string or an item to a list.

appendage: see *I/O appendage.*

appendage task: a task assigned the highest-level dispatching priority by the network control program. see also *immediate task, nonproductive task, productive task.*

application: the use to which a dataprocessing system is put; for example, a payroll application, an airline reservation application, a network application.

application developer: an individual responsible for tailoring the basic capabilities of the information system into a form suitable for endusers, mainly through the design and implementation of application programs.

application layer: in open systems architecture, the highest layer explicitly defined by end-users, that provides all the functions needed to execute their application programs or processes. (E) deprecated term for *end-user.*

application-oriented language

(1) a programming language that has facilities or notations useful for solving problems in one or more specific classes of applications, such as numerical scientific, business data processing, civil engineering, simulation; for example, FORTRAN, COBOL, COGO, SIMSCRIPT. synonymous with *problem-oriented language.* (E)

(2) a problem-oriented language whose statements contain or resemble the terminology of the occupation or profession of the user, for example, a report program generator.

application package: a series of interrelated routines and subroutines designed to perform a specified task.

application program (AP)

(1) a program written for or by a user that applies to the user's work.

(2) a program used to connect and communicate with stations in a network, enabling users to perform application-oriented activities.

application-required language: a problem-oriented language whose statements contain or resemble the terminology of the occupation or profession of the user; for example, a report program generator. (A)

applications package: a package designed for an application.

applications software (ASW): programs and packages designed to satisfy applications. cf. *systems software.*

applique: circuit components added to an existing system to provide additional or alternate functions.

APR: see *alternate path retry.*

APT (automatically programmed tools): a programming language for numerically controlled machine tools. (E)

AQL: see *acceptable quality level.*

arbitrary access: equal access time to all memory locations, independent of the location of the previous memory reference.

arbitrary sequence computer: a computer in which each instrument explicitly determines the location of the next instruction to be executed. (A) (B)

arbitration: management of competing claims of multiple systems or processes for a limited resource.

architecture: a specification which determines how something is constructed, defining functional modularity as well as the protocols and interfaces which allow communication and cooperation among modules. see *computer architecture, network architecture.*

archival storage: see *backing storage.*

archive: used as a verb or noun showing the process of storing data files in a retrieval form or the data files so stored.

archive diskette: synonymous with *diskette* and *floppy disk.*

archiving: the storage of backup files and associated journals, usually for a given period of time. (E)

area: in PL/1, a declared portion of contiguous internal storage identified by an area variable and reserved, on allocation of based variables. see *clear area, image area, input area, output area, save area.*

area transfer: the process of assigning a group of customers to a new wire center. (F)

area code: a three-digit number identifying one of 152 geographic areas of the United States and Canada to permit direct distance dialing on the telephone system. See also *direct distance dialing, numbering plan.*

area search: in information retrieval, a search of items within a database which make up a single group or category.

area variable: in PL/1, a variable with the AREA attribute; its values may only be areas.

ARG: see *argument.*

argument (ARG)
(1) an independent variable. (A) (B)
(2) any value of an independent variable. (A) (B)
(3) a parameter passed between a calling and a called program.
(4) in FORTRAN, a parameter passed between a calling program and a subprogram or statement function.
(5) in PL/1, an expression and argument list that is part of a procedure reference.

argument addresses: a single instruction to resolve any number of argument addresses, storing the results in the stack for use by the subroutines needed.

argument list
(1) a string of arguments.
(2) in PL/1, a parenthesized list of one or more arguments, separated by commas, following an entry-name constant, an entry-name variable, a generic name, or a built-in function name. The list is passed to the parameters of the entry point.

arithmetical instruction: synonym for *arithmetic instruction.* (A) (B)

arithmetic and logic unit (ALU): a part of a computer that performs arithmetic operations, logic operations, and related operations. (A) (B)

arithmetic check: synonym for *mathematical check.* (A)

arithmetic constant: in PL/1, a fixed-point constant or a floating-point constant. Although most arithmetic constants can be signed, the sign is not part of the constant.

arithmetic conversion: the transformation of a value from one arithmetic representation to another.

arithmetic data: in PL/1, data that has the characteristics of base, scale, mode, and precision. It includes coded arithmetic data, pictured numeric character data, and pictured numeric bit data.

arithmetic exception: an overflow, underflow, or divide check exception.

arithmetic expression
(1) an expression that contains arithmetic operations and operands and that can be reduced to a single numeric value. (E)
(2) in assembler programming, a conditional assembly expression that is a combination of arithmetic terms, arithmetic operators, and paired parentheses.
(3) in COBOL, a statement containing any combination of data names, numeric literals, and figurative constants, joined together by one or more arithmetic operators in such a way that the statement as a whole can be reduced to a single numeric value.
(4) in FORTRAN, a combination of arithmetic operators and arithmetic

primaries.

arithmetic instruction: an instruction in which the operation part specifies an arithmetic operation. synonymous with *arithmetical instruction*. (*A*) (B)

arithmetic logic unit: the element able to perform basic data manipulations in the central processor; usually the unit can add, subtract, complement, negate, rotate, AND and OR.

arithmetic operation: an operation that follows the rules of arithmetic. (B) see *binary arithmetic operation*. (*A*)

arithmetic operator

(1) in assembler programming, an operator that can be used in an absolute or relocatable expression, or in an arithmetic expression to indicate the actions to be performed on the terms in the expression. The arithmetic operators allowed are: $+, -, *, /$. see *binary operator, unary operator*.

(2) in COBOL and FORTRAN, a symbol that directs the system to perform an arithmetic operation. The arithmetic operators are:

Meaning	Symbol
addition	+
subtraction	−
multiplication	*
division	/
exponentiation	**

arithmetic overflow

(1) that portion of a numeric word expressing the result of an arithmetic operation by which its word length exceeds the word length provided for the number representation. synonymous with *overflow*. (B)

(2) that portion of a word expressing the result of an operation by which its word length exceeds the storage capacity of the intended stor-

age device. (*A*) (B)

arithmetic picture data: decimal picture data or binary picture data.

arithmetic primary: in FORTRAN, an irreducible arithmetic unit; a single constant, variable, array element, function reference, or arithmetic expression enclosed in parentheses.

arithmetic register: a register that holds the operands or the results of operations such as arithmetic operations, logic operations, and shifts. (A) (B)

arithmetic relation: two arithmetic expressions separated by a relational operator.

arithmetic section: that part of the hardware of a computer where arithmetic and logical operations are performed.

arithmetic shift: a shift, applied to the representation of a number in a fixed-radix numeration system and in a fixed-point representation system, in which only the characters representing the absolute value of the number are moved. An arithmetic shift is usually equivalent to multiplying the number by a positive or a negative integral power of the radix except for the effect of any rounding. (A) (B)

arithmetic statement: any instruction specifying an arithmetic operation.

arithmetic term: a term that can be used only in an arithmetic expression.

arithmetic underflow: in an arithmetic operation, a result whose absolute value is too small to be represented within the range of the numeration system in use. For example, the condition existing, particularly when a floating-point representation system is used, when the result is smaller than the nonzero quantity that can be represented; the result may underflow because of the generation of a negative exponent that is outside the permissible range. (A) (B)

arithmetic unit (AU): a part of a computer that performs arithmetic operations, and related operations. (A) (B)

armed interrupt: accepts and holds the interruption signal; it may be enabled or disabled. An interrupt signal for an enabled condition causes certain hardware processing to take place; a disabled interrupt is held waiting for enablement.

ARQ: see *automatic request for repetition.*

array

(1) an arrangement of elements in one or more dimensions. (A) (E)

(2) in assembler programming, a series of one or more values represented by a SET symbol.

(3) in FORTRAN, an ordered set of data items identified by a single name.

(4) in PL/1, a named, ordered collection of data elements, all of which have identical attributes. An array has dimensions specified by the dimension attribute, and its individual elements are referred to by subscripts. An array can also be an ordered collection of identical structures.

(5) in APL, BASIC, and RPGII, a systematic arrangement of elements in a table format.

array declarator: in FORTRAN, the part of a statement that describes an array used in a program unit. It indicates the name of the array, the number of dimensions it contains, and the size of each dimension. An array declarator may appear in a DIMENSION, COMMON, or explicit specification.

array element: in FORTRAN, a data item in an array, identified by the array name followed by a subscript indicating its position in the array.

array expression: in PL/1, an expression whose evaluation yields an array value.

array name: the name of an ordered set of data items.

array of structures: in PL/1, an ordered collection of identical structures specified by giving the dimension attribute to a structure name.

array pitch: synonym for *row pitch.* (A)

artificial cognition: a machine's ability to sense a character by optical means, and subsequently to determine its nature by comparing it with a set of standard characters.

artificial intelligence (AT): the capability of a device to perform functions that are normally associated with human intelligence, such as reasoning, learning, and self-improvement. see also *machine learning.* (A)

artificial language: a language whose rules are explicitly established prior to its usage. cf. *natural language.* (A) (B)

ARU: see *audio response unit.*

AS: see *auxiliary storage.*

ASA: American Standards Association; former name of the American National Standards Institute. see *American National Standards Institute.*

ASA control characters: see *American National Standard control characters.*

ASA label: see *American National Standard label.*

ASAP: as soon as possible.

ascender: the part of a lowercase letter, such as "b," that extends above the main part of the character. see also *descender.*

ascending sort: a sort where the final sequence of records is such that successive keys compare "greater than or equal to."

ASCII: American National Standard Code for Information Interchange. The standard code, using a coded character set consisting of seven-bit coded characters (eight bits including parity check), used for information interchange among data-processing systems, data-communication systems, and associated equipment. The ASCII set consists of control characters and graphic characters. (A)

ASCII control characters: deprecated term for *American National Standard control characters.*

ASCII keyboard: a keyboard including keys for all of the characters of the ASCII character set. Usually includes three cases for each alpha character: upper case, lower case and control.

ASCII label: deprecated term for *American National Standard label.*

ASID: see *address space identifier.*

ASIS: see *ADI.*

ASM: see *assembler.*

ASP: see *attached support processor.*

aspect: in information retrieval, those features of the contents of documents which are represented by index term, descriptors, and so on.

aspect card: a card with numbers which record the location of documents used in an information retrieval system.

ASR: see *automatic send/receive.*

assemble
(1) to translate a program expressed in an assembly language into a computer language and perhaps to link subroutines. Assembling is usually accomplished by substituting the computer language operation code for the assembly-language operation code and by substituting absolute addresses, immediate addresses, relocatable addresses, or virtual addresses for symbolic addresses. (B)
(2) to prepare a machine-language program from a symbolic language program by substituting absolute operation codes for symbolic operation codes and in absolute or relocatable addresses for symbolic addresses. (*A*) (B)

assemble-and-go: an operating technique in which there are no stops between the assembling, loading, and execution of a computer program. (A)

assembled origin
(1) the computer program origin assigned by an assembly program, a compiler, or linkage editor.
(2) the address of the initial storage location assigned to a computer program by an assembler, a compiler, or a linkage editor. (*A*)

assemble duration: synonym for *assembling time.* (A) (B)

assembler (ASM): a computer program used to assemble. synonymous with *assembly program.* (*A*) (B)

assembler directives: controls or directs the assembly processor as operation codes control or direct the central computer. These directives are represented by mnemonics.

assembler language (AL): a source language that includes symbolic machine-language statements in which there is a one-to-one correspondence with the instruction formats and data formats of the computer.

assembling: composing or integrating instructions into subroutines or main routines for acceptance and use by computing units.

assembling phase: synonym for *assembly phase*. (A) (B)

assembling time: the elapsed time taken for the execution of an assembler. synonymous with *assemble duration*. (A) (B)

assembly: utilizing an assembler to produce a machine-language program.

assembly language

(1) a computer-oriented language whose instructions are usually in one-to-one correspondence with computer instructions and that may provide facilities such as the use of macroinstructions. (B)

(2) a computer programming language whose statements may be instructions or declarations. The instructions usually have a one-to-one correspondence with machine instructions.

(3) synonymous with *computer-dependent language, computer-oriented language*. (A)

assembly listing: the output of an assembler.

assembly phase: in a run, the logical subdivision that includes the execution of the assembler. synonymous

with *assembling phase*. (A) (B)

assembly program: synonym for *assembler*. (A) (B)

assembly routine

(1) a procedure that directs the conversion of a program written in relative or symbolic form into a machine-language program, most often on an instruction-by-instruction design.

(2) a computer program operating on symbolic input data to produce from such data-machine instructions.

assembly time: the time at which an assembler translates the symbolic machine-language statements into their object code form (machine instructions). see also *preassembly time*.

assembly unit: a portion of a program that is incorporated into a large program utilizing an assembler; for example, a library subroutine.

assignment indexing: a form of automatic indexing where extracted terms are used in conjunction with some form of thesaurus to yield a list of index terms chosen from a controlled vocabulary list. The index terms are assigned. cf. *extraction indexing*.

assignment statement

(1) in a high-level language, a statement used to bind variables. (E)

(2) an instruction used to express a sequence of operations, or used to assign operands to specified variables, or symbols, or both.

(3) in COBOL, a statement used to associate a file with the symbolic name of a device. (A)

(4) in FORTRAN, an arithmetic or logical variable or array element, fol-

lowed by an equal sign (=), followed by an arithmetic or logical expression.

ASSM: see *assembler.*

Association for Computer Machinery: see *ACM.*

associative array register: a special purpose device used to compensate for inherent delays of segment or page table translation.

associative storage: a storage device whose storage locations are identified by their contents, or by part of their contents, rather than by their names or positions. synonymous with *content-addressed storage.* (A) (B)

assumed decimal point: in COBOL, a decimal point position that does not involve the existence of an actual character in a data item. It does not occupy an actual space in storage.

asterisk protection: inserting a series of asterisks on the left of the most important digit.

ASW: see *applications software.*

"A" switchboard: a manual telephone switchboard in a local central office, used primarily to receive subscribers' calls and to complete connections either directly or through some other switching equipment.

asymmetric devices: in multiprocessing, devices that have only one path to or from a multiprocessor. They are physically attached to only one processing unit.

asymmetric I/O: I/O devices physically attached to only one processing unit, that are available to jobs executing on another processing unit.

ASYNCH: see *asynchronous.*

asynchronous (A) (ASYNCH): without regular time relationship; unexpected or unpredictable with respect to the execution of a program's instructions.

asynchronous computer: a computer in which each event or the performance of each operation starts as a result of a signal generated by the completion of the previous event or operation, or on the availability of the parts of the computer required by the next event or operation. (B) cf. *synchronous computer.* (A)

asynchronous data transfer: a physical transfer of data to or from a device that occurs without a regular or predictable time relationship following the execution of an I/O request. cf. *synchronous data transfer.*

asynchronous device: a device having an operating speed not related to any specific frequency of the system to which it is connected.

asynchronous operation

(1) an operation that occurs without a regular or predictable time relationship to a specified event; for example, the calling of an error diagnostic routine that may receive control at any time during the execution of a computer program.

(2) a sequence of operations in which operations are executed out of time coincidence with any event. (A)

(3) synonymous with *asynchronous working.*

(4) cf. *synchronous operation.*

asynchronous signaling: codes used in signaling, where characters provide their own start and stop indicators.

asynchronous time-division multiplexing (ATDM): an asynchronous signal transmission mode that makes use of time-division multiplexing.

asynchronous transmission

(1) transmission in which the time of occurrence of the start of each character, or block of characters, is arbitrary; once started, the time of occurrence of each signal representing a bit within the character, or block, has the same relationship to significant instants of a fixed time frame. see also *anisochronous transmission.* (E)

(2) transmission in which each information character is individually synchronized (usually by the use of start elements and stop elements).

asynchronous working: synonym for *asynchronous operation.* (A)

asyndetic

(1) omitting conjunctions and connectives.

(2) pertaining to a catalog without cross-references.

AT: see *address translator.*

ATDM: see *asynchronous time-division multiplexing.*

ATLAS: Automatic Tabulating, Listing and Sorting System; a software package used for the purposes indicated.

ATR: see *attribute.*

attach: in programming, to create a task that can be executed asynchronously with the execution of the mainline code.

attached processing: where an arbitrary number of compact, inexpensive computers are linked together to form a large-scale computing facility.

attached processor (AP): a processor affixed to a central processor, often sharing its memory.

attached support processor (ASP): using multiple computers, usually two, connected via channel-to-channel adaptors, to increase the efficiency in processing many short duration jobs.

attempts per circuit per hour (ACH): an indication of calling pressure. see *connections per circuit per hour.*

attended operation: an application in which individuals are required at both stations to establish the connection and transfer the modems from talk (voice) mode to data mode. cf. *unattended operation.*

attended trail printer: in word processing, a trail printer that has no paper handling device and therefore requires operator intervention before and after printing each page. (D)

attention (ATTN): an occurrence, external to an operation, that could cause an interruption of the operation.

attention interruption: an I/O interruption caused by a terminal user pressing an attention key, or its equivalent. see *simulated attention.*

attention key: a function key on terminals that, when pressed, causes an I/O interruption in the processing unit.

attenuation: a decrease in magnitude of current, voltage, or power of a signal in transmission between points. It may be expressed in decibels or nepers.

attenuation constant: the real part of the propagation constant of a transmission line (the imaginery part is the phase constant). It is a ratio equal to the decrease (attenuation) in amplitude of a sinusoidal wave as it traverses a unit length of a transmission line. (F)

attenuation distortion: the change in attenuation with frequency relative to the attenuation at a reference frequency; for example, the change in attenuation with frequency within a voice band relative to the attenuation at 1 kHz. (F)

attenuation equalizer: synonym for *equalizer.*

attenuator: synonym for *pad.*

attestation: a program designed to allow direct electrical connection to the public telephone network of certain types of customer-provided equipment having a low potential for network harm. (F)

ATTN: see *attention.*

attribute (A) (ATR)

(1) a property or characteristic of one of more entities, for example, color, weight, sex.

(2) in PL/1, a descriptive property associated with a name to describe a characteristic of items that the name may represent, or a descriptive property used to describe a characteristic of the result of evaluation of an expression.

(3) see *data attribute, display attribute, user attribute.*

A-type address constant: in the assembler language, an address constant used for branching within a module or for retrieving data. see also *V-type address constant.*

AU: see *arithmetic unit.*

audible alarm: an alarm that is activated when predetermined events occur that require operator attention or intervention for system operation.

audio cassette: a small cartridge having magnetic recording tape mounted on rotatable reels. Its size is standardized allowing interchange between a wide variety of units.

audio inquiry: keying or dialing data into a computer that has an audio response unit attached to provide an audible response.

audio line: a switched telecommunication line attached to an audio response unit.

audio response: a form of output that uses verbal replies to inquiries. The computer is programmed to seek answers to inquiries made on a time-shared on-line system and then to utilize a special audio response unit which elicits the appropriate prerecorded response to the inquiry.

audio response message: an audible response generated by an audio response unit from output accepted from a computer.

audio response unit (ARU): an output device that provides a spoken response to digital inquiries from a telephone or other device. The response is composed from a prerecorded vocabulary of words and can be transmitted over telecommunication lines to the location from which the inquiry originated.

audiotape storage unit: a device able to store computer programs and/or data on ordinary audio cassette tape; audio tones are utilized to represent binary data.

audio telecommunication line: a telecommunication line attached to an audio response unit. An audio telecommunication line is always a switched line.

audio terminal: a unit of equipment associated with an audio response unit at which keyed or dialed data is entered for transmission to the computer; an associated audio response unit produces an audible response.

audit: to review and examine the activities of a data-processing system mainly to test the adequacy and effectiveness of procedures for data security and data integrity. see also *audit-review file*, *audit trail*. (E)

audit command language: see *ACL*.

audit in depth: the detailed examination of all manipulations performed on a single transaction or piece of information.

auditing: processing, employing techniques and information sources, by which source data, methodology, and report conclusions and sums are checked for accuracy and validity as well as credibility.

audit programming: application of a program designed to enable use of the computer as an auditing tool.

audit-review file: a file created as a result of running auditor-determined program modules that are incorporated into a normal processing program. (E)

audit trail: a manual or computerized means for tracing the transactions affecting the contents of a record. (E)

augend: in an addition operation, a number or quantity to which numbers or quantities are added. (A) (B)

augment: increasing a quantity to bring it to its full value.

augmenter: the quantity added to another to bring it to its full value. Usually positive, however, when an augmenter is added, a negative quantity is also called an *augmenter*.

authority: see *access authority*, *group authority*.

authority file: a set of records identifying a standard for established forms of headings, index terms, or other items, that are used for information retrieval. An authority file may also contain established cross-refer-ences, that is, a thesaurus.

authorization: the right granted to a user to communicate with or make use of a computer system. (E)

authorization code: a code made up of user identification and password, used to protect against unauthorized access to data and system facilities.

authorized library: a library that can contain authorized programs.

authorized program: a system program or user program that is allowed to use restricted functions.

authorized program facility: a facility that permits the identification of programs that are authorized to use restricted functions.

authorized stated: a condition in which a problem program has access to resources that would otherwise not be available.

auto-abstract

(1) pertaining to the material abstracted from a document by machine methods.

(2) to select keywords from a document by machine methods.

autoanswer: an instrument which automatically answers calls via a telephone network.

auto bypass: a capability that allows continuous operation of downstream terminals when another terminal in the daisy chain is powered down.

auto-call: synonymous with *automatic calling*.

autocode: using the computer itself to develop the machine-coded program from macrocodes, that is, the conversion of symbolic codes for operations and addresses.

autocoder: an IBM programming language.

autodial: see *auto dialler*.

auto dialler: a device permitting automatic dialing of calls via the telephone network.

auto-index: to prepare an index by a machine method.

auto-indexed addressing: an addressing mode resulting in the contents of an index register to be automatically altered by a specified amount each time such an instruction is actually executed.

autokey: in word processing, a control that starts the continuous printout or scanning of selected recorded text. (D)

automan: a type of locking switch that indicates and controls methods of operation, such as automatic or manual.

automata theory: theory that relates the study of principles of operations and applications of automatic devices to various behaviorist concepts and theories.

automate: to convert a process or equipment to automatic operations.

automated bibliography: a bibliography stored within a computer file.

automated data medium: synonym for *machine-readable medium*. (A)

automated dictionary: an automated lexicon used in machine-aided translation systems, listing roots. cf. *automated glossary*.

automated glossary: an automated lexicon used in machine-aided translation systems, containing entire words and thus presents numerous variations of a generic root. cf. *automated dictionary*.

automated lexicon: the generic term for all forms of automated dictionary and automated glossary. These lexicons constitute the primary compo-

nent within a machine-aided translation system.

automated logic diagram (ALD): a computer generated diagram that represents functioning circuitry in terms of logic blocks, interconnecting conductor networks, and input-output terminals.

automated management: types of management completed with the assistance of data-processing equipment.

automated operator user-exit routine: a user-exit routine that is passed a copy of system messages destined for the master terminal, operator-entered commands, and command responses. The user-exit routine may examine the commands and command responses and write a message to any terminal or to a queue for processing by an application program.

automated production management: management with the aid of under the control of data-processing equipment relating to production planning, scheduling, design or change, and control of output.

automated stock control: using software on a computer to check on receipt and delivery of items, including keeping accounts and forecasting demand.

automated thesaurus: a computer-based thesaurus used along with an automated lexicon within a machine-aided translation system.

automatic: pertaining to a process or device that, under specified conditions, functions without human intervention. (E)

automatic abstract: synonymous with *auto-abstract*.

automatic abstracting: seeking the criteria by which people judge what should be abstracted from a document, as programmed.

automatic answering

(1) answering in which the called data-terminal equipment (DTE) automatically responds to the calling signal; the call may be established whether or not the called DTE is attended. (E)

(2) a machine feature that allows a transmission control unit or a station to respond automatically to a call that it receives over a switched line.

(3) see also *manual answering.* cf. *automatic calling.*

automatic call distributor (ACD): a system for automatically providing even distribution of incoming calls to operator or attendant positions; calls are served in the approximate order of arrival and are routed to positions in the order of their availability for handling a call. (F)

automatic calling

(1) calling in which the selection signal is entered contiguously at the full data-signaling rate. The selection signal is generated by the data-terminal equipment (DTE). A limit may be imposed by the design criteria of the network to prevent more than a permitted number of unsuccessful call attempts to the same address within a specified period. (E)

(2) a machine feature that allows a transmission control unit or a station to initiate a call automatically over a switched line.

(3) synonymous with *auto-call.* see also *manual calling.* cf. *automatic answering.*

automatic calling unit (ACU): a dial-ing device that permits a business machine to automatically dial calls over a network. see also *automatic dialing unit.*

automatic carriage: a control mechanism for a typewriter or other listing device that can automatically control the feeding, spacing, skipping, and ejecting of paper and preprinted forms. (A)

automatic check: a check performed by equipment built in specifically for checking purposes. synonymous with *built-in check, hardware check.* cf. *programmed check. (A)*

automatic coding: type of automatic programming in which a computer is used to prepare computer instruction code. (E)

automatic constant: on a calculator, a number automatically held in the machine for repeated use. (D)

automatic control engineering: that branch of science and technology which deals with the design and use of automatic control devices and systems. (B)

automatic data processing (ADP)

(1) data processing performed by computer systems. (E)

(2) data processing largely performed by automatic means. (B)

(3) the branch of science and technology concerned with methods and techniques relating to data processing largely performed by automatic means. (B)

(4) pertaining to data-processing equipment such as electrical accounting machines and electronic data-processing equipment.

(5) data processing by means of one or more devices that: (a) use common storage for all or part of a

program and also for all or part of the data necessary for execution of the program, (b) execute user-written or user-designated programs, (c) perform user-designated symbol manipulation such as arithmetic operations, logic operations, or character-string manipulations, and (d) can execute programs that can modify themselves during their execution.

automatic data-processing system: an interacting assembly of procedures, processes, methods, personnel, and automatic data-processing equipment to perform a series of data-processing operations. see *automatic data processing.*

automatic decimal alignment: in word processing, the feature of a machine that enables numbers to be automatically aligned on either side of a decimal marker. (D)

automatic dialing unit (ADU): a device capable of automatically generating dialing digits. see also *automatic calling unit.*

automatic dictionary: the component of a language-translating machine that provides a word-for-word substitution from one language to another.

automatic electronic data-switching center: communications center designed for relaying digitized information through automatic electronic means.

automatic equalization: the process of automatically compensating for linear distortion. This is generally accomplished by an adaptive transversal equalizer. (F)

automatic error correction: a technique applying error-detecting codes and error-correcting codes.

automatic-feed punch: a keypunch that automatically moves punch cards from a card hopper, along a card path, and to a card stacker. (A)

automatic field duplication: a data-file utility feature that allows one or more fields to be copied from one record to another.

automatic function: on a calculator, a machine function or series of machine functions controlled by the program cycle and carried out without the assistance of the machine operator. (D)

automatic indexing: an automatic production of an index for document in any data-base.

automatic intercept center (AIC): a centrally located set of equipments that is a part of an automatic intercept system and provides arrangements, having stored program control, whereby the calling customer is automatically advised, by means of either recorded or electronically assembled announcements, of the prevailing situation that prevents completion of connection to the called number. (F)

automatic intercept system (AIS): a type of traffic service system consisting of one or more automatic intercept centers and a centralized intercept bureau for handling intercept calls. (F)

automatic library call: the process whereby control sections are processed by the linking editor or loader to resolve references to members of partitioned data sets.

automatic logon (log on): a facility of intelligent terminals used for on-line searching where passwords and addresses needed are stored at the terminal so that the log on process is carried out with one, or a few, key strokes.

automatic message accounting (AMA): a process that automatically records all data of customer-dialed long distance calls needed for billing purposes.

automatic message routing (AMR): the automatic directing of incoming messages to one or more outgoing circuits according to the message's content.

automatic number identification (ANI): the automatic identification of a calling station, usually for automatic message accounting. (F)

automatic pagination: i word processing, automatically printing page numbers at the bottom, top, left, or right side of each page. Like most features, it can be switched off so that no page numbers appear.

automatic paper carriage: a unit for holding paper prior to printing. The carriage feeds sheets, or continuous paper, to the writing heads.

automatic polling: see *auto-poll*.

automatic programming: the process of using a computer to perform some stages of the work involved in preparing a computer program. (A)

automatic programming language: see *APL*.

automatic punch: synonym for *card punch*. (A)

automatic recovery program: a program enabling a system to remain functioning while equipment has failed. The automatic recovery program activates duplex circuitry, a standby computer, or switches to a mode of degraded operation.

automatic request for repetition (ARQ): a feature that automatically initiates a request for retransmission when an error in transmission is detected.

automatic restart: a restart that takes place during the current run, that is, without resubmitting the job. An automatic restart can occur within a job step or at the beginning of a job step. cf. *deferred restart*.

automatic ringdown: a technique for supervision alerting on a nondial trunk in which the application of a two-second burst of ringing at the originating end results in a supervisory signal at the terminating manual PBX. see *ringdown*. (F)

automatic routine: a routine that is independently executed of manual operations, but only if specific conditions occur within a program or record, or during some other process.

automatic send/receive (ASR): a teletypewriter unit with keyboard, printer, paper tape, reader/transmitter, and paper tape punch. This combination of units may be used on line or off line and, in some cases, on line and off line concurrently.

automatic sequencing: the ability of equipment to put information in order or in a connected series without human intervention.

automatic sequential operation: to develop a series or family of solutions from a set of equations, various initial conditions are recalculated with other parameters.

automatic stop: a halt programmed to take place when an error is detected by an automated check.

automatic switchover: an operating system that has a standby machine that detects when the on-line machine is faulty and once this determination is made, switches this operation to itself.

automatic variable: in PL/1, a variable that is allocated at the activation of a block and released at the termination of that block. cf. *controlled variable*.

automatic volume recognition (AVR): a feature that allows the operator to mount labeled volumes on available I/O devices before the volumes are needed by a job step.

automatic volume switching: facility that provides access to a sequential data set that extends across two or more volumes, and to concatenated data sets stored on different volumes.

automation

(1) the implementation of processes by automatic means. (B)

(2) the conversion of a procedure, a process, or equipment to automatic operation. (B)

(3) the theory, art, or technique of making a process more automatic.

(4) the investigation, design, development, and application of methods of rendering processes automatic, self-moving, or self-controlling. (*A*)

automaton: a machine designed to simulate the operations of living things, or to respond automatically to predesigned programs, stimuli, or signals.

automonitor: see *monitor*.

automonitor routine: an executive program or routine that develops a selective record of a computer's execution of another program to be completed.

autonomous working: the initiation and execution of a part of a computer or automation system independent and separate from other operations being performed on other parts of the system.

autopiler: a specific automatic compiler.

autoplotter: a system designed to permit the user to automatically generate a variety of plotted data with a minimum of control in a wide variety of input and output formats. It plots paragraphs, histograms, point and line graphs, and so on.

autopoll: a machine feature of a transmission control unit that permits it to handle negative responses to polling without interrupting the processing unit.

autoscore: the automatic underlining of text.

auxiliary console: a console other than the main console.

auxiliary equipment: equipment not under direct control of the processing unit. synonymous with *ancillary equipment*.

auxiliary operation: an off-line operation performed by equipment not under control of the processing unit. (A)

auxiliary routine: a routine designed to assist in the operation of the computer, and in debugging other routines.

auxiliary storage (AS)

(1) a storage device that is not main storage. (B)

(2) storage that supplements another storage. (*A*)

(3) data storage other than main storage; for example, storage on magnetic tape or direct-access devices. synonymous with *external storage, secondary storage*.

(4) cf. *main storage*.

auxiliary store: synonymous with *backing store*.

availability: the degree to which a system or resource is ready when needed to process data.

available machine time: the elapsed time when a computer is in operating condition, whether or not it is in use.

available point: in computer graphics, an addressable point at which characteristics such as color, intensity, or on/off condition, may be changed. (E)

available time: the time during which a functional unit can be used. synonymous with *up time*. (B) cf. *maintenance time*. (*A*)

average access time: the average time between the instant of request and the delivery from a storage device.

average conditional information content: synonym for *conditional entropy*. (A) (B)

average edge line: an imaginary line, in OCR, that traces and smooths the form of the printed or handwritten character to better convey the intended form.

average information content: synonym for *entropy*. (A) (B)

average information rate: in information theory, the mean entropy per character per time unit. The average information rate may be expressed in a unit such as Shannon per second. (A) (B)

average transinformation content: synonym for *mean transinformation content*. (A) (B)

average transinformation rate: in information theory, the mean transinformation content per character per time unit. The average transinformation rate per time may be expressed in a unit such as Shannon per second.

AVR: see *automatic volume recognition*.

awaiting repair time: the interval of time when the operator reports a fault or failure until the time when the maintenance man or engineer commences to repair the device. If no fault is found, this time interval is then called operating delay.

awareness network: the condition where the central processor is cognizant of the status of the network.

AWT: see *actual work time*. (F)

B

(1) see *base*.
(2) see *batch*.
(3) see *bel*.
(4) see *binary*.
(5) see *bit*.
(6) see *block*.
(7) see *boolean*.
(8) see *bus*.
(9) see *byte*.

babble: the aggregate cross talk from a large number of interfering channels.

Baby Bell: see *American Bell*.

backbone: a common distribution core which provides all electrical power, gases, chemicals, and other services to the sectors of an automated wafer processing system.

background (BG) (BKGRD)
(1) pertaining to a low-priority job that the computer works on when it is not occupied by more pressing matters.
(2) in multiprogramming, the conditions under which low-priority programs are executed. see *program level*. cf. *foreground*.

background display image: synonym for *static display image*.

backgrounding: synonymous with *background processing*.

background ink: in optical character recognition, a type of ink with high reflective characteristics that is not detected by the scan head, and thus is used for print location guides, logotypes, instructions, and any other desired preprinting that would otherwise interfere with reading.

background job: a low-priority job, usually a batched or noninteractive job.

background noise
(1) extra bits or words ignored or removed from the data at the time it is used.
(2) errors introduced into the data in a system.
(3) any disturbance tending to interfere with the normal operation of a system or unit.

background printing: see *simultaneous input-output.*

background processing

(1) the execution of lower-priority computer programs when higher-priority programs are not using the system resources. (A) (B)

(2) in word processing, the execution of an operator's request such as printing a document while the operator is performing other tasks.

(3) cf. *foreground processing.*

(4) synonym for *backgrounding.*

background program: in multiprogramming, the program with the lowest priority. Background programs are executed from batched or stacked job input.

background reader: a system task started by the operator to process foreground-initiated background jobs.

background region: a region to which a background job is assigned.

backing storage: synonymous with *backing store.*

backing store: a storage that supports the main memory. Backing store has greater capacity than memory and is less expensive, but has slower access time. synonymous with *auxiliary store, backing storage, bulk storage, bulk store, secondary store.*

back-mounted: a connector attached from the inside of a box, having mounting flanges placed on the inside of the machines.

back plane: the area where the boards of a system are plugged. synonymous with *mother board.*

backspace

(1) to move back the reading or display position according to a prescribed format.

(2) to move a data carrier backward a specific distance. (B)

backspace character (BS): a format effector that causes the print or display position to move one position backward along the line without producing the printing or display of any graphic. (A) (B) see also *numeric backspace character, unit backspace character.*

backtracking: processing a list of names, addresses, and so on, in reverse order.

backup (BAK): pertaining to a system, device, file, or facility that can be used in the event of a malfunction or loss of data. see *switched network backup.*

backup copy: a copy of a file or data set that is kept for reference in case the original file or data set is destroyed.

backup diskette: a diskette that contains information that was copied from another diskette or the disk. It is used in case the original information is unintentionally altered or destroyed.

backup file: a complete or partial copy of a file made for possible later reconstruction of the file. synonymous with *job-recovery control file.* (E)

backup store: a supermarket system that provides backup for the supermarket terminals on store loops (a maximum of two) normally supported by the store controller in the store that is backed up.

Backus Naur form (BNF): a metalanguage used to specify or describe the syntax of a language in which each symbol, by itself, represents a set of strings of symbols. synonymous with *Backus normal form.* (*A*)

Backus normal form (BNO): synonym for *Backus Naur form.* (A)

backward channel: a data-transmission channel, associated with the forward channel, used for supervisory or error-control signals, but with a direction of transmission opposite to that in which user information is being transferred. (E)

backward file recovery: the return of a file to a previous state by using data that have been recorded in a journal. cf. *forward file recovery.* (E)

backward recovery: see *backward file recovery.*

backward supervision: the use of supervisory sequences sent from the slave to the master station. cf. *forward supervision.*

BAK: see *backup.*

balance

(1)   to distribute traffic over the line terminals at a central office as uniformly as possible. Without load balancing, a portion of the switching equipment may become overloaded even though the total capacity of the system has not been exceeded. (F)

(2)   to adjust the impendance of circuits and balance networks to achieve specified return loss objectives at junctions of two-wire and four-wire circuits. (F)

balanced circuit: a circuit that is terminated by a network whose impedence balances the impedance of the line so that the return losses are infinite.

balanced error:

(1)   an error relating to a range having a balance of zero, or a mean value of zero.

(2)   a set of errors, the distribution of

which has the mean value zero. (A) (B)

balanced merge: an external sort that places strings created by an internal sort phase on half of the available storage devices and then merges strings by moving them back and forth between an equal number of devices until the merging process is complete. (A)

balanced merge sort: a merge sort, which is an external sort, such that the sorted subsets created by the internal sorts are equally distributed among half of the available auxiliary storage devices. The subsets are merged onto the other half of the auxiliary storage devices and the process is repeated until all items are in one sorted set. cf. *unbalanced merge sort.* (*A*)

balanced sorting: a technique used in a sort program to merge strings of sequenced data.

balanced station: synonym for *combined station.*

balance network: an adjustable impedance used to terminate one port of a hybrid such that the hybrid characteristics approach the ideal when used to provide two-wire to four-wire conversion. (F)

band

(1)   a group of tracks on a magnetic drum or on one side of a magnetic disk. (B)

(2)   in data communication, the frequency spectrum between two defined limits. (*A*)

bandwidth: the maximum number of data units that can be transferred along a channel per second.

bank

(1)   an aggregation of similar de-

vices, such as transformers or lamps, connected to each other and used in cooperation.

(2)   in automatic switching, a bank is an assemblage of fixed contacts used to establish electrical connections.

(3)   see *data bank*.

BAM: see *basic access method*.

band-pass: the range of signal frequencies passed by a filter free of significant attenuation.

bandpass filter: a device which allows signal passage to frequencies within its design range and which effectively bars passage to all signals outside that frequency range.

band-stop filters: a filter having a single attentuation band, neither of the cut-off frequencies being zero or infinite.

banking: in optical character recognition, a misalignment of the first character of a line with respect to the left margin.

bank on-line teller system: transactions handled in real time by an on-line bank teller system. Teller consoles at office windows can be linked to the computer and the on-line central file.

banner word: in a file record, the first word.

BAR: see *base address register*.

bar: see *type bar*.

bar-code: a code on labels to be ready by a wand or bar-code scanner. see *bar-code scanner*.

bar-code scanner: an optical device that reads data from documents having characters recorded in the form of parallel bars. The characters are translated into digital signals for storage or processing.

bar printer: an impact printer in which the type slugs are carred on a type bar. (A)

base (B)

(1)   in the numeration system commonly used in scientific papers, the number that is raised to the power denoted by the exponent and then multiplied by the mantissa to determine the real number represented. (B)

(2)   a number that is multiplied by itself as many times as indicated by an exponent.

(3)   a reference value. (*A*)

(4)   the number system in terms of which an arithmetic value is represented.

(5)   see *complement base, data base, floating-point base*. cf. *radix*.

base address

(1)   a numeric value that is used as a reference in the calculation of addresses in the execution of a computer program. (B)

(2)   a given address from which an absolute address is derived by combination with a relative address. (*A*)

base address register (BAR):   a register that holds a base address. synonymous with *base register*. (*A*) (B)

base band: the frequency band occupied by one or more information signals that either modulate a carrier or are transmitted at base band frequency over a suitable medium. (F)

base band channel: connotes that modulation is used in the structure of the channel, as in a carrier system. The usual consequence is phase or frequency offset. The simplest example is a pair of wires that transmits direct current and has no impairments such as phase offset or frequency offset that would destroy waveform.

No modulation is needed to send pulse streams or visual signals. (F)

based storage allocation: in PL/1, the allocation of storage for based variables.

based variable: in PL/1, a variable whose generations are identified by locator variables. A based variable can be used to refer to values of variables of any storage class; it can also be allocated and freed explicitly by use of the ALLOCATE and FREE statements.

base element: in PL/1, the name of a structure member that is not a minor structure.

base item: in PL/1, the automatic, controlled, or static variable or the parameter upon which a defined variable is defined. The name may be qualified, subscripted, or both.

base mass storage volume: see *base volume*.

base notation

(1) a notation consisting of a decimal number, in parenthesis, written as a subscript suffix to a number, its decimal value indicating the radix of the number.

(2) a number written without its radix notation is assumed in the radix of ten.

base number: a quantity that specifies a system of representation for numbers. see *radix numeration system*.

base register (BR): synonym for *base address register*.

base volume: a mass storage volume that can have copies or duplicates.

BASIC (beginner's all-purpose symbolic instruction code): a programming language with a small repertoire of commands and a simple syntax, primarily designed for numerical application.

basic access method (BAM): any access method in which input-output statement causes a corresponding machine input/output operation to occur. cf. *queued access method*.

basic code: synonymous with *absolute code*.

basic controller: the part of a communication controller that performs arithmetic and logic functions.

basic direct access method (BDAM): an access method used to directly retrieve or update particular blocks of a data set on a direct access device.

basic exchange format: a format for exchanging data on diskettes between systems or devices.

basic indexed sequential access method (BISAM): an access method used in one form to directly retrieve or update particular blocks of a data set on a direct access device, using an index to locate the data set. The index is stored in direct access storage along with the data set. Other forms of this method can be used to store or retrieve, in a continuous sequence, blocks of the same set.

basic instruction: in program modification, the instruction that is modified to obtain the instruction that is to be followed. synonymous with *presumptive instruction, unmodified instruction*.

basic linkage: a linkage used repeatedly in one routine, program, or system and that follows the same set of rules every time. see also *linkage*.

basic partitioned access method (BPAM): an access method that can be applied to create program libraries, in direct-access storage, for convenient storage and retrieval of programs.

basic real constant: in FORTRAN, a string of decimal digits containing a decimal point.

basic sequential access method (BSAM): an access method for storing or retrieving data blocks in continuous sequences, using either a sequential-access or a direct-access device.

basic service: at one time this phrase meant plain old telephone service. (P.O.T.S.) The most common usage now is that provided by the FCC in the Second Computer Inquiry—basic service is the common carrier offering of transmission capacity for the movement of information between two or more points. Most authorities on the issue have agreed that the term *basic service* covers both exchange and interexchange offerings. (G)

basic telecommunications access method (BTAM): an access method that permits read/write communications with remote devices.

basis weight: the weight in pounds of a ream (500 sheets) of paper cut to a given standard size for that grade. The basis weight of continuous forms for computer output is based on the size for bond papers.

BAT: see *batch*.

Batab: a U.S. teleordering system.

batch (B) (BAT)
(1) an accumulation of data to be processed.
(2) a group of records or data-processing jobs brought together for processing or transmission.

batched communication: the sending of a large body of data from one station to another station in a network, without intervening responses from the receiving unit. cf. *inquiry/response operation*.

batched job
(1) a job that is grouped with other jobs as input to a computing system.
(2) a job whose job control statements are grouped with job control statements of other jobs as input to a computing system. synonymous with *stacked job*.

batch-header document: a document that accompanies a batch of input documents, used to validate data. For example, a document that includes balances, control totals, hash totals, or check sums. (E)

batch partition: partition in which batch processing takes place.

batch processing (BP)
(1) the processing of data or the accomplishment of jobs accumulated in advance in such a manner that each accumulation thus formed is processed or accomplished in the same run. (B)
(2) the processing of data accumulated over a period of time.
(3) loosely, the execution of computer programs serially.
(4) pertaining to the technique of executing a set of computer programs such that each is completed before the next program of the set is started.
(5) pertaining to the sequential input of computer programs or data. (*A*)
(6) in real-time systems, the processing of related transactions that have been grouped together.
(7) see *remote batch processing, sequential batch processing*. see also *stacked job processing*.

batch-processing interrupt: a major feature of a real-time system made possible through a unique feature permitting remote external units with information of high precedence to interrupt computer processing.

batch region: in a multiprogramming environment, one of several regions controlled by the operating system where batch processing can be performed. There may be several batch regions, which normally run at low priority compared to interactive regions.

batch save/restore: an optional facility of a partitioned outline batch system. It allows a real-time job to preempt on the basis of assigned priorities a partition being used for batch processing. Upon preemption, the batch program is saved on direct-access storage and when the real-time program is completed, the batch program is loaded into storage and execution is resumed.

batch session: a session established between a communication controller and the host system for the purpose of transmitting batches of records or messages.

batch terminal: a terminal that handles a large number of off-line users via high-speed input/output units, typically card readers and line printers.

batch ticket: a control document that summarizes the control totals and identifies the appropriate group of source documents.

batch total

(1) the sum of certain quantities pertaining to batches of unit records, used to verify accuracy of operations on a particular batch of records.

(2) each or any of a number of sums that can be calculated from a series of records which are intended to serve as aids to verify the accuracy of computer activities.

batch transaction files: transactions accumulated as a batch ready for processing against the master file.

batten system: synonymous with *Cordonnier system.*

baud

(1) a unit of signaling speed equal to the number of discrete conditions or signal events per second. For example, one baud equals one-half dot cycle per second in Morse code, one bit per second in a train of binary signals, and one three-bit value per second in a train of signals each of which can assume one of eight different states. (A)

(2) a unit of digital signaling rate. The signaling rate in bauds is equal to the reciprocal of the length in seconds of the signal element when all signal elements have equal lengths. (F)

(3) in asynchronous transmission, the unit of modulation rate corresponding to one unit interval per second; that is, if the duration of the unit interval is 20 milliseconds, the modulation rate is 50 baud. (A)

Baudot code (BAUD): a code for the transmission of data in which five equal-lengths bits represent one character. This code is used in some teletypewriter machines where one start element and one stop element are added. Depending on the system, the stop element may be 1-, 1.42-, or 2-unit intervals in duration.

baud rate: the transmission rate that is in effect synonymous with signal events, usually bits per second.

B-Box (Register): see *index register.*

BC: see *Bliss classification.*

BCC: see *block-check character.*

BCD: see *binary-coded decimal notation.* (A)

BCDIC: see *extended binary coded decimal interchange code.*

BCH: see *block control header.*

BCO: see *binary coded octal.*

BCP: byte control protocol.

BCU: see *block control unit.*

BDAM: see *basic direct method.*

BDRY: see *boundary.*

bead: a small program module written to perform a specific operation. Beads prepared and tested can be strung together and tested in groups known as threads.

beam deflection: on a CRT display device, the process of changing the orientation of the electron beam.

beam store: a magnetic storage unit where electron beams are used for the activation of storage cells. A CRT store is a beam store.

beamwidth: the angular extent over which an antenna detects or transmits a signal.

beat: a fundamental state of the control unit of the computer or the duration of such a state.

begin: a procedure delimiter in the ALGOL language.

begin block: in PL/1, a collection of statements headed by a BEGIN statement and ended by an END statement that is a part of a program that delimits the scope of names and that is activated by normal sequential flow of control, including any branch resulting from a GO TO statement.

beginning of a file label: the record at the beginning of a file which shows information about the file's content and boundaries.

beginning of information marker (BIM): a reflective spot on the rear of a magnetic tape, 10 feet from the physical beginning of the tape, that is sensed photoelectrically to show the point on tape at which recording begins.

beginning-of-tape mark: a mark on a magnetic tape used to indicate the beginning of the permissible recording area; for example, a photoreflective strip, a transparent section of tape. (B) cf. *end-of-tape mark.* (A)

beginning-of-volume label (VOL): an internal label that precedes and indicates the beginning of the set of data contained in a volume. synonymous with *volume label.* (E)

BEL: see *bell character.* (A)

bel (B): 10 decibels.

bell character (BEL): a control character that is used when there is a need to call for human attention and that may activate an alarm or other attention devices. (A) (B)

bellfast: a leased teletypewriter switching system formerly marketed by AT&T.

benchmark (BM): a point of reference from which measurements can be made. see also *benchmark test.*

benchmark problem

(1) a problem used to evaluate the performance of hardware or software or both.

(2) a problem used to evaluate the performance of several computers relative to each other, or a single computer relative to system specifications. (*A*)

benchmark routine: a set of routines or problems that help determine the performance of a given piece of equipment.

benchmark test: a procedure using a set of programs and files designed to evaluate the performance of the hardware and software of a computer in a given configuration. (E)

BEX: *broadband exchange.*

BF: see *blocking factor.*

BG: see *background.*

Bi: see *input blocking factor.* ·

bias

(1) a systematic deviation of a value from a reference value. (B)

(2) the amount by which the average of a set of values departs from a reference value. (*A*)

(3) in teletypewriter applications, the uniform shifting of the beginning of all marking pulses from their proper positions in relation to the beginning of the start pulse.

(4) a type of telegraph distortion resulting in which the significant intervals of the modulation do not all have their exact theoretical duration.

(5) see *ordering bias.*

bias distortion: see *distortion.*

biased data: distribution of file records which is nonrandom with respect to the sequencing or sorting criteria. Biased data impacts on sorting time, depending on the approach used during the first pass on the data.

bias testing: see *marginal check.*

bibliographic(al): relating to the description of documents.

biconditional operation: synonymous with *equivalence operation, exclusive-NOR.*

bid

(1) in the contention form of invitation or selection, an attempt by the computer or by a station to gain control of the line so that it can transmit data.

(2) an attempt to obtain a circuit in a circuit group. A bid may be successful or unsuccessful in seizing a circuit in that group. (C)

bidirectional bus: a bus that can carry signals in either direction. The bus also carries special signals that tell the devices connected to it which way data are passing.

bidirectional flow: flow in either direction represented on the same flow line in a flowchart. (E)

bidirectional printing: alternately printing in either direction. A line printed left-to-right is followed by a line printed right-to-left thereby avoiding usual carriage return delays, greatly increasing throughput.

bifurcation: a logic condition where only two states are possible. This is the basic logic pattern of binary digital computers.

Big Blue: the name competitors call International Business Machines Corporation.

billi-: prefix denoting 10^9, as in billibit, synonymous with *giga-.*

BIM: see *beginning of information marker.*

BIN: see *binary.*

binary (B) (BIN)

(1) pertaining to a selection, choice, or condition that has two possible values or states. (B)

(2) pertaining to a fixed-radix numeration system having a radix of two. (B)

(3) see *Chinese binary, column binary, row binary.* (*A*)

binary arithmetic operation: an arithmetic operation in which the operands and the result are represented in the pure binary numeration system. (B) synonym for *dyadic operation*. (*A*)

binary boolean operation: deprecated term for *dyadic boolean operation*. (A) (B)

binary card: a card containing data in column binary or row binary form. (A)

binary cell: a storage cell that holds one binary character. (A) (B)

binary chain: a series of binary circuits arranged so that each chain will impact on the following circuit.

binary chop: a means of searching a table ordered in a known sequence by comparing the required key with a key midway in the table. synonymous with *binary search, dichotomizing search*.

binary code: a code that makes use of exactly two distinct characters, usually 0 and 1. (A) see also *gray code*.

binary-coded decimal character code: a character set containing 64 6-bit characters. see also *extended binary-coded decimal interchange code*.

binary-coded decimal code: synonym for *binary-coded decimal notation*. (A)

binary-coded decimal interchange code (BCDIC): see *extended binary-coded decimal interchange code*. (A)

binary-coded decimal notation (BCD): a binary-coded notation in which each of the decimal digits is represented by a binary numeral; for example, in binary-coded decimal notation that uses the weights 8-4-2-1, the number "23" is represented by 00100011 (compare its representation 10111 in the pure binary numeration system). synonymous with *binary-coded decimal code, binary-coded decimal representation, coded decimal notation*. (*A*) (B)

binary-coded decimal representation: synonym for *binary-coded decimal notation*. (A)

binary-coded notation: a binary-coded notation in which each of the decimal digits is represented by a binary numeral (A) (B)

binary-control octal (BCO): a system where binary numbers are used to represent the octal digits of an octal number.

binary counter: a counter that counts according to the binary number system.

binary digit (BIT): in binary notation, either of the characters 0 or 1. (A) (B) see *equivalent-binary-digit factor*. synonymous with *bit*.

binary digit characters: in PL/1, the picture specification characters 1, 2, and 3.

binary element: a constituent element of data that takes either of two values or states. The term *bit*, originally the abbreviation for the term *binary digit*, is misused in the sense of binary element or in the sense of Shannon. (A) (B)

binary element string: a string consisting solely of binary elements. (A) (B)

binary half-adder: a half-adder with digits representing binary signals that receive two inputs and delivers two outputs.

binary incremental representation: incremental representation in which the value of an increment is rounded to one of the two values of plus or minus one quantum and is represented by one binary digit. (B)

binary notation

(1) any notation that uses two dif-

ferent characters, usually the binary digits 0 and 1, for example, the gray code. The gray code is a binary notation but not a pure binary numeration system. (B)

(2) fixed-radix notation where the radix is two. For example, in binary notation the numerical 110.01 represents the number 1×2 squared plus 1×2 to the first power plus 1×2 to the minus 2 power, that is, $6\frac{1}{4}$.

(3) a binary number. Loosely, a binary numeral. (*A*)

binary number: a component of computer language, which usually contains more than one figure. The numbers allowed are 0 and 1. see *binary numeral*.

binary numeral

(1) a numeral in the pure binary numeration system; for example, the binary numeral 101 is equivalent to the Roman numeral V. (B)

(2) a binary representation of a number; for example, 101 is a binary numeral and V is the equivalent Roman numeral. (*A*)

binary numeration system: synonym for *pure binary numeration system*. (A)

binary operation: deprecated term for *binary arithmetic operation, boolean operation*. (A) (B)

binary operator: an arithmetic operator having two terms. The binary operators that can be used in absolute or relocatable expressions and arithmetic expressions are: addition (+), subtraction (−), multiplication (*), and division (/). synonym for *dyadic operator*. (A) cf. *unary operator*.

binary pair: a circuit having two states, each needing an appropriate trigger for excitation and transition

from one state to the other.

binary picture data: in PL/1, arithmetic picture data specified by picture specifications containing the following types of picture specification characters: binary digit characters; the virtual point picture character; the exponent character, K; and the sign character, S.

binary point: the point in a binary number separating the integral from the fractional part.

binary search: a dichotomizing search in which, at each step of the search, the set of items is partitioned into two equal parts, some appropriate action being taken in the case of an odd number of items. (A) (B) synonymous with *binary chop*.

binary serial signaling rate: in two-state serial transmission, the reciprocal of the unit interval measured in seconds and expressed in bits per second. (E)

binary signaling: a communications mode where information is passed by the presence and absence, or plus and minus variations, of one parameter of the signaling medium only.

binary symmetric channel: a channel designed to convey messages consisting of binary characters and that has the property that the conditional probabilities of changing any one character to the other character are equal. (A) (B)

binary synchronous communication (BSC)

(1) communication using binary synchronous line discipline.

(2) a uniform procedure, using a standardized set of control characters and control character sequences, for synchronous transmis-

sion of binary-coded data between stations.

binary synchronous transmission: data transmission in which synchronization of characters is controlled by timing signals generated at the sending and receiving stations. see also *start-stop transmission*.

binary-to-decimal conversion: conversion of a binary number to the equivalent decimal number, that is, a base-two number to a base-ten number.

bind

(1) to assign a value to a variable; in particular, to assign a value to a parameter. (A) (B)

(2) to associate an absolute address, virtual address, or device identifier with a symbolic address or label in a computer program. (B)

binder group: a group of cable pairs within a cable sheath that are twisted and bound together during cable construction. (F)

binder-hole card: a card that contains one or more holes for binding. (A)

bionics: a branch of technology relating the functions, characteristics, and phenomena of living systems to the development of mechanical systems. (A)

bipolar: pertaining to ordinary transistors and integrated circuits.

bipolar signal: a digital signal technique that uses either a positive or a negative excursion (always alternating) for one state and ground for the other state. (F)

bipolar transmission: synonym for *polar transmission*.

biquinary code: a notation in which a decimal digit n is represented by a pair of numerals, a being 0 or 1, b being 0, 1, 2, 3, or 4, and ($5a + b$) being equal to n. The two digits are often represented by a series of two binary numerals. (A) (B)

BIS: see *business information system*.

BISAM: see *basic indexed sequential access method*.

bistable:. pertaining to a device capable of assuming either one of two stable states. (A)

bistable circuit: a trigger circuit that has two stable states. (A) (B) synonymous with *bistable trigger circuit, flip-flop*.

bistable multivibrator: synonymous with *flip-flop*.

bistable trigger circuit: synonym for *bistable circuit*. (A)

bisynchronous: the continuous exchange of synchronization signals between communications units.

bit (B)

(1) in the pure binary numeration system, either of the digits 0 and 1. synonymous with *binary digit*. (B)

(2) the smallest possible unit of information. One bit is enough to tell the difference between two opposites such as yes or no.

(3) deprecated term for *binary element, Shannon*. (A) (B)

(4) see *check bit, information bits, parity bit, redundancy check bit, sign bit*.

bit bumming: attempting to squeeze the required software into the minimum amount of memory in a microcomputer system.

bit density: a measure of the number of bits received per unit of length or area.

bite: alternative spelling of *byte*.

bit grinding: slang, the processing of data-processing instructions.

bit location: a storage position located on a record capable of storing one bit.

bit parallel: a means of simultaneous movement or transmission over individual wires of all bits in a contiguous set of bits.

bit pattern: a combination of n binary digits representing 2 to the n (2^n) possible choices; for example, a three-bit pattern represents eight possible combinations.

bit position: a character position in a word in a binary notation. (A) (B)

bit rate: the speed at which bits are transmitted, usually expressed in bits per second. see also *baud*.

bit serial: the sequential transmission of the bits in a group through one channel.

bit slice microprocessor: microprocessors; for example, of two- or four-bit word length, chained together and microprogrammed to form processors of long word length. Each bit slice performs a unique function within the chain.

bit-slicing processing: microprocessors that permit large scale parallel data processing, that is, allowing many jobs to be done at the same time.

bits per second (BPS) (B/S): digital information rate expressed as the number of binary information units transmitted per second. *see symbol.* (F)

bit stream: a binary signal without regard to group by character.

bit string: a string consisting solely of bits. (A) (B)

bit-string operators: in PL/1, the logical operators − (not), & (and), and / (or).

bit track: a track on a magnetic drum or disk where bits are recorded or read by a read/write head. cf. *logical track.*

bit twiddler: slang, an operator of computer equipment.

BKGRD: see *background.*

black box: slang, a device that performs a specific function, but whose detailed activity is not known, or not specified, in the context of the discussion.

black box approach: acceptance of computed results without questioning the method of working of the computer.

"black recording"

(1) in facsimile systems using amplitude-modulation, that form of recording in which the maximum received power corresponds to the maximum density of the record medium.

(2) in a facsimile system using frequency modulation, the form of recording in which the lowest received frequency corresponds to the maximum density of the record medium.

blank

(1) a part of a data medium in which no characters are recorded. (A)

(2) in computer graphics, to suppress the display of all or part of a display image.

blank character: a graphic representation of the space character. (A)

blank coil: a tape (for perforation) with only the feed holes punched.

blank common: in FORTRAN, an unlabeled (unnamed) common block.

blank deleter: a device that eliminates the receiving of blanks in perforated paper tape.

blank diskette: see *unformatted diskette.*

blanking: in computer graphics, the suppression of the display of one or more display elements or display groups. (E)

blank instruction: synonymous with *do-nothing operation*.

blank medium: various types or blank forms of media.

blast: to release internal or external memory area under dynamic storage allocation. synonymous with *blow*.

bleed: in optical character recognition, spreading of ink beyond the edges of a printed character.

blind: to make a device nonreceptive to unwanted data, through recognition of field definition characters in the received data. see also *lockout, polling, selection*.

blind keyboard

(1) a keyboard that does not produce a visual display.

(2) hardcopy of data entered through a keyboard.

b-line: synonymous with *index register*.

blinking: in computer graphics, an intentional regular change in the intensity of a display element or a display group on a display space. (E)

blip: synonym for *document mark*. (A) (B)

blip counting: a position-sensing approach based on adding or deleting one from a location register, based on the direction in which each position mark (blip) passes a sensor.

Bliss classification (BC): a classification scheme using 26 alphabetic classes (A-Z) with subunits of each main class shown by the addition of further letters.

BLK: see *block*.

block (B) (BLK)

(1) a string of records, a string of words, or a character string formed for technical or logic reasons to be treated as an entity. (B)

(2) a set of things, such as words, characters, or digits, handled as a unit.

(3) a collection of contiguous records recorded as a unit. Blocks are separated by interblock gaps and each block may contain one or more records.

(4) a group of bits, or n-ary digits, transmitted as a unit. An encoding procedure is generally applied to the group of bits or n-ary digits for error-control purposes. (*A*)

(5) in word processing, the ability to define information so as to move it from one point to another within a text element or into another text element, or to edit it. (D)

(6) in word processing, a sequential string of text whose end points are defined by the user with cursor movement keys at a display work station.

(7) in PL/1, a begin block or procedure block.

(8) to record data in a block.

(9) see *program block, record blocking*.

block cancel character: a cancel character used to indicate that the preceding portion of the block, back to the most recently occurring block mark, is to be disregarded. synonymous with *block ignore character*. (*A*) (B)

block character: see *end-of-transmission-block character*. (A)

block check: that part of the error-control procedure used for determining that a data block is structured according to given rules. (E)

block-check character (BCC): in longitudinal redundancy checking and cyclic redundancy checking, a character that is transmitted by the sender after each message block and is compared with a block-check character computed by the receiver to determine if the transmission was successful.

block-check procedure: that part of the error-control procedure used for determining that a data block is structured according to given rules. (E)

block control: a storage location holding information in condensed, formalized form needed for the control of a task, function, operation, or quantity of information.

block control header (BCH): see *block control unit.*

block control unit (BCU): a network control program data area built by the channel manager and other routines such as the block handling and control command routines. Used to request work, it contains a buffer prefix, an event control block, a work area, and a basic transmission unit.

block copy: to copy a file, from one medium to another, without altering its contents. see *block transfer.*

block diagram: a diagram of a system, a computer, or a device, in which the principal parts are represented by suitably annotated geometrical figures to show both the basic functions of the parts and their functional relationships. (B) cf. *flowchart.*

block-error rate: the ratio of the number of blocks incorrectly received to the total number of blocks sent. (C)

blockette: a subdivision of a block which is input and output as a single unit or block in its own right.

block gap: deprecated term for *inter-block gap (2).*

block header: data appearing at the beginning of a block that describes the organization of the file and relationship between blocks.

block heading statement: in PL/1, the PROCEDURE or BEGIN statement that heads a block of statements.

block ignore character: synonym for *block cancel character.* (A)

blocking
(1) the process of combining two or more records into one block.
(2) the process of combining incoming messages into a single message. see also *concentrator.*
(3) in a telephone switching system, inability to make a connection or obtain a service because the devices needed for the connection or service are in use.
(4) synonym for *concentration.*
(5) cf. *deblocking.*

blocking factor (BF): the number of logical records in each block. see also *input blocking factor, output blocking factor.* (B)

blocking of records: synonymous with *grouping of records.*

block length
(1) the number of records, words, or characters in a block. (B)
(2) a measure of the size of a block, usually specified in units such as records, words, computer words, or characters. (A)
(3) synonymous with *block size.*

block list: a printout of a file's content where records are listed in the sequence in which they appear.

block loading: bringing the control sections of a load module into adjoining positions of main storage. cf. *scatter loading.*

block movement: in word processing, the ability to move a block of information from one point to another within a document or into another document. (D)

block multiplexer channel: a multiplexer channel that interleaves blocks of data. see also *byte multiplexer channel*. cf. *selector channel*.

block multiplexer mode: a data transfer mode that permits interleaving of records in block form. cf. *byte multiplexer mode*.

block paging: paging of multiple pages simultaneously to or from real or external storage.

block parity system: a system using an additional bit to a block of information to find single-bit errors in the entire block.

block prefix: an optional, variable length field that may precede unblocked records or blocks of records recorded in American National Standard Code for Information Interchange (AS-CII) on magnetic tapes.

block record: a specific storage area of a fixed size containing a main memory or file storage, set into standard blocks to permit more flexibility in storage allocation and control.

block separation: information indicating that the next character is the first character of a block of supplementary information. (C)

block separator: the character indicating that the next character is the first of a block of supplementary information. (C)

block size: synonymous with *block length*.

block sort: a sort that separates a file into segments, using the highest-or-der portion of the key, orders the segments separately, and then joins them.

block structure: a hierarchy of program blocks. (A)

block transfer: the process, initiated by a single action, of transferring one or more blocks of data. (A) (B)

blow: pertaining to the writing into a programmable read-only memory (PROM), or variants, such as EPROM. cf. *zap*. synonymous with *blast*, *burn*.

blow back: synonym for *reenlargement*. (E)

blowing: programming read only memory (ROM) utilizing special devices; as in PROM blowing.

blue ribbon program: a program that runs effectively upon first try. synonymous with *star program*.

BM

(1) see *benchmark*.

(2) see *business machine*.

BNF

(1) see *Backus Naur form*.

(2) see *Backus normal form*. (A)

(3) see *normal form Backus*.

BNO: see *Backus normal form*.

Bo: see *output blocking factor*.

board: an electrical panel that can be changed with an addition or deletion of external wiring. synonym for *panel*, *plugboard*, *wire board*.

board tester: a unit, usually computer controlled, which performs electronic tests on printed circuit boards.

BOCs: 22 operating companies of the Bell System.

boldface: in word processing, typing each character twice, but the second impression is slightly to one side of the first.

bomb: deprecated term for when a

program fails spectacularly.

book: a group of source statements written in the assembler or COBOL language.

book message: a message to be sent to two or more destinations.

BOOL: see *boolean.*

boolean (B) (BOOL)

(1) pertaining to the processes used in the algebra formulated by George Boole. (A)

(2) a value of 0 or 1 represented internally in binary notation.

boolean ADD: synonym for *OR* (3). (A)

boolean complementation: deprecated term for *negation.* (A)

boolean connective: a symbol used to connect the operands in a statement of a boolean operation, showing which type of operation is involved.

boolean function: a switching function in which the number of possible values of the function and each of its independent variables is two. (A)(B)

boolean operation

(1) any operation in which each of the operands and the result take one of two values. (B)

(2) an operation that follows the rules of boolean algebra. (B)

(3) see *dyadic boolean operation, n-adic boolean operation, n-ary boolean operation.* (A)

boolean operation table: an operation table in which each of the operands and the result take one of two values. (A) (B)

boolean operator: an operator, each of the operands of which and the result of which take one of two values. (B) see *dyadic operator, monadic operator.* (A)

BOOT: see *bootstrap.*

bootleg program: a conventional rou-tine or stop-gap program that begins, captures, and processes information in a specifically prescribed form, usually to start or initiate the reading of a program by means of its own action.

bootstrap (BOOT)

(1) an existing version, perhaps a primitive version, of a computer program that is used to establish another version of the program. (B)

(2) a technique or device designed to bring itself into a desired state by means of its own action; for example, a machine routine whose first few instructions are sufficient to bring the rest of itself into the computer from an input device.

(3) that part of a computer program used to establish another version of the computer program.

(4) to use a bootstrap. (B)

(5) see also *bootstrap loader, initial program loader.* (A)

bootstrap loader: an input routine in which simple present computer operations are used to load instructions which in turn cause further instructions to be loaded until the complete computer program is in storage. (B) see also *bootstrap, initial program loader.* (A)

bootstrap memory: a time-saving unit built into the main computer.

borrow: an arithmetically negative carry. see *end-around borrow.* (A)

borrow digit: a digit that is generated when a difference in a digit place is arithmetically negative and that is transferred for processing elsewhere. In a positional representation system, a borrow digit is transferred to the digit place with the next higher weight for processing there. (A) (B)

BOT: beginning of tape.

both-way communication: synonym for *two-way simultaneous communication.*

both-way operation: synonym for *duplex operation.*

bounceless contact: a mechanical contact conditioned by means of a flip-flop or a device with only one stable state to eliminate all noise during contact.

bouncing: vibration of mechanical switch contacts following closure, which results in a short period of intermittent conduction.

bouncing busy hour: see *busy hour, bouncing.*

bound: in PL/1, the upper or lower limit of an array dimension.

boundary (BDRY): see *character boundary, integral boundary.*

boundary alignment: the positioning in main storage of a fixed-length field, such as a half-word or double-word, on an integral boundary for that unit of information.

BP: see *batch processing.*

BPAM: see *basic partitioned access method.*

BPI: bytes per inch.

bpi: bits per inch.

"B" pins: module pins used only for stacking purposes and located in the top substrate.

BPS

(1) bits per second. In serial transmission, the instantaneous bit speed with which a device or channel transmits a character.

(2) bytes per second.

BR

(1) see *base register.*

(2) see *break.*

branch

(1) a set of instructions that are executed between two successive branch instructions. (A)

(2) in a network, a direct route between two adjacent nodes. (E)

(3) loosely, a conditional jump. (A)

(4) in the execution of a computer program, to select one from a number of alternative sets of instructions. (A) (B)

(5) to select a branch as in (1). (A)

(6) deprecated term for *jump.* (A) (B)

branch cable: a cable that diverges from a main cable to reach some secondary point.

branching: a computer operation, like switching where a selection is made between two or more possible courses of action depending upon some related fact or condition.

branching networks: electrical networks, such as filters, isolators, and circulators, used for transmission or reception of signals over two or more channels on one antenna.

branch instruction: an instruction that controls branching. synonymous with *decision instruction.* deprecated term for *jump instruction.* (A) (B)

branchpoint

(1) a point in a computer program at which branching occurs, in particular the address or the label of an instruction. (B)

(2) a place in a routine where a branch is selected. (A)

branch table: a table of arguments and related addresses to which control can be passed on the basis of tests.

breadboard: an experimental model of a unit used to test the parameters of the design.

break (BR):
(1) to interrupt the sending end and take control of the circuit at the receiving end.
(2) a separation of continuous paper forms, usually at the perforation.

break key: synonym for *stop key*. (D)

breakpoint
(1) a place in a computer program, usually specified by an instruction, where its execution may be interrupted by external intervention or by a monitor program. (A) (B)
(2) an instruction address stop that can be established by command. see *instruction address stop*.

breakpoint halt: a closed loop consisting of a single jump instruction that effects a jump to itself, often used to achieve a breakpoint. synonymous with *breakpoint instruction*, *dynamic stop*. (*A*) (B)

breakpoint instruction: synonym for *breakpoint halt*. (A) (B)

breakpoint switch: a manually operated switch that controls conditional operations at breakpoints; used primarily in debugging.

break sequence: in start-stop protocol, the transmission of all O bits.

b-register: deprecated term for *index register*. (A) (B)

bridged tap: a cable pair connected in parallel with a customer loop. The connection (tap) may occur at the central office or at some point along a cable route. (F)

bridgeware: hardware or software, used to transcribe data files or programs written for one type of computer into a format that can be used with another type of computer.

bridging: in optical character recognition, a combination of peaks and smudges that may close or partially close a loop of a character.

brightness ratio: a measure of contrast; the ratio between the brightest and darkest parts of a printed paper sheet.

broadband: synonymous with *wide band*.

broadcast: the dissemination of information to several receivers simultaneously, usually via electromagnetic signals.

broadcast satellite: frequency allocation for communications satellites which identifies the uplink stations only.

brush: an electrical apparatus for reading information from a punched card.

brute-force approach: an attempt to comprehend with existing equipment the size of problems that do not use precise computation or logical manipulations.

BS: see *backspace character*. (A)

B/S: see *bits per second*.

BSAM: see *basic sequential access method*.

BSC: see *binary synchronous communication*.

BSC or SS line: a line that uses binary synchronous or start-stop protocols.

b-store: synonymous with *index register*.

BTAM: see *basic telecommunications access method*.

BTE: see *business terminal equipment*. (F)

BTU: British thermal unit.

bubble memory: a memory device placed on a chip. The bubbles are microscopically small, magnetized domains that can be moved across a thin magnetic film by a magnetic field. Magnetic-bubble chips that store a million bits of information have been fabricated. Magnetic bubble memory is not as fast as RAM or ROM, but many times faster than mass memory devices such as tapes and disks.

bubble sort: an exchange sort in which the sequence of examination of pairs of items is reversed whenever an exchange is made. synonymous with *sifting sort.* (A)

bucket: in random-access memory, a unit or place of storage.

BUF: see *buffer.*

buffer (BUF)

(1) a routine or storage used to compensate for a difference in rate of flow of data, or time of occurrence of events, when transferring data from one device to another.

(2) an isolating circuit used to prevent a driven circuit from influencing the driving circuit.

(3) to allocate and schedule the use of buffers. (*A*)

(4) an area of storage that is temporarily reserved for use in performing an input/output operation, into which data is read or from which data is written. synonymous with *I/O area.*

(5) a portion of storage for temporarily holding input or output data.

buffer channel: a means of interfacing devices with a computer, which contains memory addressing potential and an ability to transfer words.

buffered amplifier: an amplifier designed to isolate a preceding circuit from the effects of a following circuit.

buffered computer: a computer system with a storage unit that allows for input and output data to be stored

temporarily in order to match the slow speed of input-output devices with the higher speeds of the computer.

buffered device: a device that has I/O elements queued to a direct access device before being written.

buffered input: the ability to enter new items or function instructions into the machine before current operations are completed. (D)

buffering: see *anticipatory buffering.* (A)

buffer management: a portion of the network control program supervisor that controls buffer chains, senses critical storage usage requirements, and initiates recovery procedures.

buffer output: a buffer developed to receive and store data being transmitted into a computer, and that usually includes instructions.

buffer pad characters: a sequence of characters that the network control program sends to an access method buffer preceding message data, to allow space for the host access method to insert message prefixes.

buffer pool: an area of storage in which all buffers of a program are kept.

buffer prefix: an area within a buffer that contains buffer control information. A user must allow space for the buffer prefix when specifying buffer size.

buffer storage

(1) a storage device that is used to compensate for differences in the rate of flow of data between components of an automatic data-processing system, or for the time of occurrence of events in the components. (A) (B)

(2) in word processing, a temporary storage in which text is held for processing or communication. (D)

buffer store: see *buffer storage*.

bug

(1) a mistake or malfunction. (A)

(2) an error in a program.

built-in adapter: deprecated term for *integrated adapter*.

built-in check: synonym for *automatic check*. (A)

built-in function: a function that is supplied by a language.

bulk storage: deprecated term for *mass storage*. (B)

bulk store: synonymous with *backing store*.

burn: synonymous with *blow*.

burn-in: the phase of component testing where basic flaws or early failures are screened out by running the circuit for a specified length of time, such as a week, generally at increased temperatures in some sort of oven.

burst

(1) in data communication, a sequence of signals counted as one unit in accordance with some specific criterion or measure.

(2) to separate continuous-form paper into discrete sheets.

(3) see *error burst*. (A)

burst isochronous: synonym for *burst transmission*. (E)

burst mode: a mode in which data is transmitted by means of burst transmission.

burst modem: in satellite communications, each station sends high-speed bursts of data which are interleaved with one another. These bursts must be precisely timed, and consequently are sent using a burst modem.

burst traffic: transmission of data in bursts, instead of continuously as in the exchange of information in a telephone conversation.

burst transmission: data transmission at a specific data signaling rate during controlled intermittent intervals. synonymous with *burst isochronous*. (E)

bus (B): one or more conductors used for transmitting signals or power. (A)

bus bar: deprecated term for *bus*.

bus controller: the unit in charge of generating bus commands and control signals.

bus driver: a power amplifier used to drive logic elements with a conductor or bus. synonymous with *line driver*.

bus extender: a device permitting additional cards to be plugged into a computer's bus.

business data processing: data processing for business purposes, for example, recording and summarizing the financial transactions of a business. synonym for *administrative data processing*. (A) (B)

business information system (BIS): a combination of people, data processing equipment, input/output devices, and communications facilities. The system must accept information at the point where it is generated, transport it to the point where it is processed, process it, and finally deliver the information to the point where it is to be used.

business machine (BM): a machine designed to facilitate clerical operations in commercial or scientific activities.

business machine clocking: a time-base oscillator supplied by the business machine for regulating the bit rate of transmission. synonymous with *nondata-set clocking*. cf. *data-set clocking*.

business service: telecommunications service used in a business environment. (F)

business terminal equipment (BTE): terminal equipment used by business customers including teletypewriter machines, data serts, key telephone systems, PBXs, and so forth. (F)

bussback: the connection, by a common carrier, of the output portion of a circuit back to the input portion of a circuit. see also *loopback test*.

bust: the malperformance of a programmer or machine operator.

bus termination: the electrical means of preventing reflections at the end of a bus that is only needed in high-speed systems or poorly designed low-speed systems.

bust this: a phrase used instead of a normal message ending to indicate that the entire message, including heading, is to be disregarded. see also *CANTRAN*.

bus wire: a group of wires that permits the memory, the CPU, and the input-output devices to exchange words.

busy hour: that hour during which the portion of the telephone network in question carries the most traffic. Traffic peaks caused by holidays or special events are not considered. Switching systems and trunk groups are normally sized for the busy hour. see *peak load*. (F)

busy hour, bouncing: the highest load may not occur at the same hour on all days. If the highest load is selected for each day without regard to

the hour in which is occurs, the average of these loads is said to occur in the bouncing busy hour. Traffic measurements are usually made over the five working days of each week. see *busy hour*. (F)

busy hour, fixed: when the hourly loads are averaged across days for each hour of the day, the maximum of these averages defines the fixed busy hour. Traffic measurements are usually made over the five working days of each week. synonymous with *time-consistent busy hour*. see *busy hour*. (F)

busy tone: an audible signal indicating a call cannot be completed because the called line is busy. The tone is applied 60 times per minute. (F)

bypass procedure: a procedure used to get the most information into the main computer when the line control computer fails.

byproduct: data developed without further effort from a unit whose basic purpose is to perform some other operation.

byte (B)
(1) a binary character operated upon as a unit and usually shorter than a computer word. (A)
(2) the representation of a character.
(3) see *n-bit byte*. (A)

byte manipulation: manipulating, as individual instructions, groups of bits, such as characters.

byte mode: synonym for *multiplex mode*.

byte multiplexer channel: a multiplexer channel that interleaves bytes of data. see also *block multiplexer channel*. cf. *selector channel*.

byte multiplexer mode: a data transfer mode that permits interleaving of bytes of data. cf. *block multiplexer mode.*

byte multiplexing: the process where time slots on a channel are delegated to individual slow input-output devices so that bytes from one after another can be interlaced on the channel to or from main memory.

byte-serial transmission: transmission in which successive bytes follow one another in sequence. (C)

C

  (1) see *capacitor*.
  (2) see *carry*.
  (3) see *centi*.
  (4) see *clear*.
  (5) see *clock*.
  (6) see *computer*.
  (7) see *constant*.
  (8) see *control*.
  (9) see *controller*.
  (10) see *counter*.

CA: see *control area*.

cable: one or more conductors found within a protective sheathing. When multiple conductors exist, they are electrically isolated from each other.

cable casting: the dissemination of information via cables.

cable fill: the percentage of pairs in a cable sheath actually assigned and used. (F)

cable television service: the reception and retransmission of broadcast television and radio signals and the origination of television and radio programming which is selected by the cable television service for mass distribution to multiple subscribers who pay to receive such services. (G)

cable vault: an area, generally on the lower level of a telephone company building, where cables enter the building. (F)

cache: in a processing unit, a high-speed buffer storage that is continually updated to contain recently accessed contents of main storage. Its purpose is to reduce access time.

CAD: see *computer-aided design*.

CAD/CAM: an acronym for computer-aided design/computer-aided manufacturing. CAD permits the design and testing of a product on a computer screen in simulation. CAM permits a computer to direct the manufacture and assembly of a product.

CAE: see *computer-aided engineering*.

CAI: see *computer-assisted instruction*.

CAL: see *Conversational Algebraic Language*.

calculating punch: a calculator with a card reader and a card punch that reads the data on a punched card, performs some arithmetic operations or logic operations on the data, and punches the results on the same or another punched card. synonymous with *multiplying punch*. (*A*) (B)

calculator: a device that is especially suitable for performing arithmetic operations, but that requires human intervention to alter its stored program, if any, and to initiate each operation or sequence of operations. (E)

calculator chip: a chip with a microprocess that has a built-in microprogram to solve arithmetic functions.

calculator for extensive use: a calculator intended for continuous operation, in the design of which ergonomic factors are a prime consideration. (D)

calculator for occasional use: a calculator intended for occasional operation, in the design of which ergonomic factors do not constitute a major consideration. (D)

calculator with algebraic logic: a machine in which the operating rule for addition and subtraction is such that the operating instruction is given before the input of the relevant item. When combining addition and subtraction with multiplication and division it is unnecessary to take interim totals. (D)

calculator with arithmetic logic: a machine in which the operating rule for addition and subtraction is such that the operating instruction is given after the input of the relevant item. When combining addition and subtraction with multiplication and division it is necessary to take interim totals. (D)

calculator with keyboard-controlled addressable storage: a machine allowing keyboard-controlled storage and accumulation of data, the data in the storage device being changed only by program operations addressed to those devices. (D)

calculator without addressable storage: a machine in which data cannot be stored without being cleared by subsequent operations, but which may or may not have a constant facility. (D)

calculator without programmability: a machine whose program cannot be changed by the operator. (D)

calculator with program-controlled addressable storage: a machine allowing only program-controlled storage and accumulation of data, the data in the storage devices being changed only by program operations addressed to those devices. (D)

calculator with programmability: a machine whose program can be changed by the operator. (D)

calculator with specified data storage capacity: a machine capable of storing a stated maximum number of digits in each of a stated number of storage devices. (D)

calculator with specified entry capacity: a machine capable of accepting entry of a stated maximum number of digits. (D)

calculator with specified numerical data processing capacity: a machine capable of processing a stated maximum number of digits. (D)

calculator with specified output capacity: a machine capable of displaying and/or printing a stated maximum number of digits. (D)

calculus of variations: the theory of maxima and minima of definite integrals whose integrand is a function of the dependent variables, the independent variables, and their derivates. (A)

call

(1) the action of bringing a computer program, a routine, or a subroutine into effect, usually by specifying the entry conditions and jumping to an entry point. (B)

(2) in computer programming, to execute a call. (*A*) (B)

(3) in data communication, the action performed by the calling party, or the operations necessary in making a call, or the effective use made of a connection between two stations.

(4) a transmission for the purpose of identifying the transmitting station for which the transmission is intended.

(5) an attempt to reach a user, whether or not successful. (C)

(6) to transfer control to a specified closed subroutine. (A)

(7) see *subroutine call.* (A)

(8) synonymous with *cue.* (A)

call by reference: a subroutine or procedure call where the addresses of the parameter's storage locations are passed to the subroutine.

call by value: a subroutine or procedure call in where the actual values of the parameters are passed to the subroutine.

call directing code (CDC): a Bell System term for an identifying call, which is transmitted on an outlying telegraph receiver and automatically turns on its printer. see also *selective calling, station selection code.*

call establishment: the sequence of events for the establishment of a data connection.

call forwarding: when activated by a customer, all calls to that line are automatically routed to another line designated during activation. (F)

calligraphic plotter: in computer graphics, a plotter that draws an image on a CRT consisting of lines alone.

calling: the process of transmitting selection signals in order to establish a connection between data stations. (C)

calling sequence

(1) an arrangement of instructions, and in some cases of data also, that is necessary to perform a call. (A) (B)

(2) a polling list. see also *polling.*

call not accepted signal: a call control signal sent by the called data-terminal equipment (DTE) to indicate that it does not accept the incoming call. (E)

call number: a group of characters identifying a subroutine.

call processor (CP): a subsystem consisting of a microcomputer, a synchronizer, and a random access memory. Contains sufficient memory to accommodate the call-processing program and its data base.

call progress signal: a call control signal transmitted from the data circuit-terminating equipment (DCE) to the calling data-terminal equipment (DTE) to indicate the progress of the establishment of a call, the reason why the connection could not be established, or any other network condition. (E)

call store: the equipment unit of an electronic switching system that provides temporary memory storage of information pertaining to call processing and maintenance. (F)

call waiting: a custom calling service that provides a tone burst to a customer on an established call when a second call has been directed to that line. The notification tone is heard only by the called customer, whereas the incoming caller hears regular audible ringing. (F)

CAM: computer-aided manufacturing. see *CAD/CAM*.

CAMA: see *centralized automatic message accounting*. (F)

CAMA-ONI: see *centralized automatic message accounting-operator number identification operator*. (F)

camp-on: a method of holding a call for a line that is in use and of signaling when it becomes free. see *call waiting*. synonymous with *clamp-on*.

CAN: see *cancel character*. (A)

cancel (CNCL): when used, cancels the execution of the current job in the partition in which the command was given.

cancel character (CAN)

(1) a control character used by some convention to indicate that the data with which it is associated are in error or are to be disregarded. synonymous with *ignore character*. (B)

(2) an accuracy control character used to indicate that the data with which it is associated are in error or are to be disregarded.

(3) see *block cancel character*. (A)

cancel key: synonym for *stop key*. (D)

canned paragraphs: in word processing, describes pre-recorded paragraphs in frequent usage, and combined in various ways.

canned software: synonymous with *package*.

CANTRAN: cancel transmission. see also *bust this*.

CAP: see *capacity*.

capacitance: a measure of the ability to store electric charge.

capacitor (C): an electronic unit with the properties of capacitance.

capacitor storage: a storage device that uses the capacitive properties of certain materials. (A) (B)

capacity (CAP): see *channel capacity, storage capacity*. (A)

capstan: a small cylindrical pulley used to regulate the speed of magnetic tape in a tape drive.

capture: in optical character readers, to gather picture data from a field on an input document, using a special scan.

card (CD): see *aperture card, binary card, binder-hole card, check card, double card, edge-coated card, edge-notched card, edge-punched card, flash card, header card, Hollerith card, laced card, magnetic card, mark-sensing card, punch card, punched card, scored card, short card, source data card, stub card, trailer card*. (A)

card cage: a chassis or frame that holds a central processor, memory cards and interfaces. synonymous with *card chassis*.

card chassis: synonymous with *card cage*.

card checking: checking the validity of a card image transfer.

card code: the combinations of punched holes that represent characters (e.g., letters, digits) in a punched card.

card column
(1)   a line of punch positions parallel to the storage edges of a punch card. (B)
(2)   a line of punch positions parallel to the Y datum in line of a punch card. (*A*)

card cycle: time needed to read and/or punch a card.

card deck: a group of punched cards. synonymous with *card pack*. (B)

card feed: the mechanism that moves punch cards from the card hopper to the card path. (E)

card field: a specific combination of punch positions, mark-sensing positions, or both, on a card. (A)

card form: see *printed card form*. (A)

card format: pertaining to the columns and fields of data in a punched card.

card hopper: the part of a card-processing device that holds the cards to be processed and makes them available to a card-feed mechanism. (B) cf. *card stacker*. (*A*)

card image: a one-to-one representation of the hole patterns of a punched card; for example, a matrix in which a 1 represents a punch and a 0 represents the absence of a punch. (A)

card input: the introduction of information to a processing unit with punched cards. The data channel used to feed card information into a device.

card jam: a malfunction of a card-processing device in which cards become jammed. (A)

card loader: a routine used to load a program from punched cards into store.

card pack: synonym for *card deck*.

card path: the part of a card-process-ing device that moves and guides the card through the device. (B)

card-programmed computer: either a mini-sized computer or an older computer, limited in input operation in gathering information from punched, wired, or magnetic cards or as preprogrammed computers.

card punch (CP)
(1)   a computer-actuated punch that punches holes in a punch card or punched card. (B)
(2)   a device that punches holes in a card to represent data. (A)
(3)   synonymous with *automatic punch*.
(4)   deprecated term for *keypunch*. (B)

card reader (CDR) (CR)
(1)   a device that reads or senses the holes in a punched card, transforming the data from hole patterns to electrical signals. (B)
(2)   an input device that senses hole patterns in a punched card and translates them into machine language. synonymous with *punched card reader*. (*A*)

card reproducer: a device that reproduces a punch card by punching another similar card.

card row
(1)   a line of punch positions parallel to the longer edges of a punch card. (B)
(2)   a line of punch positions parallel to the X datum line of a punch card. (*A*)

cards: see *continuous-form cards*. (A)

card set: cards and forms, bound in a manner that provides multiple copies of source data. (A)

card sorter: a device that deposits

punched cards in pockets selected according to the hole patterns in the cards. (B)

card stacker: the part of a card-processing device that receives the cards after they have been processed. (B) cf. *card hopper.* (A)

card storage: see *magnetic card storage.* (A)

card-to-tape: pertaining to equipment that transfers information directly from punched cards to punched or magnetic tape.

card track: the part of a card-processing device that moves and guides the card through the device. (A)

card verifying: a way of checking the accuracy of key punching and is a duplication check. A second operator verifies the original punching by depressing the keys of a verifier while reading the identical source data, and the machine compares the key depressed with the hole already punched in the card.

caret: a symbol (^) used to indicate the location of a decimal point.

carousel: the rotary device that shows a data medium such as microfilm at an identified position for reading or recording.

CARR: see *carrier.*

carriage: see *automatic carriage.* (A)

carriage control character: the first character of an output record (line) that is to be printed; it determines how many lines should be skipped before the next line is printed.

carriage control tape
(1) a tape that is used to control vertical tabulation of printing positions or display positions.
(2) a tape that contains line-feed control data for a printing device. (*A*)

carriage return (CR): the operation that prepares for the next character to be printed or displayed at the specified first position on the same line. (A)

carriage return character
(1) a format effector that causes the print or display position to move to the first position on the same line. (A) (B).
(2) a format effector that causes the location of the printing or display position to be moved to the first space on the same printing or display line.
(3) cf. *carrier return character, newline character.*

CARR: see *carrier.*

carried load: the average number of calls that are in progress. The unit, one call, is an Erlang. (F)

carrier (CARR): a continuous frequency capable of being modulated or impressed with a second (informative carrying) signal. see *communication common carrier, data carrier.* see also *automatic carriage.*

carrier holes: the holes in the side margins on continuous forms paper. When placed on the tractor pins, the holes maintain printer alignment and registration and control movement of the paper. synonymous with *tractor holes.*

carrier return character (CRC): a word-processing formatting control that moves the printing or display point to the first position on the next line. Carrier return may be ignored during text adjust mode operations. synonymous with *new-line character.* see *required carrier return character.* cf. *carriage return character.*

carrier's carrier: see *underlying carrier.* (G)

carrier signal: a signal which carries packages, or streams of information.

carrier system: a system for transmitting one or more channels of information by processing and converting to a form suitable for the transmission medium used by the system. Many information channels can be carried by one broad-band carrier system. Common types of carrier systems are frequency division, in which each information channel occupies an assigned portion of the frequency spectrum, and time division, in which each information channel uses the transmission medium for periodic assigned time intervals. (F)

carrier-to-noise ratio: the ratio of received carrier power to the noise level in a given bandwidth, expressed in dB.

carrier wave: an electromagnetic signal to which information can be added by the process of modulation.

carry (C) (CY)

(1)   the action of transferring a carry digit. (B)

(2)   one or more digits, produced in connection with an arithmetic operation on one digit place of two or more numerals in positional notation, that are forwarded to another digit place for processing there.

(3)   the number represented by the digit or digits in (2).

(4)   most commonly, a digit as defined in (2), that arises when the sum or product of two or more digits equals or exceeds the radix of the number representation system.

(5)   less commonly, a borrow.

(6)   the command directing that a carry be forwarded.

(7)   to transfer a carry digit.

(8)   to forward a carry.

(9)   see *addition without carry, cascaded carry, complete carry, end-around carry, high-speed carry, partial carry, standing-on-nines carry.* (*A*)

carry-complete signal: an adder's signal showing that all carriers needed for an operation have been made.

carry digit: a digit that is generated when a sum or a product in a digit place exceeds the largest number that can be represented in that digit place and that is transferred for processing elsewhere. In a positional representation system, a carry digit is transferred to the digit place with the next higher weight for processing there. (A) (B)

carry flag: an indicator signaling when a register overflow or underflow condition exists during mathematical operations with an accumulator.

carry/link bit: on some systems, a bit set if a carry from the most significant bit occurs during an add, a complement-and-add, or a decimal-add instruction. The bit is included in the shift right with link and the rotate right with link instructions.

carry look-ahead: a circuit that predicts the final carry from propagate and generate signals supplied by partial adders; used to speed up significantly binary addition by eliminating the carry propagation (or ripple) delay.

carry time: time needed for transferring all the carry digits to higher columns and adding them for all digits in the number.

CART: see *cartridge.*

Carterfone decision: a decision made by the Federal Communications Commission in 1968 to the effect that telephone company customers should be permitted to connect their own equipment (e.g., data modems) to the public telephone network provided that this interconnection does not adversely affect the telephone companies' operations or the utility of the telephone system to others. Prior to this decision, only telephone company–provided equipment could be connected to the network. (F)

cartridge (CART): a container holding a supply reel with a length of magnetic tape. (D) see also *cassette, magnetic tape cartridge.* synonymous with *strap.*

cartridge disk: a type of hard disk that can be removed from its drive.

cascade control: a system of organizing control units in sequence so that each unit controls the function of its successor and is in turn regulated by its predecessor.

cascaded carry: in parallel addition, a procedure in which the addition results in a partial sum numeral and a carry numeral which are in turn added; this process is repeated until a zero carry is generated. (B) cf. *high-speed carry. (A)*

cascaded merging: a technique used in a sort program to merge strings of sequenced data and performed a T-1 on part of the data, T-2 on parts of the data, and so on.

cashlike document: a document such as a check, gift, or certificate that is used in the same manner as cash, for payment of merchandise. synonymous with *cashlike tender.*

cashlike tender: synonym for *cashlike document.*

Cassegrain feed system: a radiating system which includes a primary reflector (dish), secondary reflector, and feed horn. Named for Nicholas Cassegrain, 17th century French physician who invented a telescope using this principle.

cassette: a container holding a supply reel with its length of magnetic tape and a pickup spool. (D) see also *cartridge, magnetic tape cassette.*

casting-out-nines: utilizing a remainder from the operand by dividing by nine and carrying out the same operations on the remainders as are performed on the operands.

CAT: computer aided testing.

catalanguage: synonymous with *object language.*

catalog (CATLG)

(1) a directory of locations of files and libraries. (B)

(2) an ordered compilation of item descriptions and sufficient information to afford access to the items. (A)

(3) the collection of all data set indexes that are used by the control program to locate a volume containing a specific data set.

(4) to enter information about a file or a library into a catalog. (B)

(5) to include the volume identification of a data set in the catalog.

catalog directory: a table in a catalog that identifies items in the catalog.

cataloged data set: a data set that is represented in an index, or hierarchy of indexes, in the system catalog; the indexes provide the means for locating the data set.

cataloged procedure: a set of control statements that has been placed in a library and can be retrieved by name.

catalogue: see *catalog.*

catastrophic errors: in a situation where so many errors have occurred, no more useful diagnostic information can be produced and the compilation is ended.

catena: a series of items linked in a chained list; specifically, a string of characters in a word.

catenate: pertaining to the arrangement of a series of items in a catena. synonymous with *concatenate.*

cathode-ray storage: an electrostatic storage that uses a cathode-ray beam for access to data. (A) (B)

cathode-ray tube (CRT): a vacuum tube display in which a beam of electrons can be controlled to form alphanumeric characters or symbols on a luminescent screen, for example, by use of a dot matrix. (D)

cathode-ray tube display (CRT display)

(1) a device that presents data in visual form by means of controlled electron beams.

(2) the data display produced by the device as in (1). (*A*)

CATLG: see *catalog.*

caveman: slang, referring to an antiquated computer; any obsolete data-processing equipment.

CAW: see *channel address word.*

CAX: see *community automatic exchange.*

CBA: see *computer-based automation.*

CBEMA: Computer and Business Equipment Manufacturers Association.

CC

(1) see *cluster controller.*

(2) see *command chain.*

(3) see *communication controller.*

(4) see *control counter.*

CCA: see *common communication adapter.*

CCD: see *charge couple device.*

CCH: see *connections per circuit per hour.*

CCHS: see *cylinder-cylinder-head sector.*

CCIS: see *common channel interoffice signaling.*

CCITT: see *Consultive Committee International Telegraph and Telephone.*

CCS: see *hundred call seconds.*

CCSA: see *common-control switching arrangement.*

CCU: see *central control unit.*

CCW: see channel command word.

CCW translation: see *channel program translation.*

CD: see *card.*

CDC: see *call directing code.*

CDF: see *combined distribution frame.*

CDO: see *community dial office.*

CDR: see *card reader.*

ceefax: a system by which data is transmitted on television picture lines in the vertical blanking interval, which are not ordinarily visible.

cell: see *binary cell, data cell, magnetic cell,* storage cell. see also *circuit unit assembly.*

cellular mobile telephone networks: see *cellular radio.*

cellular radio: a mobile communications service that offers sharply expanded mobile phone service by dividing an area into many small districts or "cells," each with its own transmitting stations. Sophisticated computer technology automatically switches a caller from one radio frequency to another as the caller moves from cell to cell. The mobile units can be carried in automobiles, around the home or office, or walking down the street.

cellular splitting: a technique for accommodating further information in a system that allocates storage in units of cells.

centering: in word processing, the positioning of a text string so that its midpoint is aligned with a given reference point position. (D)

center line: see *stroke center line*. (A)

centi (C): hundred or one hundredth.

centimeter (CM): one hundredth of a meter; 0.39 inch.

central computer: deprecated term for *host computer*.

central control unit (CCU): the communication controller hardware unit that contains the circuits and data flow paths needed to execute instructions and to control its storage and the attached adapters.

centralization: concentration of problem solving within an organization structure; often takes place to make optimum use of a computer-based information system. Centralization enables management to weigh all the relevant data, whereas a fragmented system cannot.

centralized automatic message accounting (CAMA): a process using centrally located equipment, including a switchboard or a traffic service position, associated with a tandem or toll switching office, for automatically recording billing data for customer-dialed extra-charge calls originating from several local central offices. A tape record is processed at an electronic data-processing center. (F)

centralized automatic message ac-

counting-operator number identification (CAMI-ONI) operator: an operator located at a position that is connected temporarily on a customer-dialed station-to-station call. The operator secures the calling number from the customer and keys the number into the centralized automatic message accounting equipment. (F)

centralized data processing: data processing performed at a single, central location on data from several regional locations or managerial levels.

centralized intercept bureau (CIB): that type of bureau that is part of an automatic intercept system and is associated with one or more automatic intercept centers. It provides facilities whereby operators situated at auxiliary service positions furnish assistance to calling customers whose calls have been intercepted and who require help beyond that furnished by an automatic intercept center. (F)

centralized network: synonym for *star network*. (E)

central office (CO): a switching system that connects lines to lines and trunks to trunks. The term is sometimes used loosely to refer to a telephone company building in which a switching system is located and to include other equipment (such as transmission system terminals) that may be located in such a building. (F)

central office code: a three-digit identification under which up to 10,000 station codes are subgrouped. Exchange area boundaries are associated with the central office code which accordingly has billing significance. Note that several central office codes may be served by a central office. synonymous with *NNX code.* (F)

central office work order: an order for work to be done in the operating company to make or change equipment assignments for switching system line or trunk access. (F)

central processing unit (CPU): a unit of a computer that includes circuits controlling the interpretation and execution of instructions. synonymous with *central processor, main frame.* (B) deprecated term for *processing unit.* (E)

central processing unit loop: the main routine or a control program and that which is associated with the control of the internal status of the processing unit.

central processor (CP): synonymous with *central processing unit.*

central scanning loop: a loop of instructions that determine which task is to be performed next.

central station: deprecated term for *control station.*

centrex: central office telephone equipment serving subscribers at one location on a private automatic branch exchange basis. The system allows such services as direct inward dialing, direct distance dialing, and console switchboards.

certified tape: computer tape that is machine-verified on all tracks throughout each roll and certified by the supplier to have less than a specific total number of errors or to have no errors.

CESD: see *composite external symbol dictionary.*

CFIA: see *component failure impact analysis.*

CG: see *computer graphics.*

CH: see *channel.*

chad

(1) the material separated from a data carrier when forming a hole. (E)

(2) the residue separated from the carrier holes in continuous forms paper.

(3) synonymous with *chip.*

chadded: pertaining to the punching of tape in which chad results.

chadless tape: punched tape that has been punched in such a way that chad is not formed. (A)

chain: see *Markov chain.* see also *chained list.*

chain additions program: an instruction set that will permit new records to be added to a file.

chain code: an arrangement in a cyclic sequence of some or all of the possible different n-bit words, in which adjacent words are related such that each is derivable from its neighbor by displacing the bits on digit position to the left, or right, dropping the leading bit and inserting a bit at the end. The value of the inserted bit needs only to meet the requirement that a word must not recur before the cycle is complete, for example, 000 001 010 101 011 111 110 100 000 . . . (A)

chained file: a computer file arranged so that each data item or key in a record in a chain has the address of another record with the same data or key.

chained list: a list in which the items may be dispersed but in which each item contains an identifier for locating the next item. (A) (B)

chained record: a record in a chained file.

chaining: a method of storing records in which each record belongs to a list or group of records and has a linking field for tracing the chain.

chaining overflow: on a direct-access storage device, the writing of overflow records on the next higher available track; each track contains a record that provides a link between the home track and the overflow track. cf. *progressive overflow*.

chaining search: a search in which each item contains the means for locating the next item to be considered in the search. (A) (B)

chain links

(1) various series of linked data items.

(2) in sequential processing, successive program segments, each of which relies on the previous segment for its input.

chain maintenance program: an instruction set permitting the deletion of records from a file.

chain printer: an impact printer in which the type slugs are carried by the links of a revolving chain. (A) (B)

change character: see *font change character*. (A)

change dump: a selective dump of those storage locations whose contents have changed. (A) (B)

change file: a file of transactions forming change records; used to update a master file during batch processing. synonymous with *detail file*, *transaction file*.

change record: a record which results in the modification of some of the information in the corresponding master file record.

change sign: the reversal of a sign of a number held in the machine. (D)

change tape: synonymous with *transaction tape*.

channel (CH) CHNL)

(1) in information theory, that part of a communication system that connects the message source with the message sink. Mathematically, this part can be characterized by the set of conditional probabilities of occurrence of all the possible messages received at the message sink when a given message emanates from the message source. (B)

(2) a path along which signals can be sent, for example, data channel, output channel.

(3) the portion of a storage medium that is accessible to a given reading or writing station, for example, track, band. (*A*)

(4) in data communications, a means of one-way transmission. cf. *circuit*.

(5) see *backward channel*, *binary symmetric channel*, *data channel*, *data communication channel*, *forward channel*, *information bearer channel*, *information channel*, *input channel*, *input/output channel*, *output channel*.

channel adapter: a unit permitting the connection between data channels of differing devices. The unit permits data transfer at the rate of the slower channel.

channel address word (CAW): an area in storage that specifies the location in main storage at which a channel program begins.

channel-attached

(1) pertaining to the attachment of devices directly by data channels (I/O channels) to a computer.

(2) pertaining to devices that are at-

tached to a controlling unit by cables, rather than by telecommunications lines.

(3) synonymous with *local, locally attached.* cf. *link-attached.*

channel-attached station: a station that is attached by a data channel to a host node. synonymous with *local station.* cf. *link-attached terminal.*

channel bank: channel terminal equipment used for combining (multiplexing) channels on a frequency-division or time-division basis. Voice channels are combined into 12- or 24-channel groups. (F)

channel busy tone: an audible signal indicating that a call cannot be completed because of trunk or switching system blocking. The tone is applied 120 times per minute. synonymous with *fast busy* and *reorder tone.* (F)

channel capacity: in information theory, the measure of the ability of a given channel subject to specific constraints to transmit messages from a specified message source expressed as either the maximum possible mean transinformation content per character, or the maximum possible average transinformation rate. (A) (B)

channel command: an instruction that directs a data channel, control unit, or device to perform an operation or set of operations.

channel command word (CCW): a double-word at the location in main storage specified by the channel address word. One or more CCWs make up the channel program that directs data-channel operations.

channel controller (CC): provides an independent data path to storage and assures multiprocessor systems maximum availability, permitting each processing unit access to each channel within the system.

channelize: a procedure employed to divide a communications circuit into a number of channels.

channel overload: a state in which data transfer to or from the processor and I/O devices reaches a rate that approaches the capacity of the data channel.

channel program: one or more channel command words that control a specific sequence of data-channel operations. Execution of the specific sequence is initiated by a single start I/O instruction.

channel program translation: in a channel program for a virtual storage system, replacement by software of virtual storage addresses with real addresses.

channel queue: a queue of data or requests waiting to be processed on a channel.

channel reliability: the percentage of time the channels meet all arbitrary standards.

channel service unit (CSU): an American Telephone and Telegraph (AT&T) unit that is part of the AT&T nonswitched digital data system.

channel set: a collection of channels that can be concurrently addressed by a processor.

channel status word (CSW): an area in storage that provides information about the termination of input-output operations.

channel synchronizer: a unit providing the proper interface between the central computer and peripheral devices.

channel-to-channel adapter (CTCA): a hardware device that can be used to connect two channels on the same computing system or on different systems.

chapter: deprecated term for *segment.* (A)

CHAR: see *character.*

character (CHAR) (CHR)

(1) a member of a set of elements upon which agreement has been reached and that is used for the organization, control, or representation of data. Characters may be letters, digits, punctuation marks, or other symbols, often represented in the form of a spatial arrangement of adjacent or connected strokes or in the form of other physical conditions in data media. (A) (B)

(2) a letter, number, punctuation mark, or special graphic used for the production of text. (D)

(3) a letter, digit, or other symbol that is used as part of the organization, control, or representation of data. A character is often in the form of a spatial arrangement of adjacent or connected strokes. (A)

(4) see *accuracy control character, acknowledge character, alphanumeric character set, backspace character, bell character, blank character, block cancel character, cancel character, carriage return character, carrier return character, check character, code extension character, control character, cyclic redundancy check character, data-link escape character, delete character, device control character, end-of-medium character, end-of-text character, end-of-transmission character, enquiry character, erase character, escape character, font change character, form feed character, gap character, graphic character, horizontal tabulation character, illegal character, indent tab character, index character, index return character, line feed character, longitudinal redundancy check character, negative acknowledge character, new-line character, null character, numeric backspace character, numeric space character, print control character, redundancy check character, repeat character, required carrier-return character, required hyphen character, required page-end character, required space character, shift-in-character, space character, special character, start-of-heading character, start-of-text character, start-stop character, stop character, substitute character, superscript character, switch character, syllable hyphen character, synchronous idle character, transmission control character, unit backspace character, vertical tabulation character, word underscore character.*

character addressing: the process of gaining access to a character position by using an address.

character arrangement: an arrangement composed of graphic characters from one or more modified or unmodified character sets.

character assembly: the process by which bits are put together to form characters as the bits arrive on a data link. In the communication controller, character assembly is performed either by the control program or by the communication scanner, depending on the type of scanner installed. cf. *character disassembly.*

character-at-a-time printer: synonym for *character printer*. (A)

character average information content: synonym for *character mean entropy*. (A)

character blink: part of a terminal device that permits one or more characters to blink together with the main cursor or out of synchronization with the main cursor.

character boundary: in character recognition, the largest rectangle, with a side parallel to the document reference edge, each of whose sides is tangential to a given character outline. (A)

character cell: the maximum physical boundary of a single character.

character check: a check that verifies the observance of rules for the formation of characters. (A)

character crowding: the reduction of the appropriate interval between characters on a magnetic medium. see *pack*.

character-deletion character: a character within a line of terminal input specifying that it and the immediately preceding character are to be removed from the line. see also *line-deletion character*.

character density: a measure of the horizontal spacing of characters.

character device control: a control character used to control devices associated with computing or telecommunication systems; for example, the switching on to or off of these devices.

character disassembly: the process by which characters are broken down into bits for transmission over a data link. In the communication controller, character disassembly is performed either by the control program or by the communication scanner, depending on the type of scanner installed. cf. *character assembly*.

character display device: a display device that gives a representation of data only in the form of characters. (A) (B) synonymous with *alphanumeric display device*, *read-out device*.

character edge: in optical character recognition, the imaginary edge running along the optical discontinuity between the printed area and the unprinted area of a printed symbol or character.

character element: a basic information element as transmitted, printed, displayed, and so forth, or used to control communications, when used as a code.

character emitter: an electromechanical unit that emits a timed pulse or group of pulses in a code.

character error rate: the ratio of the number of characters incorrectly received to the total number of characters sent. (C)

character expression: in assembler programming, a character string enclosed by apostrophes. It can be used only in conditional assembly instructions. The enclosing apostrophes are not part of the value represented. cf. *quoted string*.

character fill: to insert as often as necessary into a storage medium the representation of a specified character that does not itself convey data but may delete unwanted data. (A) (B)

character format memory: memory-storing approach for storing one character in each addressable location.

character generator

(1) in computer graphics, a functional unit that converts the coded representation of a graphic character into the shape of the character for display. see also *stroke character generator*. (E)

(2) in word processing, the means within equipment for generating visual characters or symbols from coded data. (D)

character information rate: synonym for *character mean entropy*. (A)

characteristic

(1) in a floating-point representation, the numeral that represents the exponent. (B)

(2) the integer part, which may be positive or negative, of the representation of a logarithm. (*A*) (B)

(3) distortion caused by transients which, as a result of the modulation, are present in the transmission channel and depend on its transmission qualities.

(4) cf. *mantissa*.

characteristic distortion: see *distortion*.

characteristic impedance: synonymous with *line impedance*.

character key: in word processing, a control used to process text one character at a time. (D)

character manipulation: the operations and techniques for handling strings of alphanumeric information, including searching, sorting, and reorganization of names, words, phrases, and textual information.

character mean entropy: in information theory, the mean per character of the entropy for all possible messages from a stationary message source. synonymous with *character average information content, character mean information content, character information rate*. (*A*) (B)

character mean information content: synonym for *character mean entropy*. (A) (B)

character modifier: a constant utilized in address modification to reference the location of the character.

character oriented: pertaining to a computer where character locations rather than words are addressed.

character-oriented word-processing programs: programs that display the words in the order, but not necessarily the format, in which they will be printed.

character outline: the graphic pattern established by the stroke edges of a character. (A)

character position: synonym for *display position*.

character printer (CP): a device that prints a single character at a time, for example, a typewriter. synonymous with *character-at-a-time printer, serial printer*. cf. *line printer*. (*A*)

character reader: an input unit that performs character recognition. (A) (B)

character recognition

(1) the identification of characters by automatic means. see *magnetic ink character recognition, optical character recognition*. (B)

(2) the identification of geographic, phonic, or other characters by various means including magnetic, optical, or mechanical. (*A*)

character relation: in assembler programming, two character strings separated by a relational operator.

character repertoire: the set of characters available in a specific code.

character row: synonym for *display line*.

character set

(1) a finite set of different characters upon which agreement has been reached and that is considered complete for some purpose. (B)

(2) a set of unique representations called characters; for example, the 26 letters of the English alphabet, 0 and 1 of the boolean alphabet, the set of signals in the Morse code alphabet, and the 128 ASCII characters. (*A*)

(3) a defined collection of characters.

(4) see *alphabetic character set, alphabetic-coded character set, alphanumeric character set, alphanumeric-coded character set, coded character set, numeric character set, numeric-coded character set.*

character size: the number of binary digits in a single character in the storage unit.

character skew: in optical character recognition, the angular rotation of a character relative to its intended or ideal placement.

character spacing reference line: in character recognition, a vertical line that is used to evaluate the horizontal spacing of characters. It may be a line that equally divides the distance between the sides of a character boundary or that coincides with the center line of a vertical stroke. (A)

character string

(1) a string consisting solely of characters. (A) (B)

(2) a connected sequence of characters.

character stroke: OCR lines, points, arcs, and other marks used as parts or portions of graphic characters. The dot over the letter *i* or the cross of a *t* is a stroke.

character style: in OCR, a distinctive construction, with no restriction as to size that is common to a group of characters.

character subset: a selection of characters from a character set, comprising all characters that have a specified common feature; for example, in each of the character sets of International Standards Organization (ISO) Recommendation R646 "6- and 7-bit coded character sets for information processing interchange," the digits 0 and 9 may constitute a character subset. (B) see *alphabetic character subset, alphanumeric character subset, numeric character subset.* (*A*)

character tape: information composed of bits kept across the several longitudinal channels of a tape.

charge couple device (CCD): a memory unit with high packing density and low power consumption. synonymous with *image sensor.*

chart: see *data flowchart, flowchart, plugboard chart.* (A)

chassis: the frame on which boards are mounted. see *hot chassis.*

chassis assembly: a structure permitting mounting locations for the processor, power supply, and peripheral interface cards; designed using a printed circuit back plane for interconnecting wiring.

check (CHK): a process for determining accuracy. (A) see *automatic check, character check, completeness check, consistency check, cyclic redundancy check, duplication* *check, echo check, expiration check, format check, limit check, longitudinal parity check, marginal check, mathematical check, modulo check, modulo-N check, overflow check, parity check, programmed check, range check, reasonableness check, redundancy check, selection check, sequence check, sight check, summation check, transfer check, transverse parity check.* see also *check digit, check key, check problem, check sum, desk checking, machine check interruption.*

check bit

(1) a binary check digit; for example, a parity bit. see *redundancy check bit.* (*A*)

(2) a bit associated with a character or block for the purpose of checking the absence of error within the character or block. (C)

check bus: a set or group of parallel lines for transmission of data to a specific checking unit such as a check register, a parity checker, or a comparator.

check card

(1) a punched card suitable for use as a bank check.

(2) a punch card used for checking. (*A*)

check character

(1) a character used for the purpose of performing a check. (A)

(2) a character of a check key. (E)

check code: to isolate and remove mistakes from any routine.

check diagnostic: a routine designed to locate a malfunction or error in a computer.

check digit

(1) a digit used for the purpose of performing a check. (A)

(2) a digit of a check key. (E)

check indicator: a device that can display or announce when an error has been made or a malfunction has occurred.

check indicator instruction: an instruction directing a signal device that is turned on to call the operator's attention to the fact that there is some discrepancy in the instruction presently in use.

checking program: a computer program that examines other computer programs or sets of data for mistakes of syntax. (A) (B)

check key: a group of characters, derived from and appended to a data item, that can be used to detect errors in the data item during processing. (E)

check number: synonymous with *check digit.*

check out: synonym for *debug.*

check-out routine: various routines assisting programmers in the debugging of routines.

checkpoint (CHKPT)

(1) a place in a computer program at which a check is made, or at which a recording of data is made for restart purposes. (A)(B)

(2) a point at which information about the status of a job and the system can be recorded so that the job step can be later restarted.

(3) to record such information.

checkpoint data set: a data set that contains checkpoint records.

checkpoint dump: recording data at a checkpoint.

checkpoint records: records that contain the status of a job and the system at the time the records are written by the checkpoint routine.

These records provide the information necessary for restarting a job without having to return to the beginning of the job. see also *control record*.

checkpoint restart: the process of resuming a job at a checkpoint within the job step that caused abnormal termination. The restart may be automatic or deferred, where deferred restart involves resubmitting the job. see also *automatic restart*, *deferred restart*. cf. *step restart*.

checkpoint routine: a series of instructions that generate information for future verification.

checkpoint sorting: the point at which a restart, or rerun can be initiated. Memory, registers, and the position of tapes are recorded at this point.

check problem: a problem whose previously evaluated solution is used to determine whether a functional unit is operating correctly. (E)

check register: a register where data is stored temporarily prior to making a comparison with the same data input at a differing time or by a differing path.

check reset key: a push button that shows an error and resets the error detection mechanism indicated by the check light; required to restart a program following the making of an error found in a batch mode.

check solution: the solution to a problem drawn by independent means to verify a computer solution.

check sum: the sum of a group of data ited items associated with the group for checking purposes. The data items are either numerals or other character strings regarded as numerals during the process of cal-

culating the check sum. (E)

check total: one of a large number of totals or sums that can be correlated as a check for the consistency of reconciliation in a set of calculations.

check trunk: a set or group of parallel lines for transmission of data to a specific checking unit such as a check register, a parity checker, or a comparator.

check word: the machine word used to represent a check symbol and is affixed and printed to the block thereby signifying the check.

child segment: in a data base, a segment immediately below another segment in a hierarchy. A child segment has only one parent segment. see also *parent segment*.

Chinese binary: synonym for *column binary*. (A)

chip

(1) in micrographics, a piece of microform that contains both microimages and coded identification.

(2) a minute piece of semiconductive material used in the manufacture of electronic components. (A)

(3) an integral circuit on a piece of semiconductive material. (A)

(4) synonym for *chad*. (A)

chip carrier: a plug-in unit for mounting LSI chips on circuit boards.

chip microprocessor: LSI circuits residing on a single silicon chip, able to perform the necessary activities of a computer; popularly called "computer on a chip."

chip processes: processes involved in producing integrated circuits.

chip register architecture: the arrangement of registers on a chip, including the number and function of on-chip registers, the type and depth of the stack register, interrupt capability, and the direct-memory-access feature.

chip select: each large scale integration chip usually has one or more chip selects. The chip select line is used to activate one chip among many which receive similar signals. When chosen, the chip examines the rest of its pins, in particular the address bus, which specifies a location/register within the chip.

CHK: see *check*.

CHKPT: see *checkpoint*.

CHNL: see *channel*.

choice device: in computer graphics, an input device that provides integers specifying alternatives. see also *locator device, pick device, valuator device*. (E)

CHR: see *character*.

CIB: see *centralized intercept bureau*.

CICS: see *customer information control system*.

CIF: computer-integrated factory.

CIM: computer-integrated manufacturing.

cine-oriented image: in micrographics, an image appearing on a roll of microfilm in such a manner that the top edge of the image is perpendicular to the long edge of the film. cf. *comic-strip oriented image*. (A)

ciphertext: synonym for *enciphered data*.

CIR: see *current instruction register*.

circuit: in data communications, a means of two-way communication between two data terminal installations. cf. *channel*. see *bistable circuit, combinational circuit, data circuit, monostable circuit, physical circuit, sequential circuit, trigger cir-*

cuit, virtual circuit.

circuit board: a board to which is affixed the circuitry of a microprocessor. synonymous with *card, circuit card*.

circuit breaker: a manual or automatic protective device for closing and opening a circuit between separable contacts under both normal and abnormal conditions.

circuit card: synonymous with *circuit board*.

circuit grade: the information-carrying capability of a circuit, in speed or type of signal. The grades of circuits are broad band, voice, subvoice, and telegraph. For data use, these grades are identified with certain speed ranges.

circuit load: synonym for *line load*.

circuit order: the document used to transmit engineering design of a public telephone network trunk or special-service circuit to the department that implements the design. (F)

circuit reliability: the percentage of time the circuit meets arbitrary standards set by the user.

circuit switch: a method of switching in which a path or circuit is established between origin and destination and held available for as long as required by the users, whether information is passing or not.

circuit-switched connection: a connection that is established and maintained on demand between two or more data stations in order to allow the exclusive use of a data circuit until the connection is released. (E)

circuit-switched data-transmission service: a service using circuit switching to establish and maintain a connection before data can be transferred between data-terminal equipments (DTEs). (E)

circuit switching: a process that, on demand, connects two or more data-terminal equipments (DTEs) and permits the exclusive use of a data circuit between them until the connection is released. synonymous with *line switching*. see also *message switching, packet switching*. (E)

circuit switching unit (CSU): that equipment used for directly connecting two compatible data terminals for end-to-end data exchanges. Also used to connect a data terminal to a store-and-forward switch.

circuit unit assembly (CUA): a subassembly within an equipment cabinet. synonymous with *cell*.

circular list: a chained list, which, following the processing of all items from any starting place, permits a return to the item preceding the starting point.

circular shift: synonym for *end-around shift*. (A)

circulating register: a shift register in which data moved out of one end of the register are reentered into the other end as in a closed loop. (A)

circulating storage: dynamic storage involving a closed loop. synonymous with *cyclic storage*. (A)

citation: a statement of reference relating to other sources of data or special notes concerning the data found on punched cards.

city-call: an intercity MTS-like service offered by United States Transmission Systems, Inc. (USTS), a subsidiary of ITT. see *MTS/WATS-like services*. (G)

CIU: see *computer interface unit*.

CKD: see *count-key-data device*.

CL: see *command language*.

cl: centiliter.

cladding: a sheathing or covering, usually of glass, fused to the core of an optical fiber.

clamp: an electronic circuit which holds the output of a circuit at some constant value. A clamp is used in some data sets to hold receiver output constant and avoid troublesome noise interference when no data signals are being received.

clamp-on: synonym for *camp-on*.

class: a means of grouping jobs that require the same set of resources for their execution. There are two classes: input class and output class.

class condition: in COBOL, a statement that the content of an item is wholly alphabetic or wholly numeric. It may be true or false.

class 5 office: a local central office that serves as the network entry point for station loops and certain special-service lines. Other offices, classes 1, 2, 3, and 4, are toll offices in the telephone network. synonymous with *end office*. (F)

classification: the arrangement of data in classes or groups; needed to produce summary reports.

classify: the arrangement of data into classes or groups according to a definite plan or method.

clause: in COBOL, a set of consecutive words whose purpose is to specify an attribute of an entry. There are three types of clauses: data, environment, and file.

clear (C) CLR)

(1) to put one or more storage locations or registers into a prescribed state, usually that denoting zero. (B)

(2) to cause one or more storage lo-

cations to be in a prescribed state, usually that corresponding to zero or that corresponding to the space character. (A) (B)

(3) in a calculator, the cancellation of data in the working registers of the machine. (D)

clear all: in a calculator, the cancellation of data in the working registers and storage devices. (D)

clear area: in character recognition, a specified area that is to be kept free of printing or any other markings not related to machine reading. (A)

clear band: in optical character recognition, the area on a document that must be kept free of printing. synonymous with *clear area.*

clear data: data that is not enciphered. synonymous with *plaintext.*

clear display: the action of deleting all information from a display. (D)

clear entry: in a calculator, the cancellation of data entered into the machine but not yet processed. (D)

clear memory: deprecated term for *clear storage.*

clear session: a session in which only clear data is transmitted or received.

clear storage: in a calculator, the cancellation of data in the storage devices to which the keys refer. (D)

clipping: synonym for *scissoring.*

CLK: see *clock.*

clock (C) (CLK)

(1) a device that measures and indicates time.

(2) a register whose content changes at regular intervals in such a way as to measure time. (A)

(3) a device that generates periodic signals used for synchronization. (E)

(4) equipment that provides a time base used in a transmission system

to control the timing of certain functions such as sampling and to control the duration of signal elements. (C)

(5) deprecated term for *timer.* (A) (B)

clock counter: a memory location that records real-time progress, or its approximation, by accumulating counts produced by a clock count pulse interrupt.

clock frequency: see *clock rate.*

clocking: in binary synchronous communication, the use of clock pulses to control synchronization of data and control characters.

clock pulse: a synchronization signal provided by a clock. synonym for *clock signal.* (A) (B)

clock rate: the time rate at which pulses are emitted from the clock; determines the rate at which logical or arithmetic gating is performed with a synchronous computer.

clock register: synonym for *timer.* (A) (B)

clock signal: the output of a device that generates periodic signals used for synchronization. synonymous with *clock pulse.* (A) (B)

clock track: a track on which a pattern of signals is recorded to provide a timing reference. (B)

close: to call a subroutine to terminate the reading from or writing to a file by a program.

close classification: the arrangement of subjects into a classification system involving small subdivisions.

closed array: an array that cannot be extended at either end.

closed loop: a loop that has no exit and whose execution can be interrupted only by intervention from outside the computer program in which the loop is included. (A) (B)

closed loop (control) system: a control system with feedback characteristics.

closedown: the deactivation of a device, program, or system.

closed routine: a routine that is not inserted as a block of instructions within a main routine, but is instead entered by basic linkage from the main routine.

closed shop: pertaining to the operation of a computer facility in which most productive problem programming is performed by a group of programming specialists rather than by the problem originators. The use of the computer itself may also be described as closed shop if full-time trained operators, rather than user/programmers, serve as the operators. cf. *open shop.* (A)

closed subroutine: a subroutine of which one replica suffices for the subroutine to be linked by calling sequences for use at more than one place in a computer program. (B) cf. *open subroutine.* (A)

closed-user group: in a group of users, a subgroup that is assigned a facility that enables a member of one subgroup to communicate only with other members of the subgroup. (E)

closed-user group with outgoing access: a closed-user group that has a user assigned a facility which enables that user to communicate with other users of a public data network transmission service, where appropriate, or with users having a data-terminal equipment (DTE) connected to any other public switched network to which interworking facilities are available. (C)

closing a terminal: performing the store and equipment procedures necessary to shut down the point of sale terminal at the close of a sales period or at the close of a particular program. see also *opening a terminal.*

closing of a file: the disassociation of a file from a data set.

CLP: see *current line pointer.*

CLR: see *clear.*

cluster: a station that consists of a control unit (cluster controller) and the terminals attached to it.

cluster controller: a device that can control the input-output operations of more than one device connected to it. A cluster controller may be controlled by a program stored and executed in the unit. see also *cluster, cluster controller node.* synonymous with *cluster control unit.*

cluster controller node: a peripheral node that can control a variety of devices. see also *host node, terminal node.*

cluster control unit: synonym for *cluster controller.*

CM: centimeter.

CML: see *current mode logic.*

CMND: see *command.*

CMOD: a user-written module for a subsystem controller.

C-MOS: complementary metal-oxide semiconductor; chips that use far less electricity than other types where circuits are relatively immune to electrical interference and operate in a wide range of temperatures. In C-MOS, transistors on the chip are paired, with one requiring positive voltage to work and the other negative. The transistors thus offset, or complement each other's power requirements. see also *MOS*.

CNC: computer numerical control.

CNCL: see *cancel*.

CNET: see *communication network*.

CNT: see *count*.

CNTL: see *control*.

CNTR: see *counter*.

CNTRL: see *control*.

CO: see *central office*.

coalesce
(1) to combine two or more sets of items into one set of any form. (B)
(2) to combine two or more files into one file. (A)

coated card: see *edge-coated card.* (A)

coax: abbreviation of *coaxial cable*.

coaxial cable: a transmission cable consisting of a conducting outer-metal tube enclosing and insulating from a common core.

COBOL
(1) common business-oriented language. An English-like programming language designed for business data processing applications.
(2) a general purpose (machine) language designed for commercial data utilizing a standard form. It is a language that can present any business program to any suitable computer and also act as a means of communicating these procedures among people.

COBOL character: any of the 51 valid characters in the COBOL character set.

CODASYL: Conference on Data Systems Languages.

code
(1) a set of unambiguous rules specifying the manner in which data may be represented in a discrete form. synonymous with *coding scheme*. (B)
(2) a set of items, such as abbreviations, representing the members of another set.
(3) to represent data or a computer program in a symbolic form that can be accepted by a data processor.
(4) to write a routine. (*A*)
(5) loosely, one or more computer programs, or part of a computer program.
(6) synonym for *coded character set, coded representation*.
(7) deprecated term for *coded representation, code set*. (B)
(8) see *alphabetic code, alphanumeric code, binary code, biquinary code, chain code, computer instruction code, data code, error detecting code, excess-three code, gray code, hamming code, in-line code, interpretive code, minimum distance code, numeric code, object code, operation code, perforated tape code, pseudocode, retrieval code, return code, skeletal code, two-out-of-five code.*

Code and Go FORTRAN: a version of FORTRAN IV for rapid compilation and execution of programs.

code area: in micrographics, a part of the film frame reserved for retrieval code. (A)

codec
(1) an assembly comprising an encoder and a decoder in the same equipment.
(2) a device that performs the dual function of encoding two-way analog data into digital data and two-way digital data into analog data.

code chain: an arrangement in a cyclic sequence of some or all of the possible different N-bit words in which adjacent words are linked by the relation that each word is derived from its neighbors by displacing the bits one digit position to the left or right, dropping the leading bit, and inserting the bit at the end.

code check: to isolate and remove errors from a routine.

code conversion: a process for changing the bit grouping for a character in one code into the corresponding bit grouping for a character in a second code.

code converter: a data converter that changes the representation of data, using one code in the place of another or one coded character set in the place of another. (A) (B)

coded: see *binary-coded decimal notation.*

coded arithmetic data: arithmetic data that is stored in a form that is acceptable, without conversion, for arithmetic calculations.

coded character set: a set of unambiguous rules that establish a character set and the one-to-one relationships between the characters of the set and their coded representations. synonymous with *code (6).* (B) see *alphabetic-coded character set, alphanumeric-coded character set, numeric-coded character set.* (A)

coded decimal notation: synonym for *binary-coded decimal notation.* (A)

code-dependent system: a system that depends, for its correct functioning, upon the character set or code used for transmission by the data terminal equipment (DTE). synonymous with *code-sensitive system.* (C)

coded graphics: deprecated term for *coordinate graphics.*

coded-image space: synonymous with *image storage space.*

code-directing characters: characters used to show the routing and destination of the message to which they are affixed.

coded program: a program expressed in the language or code of a specific machine or programming system.

coded representation: the representation of an item of data established by a code or the representation of a character established by a coded character set; for example, "ORY" as the representation of Paris (Orly) in the code for three-letter identification for airports; the seven binary elements representing the delete character in the ISO seven-bit coded character set. synonymous with *code value.* (A) (B)

coded ringing: a form of semiselective ringing. The customer is required to identify his own code by the number of rings and/or their duration. (F)

coded stop: synonymous with *program halt.*

code element: synonym for *coded representation.* (A)

code error: illegal control code on a binary card.

code extension character: any control character used to indicate that one or more of the succeeding coded representations are to be interpreted according to a different code or according to a different coded character set. (A) (B)

code frame: a set of characters that recur cyclically.

code holes: the information holes in perforated tape, as opposed to the feed or other holes.

code-independent data communication: a mode of data communication that uses a character-oriented link protocol that does not depend on the character set or code used by the data source. (E)

code-independent system: a system that does not depend, for its correct functioning, upon the character set or code used for transmission by the data-terminal equipment (DTE). synonymous with *code-insensitive system, code-transparent system.* (C)

code-insensitive system: synonym for *code-independent system.*

code key: in word processing, a key, which when operated in conjunction with another key, gives an alternate meaning to the key, such as to initiate a program or execute a function.

code level: the number of bits used to represent a character.

code line: the written form of a program instruction.

code line index: in micrographics, a visual index consisting of an optical pattern of clear and opaque bars parallel to the long edge of the role of microfilm and located between the images. (A)

code-point translator: the facility for interpreting incoming digits to determine proper disposition of service requests.

code position: synonym for *punch position.* (A) (B)

coder: a person who writes but does not usually design computer programs. (A) (B)

code-sensitive system: synonym for *code-dependent system.*

code set: the complete set of representations defined by a code, or by a coded character set; for example, all of the three-letter international identifications for airports. synonymous with *code (6).* (A) (B)

code-transparent data communication: a mode of data communication that uses a bit-oriented link protocol that does not depend on the bit sequence structure used by the data source. (E)

code-transparent system: synonym for *code-dependent system.*

code value: one element of a code set; for example, the eight-binary digit code value for the delete character. synonym for *coded representation.* (B)

coding: see *relative coding, straight-line coding, symbolic coding.* (A)

coding check: a test used to determine that a program is error free.

coding scheme: synonym for *code(1).* (A)

coding sheet: a pre-printed form on which program instructions are written.

coefficient unit: a functional unit whose output variable equals the input variable multiplied by a constant. (B)

coffret: a transmission interface used to connect with the French telephone network.

COGO (coordinate geometry): a programming language designed for coordinate geometry problems in civil engineering. (E)

coherent: a fixed-phase relationship that provides certain advantages in signal detection. (F)

coherent modulation system: a modulation system that requires a carrier, either transmitted or locally derived and having the same frequency and phase as that associated with the received signal, for recovering the original modulating signal. (F)

coherent phase-shift keying (CPSK): modulation techniques for transmitting digital information in which that information is conveyed by selecting discrete phase changes of the carrier relative to a reference. see *coherent modulation system.* (F)

coincidence circuit: synonymous with *AND element.*

coincidence element: synonymous with *AND element.*

coincidence error: the error caused by a time difference in switching different integrators to the computer mode or to the holding mode. (B)

coincidence gate: synonymous with *AND element.*

coincident-current selection: in an array of magnetic storage cells, the selective switching of one cell in the array by the simultaneous application of two or more currents such that the resultant magnetomotive force exceeds a threshold value only in the selected cell. (B)

coin-first service: coin telephone service in which an initial rate deposit is required to obtain dial tone. (F)

coin relay: a relay in a coin telephone that collects or returns the coins under the control of the central office.

COL: see *column.*

cold fault: a computer fault determined at the time the machine is turned on.

cold restart: synonym for *initial program load.* see also *checkpoint restart, system restart.*

COLL: see *collator.*

collate: to alter the arrangement of a set of items from two or more ordered subsets to one or more other subsets each containing a number of items, commonly one, from each of the original subsets in a specified order that is not necessarily the order of any of the original subsets (B). see also *merge.* (*A*)

collating sequence

(1)   a specified arrangement used in sequencing. synonymous with *sequence.* (B)

(2)   an ordering assigned to a set of items, such that any two sets in that assigned order can be collated.

(3)   deprecated term for *order(1).* (*A*) (B)

collating sorting: a sort that utilizes the technique of continuous merging of data until one sequence is developed. see *collating sequence.*

collator (COLL): a device that collates, merges, or matches sets of punched cards or other documents. (A) (B)

color: in optical character recognition, the spectral appearance of the image dependent upon the spectral reflectance of the image, the spectral response of the observer, and the spectral composition of incident light. (A)

color bars: standards established to ensure that color television and computer terminal equipment perform effectively together.

column (COL): a vertical arrangement ·of characters or other expressions. see *card column, mark-sensing column, punch column.* cf. *row.* (*A*)

column binary: pertaining to the binary representation of data on cards in which the weights of punch positions are assigned along card columns.

For example, each column in a 12-row card may be used to represent 12 consecutive bits. synonymous with *Chinese binary.* cf. *row binary.* (*A*)

column move: in word processing, a process in which a vertical column of text or numbers is moved from one part of a document to another, or from one document to another.

column split: the capability of a card-processing device to read or punch two parts of a card column independently. (B)

COM

(1) see *computer output microfilm.*

(2) see *computer output microfilmer.* (*A*)

COMB: see *combination.*

combination (COMB): a given number of different elements selected from a set without regard to the order in which the selected elements are arranged (B). see *forbidden combination.* cf. *permutation.* (*A*)

combinational circuit: a logic device whose output values, at any given instant, depend only upon the input values at that time. A combinational circuit is a special case of a sequential circuit that does not have a storage capability. synonymous with *combinatorial circuit.* (*A*) (B)

combinational logic element: a device having at least one output channel and zero or more input channels, all characterized by discrete states, such that any instant the state of each output channel is completely determined by the states of the input channels at the same instant. cf. *sequential logic element.* (*A*)

combination hub: an electrical jack connection that emits or receives electrical impulses on a control panel.

combinatorial circuit: synonymous with *combinational circuit.* (*A*)

combined distribution frame (CDF): a distribution frame combining the functions of the main distribution frame and intermediate distribution frame.

combined head: synonym for *read/write head.* (*A*) (B)

combined read/write head: synonym for *read/write head.*

combined station: in high-level data-link control (HDLC), the data station that includes both a primary and a secondary. synonymous with *balanced station.* (E)

combiner: a functional block that groups several inputs that are separated by space to form a single output.

comic-strip oriented image: in micrographics, an image appearing on roll microfilm in such a manner that the top edge of the image is parallel to the long edge of the film. cf. *cine-oriented image.* (*A*)

command (CMND)

(1) a control signal.

(2) loosely, a mathematical or logic operator; an instruction. (*A*)

(3) a request from a terminal for the performance of an operation or the execution of a particular program.

(4) a character string from a source external to a system that represents a request for system action.

(5) deprecated term for *instruction.* (*A*)

(6) see *absolute command, channel command, display command, operator command, relative command, subcommand.*

command chain (CC): the sequence

of input-output instructions that can be executed independently of the process of which they form a part.

command control program: a program that handles all commands addressed to the system from the user-consoles.

command double-word: a double-word containing detailed information concerning a part of an input-output operation.

command functions: instructions used by the CPU to govern the circuitry to carry out a specific action.

command language (CL): a source language consisting primarily of procedural operators, each capable of invoking a function to be executed. (A) synonymous with *query language* and *search language*.

command list: a sequence of steps, generated by the central processing unit, pertaining to the performance of an I/O operation.

command name: the first term in a command, usually followed by operands.

command pointer: a specific multiple-bit register that shows the memory location being accessed in the control store.

command processing: the reading, analyzing, and performing of commands issued via a console or through an input system.

command processor (COMPROC) (CP): a problem program executed to perform an operation specified by a command.

command retry: a channel and control unit procedure that causes a command to be retried without requiring an I/O interruption.

command statement: a job control statement that is used to issue commands to the system through the input stream.

comment
(1) a description, reference, or explanation, added to or interspersed among the statements of the source language, that has no effect in the target language. (A) (B) synonymous with *computer program annotation*.
(2) a statement used to document a source program. Comments include information that may be helpful in running a job or reviewing an output listing.

comment field: the field within an instruction, used for explanations and remarks, which are ignored by the compiler or the assembler.

comment statement: a source language statement that has no effect other than to cause itself to be reproduced on an output listing.

commercial character: in PL/1, the following picture specification characters: (1) CR (credit), (2) DB (debit), (3) T, I, and R, the overpunched-sign characters, which indicate that the associated position in the data item contains or may contain a digit with an overpunched sign and that this overpunched sign is to be considered in the character string value of the data item.

commercial instruction set: a combination of instructions of the standard instruction set and the decimal feature.

common area: a control section used to reserve a main storage area that can be referred to by other modules.

common battery: a battery (usually 48V) which serves as a central source of energy for many similar circuits.

common block: in FORTRAN, a storage area that may be referred to by a calling program and one or more subprograms.

Common Business-Oriented Language: see *COBOL*.

common carrier: see *communication common carrier*.

common carrier bureau: the bureau within the FCC which is responsible for the regulation of telecommunications. The FCC staff is divided into several bureaus, each responsible for a different form of communications. The bureau staff conducts research and makes recommendations. (G)

common channel interoffice signaling (CCIS): an electronic means of signaling between any two switching systems independent of the voice path. The use of CCIS makes possible new customer services, versatile network features, more flexible call routing and faster call connections. By interacting with communications processors that control data bases incorporated into the system, CCIS can be used to store and provide access to large amounts of information for vast numbers of terminals. (G)

common command language: a command language created for the searching of more than one host, where the searcher can easily switch from host to host during a search.

common communication adapter (CCA): a general purpose adapter that inserts or removes control information and converts message data into an appropriate form for the terminal in which it is used.

common control: an automatic arrangement in which items of control equipment in a switching system are shared; they are associated with a given call only during the periods required to accomplish the control functions. (F)

common-control switching arrangement (CCSA): an arrangement in which switching for a private network is provided by one or more common-control switching systems. The switching systems may be shared by several private networks and also may be shared with the public telephone network. (F)

common control system: automatic switching system that makes use of common equipment to establish a connection. The common equipment then becomes available to establish other connections.

common error: the maximum size of common was not specified in the first loaded program.

common field: a field that can be accessed by two or more independent routines. (A)

common hub: a common connection such as a ground voltage that provides this voltage to other circuits that are connected.

common language: a language in a machine-sensible form that is common to a group of computers and associated equipment.

common language code: codes used to ensure uniform abbreviation of equipment and facility names, place names, and so forth.

common segment: in an overlay structure, an overlay segment upon which two exclusive segments are dependent.

common software: computer programs and routines in a language common to a number of computers and users.

common storage area: synonymous with *common area*.

common target machine: see *target computer*.

common user circuit: a circuit designated to furnish a communications service to a number of users.

common user network: a system of circuits or channels allocated to furnish communication paths between switching centers to provide communication service on a common basis to all connected stations or subscribers. It is sometimes described as a general purpose network.

communality: that proportion of one correlated variance held in common with other measures in the same set.

communicating word-processing equipment: word-processing equipment capable of transmission and reception of text, data, or both, using telecommunication techniques. (D)

communication: see *data communication*. (A)

communication adapter: an optional hardware feature, available on certain processors, that permits telecommunication lines to be attached to the processors.

communication channel: see *data communication channel*.

communication common carrier: in the USA and Canada, a public data transmission service that provides the general public with transmission service facilities; for example, a telephone or telegraph company. see also *Post Telephone and Telegraph Administration, public data network,*

Recognized Private Operating Agency, telecommunication administration.

communication control character: synonym for *data-link control character, transmission control character*. (A) (B)

communication controller (CC): a type of communication control unit whose operations are controlled by one or more programs stored and executed in the unit. see also *cluster controller, communication controller node, transmission control unit*.

communication controller node: a subarea node that does not contain a system services control point (SSCP). see also *NCP node*.

communication data system: a real-time system that interfaces between teletypewriter stations and a computer.

communication facility: see *telecommunication facility*.

communication interface (CI): see *transmission interface*.

communication line: deprecated term for *telecommunication line, transmission line*.

communication line adapter: deprecated term for *line set*.

communication link: deprecated term for *data link*.

communication mix: a combination of communication media and/or techniques.

communication network (CNET): see *data network, distributed data-processing network, path control network, public network, remote-access data-processing network, user application network*.

communications: see *data communication*.

Communications Act of 1934: this Act, passed by Congress in 1934, established a national telecommunications goal of high quality, universally available telephone service at reasonable cost. The act also established the FCC and transferred federal regulation of all interstate and foreign wire and radio communications to this commission. It requires that prices and regulations for service by just, reasonable, and not unduly discriminatory. (G)

communication scanner: a communication controller hardware unit that provides the connection between lines and the central control unit. The communication scanner monitors telecommunication lines and data links for service requests.

communications center: a facility responsible for the reception, transmission, and delivery of messages. Its normal elements are a message center section, a cryptographic section, and a sending and receiving section, using electronic communications devices.

communications computer: a computer that acts as the interface between another computer or terminal and a network, or which controls data flow in a network.

communications controller: see *communication controller.*

communications satellite: an artificial satellite which amplifies and converts the frequency of signals received from earth stations. The resulting signal is retransmitted back to ground-based receivers.

Communications Satellite Corporation (COMSAT): created by authorization of Congress in the Communications Act of 1962. This private corporation (not an agency of the United States government, although subject to governmental regulation) was created primarily to provide for the establishment, operation, and management of a commercial communications satellite system. COMSAT presently acts as manager for INTELSAT and also represents the United States in INTELSAT. (F)

communications security equipment: equipment designed to provide security to telecommunications, by converting information to a form unintelligable to an unauthorized interceptor, and by reconverting such information to its original form for authorized recipients, as well as equipment designed specifically to aid in, or an essential element of, the conversion process.

communications terminal: any device which generates electrical or tone signals that can be transmitted over a communications channel.

communication subsystem: the standard communication subsystem permitting the real-time system to transmit and receive data by way of any common carrier in any of the standard codes and at any of the standard rates of transmission, up to 4800 bits per second.

communication theory: the mathematical discipline dealing with the probablistic features of the transmission of data in the presence of noise. (B) deprecated term for *information theory.*

community automatic exchange (CAX): a small dial telephone office serving a community.

community dial office (CDO): a small

automatic switching system that serves a separate exchange area having its own numbering plan and ordinarily having no operating or maintenance force located in its own building; operation is handled and maintenance is directed from a conveniently located point referred to as an operator office. (F)

commutator pulse: a pulse issued at a particular moment to define a specific binary digit in a word, establishing the limits of a digit period. synonymous with *position pulse, p-pulse.*

COMP: see *compatible.*

compaction algorithm: an algorithm to achieve data compaction, that is, reducing data to a more compact form requiring fewer bits.

compaction of file records: the reduction of space required for records by compressing or compacting them by means of specialized coding and formatting under a programmed routine.

companding: compressing and expanding.

compandor (compression-expandor): equipment that compresses the outgoing speech volume range and expands the incoming speech volume range on a long distance telephone circuit. see also *compressor, expandor.*

compandor mistracking: mistracking refers to the failure of the expandor characteristic of a compandor to complement exactly the compressor characteristic, thereby causing signal distortion. (F)

companion store backup: see *backup.*

comparator
(1) a functional unit that compares

several items of data and indicates the result of that comparison. (B)
(2) a device for determining the dissimilarity of two items, such as two pulse patterns or words. (*A*)

compare: to examine two items to discover their relative magnitudes, their relative positions in an order or in a sequence, or whether they are identical in given characteristics. (A) (B)

comparing unit: synonymous with *comparator.*

comparison: the process of examining two or more items for identity, similarity, equality, relative magnitude, or for order in a sequence. see *logical comparison.* (*A*)

comparison test: a test that compares one value to another. A comparison test is performed within a procedure; the next action performed by the procedure usually depends upon the result of the test.

compatibility: the ability of two units to work in harmony, usually software and hardware. In most cases, computer compatibility refers to software compatibility.

compatibility test: tests conducted to check acceptability of both software and hardware as a system, that is, to test component workability.

compatible (COMP): pertaining to computers on which the same computer programs can be run without appreciable alteration. see also *upward compatible.*

compile
(1) to translate a computer program expressed in a problem-oriented language into a computer-oriented language. (B)
(2) to prepare a machine language program from a computer program

written in another programming language by making use of the overall logic structure of the program, or generating more than one computer instruction for each symbolic statement, or both, as well as performing the function of an assembler. (*A*).

compile and go: an operating technique in which there are no stops between the compiling, loading, and execution of a computer program. (A)

compile duration: synonym for *compiling time.* (A) (B)

compile phase: the logical subdivision of a run that includes the execution of the compiler. synonymous with *compiling phase.* (*A*) (B)

compiler: a program that decodes instructions written as pseudocodes and produces a machine language program to be executed at a later time. synonymous with *compiling program.* (B)

compiler-compiler: a machine-independent language that generates compilers for any specific machine.

compiler directing statement: synonym for *compiler directive.*

compiler directive

(1) a nonexecutable statement that supplies information to a compiler to affect its action but which usually does not directly result in executable code; for example, all declarations, symbols used to indicate a macrocall, symbols used to indicate a comment. (E)

(2) in COBOL, a statement that causes the compiler to take a specific action at compile time, rather than causing the object program to take a particular action at execution time.

(3) synonymous with *compiler directing statement.*

compiler generator: a translator or an interpreter that is used to construct compilers. (A) (B)

compiler interface: functions carried out by an operating system to provide supporting capability for a compiler.

compiler manager: software, often part of an operating system, that controls the process of compiling.

compiler options: key words that can be specified to control certain aspects of compilation. Compiler options can control the nature of the load module generated by the compiler, the types of printed output to be produced, the efficient use of the compiler, and the destination of error messages.

compile time: see *compiling time.*

compile-time statement: see *preprocessor statement.*

compiling duration: time needed to translate one computer program into an acceptable language for another computer, or to translate to an assembly program, or to generate and diagnose programs.

compiling phase: synonym for *compile phase.* (A) (B)

compiling program: synonym for *compiler.* (A) (B)

compiling time: the elapsed taken for the execution of a compiler. synonymous with *compile duration.* (*A*) (B)

complement

(1) in a fixed-radix numeration system, a numeral that can be derived from a given numeral by operations that include subtracting each digit of the digital representation of the given number from the corresponding digit of the digital representation of a specified number. (B)

(2) a number that can be derived from a specified number by subtracting it from a second specified number. For example, in radix notation, the specified number may be a given power of the radix or one less than a given power of the radix. The negative of a number is often represented by its complement.

(3) see *diminished radix complement, nines complement, ones complement, radix complement, tens complement, twos complement.* (*A*)

complementary metal-oxide semiconductor: see *C-MOS.*

complementary operation: in a boolean operation, another boolean operation whose result, when it is performed on the same operands as the first boolean operation, is the negation of the result of the first boolean operation. (A) (B)

complementary operator: the logic operator whose result is the NOT of a given logic operator. (A)

complement base: in a fixed-radix numeration system, the specified number whose digital representation contains the digits from which the corresponding digits of the given number are subtracted in obtaining a complement of the given number. (A) (B)

complementer: a device whose output data are a representation of the complements of the numbers represented by its input data. (A) (B)

complementing: pertaining to the carrying out of a complementary operation.

complement-on-nine: synonym for *nines complement.* (A) (B)

complement-on-one: synonym for *ones complement.* (A) (B)

complement-on-ten: synonym for *tens complement.* (A) (B)

complement-on-two: synonym for *twos complement.* (A) (B)

complete carry: in parallel addition, a procedure in which each of the carriers is immediately transferred. (B) cf. *partial carry.* (A)

completeness check: a check for the presence of data in fields that should not be empty. (E)

complete operation: implementation of an instruction that includes the getting of the instruction, interpreting it, finding the needed operands, executing the instruction, and placing the results in store.

complete routine: a routine that does not require modification before it is used. Such routines are usually found in company libraries.

completion code: a code communicated to the job stream processor by batch programs to influence the execution of succeeding steps in a job in the input stream. see also *return code (2).*

complex constant: in FORTRAN, an ordered pair of real constants separated by a comma and enclosed in parentheses. The first real constant represents the real part of the complex number; the second represents the imaginary part.

complex data: arithmetic data, each item of which consists of a real part and an imaginary part.

complex decision-making simulation: a process allowing people to make certain decisions which are difficult to define sufficiently rigorous for incorporation into the computer-based portion of the model.

complex number: a number consisting of an ordered pair of real numbers, expressible in the form $a + bi$, where a and b are area numbers and i squared equals minus one. (A) (B)

complex relocatable expression: in assembler programming, a relocatable expression that contains two or more unpaired relocatable terms or an unpaired relocatable term preceded by a minus sign, after all unary operators have been resolved. A complex relocatable expression is not fully evaluated until program fetch time.

component: a functional part of an operating system; for example, the scheduler or supervisor. see *terminal component, solid state component.*

component address: the fixed address of a terminal component, as opposed to the address of the terminal itself.

component failure impact analysis (CFIA): an account management technique that determines the impact of a critical system component failure.

composite console: a console consisting of two different physical devices that are considered as one unit. One device is used for input and the other for output, such as a reader and printer.

composite data service vendor: a value-added carrier that has been certificated by the FCC to acquire services from common carriers and operate those services to perform data switching for others. (G)

composited circuit: a circuit that can be used simultaneously for telephone and direct-current telegraph or signaling applications, separation between the two being accomplished by frequency discrimination.

composite external symbol dictionary (CESD): control information associated with a load module that identifies the external symbols in the module.

composite module data set: a disk-resident or diskette-resident data set that contains composite modules.

composite module library: a partitioned data set (PDS) containing multiple composite modules, in which each composite module is a member of the PDS.

composite modules: object modules (programs) structured into a resident segment and optional overlay segments. A composite module is in relocatable format; that is, its address constants can be modified to compensate for a change in its origin.

composite operator: an operator composed of two operator symbols; for example, ->.

composition file: the filing of records within a storage unit.

compound condition: in COBOL, a statement that tests two or more relational expressions. It may be true or false.

compound logical element: computer circuitry that provides an output resulting from multiple inputs.

compound statement
(1) two or more statements that may be treated as a single executable statement. (F)
(2) a statement whose statement body contains one or more other statements.

compress: reduction of a signal's parameter, such as bandwidth, amplitude variation, duration, and so on, but with the preservation of the basic information content and purpose.

compressor: an electronic device that compresses the volume range of a signal. see also *compandor, expandor.*

COMPROC: see *command processor.*

compromise net: a network, used in conjunction with a hybrid coil to balance a subscriber's loop, that is adjusted for an average loop length or an average subscriber's set, or both, to secure compromise (not precision) isolation between the two directional paths of the hybrid.

computational stability: the degree to which a computational process remains valid when subjected to effects such as errors, mistakes, or malfunctions. (A)

compute limited: a restriction found in computing units limiting the output because operations are delayed awaiting completion of a computation operation.

compute mode: an operating mode of an analog computer during which the dynamic solution is in progress. synonymous with *operate mode.* (B)

computer (C): a functional unit that can perform substantial computation, including numerous arithmetic operations or logic operations, without intervention by a human operator during a run. (E) see *analog computer, arbitrary sequence computer, asynchronous computer, consecutive sequence computer, digital computer, general-purpose computer, hybrid computer, parallel computer, self-adapting computer, self-organizing computer, sequential computer, serial computer, simultaneous computer, special-purpose computer, stored program computer, synchronous computer.* see also *computer system.*

computer administrative records: records showing the source of statistics that tell how the computer use is distributed, that is, by department, by programmer, by application, and by time.

computer-aided design (CAD): a system where engineers create a design and see the proposed product in front of them on a graphics screen or in the form of computer printout. see also *CAD/CAM.*

computer-aided engineering (CAE): essentially computer software purporting to use the computer to predict how the part, machine or manufacturing process can perform.

computer-aided manufacture (CAM): see *CAD/CAM.*

computer architecture: the specification of the relationships between the parts of a computer system. (A)

computer-assisted instruction (CAI): a data-processing application in which a computing system is used to assist in the instruction of students. The application usually involves a dialog between the student and a computer program which informs the student of mistakes as they are made.

computer-assisted management: management performed with the aid of automatic data processing. (A) (B)

computer-based automation (CBA): concept describing the potential speed and accuracy of an adequately programmed digital computer to accomplish automated operating objectives in place of noncomputerized methods.

computer bureau: an agency which runs other people's work on its own computer and often provides other consulting and assistance services.

computer capacity: the span, dimension, or range of values that a number (variable) can assume in a computer, frequently expressed within beginning and ending limits of using N, when such limits are unknown.

computer code: synonymous with *machine code*.

computer conferencing: the interchange of messages on a specific topic via a computer network.

computer configuration: equipment connected to form a single computer center or system for various computer runs.

computer console: a part of a computer used for communication between operator or maintenance engineer and the computer.

computer control: a computer designed so that inputs from and outputs to a process directly control the operation of elements in that process.

computer-dependent language: synonym for *assembly language*. (A)

computer duplex: a pair of usually identical computers that operate so that if and when one is shut down for maintenance, checkouts, and so forth, the other can operate without a reduction in capability of the total system.

computer equation: an equation derived from a mathematical model for more convenient use on a computer. synonymous with *machine equation*.

computerese: slang, language used by computer specialists.

computer-generated map: a map constructed through mathematical projections using a computer.

computer graphics (CG): methods and techniques for converting data to or from graphic display via computers. (E)

computer-independent language: a programming language that is not a computer language, but instead one requiring translation or compiling to any one of a variety of computer languages. The language which is a particular language of that machine or one which has compilers for translating to its own machine language.

computer instruction: an instruction that can be recognized by the processing unit of the computer for which it is designed. synonymous with *machine instruction*. (A) (B)

computer instruction code: a code used to represent the instructions in an instruction set. (B) synonymous with *machine code, instruction code.* synonym for *operation code.* (A)

computer instruction set: a complete set of the operators of the instructions of a computer together with a description of types of meanings that can be attributed to their operands. synonymous with *machines instruction set.* (A)

computer interface unit (CIU): a device which interfaces with the central processing unit and peripheral devices such as disks or printers.

computerized foreman: computers used to minimize inventory and production bottlenecks on the factory floor. If orders or materials change, or if machines break down, these systems will automatically change the schedule.

computerized hyphenation: in word

processing, a feature that allows units to use standard rules of grammar to automatically hyphenate most words at the end of a typing line.

computer language: a computer-oriented language whose instructions consist only of computer instructions. synonymous with *machine language*. deprecated term for *computer-oriented language* (*A*) (B)

computer language symbols: prescribed graphical special meanings or functions in any computer program.

computer learning

(1) the process by which a computer modified programs according to its own memory or experience, that is, changes of logic paths, or parameters values. An example is a chess-playing computer.

(2) in process control, an analog computer is able to change its parameters by a continuous process according to temperatures, or other gauge reports it receives.

computer letter: a letter of standard form into which personal information, that is, names and addresses, are inserted using word processing software.

computer-limited: on buffered computers, a section of a routine in which the time required for computation exceeds the time required to read and write to or from input-output devices.

computer micrographics: methods and techniques for converting data to or from microform with the assistance of a computer. (E)

computer network: a complex consisting of two or more interconnected computing units. (A) synonym for *user-application network*. (E)

computer numerical control: a state in which a number of numerical control devices are linked together via a data transmission network and brought under the control of a single numerical control machine. see also *direct numerical control.*

computer operation: one of the elementary operations which a computer is designed to perform. synonymous with *machine operation*. (*A*)

computer-oriented language

(1) a programming language that reflects the structure of a given computer or that of a given class of computers. (B)

(2) a programming language whose words and syntax are designed for use on a specific class of computers. synonymous with *machine-oriented language.*

(3) see also *computer language*. (*A*)

computer output microfilm (COM): microfilm that contains data that are recorded directly from computer-generated signals. (B)

computer output microfilmer (COM): a recording device that produces computer output microfilm. (A)

computer peripherals: the auxiliary devices under control of a central computer, such as card punches and readers, high-speed printers, magnetic tape units, and optical character readers.

computer program: a sequence of instructions suitable for processing by a computer.

computer program annotation: synonym for *comment*. (A) (B) (E)

computer program origin: the address assigned to the initial storage location of a computer program in main storage. (A)

computer sciences (CS): the branch of science and technology that is concerned with methods and techniques relating to data processing performed by automatic means. (E)

computer simulator: a computer program that translates computer programs prepared for a computer of one model for execution on a computer of a different model. (A) (B)

computer system: a functional unit, consisting of one or more computers and associated software, that uses common storage for all or part of a program and also for all or part of the data necessary for execution of the program; executes user-written or user-designated programs; performs user-designated data manipulation, including arithmetic operations and logic operations; and that can execute programs that modify themselves during their execution. synonymous with *ADP system, computing system.* (E)

computer system audit: an audit of the controls throughout a computer system to evaluate their effectiveness and to recommend improvements. (E)

computer time: in simulation, the time required to process the data that represents a process or that represents a part of a process. (A)

computer utility: a time-shared computer system providing computational and processing ability, generally accessed by means of data-communications subsystems. Certain data and programs are shared by all users of the service who may have their own programs immediately available in the CPU, may have them on call at the computer utility, or may load

them by transmitting prior to use.

computer word: a word stored in one computer location and capable of being treated as a unit. synonymous with *machine word.* (B) see also *half-word.* (A)

computing element: a computer component that performs the mathematical operations required for problem solutions.

computing power: the speed with complex operations can be performed in a computing system. see also *supercomputer.*

computing system: synonym for *computer system.* (E)

COMSAT: see *Communications Satellite Corporation.*

concatenate: to connect in a series. synonymous with *catenate.*

concatenated data sets: a group of logically connected data that are treated as one data set for the duration of a job step.

concatenated key: a key constructed to access a particular segment; consisting of the key fields, including that of the root segment and successive segments, down to the root segment.

concatenation: in PL/1, the operation that joins two strings in the order specified, thus forming one string whose length is equal to the sum of the lengths is equal to the sum of the lengths of the two strings. It is specified by the operator.

concatenation character: in assembler programming, the period (.) that is used to separate character strings that are to be joined together in conditional assembly processing.

concentrated messages: incoming messages from a group of terminals directed to a remote device that combined them into a single physical message for forwarding to the processing unit. Or, conversely, a single physical message made up of a group of messages for a group of terminals that is sent by the processing unit to a remote device for deconcentration.

concentration: the process of combining multiple messages into a single message for transmission. synonym for *blocking*. cf. *deconcentration*.

concentrator

(1) in data transmission, a functional unit that permits a common transmission medium to serve more data sources than there are channels currently available within the transmission medium. (E)

(2) any device that combines incoming messages into a single message (concentration) or extracts individual messages from the data sent in a single transmission sequence (deconcentration).

(3) see also *blocking, deblocking.*

concentrator terminal buffer (CTB): a main storage area that contains a segment of a physical message transmitted to or from a concentrator that pertains to one attached terminal.

conceptual model: in a data base, a collection of entities and their relationships that describe and represent an enterprise or an organization. (E)

concordance: an alphabetical list of words appearing in a document, with an indication of the place where they appear.

concordant: an arrangement of information or data into fixed or harmoni-

ous locations on particular documents.

concurrent: pertaining to the occurrence of two or more activities within a given interval of time. (B) cf. *consecutive, sequential, simultaneous.* (A)

concurrent operation: a mode of operations which includes the performance of two or more operations within a given interval of time. (A)

concurrent peripheral operations (CPO): synonym for *spooling.*

concurrent processing

(1) the ability to carry out more than one program at a time.

(2) the processing of more than one independent task simultaneously by a single computing system involving interlaced timesharing of at least one section of hardware, usually the control unit and memory-address register or the multiplexing unit, for selecting individual control units and memory-address registers for each task.

COND: see *condition.*

condensing routine: a routine that converts machine language, that is, the one-instruction-per-card output format, from an assembly program or system into several instructions per card.

condition (COND)

(1) one of a set of specified values a data item can assume.

(2) in COBOL, a simple conditional expression: relation condition, class condition, condition-name condition, sign condition, switch-name condition, sign condition, switch-status condition, NOT condition.

(3) see *on condition, restart condition.*

conditional assembly: an assembler facility for altering at preassembly time the content and sequence of source statements that are to be assembled.

conditional assembly expression: an expression that an assembler evaluates at preassembly time.

conditional assembly instruction: an assembler instruction that performs a conditional assembly operation. Conditional assembly instructions are processed at preassembly time.

conditional branch instruction: deprecated term for *conditional jump instruction.* (A) (B)

conditional breakpoint: a breakpoint where the setting of certain conditions permit variation in the particular program sequence.

conditional breakpoint instruction: an instruction at a breakpoint that serves as a conditional branch instruction following the intervention resulting in the breakpoint has occurred.

conditional control transfer instruction: deprecated term for *conditional jump instruction.* (A) (B)

conditional entropy: in information theory, the mean of the measure of information conveyed by the occurrence of any one of a finite set of mutually exclusive and jointly exhaustive events of definite conditional probabilities, given the occurrence of events of another set of mutually exclusive events. synonymous with *average conditional information content, mean conditional information content.* (A) (B)

conditional expression: in COBOL, an expression having the particular characteristic that, taken as a whole,

it may be either true or false, in accordance with the rules.

conditional implication operation: synonym for *implication.* (A) (B)

conditional information content: in information theory, a measure of information conveyed by the occurrence of an event of a definite conditional probablity, given the occurrence of another event. (B) see *average conditional information content, mean conditional information content.* (A)

conditional jump: a jump that takes place only when the instruction that specifies it is executed and specified conditions are satisfied. (A) (B)

conditional jump instruction: an instruction that specifies a conditional jump and the conditions that have to be satisfied for the conditional jump to occur. (A) (B)

conditional statement

(1) a statement that permits the execution of one of a number of possible operations, with or without a transfer of control; for example, a case statement, a computed GOTO in FORTRAN, an IF statement. (E)

(2) a statement used to express an assignment or branch, based on specified criteria; for example, an IF-THEN statement. (A)

(3) in COBOL, a statement made up of data names, literals, figurative constants, logical operators, or a combination of such operators, so constructed that it tests a truth value. The subsequent action of the object program is dependent on this truth value.

conditional stop instruction: an instruction that causes a program to be halted on the detection of a condition such as the setting of a console switch by the operator.

conditional transfer instruction: deprecated term for *conditional jump instruction, jump instruction.* (A) (B)

conditional variable: in COBOL, a data item that can assume more than one value; one or more of the values it assumes has a condition name assigned to it.

condition code: a code that reflects the result of a previous input-output, arithmetic, or logical operation.

conditioned circuit: a circuit which has conditioning equipment to obtain the desired characteristics for voice or data transmission.

conditioning: the addition of equipment to leased voice-grade channel to provide minimum values of line characterics required for data transmission.

conditioning equipment

(1) at junctions of circuits, equipment used to match transmission levels and impedances and also to provide equalization between facilities.

(2) corrective networks used to equalize the insertion loss-versus-frequency characteristic and the envelope delay distortion over a desired frequency range in order to improve data transmission.

condition list: in PL/1, a list of one or more condition prefixes.

condition name

(1) in COBOL, the name assigned to a specific value, set of values, or range of values, that a data item may assume.

(2) in PL/1, a language key word (or CONDITION followed by a parenthesized programmer-defined name)

that denotes an on condition that might arise within a task.

condition-name condition: in COBOL, a statement that the value of a conditional variable is one of a set (or range) of values of a data item identified by a condition name. The statement may be true or false.

condition prefix: in PL/1, a parenthesized list of one or more language condition names, prefixed to a statement. It specifies whether the named on conditions are to be enabled.

conditions: see *entry conditions.* (A)

cone of nulls: a conical surface formed by directions of negligible radiation.

conference control: synonym for *sensitivity control.*

confidence level: a degree of probability and/or of certainty that can be expressed as a percentage.

configuration

(1) the arrangement of a computer system or network as defined by the nature, number, and the chief characteristics of its functional units. More specifically, the term *configuration* may refer to a hardware configuration or a software configuration. (E)

(2) the devices and programs that make up a system, subsystem, or network.

configuration section: a section of the environment division of a COBOL program. It describes the overall specification of computers.

configure: to plan the needed component parts of a computer system to fulfill the requirements of a specified application or group of applications.

confirmation: a type of response by a receiver that permits a sender to continue.

congestion: see *reception congestion.*

conjunction: the boolean operation whose result has the boolean value 1 if and only if each operand has the boolean value 1. synonymous with *AND operation, intersection, logical product.* (B) cf. *nonconjunction.* (A)

connected reference: in PL/1, a reference to connected storage; it must be apparent, prior to execution of the program, that the storage is connected.

connected storage: in PI/1, internal storage of an interrupted linear sequence of items that can be referred to by a single name.

connecting arrangement: the implementation for connecting arrangement service. A connecting arrangement consists of an interconnecting unit, a technical reference, and a tariff offering. (F)

connecting arrangement service: a service providing electrical connection to the public telephone network of customer-provided equipment. (F)

connection: an association established between functional units for conveying information. (C) synonym for *connection.* see *data connection, dedicated connection, multipoint connection, point-to-point connection, switched connection.*

connections per circuit per hour (CCH): an indication of holding time of calls. (F)

connective: in COBOL, in word or a punctuation character that associated a data name or paragraph name with its qualifier, links two or more operands in a series, or forms a condition expression.

connector

(1) a flowchart symbol that represents a break in a flow line and that indicates where the flow line is continued. (E)

(2) in step-by-step switching systems, a two-motion electromechanical switch that operates on the last two digits of the telephone number to connect from a selector to any one of 100 customer loops. (F)

(3) see also *inconnector, outconnector.*

connect time: time that elapses while the user of a remote terminal is connected to a time-shared system; measured by the duration between sign-on and sign-off.

CONS: see *console.*

consecutive: pertaining to the occurrence of two sequential events without the intervention of any other such event. (B) cf. *sequential.* see also *concurrent, simultaneous.* (A)

consecutive operation: synonym for *sequential operation.* (A)

consecutive sequence computer: a computer in which instructions are executed in an implicitly defined sequence unless a jump instruction specifies the storage location of the next instruction to be executed. (A) (B)

consistency check: a check to determine whether specific data items are compatible; for example, a check to determine whether two occurrences of a data item are equal. (E)

console (CONS)

(1) a part of a computer used for communication between the operator or maintenance engineer and the computer. (A)

(2) a COBOL mnemonic name as-

sociated with the console typewriter.
(3) see *operator console*. (A)

Console   Command-Device   Down:
see *DVCDN*.

Console Command-Device Up: see
DVCUP.

console word-processing equipment:
word-processing equipment incorporated into a larger unit containing
other equipment. If it is not integrated
word-processing equipment, its control unit is usually designed also to fit
into the unit. (D)

CONST: see *constant*.

constant (C) (CONST)

(1) in a calculator, a number entered and held in the machine for repeated use. (D)

(2) a fixed or invariable value or
data item.

(3) see *figurative constant, hexadecimal constant, literal constant,
logical constant.*

constant area: an area of store allocated by a program, used to hold
constants.

constant instruction: an instruction
not intended to be executed as an instruction, written in the form of a constant.

constant length field: an entry on a
document or card requiring a fixed
number of alphanumeric characters.

constant ratio code: a code in which
all characters are represented by
combinations having a fixed ratio of
ones to zeroes.

constant storage: a part of storage
designated to store the invariable
quantities needed for processing.

constant words: descriptive data that
is fixed and does not generally appear as an element of input.

constraint: an equation or inequality

relating the variables in an optimization problem.

constructing: synonym for *blocking*.

**Consultive Committee International
Telegraph and Telephone (CCITT):**
an advisory committee established
under the United Nations within the
International   Telecommunication
Union (ITU) to recommend worldwide standards.

CONT: see *controller*.

contained text: in PL/1, all text in a
procedure (including nexted procedures) except its entry names and
condition prefixes of the PROCE-
DURE statement; all text in a begin
block except labels and conditions
prefixes of the BEGIN statement that
heads the block. Internal blocks are
contained in the external procedure.

content: see *conditional information
content, decision content, information content, joint information content, mean transinformation content,
transinformation content*. (A)

content-addressed storage: synonym
for *associative storage*. (A)

contention

(1) a condition arising when two or
more data stations attempt to transmit at the same time over a shared
channel, or when two data stations
attempt to transmit the same time in
two-way alternate communication.

(2) a line-control scheme in which
stations on a line compete for the use
of that unused line; the station that is
successful in gaining control of the
line is able to transmit.

contention system: a system in which
one or more terminals and the computer compete for use of the line.

contents list: in word processing, the
display or printout of a list of available

stored information for selection by the operator. (D)

context: words of text that occur prior to and following a particular group of words.

context editing: a method of editing a line without using line numbers. To refer to a particular line, all or part of the contents of that line are specified.

çontextual declaration: in PL/1, the appearance of an identifier that has not been explicitly declared, in a context that allows the association of specific attributes with the identifier.

contiguous: touching or joining at the edge or boundary; adjacent. For example; an unbroken consecutive series of storage locations.

contingency procedure: a procedure that is an alternative to the normal path of a process if an unusual but anticipated situation occurs. A contingency procedure may be triggered by events such as an overflow or an operator intervention. (E)

continuation card: a punched card that holds data that has been started on a previous card. This is permitted in many compilers such as FORTRAN.

continuation line: a line of a source statement into which characters are entered when the source statement cannot be contained on the preceding line or lines.

continuity check: a check made of a circuit or circuits in a connection to verify that a path (for transmission such as data or speech) exists. (C)

continuous-form cards: special cards attached together in continuous strips to facilitate printing. They can be separated into individual punched cards. (A)

continuous forms: a series of connected paper forms that feed continuously through a printing device. The connection between the forms is perforated to allow the user to tear them apart. Prior to printing, the forms are folded in a stacked arrangement, with the folds along the perforations. cf. *cut form.*

continuous forms paper: a continuous length of single-ply, fanfolded paper with both edges punched for tractor feeding and with perforation between pages. There are various sizes and basis weights.

continuous items: in COBOL, consecutive elementary or group items in the data division that have a definite relationship with each other.

continuous simulation: simulation represented by continuous variables. The system becomes suitable for representation by a set of differential equations, classified as linear or nonlinear.

continuous-tone original: an original in which the subject matter consists of areas of actual tonal graduation. synonymous with *full-tone original.* (D)

contrast

(1) in optical character recognition, the difference between color or shading of the printed material on a document and the background on which it is printed. see *print contrast ratio* (A)

(2) in computer graphics, the difference in brightness or color between a display image and the area in which it is displayed. (E)

control (C) (CNTL) (CNTRL) (CTRL): the determination of the time and order in which the different parts of a data processing system and the devices that contain those parts perform the input, processing, storage, and output functions. see *loop control, numerical control, process control, real-time control, sequential control.*

control area (CA): see *control block.*

control ball: in computer graphics, a ball, movable about its center, that is used as a locator device. synonymous with *track ball.* (E)

control block: a storage area used by a computer program to hold control information. synonymous with *control area.* (B)

control bus: control lines (paths) usually from 10 to 100, with a function to carry the synchronization and control information needed to the computer system.

control bytes: bytes associated with a physical record that serve to identify the record and indicate characteristic such as its length and blocking factor.

control card: a punched card containing input data or parameters for initiating or modifying a program.

control character: a character whose occurrence in a particular context initiates, modified, or stops a control operation. A control character may be recorded for use in a subsequent action, and it may have a graphic representation in some circumstances. (E) see *accuracy control character, device control character, print control character, transmission control character.*

control circuits: circuits in a control unit that carry out the operations begun by instructions.

control clerk: a worker responsible for the integrity of the data received,

processed, and dispatched from the data-processing department.

control computer: a computer which, by means of inputs from and outputs to a process, directly control the operation of elements in that process.

control counter (CC): synonym for *instruction address register.* (B)

control cycle: a specific cycle of a punch card machine's main shaft during which the feeding is stopped due to a control change.

control data: items of data, used to select, execute, identify, or modify another routine, record, file, operation, or data value.

control dictionary: the external symbol dictionary and the relocation dictionary, collectively, of an object or load module. see also *dictionary.*

control engineering: see *automatic control engineering.* (A)

control field

(1) a field that is compared with other fields to determine the record sequence in the output file.

(2) a field in a record that identifies the relationship of the record to other records (such as a part number in an inventory record). Control fields determine when certain operations are to be performed.

(3) in sorting or merging records, a group of contiguous bits in a control word used in determining sequence.

control format item: in PL/1, a specification used in edit-directed transmission to specify positioning of a data item within the stream or printed page.

control function: synonym for *control operation.* (A)

control heading: a title or short definition of a control group of records which appear in front of each such group.

control hole: synonym for *designation hole.* (A) (B)

control instruction: instruction used to manipulate data within the main memory and the control unit, to ready main memory storage areas for the processing of data fields and to control the sequential selection and interpretation of instructions in the stored program.

control instruction register: deprecated term for *instruction address register.* (A) (B)

control language: see *job control language.* (A)

controlled parameter: in PL1, a parameter for which the CONTROLLED attribute is specified; it can be associated only with arguments that have the CONTROLLED attribute.

controlled storage allocation: the allocation of storage for controlled variables.

controlled variable: in PL1, a variable whose allocation and release are controlled by the ALLOCATE and FREE statements, with access to only the current generation. cf. *automatic variable.*

controlled vocabulary: a fixed listing of terms used to index records for storage and retrieval, usually required in on-line searching.

controller: a device that directs the transmission of data over the data links of a network; its operation may be controlled by a program executed in a processor to which the controller is connected or they may be controlled by a program executed within the device. (E) see *communication controller, input-output controller,*

store controller, subsystem controller.

controller functions: an action or series of actions built into a controller and taken by the controller in response to a request from a terminal, another controller function, or a host system.

control line: the randomly timed cycle control that tells each terminal in a reel when to begin transmitting.

control logic: steps needed to perform a specific function.

control loop: synonymous with *control tape.*

control mark: synonymous with *tape mark.*

control-message display: a machine that displays information in plain language; for example, a display on the screen of a terminal.

control mode

(1) the state that all terminals on a line must be in to allow line discipline, line control, or terminal selection to occur.

(2) a mode in which a tributary station can be polled or addressed by a control station.

control number: the quantity or number (value) that is the result of a process or problem needed to prove the accuracy of a process or problem.

control objectives: criteria required to obtain an acceptable level of integrity required for a data-processing system. (E)

control operation: an action that affects the recording, processing, transmission, or interpretation of data; for example, starting or stopping a process, carriage return, font change, rewind, and end of transmission. synonymous with *control function*. (A) (B)

control operator: the person who generally performs special administrative, control, and testing functions.

control operator's terminal: the terminal at which the control operator has logged on.

control panel: a part of a computer console that contains manual controls. synonym for *plugboard*. see *operator control panel*. (A)

control printing: a list of the control group for purposes of identification without the list of the detail records.

control program (CP): a computer program designed to schedule and to supervise the execution of programs of a computer system. (E)

control program generation language: the set of macroinstructions and associated operands with which a user defines the network configuration for a communication controller.

control program generation procedure: a two-stage process that creates a control program load module for a communication controller based on parameters specified by a user through the control program generation language.

control punch: synonym for *designation hole*. (A) (B)

control record: a checkpoint record that contains data used to initiate, modify, or stop a control operation, or to determine the manner in which data is processed.

control register: deprecated term for *instruction address register*. (A) (B)

control routine

(1) a routine that controls loading and relocation of routines and can make use of instructions that are un-

known to the general programmer.

(2) a set of coded instructions designed to process and control other sets of coded instructions.

(3) a set of coded instructions used in realizing automatic coding.

control section (CSECT): that part of a program specified by the programmer to be a relocatable unit, all elements of which are to be loaded into adjoining main storage locations.

control sequence: the usual order in which instructions are executed.

control specifications: a statement of the rules and regulations to be applied within a data-processing system in order to ensure the required level of integrity. (E)

control stack: a number of storage locations for providing control in the dynamic allocation of work space.

control standards: control specifications accepted as criteria for preventing, detecting, and correcting errors or omissions. (E)

control statement

(1) a statement that controls or affects the execution of a program in a data processing system.

(2) in programming languages, a statement that is used to alter the continuous sequential execution of statements; a control statement may be a conditional statement such as IF, or an imperative statement such as STOP. (E)

(3) see *job control statement, linkage editor, operation control statement.*

control station

(1) in basic mode link control the data station in a multipoint connection or a point-to-point connection that nominates the master station

and supervises polling, selecting, interrogating, and recovery procedures. (E)

(2) a station that can poll or address tributary stations.

control storage: a portion of storage that contains microcode.

control storage save: the automatic writing of critical areas of store controller storage onto areas of the integrated disk unit when a power failure is detected or when certain machine errors occur.

control system: a system of the closed-loop type in which the computer is used to govern external processes.

control tape: see *carriage control tape.* (A)

control techniques: procedures, in a given computer installation, some or all of which may be appropriate to maintain integrity. (E)

control terminal: any active terminal at which the user is authorized to enter commands affecting system operation.

control total: a sum, resulting from the addition of a specified field from each record in a group of records, that is used for checking machine, program, and data reliability. synonymous with *hash total.*

control transfer statement: a statement that causes the execution of a statement other than the next statement written in the source program. (E)

control unit (CU): a device that controls input-output operations at one or more devices. see *device control unit, instruction control unit, main control unit, peripheral control unit, transmission control unit.*

control variable: in PL/1, a variable used to control the iterative execution of a group. see *loop-control variable.*

control volume: a volume that contains one or more indexes of the catalog.

control word (CW): all control fields used to sort or merge a particular group of records; the major field appears first and other fields follow in descending order of importance.

CONV: see *conversion.*

convention: specific standard and accepted procedures in programs and systems analysis; the abbreviations, symbols, and their meanings as developed for particular systems and programs.

convention equipment: devices considered to be part of the computer system but which are not specifically part of the computer itself.

convergence: the joining together of technologies that were previously thought to be distinct, that is, computers, telecommunications, to produce integrated systems.

conversation: a dialog between a user and an interactive data-processing system.

conversational: pertaining to a program or a system that carries on a dialog with a terminal user, alternately accepting input and then responding to the input quickly enough for the user to maintain his train of thought. see also *interactive.*

Conversational Algebraic Language (CAL): a general purpose language designed to be used extensively in time sharing; developed at the University of California; similar in usage to BASIC.

conversational language: a language using a near-English character set which aids communication between user and the computer.

conversational mode

(1) a mode of operation of a data-processing system in which a sequence of alternating entries and responses between a user and the system takes place in a manner similar to a dialog between two persons. synonymous with *interactive mode.* (E)

(2) a mode in which the next message received by a station after it enters an inquiry message is a reply to that message.

conversational remote job entry (CRJE): an operating system facility for entering job control language statements from a remote terminal, and causing the scheduling and execution of the jobs described in the statements. The terminal user is prompted for missing operands or corrections.

conversational time sharing: the simultaneous use of a computer system by multiple users at remote locations, each equipped with a remote terminal.

conversion (CONV)

(1) the process of changing from one method of data processing to another or from one data-processing system to another.

(2) the process of changing from one form of representation to another; for example, to change from decimal representation to binary representation. see also *translation.*

(3) in signaling, the substitution of one, two, or three digits for received digits for the purpose of directing the call through the next office. (F)

conversion costs: one-time expenses, which are incurred when an organization installs a computer for the first time or when it applies an existing system to a new application area.

conversion device: a piece of peripheral equipment that converts data from one form into another form or medium, without changing the date, content, or information.

conversion mode: communication between a terminal and the computer in which each entry from the terminal elicits a response from the computer and vice versa.

conversion routine: a flexible program that is used by a programmer to alter the presentation of data from one form to another, such as from card to disk.

convert: to change the representation of data from one form to another, without changing the information they convey; for example, radix conversion, code conversion, conversion from punched cards to magnetic tape, analog to digital conversion. (B) synonymous with *transform.* see also *copy, duplicate. (A)*

converter: a device capable of converting impulses from one mode to another, such as analog to digital, or parallel to serial, or from one code to another. see *code converter, data converter.*

converting: transferring data from one form to a different one.

convex programming: in operations research, a particular case of non-linear programming in which the function to be maximized or minimized and the constraints are appropriately convex or concave functions of the controllable variables. (B) cf. *dynamic programming, integer programming, linear programming, mathematical programming, nonlinear programming, quadratic programming. (A)*

coordinate: see *absolute coordinate, device coordinate, normalized device coordinates, relative coordinate, user coordinate, world coordinates.*

coordinate data: data that specifies a location within a display space or an image space. see also *absolute data, relative data.*

coordinated time scale: a time scale generated by electronic or mechanical devices, such as electronic clocks driven by crystal or atomic oscillators, which is coordinated by international agreement to approximate Universal Time (UT).

coordinate graphics: computer graphics in which display images are generated from display command coordinate data. (E)

coordinate network: a switching network consisting of incoming and outgoing talking paths arranged at right angles to each other with fine-motion or electronic switching elements at intersections. (F)

copy
(1) to read data from a source, leaving the source data unchanged, and to write the same data elsewhere in a physical form that may differ from that of the source; for example, to copy a deck of punched cards onto magnetic tape. The degree of editing that may be carried out at the same time depends upon the circumstances in which the copying is performed. (A) (B)

(2) in word processing, the reproduction of selected recorded text from storage or from a recording medium to another recording medium. (D)

(3) see *hard copy, soft copy.*

CORAL: Computer On-Line Real-time Applications Language, a high-level language designed for real-time applications.

cordless plugs: on patch cords, if connectors do not include a flexible portion, they are termed cordless plugs.

Cordonnier system: an information-retrieval system using peek-a-boo cards; that is, cards with small holes drilled at intersections of coordinates (column and row designations) to represent document numbers. synonymous with *batten system.*

core
(1) deprecated term for *tape spool.* (A) (B)

(2) deprecated term for *main storage.*

(3) see *magnetic core, multiple aperture core, switch core.*

core dump: a listing of the selected parts or contents of a storage device. synonymous with *memory dump, memory printout.*

core image: the form in which a computer program and related data exist at the time they reside in main storage. (B)

core image library: a library of phases that have been produced as output from link editing. The phases in the core image library are in a format that is executable either directly or after processing by the relocating loader in the supervisor.

core memory (CM): a storage device

consisting of ferromagnetic cores, or an apertured ferrite plate, through which sense windings and select lines are threaded.

core network: a regulated system of transmission and switching facilities planned, owned, and operated by a partnership of Bell and Independent Telephone Companies for the purpose of providing basic universal telecommunications service. The boundary of the core network is determined by the FCC under public interest criteria. (G)

co-resident: pertaining to the condition in which two or more modules are located in main storage at the same time.

core storage

(1) a magnetic storage in which the magnetic medium consists of magnetic cores. (A)

(2) deprecated term for *main storage.*

(3) see *magnetic core storage.*

corner cut: a corner removed from a card for orientation purposes.

correct and copy: a designated record is copied from one tape to another with specified corrections. In manipulating magnetic tapes, either a record-counting method or a file-identification method is used. The file option provides further convenience in that it allows operation over an entire tape or file, rather than over a specified number of records.

correcting feature (printing process only): in word processing, a facility for removing or blocking out type characters during the editing process. (D)

correction: a quantity (equal in absolute value to the error) that is added to a calculated or observed value to obtain the true value.

corrective maintenance: maintenance specifically intended to eliminate an existing fault. cf. *preventive maintenance. (A)*

corrective maintenance time: time, either scheduled or unscheduled, used to perform corrective maintenance. (A)

corruption: the mutilation of code or data caused by hardware or software failure.

cost-center accounting: financial accounting where charges are recorded, keypunched, edited, sorted, and posted. This information is then used as input to the computer to post the required formal ledgers.

count (CNT): the cumulative total of the number of times a specific event occurs, kept as a factual record.

counter (C) (CNTR) (CT) (CTR): a device whose state represents a number and that, on receipt of an appropriate signal, causes the number represented to be increased by unity or by an arbitrary constant; the device is usually capable of bringing the number represented to a specified value, for example, zero. (A) (B) see *instruction counter, modulo-N counter, reversible counter.*

counter inhibit: the bit, in the program status double-word, that shows whether (if one) or not (if zero) all (clock) count zero interrupts are inhibited.

count-key-data (CKD) device: a disk storage device that stores data in the format count field, usually followed by a key field, followed by the actual data of a record. The count field contains, among others, the address of the record in the format CCHHR (CC = cylinder number, HH = head number, R = record number) and the length of the data; the key field contains the record's key (search argument).

count modulo-N: when a number in a counter reverts to zero in the counting sequence after reaching a maximum value of (N-1), the counter is said to count modulo-N.

country code: the one-, two-, or three-digit number that, in the world numbering plan, identifies each country or integrated numbering plan in the world. The initial digit is always the world-zone number. Any subsequent digits in the code further define the designated geographic area (normally identifying a specific country). On an international call, the country code is dialed before the national number. (F)

coupler: synonym for *interconnecting unit.*

CP
(1)   see *call processor.*
(2)   see *card punch.*
(3)   see *central processor.*
(4)   see *character printer.*
(5)   see *command processor.*
(6)   see *control program.*

CPE: see *customer premises equipment.*

CPI: characters per inch.

"C" pins: module exit pins, used for circuit-board connections. These are usually located around the periphery of the substrate.

CP/M: control program microcomputer; a common disk operating system used by many microcomputers.

CPO: see *concurrent peripheral operations.* synonym for *spooling.*

CPS: characters per second.

CPSK: see *coherent phase-shift keying.*

CPU: see *central processing unit.* deprecated term for *processing unit.* (B)

CR
(1)   see *card reader.*
(2)   see *carriage return.*

crash: a computer system is said to "crash" when it stops working for some reason and must be restarted by the operator.
see *carrier return character.*

CRC: see *cyclic redundancy check.* (A)

CRE: see *carrier return character.*

cream skimming: a situation in which market suppliers can selectively choose to serve only the more profitable areas (or the "cream") of the communications market. For example, cream skimming occurs when an Other Common Carrier (OCC) offers private-line service along high-volume, lower-costs routes, while ignoring areas in which it costs more to provide service. The common carriers are required by law to service all routes, even the high-cost, low-volume routes. Since the established telephone common carriers charge uniform prices based on average costs over all their routes, their lower-cost routes are vulnerable to cream-skimming competition. (G)

CR-hi: channel request high priority; the first level of priority.

CRJE: see *conversational remote job entry.*

CR-lo: channel request low priority; the third level of priority.

CR-med: channel request medium priority; the second level of priority.

cross assembler: a program run on

one computer for the purpose of translating instructions for a different computer.

crossbar switch: a relay-operated device that makes a connection between one line in each of two sets of lines. The two sets are physically arranged along adjacent sides of a matrix of contracts or switch points. see also *line switching, step-by-step system.*

crossbar system: a type of line-switching system that uses crossbar switches. see also *step-by-step switch.*

cross check: checking the result of a calculation by obtaining a solution by a different method and comparing the results.

cross compiler: a compiler that yields object code suitable for a different computer from the one on which the compiler is used.

cross-domain communication: synonym for *networking.*

cross-domain link
(1) a subarea link connecting two subareas that are in different domains.
(2) a link physically connecting two domains.

cross-domain subarea link: a link between two subarea nodes in different domains.

crossfire: interference from one telegraph circuit to another telegraph circuit or into telephone circuits.

crossfoot: to add across several domains of numerical information.

crossfooting test: a check based on the comparison of two totals obtained by adding the same set of numbers in different sequences. (E)

cross-point array: an arrangement of

switching elements used in some switching networks, characterized by incoming and outgoing talking paths arranged at right angles to each other, with switching elements at intersections. (F)

cross-sectional testing: a series of tests required to obtain a representative sampling of system performance.

cross section of an array: in PL/1, the elements represented by the extent of at least one dimension (but not all dimensions) of an array. An asterisk in the place of a subscript in an array reference indicates the entire extent of that dimension.

cross software: software allowing users to develop programs for a target computer on a host computer.

cross-subarea link: synonym for *subarea node.* see also *cross-domain link.*

crosstalk
(1) the unwanted energy transferred from one circuit, called the disturbing circuitry, to another circuit, called the disturbed circuit. (A)
(2) undesired power coupled into a communications circuit from other communications circuits. Telephone cross talk may be either intelligible or unintelligible. (F)

cross tracking: a specific crosslike array of bright dots on the cathode-ray tube display used for locating points and lines or for drawing curves.

crowding: in optical character recognition, the insufficient horizontal spacing between characters.

CRT: see *cathode-ray tube.*

CRT display
(1) cathode-ray tube display. (A)
(2) a display device that uses a cathode-ray tube.

CRT display device: a display device in which display images are produced on a cathode-ray tube.

cryogenics: the study and use of devices utilizing properties of materials near absolute zero in temperature. (A)

cryogenic storage: a storage device that uses the superconductive and magnetic properties of certain materials at very low temperatures. synonymous with *cryogenic store*. (A) (B)

cryogenic store: synonym for *cryogenic storage*. (B)

cryostat: a device designed to use evaporative and condensing cycles to achieve extremely low temperatures, and often used to liquify gases.

cryotron: a device that makes use of the effects of low temperatures on conductive materials such that small magnetic field changes can control large current changes. (A)

cryptographic: pertaining to the transformation of data to conceal its meaning. see also *decipher, encipher*.

cryptographic algorithm: a set of rules that specify the mathematical steps required to encipher and decipher data.

cryptography: the transformation of data to conceal its meaning.

crystal: a quartz crystal whose piezoelectric vibrational modes provide a highly accurate frequency for clock timing.

CS: see *computer science*.

CSECT: see *control section*.

CSU

(1) see *channel service unit*.

(2) see *circuit switching unit*.

CSW: see *channel status word*.

CT: see *counter*.

CTB: see *concentrator terminal buffer*.

CTCA: see *channel-to-channel adapter*.

CTR: see *counter*.

CTRL: see *control*.

CU: see *control unit*.

CUA: see *circuit unit assembly*.

cue: synonym for *call*. (A)

cumulative index: an index showing all items appearing in a number of separate indexes.

currency symbol: a graphic character used to designate monetary quantities; for example, $.

current beam position: on a CRT display device, the coordinates on the display surface at which the electron beam is aimed. synonymous with *starting point*.

current connect group: the group to which a user is associated during a terminal session or batch job.

current generation: in PL/1, that generation of an automatic on or controlled variable currently available by reference to the name of the variable.

current instruction register (CIR): the control section register which contains the instruction currently being executed after it is brought to the control section from memory. synonymous with *instruction register*.

current line pointer (CLP): in systems with time sharing, a pointer that indicates the display line on which operations are being performed.

current loop: the means of communicating data via presence or absence of current on a two-wire cable.

current mode logic (CML): logic in which transistors operate in the unsaturated mode as distinguished from most other logic types which operate in the saturation region. This logic possesses fast switching speeds and low logic swings.

current record: the record pointed to by the current line pointer.

cursor

(1) in computer graphics, a movable marker that is used to indicate a position on a display space. (E)

(2) a displayed symbol that acts as a marker to help the user locate a point in text, in a system command, or in storage. (D)

(3) a movable spot of light on the screen of a display device, usually indicating where the next character is to be entered, replaced, or deleted.

cursor control keys: the keys that control the movement of the cursor. (D)

curtate: a group of adjacent card rows. see *lower curtate, upper curtate. (A)*

curve follower: an input unit that reads data represented by a curve. (A) (B)

curve generator: in computer graphics, a functional unit that converts a coded representation into the shape of a curve. (E)

cushion: a contiguous address space in dynamic storage that is held in reserve and not normally used to satisfy a request for storage until such requests cannot be satisfied from other areas of dynamic storage.

customer access area: a specifically designated area of a machine or system to which the customer has access to connect, install, and maintain signals, control, power, or other utilities.

customer information control system (CICS): a program product that en-ables transactions entered at remote terminals to be processed concurrently by user-written application programs. It also includes facilities for building, using, and maintaining data bases.

customer premises equipment (CPE): all telecommunciations terminal equipment located on the customer premises, both state and interstate, and encompassing everything from black telephones to the most advanced data terminals and PBXs. (G)

customer switching system: a switching system that provides service for a customer, typically a business customer. Systems in this category include key telephone systems, private branch exchanges, automatic call distributors, and telephone answering systems. The term is replacing *business communications system.* (F)

customization: the process of designing a data-processing installation or network to meet the requirements of particular users.

cut form: a single form, not connected to other forms. The form may have more than one part; that is, it may have an original and one or more copies. cf. *continuous forms.*

cut-forms mode: a mode in which a printer produces one form at a time.

cutoff: the point of degradation, due to attenuation or distortion, at which a signal becomes unusable.

cutout: a part of a form that has been eliminated or perforated for subsequent removal.

CUTS: cassette user tape system.

cut-to-tie ratio: the length of the cut and the tie associated with perforations. If the length of the cut is less than the length of the tie, it is reasonable to assume that the perforation has greater strength than a perforation with the opposite case. see also *perforation, tie.*

CV: constant value.

CW

(1) clockwise.

(2) see *control word.*

CY: see *carry.*

cybernation: automation through the use of computers. see also *cybernetics.*

cybernetics: the branch of learning that brings together theories and studies on communication and control in living organisms and in machines. see also *cybernation.* (*A*) (B)

cycle

(1) an interval of space or time in which one set of events or phenomena is completed.

(2) any set of operations that is repeated regularly in the same sequence. The operations may be subject to variations on each repetition. (*A*)

(3) see *display cycle, search cycle.*

cycle count: the number of times a cycle has been performed.

cycle index: the number of times a cycle of instructions has been or remains to be completed.

cycle reset: the setting of a cycle index or cycle count to its initial value or to another specified value.

cycle sharing: the process by which a device utilizes machine cycles of another device or processing unit. synonymous with *cycle stealing.*

cycles per second (cps): synonym for *hertz.*

cycle steal: a hardware function that allow I/O devices to access storage directly.

cycle stealing: synonym for *cycle sharing.*

cycle time: the minimum time interval between the starts of successive read write cycles of a storage device. (E) see *display cycle time, read cycle time, write cycle time.*

cyclic code: a code in which every cyclic shift of a code word is in itself a code word (C).

cyclic redundancy check (CRC)

(1) a redundancy check in which the check key is generated by a cyclic algorithm. (E)

(2) a system or error checking performed at both the sending and receiving station after a block check character has been accumulated. see also *longitudinal redundancy check, vertical redundancy check.*

cyclic redundancy check character: a character used in a modified cyclic code for error detection and correction. (A)

cyclic shift: synonym for *end-around shift.* (A)

cyclic storage: synonym for *circulating storage.* (A)

CYL: see *cylinder.*

cylinder (CUL)

(1) in a disk pack, the set of all tracks with the same nominal distance from the axis about which the disk pack rotates. (B)

(2) the tracks of a disk storage device that can be accessed without repositioning the access mechanism.

cylinder concept: a concept that data on all tracks above and below the one currently in use is available by merely switching read/write heads. Permits access to large amount of information with no extra movement of the access unit.

cylinder-cylinder-head-sector (CCHS): the representation of the address of a data field on a disk.

cylinder scanning: scanning used in facsimile transmission, where the object image is wrapped around a rotating cylinder that can be scanned by a photosensitive unit. synonymous with *drum scanning*.

D

  (1) see *data*.
  (2) deci. Ten or tenth part.
  (3) see *decimal*.
  (4) see *destination*.
  (5) see *digit*.
  (6) see *digital*.
  (7) see *displacement*.
  (8) see *domain*.

DA

  (1) see *data administrator*.
  (2) see *deka*.
  (3) see *destination address*.
  (4) see *directory assistance*.

D/A: digital-to-analog.

DAA

  (1) see *data access arrangement*.
  (2) see *direct access arrangement*.

DAC: see *digital-to-analog converter*.

dagger operation: synonymous with *NOR operation*.

daisy chain: the movement of signals from one device to another in a serial fashion.

daisy print wheel: a plastic or metal print wheel found in word-processing printers that makes the typing impression on paper. Its unique circular design allows these units to print up to 540 words per minute.

daisy wheel (DW): a serrated plastic disk around which is arranged a set of print characters.

DAMA: see *demand assigned multiple access*.

damping: a characteristic built into electrical circuits and mechanical systems to prevent unwanted oscillatory conditions.

dark trace tube: in computer graphics, a type of cathode-ray tube whose electron beam causes the phosphorescent surface of the tube to darken rather than to brighten. (E)

DASD: see *direct-access storage device*.

DASD queue: a queue that resides on a direct-access storage device.

DASM: see *direct access storage media*.

data (D)

  (1) a representation of facts, con-

cepts, or instructions in a formalized manner suitable for communication, interpretation, or processing by human or automatic means. (B)

(2) any representations such as characters or analog quantities to which meaning is, or might be, assigned. (A)

(3) see *absolute data, alphanumeric data, analog data, digital data, discrete data, input data, numeric data, output data, relative data, test data.*

(4) see also *information.*

data above voice (DAV): a transmission system carrying digital data on a portion of the microwave radio spectrum above the frequency used for voice transmission.

data access arrangement (DAA): equipment that permits attachment of privately owned data-terminal equipment and telecommunication equipment to the network.

data acquisition: the process of identifying, isolating, and gathering source data to be centrally processed. see also *data collection.*

data adapter unit (DAU): a unit that allows the central processor to be connected to a number of data-communications channels.

data administrator (DA):

(1) a control element from a database management system.

(2) an individual responsible for data definition and control of the data-base management system.

data aggregate

(1) in a data base, a named collection of data items. (E)

(2) a logical collection of two or more data items that can be referred to either collectively or individually; an array of structure. see also *data array.*

data area: a storage area used by a program to hold information.

data array: a representation of data in the form of signs, symbols, special characters as recorded on cards, tapes, and so on. see also *data aggregate.*

data attribute: a characteristic of a unit of data such as length, value, or method of representation. (A)

data bank

(1) a set of libraries of data. (B)

(2) a comprehensive collection of libraries of data. For example, one line of an invoice may form an item, a complete invoice may form a record, a complete set of such records may form a file, the collection of inventory control files may form a library, and the libraries used by an organization are known as its data bank. (*A*)

data base (DB)

(1) a collection of data fundamental to a system.

(2) a collection of data fundamental to an enterprise. (A)

(3) a set of data that is sufficient for a given purpose or for one or several given data-processing systems. (E)

(4) a collection of interrelated or independent data items stored together without unnecessary redundancy, to serve one or more applications.

(5) see *relational data base, sub-data base.*

data-base administrator (DBA)

(1) an individual responsible for the design, development, operations, safeguarding, maintenance, and use of a data base. (E)

(2) a person who is responsible for a data-base system, particularly for defining the rules by which data is ac-

cessed and stored. The data-base administrator is usually responsible also for data-base integrity, security, performance, and recovery.

data-base management system (DBMS): a software system facilitating the creation and maintenance of a data base and the execution of computer programs using the data base.

data block: see *block.*

data break: synonymous with *direct memory access.*

data buffer register: a temporary storage register in a CPU or a peripheral unit able to receive or transmit data at varying input and output rates.

data bus (DB): see *bus.*

data capture: the act of collecting data into a form that can be directly processed by a computer system. Some electronic funds transfer systems are designed to capture transaction data at the precise time and place the transaction is consummated.

data card: see *source data card.* (A)

data carrier: material that serves as a data medium or to which a data medium is applied, and that is designed to facilitate the transport of data. For example, a punch card or paper tape; a disk, drum, tape, or employee badge with a magnetizable surface that serves as the data medium. see also *data medium.*

data cell: a direct-access storage volume containing strips of tape on which data is stored.

data channel (DC) (DCH): a device that connects a processor and main storage with I/O control units. synonymous with *input-output channel.* cf. *data-communication channel.*

data-channel multiplexor: a multiplexor that services communications channels operating at high speeds to service these channels successively, a character at a time. see *multiplexer.*

data circuit: associated transmit and receive channels that provide a means of two-way data communications. (E) synonym for *link connection.* see *tandem data circuit.* see also *physical circuit, virtual circuit.*

data circuit-terminating equipment (DCE): the equipment installed at the user's premises that provides all the functions required to establish, maintain, and terminate a connection, and the signal conversion and coding between the data terminal equipment (DTE) and the line. (E)

data-circuit transparency: the capability of a data circuit to transmit all data without changing the data content or structure. (E)

data code (DC)
(1) a structured set of characters used to represent the data items; for example, the codes 01, 02, . . . 12 may be used to represent the months January, February, . . . December of the data element months of the year. (A)
(2) in data communications, a set of rules and conventions according to which the signals representing data should be formed, transmitted, received, and processed. (B)
(3) deprecated term for *code set.* (A) (B)
(4) see *numeric code.* (A)

data collection
(1) a facility for gathering small quantities of data from a nominated group of addresses, assembling them within the network into a single

message for delivery to another nominated address. (C)

(2) an application in which data from several locations is accumulated at one location (in a queue or on a file) before processing. see also *data acquisition.*

data-collection station: synonym for *data-input station.* (A) (B)

DATACOM: see *data communication.*

data communication (DATACOM) (DC)

(1) the transmission and reception of data.

(2) the transmission, reception, and validation of data. (*A*)

(3) data transfer between data source and data sink via one or more data links according to appropriate protocols. (E)

(4) in telephone company terminology, refers to end-to-end transmission of any kind of information other than sound (including voice) or video. (F)

(5) see also *transmission.*

data-communication channel: a means of one-way transmission. (E) cf. *data channel.*

data-communication interface: see *transmission interface.*

data-communication network: see *network, public network, user-application network.*

data communications: see *data communication.*

data-communication service: see *transmission service.*

data communications equipment: the interfacing equipment sometimes required to couple the data terminal equipment into a transmission circuit or channel and from a transmission circuit or channel into the data terminal equipment.

data-communication terminal: see *data terminal.*

data compaction: any method for encoding data to reduce the storage it requires. see also *null suppression.*

data compression: a technique that saves storage space by eliminating gaps, empty fields, redundancies, or unnecessary data to shorten the length of records or blocks.

data concentrator: see *concentrator.*

data conferencing network: a device that enables a predetermined group of users to operate such that if any one user transmits a message it will be received by all others in the group.

data connection: the interconnection of two data-terminal equipments (DTEs) by means of switched tandem data circuits. (E)

data connector: a device which permits connection of customer-owned modems or data sets to the regular telephone network. It limits the power applied to the line and provides network control and signaling functions.

data constant: see *figurative constant.*

data contamination: synonym for *data corruption.*

data control: the organization of data entering or leaving the system.

data control block (DCB): a control block used by access method routines in storing and retrieving data.

data conversion: the process of changing data from one form or representation to another.

data converter: a device whose purpose is to convert data. (A) (B)

data corruption: a deliberate or accidental violation of data integrity. synonymous with *data contamination.* (E)

data declaration: a nonexecutable statement that describes the characteristics of the data to be operated upon; for example, PICTURE clause, DIMENSION. (E)

data-declaration statement: synonym for *data declaration*. (E)

data definition (DD): a program statement that describes the features of, specifies relationships of, or establishes context of data. (A)

data-definition name (ddname): the name of a data-definition (DD) statement that corresponds to a data-control block that contains the same name.

data-definition (DD) statement: a job control statement that describes a data set associated with a particular job step.

data delay: measured time concerned in the waiting period for information before another process can be performed.

data delimiter: synonymous with *delimiter*.

data density: on magnetic tape, the number of bytes of data per inch (bpi).

data-description entry: in COBOL, an entry in the data division that is used to describe the characteristics of a data item. It consists of a level number, followed by an optional data name, followed by data clauses that fully describe the format the data will take. An elementary data-description entry (or item) cannot logically be subdivided further. A group data-description entry (or item) is made up of a number of related group items, elementary items, or both.

data-description language (DDL): a language that provides a facility for describing data and their relationships in a data base. (E)

data design: a layout or format of computer storage or machine storage allocation, that is, for input and output.

data dictionary (DD): a centralized repository of information about data such as meaning, relationships to other data, origin, usage, and format. It assists company management, data base administrators, systems analysts, and application programmers in effectively planning, controlling, and evaluating the collection, storage, and use of data. see also *dictionary*.

data-directed transmission: in PL/1, the type of stream-oriented transmission in which data is transmitted as a group, comprising one or more items separated by commas, terminated by a semicolon, where each is of the form *name = constant*. The name can be qualified, subscripted, or both.

data display unit: synonymous with *terminal*.

data division (DD): one of the four main component parts of a COBOL program. The data division describes the files to be used in the program and the records contained within the files. It also describes any internal working-storage records that will be needed. synonym for *data item*.

data element: a set of data items to be considered in a given situation as a unit. synonym for *data item*.

data-element chain: an ordered set of two or more data elements used as one data element. synonymous with *macroelement*.

data-encrypting key: a key used to

encipher and decipher data transmitted in a session that uses cryptography. cf. *key-encrypting key.*

data-encryption standard (DES): see *DES.*

data-encryption standard (DES) algorithm: a cryptographic algorithm designed to encipher and decipher data using 64-bit cryptographic key, as specified in the Federal Information Processing Standard Publication 46, January 15, 1977.

data entry (DE)

(1) a catalog entry that describes a cluster's or catalog's data component. A data entry contains the data component's attributes, allocation and extent information, and statistics. A data entry for a cluster's or catalog's data component can also contain the data component's passwords and protection attributes.

(2) the method of entering data into a computer system for processing, usually via terminal applications.

(3) the entry of data into a computer by an operator from a single data device, such as a card reader, badge reader, keyboard, or rotary switch.

data error: a deviation from correctness in data, often an error, which occurred before the processing of the data.

data evaluation: the review and analysis of data so as to make an assessment of its inherent meaning, probable accuracy, relevancy, and relation to given situations.

data-examination clerk: the individual who is responsible for maintaining accuracy, correctness, and appropriateness of input-output data.

data exchange: the use of data by more than one computer program or system. Data that is recorded or transmitted in a format is referred to as exchange data. see also *data interchange.*

data-extent block (DEB): an extension of the data-control block that contains information about the physical status of the data set being processed.

data field (DF): any designated portion of a data-base segment. A segment may contain one or more data fields.

data file: a collection of related data records organized in a specific manner; for example, a payroll file (one record for each employee, showing such information as rate of pay and deductions) or an inventory file (one record for each inventory item, showing such information as cost, selling price, and number in stock). see also *data set (1), file, logical file.*

data flow: the type of route or extended route that a message takes from the originating station or application program to its destination, including the host nodes that process the message while it is enroute to its destination.

data flowchart: a flowchart that represents the path of data in the solving of a problem, and that defines the major phases of the processing as well as the various data media used. synonymous with *data flow diagram.* (A) (B)

data-flow control (DFC): the layer within a half-session that controls whether the half-session can send, receive, or concurrently send and receive, request units (RUs); group related RUs into RU chains; delimits transactions via the bracket protocol;

controls the interlocking of requests and responses in accordance with control modes specified at session activation; generates sequence numbers; and correlates requests and responses.

data-flow control protocol: the sequencing rules for requests and responses by which network addressable units (NAUs) in a session coordinate and control data transfer and other operations; for example, bracket protocol.

data-flow diagram: synonym for *data flowchart* (A) (B)

data format: procedures and rules that describe the way data is retained in file or record, whether in character form, as binary numbers, and so forth.

data-format item: in PL/1, a specification used in edit-directed transmission to describe the representation of a data item in the stream.

data gathering: see *data acquisition, data collection.*

data generator: a data-set utility program that creates multiple data sets within one job for the sequential and partitioned access methods.

datagram (DG): in packet switching, a self-contained packet that is independent of other packets, that does not require acknowledgment, and that carries information sufficient for routing from the originating data-terminal equipment (DTE) to the destination DTE without relying on earlier exchanges between the DTEs and the network. (E)

datagram service: in packet switching, a service that routes a datagram to the destination identified in its address field without reference by the

network to any other diagram.

data handling
(1) the production of records and reports.
(2) the performance of data-processing activities, that is, sorting, input-output operations, and report generation.

data hierarchy: a data structure consisting of sets and subsets such that every subset of a set is of lower rank than the data of the set. (A)

data host: a host that is dedicated to processing applications and does not control network resources, except its locally attached devices.

data independence
(1) the property of a data-base management system that enables data to be processed independently of access mode, storage method, or arrangement of data. (E)
(2) the definition of logical and physical data so that application programs do not depend on where physical units of data are stored; data independence reduces the need to modify application programs when data storage and access methods are modified.

data input: data ready for processing, such as coding, sorting, computing, summarizing, and reporting, recording, and communication.

data-input station: a user terminal primarily for the insertion of data into a data-processing system. synonymous with *data-collection station.* (A) (B)

data integrity
(1) the quality of data that exists as long as accidental or malicious destruction, alteration, or loss of data are prevented. (E)

(2) preservation of data for its intended purpose.

data interchange: the use of data by systems of different manufacture. see also *data exchange.*

data in voice (DIV): transmission where digital data displaces voice circuits in a microwave channel.

data item

(1) the smallest unit of named data that has meaning in the schema or subschema. synonymous with *data element.* (E)

(2) in COBOL, a unit of recorded information that can be identified by a symbolic name or by a combination of names and subscripts. Elementary data items cannot logically be subdivided. A group data item is made up of logically related group items, elementary items, or both, and can be a logical group within a record or can itself be a complete record.

(3) in FORTRAN, a constant, variable, or array element.

(4) in PL/1, a single unit of data. synonymous with *element.*

data level: the position of a data element in relation to other elements specified as part of the same record in a source language.

data library: a collection of related files; for example, in stock control, a collection of inventory control files. (A) (B)

data link (DL)

(1) the physical means of connecting one location to another for the purpose of transmitting and receiving data. (A)

(2) the assembly of parts of two data-terminal equipments (DTEs) that are controlled by a link protocol, and that, together with the intercon-

necting data circuit, enables data to be transferred from a data source to a data sink. (E)

(3) the interconnecting data circuit between two or more equipments operating in accordance with a link protocol; it does not include the data source and the data sink.

(4) see also *multiplex.*

(5) cf. *telecommunication line.*

data-link control character: a control character intended to control or facilitate transmission of data over a network. synonymous with *communication control character.*

data-link control protocol: synonymous with *line code.*

data-link escape character (DLE): a transmission control character that changes the meaning of a limited number of contiguously following characters or coded representations and that is used exclusively to provide supplementary transmission control characters. (A) (B)

data-link layer: in open systems architecture, the layer that provides the functions and procedures used to establish, maintain, and release data link connections between elements of the network. (E)

data list (DL): in PL/1, a parenthesized list of expressions or repetitive specifications, separated by commas, used in a stream-oriented input or output specifications that represents storage locations to which data items are to be assigned during input, or values which are to be obtained for output.

data logging: the recording of data about events that occur in time sequence. (A)

data-loop transceiver (DLT): a station

arrangement (data set) for Western Union's Class D leased data channels. see also *data set, station arrangement.*

data management (DM)

(1) the function of controlling the acquisition, analysis, storage, retrieval, and distribution of data.

(2) in an operating system, the computer programs that provide access to data, perform or monitor storage of data, and control input-output devices. (*A*)

data-management programming system: programs designed to provide an operator with the capability for querying, augmenting, and manipulating large computer-stored data bases in a natural language.

data-manipulating language (DML): a set of statements usually embedded in a host programming language that a programmer uses to transfer data between the data base and computer programs. (E)

data manipulation: defining operations needed by users in processing data followed by carrying out the operations.

datamation: a shortened term for automatic data processing; taken from *data* and *automation*. see both terms.

data medium: the material in or on which data may be represented. (E) see also *data carrier.*

data migration: the moving of data from an on-line device to an off-line or low-priority device, as determined by the system or as requested by the user. cf. *staging.*

data mode: a move mode in which the data portions of all segments of a spanned record are accessed.

data multiplexer (DMX): a functional unit that permits two or more data sources to share a common transmission medium such that each data source has its own channel. (E)

data name (DN)

(1) a character or group of characters used to identify an item of data. (A) (B)

(2) in COBOL, a name assigned by the programmer to a data item in a program. It must contain at least one alphabetic character.

DATANET: see *data network.*

data network (DATANET): the assembly of functional units that establishes data circuits between data-terminal equipments (DTEs). see also *synchronous data network.* (E)

data organization: see *data set organization.*

data origination: the translation of information from its original form into a machine-readable form or directly into electrical signals.

data output: data obtained from a unit, such as a logic element, or the output channel of a logic element.

data phase: that phase of a data call during which data signals may be transferred between data-terminal equipments (DTEs) that are interconnected via the network. see also *network control phase.* (C)

data phone: a unit that permits data to be transferred over a telephone line.

DATA-PHONE: both a service mark and a trademark of AT&T and the Bell System. As a service mark, it indicates the transmission of data over the telephone network. As a trademark, it identifies the telecommunication equipment furnished by the Bell System for transmission services. see *Dataphone digital service.*

Dataphone digital service (DDS): AT&T's private-line service, filed in 1974, for transmitting data over a digital system. The digital transmission system transmits electrical signals directly, instead of translating the signals into tones of varied frequencies as with the traditional analog transmission system. The digital technique provides more efficient use of transmission facilities, resulting in lower error rates and costs than analog systems. (G)

data plotter: a unit providing a visual display in the form of a graph on paper.

data pointer: a specific register holding the memory address of the data to be utilized by the instruction. The register "points" to the memory location of the data.

data preparation: pertaining to the conversion to machine-readable form data.

data processing (DP): the systematic performance of operations upon data, for example, handling, merging, sorting, computing. synonymous with *information processing*. (E) see *administrative data processing, automatic data processing, business data processing, distributed data processing, electronic data processing, integrated data processing, remote-access data processing*.

data processing cycle: the sequence of operations associated with data processing, from the collection of data to displaying and storing the results of all machine activities.

data-processing machine: a generic name for a device that can store and process numeric and alphabetic information.

data-processing node: a node at which data-processing equipment, such as processors, controllers, or terminals, and associated software, may be situated. (E)

data-processing station: one or more devices and associated software that provide one of the input-output points of a user-application network; for example, one or more terminals, processors, or input-output devices at a particular location. (E)

data-processing system (DPS): a system, including computer systems and associated personnel, that performs input, processing, storage, output, and control functions to accomplish a sequence of operations on data. see also *computer, computer system*. (E)

data-processing system security: all of the technological and managerial safeguards established and applied to a data-processing system to protect hardware, software, and data from accidental or malicious modifications, destruction, or disclosure. (E)

data processor (DP): a device capable of performing data processing, such as a desk calculator, a punched card machine, or a computer. (B) see *processor*.

data protection: a safeguard against the loss or destruction of data. see also *data integrity, security*.

data purification: validating and correcting data to reduce errors entering a data-processing system.

data radio: transmission of data utilizing radio waves.

data receiver: a device that converts data from analog representation as transmitted on telecommunications facilities to digital representation for use in digital computers.

data record: a record containing data to be processed by a program.

data reduction: the transformation of raw data into a more useful form, for example, smoothing to reduce noise. (A)

data registers: registers found in many microprocessors for the temporary storage of data.

data reliability: the ratio that relates the extent to which data meets a given standard, usually concerning the accuracy of data, or the degree to which data is error free.

data retrieval: the return of data by selecting, searching, or retransmission of information from a file data bank, or storage unit.

data scaling: see *scaling*.

data security: the protection of data against unauthorized disclosure, whether accidental or intentional. see also *data-processing system security*. (C)

data separator: a circuit in disk controllers that separates the data from the carrier in the signals read from the disk surface.

data set (DS)

(1) the major unit of data storage and retrieval, consisting of a collection of data in one of several prescribed arrangements and described by control information to which the system has access. see *direct data set, partitioned data set, sequential data set*.

(2) deprecated term for *modem*. (E)

(3) see also *file*.

data set adapter: a unit for interfacing a computer and a modem by breaking down bytes from the computer in-

to bits for serial transmission. For received signals the process is reversed.

data-set clocking: a time-base oscillator supplied by the data set for regulating the bit rate of transmission. cf. *business machine clocking*.

data-set control block (DSCB): a data set label for a data set in direct-access storage.

data-set definition table (DSD table): a table that contains parameters for data sets.

data-set label

(1) a collection of information that describes the attributes of a data set and is normally stored on the same volume as the data set.

(2) a general term for data-set control blocks and tape data-set labels.

data-set name (DSN) (DSNAME): the term or phrase used to identify a data set. see also *qualified name*.

data-set organization (DSORG): the arrangement of information in a data set; for example, sequential organization or partitioned organization.

data-set reference number: in FORTRAN, a constant or variable in an input-output statement, which specifies the data set that is to be operated upon. synonymous with *external unit identifier*.

data-set security: see *data security*.

data-set utility programs: programs that can be used to update, maintain, edit, and transcribe data sets.

data signal: a signal representing a set of digits used to convey information, service functions, or both, and which may include check digits. (C)

data signaling rate: the aggregate signaling rate in the transmission path of a data-transmission system, expressed in normalized form in binary digits (bits) per second. cf. *actual data-transfer rate, effective data-transfer rate.* (E)

data sink

(1) a functional unit that accepts data after transmission. It may originate error control signals. (E)

(2) that part of a data terminal equipment (DTE) that receives data from a data link.

(3) cf. *data source.*

data source

(1) a functional unit that supplies data for transmission. (E)

(2) that part of data terminal equipment (DTE) that enters data into a data link.

(3) cf. *data sink*

data specification: in PL/1, the portion of a stream-oriented data transmission statement that specifies the mode of transmission (DATA, LIST, or EDIT) and includes the data list (or lists) and, for edit-directed mode, the format list (or lists).

DATASPEED: a Bell System marketing term for a family of medium-speed paper-tape transmitting and receiving units. Similar equipment is also marketed by the Western Union Telegraph Company.

data station: the data terminal equipment (DTE), the data circuit-terminating equipment (DCE), and any intermediate equipment. synonymous with *data-terminal installation.* (E)

data storage: the use of any medium for storing data.

data stream

(1) all data transmitted through a data channel in a single read or write operation.

(2) a continuous stream of data elements being transmitted, or intended for transmission, in character or binary-digit form, using a defined format.

data structure: the syntactic structure of symbolic expressions and their storage allocation characteristics. (E)

data switch: a location where an incoming data message is automatically or manually directed to one or more outgoing circuits, according to the intelligence contained in the message.

data-switching exchange (DSE): the equipment installed at a single location to provide circuit switching, pocket switching, or both. see also *digital data switching.* (E)

data tablet: a unit with which to input graphics, making it possible to draw images directly into the computer.

data terminal (DT): a device, associated with a computer system for data input and output, that may be at a location remote from the computer system, thus requiring data transmission. (F) see *terminal.* see also *data station, data terminal equipment, station, work station.*

data-terminal equipment (DTE): that part of a data station that serves as a data source, data sink, or both, and provides for the data-communication control function according to protocols. (E)

data-terminal installation: synonym for *data station.*

data time: the unit of time needed to fulfill a single instruction.

data transfer

(1) the result of the transmission of data signals from any data source to

a data sink. (C)

(2) the movement, or copying, of data from one location and the storage of the data at another location.

data-transfer phase: that phase of a data call during which data signals may be transferred between data-terminal equipments (DTEs) that are interconnected via the network.

data-transfer rate: the average number of bits, characters, or blocks per unit of time transferred from a data source to a data sink. The rate is usually expressed as bits, characters, or blocks per second, minute, or hour. (C) see *actual data-transfer rate*, *effective data-transfer rate*. synonymous with *data-signaling rate*.

data-transfer register: a temporary storage unit that eases the shifting of data within the computer.

data transmission: synonym for *transmission*. (A)

data transmission channel: the transmission media and intervening equipment involved in the transfer of data between data terminal equipment.

data-transmission facility: see *telecommunication facility*.

data-transmission interface: see *transmission interface*.

data-transmission line: synonym for *telecommunication line*.

data-transmission service: see *transmission service*.

data-transmission trap: a special conditional jump, frequently nonprogrammed, to specified locations as automatically set to give communication or signaling between input-output programs and routines.

data-transmission utilization measure: the ratio of useful data output of a data-transmission system, to the total data input.

data-transmission video display unit: input-output device with a special feature of displaying information on a screen, usually a cathode-ray tube.

data type

(1) the structural characteristics, features, and properties of data that may be directly specified by a programming language; for example, integers, real numbers in FORTRAN; arrays in APL; linked lists in LISP; character string in SNOBOL. (E)

(2) the mathematical properties and internal representation of data and functions. The four basic types are integer, real, complex, and logical.

data under voice (DUV): an arrangement for transmitting 1.544-megabit-per-second data streams in the bandwidth available underneath the portion of the base band used for voice channels on existing microwave systems. (F)

data unit: a group of characters related so that they form a whole.

data word: a unit of data stored in a single word of a storage medium.

dating routine: a routine which computes and/or stores, where needed, a data such as current day's date, expiration date of a tape, and so forth.

datum: the singular form of "data."

datum line: see *X-datum line*, *Y-datum line*. (A)

DAU: see *data adapter unit*.

DAV: see *data above voice*.

DB

(1) see *data base*.

(2) see *data bus*.

(3) see *decibel*.

DBA

(1) adjusted decibels.

(2)   see *data-base administrator*.

dBm: decibel based on one milliwatt.

dBrnC: a power level in dB relative to a noise reference of −90 dBm, as measured with a noise meter, weighted by a special frequency function called C-message weighting that expresses average subjective reaction to interference as a function of frequency. (F)

dBrnCO: N noise measured in dBrnC and referred to the O transmission level point. (F)

DBS: direct broadcast system.

D-bus: internal destination bus in a central processing unit, from the arithmetic and logic unit to the registers.

DC

(1)   see *data channel*.

(2)   see *data code*.

(3)   see *data communication*.

(4)   see *direct current*.

DCB: see data control block.

DCE: see *data circuit-terminating equipment*.

DCH: see *data channel*.

DCL: see *declaration*.

DC1, DC2, DC3, DC4:   see *device control character*. (A)

dc patch bay: a patch bay in which direct-current circuits are grouped.

DC signaling: a variety of techniques for transmitting signaling information using direct current over metallic circuits; for example, loop-reverse battery, loop-start, or duplex (DX) signaling. DC signaling is a subset of out-of-band signaling. (F)

DD

(1)   see *data definition*.

(2)   see *data dictionary*.

(3)   see *data division*.

DDA: see *digital differential analyzer*

(A).

DDC: see *direct digital control*.

DDD: see *direct distance dialing*.

DDL: see *data-description language*.

ddname: see *data-definition name*.

DDP: see *distributed data processing*.

DDR: see *dynamic device reconfiguration*.

DDS

(1)   see *Dataphone digital service*.

(2)   see *digital data system*.

DD statement: see *data-definition statement*.

DE: see *data entry*.

deactivated: in PL/1, the state in which a preprocessor variable or entry name is said to be when its value cannot replace the corresponding identifier in source program text.

deactivation: in a network, the process of taking any element out of service, rendering it inoperable, or placing it in a state in which it cannot perform the functions for which it was designated.

dead band: synonymous with *dead zone*.

dead file: any file that is not in current use but which is kept.

dead halt: see *drop-dead halt*.

deadlock

(1)   unresolved contention for the use of a resource.

(2)   an error condition in which processing cannot continue because each of two elements of the process is waiting for an action by or a response from the other.

deadly embrace: synonymous with *deadlock*.

dead time

(1)   any definite delay deliberately placed between two related actions in order to avoid overlap that can

confuse or permit a particular different event, such as a control decision, switching event, or similar action, to take place.

(2) the delay between two related actions, measured in units of time for efficiency study.

dead zone: the range of input values for a signal that can be altered but have no impact on the output signal. synonymous with *dead band*.

dead zone unit: a functional unit whose output variable is constant over a particular range of the input variable. (B)

deallocate: to release a resource that is assigned to a specific task.

DEB: see *data-extent block*.

deblock: to separate the parts of a block, for example, to select records from a block. (A)

deblocking: the process of removing each logical record from a block. see also *deconcentration*. cf. *blocking*.

debouncing: eliminating the rapid signal fluctuations that accompany a change of state in mechanical switches.

debug: to detect, to trace, and to eliminate mistakes in computer programs or in other software. synonymous with *checkout*. (*A*) (B)

debugger: an essential program purporting to aid software debugging, providing breakpoints, dump facilities, register and memory examine/modify, usually in symbolic form.

debugging aid routine: a routine used for testing programs.

debug macros: aids within a program added by the applications programmer in addition to those supplied by the supervisory program: a form of

unit testing.

debug statements: in FORTRAN, the statements DEBUG, AT, TRACE ON, and TRACE OFF.

DEC
(1) see *decimal*.
(2) see *decoder*.
(3) see *decrement*.

deca: see *deka*.

decade: a group of ten items; for example, a group of ten storage locations.

decade counter: a counter advancing in increments of ten.

decelaration time: time that elapses between finishing the reading or writing of a tape record and the time when the tape stops moving. synonymous with *stop time*.

decentralized information system: two or more sets of information-processing equipment operated by the same enterprise to perform processing, but without any implied cooperation among the sets.

deci: tenth part.

decibel (DB)
(1) a unit that expresses the ratio of two power levels on a logarithmic scale.
(2) a unit for measuring relative power. The number of decibels is ten times the logarithm (base 10) of the ratio of the measured power levels; if the measured levels are voltages (across the same or equal resistance), the number of decibels is 20 times the log of the ratio. see also *neper, power level*.

decimal (D) (DEC)
(1) pertaining to a selection, choice, or condition that has ten possible different values or states. (B)
(2) pertaining to a fixed-radix nu-

meration system having a radix of ten. (B)

(3) see *binary-coded decimal notation.* (*A*)

decimal alignment: the feature of a machine that enables members to be automatically aligned on either side of a decimal marker. (D)

decimal arithmetic operation: a type of arithmetic operation whereby data enters and leaves the system as zoned decimal and is processed as packed decimal.

decimal digit: in decimal notation, or in the decimal numeration system, one of the digits 0 to 9. (A) (B)

decimal marker: on a calculator, a visual indication of the position of the decimal point or decimal comma in a number. (D)

decimal notation: a notation that uses ten different characters, usually the decimal digits, for example, the character string 196912312359, construed to represent the date and time one minute before the start of the year 1970; the representation used in the Universal Decimal Classification (UDC). (B) cf. *decimal numeration system.* (*A*)

decimal numeral: a numeral in the decimal numeration system. (A)

decimal numeration system: the fixed-radix numeration system that uses the decimal digits and the radix 10 and in which the lowest integral weight is 1. (B) cf. *decimal notation.* (*A*)

decimal picture data: in PL/1, arithmetic picture data specified by picture specifications containing the following types of picture specification characters: decimal digit characters, the virtual point picture character, zero-suppression characters, sign and currency symbol characters, insertion characters, commercial characters, and exponent characters.

decimal point: the radix point in the decimal numeration system. The decimal point may be represented, according to various conventions, by a comma, by a period, or by a point at the mid-height of the digits. (A) (B)

decimal symbol: a graphic symbol, usually a period or comma, used to separate the fractional part of a decimal number from the whole part of a decimal number.

decimal to binary conversion: converting a number written to the base of ten, or decimal, into the equivalent number written to the base of two, or binary.

decimeter (DM): one tenth of a meter. 3.94 inches.

decipher: to convert enciphered data into clear data. synonymous with *decrypt.* cf. *encipher.*

decision: see *leading decision, trailing decision.* (A)

decision box: in flowcharting, a symbol used to indicate a choice of branching in the information-processing path.

decision circuit: a circuit that measures the probable value of a signal element.

decision content: in information theory, a logarithmic measure of the number of decisions needed to select a given event among a finite number of mutually exclusive events; in mathematic notation, this measure is $H = \log_2 n$, where n is the number of events. In information theory, the term *event* is to be understood as used in the theory of probability. For instance, an event may be the presence of a given element of a set, the occurrence of a specified character or of a specified word in a given position of a message. (A) (B)

decision element: synonymous with *threshold element.*

decision instruction: deprecated term for *discrimination instruction.* synonym for *branch instruction.* (*A*) (B)

decision logic: a decision made in a computing system as a result of the internal organization of that system, where one of the binary, or yes or no type, and basically relating to questions of equality, inequality, or relative magnitude, is the result of a particular computation less than, equal to, or greater than some reference point or number.

decision mechanism: the component part of a character reader, in character recognition, that receives the finalized version of the input character, and makes a determination as to its probable identity.

decision rules: the programmed criteria which an on-line, real-time system uses to make operating decisions.

decision table (DETAB)
(1) a presentation in either matrix or tabular form of a set of conditions and their corresponding actions. (A)
(2) a table of all contingencies that are to be considered in the description of a problem, together with the actions to be taken for each set of contingencies. (E)

decision theory: the formal specifications and analysis of choice situations in terms of the alternative actions available to the decision maker, the likely outcomes, and the preference ordering of all possible consequences.

deck: see *card deck.* (A)

declaration (DCL)
(1) In a programming language, a meaningful expression that affects the interpretation of other expressions in that language. synonymous with *directive.* (A) (B)
(2) in PL/1, the establishment of an identifier as a name and the construction of a set of attributes (partial or complete) for it. Also, a source of attributes of a particular name.
(3) a nonexecutable statement that supplies information about data or about particular aspects of a computer program. synonymous with *declarative statement.* (E)

declarative: deprecated term for *declaration.* (B)

declaratives: a set of one or more compiler-directing sections written at the beginning of the procedure division of a COBOL program. The first section is preceded by the header DECLARATIVES. The last section is followed by the header END DECLARATIVES.

declarative statement: synonym for *declaration.*

declare: in assembler-language programming, to identify the variable symbols to be used by the assembler at preassembly time.

decliter (dl): one tenth of a liter; 0.21 pints.

decode
(1) to convert data by reversing the effect of some previous encoding. (B)
(2) to interpret a code. see *decoding.*
(3) cf. *encode.* (A)

decoder (DEC)

(1) a device that decodes data. (B)

(2) a device that has a number of input lines of which any number may carry signals and a number of output lines of which not more than one may carry a signal, there being a one-to-one correspondence between the output and the combinations of the input signals. (B)

(3) cf. *encoder.*

(4) see *operation decoder.* (*A*)

decoding

(1) internal hardware operations by which the computer determines the meaning of the operation code of an instruction. Also sometimes applied to *addresses.*

(2) in interpretive routines, some subroutines, and elsewhere, an operation by which a routine determines the meaning of parameters. see also *decode.*

decollate: to separate the plies of a multipart form or paper stock. synonymous with *deleave.* (*A*)

decollator: a device that combines the removal of carbon paper and separation of various copies of a standard multipart continuous form.

deconcentration: the process of extracting individual messages from data sent in a single transmission sequence. cf. *concentration.* see also *concentrator, deblocking.*

deconcentrator: any device that extracts individual messages from data sent in a single transmission sequence.

DECR: see *decrement.*

decrement (DEC) (DECR)

(1) the quantity by which a variable is decreased.

(2) in some computers, a specific part of an instruction word.

(3) to decrease the value of a number.

decrypt: synonym for *decipher.*

decurl: in a printer, to remove abnormal curving of the paper.

dedicated: machines, programs, or procedures designed or set apart for special or continued usage.

dedicated channel: a channel that is not switched.

dedicated circuit: a circuit designated for exclusive use by two users.

dedicated connection: deprecated term for *nonswitched connection.*

dedicated device: a device that cannot be shared among users.

dedicated line: deprecated term for *nonswitched line.*

dedicated port: the access point to a communication channel used only for one specific type of traffic.

dedicated register: a register used to contain a specific item.

dedication: pertaining to the assignment of a system resource—an I/O device, a program, or a whole system—to one application or purpose.

DEF: see *definition.*

default: an alternative value, attribute, or option that is assumed when none has been specified.

default group: the group to which a user is associated when a group name is not specified on the TSO LOGON command or batch JOB statement.

default option: the implicit option that is assumed when no option is explicitly stated. (A)

default parameters: parameter values supplied by a computer system when no explicit values are provided by a program.

default value: the choice among exclusive alternatives made by the system when no explicit choice is specified by the user.

deferred addressing: a method of addressing in which one indirect address is replaced by another to which it refers a predetermined number of times or until the process is terminated by an indicator. (A) (B)

deferred entry: an entry into a subroutine that occurs as a result of a deferred exit from the program that passed control to it.

deferred exit: the passing of control to a subroutine at a time determined by an asynchronous event rather than at a predictable time.

deferred maintenance: maintenance specifically intended to eliminate an existing fault that did not prevent continued successful operation of the device or computer program. (A)

deferred maintenance time: time, usually unscheduled, used to perform deferred maintenance. (A)

deferred processing: processing that can be delayed or considered low priority and is completed when computer time is at nonpeak periods.

deferred restart: a restart performed by the system on resubmission of a job by the programmer. The operator submits the restart deck to the subsystem through a system input reader. cf. *automatic restart.*

define: establishing a value for a variable or symbol or establishing what the variable represents.

defined item: in PL/1, a variable declared to represent part or all of the same storage as that assigned to another variable known as the base item.

definition (DEF): see *data definition, macrodefinition.* (A)

deflection plates: plates used to evolve electrostatic deflection in a cathode ray tube.

degauss: to demagnetize a magnetic tape by use of a degausser.

degausser: a coil momentarily energized by an alternating current that rearranges signals on a magnetic tape.

degeneracy: the condition created by negative feedback.

degradation factor: a measure of the loss in performance that results from the reconfiguration of data-processing system; for example, a slowdown in run time due to a reduction in the number of processing units.

degree of multiprogramming: the number of transactions handled in parallel by the systems involved in a multiprogram.

deka (DA): ten.

dekaliter (dal): ten liters. 2.64 gallons.

dekameter (dam): ten meters. 32.81 feet.

DEL

 (1) see *delete.*

 (2) see *delete character.* (A)

delay: the amount of time by which an event is retarded. (A)

delay counter: a counter for inserting a deliberate time delay allowing an operation external to the program to occur.

delay differential: the difference between the maximum and minimum frequency delays occurring across a band.

delay digit: a logic element which delays its input signal by one digit period.

delay distortion: see *distortion.*

delay element: an element that delays a signal by introducing a time delay.

delay equalizer: a corrective network that is designed to make the phase delay or envelope delay of a circuit or system substantially constant over a desired frequency range. see also *equalizer.*

delay line

(1) a line or network designed to introduce a desired delay in the transmission of a signal, usually without appreciable distortion. (B)

(2) a sequential logic element with one input channel and in which an output channel state at any one instant, T, is the same as the input channel state at the instant T-N, where N is a constant interval of time for a given output channel; for example, an element in which the input sequence undergoes a delay of N time units.

(3) see *acoustic delay line, electromagnetic delay line, magnetic delay line.* (A)

delay line storage: a storage device that uses delay lines. (A) (B)

delay loop stores: an approach for storing information by transmitting bits or no bits serially through a loop.

delay programming: see *minimum delay programming.*

delay time: the amount of elapsed time between the end of one event and the beginning of the next sequential event.

delay unit: a device that yields, after a given time interval, an output signal essentially similar to a previously introduced input signal. (A) (B)

deleave: synonym for *decollate.* (A)

delete (DEL)

(1) to remove or eliminate an item, record, or group of records from a file.

(2) to erase a program from memory.

(3) in word processing, a function that enables text held in storage to be deleted. (D)

delete character (DEL): a control character used primarily to obliterate an erroneous or unwanted character; on perforated tape, this character consists of a car hole in each punch position. synonymous with *erase character.* (A) (B)

delete key: in word processing, a control that enables text already recorded on the recording medium or in storage to be deleted.

deletion of an I/O device: removal of the I/O unit from the supervisor configuration tables.

deletion record: a new record that replaces or removes an existing record of a master file.

delimiter

(1) a flag that separates and organizes items of data. synonymous with *punctuation symbol, separator.* (A)

(2) a string of one or more characters used to separate or organize elements of computer programs or data; for example, parentheses, blank character, arithmetic operator, if, "BEGIN". (E)

(3) a character that groups or separates words or values in a line of input.

(4) in PL/1, all operators, comments, and the following characters: percent, parentheses, comma, period, semicolon, assignment symbol, and blank; they define the limits of identifiers, constants, picture specifi-

cations, and key words.

delimiter statement: a job control statement used to mark the end of data.

delivery time: the time interval between the beginning of transmission at an initiating terminal and the completion of reception at a receiving terminal.

delta modulation: conversion of an analog signal, such as voice, to a digital format in which the amplitude difference between successive samples of the analog signal is represented by a set of digits coded to express the quantized amplitude difference. In its simplest form, the quantized magnitude of the amplitude difference can have only one value other than zero. (F)

delta noise: the difference between the 1-state and the 0-state half-selected noise.

demand: an input-output coding technique in which a read or write order is initiated as the need to read a new block or write a new block of data occurs. Operations do not take place in parallel.

demand assigned multiple access (DAMA): trunks at each station in a satellite network that may initiate traffic to any other station.

demand fetching: a memory multiplexing design in which segments are kept on a backing storage and only placed in an internal storage when computations refer to them.

demand paging: the transfer of a page from auxiliary storage to real storage at the moment of need. (E)

demand processing: the processing of data as rapidly as it becomes available or ready. This is real time and avoids the need for storage of any appreciable amount of unprocessed data.

demand staging: moving data from disk to main memory when requested by an applications program and not before, as opposed to anticipatory staging.

demarcation strip: usually a terminal board acting as a physical interface between the business machine and the common carrier. see also *interface*.

demodulation: the process of retrieving intelligence (data) from a modulated carrier wave; the reverse of modulation.

demodulator: a functional unit that converts a modulated signal into the original signal. cf. *modulator*. (E)

demount: to remove a volume from a tape unit or a direct-access device.

demultiplexing: dividing one or more information streams into a larger number of streams.

denary: synonym for *decimal (2)*. (A) (B)

dense list: a list of the contents of contiguous storage areas. synonymous with *linear list*.

density: the closeness of space distribution on a storage medium.

dependent segment
(1) in a tree structure, a segment that relies on at least the root segment and possibly other dependent segments for its full meaning.
(2) in a data base, a segment that relies on a higher level segment for its full hierarchical meaning.

deposit: synonymous with *dump*.

DEQ: see *dequeue*.

dequeue (DEQ): to remove items from a queue. cf. *enqueue*.

derail: an instruction to go to a subroutine.

DES: the *National Bureau of Standards Data Encryption Standard.*

descender: the part of a letter, such as "j" or "y", that extends below the main body of a character; easier to read on some printers than others. see also *ascender.*

descending sort: a sort in which the final sequence of records is such that all successive keys compare "less than" or "equal to."

description: see *problem description.*

description list: a list of data elements and their attributes.

descriptor: in information retrieval, a word used to categorize or index information. synonymous with *key word.* (A) see *parameter descriptor.*

deserialize: to change from serial-by-bit to parallel-by-byte. cf. *serialize.*

deserializer: synonym for *serial-to-parallel converter.* (C)

design: see *functional design, logic design.*

designating device: a unit on some tabulators that permits the first item of a series of similar data to be printed, and inhibits some or all printing of the rest of the series.

designation hole: a hole punched in a punch card to indicate the nature of the data on the card, or the functions that a machine is to perform. (B) synonymous with *control hole, control punch.* (A) (B)

designator: any part that classifies.

desired value: synonymous with *input reference.*

desk checking: checking for errors in software by manual simulation of the application process. (E)

desk-mounted word processing equip-ment: word-processing equipment that is mounted into a specially designed or adapted desk or table. (D)

desktop computer: another name for microcomputer.

despatch: to allocate time of a CPU to a specific job. see *dispatch.*

DEST: see *destination.*

destination (D) (DEST): in a network, any point or location, for example, a node, a station, or a terminal, to which data is to be sent.

destination address (DA): information sent in the forward direction consisting of a number of address signals indicating the complete address of the called customer. (C)

destination code: synonym with *address (5).*

destination field (DF): a field in a message header that contains the destination code.

destination file: a CRAM deck or magnetic tape designated to receive the file of information which is output from a computer run.

destination station: a station to which a message is directed.

destructive addition: addition after which the sum appears in the location previously occupied by an operand, usually the augend; thus destroying the operand.

destructive cursor: on a CRT display device, a cursor that erases any character through which it passes as it is advanced, backspaced, or otherwise moved. cf. *nondestructive cursor.*

destructive read: reading that erases the data in the source location. (A) (B)

destructive storage: a storage unit where read operations are destructive and the contents must be regenerated after being read if they are required at the same location following a read operation. see *destructive read*.

DETAB: see *decision table*.

detail card: synonym for *trailer card*.

detail file: synonym for *transaction file*. (A) (B)

detectable element: in computer graphics, a display element that can be detected by a pick device. (E)

development system: a computer system with needed facilities for appropriate software and hardware application development.

development time: that part of operating time used for debugging new routines or hardware. see *program development time*. cf. *makeup time*. (*A*)

development tools: hardware and software aids used in evolving programs and/or electronic systems.

deviation from linearity: concerns the maximum deviation of output from the most favorable straight line that can be drawn through the input-output curve. The method of determining the most favorable line has to be given, to be expressed in percent of output full scale.

device (DVC): a mechanical, electrical, or electronic contrivance with a specific purpose. see *character display device, choice device, display device, locator device, logic device, mass storage device, pick device, raster display device, storage device, valuator device*. see also *device type, end-user device*.

device address: see *logical device address*.

device backup: pertaining to the as-

signment of alternate devices.

device control character: a control character used for the control of ancillary devices associated with a data-processing system or data-communication system; for example, for switching such devices on or off. (A) (B)

device controller: a hardware unit that electronically supervises one or more peripheral devices. It acts as the link between the CPU and the I/O devices.

device control unit: a hardware device that controls the reading, writing, or displaying of data at one or more input-output devices or terminals. see also *transmission control unit*.

device coordinate: in computer graphics, a coordinate specified in a coordinate system that is device dependent. (E) see *normalized device coordinates*.

device-dependent: pertaining to an application program that is responsible for controlling the terminal to which it is connected. The application program is not responsible for controlling the use of the line by which the terminal is attached.

device-dependent program: a program that must consider the characteristics of a specific type of I/O device when processing an I/O request.

device flag (DF): a register with one bit for recording the status of a peripheral unit.

device independence (DI): the capability to write application programs so that they do not depend on the physical characteristics of devices.

device-independent: pertaining to the

ability to request I/O operations without regard for the characteristics of specific types of input-output devices. see also *symbolic I/O assignment.*

device-independent program: a program that does not consider the characteristics of a specific type of input-output device when processing an input-output request.

device line: synonym for *display line.*

device media control language: a language for specifying the physical implementation of the data-base logical data structure.

device name: the logical name assigned to a device.

device number: the reference number assigned to any external device.

device queue: a queue of requests to use a unit.

device status word: a word in which the condition of the bits indicates the status of peripheral units. see *device flag.*

device type: the general name for a kind of device; for example, 2311, 2400, 2400-1. see also *group name, unit address.*

DF
   (1)   see *data field.*
   (2)   see *destination field.*
   (3)   see *device flag.*

DFC: see *data-flow control.*

D flip-flop: a flip-flop with a delayed reaction where the output is conditioned by previous input.

DFT
   (1)   see *diagnostic function test.*
   (2)   see *digital facility terminal.*

DG: see *datagram.*

DI: see *device independence.*

diad: synonymous with *doublet.*

diadic boolean operation: synonymous with *binary boolean operation.*

diagnosis: locating and explaining detectable errors in a computer routine or hardware component.

diagnostic: pertaining to the detection and isolation of a malfunction or mistake. (A)

diagnostic check: a specific routine designed to locate a malfunction in a computer.

diagnostic function test (DFT): a program to test overall system reliability.

diagnostic program: a computer program that recognizes, locates, and explains either a fault in equipment or a mistake in a computer program. (A) (B)

diagnostic routine: a routine designed to locate a malfunction, either in other routines or in the computer hardware.

diagnostics: mechanisms built into hardware and software to inform users that an error has prevented the program from running properly. Systems which locate malfunctioning sections of a computer.

diagnostic test: the running of a machine program or routine for the purpose of discovering a failure or potential failure of a machine element, and to determine its location or its potential location.

diagram: see *block diagram, functional diagram, logic diagram, setup diagram, Veitch diagram, Venn diagram. (A)*

dial: to use a dial or push-button telephone to initiate a telephone call. In telecommunication, this action is taken to attempt to establish a connection between a terminal and a telecommunication device over a switched line.

dialectic sensors: an approach used in reading data from paper tape by a special sensor.

dialed line: synonym for *switched connection*.

dial exchange: an exchange where all subscribers can originate calls by dialing.

dialing: deprecated term for *calling*.

dial line: synonym for *switched connection*.

dialog: in an interactive system, a series of interrelated inquiries and responses analogous to a conversation between two people.

dial long-line circuit: a circuit, usually located in a central office, that extends the dialing, supervision, and other signaling range of a loop. (F)

dial pulse: an interruption in the loop of a calling telephone. The interruption is produced by the breaking and making of the dial pulse contacts of a calling telephone when a digit is dialed. The loop current is interrupted once for each unit of value of the digit.

dial repeating trunks: PBX tie trunks used with terminating PBX equipment capable of handling PBX station signaling information without attendant assistance. (F)

dial service assistance (DSA) switchboard: a switchboard associated with the switching center equipment to provide operator services such as information, intercepting, conferencing, and precedence calling assistance.

dial tone (DT): an audible signal indicating that a device is ready to be dialed.

dial tone delay: a measure of time required to provide dial tone to custom-

ers. This measures one aspect of the performance of a switching system. (F)

dial-tone-first coin service: a coin service that allows customers to obtain dial tone before money is deposited into the coin telephone. (F)

dial transfer: a service available with some PBXs that enable a station receiving a call to transfer it to another station in the same group without the assistance of an attendant. synonymous with *call transfer*. (F)

dial-up: the use of a dial or push-button telephone to initiate a station-to-station telephone call.

dial-up terminal: a terminal on a switched line.

dibit: a group of two bits. In four-phase modulation, each possible dibit is encoded as one of four unique carrier phase shifts. The four possible states for a dibit are 00, 01, 10, and 11.

DIBOL: Digital Business Oriented Language.

dichotomizing search: a search in which an ordered set of items is partitioned into two parts, one of which is rejected, the process being repeated on the accepted part until the search is completed. see also *binary search*. (*A*) (B)

dichotomy: a division into subordinate units or classes, that is, all white and all nonwhite, or all zero and all nonzero.

DICT: see *dictionary*.

dictionary (DICT): synonym for *proofreader, spell check, table*. see *composite external symbol dictionary, data dictionary, external symbol dictionary, relocation dictionary*.

die/dice: circuit elements built on

small rectangles of silicon on a wafer. Each wafer contains several dozen to more than a hundred rectangles–dice. When packaged, they are referred to as *chips*.

DIFF: see *difference*.

difference (DIFF): in a subtraction operation, the number or quantity that is the result of subtracting the subtrahend from the minuend. (A) (B)

difference engine: a forerunner to the computer, it is the machine designed and developed by Charles Babbage to solve polynominal expressions or equations by the difference method.

difference report: a report showing resultant changes from an original computer program and a program change.

differential analyzer: an analog computer using interconnected integrators to solve differential equations. (B) see *digital differential analyzer*. (*A*)

differential delay: the difference in the delays experienced by two sinusoids of different frequencies in passing through a communications channel. (F)

differential gear: in analog computers, a mechanism that relates the angles of rotation of three shafts, usually designed so that the algebraic sum of the rotation of two shafts is equal to twice the rotation of the third. A differential gear can be used for addition or subtraction. (A)

differential modulation: a type of modulation where the choice of the significant condition for any signal element is dependent on the choice of the previous signal element.

differential phase-shift keying (DPSK): a modulation technique in which the

relative changes of the carrier signal phase are coded according to the data to be transmitted.

differentiator: a device whose output function is proportional to the derivative of the input function with respect to one or more variables; for example, a resistance-capacitance network used to select the leading and trailing edges of a pulse signal. (A)

diffusion: in semiconductor production, introducing small quantities of impurity into a substrate material, such as silicon, permitting the impurity to spread into the substrate.

DIG: see *digit*.

digit (D) (DIG)

(1) a graphic character that represents an integer; for example, one of the characters 0 to 9. (B)

(2) a symbol that represents one of the nonnegative integers smaller than the radix; for example, in decimal notation, a digit is one of the characters from 0 to 9.

(3) synonymous with *numeric character*.

(4) see *binary digit, borrow digit, carry digit, check digit, decimal digit, sign digit, significant digit*. (A)

digital (D): pertaining to data in the form of digits. cf. *analog*.

digital adder: see *adder*.

digital/analog converter: a unit capable of converting digital signals into a continuous signal ready for input into an analog computer.

digital block: a set of multiplexed equipment that includes one or more data channels and associated circuitry. Digital blocks are usually designated in terms of signaling speed.

digital carrier system: a common carrier communication system that handles digital data.

digital computer

(1) a computer that operates on discrete data by performing arithmetic and logic processes on these data. (A)

(2) a computer that consists of one or more associated processing units and peripheral equipment and that is controlled by internally stored programs. (E)

(3) see also *analog computer, hybrid computer.*

digital data: data represented by digits, perhaps with special characters and the space characters. (A) (B)

digital data switching: see *digital switching.*

digital data system (DDS): a nationwide private-line synchronous data-communications network formed by interconnecting digital transmission facilities and providing special maintenance and testing capabilities. Customer channels operate at 2.4, 4.8, 9.6, 56, or 1544 kilobits per second. (F)

digital differential analyzer (DDA)

(1) an incremental computer in which the principal type of computing unit is a digital integrator whose operation is similar to the operation of an integrating mechanism. (B)

(2) a differential analyzer that uses digital representations for the analog quantities. (*A*)

digital facility: a switching or transmission facility designed specifically to handle digital signals. (F)

digital facility terminal (DFT): a voice-frequency terminal that performs signaling and transmission functions and includes digital banks. It inter-faces between a digital carrier system and a switching system, a metallic facility, an analog facility terminal, or another digital facility terminal. (F)

digital filter: a filtering process performed on a digitized signal by a general- or special-purpose computer.

digital incremental plotter: an output unit that accepts digital signals from the CPU and uses them to activate a plotting pen and paper-carrying drum.

digital inquiry-voice answerback (DI-VA): a data-communications system in which data are entered by means of a TOUCH-TONE dial and in which the answer comes back in the form of a computer-controlled audio response. (F)

digital line path: two or more digital line sections interconnected in tandem in such a way that the specified rate of the digital signal transmitted and received is the same over the whole length of the line path between the two terminal distribution frames or their equivalents.

digital line section: two consecutive sets of line terminal equipment, their interconnecting transmission medium, the in-station cabling between them, and their adjacent digital distribution frames (or equivalents) which together provide the whole of the means of transmitting and receiving data between two consecutive digital distribution frames (or equivalents) at a specified rate.

digital multiplex equipment: equipment for combining, by time division multiplexing, a defined integral number of digital input signals into a single digital signal at a defined digit rate and also for carrying out the inverse function (demultiplexer).

digital multiplex switching system (DMS): a family of switching systems utilizing new technology that will provide digital circuit switched service for voice and data transmission. DMS is characterized by the use of pulse code modulation and time division multiplexing through the switched network. The system allows the direct switching of pulse code modulation signals used in transmission systems without their conversion to analog format.

digital optical recording: recording of digital information using optical techniques.

digital radio path: two or more digital radio sections interconnected in tandem in such a way that the specified signaling rate of the digital signals transmitted and received is the same over the whole length of the radio path between the two terminal digital distribution frames (or equivalents).

digital radio section: two consecutive sets of radio terminal equipment and their interconnecting transmission medium which together provide the means of transmitting and receiving, between two consecutive digital distribution frames (or equivalents), digital signals at a specified rate.

digital read-out: an immediate display of data in digital form.

digital recorder: a peripheral device that records data as discrete numerically defined points.

digital representation: a discrete representation of a quantized value of variable, that is, the representation of a number of digits, perhaps with special characters and the space character. (A) (B)

digital section: the equipment or circuits used for transmitting and receiving digital signals at a specified rate between two consecutive digital distribution frames (or equivalent points).

digital signal: a discrete or discontinuous signal; one whose various states are discrete intervals apart.

digital signature: a numerical representation of a set of logic states, typically used to describe the logic-state history at one output of the unit under test during the complete test program.

digital sort: an ordering or sorting first according to the least significant, followed by a resort on each next higher order digit until all the items are completely sorted; most often used in punched card sorting.

digital switching: a process in which connections are established by operations on digital signals without converting them to analog signals. (C)

digital termination systems (DTS): a wide-band local distribution system for use in Electronic Message Service. The FCC has authorized usage in the 10.6 GHz band and it is likely that cellular technology will be used. (G)

digital-to-analog converter (DAC)
(1) a functional unit that converts digital data to analog signals. (B)
(2) a device that converts a digital value to a proportional analog signal.

digital transmission: a mode of transmission in which all information to be transmitted is first converted to digital form and then transmitted as a serial stream of pulses. Any signal—voice, data, television—can be converted to digital form. (F)

digit arithmetic: see *significant digit arithmetic.*

digit compression: a technique for increasing the number of digits stored in a storage area, thereby decreasing the size of a file.

digit delay element: a logic device for introducing a delay element of one digit period.

digitize: to express or represent in a digital form data that are not discrete data; for example, to obtain a digital representation of the magnitude of a physical quantity from an analog representation of that magnitude. (A) (B)

digitizer: a unit that converts an analog measurement to digital form.

digit period: the time interval for the single digital signal in a series, determined by the pulse repetition frequency of the computer. synonymous with *digit time.*

digit place: in a positional representation system, each site that may be occupied by a character and that may be identified by an ordinal number or by an equivalent identifier. synonymous with *digit position, symbol rank.* (A) (B)

digit position: synonym for *digit place.* (A) (B)

digit punch: a punch in rows 1, 2 . . . . 9 of a punched card. see also *eleven punch, twelve punch.* cf. *zone punch.* (A)

digit time: synonymous with *digit period.*

digroup: a digitally multiplexed group of 24 channels. Digroup usually refers to the T1 carrier line signal of 1.544 megabits per second; however, the term also is used to refer to the digital channel bank that provides the 24-channel mul-

tiplexing function. (F)

dimension: in assembler-language programming, the maximum number of values that can be assigned to a SET symbol representing an array.

dimensionality: in PL/1, the number of bound specifications in an array declaration.

diminished radix complement: a complement obtained by subtracting each digit of the given number from the number that is one less than the radix of that digit place. synonymous with *radix-minus-one complement.* (A) (B)

diode: an electronic device used to permit current flow in one direction and to inhibit current flow in the other.

DIP: see *dual in-line package.*

diplexer: a multicoupler device for permitting the simultaneous use of several transmitters or several receivers in connection with a common element such as an antenna system; the diplexer does not permit simultaneous transmit and receive.

dipole antenna: a straight, center-fed, one-half wavelength antenna.

dipole modulation: synonym for *nonpolarized return-to-zero recording.* (A)

DIR: see *directory.*

direct access: the facility to obtain data from a storage device, or to enter data into a storage device in such a way that the process depends only on the location of that data and not on a reference to data previously accessed. (B) cf. *serial access.* (A)

direct access arrangement (DAA): a unit that protects the telephone network from high voltages, or large signals which can be produced by the attachment to the network of consumers' equipment.

direct-access hash: pertaining to indexing, a hash algorithm that precludes collision, where no two elements have the same hash indices.

direct access inquiry: a storage approach allowing direct information inquiry from temporary or permanent storage devices.

direct-access storage

(1) a storage device in which the access time is in effect independent of the location of the data. (A)

(2) a storage device that provides direct access to data. (E)

(3) see also *immediate-access storage.*

direct access storage device (DASD): a device in which the access time is effectively independent of the location of the data.

direct access storage media (DASM): media capable of storing programs and data so that the time needed to access specific elements is quick and independent both of their location, and of the location of the last data element accessed. see *memory.*

direct address: an address that designates the storage location of an item of data to be treated as an operand. synonymous with *one-level address.* (B) cf. *indirect address.* (A)

direct addressing: a method of addressing in which the address part of an instruction contains a direct address. (B) cf. *indirect addressing.* (A)

direct call: a facility that does not require the use of address selection signals; the network interprets the call-request signal as an instruction to establish a connection to one or more predetermined data stations. (E)

direct code: synonymous with *absolute code.*

direct coding: instructions written in absolute code.

direct-coupled flip-flop: a flip-flop composed of electronic circuits in which the active elements are coupled with transistors. see also *flip-flop.*

direct coupling: a means of connecting electronic circuits or components so that the amplitude of currents within each are independent of the frequency of those currents.

direct current (DC): a unidirectional current of effectively constant value.

direct data organization: the organization of records in a nonsequential order. Each record is located at an address which is computed by a randomizing process.

direct data set: a data set whose records are in random order on a direct-access volume. Each record is stored or retrieved according to its actual address or its address relative to the beginning of the data set. cf. *sequential data set.*

direct digital control (DDC): a computer-control technique where a time-shared digital computer is substituted for a portion of or all of the analog simulator, thereby lowering capital investment and permitting greater facility in transferring a program from one system to another.

direct distance dialing (DDD): a telephone exchange service that enables the telephone user to call subscribers outside of his local area without operator assistance. see also *area code, numbering plan.*

directed-beam scan: in computer graphics, a technique of generating or recording the display elements of a display image in any sequence. synonymous with *directed scan, random scan.* (E)

directed scan: synonym for *directed-beam scan.*

direct insert routine: synonym for *open routine.*

direct insert subroutine: synonym for *open subroutine.* (A) (B)

direct instruction: an instruction that contains the direct address of an operand for the operation specified. (A) (B)

direction: see *flow direction.*

directional coupler: a transmission coupling device for separately (ideally) sampling (through a known coupling loss for measuring purposes) either for the forward (incident) or the backward (reflected) wave in a transmission line. It may be used to excite in the transmission line either a forward or backward wave.

directive: synonym for *declaration.* (A) (B)

direct memory access (DMA): high-speed data transfer direct between an input/output channel and memory. synonymous with *cycle stealing, data break.*

direct numerical control: a situation where a number of numerical control units are connected via a data transmission network. They can be under the direct control of a central computer, with or without the aid of an operator. In the latter situation, the system is referred to as *computer numerical control.*

directory (DIR)

(1) a table of identifiers and refer-ences to the corresponding items of data. (A) (B)

(2) an index that is used by a control program to locate more blocks of data that are stored in separate areas of a data set in direct-access storage.

directory assistance (DA): a service in which a customer will be connected to an operator at a directory assistance bureau by dialing the proper service code or number and will be told the directory number of the customer whom he desires to call, provided that the customer's number is, or will be, published (listed) in the telephone directory. Formerly called *information service.* (F)

directory assistance bureau: a bureau in which directory assistance service is rendered to customers. The operators in attendance obtain the desired telephone numbers from telephone directories or similar media. (F)

directory assistance operator: a person who handles directory assistance calls. (F)

directory devices: a unit that contains a table of contents with critical information about the files on that machine. Besides the file name and data of creation or modification, the directory has the size and address of the file on the device, although the directory listing on the terminal may not show all of this information.

direct outward dialing: a facility that allows an internal caller at an extension to dial an external number without going through an operator.

direct percentage: on a calculator, the calculation directly of a percentage markup or discount value by the implied use of multiplication and division functions. (D)

direct-point repeater: a telegraph function in which the receiving relay controlled by the signals received over a line repeats corresponding signals directly into another line or lines without the interposition of any other repeating or transmitting apparatus.

direct transmission satellite: a communications satellite which transmits messages to single receiving sets.

direct voice input: input of information into a unit directly using the human voice, without an intermediate stage of keyboarding.

DIS: see *disconnect.*

disabled

(1) pertaining to a state of a processing unit that prevents the occurrence of certain types of interruptions. synonymous with *masked.*

(2) pertaining to the state in which a transmission control unit or audio response unit cannot accept incoming calls on a line.

(3) not selectable.

(4) in PL/1, the state in which a particular on condition does not result in an interrupt.

disabled module: a module that cannot be interrupted during its execution. It must be executed from beginning to end once it has gained control. cf. *enabled module.*

disaggregation: separation of existing rate structures into stand-alone component rate elements. Under the disaggregation concept, the rate for local exchange service, for example, is separated into two elements—one applicable to the exchange access line and one applicable to the telephone instrument. (G)

disarm: to disallow an interrupt.

disassembler: a program that translates from machine language to assembly language, often to decipher existing machine language programs by generating symbolic code listings.

disaster dump: a dump made when a nonrecoverable computer program error occurs. (A)

disc (DSK): alternate spelling for disk. (A) see *magnetic disk.*

disconnect (DIS): to disengage the apparatus used in a connection and to restore it to its ready condition when not in use. synonymous with *release.*

disconnect signal: a signal transmitted from one end of a subscriber line or trunk to indicate at the other end that the established connection is to be disconnected.

disconnect timeout: an indication that a station has gone on-hook.

discrete: pertaining to data in the form of distinct elements such as characters, or to physical quantities having distinctly recognizable values. cf. *analog.*

discrete data: data represented by characters. (A) (B)

discrete programming: synonym for *integer programming.* (A)

discrete representation: a representation of data by characters, each character or a group of characters designating one of a number of alternatives. (A) (B)

discretionary hyphen: in word processing, a hyphen inserted by an operator to divide a word when there is insufficient space to produce the whole of that word at the end of a line.

synonymous with *syllable hyphen.* see also *required hyphen.* (D)

discrimination: skipping of various instructions as developed in a predetermined set of conditions as programmed.

discrimination instruction: an instruction of the class of instructions that comprises branch instructions and conditional jump instructions. (A) (B)

discriminator: that part of an FM receiver circuit which extracts the desired signal from an incoming frequency-modulated carrier wave by changing frequency variations into amplitude variations.

dish (antenna): a transmitting or receiving aerial shaped as a dish; used to receive radio and television signals from a communications satellite.

disjunction: the boolean operation whose result has the boolean value 0 if and only if each operand has the boolean value 0. synonymous with *inclusive-OR operation, logical ADD, OR operation.* (B) cf. *nondisjunction.* (A)

disk: loosely, a magnetic disk unit. see *integrated disk, magnetic disk.*

disk accessing: the process used in transferring data to and from a disk file.

disk-based operating system: a system where software is held on one, or more magnetic disks.

disk controller card: a printed-circuit board which interfaces disk storage hardware to the CPU of a computer.

disk drive: a mechanism for moving a disk pack or a magnetic disk and controlling its movements; deprecated term for *magnetic disk unit.*

diskette: a thin, flexible magnetic disk and a semirigid protective jacket, in which the disk is permanently enclosed. see *unformatted diskette.* synonymous with *flexible disk.*

diskette 1: any diskette that is the medium used to record single-density information on one side.

diskette 2: any diskette that is the medium used to record single-density information on both sides.

diskette 2D: any diskette that is the physical medium used to record double-density information on both sides.

diskette drive: see *diskette storage drive.*

diskette-formatted tape: a tape that is formatted so that it can be read by a data converter unit, which transfers the data written on it to a diskette.

diskette hard-holes: small mylar doughnuts affixed to the center hole of a diskette for additional protection.

diskette-only feature: a special feature or a specify feature that, through macroinstructions or microinstructions on diskette, either: (1) activates, suppresses, or adapts product application functions; or (2) simulates functions to enhance the capability, storage capacity, or performance of the product. For example, a feature on diskette that enables a processor to execute the instructions of some other machine.

diskette slot: see *slot.*

diskette storage: storage on magnetic diskettes.

diskette storage device: a direct-access storage device that uses diskettes as the storage medium.

diskette storage drive: a device that

rotates diskette disks in a diskette storage device. deprecated term for *diskette storage device.*

disk file: an associated set of records of the same format, identified by a unique label.

disk file controller: a unit that controls the transfer of data between a number of magnetic disk units and main memory.

disk operating system: see *DOS.*

disk overlay: deprecated term for *overlay.*

disk pack
(1) a removable assembly of magnetic disks. (B)
(2) a portable set of flat, circular recording surfaces used in a disk storage device. (*A*)

disk sector: a 512-byte area of disk storage. Each disk sector contains two 256-byte disk data blocks.

disk sorting: a sort program that utilizes disk-type memory for auxiliary storage during sorting.

disk storage: see *magnetic disk storage.*

disk storage device: see *magnetic disk unit.*

disk storage drive: see *disk drive.*

disk storage module: a nonremovable assembly of magnetic disks serviced by two access mechanisms.

disk unit: see *magnetic disk unit.* (B)

disk volume: a disk pack or part of a disk storage module.

dismount: deprecated term for *demount.*

dispatch
(1) to allocate time on a processor to jobs or tasks that are ready for execution. (E)
(2) the process of sending a craftsperson to an equipment location

such as an outside plant location or to a customer's premises for maintenance or trouble diagnostic purposes. (F)

dispatcher
(1) the program in an operating system that places jobs or tasks into execution.
(2) the routing or controlling routines of Subsystem Support Services. This routine provides multitasking and control support, on a priority basis, for all Subsystem Support Services functions.

dispatching priority: a number assigned to tasks, used to determine the order in which they use the processing unit in a multitasking situation.

disperse: pertaining to the distribution of items from an input record to locations in one or more output records.

dispersed intelligence: synonymous with *distributed intelligence.*

dispersion: synonymous with *NOT-AND operation.*

DISP
(1) see *displacement.*
(2) see *display.*

displacement (D) (DISP): the distance from the beginning of a record, block, or segment to the beginning of a particular field. synonym for *relative address.*

display (DISP) (DSPL)
(1) a visual presentation of data. (A) (B)
(2) in word processing, a device for visual presentation of information on any temporary character-imaging device. (D)
(3) loosely, a display device. (B)
(4) see *cathode ray tube display.*
(5) see also *display device, raster*

display device.

display and printing calculator: a machine that provides the data output facilities of a display calculator and of a printing calculator, which may be selected at the user's option. (D)

display attribute: in computer graphics, a particular property that is assigned to all or part of a display; for example, low intensity, green color, blinking status. (E)

display background: see *static display image.*

display-based word-processing equipment: word-processing equipment that can electronically display text and other graphics, using, for example, a cathode ray tube (CRT), light emitting diode (LED), or gas plasma display. cf. *non-display-based word-processing equipment.* (D)

display calculator: a machine in which the data output is shown in the form of illuminated characters. (D)

display center: the position on a display screen for duplicating data or information to an advantage.

display character generator: on a CRT display device, a hardware unit that converts the digital code for a character into signals that cause the electron beam to create the character on the screen.

display column: in computer graphics, all display positions that constitute a full-length vertical line on the display surface. synonymous with *addressable vertical positions.* cf. *display line.*

display command: in computer graphics, a command that controls a display device. (E)

display component: a terminal component capable of displaying information on a viewing surface; for example, a cathode ray tube or a gas panel.

display console: a console that must include at least one display device and may also include one or more input units such as an alphanumeric keyboard, function keys, a job stick, a control ball, or a light pen. (E)

display cycle: in computer graphics, the sequence of events needed to generate a display image once. (E)

display cycle time: in computer grahics, the minimum time interval between the starts of successive display cycles.

display device
(1) an output unit that gives a visual representation of data. (A) (B)
(2) in computer graphics, a device capable of presenting display elements on a display surface; for example, a cathode ray tube, plotter, microfilm viewer, printer.
(3) see *character display device, raster display device.*

display drum: a magnetic, digital, data buffer storage drum that stores data to be used for display on a visual unit.

display element: in computer graphics, a basic graphic element that can be used to construct a display image; for example, a dot, a line segment, a character. synonymous with *graphic primitive, output primitive.* (E)

display entity: in computer graphics, a collection of display elements that can be manipulated as a unit.

display field: in computer graphics, an area in a display buffer or on a display space that contains a set of characters that can be manipulated or operated upon as a unit. (E)

display foreground: see *dynamic display image.*

display frame:

(1) in computer graphics, an area in storage in which a display image can be recorded.

(2) in computer micrographics, an area on a microform in which a display image can be recorded.

display group: in computer graphics, a collection of display elements that can be manipulated as a unit and that can be further combined to form larger groups. synonymous with *display segment.* (E)

display image: in computer graphics, a collection of display elements or display groups that are represented together at any one time in a display space. see *dynamic display image, static display image.* see also *screen image.* (E)

display line: in computer graphics, all display positions that constitute a full-length horizontal line on a display surface. synonymous with *addressable horizontal positions.* cf. *display column.*

display order: synonym for *display command.*

display panel: synonym for *panel.*

display position: in computer graphics, any position in a display space that can be occupied by a picture element or a display element. (E)

display recall control: on a battery-powered calculator, a control for recalling a display that has been blanked out by battery-saving circuitry. (D)

display segment: synonym for *display group.*

display space: in computer graphics, that portion of a display surface available for a display image. The display space may be all or part of the display surface. synonymous with *operating space.* see also *image storage space.* (E)

display surface: in computer graphics, that medium on which display images may appear; for example, the entire screen of a cathode-ray tube. (E)

display tube: a tube, usually a cathode-ray tube, used to display data.

dissuasion tone: in telephony, an audible signal indicating that the requested extension is out of order or does not exist, or that the type of call requested is not allowed with a particular class of service.

distance: synonymous with *Exclusive-OR operation.*

distinctive ringing: a ringing cadence indicating whether a call is internal or external.

distortion: the unwanted change in wave form that occurs between two points in a transmission system. The six major forms of distortion are: bias, characteristic, delay, end, fortuitous ("jitter"), and harmonic.

distributed data processing (DDP): data processing in which some or all of the processing, storage, and control functions, in addition to input-output functions, are situated in different places and connected by transmission facilities. see also *remote-access data processing.*

distributed data-processing network: a network in which some or all of the processing, storage, and control functions, in addition to input-output functions, are dispersed among its nodes.

distributed function

(1) the use of programmable terminals, controllers, and other devices to perform operations that were previously done by the processing unit, such as managing data links, controlling devices, and formatting data.

(2) functions, such as network management, processing, and error recovery operations, that are dispersed among the nodes of a network, as opposed to functions that are concentrated at a central location.

distributed intelligence: deprecated term for *distributed data processing, distributed function.*

distributed logic: systems were where logic, or intelligence, is distributed within the system instead of being located centrally, that is, word processing systems linking intelligent terminals to make shared use of other resources, such as storage, printer.

distributed processing: a technique for implementing a set of information processing functions within multiple physically separated physical devices.

distributed processing network: see *distributed data-processing network.*

distributed system: see *distributed data processing, distributed function.*

Distributed Systems Environment (DSE): Honeywell's broad arena of information-processing capabilities, governed by a set of unifying design concepts, allowing users flexibility in the implementation of distributed system configurations.

distributing frame: a structure for terminating permanent wires of a telephone central office, private branch exchange, or private exchange, and for permitting the easy change of connections between them by means of cross-connecting wires.

distribution: in a switching network, distribution refers to the capability of connecting an input to any one of several outputs. In a traffic network, distribution refers to separating calls on incoming trunk groups at a toll or tandem office and recombining them on other outgoing trunk groups. (F)

distribution cable: part of the outside cable plant connecting feeder or subfeeder cables to drop wires or buried service wires that connect to the customer's premises. Distribution cable usually contains fewer than 300 twisted wire pairs. (F)

distribution frame: a structure with terminations for connecting the permanent wiring in such a manner that interconnection by cross-connections may be made readily.

DIV: see *data in voice.*

DIVA: see *digital inquiry-voice answerback.*

diversity

(1) a method of radio transmission and/or reception in which a single information channel is derived or selected from a plurality of received channels. Diversity may take the form of frequency diversity, the use of more than one frequency; polarization diversity, the use of more than one polarization for transmission; space diversity, the use of two or more antennas at different locations at the transmitter and/or receiver; and angle diversity, antennas pointed in slightly different directions. (F)

(2) a method of transmitting a single information channel over sepa-

rate geographic routes to provide a high degree of service continuity. (F)

diversity combiner: a circuit or device for combining two or more signals carrying the same intelligence received via separate paths or channels with the objective of providing a single resultant which is superior in quality to any of the contributing signals.

divide check: an indicator denoting that an invalid division has been attempted or has occurred.

divided slit scan: a device, in OCR, that scans an input character at given intervals to obtain its horizontal and vertical components; consists of a narrow column of photoelectric cells.

division: the parts into which a COBOL program is organized; identification division provides information to identify the source and object programs.

division header: the COBOL words that indicate the beginning of a particular division of a COBOL program. The four division headers are: identification division, environment division, data division, and procedure division.

divisor (DR): in a division operation, the number or quantity by which the dividend is divided. (A) (B)

DL
(1) see *data link*.
(2) see *data list*.

dl: see *deciliter*.

DLE: the *data-link escape character*. (A)

DLT: see *data-loop transceiver*.

DM:
(1) see *data management*.
(2) see *decimeter*.

dm: see *decimeter*.

DMA: see *direct memory access*.

DML: see *data manipulating language*.

DMP: see *dump*.

DMS: see *digital multiplex switching system*.

DMX: see *data multiplexer*.

DN: see *data name*.

document
(1) a data medium and the data recorded on it, that generally has permanence and that can be read by man or machine. (A) (B)
(2) a unified collection of information pertaining to a specific subject or related subjects.
(3) in word processing, a collection of one or more lines of text that can be named and stored as a separate entity.

document assembly (printing process only): in word processing, the process of merge and output of recorded text in a predetermined sequence to form a complete, distinct document. (D)

documentation
(1) the management of documents, which may include the actions of identifying, acquiring, processing, storing, and disseminating them. (B)
(2) a collection of documents on a given subject. (*A*) (B)

documentation book: a collection of all documentation relevant to a specific system or program.

document fulfilment agency: an agency providing copies of documents ordered by users. Requests are generated following an on-line search and transmitted to the agency via a computer network.

document handling: a procedure system or process for loading, feeding, transporting, and unloading a cut-form document submitted for character recognition.

document leading edge: the edge which is first encountered during the reading process in character recognition, and whose relative position shows the direction of travel.

document mark: in micrographics, an optical mark, within the recording area and outside the image on a roll of microfilm, used for counting images or film frames automatically. synonymous with *blip*. (*A*)

document reference edge: in character recognition, a specified document edge with respect to which the alignment of characters is defined. (A)

document retrieval: a system for indexing, searching and identifying documents, from which information is requested.

docuterm: a word or phrase used to describe the contents within a document and can be used in future retrieval as a data name.

DO group: in PL/1, a sequence of statements headed by a DO statement and ended by its corresponding END statement, used for control purposes.

DO loop: in FORTRAN, repetitive execution of the same statement or statements by use of a DO statement.

domain (D)

(1) in a network, the resources that are under the control of one or more associated host processors. (E)

(2) the network resources that are under the control of a particular system services control point (SSCP).

domestic satellite carrier: an intercity carrier which provides communications service within the United States via a domestic satellite (DOMSTAT). see other *common carriers*. (G)

dominant carrier: in legislative proposals to rewrite or amend the Communication Act of 1934 it is used to describe a carrier having control over a substantial portion or subportion of the telecommunications market. A dominant carrier would be subject to special restrictions, usually including a requirement to establish a fully separated subsidiary for offering other than basic services. FCC Docket 79-252 defines a dominant carrier as one having significant market power. This includes AT&T and all the independent telephone companies in the voice market, and Western Union in the domestic record market, which are subject to more stringent rules regarding tariffs and regulatory oversight. (G)

donor: an element introduced in small quantities as an impurity to a semiconducting material.

do-nothing operation: synonym for *no-operation instruction*. (A) (B)

dopant: a chemical impurity added to a semiconductor material to change its electrical characteristics.

doped: subjected to *dopant*.

DOS (disk operating system): a program that controls the computer's transfer of data to and from a hard or floppy disk. Frequently combined with the main operating system.

DO statement: a statement used to group a number of statements in a procedure.

dot matrix

(1) in computer graphics, a two-dimensional pattern of dots used for constructing a display image. This type of matrix can be used to represent characters by dots. (E)

(2) in word processing, a pattern of dots used to form characters. This term normally refers to a small section of the set of addressable points; for example, a representation of characters by dots. (D)

(3) in micrographics, a method of generating characters using a matrix of dots so that the combination of energized dots produces a human-readable character. (B)

dot matrix character generator: in computer graphics, a character generator that generates character images composed of dots. (E)

dot printer: synonym for *matrix printer*. (A) (E)

double card: a special card that is approximately twice the length of a general-purpose paper card. A double card usually consists of two separable general-purpose paper cards. (A)

double-dense recording: synonymous with *modified frequency modulation*.

double-density recording: synonymous with *modified freqency modulation*.

double-ended queue: a list of variable length, whose content may be changed by adding or removing items at either end. (A)

double-entry card: a particular punched card designed to hold data for entry into two different accounts, that is, a card contaning both payroll and labor distribution information.

double-length register: two registers that function as a single register. Each register may be individually accessed. For example, a double-length register may be used in exact multiplication for storing the result, in exact division for storing the partial

quotient and remainder, in character manipulation for shifting character strings, and for accessing the left or right portion. synonymous with *double register*. (A) (B)

double precision: pertaining to the use of two computer words to represent a number in accordance with the required precision. (A) (B)

double-pulse recording: phase modulation recording magnetized in opposite polarity with unmagnetized regions on each end. A zero may be represented by a cell composed of a negative region followed by a positive region, and a one by a positive region followed by a negative region, or vice versa. (A) (B)

double punch: more than one numeric punch in any one column of a punched card.

doubler: an internal component that doubles a given digit and is used in the multiplication routine.

double-rail logic: pertaining to self-timing asynchronous circuits in which each logic variable is represented by two electrical lines which together can take on three meaningful states: zero, one, and undecided. (A)

double register: synonym for *double-length register*. (A) (B)

double-sheet detector: in a duplicator, a device that senses the presence of two or more superimposed sheets during the feeding process. (D)

double-sheet detector control: in a duplicator, a means of adjusting the double-sheet detector. (D)

double-sheet ejector: in a duplicator, a mechanism that, when triggered by the double-sheet detector, diverts the double sheets away from the normal path of the paper through the machine. (D)

double-sided disk: a disk with both surfaces available for the storage of data.

double strike: in word processing, typing each character twice, which gives a darker, more solid impression. It is useful for preparing copy that will be printed.

doublet: a byte composed of two binary elements. synonymous with *two-bit byte*. (*A*) (B)

double-word (DW): a contiguous sequence of bits or characters that comprises two computer words and is capable of being addressed as a unit. (A)

DO variable: in FORTRAN, a variable, specified in a DO statement, which is initialized or incremented prior to each execution of the statement or statements within a DO loop. It is used to control the number of times the statements within the DO loop are executed.

down: a computer is "down" when it is not running. It may be shut down for maintenance, there may be a hardware failure, or the operating system may have been disarranged by a runaway program.

downconverter: a type of converter which is characterized by the frequency of the output signal being lower than the frequency of the input signal. It is the converse of an "up" converter.

down link: the communications link from the satellite to the receiving earth station.

down loaded: a programming method in which the program to be used in a remote terminal is sent down the line from central location to that terminal and stored there for local use.

downtime: the time interval during which a functional unit is inoperable due to a fault. (A)

downward compatibility: the capability of an advanced system to interact with a lesser advanced one.

downward reference: in an overlay structure, a reference made from a segment to a segment lower in the path, that is, farther from the root segment.

DP
(1) see *data processing*.
(2) see *data processor*.

DPS: see *data-processing station*.

DPSK: see *differential phase-shift keying*.

DR: see *divisor*.

draft copy: in word processing, a printout prepared for approval or editing. see also *edited copy, final copy*. (D)

dragging: in computer graphics, moving all or part of a display group in a display space in such a way that the group continuously follows the pointer as though it were attached. (E)

drift: a change in the output of a circuit that occurs slowly.

drift error: in analog computers, an error caused by a drift.

drifting characters: see *sign and currency symbol characters*.

drive: see *disk storage drive, media drive, tape drive*.

driver: a program that controls a peripheral unit connected on line.

drop (subscribers): the line from a telephone cable to a subscriber's building.

drop-dead halt: a machine halt from which there is no recovery.

drop-in

(1) the reading of a spurious signal whose amplitude is greater than a predetermined percentage of the nominal signal. (A)

(2) an error in the storage into or in the retrieval from a magnetic storage device, revealed by the reading of a binary character not previously recorded. Drop-ins are usually caused by defects in, or the presence of particles on, the magnetic surface layer. (E)

drop-out

(1) in magnetic tape a recorded signal whose amplitude is less than a predetermined percentage of a reference signal.

(2) in data communication, a momentary loss in signal, usually due to the effect of noise or system malfunction.

(3) a failure to read a bit from magnetic storage. *(A)*

(4) an error in the storage into or the retrieval from a magnetic storage device, revealed by a failure to read a binary character. Drop-outs are usually caused by defects in, or the presence of particles on, the magnetic surface layer. (E)

drop repeater: a repeater that is provided with the necessary equipment for local termination (dropping) of one or more channels of a multichannel system.

drop wire: a relatively short pair of wires connecting an aerial distribution cable pair to a customer's premises. (F)

drum: see *magnetic drum*.

drum drive: a mechanism for moving a magnetic drum and controlling its movement. (B)

drum plotter: in computer graphics, a plotter that draws a display image on a display surface mounted on a rotating drum. see also *flatbed plotter*. (E)

drum printer: a line printer in which the type is mounted on a rotating drum that contains a full character set for each printing position. (A)

drum scanning: in facsimile transmission, scanning where the object to be imaged, is wrapped around a drum, which then rotates past an optical sensing unit. synonymous with *cylinder scanning*.

drum storage: see *magnetic drum storage*. (A)

drum unit: see *magnetic drum unit*.

dry running: the examination of the logic and coding of a program from a flowchart and written instructions, and record of the results of each step of the operation before running the program on the computer.

DS: see *data set (2)*.

DSBAM: double sideband amplitude modulation.

DSCB: see *data-set control block*.

DSDT: see *data-set definition table*.

DSD table: see *data-set definition table*.

DSE

(1) see *data-switching exchange*.

(2) see *Distributed Systems Environment*.

DSECT: see *dummy control section*.

DSK: see *disc*.

DSN: see *data-set name*.

DSNAME: see *data-set name*.

DSPL: see *display*.

DSS: see *dynamic support system*.

DT
  (1) see *data terminal*.
  (2) see *dial tone*.
DTE: see *data-terminal equipment*.
DTS: see *digital termination systems*.
dual density: a feature that allows a program to use a tape unit in either 800- or 1600-byte-per-inch recording.
dual intensity: printers or display units that can produce symbols in regular and bold-faced formats.
dual operation: of a boolean operation, another boolean operation whose result, when it is performed on operands that are the negation of the operands of the first boolean operation, is the negation of the result of the first boolean operation. For example, disjunction is the dual operation of conjunction. (A) (B)
dual port memory: a memory unit having dual data and address connections suitable for low-level communication.
dual processor system: a configuration including two central processors, each receiving the same input and executing the same routines. synonymous with *dual system*.
dual system: synonymous with *dual processor system*.
ducol-punched card: a punched card with 12 rows of punching positions in each column, that is, zero through 9, an X and Y, representing numerals zero to 99 using multiple punching in each column and using a punch or no punch in the X and Y positions, lower-value digit positions are the ten digit, higher positions, the units.
dumb terminal: a terminal with no independent processing ability of its own which can only carry out operations when connected to a computer.
dummy: pertaining to the characteristic of having the appearance of a specified thing but not having the capacity to function as such: for example, a dummy character, dummy plug, or a dummy statement. (A)
dummy address: an artificial address used for illustration or instruction purposes.
dummy argument
  (1) in FORTRAN, a variable within a FUNCTION or SUBROUTINE statement or statement function definition, with which actual arguments from the calling program or function reference are associated.
  (2) in PL/1, temporary storage that is created automatically to hold the value of an argument that is constant, an operational expression, a variable whose attributes differ from those specified for the corresponding parameter in a known declaration, or an argument enclosed in parentheses.
dummy check: a check consisting of adding all the digits during dumping, and verifying the sum when retransferring.
dummy control section (DSECT): a control section that an assembler can use to format an area of storage without producing any object code. synonymous with *dummy section*.
dummy data set
  (1) a data set for which operations such as disposition processing, input-output operations, and allocation are bypassed.
  (2) data sets, created by the programmer and used during the testing phase of program validation services, that represent the data sets

that the program would use during normal execution.

dummy instruction: an item of data in the form of an instruction that is inserted in a set of instruction, but is not intended to be executed. (A) (B)

dummy section: synonym for *dummy control section.*

dummy variable: a symbol inserted at definition time, which will be replaced at a future time by the actual variable.

dump (DMP)

(1) data that have been dumped. (B)

(2) to write the contents of a storage, or of part of a storage, usually from an internal storage to an external medium, for a specific purpose such as to allow other use of the storage as a safeguard against faults or errors, or in connection with debugging. (B)

(3) see *change dump, disaster dump, dynamic dump, postmortem dump, selective dump, snapshot dump, static dump.* (A)

dump and restart: approaches used to ensure that a run is satisfactorily restarted following a dump.

dump check: a check used to ensure that a dump has been correctly made or properly restarted.

dump point: that step in a program at which a dump is started.

dump routine: a utility routine that dumps. (A) (B)

duodecimal

(1) characterized by a selection, choice, or condition that has 12 possible different values or states. (B)

(2) pertaining to a fixed-radix numeration system having a radix of 12. (A) (B)

DUP: see *duplicate.*

duplex: in data communication, per-

taining to a simultaneous two-way independent transmission in both directions. synonymous with *full duplex.* (A) see also *duplex transmission.* cf. *half-duplex.*

duplex channel: a channel permitting simultaneous transmission in both directions. see *duplex.*

duplex circuit: a communications circuit capable of transmission in two directions.

duplex console: a switchover console connecting two or more computers for on-line control.

duplexed system: a system with two distinct and separate sets of facilities, each of which is capable of assuming the system function while the other assumes a standby status. Usually, the sets are identical.

duplexer: a device that permits the simultaneous use of a transmitter and a receiver in connection with a common element such as an antenna system.

duplexing: utilizing duplicate components, so that, should one fail, the system can continue to function with the other.

duplex operation

(1) in data transmission, a method of working between two data-terminal equipments (DTEs) in which the transmission of digital data may take place simultaneously in both directions. (C)

(2) a mode of operation of a data link in which data may be transmitted simultaneously in both directions over two channels. synonymous with *both-way operation, full-duplex operation.*

duplex transmission: data transmission in both directions at the same time. see also *half-duplex transmission, simplex transmission.* (E)

duplicate (DUP): to copy from a source to a destination that has the same physical form as the source; for example, to punch new punched cards with the same pattern of holes as an original punched card. synonymous with *reproduce.* (*A*) (B)

duplicate key: in word processing, a control that initiates the duplication process. (D)

duplicate mass storage volume: see *duplicate volume.*

duplicate volume: an inactive mass storage volume that has the same identification as another mass storage volume and is not a copy.

duplication: in word processing, the reproduction of the entire recorded text from one element of recording medium to another. (D)

duplication check: a check based on the consistency of two independent performances of the same task. (A)

duplication factor: in assembler programming, a value that indicates the number of times that the data specified immediately following the duplication factor is to be generated.

duplication of facilities: the provision of similar types of transmission facilities over similar routes by more than one carrier. In intercity transmission, for example, this practice is wasteful because it fragments user demand, thereby preventing full realization of the economies of scale inherent in a single unified transmission facility. (G)

duplicator: a machine that uses direct litho duplicating, offset litho duplicating, spirit (or other fluid) duplicating, or stencil duplicating to produce mul-

tiple copies from a master. see also *duplicator with automatic feed, duplicator with hand feed, duplicator with manual master change, duplicator with semiautomatic master change.* (D)

duplicator with automatic feed: a duplicator into which the copy paper is fed automatically by mechanical means. (D)

duplicator with hand feed: a duplicator into which the copy paper is fed manually sheet by sheet. (D)

duplicator with manual master change: a duplicator in which the master is introduced manually to the attachment device and is removed either by hand or automatically. (D)

duplicator with semiautomatic master change: a duplicator in which masters are fed individually by hand into a loading device, are then introduced automatically to the attachment device, and are finally removed, either automatically or by hand.

duration: see *assemble duration, compile duration, response duration, run duration, translate duration.* (D)

DUV: see *data under voice.*

DVC: see *device.*

DVCDN: Console Command-Device Down. Informs the system that a device is no longer physically available for system operation.

DVCUP: Console Command-Device Up. Informs the system that a device is available for system or operation after the device has been down.

DW

(1) see *daisy wheel.*

(2) see *double-word.*

dwell: a programmed time delay of variable duration.

DX signaling: a facility signaling system and range extension technique for long metallic trunks that use bridge-type detection of small changes. (F)

dyadic boolean operation: a boolean operation on two and only two operands. (A) synonymous with *binary boolean operation.*

dyadic operation: an operation on two and only two operands. (A) (B)

dyadic operator: an operator that represents an operation on two and only two operands. The dyadic operators are AND, equivalence, exclusion, exclusive OR, inclusion, NAND, NOR, OR. synonymous with *binary operator.* (*A*) (B)

dynamic: of occurring at the time execution.

dynamic accuracy: accuracy determined with a time-varying output.

dynamic allocation

(1) an allocation technique in which the resources assigned for the execution of computer programs are determined by criteria applied at the moment of need.

(2) assignment of system resources to a program at the time the program is executed rather than at the time it is loaded into main storage. see also *dynamic storage allocation.*

dynamic buffer allocation: synonym for *dynamic buffering.*

dynamic buffering

(1) a dynamic allocation of buffer storage. (E)

(2) allocating storage for buffers as they are needed for incoming data during program execution.

dynamic control function: one of the network control program functions initiated by a control command from the host access method. Dynamic

control functions include activating and deactivating telecommunication lines, requesting the status of a telecommunication line, and switching channel adapters.

dynamic data set definition: the process of defining a data set and allocating auxiliary storage space for it during job-step execution rather than before job-step execution.

dynamic debug: debug programs designed for interactive debugging of user-written programs.

dynamic device reconfiguration (DDR): a facility that allows a demountable volume to be moved, and repositioned if necessary, without abnormally terminating the job or repeating the initial program load procedure.

dynamic display image: in computer graphics, that part of a display image that can be frequently changed by the user during a particular application. synonymous with *foreground display, image.* cf. *static display image.* (E)

dynamic dump: dumping performed during the execution of a computer program, usually under the control of that computer program. (A) (B)

dynamic instructions: the sequence of machine steps performed by the computer in real-time or simulated environment.

dynamicizer: synonym for *parallel-to-serial converter, serializer.* (A) (B)

dynamic loading: the loading of routines into main storage as needed by an executing program. Dynamically loaded routines are not part of the executing program's load module.

dynamic memory: synonymous with *dynamic storage.*

dynamic memory allocation: the time-varying allocation of a limited main memory among competing processes according to some system-dependent strategy.

dynamic parameter: synonym for *program-generated parameter*. (A) (B)

dynamic printout: a printout of data occurring as one of the sequential operations during the machine run.

dynamic programming: in operations research, a procedure for optimization of a multistage problem solution wherein a number of decisions are available at each stage of the process. (B) cf. *convex programming, integer programming, linear programming, mathematical programming, nonlinear programming, quadratic programming*. (*A*)

dynamic RAM: see *dynamic storage*.

dynamic range: a range from weakest to strongest signals that a receiver is able to accept as input.

dynamic relocation: a process that assigns new absolute addresses to a computer program during execution so that the program may be executed from a different area of main storage. (A)

dynamic response: the behavior of the output of a device as a function of the input, with respect to time.

dynamic scheduling: scheduling that changes with the different demands that are made on the system rather than being fixed as in conventional applications.

dynamic stop: synonym for *breakpoint halt*. (A) (B)

dynamic storage

(1) a device storing data in a manner that permits the data to move or vary with time such that the specified data are not always available for recovery. Magnetic drum and disk storage are dynamic nonvolatile storage. An acoustic delay line is a dynamic volatile storage. (A)

(2) the available storage left within the partition after the task set is loaded.

(3) synonymous with *dynamic memory*.

dynamic storage allocation (DYSTAL): a storage allocation technique in which the storage assigned to computer programs and data is determined by criteria applied at the moment of need. (A) (B)

dynamic subroutine: a subroutine in skeletal form with regard to certain features, such as the number of repetitions, decimal point position, or item size, that are selected or adjusted in accordance with the data-processing requirements. (A)

dynamic support system (DSS): an interactive debugging facility that allows authorized maintenance personnel to monitor and analyze events and alter data.

DYSTAL: see *dynamic storage allocation*.

E
- (1) see *error*.
- (2) see *execute*.
- (3) see *execution*.
- (4) see *exponent*.
- (5) see *expression*.

EA: see *effective address*.

EADAS: see *Engineering and Administration Data Acquisition System*. (F)

EAM: see *electrical accounting machine*. (A)

earth segment: in satellite communications, the earth or ground, as opposed to the satellite itself.

earth station: a terminal capable of transmitting, receiving and processing data communicated by satellite.

EAX: see *electronic automatic exchange*.

EBCDIC: extended binary-coded decimal interchange code. A coded character set consisting of eight-bit coded characters. (A)

E beam: electron beam.

E-beam bonding: formation of interconnection bonds by electron beam welding.

EBR: see *electron beam recording*. (A)

ECB: see *event control block*.

ECC: see *error checking and correction*.

echo: an attenuated signal derived from a primary signal by reflection at one or more impedance discontinuities and delayed relative to the primary signal. (F)

echo check: a check to determine the correctness of the transmission of data in which the received data are returned to the source for comparison with the originally transmitted data. (E)

echo suppressor: a device that detects speech signals transmitted in either direction on a four-wire circuit and introduces loss in the opposite direction of speech transmission for suppressing echos. In the public telephone network, echo suppressors are used typically in trunks longer than 1850 miles. (F)

echo, talker: an echo of a talker's voice that is returned to the talker. When there is delay between the original signal and the echo, the affect is disturbing unless the echo is attenuated to a tolerable level. (F)

echo test: synonym for *echo check.*

ECMA: European Computer Manufacturer's Association.

economy of scale: as the need for increasing capacity in switching and transmission facilities develops, due either to growth or concentration, the cost per unit of capacity may decrease because of two factors: (a) fixed start-up costs that are spread over an increasing number of units; and (b) technological advantages that can be achieved when designing for large capacity. (F)

EC pads: the plated areas around a chip site that are in series with I/O circuits of the chips. Each pad provides a wiring function where two discrete wires may be bonded, plus a delete area for repairs, ECs, and test probing.

ED: see *editor.*

edge: see *document reference edge, reference edge, stroke edge.* (A)

edge-coated card: a card that has been strengthened by treating one or more edges. (A)

edge-notched card: a card in which notches representing data are punched around the edges. Usually long needles are used to select a specified set. (B)

edge-punched card:

(1) a card that is punched with hole patterns in tracks along the edges. Usually the hole patterns are in punch tape code. synonymous with *verge-punched card.* (A)

(2) in word processing, a card in which holes, similar to those used in punched tape, are located along one or more edges. (D)

EDI: see *editor.*

edit

(1) to prepare data for a later operation. Editing may include the rearrangement or the addition of data, the deletion of unwanted data, format control, code conversion, and the application of standard processes such as zero suppression. (A) (B)

(2) to enter, modify, or delete data.

edit-directed transmission: in PL/1, the type of stream-oriented transmission in which data appears as a continuous stream of characters and for which a format list is required to specify the editing desired for the associated data list.

edited copy: in word processing, a draft copy marked up with corrections or amendments. see also *final copy,* (D)

editing character: in COBOL, a single character or a fixed two-character combination used to create proper formats for output reports.

editing session: a period of time beginning when the editor is invoked and ending when the editor has completed processing.

editing statement: a statement that specifies syntactic and formatting operations to be performed on data. (E)

editing symbol: in micrographics, a symbol on microfilm that is readable without magnification and that provides cutting, loading, and other preparation instructions. (A)

edit mode: in systems with time sharing, an entry mode in which a user may issue subcommands to enter, modify, delete, or rearrange data.

editor (ED) (EDI) EDT):   see *linkage editor.* (A)

editor program: a computer program designed to perform such functions as the rearrangement, modification, and deletion of data in accordance with prescribed rules. cf. *linkage editor.* (*A*)

EDP: see *electronic data processing.*

EDPM: electronic data-processing machine.

EDT: see *editor.*

edulcorate
(1)   to improve by eliminating worthless information.
(2)   to weed out.

EE-PROMs: electrically erasable, programmable read-only memories. synonymous with *E²-PROMs*. See *erasable programmable read-only memory.*

effective address (EA)
(1)   the contents of the address part of an effective instruction. (B)
(2)   the address that is derived by applying any specified indexing or indirect addressing rules to the specified address and that is actually used to identify the current operand. (*A*).

effective byte: the byte actually accessed in an operation on a single byte or byte string.

effective data-transfer rate: the average number of bits, characters, or blocks per unit time transferred from a data source to a data sink and accepted as valid. It is expressed in bits, characters, or blocks per second, minute, or hour. (E)

effective double-word: the double-word accessed in a double-word operation.

effective half-word: the half-word accessed in a half-word operation.

effective instruction: an instruction that may be executed without modification. (A) (B)

effective isotropic radiated power (EIRP):   power level of a signal leaving an earth station antenna or leaving the satellite antenna.

effective operand address: an address obtained at the time of execution by a computer giving the actual operand address.

effective speed: speed (less than rated) that can be sustained over a significant span of time and that reflects slowing effects such as those caused by control codes, timing codes, error detection, retransmission, tabbing, or hand keying.

effective transmission speed: the rate at which information is processed by a transmission facility, expressed as the average rate over a significant time interval; expressed as average characters per unit of time, or average bits per unit of time.

effective word: the word accessed in an operation on a single word.

effective word location: the storage location pointed to by the effective virtual address of a word-addressing instruction.

EFTS: see *electronic funds transfer system(s).*

EI: see *error indicator.*

eight-bit byte: synonym for *octet.* (A) (B)

EIRP: see *effective isotropic radiated power.*

either-or operation: deprecated term for *disjunction.* (A) (B)

either-way communication: synonymous with *two-way alternate communication*.

either-way operation: synonym for *half-duplex operation*. (E)

eject key: in word processing, a control that releases or moves the recording medium to a position for easy removal from the equipment. (D)

elastic buffer (store): a buffer store holding a variable amount of data.

electrical accounting machine: pertaining to data-processing equipment that is predominantly electromechanical such as a keypunch, mechanical sorter, collator, and tabulator.

electrically alterable memory: a memory unit whose contents are revised with electrical signals.

electromagnet: a device consisting of a ferromagnetic core and a coil that produces appreciable magnetic effects only when an electric current exists in the coil.

electromagnetic delay line: a delay line whose operation is based on the time of propagation of electromagnetic waves through distributed or lumped capacitance and inductance. (A)

electromagnetic relay: an electromagnetic switching unit having multiple electrical contacts operated by an electrical current through a coil; used to complete electrical circuits with an applied control current, and also as a mechanical binary counter.

electromagnetic wave: electrical and magnetic vibrations at right angles to each other which move together in space.

electromechanical switching system: an automatic switching system in which the control functions are performed principally by electromechanical devices.

electron: an elementary particle circling the nucleus of an atom. A negative charge, the flow of electrons is an electrical current.

electron-beam recording (EBR): in micrographics, a specific method of computer output microfilming in which a beam of electrons is directed onto an energy-sensitive microfilm. (A)

electronic accounting machines: synonymous with *tabulating equipment*.

electronic automatic exchange (EAX): the General Telephone Company term for electronic telephone exchange equipment.

electronic cash register: a cash register in which electronic circuitry replaces electromechanical parts.

electronic data processing (EDP): data processing largely performed by electronic devices.

electronic data-processing system: a machine system that receives, stores, operates on, and records data without the intermediate use of tabulating cards, and which possesses an ability to store internally at least some instructions for data-processing functions, and the means for locating and controlling access to data stored internally.

electronic filing: in word processing, the way processors store information electronically on disks, cards, or tapes.

electronic funds transfer system(s) (EFTSs): a loose description of computerized systems that process financial transactions or process information about financial transactions, or effect an exchange of value between two parties.

electronic mailing: in word processing, the ability of processors to transmit documents over cables or phone lines.

electronic message service (EMS): the FCC has allocated a band of radio frequencies for new common-carrier Electronic Message Service. The new broad-band services will be carried over domestic satellites and Digital Termination Systems and will have the potential for becoming direct competitors with telephone companies at the local levels. see *digital termination systems.* (G)

electronic message system: communication via terminals in a communications network.

electronic printer: any computer printer; a printer for units which hold a magnetic tape record of the text and reproduces it via digitized founts.

electronic scales: microcomputer-based units with electronic weighing indicators that can handle numerous operations involved in static weighing and simple batching.

electronic statistical machine: a sorter that can print and add data while storing.

electronic stylus: an input unit permitting images to be drawn, having the form of a light pen or a purely electronic unit used in conjunction with, for example, a graphics tablet.

electronic switch: a circuit element causing a start and stop action or a switching action electronically, often at high speeds.

electronic switching system (ESS): a class of modern switching systems in which the control functions are performed principally by electronic devices. There are two types in use: time division and space division. (F)

electronic translator: equipment in a toll switching system that translates the called codes, by means of electronic circuitry and stored program control information, into information required by the system to select an available route toward the central office of the called customer. (F)

electronic tutor: a teaching unit making use of instructions within the computer to help students achieve goals; with each student communicating directly with the computer via a terminal.

electrostatic deflection: deviating a beam in a cathode ray tube by means of an electrostatic field created by deflection plates.

electrostatic printer: a unit for printing an optical image on paper, where dark and light areas of the original are represented by electrostatically charged and uncharged areas on the paper.

electrostatic storage: a storage device that uses electrically charged areas on a dielectric surface layer. (A) (B)

ELEM: see *element.*

element (ELEM) (ELT)

(1) in a set, an object, entity, or concept having the properties that define a set. synonymous with *member.* (A) (B)

(2) in PL/1, a single item of data as opposed to a collection of data items such as an array; a scalar item.

(3) the particular resource within a subarea that is identified by an element address.

(4) see *AND element, binary element, combination logic element, display element, exclusive -OR element, identity element, IF-AND-ONLY-IF element, IF-THEN element, inclusive-OR element, logic element, majority element, NAND element, NOR element, NOT element, NOT-IF-THEN element, picture element, sequential logic element.*

elementary item: in COBOL, a data item that cannot logically be subdivided.

element expression: in PL/1, an expression whose evaluation yields an element value.

element string: see *binary element string.* (A)

element variable: in PL/1, a variable that represents an element; a scalar variable.

eleven punch: a punch in the second row from the top, on a Hollerith card. synonymous with *X punch.* (A)

elimination factor: in information retrieval, the ratio obtained by dividing the number of documents that have not been retrieved by the total number of documents held within the file.

ELSE clause: that part of an IF statement used to specify the action to be performed if the comparison of operands on the IF statement is false.

ELT: see *element.*

EM: the end-of-medium character.

E&M lead signaling: a specific form of interface between a switching system and a trunk in which the signaling information is transferred across the interface via two-state voltage conditions on two leads, each with ground return, separate from the leads used for message information. The mes-sage and signaling information are combined (and separated) by a signaling system appropriate for application to the transmission facility. The term *E&M lead signaling* is used also in some special-service applications.

emboldening: in word processing, the process of intensifying the image of selected characters when displayed or printed. (D)

embossment

(1) a distortion of the surface of a document.

(2) in character recognition, the distance between the undistorted surface of a document and a specified part of a printed character. (*A*).

EMC: electromagnetic compatibility.

emergency maintenance: maintenance specifically intended to eliminate an existing fault, which makes continued production work unachievable. (A)

emergency maintenance time: time, usually unscheduled, used to perform emergency maintenance. (A)

emitter: a unit, used on punched card machines, giving timed pulses at regular intervals during a machine cycle.

empty medium: a data medium that does not contain data other than a frame of reference; for example, a preprinted form, tape punched only with feed holes, a magnetic tape that has been erased. (B)

empty set: a set that has no elements. synonymous with *null set.* (A) (B)

empty string: synonymous with *numeric string.*

EMS: see *electronic message service.*

emulate: to imitate one system with another, primarily by hardware, so that the imitating system accepts the same data, executes the same computer programs, and achieves the same results as the imitated system. cf. *simulate*. (A).

emulation

(1)   the imitation of all or part of one computer system by another, primarily by hardware, so that the imitating computer system accepts the same data, executes the same programs, and achieves the same results as the imitated computer system. (E)

(2)   the use of programming techniques and special machine features to permit a computing system to execute programs written for another system.

(3)   cf. *simulation*.

emulator

(1)   a device or computer program that emulates. (A)

(2)   the combination of programming techniques and special machine features that permits a given computing system to execute programs written for another system. see also *integrated emulator*.

emulator generation: the process of assembling and link editing an emulator program into an operating system during system generation.

enable: restoration of a suppressed interrupt feature.

enabled

(1)   pertaining to a state of the processing unit that allows the occurrence of certain types of interruptions. synonymous with *interruptible*.

(2)   pertaining to the state in which a transmission control unit or an audio response unit can accept incoming calls on a line.

(3)   in PL/1, that state in which a

particular on condition will result in a program interrupt.

enabled module: a module that can be interrupted at any time during its execution. When the interruption occurs, the enabled module waits for the external routine that interrupted it to complete its processing and then continues. cf. *disabled module*.

enabled page fault: a page fault that occurs when I/O and external interruptions are allowed by the processing unit.

enable pulse: a digit pulse that assists the write pulse, which together are strong enough to switch the magnetic cell.

enabling signal: a signal that permits the occurrence of an event. (A)

encipher

(1)   to scramble data or convert it, prior to transmission, to a secret code that masks the meaning of the data to any unauthorized recipient. see also *encode*.

(2)   to convert plaintext into ciphertext.

enciphered data: data whose meaning is concealed from unauthorized users.

encode

(1)   to convert data by the use of a code or a coded character set in such a manner that reconversion to the original form is possible. Encode is sometimes loosely used when complete reconversion is not possible. (B)

(2)   cf. *decode*. (A) (B)

(3)   see also *encipher*.

(4)   synonymous with *code*.

encoded point: in computer graphics, an addressable point in an image space.

encoded question: a question set up and encoded in an appropriate format for operating, programming, or conditioning a searching unit.

encoder

(1) a device that encodes data. (B)

(2) a device that has a number of input lines of which not more than one at a time may carry a signal and a number of output lines of which any number may carry signals, there being a one-to-one correspondence between the combinations of output signals and input signals. (B)

(3) cf. *decoder.* (*A*) (B)

encryption: coding of data for privacy protection, in particular when transmitted over telecommunication links.

END: statement showing the end of a program.

end-around borrow: the action of transferring a borrow digit from the most significant digit place to the least significant digit place. (A) (B)

end-around carry: the action of transferring a carry digit from the most significant digit place to the least significant digit place. An end-around carry may be necessary when adding two negative numbers that are represented by their diminished radix complements. (A) (B)

end-around shift: a shift in which the data moved out of one end of the storing register are reentered into the other end. synonymous with *circular shift.* (*A*)

end-data symbol: the representation showing that no more data will follow this symbol.

end distortion: see *distortion.*

end instrument: a unit connected to the terminal of a loop and capable of converting usable intelligence into electrical signals, or vice versa.

end mark: a signal or code showing termination of a unit of information.

end of address (EOA): one or more control characters transmitted on a line to indicate the end of nontext characters (for example, addressing characters).

end of block (EOB): a code that marks the end of a block of data.

end-of-data indicator: a code that signals that the last record of a consecutive data set has been read.

end office: a local switching office where loops are terminated for purposes of interconnection to each other and to trunks. End offices are designated class 5. see *toll hierarchy.* synonymous with *class 5 office.* (F) see also *exchange, exchange classes, local central office.*

end of file (EOF) label: an internal label, immediately following the last record of a file, signaling the end of that file. It may include control totals for comparison with counts accumulated during processing. (E)

end-of-file mark (EOF): a code which signals that the last record of a file has been read.

end of form: the last print position, left or right side at the bottom of a form.

end-of-medium character (EM): a control character that may be used to identify the physical end of the data medium, the end of the used portion of the medium, or the end of the wanted portion of the data recorded on the medium. (A) (B)

end-of-message code (EOM): the specific character or sequence of characters that indicates the end of a message or record.

end-of-record word: the final word of

a record on tape; having a unique bit configuration and used to define the end of a record in memory.

end-of-tape mark (EOT): a mark on a magnetic tape used to indicate the end of the permissible recording area; for example, a photoreflective strip, a particular bit pattern. (A)

end-of-tape warning: a visible magnetic strip on magnetic tape indicating that a few feet, often five, of the tape remain available.

end-of-text character (ETX): a transmission control character used to terminate text. (A)

end-of-transmission-block character (ETB): a transmission control character used to indicate the end of a transmission block of data when data are divided into such blocks for transmission purposes. (B)

end-of-transmission character (EOT): a transmission control character used to indicate the conclusion of a transmission, which may have included one or more texts and any associated message headings. (A) (B)

end-of-transmission code: the specific character, or sequence of characters, that indicates termination of sending.

end-of-volume (EOV) label: an internal label that follows and indicates the end of a set of data contained in a volume. (E)

endorser: a feature on most magnetic-ink character readers (MICRs) that is an endorsement record for a bank after the document has been read.

end point: on a display device, the coordinates on the display surface to which a display writer is to be moved.

end point node: synonym for *peripheral node*. (E)

END statement: a statement used to indicate the end of a procedure or the end of one or more DO loops.

end-to-end responsibility: the principle that assigns to communications common carriers complete responsibility for all the equipment and facilities involved in providing a telecommunications service—from one end of a connection to the other. These responsibilities include design control, installation, operation and maintenance. (G)

end-to-end signaling: a mode of network operation in which the originating central office (or station) retains control and signals directly to each successive central office (or PBX) as trunks are added to the connection. This contrasts with operation in which each office takes control in turn, called *link-by-link signaling*. (F)

end-use device: a device, such as a printer, that provides the final output of an operation without further processing.

end-user (EU)
(1) the ultimate source or destination of information flowing through a system.
(2) a person, process, program, device, or system that employs a user-application network for the purpose of data processing and information exchange. (E)

end-user device: a device such as a printer that provides the final output of an operation without further processing.

energy level diagram: a line drawing that shows increases and decreases of electrical power along a channel.

ENFIA: see *exchange network facilities for interstate access*.

engineered capacity: the highest load for a trunk group or a switching system at which service objectives are met. In general, for a switching system, carried load is equal to offered load below engineered capacity, but is less than offered load above engineered capacity. (F)

engineering and administration data-acquisition system (EADAS): a system in which traffic data are measured at switching systems by electronic devices, transmitted to a centrally located minicomputer, and recorded on magnetic tape in a format that is suitable for computer processing and analysis. (F)

engineering, communications or telephone: an activity that applies the principles of electrical communications to the solution of practical communication problems. A common use of the term refers to operating company functions, such as the final planning and sizing of trunk groups, central office equipment, and transmission facilities, or the end-to-end transmission design of loops and trunks. (F)

engineering, planning, and analysis systems (EPLANS): software systems used by operating telephone company engineering and related personnel to support their planning, record keeping, implementation, scheduling, ordering, network performance evaluation, network characterization, and other similar activities. The programs are Western Electric products and are offered as time-share or batch-run computer services by Western Electric or, in some cases, are run in telephone company data centers. (F)

engineering work order: an order for work to be done in an operating company to add, remove, or change outside plant facilities in the inventory. (F)

enhanced private switched communications service (EPSCS): a service utilizing telephone company electronic switching system (ESS) machines designed to provide customized private communications to customers who have extensive communications requirements. Switching centers that utilize the ESS machines are located on telephone company premises and may be shared with other EPSCS customers and/or other telephone company services. Private line channels between switching centers and between a switching center and a customer premise are dedicated to specific customers. Switching terminals are provided at the ESS machines to permit interconnection of voice grade channels from other EPSCS switching centers and customer locations, as well as local exchange lines, foreign exchange lines and WATS lines. A customer Network Control Center located on the customers' premises is provided as a standard feature of the service to enable the customer to monitor and select various network features and switching functions associated with his network. (G)

enlargement: see *reenlargement*.

ENQ: see *enquiry character*. (A)

enqueue: to place items on a queue. cf. *dequeue*.

enquiry character (ENQ): a transmission control character used as a request for a response from the station with which the connection has been set up; the response may include station identification, the type of equipment in service, and the status of the remote station. (A) (B)

enter: to place on the line a message to be transmitted from a terminal to the computer.

enter/inquiry mode: the use of a terminal to enter data, to request the system to provide information, or for a combination of these operations. cf. *rerun mode*.

enter key: synonymous with *start key*.

enterprise number: a unique telephone exchange number that permits the called party to be automatically billed for incoming calls. synonymous with *toll-free number*.

entity

(1) an object or an event about which information is stored in a data base; for example, a person, or a train departure time. (E)

(2) a user, group, or DASD data set that is defined to RACF.

entrance: synonym for *entry point*. (A) (B)

entropy: in information theory, the mean value of the measure of information conveyed by the occurrence of any one of a finite number of mutually exclusive and jointly exhaustive events of definite probabilities. synonymous with *average information content, mean information content, negentropy*. see *character mean entropy, conditional entropy*. (A) (B)

entry

(1) any consecutive set of descriptive clauses terminated by a period, written in the identification, environment, or procedure divisions of a COBOL program.

(2) an element of information in a table, list, queue, or other organized structure of data or control information.

(3) a single input operation on a terminal.

(4) synonym for *entry point*. (A) (B)

entry block: a block of main-memory storage assigned on receipt of every entry into a system and associated with that entry throughout its life within the system.

entry conditions

(1) the conditions to be specified on entering a computer program, a routine, or a subroutine. For example, the address of those locations from which the program, routine, or subroutine will take its operands and of those locations with which its entry points and exits will be linked. (B)

(2) the initial data and control conditions to be satisfied for successful execution of a given routine. (*A*).

entry constant: in PL/1, an entry name.

entry expression: in PL/1, an expression whose evaluation yields an entry value.

entry instruction: the first instruction to be executed in a subroutine, that is, it may have several different entry points, each of which corresponds to a differing activity of the subroutine.

entry name

(1) a name within a control section that defines an entry point and can be referred to by any control section.

(2) a programmer-specified name that establishes an entry point in a COBOL subprogram.

(3) in PL/1, an identifier that is explicitly or contextually declared to have the ENTRY attribute (unless the

VARIABLE attribute is given) or has an implied ENTRY attribute; the value of an entry variable.

entry point

(1) the address or the label of the first instruction executed upon entering a computer program, a routine, or a subroutine. A computer program, a routine, or a subroutine may have a number of different entry points, each perhaps corresponding to a different function or purpose. synonymous with *entrance, entry.* (B)

(2) in a routine, any place to which control can be passed. (*A*).

(3) in PL/1, a point in a procedure at which it may be invoked. see *primary entry point* and *secondary entry point.*

entry symbol: an ordinary symbol that represents an entry name or control section name. see also *external symbol.*

entry time: the time when control is transferred from the supervisory to the application program.

entry value: in PL/1, the entry point represented by an entry constant; the value includes activation information that is associated with the entry constant.

entry variable: in PL/1, a variable that can represent entry values.

envelope: a group of binary digits formed by a byte augmented by a number of additional bits which are required for the operation of the data network. (C)

envelope delay distortion: departure from a constant value of the envelope delay versus frequency characteristic. Envelope delay is the derivative with respect to frequency of the phase characteristic of the transfer function and should not be confused with differential delay which is the difference in delay at two frequencies. (F)

environment: the physical conditions surrounding a computer installation including heat, pressure, pollution, vibration, and so forth.

environment description statement: a nonexecutable statement that describes the hardware-software system on which an object program is to be executed; for example, the ENVIRONMENT DIVISION in COBOL. (E)

environment division: one of the four main component parts of a COBOL program. The environment division describes the computers upon which the source program is compiled and those on which the object program is executed, and provides a linkage between the logical concept of files and their records, and the physical aspects of the devices on which files are stored.

environment (of activation): in PL/1, information associated with the invocation of a block that is used in the interpretation of references, within the invoked block, to data declared outside the block. This information includes generations of automatic variables, extents of defined variables, and generations of parameters.

environment (of a label constant): in PL/1, identity of the particular activation of a block to which a reference to a statement-label constant applies. This information is determined at the time a statement-label constant is passed as an argument or is assigned to a statement-label variable, and it is passed or assigned along with the constant.

EOA: see *end of address.*

EOB: see *end of block.*

EOF: see *end of file.*

EOM: see *end-of-message code.*

EOT

(1) see *end-of-tape mark.*

(2) see *end-of-transmission character.* (A)

EOV: see *end-of-volume label.*

epilog: in PL/1, those processes that occur automatically at the termination of a block or task.

EPLANS: see *engineering, planning, and analysis systems.*

EPROM: electrically programmable, read only memory. Has permanent data electrically recorded or programmed into it and therefore can only be read.

EPSCS: see *enhanced private switched communications service.*

EQPT: see *equipment.*

equal gain combiner: a diversity combiner in which the signals on each channel are added together; the channel gains are all equal and can be made to vary equally so that the resultant signal is approximately constant.

equality: synonymous with *exclusive-NOR.*

equalization: the procedure applied to transmission media or channels in order that the amplitude and phase (or envelope delay) characteristics of a signal to be transmitted are preserved at the receiving end of the connection. (If a channel introduces phase or frequency offset, equalization does not preserve the wave form of the signal.) (F)

equalizer: any combination (usually adjustable) of coils, capacitors, or resistors inserted in a transmission or amplifier circuit to improve its frequency response. see also *delay equalizer.*

equals: on a calculator, the completion of a series of operations and the provision of the result. (D)

EQUIP: see *equipment.*

equipment (EQPT) (EQUIP): a unit of hardware, typically including apparatus units as components, that may have options to alter its function and may have changes made on the telephone companies' premises to improve existing characteristics, to correct undesirable conditions, or to provide new operating features. (F) see *data-terminal equipment, peripheral equipment.*

equipment charge: a monthly non-usage-sensitive charge, based on the amount and type of installed telephone equipment or apparatus. (F)

equipment clock: a clock which satisfies the particular needs of equipment and in some cases may control the flow of data at the equipment interface.

equipment compatibility: the characteristics of some computers where one system accepts and processes data prepared by another computer without conversion or code modification.

equipment failure: a fault in equipment, excluding all external factors, that prevents the accomplishment of a scheduled job.

equipment side: that portion of a device that looks toward the in-station equipment.

equivalence: a logic operator having

the property that if P is a statement, Q is a statement, R is a statement, then the equivalence of P,Q,R, . . . , is true if and only if all statements are true or all statements are false. (A)

equivalence operation: the dyadic boolean operation whose result has the boolean value 1 if and only if the operands have the same boolean value. synonymous with *IF-AND-ONLY-IF operations. (A)* (B)

equivalent-binary-digit factor: the average number of binary digits required to express one radix digit in a nonbinary numeration system. For example, approximately 3 1/3 times the number of decimal digits is required to express a decimal numeral as a binary numeral. (A)

equivalent four-wire system: a transmission system using frequency division to obtain full-duplex operation over only one pair of wires.

equivocation: in information theory, the conditional entropy of the occurrence of specific messages at the message source, given the occurrence of specific messages at a message sink connected to the message source by a specified channel. The equivocation is the mean additional information content that must be supplied per message at the message sink to correct the received messages affected by a noisy channel. (A) (B)

ER: see *error.*

erasable programmable read-only memory: see **EPROM**.

erasable storage: a storage device whose contents can be modified. (B) cf. *read-only storage. (A)*

erase
(1)   to remove data from a data me-

dium, leaving the medium available for recording new data. (B)
(2)   to remove all previous data from magnetic storage by changing it to a specified condition; that may be an unmagnetized state or a predetermined magnetized state.

erase character: deprecated term for *delete character.* (A) (B)

erase head: a device on a magnetic tape drive whose sole function is to erase previous information before new information is written.

EREP: the environmental recording, editing, and printing program. Keeps records of hardware error problems and determinations.

Erlang: a dimensionless unit of traffic intensity used to express the average number of calls under way or the average number of devices in use. One Erlang corresponds to the continuous occupancy of one traffic path. Traffic in Erlangs is the sum of the holding times of paths divided by the period of measurement. The term *Erlang* can be used to express the capacity of a system; for example, a trunk group of 30 trunks, which in a theoretical peak sense might carry 30 Erlangs of traffic, would have a typical capacity of perhaps 25 Erlangs averaged over an hour. (F)

Erlang B: one of the basic traffic models and related formulas used in the Bell System. The assumptions are Poisson input, negative exponential holding time, and blocked calls cleared. Used for trunk engineering. (F)

Erlang C: one of the basic traffic models and related formulas used in the Bell System. This is the queuing model with assumptions of Poisson input, negative exponential holding times, and blocked calls delayed. The queuing discipline may be arbitrary but is usually approximately first come, first served. Used for common-control engineering. (F)

ERP: see *error recovery procedures.*

ERR: see *error.*

error (E) (ER) (ERR)

(1) a discrepancy between a computed, observed, or measured value or condition and the true, specified, or theoretically correct value or condition. (B)

(2) deprecated term for *mistake.* (B)

(3) cf. *fault, malfunction, mistake.* (*A*)

(4) see *absolute error, balanced error, inherited error, irrecoverable error, relative error, rounding error, truncation error.*

(5) see also *error condition.*

error burst: in data communication, a sequence of signals containing one or more errors but counted as only one unit in accordance with some specific criterion or measure. An example of a criterion is that if three consecutive correct bits follow an erroneous bit, then an error burst is terminated. (A)

error character: synonymous with *ignore character.*

error checking and correction (ECC): the detection, in the processing unit, and correction of all single-bit errors, plus the detection of double-bit and some multiple-bit errors.

error-checking code: a general term for all error-correcting codes and all error-detecting codes. see *error code.*

error code: the marking of a specific error with a character or code. The code is usually printed out to show that an error has taken place, or can be associated on a storage device with an item of data that is in error so that the item can be corrected or ignored when the data is later processed.

error condition

(1) the state that results from an attempt to execute instructions in a computer program that are invalid or that operate on invalid data.

(2) on a calculator, the situation in which the operator attempts to carry out an impossible function on the machine.

error-condition statement: an executable statement that specifies action to be taken upon the occurrence of an event in the execution of a computer program that the programmer has chosen to call an error. (E)

error control: in data transmission, that part of a protocol that controls the detection, and possibly the correction, of errors. (E)

error-control character: synonym for *accuracy-control character.* (A)

error-correcting code

(1) an error-detecting code designed to correct certain kinds of errors. (E)

(2) a code in which each telegraph or data signal conforms to specific rules of construction so that departures from this construction in the receive signals can be automatically detected, permitting the automatic correction, at the receiving terminal, of some or all of the errors. Such codes require more signal elements than are necessary to convey the ba-

sic information. (C)

error-correcting system: a system employing an error-detecting code and so arranged that some or all of the signals detected as being in error are automatically corrected at the receiving terminal before delivery to the data sink or to the telegraph receiver. (C)

error-correction routine: a routine for the detection and correction of errors on data files.

error-correction submode: a mode of operation that provides the ability to go back in a program to a point where the environment was saved, thereby permitting correction of a previously entered field.

error detecting and feedback system: a system employing an error detecting code and so arranged that a signal detected as being in error automatically initiates a request for retransmission of that signal.

error-detecting code

(1) a code in which each element representation conforms to specific rules of construction so that if certain errors occur, the resulting representation will not conform to the rules, thereby indicating the presence of errors. synonymous with *self-checking code.* (E)

(2) a code in which each telegraph or data signal conforms to specific rules of construction, so that departures from this construction in the received signals can be automatically detected. Such codes require more signal elements than are necessary to convey the fundamental information. (C)

error diagnostics: verifying source language statements for errors during compilation, and the printing of error messages showing all found errors.

error indicator (EI): on a calculator, a visual indication that the operation has attempted to carry out an impossible mathematical function on the machine. (D)

error interrupts: an interrupt that occurs when a program or hardware malfunctions.

error list: produced by a complier that shows incorrect or invalid instructions in a source program.

error message: an indication that an error has been detected. (A)

error range: the set of values that an error may take. deprecated term for *error span.* (A) (B)

error rate: a measure of the quality of a circuit or system; the number of erroneous bits or characters in a sample, frequently taken per 100,000 characters.

error ratio: the ratio of the number of data units in error to the total number of data units. (A)

error record: a record that indicates the occurrence of errors.

error recovery: the process of correcting or bypassing a fault to restore a computer system to a prescribed condition. (E)

error-recovery procedures (ERP): procedures designed to help isolate and, where possible, to recover from errors in equipment. The procedures are often used in conjunction with programs that record the statistics of machine malfunctions.

error routine: a routine entered on the detection of an error. This routine may output an error message, correct the error, duplicate the process that caused the error, or perform any other specified action.

error signal: a signal whose magnitude and sign are used to correct the alignment between the controlling and the controlled elements of an automatic control unit.

error span: the difference between the highest and the lowest error values. (A) (B)

error tape: magnetic tape containing errors for later listing and analysis.

ESC: see *escape character.* (A)

escape: the departure from one code or language to another code or language, that is, the removal from existing pattern.

escape character (ESC): a code extension character used, in some cases, with one or more succeeding characters to indicate by some convention or agreement that the coded representations following the character or the group of characters are to be interpreted according to a different code or according to a different coded character set. (B) see *data-link escape character.* (A)

escape code: a code used with text input to show that the next character (or characters) will represent a function code.

ESD: see *external symbol dictionary.*

ESI communications (externally specified index): an index that permits a number of communications networks to function concurrently on a pair of I/O channels.

ESS: see *electronic switching system.*

ETB: see *end-of-transmission-block character.* (A)

E-time: execution time.

ETP: see *electrical tough pitch.*

E² PROMs: synonymous with *EE-*

PROMs.

ETX: see *end-of-text character.* (A)

EU: see *end-user.*

EUROMICRO: European Association for Microprocessing and Microprogramming.

evaluation: in PL/1, reduction of an expression to a single value (which may be an array or structure value).

even parity check: a parity check where the number of ones (or zeroes) in a group of binary digits is expected to be even. cf. *odd-parity check.*

event

(1) an occurrence or happening.

(2) an occurrence of significance to a task; typically, the completion of an asynchronous operation, such as an input-output operation.

(3) in PL/1, an activity in a program whose status and completion can be determined from an associated event variable.

event chain: a series of actions resulting from an initial event.

event-control block (ECB): a control block used to represent the status of an event.

event posting: the saving of a computer program and data context of a task and establishing the program and data of another task to which control is to be passed, based on an event such as completion of loading of data into main storage. (A)

event variable: in PL/1, a variable with the EVENT attribute, which may be associated with an event; its value indicates whether the action has been completed and the status of the completion.

EX: see *execute.*

exceed capacity: the generating of a word, the magnitude or length of which is too great or too small to be represented by a computer, such as in an attempt to divide by zero.

except gate: synonymous with *exclusive-OR element*.

exception: an abnormal condition such as an I/O error encountered in processing a data set or a file. see *overflow exception, underflow exception*.

exception message: in communicating with a logical unit, a message that indicates an unusual condition such as a sequence number being skipped.

except operation: deprecated term for *exclusion*. (A) (B)

excess fifty: a binary code where the number n is represented by the binary equivalent of n + 50.

excess 64 binary notation: in assembler programming, a binary notation in which each component of a floating-point number E is represented by the binary equivalent of E plus 64.

excess-three code: the binary-coded decimal notation in which a decimal digit n is represented by the binary numeral that represents (n + 3). (A) (B)

exchange: a room or building equipped so that telecommunication lines terminated there may be interconnected as required. The equipment may include manual or automatic switching equipment. see *data-switching exchange, private automatic branch exchange, private automatic exchange, private branch exchange, trunk exchange*. (C) see also *exchange area, exchange area facilities*.

exchangeable disk storage (EDS): a backing store device using magnetic disks loaded in a disk drive; the operator can replace capsules of, for example, six disks during operation.

exchange area: an area within which there is a single uniform set of charges for telephone service. An exchange area may be served by a number of central offices. A call between any two points within an exchange area is a local call. (F)

exchange area facilities: transmission facilities within an exchange area used for loops, trunks, and special-service circuits. The term commonly refers to facilities used for trunks between class 5 offices, between tandems and class 5 offices or other tandems, and between class 5 offices and toll offices over distances up to approximately 100 miles. T1 carrier is an example of an exchange area facility. (F)

exchange buffering: a technique using data chaining to avoid moving data in main storage, in which control of buffer segments and user program work areas is passed between data management and the user program.

exchange classes: class 1 (see *regional center*), class 2 (see *sectional center*), class 3 (see *primary center*), class 4 (see *toll center*), class 5 (see *end office*).

exchange instruction: an instruction to replace the contents of one register (or registers) with the contents of another, and vice versa.

exchange network facilities for interstate access (ENFIA): an interstate tariff offering access to exchange network facilities to complete OCCs public-switched voice message interstate services, when such OCCs are duly authorized by the FCC to furnish end-to-end public-switched interstate service. The tariff includes a schedule of interim charges negotiated by the industry and OCCs and approved by the FCC. see *access charge*. (G)

exchange memory

(1) the interchange of the contents of two storage devices or locations, such as two registers.

(2) a switching device capable of controlling and handling the exchange of data between storage units or other elements within the system.

exchange service: the furnishing of ordinary voice-grade telecommunications service under regulation within a specified geographical area. see *exchange*. (G)

exchange sort: a sort in which succeeding pairs of items in a set are examined; if the items in a pair are out of sequence according to the specified criteria, the positions of the items are exchanged; for example, a bubble sort. This process is repeated until all items are sorted. (A)

exchange-test string: in word processing, a function that enables a text string to be changed for another text string at one or a number of points throughout the text. (D)

exclusion

(1) the dyadic boolean operation whose result has the boolean value if and only if the first operand has the boolean value 1 and the second has the boolean value 0. (B)

(2) a logic operator having the property that if P is a statement and Q is a statement, then P exclusion Q is true if P is true and Q is false, false if P is false, and false if both statements

are true. P exclusion Q is often represented by a combination of "AND" and "NOT" symbols, such as P̄ Q. (*A*)

(3) synonymous with *NOT-IF-THEN, NOT-IF-THEN operation*. (E)

exclusive-NOR: a boolean operation on two operands (p and q), the result (r) being as follows:

Operands		Result
p	q	r
0	0	0
1	0	1
0	1	1
1	1	0

synonymous with *bi-conditional operation, equality, nonequivalence*.

exclusive-OR: a logic operator having the property that if P is a statement and Q is a statement, then P exclusive-OR Q is true if either but not both statements are true, false if both are true or both are false. cf. *OR*. (*A*)

exclusive-OR element: a logic element that performs the boolean nonequivalence operation. synonymous with *exclusive-OR gate*. (*A*) (B)

exclusive-OR gate: synonym for *exclusive-OR element*. (A) (B)

exclusive reference: a reference from a segment in storage to an external symbol in a segment that will cause overlaying of the calling segment.

exclusive segments: segments in the same region of an overlay program, neither of which is in the path of the other. They cannot be in main storage simultaneously.

EXEC: see *execute*.

exec statements: a console-entered statement which initiates the program from the library for processing.

EXECUNET: an intercity public switched-voice message service, introduced by MCI in 1975. see *MTS/ WATS-like services.* (G)

executable program: a program that has been link edited and is therefore capable of being run in a processor.

executable statement

(1) a statement that specifies one or more actions to be taken by a computer program at execution time; for example, instructions for calculations to be performed, conditions to be tested, flow of control to be altered. (E)

(2) in FORTRAN, a statement that specifies action to be taken by the program; for example, calculations to be performed, conditions to be tested, flow of control to be altered.

execute (E) (EX) (EXEC)

(1) to perform the execution of an instruction or of a computer program. (A) (B)

(2) in programming, to change the state of a computer in accordance with the rules of the operations it recognizes. (B)

execute key: synonymous with *start key.*

execute phase: the logical subdivision of a run that includes the execution of the target program. synonymous with *executing phase.* (A) (B)

execute (EXEC) statement: a job control language (JCL) statement that marks the beginning of a job step and identifies the program to be executed or the cataloged or in-stream procedure to be used.

executing phase: synonym for *execute phase.* (A) (B)

execution (E)

(1) the process of carrying out an instruction by a computer. (A) (B)

(2) in programming, the process by which a computer program or subroutine changes the state of a computer in accordance with the rules of the operations that a computer recognizes. (B)

(3) the process of carrying out the instructions of a computer program by a computer. (B)

execution cycle: that part of a machine cycle during which the actual execution of the instruction occurs.

execution-error detection: detection concerned with errors found during the execution of the user's program.

execution path: the major course or line of direction taken by a computer in the execution of a routine, directed by the logic of the program and the nature of the data.

execution time (E-time)

(1) the time during which an instruction is decoded and performed. see also *instruction time.*

(2) in COBOL, the time at which an object program performs the instructions coded in the procedure division, using the data provided.

executive cycle: synonymous with *execute phase.*

executive program: synonym for *supervisory program.* (A) (B)

executive routine: synonym for *supervisory routine.* (A) (B)

executive supervisor: the executive-system component that controls the sequencing, setup, and execution of all runs entering the computer.

executive system: an integrated collection of service routines for supervising the sequencing of programs by a computer.

executive termination: the normal or abnormal termination of an operating program and its return of assigned facilities to an available status.

exerciser: a test or program to find malfunctions in a memory, disk, or tape unit prior to use.

EXF: see *external function.*

exhaustivity: the number of keywords assigned to a record in a file with any information retrieval system.

exit: any instruction in a computer program, in a routine, or in a subroutine after the execution of which control is no longer exercised by that computer program, that routine, or that subroutine. (A) (B)

exit macroinstruction: a supervisory program macroinstruction that is the last instruction in an application program, showing that processing is over.

exit point: the instruction that transfers control from a main routine to a subroutine. see *exit routine.*

exit routine
(1) a routine that receives control when a specified event occurs, such as an error.
(2) any of several types of user-written routines.

EXP
(1) see *exponent.*
(2) see *expression.*

expandor: in a compander, an electronic device able to expand the volume range of a signal.

expansion: term applied to a switching network (or portion of one) that has more outputs than inputs. (F)

expansion board: a printed-circuit board which accommodates addi-

tional components or cards for expanding a computer.

expansion cascading: shifting from a fine level of detail to increasingly broader levels.

expansion interface: a device to expand the functional capacity of a computer by containing additional memory or controlling more peripherals.

expert programs: computers acting as intelligent assistants, providing advice and making judgments in specialized areas of expertise. see also *Xcon.*

expiration check: a comparison of a given date with an expiration date associated with a transaction, record, or file. synonymous with *retention period check.* (E)

expiration date: the date set at which a file is no longer protected from automatic deletion by the system.

explicit address: synonym for *absolute address.* (A) (B)

explicit declaration: in PL/1, the appearance of an identifier in a DECLARE statement, as a label prefix, or in a parameter list.

explicit specification statement: an INTEGER, REAL, DOUBLE PRECISION, or LOGICAL statement, which specifies data type.

exponent (EX)
(1) in a floating-point representation, the numeral denotes the power to which the implicit floating-point base is raised before being multiplied by the fixed-point part to determine the real number represented; for example, a floating-point representation of the number 0.0001234 is $0.1234 - 3$, where 0.1234 is the fixed-point part and -3 is the exponent.

(A) (B)

(2) a number indicating how many times another number (the base) is to be repeated as a factor. Positive exponents denote multiplication, negative exponents denote division, fractional exponents denote a root of a quantity. In COBOL, exponentiation is indicated with the symbol **, followed by the exponent.

exponent characters: in PL/1, the following picture specification characters, (1) K and E, which are used in floating-point picture specifications to indicate the beginning of the exponent field; (2) F, the scaling-factor character, specified with an integer constant which indicates the number of decimal positions the decimal point is to be moved from its assumed position to the right (if the constant is positive) or to the left (if the constant is negative).

EXPR: see *expression.*

expression (E) (EX) EXPR)

(1) a configuration of signs. (A)

(2) a source-language combination of one or more operations.

(3) in assembler programming, one or more operations represented by a combination of terms and paired parentheses.

(4) a notation, within a program, that represents a value; a constant or a reference appearing alone, or combination of constants and references with operators.

(5) see *absolute expression, arithmetic expression, character expression, complex relocatable expression, relocatable expression.*

express order wire: a permanently connected voice circuit between selected stations for technical control

purposes.

extended area service: a telephone exchange service, without toll charges, that extends over an area where there is a community of interest in return for a somewhat higher exchange service rate.

extended binary-coded decimal interchange code (EBCDIC): see *EBCDIC.* see also *binary-coded decimal character code.*

extended floating-point numbers: floating-point operand fractions extended for greater precision.

extended format diskette: a diskette in 256-byte format.

extended mnemonic: an operation code that is an extension to an instruction.

extended-precision floating point: a feature that permits floating-point operand fractions to be 112 bits long for greater precision that in short or long floating-point arithmetic.

extended range (of a DO statement): in FORTRAN, those statements that are executed between the transfer out of the innermost DO of a completely nested group of DO statements and the transfer back into the range of the innermost DO.

extended-result output: on a calculator, the facility for displaying or printing the result of a calculation in successive operations where the number of digits in the result exceeds the output capacity of the machine to the right of the decimal marker. (D)

extended-time scale: the time scale used in data processing when the time-scale factor is greater than one. synonymous with *slow-time scale.* cf. *fast time scale.* (A)

extensible language: a programming

language that permits the user of the language to define new elements such as data types, new operators, types of statements, or control structures in terms of existing elements of the language; for example, ALGOL 68. (E)

extension

(1) additional equipment on the same line and on the same premises, but at a location other than the main station.

(2) each telephone served by a private branch exchange.

extension character: see *code extension character.* (A)

extension memory: synonymous with *external store.*

extension station: an extra telephone set associated with a main telephone station by means of an extension on the same subscriber line and having the same call number designation as the associated main station. see also *main station.*

extent

(1) a continuous space on a direct-access storage volume, occupied by or reserved for a particular data set, data space, or file.

(2) in PL/1, the range indicated by the bounds of an array dimension, the range indicated by the length of a string, or the range indicated by the size of an area.

(3) see also *primary space allocation.*

exterior label: a label affixed to the outside of a reel. cf. *interior label.*

external call: a call involving a public exchange or tie line.

external delays: time lost due to circumstances beyond the control of the operator or maintenance engi-

neer; for example, failure of external power source. (A)

external device address: specifies which external device a particular instruction is referring to.

external error: pertaining to a specific file mark that has been incorrectly read or an end of tape that has been sensed during a loading operation.

external function (EXF): in FORTRAN, a function whose definition is external to the program unit that refers to it.

external-interrupt inhibit: the bit, in the program status double-word, that shows whether (if 1) or not (if 0) all external interrupts are inhibited.

external interruption: an interruption caused by a signal from the interruption key on the system console panel, from the timer, or from another computing system.

external-interrupt status word: a status word accompanied by an external-interrupt signal; where the signal informs the computer that the word on the data lines is a status word, and the computer puts the word into main memory.

external label: a label, usually not machine-readable, attached to a data medium container; for example, a paper sticker attached to the outside of a magnetic tape reel. cf. *internal label.* (E)

external line: a trunk or tie line.

externally specified index: see *ESI communications.*

externally stored programs: programs with instruction routines set up in wiring boards or plugboards for manual insertion in older models or small-scale processors.

external memory: synonymous with

external storage.

external merge: a sorting technique that reduces sequences of records or keys to one sequence, usually following one or more internal sorts.

external model: a collection of entities and their relationships representing a specific application or a type of application in an enterprise or organization. (E)

external modem: synonym for *stand-alone modem.* cf. *integrated modem.*

external name

(1) a name that can be referred to by any control section or separately assembled or compiled module; that is, a control section name or an entry name in another module.

(2) In PL/1, a name (with the EXTERNAL attribute) whose scope is not necessarily confined only to one block and its contained blocks.

external number: a number by which a party is called through an external line.

external-numbering plan: a numbering system for tie lines and trunks.

external-number repetition: a facility that enables a caller or an operator to store an external number in order to call it later by dialing only two digits.

external-page address: an address that identifies the location of a page in a page data set.

external procedure

(1) a procedure that is not contained in any other procedure.

(2) in FORTRAN, a procedure subprogram or a procedure defined by means other than FORTRAN statements.

external-program parameter: in a computer program, a parameter that must be bound during the calling of

the computer program. (A) (B)

external reference (EXTRN)

(1) a reference to a symbol that is defined as an external name in another module.

(2) an external symbol that is defined in another module; that which is defined in the assembler language by an EXTRN statement or by a V-type address constant, and is resolved during linkage editing. see also *weak external reference.*

external sort

(1) a sort that requires the use of auxiliary storage because the set of items to be sorted cannot be held in the available internal storage at one time.

(2) a sort program, or a sort phase of a multipass sort, that merges strings of items, using auxiliary storage, until one string is formed. (*A*)

(3) when building an alternate index, the sorting of the alternate keys into ascending sequence by using work files.

(4) see also *internal sort.*

external storage

(1) storage that is accessible by a computer only through input-output channels. (B)

(2) in a hierarchy of storage devices of a data-processing system, any storage device that is not internal storage. External storage and internal storage are terms which take on precise meanings only with reference to a particular configuration.

external symbol

(1) a control section name, entry point name, or external reference that is defined or referred to in a particular module.

(2) in assembler programming, an

ordinary symbol that represents an external reference.

(3)   a symbol in the external symbol dictionary.

(4)   see also *entry symbol.*

external symbol dictionary (ESD): control information, associated with an object or load module, that identifies the external symbols in the module.

external-unit identifier: synonym for *data-set reference number.*

extract

(1)   to select and remove from a set of items those items that meet some criteria; for example, to obtain certain specified digits from a computer word as controlled by an instruction or mask. (A) (B)

(2)   to separate specific parts of a word from the whole word.

(3)   to remove specific items from a file.

extract instruction: an instruction that requests the formation of a new expression from selected parts of given expressions. (A)

extraction: the reading of only selected parts of a record into storage.

extractor: see *filter.*

extraneous ink: ink deposited on a computer printout that is not confined to the printed characters themselves.

extremity routine: a routine used when initiating a new tape or when reaching the end of reel of a multireel file. The routine need not be included in memory if all tapes are set up or initiated automatically by the system supervisor and the open or close macros are not used. The primary value of this routine is that it performs needed tape housekeeping, checks on the operator, and provides needed information concerning the program being run.

EXTRN: see *external reference.*

F
(1) Fahrenheit.
(2) see *farad.*
(3) see *fetch.*
(4) see *file.*
(5) see *fixed.*
(6) see *flag.*
(7) see *frequency.*
(8) see *function.*

FA: see *full adder.*

FAC: see *facsimile.*

face: in OCR, a character style with given relative dimension and line thicknesses.

face-change character: synonym for *font-change character.* (A) (B)

facility
(1) an operational capability, or the means for providing such a capability. (E)
(2) a service provided by an operating system, for a particular purpose; for example, the checkpoint/restart facility.
(3) a measure of how easy it is to use a data-processing system.
(4) any one of the elements of a physical telephone plant that are needed to provide service. Thus, switching systems, cables, and microwave radio transmission systems are examples of facilities. Facility is sometimes used in a more restricted sense to mean transmission facility. (F)
(4) see also *telecommunication facility.*

facility management: a concept of overall efficient transmission system (facility) utilization, including concepts such as the use of protection channels, temporary setups for television specials, and so on. These uses are in addition to normal utilization for maintenance and restoration purposes. (F)

facility work order: an order to rearrange facilities on working services, or those for which service order work is in progress. (F)

facsimile (FAC) (FAX)
(1) an exact copy or likeness.

191

(2) a system for the transmission of images.

facsimile converter

(1) **receiving.** a facsimile device which changes the type of modulation from frequency shift to amplitude.

(2) **transmitting.** a facsimile device which changes the type of modulation from amplitude to frequency shift.

facsimile receiver: a facsimile device which converts the facsimile picture signal from the communications channel into a facsimile record of the subject copy.

facsimile recorder: that part of the facsimile receiver which performs the final conversion of the facsimile picture signal to an image of the subject copy on the record medium.

facsimile-signal level: an expression of the maximum signal power or voltage created by the scanning of the subject copy as measured at any point in a facsimile system. According to whether the system employs positive or negative modulation, this will correspond to picture white or black respectively. The level may be expressed in decibels with respect to some standard value, such as 1 milliwatt or 1 volt.

facsimile system (FAX): a system for the transmission of images. The image is scanned at the transmitter, reconstructed at the receiving station, and duplicated on some form of paper.

facsimile telegraphy: a system of telegraphy that allows the reproduction of fixed images (photographic or otherwise) in permanent form at a distance using a scanning technique.

The reproduction may be in two significant states only (for example, black and white), it may contain intermediate shades, or it may be colored. (C)

facsimile transmitter: a facsimile device which converts the subject copy into signals suitable for delivery to the communication system.

fact correlation: a process that is an integral part of linquistic analysis and adaptive learning that employs techniques of manipulating and recognizing data elements, items, or codes to examine and determine explicit and implicit relations of data in files; for example, for fact retrieval in place of document retrieval.

factor: in a multiplication operation, any of the numbers or quantities that are the operands. (A) (B) see *equivalent-binary-digit factor, multiplier factor, relocation factor, scale factor, time-scale factor.*

factorial: the product of positive integers from 1 up to and including a given integer; for example, factorial 5 is the product of $1 \times 2 \times 3 \times 4 \times 5$, or 120. (A) (B)

factoring: in PL/1, the application of one or more attributes or of a level number to a parenthesized list of names. see *level number.*

factor total: on a calculator, the facility for accumulating factors.

fade: intensity fluctuation of any or all components of a received signal.

FADS: see *force administration data system.*

fail safe: descriptive of a system which is able to close down in a controlled fashion during a serious failure, although some deterioration in performance can be expected. synonymous with *fail soft*.

fail soft:　synonymous with *fail safe*.

failure:　the termination of the capability of a functional unit to perform its required function. A failure is the effect of a fault. (B) cf. *error, fault, mistake*. (*A*)

failure analysis:　laboratory or on-the-spot analysis and study of a failure to identify the exact cause of the failure.

failure logging:　the automatic listing of failures that can be detected by a program, permitting corrective procedures to be attempted.

failure rate:　a measure of the number of a specified type or class of failures over a stated time frame.

failure recovery:　resumption of a system following a failure.

fallback

(1)　the use of a backup module in a redundant system during degraded operation.

(2)　a condition in processing when special computer or manual functions are employed as either complete or partial substitutes for malfunctioning systems.

false add:　to form a partial sum, that is, to add without carries. (A)

false code:　a code producing an illegal character.

false drop:　synonymous with *false retrievals*.

false error:　the signaling of an error when no error exists.

false retrievals:　library references that are not pertinent to, but are vaguely related to, the subject of the library search, and are sometimes obtained by automatic search methods. synonymous with *false drop*.

fan-fold paper:　continuous sheets of paper joined along perforations and folded in a zigzag manner. Usually used with printers as it can be continuously fed and folded without ongoing operator participation.

fan-in:　an electrical load presented to an output by an input.

fan-out:　an electrical load that an output is able to drive; often expressed as the number of inputs that are driven from a given output signal.

farad (F):　the measurement of the ability of two insulated bodies to hold a static charge equal to 1 coulomb at a potential difference of 1 volt between the two bodies, or 1 coulomb per volt. Usually a capacitor is measured in smaller units, called microfarads and picofarads.

fast-access storage:　the section of the storage from which data is obtained most rapidly.

fast busy:　synonymous with *channel busy tone*. (F)

fast select:　in packet switching, an option of the virtual call that allows the inclusion of data in the call setup and call clearing packets. (E)

fast-time scale:　the time scale used in data processing when the time-scale factor is less than one. cf. *extended-time scale*. (*A*)

fatal error:　an unplanned condition resulting from the execution of a program which precludes additional running of a program.

fault:　an accidental condition that causes a functional unit to fail to perform in a required manner. (B) cf. *error, failure, mistake*. see *pattern-sensitive fault, program-sensitive fault*. (*A*) see also *fault-rate threshold, fault threshold, fault trace*.

fault defect:　an anomaly preventing the correct operation of a unit.

fault dictionary: a set of fault signatures, each indicating the probable faults causing the error message from matching the signature.

fault-rate threshold: a fault threshold expressed in terms of the number of faults in a prescribed period of time. (E)

fault signature: an output response or set of responses generated when a test program is executed on a unit having a fault.

fault threshold: a prescribed limit to the number of faults in a specified category which, if exceeded, results in remedial action. The remedial action may include notifying the operators, running diagnostic programs, or reconfiguration to exclude a faulty unit. (E)

fault time: synonymous with *down time*.

fault-tolerant: a program or system that continues to function properly in spite of a fault or faults.

fault trace: a record of faults, and the circumstances of their occurrence, obtained by a monitor. (E)

FAX: see *facsimile*.

FB: see *fixed block*.

FBA: See *fixed-block architecture device*.

FC
(1) see *font-change character*.
(2) see *function code*.

FCC: see *Federal Communications Commission*.

F-conversion: one of the three types of FORMAT specification in FORTRAN; used to convert floating-point data for input-output operations.

FCT: see *function*.

FD
(1) see *file description*.

(2) see *flexible disk*.
(3) full duplex. see *duplex*.

FDM: frequency division multiplex. see *multiplexing*.

FDX: full duplex. see *duplex*.

FE: see *format effector character*. (A)

feasibility study: a preliminary investigation to determine the overall soundness of applying electronic computers to potential applications.

feature extraction: approaches for extracting significant features from a signal.

FEC: see *front-end computer*.

Federal Communications Commission (FCC): a board of commissioners appointed by the president under the Communications Act of 1934, having the power to regulate all interstate and foreign electrical telecommunication systems originating in the United States.

feed
(1) to cause data to be entered into a computer system, employing punched cards, paper tape, or other medium instead of by direct data entry.
(2) a device for causing data to be entered.

feedback: the return of part of the output of a machine, process, or system to the computer as input for another phase, especially for self-correcting or control purposes.

feedback amplifier: an amplifier in which a portion of the output signal is fed back and combined with the input signal. By proper negative feedback (opposite phase) design, the gain of an amplifier can be made essentially independent of the active elements (transistors, etc.) in the amplifier circuit. The gain can therefore be made very controllable and stable, as can input and output impedance as well as linear and nonlinear distortion. (F)

feedback loop: the components and processes involved in correcting and/or controlling a system by using part of the output as input. (A)

feedback system: see *information feedback system.* (A)

feeder cable: a large pair-size loop cable emanating from a central office and usually placed in an underground conduit system with access available at periodically placed manholes. (F)

feeder route: a network of loop cable extending from a wire center into a segment of the area served by the wire center. (F)

feeder section: a segment of a feeder route that is uniform throughout its length with respect to facility requirements and facilities in place. (F)

feed hole

(1) a hole punched in a data medium to enable it to be moved or synchronized. (A) (B)

(2) a hole punched in a data carrier to enable it to be positioned.

(3) synonymous with *sprocket hole.* (A)

feeding: a system used by character readers in character recognition, where each input document is issued to the document transport at a predetermined and fixed rate.

feed pitch: the distance between corresponding points of adjacent feed holes along the feed track. (A)

feed punch: see *automatic-feed punch.* (A)

feed reel: a specific reel from which tape is unwound throughout the processing.

feed track: the track of a data carrier that contains the feed holes. synonymous with *sprocket track.* (E)

FEFO: see *first-ended, first-out.*

FEP: see *front-end processor.*

ferreed assembly: a component consisting of two or four miniature glass-enclosed reed switches that are operated or released by controlling the magnetization of two adjacent plates. The magnetization of the plates is controlled by two windings. When both windings are energized, the reeds close and remain closed. When only one winding is energized, the reeds open. (F)

ferrite: an iron compound frequently used in the construction of magnetic cores. (A)

ferrod: a current-sensing device (ferrite rod) used in scanners for supervisory and other purposes. (F)

FET: see *field-effect transistor.*

fetch (F)

(1) to locate and load a quantity of data from storage. (A)

(2) in virtual storage systems, to bring load modules or program phases from auxiliary storage into virtual storage.

(3) a control program routine that accomplishes (1) or (2).

(4) the name of the macro instruction (FETCH) used to accomplish (1) or (2).

(5) see also *loader.*

(6) synonymous with *retrieve.*

fetch data: a command specifying the unit and file to which access is desired.

fetch phase: an alternate part of the cycle of the computer activity wherein the instruction is brought from memory into the program register.

fetch process: addressing the memory and reading into the CPU the information word or byte stored at the addressed location.

fetch protection: a storage protection feature that determines right of access to main storage by matching a protection key, associated with a fetch reference to main storage, with a storage key, associated with each block of main storage. see also *store protection.*

FF

(1) see *flip-flop.*

(2) see *form-feed character.* (A)

F format: a data-set format in which logical records are the same length.

FG: see *foreground.*

fiber bundle: a group of parallel fibers within a jacket-usually polyvinyl chloride. The number of fibers might range from a few to several hundred, depending on the application and the characteristics of the fiber.

fiber optics: the technology of guiding and projecting light for use as a communications medium. Hair-thin glass fibers which allow light beams to be bent and reflected with low levels of loss and interferences are known as "glass optical wave guides" or simply as "optical fibers." (G)

fiber-optic transmission system (FOTS): a transmission system utilizing small-diameter glass fibers through which light is transmitted. Information is transferred by modulating the transmitted light. These modulated signals are detected by light-sensitive semiconductor devices (photo-diode).

Fibonacci number: an integer in the Fibonacci series. (A)

Fibonacci search: a dichotomizing search in which the number of items in the set is equal to a Fibonacci number or is assumed to be equal to the next higher Fibonacci number and then at each step in the search a division is made in accordance with the Fibonacci series.

Fibonacci series: a series of integers in which each integer is equal to the sum of the two preceding integers in the series. (A) (B)

FIC: see *first-in-chain.*

fiche: see *microfiche.* (A)

FICON: see *file conversion.*

field (FLD)

(1) in a record, a specified area used for a particular category of data; for example, a group of card columns in which a wage rate is recorded. (B)

(2) a group of adjacent card columns on a punch card. (*A*)

(3) in a data base, the smallest unit of data that can be referred to. see also *data field.*

(4) see *card field, common field, display field.*

field checking: on some terminals, the numeric-only and alpha-only field checks that are dynamically performed to find errors as they occur.

field data code: a standardized military data transmission code consisting of 7 data bits plus 1 parity bit.

field-developed program: a licensed program that performs a function for the user. It may interact with program products, system control programming, or currently available type 1, type 2, or type 3 programs, or it may be a stand-alone program.

field effect transistor (FET): a voltage-controlled semiconductor which has a high input impedance comparable to that of a vacuum tube. Field effect transmittors are used to replace vacuum tubes in equipment for improved reliability.

field (in a data stream): in PL/1, that portion of the data stream whose width, in number of characters, is defined by a single data or spacing format item.

field length (FL): the number of characters or words in a field or a fixed-length record.

field (of a picture specification): in PL/1, any character-string picture specification or that portion (or all) of a numeric-character of numeric-bit picture specification that describes a fixed-point number.

field mark: the symbol used to show the beginning or the end of a set of data, that is, group, file, block.

field name: the symbolic name a programmer gives to a specific field of data.

field replaceable unit (FRU): an assembly that is replaced in its entirety when any one of its components fails. In some cases a field replaceable unit may contain other field replaceable units; for example, a brush and a brush block that can be replaced individually or as a single unit.

field selection: the ability of computers to isolate a specific data field within one computer word or words, without isolating the entire word.

field shifting: the process of adjustment for the address of a field to realign the item of data.

field upgrading: upgrading of devices by the insertion of functional logic boards such as expanded memory and I/O device controllers, with utilization of the appropriate program.

field utilization: using fields, or groups of computer characters as a single data item.

FIFO (first-in, first-out): a queuing technique in which the next item to be retrieved is the item that has been in the queue for the longest time. (A)

fifth-generation computers: a new family of computers to appear in the 1990s designed especially for artificial intelligence applications. The effort includes both computer hardware design and advanced computer programs. see also *artificial intelligence*.

figurative constant
(1) a data name that is reserved for a specified constant in a specified programming language. (A) (B)
(2) in COBOL, a reserved word that represents a numeric value, a character, or a string of repeated values or characters. The word can be written in a COBOL program to represent the values or characters without being defined in the data division.
(3) deprecated term for *literal*. (A) (B)

figures shift: the function performed by a teletypewriter machine causing the machine to shift to upper case for numbers, symbols, and so forth, when initiated by the figures-shift character.

file (F): a set of related records treated as a unit; for example, in stock control, a file could consist of a set of invoices. (A) (B) see *audit-review file, backup file, detail file, inverted file, master file, transaction file*. see also *data set, file cleanup*.

file activity ratio: the ratio of the number of records or other file element for which a transaction occurs during a given number of runs to the number of records or other file elements within the file.

file-address checking system: a program that checks addresses when macros instruct to write on the file, to see that the program is not writing on the incorrect area.

file attribute: any of the attributes that describe the characteristics of a file.

file cleanup: the removal of superfluous data from a file. synonymous with *file tidying.* (E)

file composition: filing of records within a storage unit.

file constant: in PL/1, a name declared for a file and for which a complete set of file attributes exists during the time that the file is open.

file control: in COBOL, the name and header of an environment division paragraph in which the data files for a given source program are named and assigned to specific input/output devices.

file control system: a system created to assist in the storage and retrieval of data without restricting the type of input/output device.

file conversion (FICON): the transformation of parts of records from their original documents into magnetic files by a computer.

file description (FD)
(1) a part of a file where file and field attributes are described.
(2) in COBOL, an entry in the file section of the data division that provides information about the identification and physical structure of a file.

file description statement: a nonexecutable statement used to specify the characteristics of a file, usually including such information as the names of logical records, header and trailer formats, and the type of device on which it is stored. (E)

file event: a single file access, either reading or writing.

file expression: in PL/1, an expression whose evaluation yields a file name.

file extent: an area with a file made up of contiguous tracks on a file storage medium.

file feed: an extension unit that increases the punch card capacity of the feed hopper peripheral units.

file gap: an area on a data medium intended to be used to indicate the end of a file and, possibly, the start of another. A file gap is frequently used for other purposes, in particular, as a flag to indicate the end or beginning of some other group of data. (A)

file insertion: in word processing, allows the user to add the contents of files B, C, and D to file A, just by pushing a few buttons, creating files of frequently used paragraphs or phrases, and adding them to letters or contracts in seconds.

file interrogation program: a program purporting to examine the contents of a computer file.

file label: a form of file identification; the initial record or block in a file is a set of characters unique to the file. synonymous with *header label.*

file layout: the arrangement and structure of data or words in a file, including the order and size of the components of the file. (A) (B)

file length: in word processing, determines the amount of text the word-processor file can contain; usually measured in kilobytes. see *kilobytes.*

file maintenance: the activity of keeping a file up to date by adding, changing, or deleting data. (A) (B)

file management: supervision and optimization of on-going work on a computer.

file management program: computer program which assigns, or recognizes, labels showing at data files, and facilitates their being called from storage when needed.

filemark: an identification mark showing that the last record in a file has been reached.

file merge: in word processing, the creating of form letters. One file contains the base document, the other the names to be plugged into specified areas in the base document. synonymous with *mail merge*.

file name

(1) a name assigned to a set of input data or output data. In COBOL, a file name must include at least one alphabetic character.

(2) a name declared for a file.

file organization: a procedure designed for organizing different information files; these files are usually random-access files to evolve maximum use of storage and swift retrieval for processing.

file-oriented programming: when I/O coding is simplified with the general file and record control program, programming is file-oriented rather than device-oriented and information is requested in device-independent fashion.

file packing density: the ratio of available file- or data-storing space to the total amount of data kept within the file.

file processing: operations connected with the evolution and utilization of files.

file protected: pertaining to a tape reel with the write-enable ring removed.

file protection: prevention of the destruction of data recorded on a volume by disabling the write head of a unit.

file purging: the erasing of the contents within a file.

file reconstitution: the recreation of a file which has been corrupted during system or failure, or other cause.

file recovery: see *backward file recovery, forward file recovery*.

file reel: a magnetic tape reel that feeds toward the rewrite head.

file section: in COBOL, a section of the data division that contains descriptions of all externally stored data (or files) used in a program. Such information is given in one or more file description entries.

file security: limiting access to computer systems by approved operators only. Passwords are frequently used in file security.

file separator character (FS): the information separator intended to identify a logical boundary between items called files. (A) (B)

file set: a collection of files forming a unit and stored consecutively on a magnetic disk unit.

file store: the files of an operating system, usually kept on a backing store.

file tidying: synonym for *file cleanup*.

file variable: in PL/1, a variable to which file constants can be assigned; it must have both the attributes FILE and VARIABLE. No file-name attributes, other than FILE, can be specified for a file-name variable.

fill: see *character fill, zero fill*.

fill character

(1) a character used to occupy an area on a human-readable medium; for example, in a business form or a legal document, dashes or asterisks used to fill out a field to ensure that nothing is added to the field once the form or document has been issued.

(2) a character used to fill a field in storage.

filler: one or more characters adjacent to an item of data that serves to bring its representation up to a specified size. (A) (B)

film: see *magnetic thin film, microfilm.*

film frame: in micrographics, that area of film exposed during each exposure, whether or not the area is filled by an image. synonymous with *recording area.* (A)

film storage: see *magnetic thin film storage.* (A)

filter: a device or program that separates data, signals, or material in accordance with specified criteria. (A)

FINAC: Fast Interline Non-active Automatic Control. A leased automatic teletypewriter system provided by AT&T.

final copy: in word processing, the final version of the text. see also *draft copy, edited copy.*

final group: a trunk group that acts as a final route for traffic. Traffic can overflow to a final group from high-usage groups that are busy. Traffic cannot overflow from a final group. (F)

final-route chain: the hierarchy of trunks and switching offices in the direct distance dialing network over which calls will be routed as a final choice when all direct or high usage paths are busy.

find text string: in word processing, a function that enables a point to be found within the text by entering a set of unique characters identifying the desired point. (D)

fine sort: usually off-line detail sorting by a sorter; for example, fine sorting could be the function of organizing bank checks and deposits into customer account number order.

firmware (FW): a computer's components that are neither hardware or software; for example, a unit for storing information used in programming the computer.

firmware circuitry: computer circuitry that performs the functions of program instructions.

firmware ROM: a ROM containing a control program.

first element of chain: deprecated term for *first RU of chain.*

first-ended, first-out (FEFO): a queuing scheme whereby messages on a destination queue are sent to the destination on a first-ended, first-out basis within priority groups. That is, higher-priority messages are sent before lower-priority messages; when two messages on a queue have equal priority, the one whose final segment arrived at the queue earliest is sent first.

first-generation computer: a computer utilizing vacuum tube components.

first-level addressing: see *level of addressing.*

FIT: a unit for expressing reliability in terms of failure rate. 1 FIT = 1 failure in 10^9 component operating hours. (F)

five-bit byte: synonym for *quintet.* (A) (B)

five-level code: a telegraph code that utilizes five impulses for describing a character. Start and stop elements may be added for asynchronous transmission. A common five-level code is Baudot code.

fix: a correction of an error in a program; usually a temporary correction or bypass of defective code. see also *fixed*.

fixed (F): synonym for *read-only* and *resident*.

fixed block (FB): the number of characters in the block determined by the logic of the computer.

fixed-block architecture (FBA) device: a disk storage device that stores data in blocks of fixed size; these blocks are addressed by block number relative to the beginning of the particular file.

fixed busy hour: see *busy, hour fixed*.

fixed-cycle operation: an operation that is completed in a specified number of regularly timed execution cycles. (A)

fixed data: in word processing, data, text, or format instructions entered initially and available for subsequent reuse in documents. (D)

fixed decimal: on a calculator, the preselection of the number of decimal places to be shown in the result of a calculation. (D)

fixed field: in word processing, preset information or an area that may be reserved by the operator for a particular purpose until no longer required. (D)

fixed-form: pertaining to entry of data or the coding of statements in a predefined state format. cf. *free-form*.

fixed-format messages: messages in which line control characters must be inserted upon departure from a terminal and deleted upon arrival at a terminal; fixed-format messages are intended for terminals with dissimilar characteristics. cf. *variable-format messages*.

fixed-function generator: a function generator in which the function to be generated is set by construction and cannot be altered by the user. (B)

fixed-head disk: a various disk unit that has read/write heads that are fixed in position. In such systems, one head is needed for each track of information recorded on a disk.

fixed-image graphics: a technique that involves the projection and positioning of selectable fixed images; for example, form flash. (E)

fixed-length record: a record having the same length as all other records with which it is logically or physically associated. cf. *variable-length record*. see also *F format*.

fixed-line number: the line number assigned to a text record and associated with that text record for the duration of the editing work session (unless specifically altered by the user).

fixed partition: a partition having a predefined beginning and ending storage address.

fixed point: the decimal point location technique in which the decimal point is not automatically located by the computer or by a routine; used primarily in contrast with floating point.

fixed-point constant: see *arithmetic constant*.

fixed-point part: in a floating-point representation, the numeral that is multiplied by the exponentiated implicit floating-point base to determine the real number represented; for example, a floating-point representation of the number 0.0001234 is 0.1234-3, where .1234 is the fixed-point part and -3 is the exponent. synonymous with *mantissa*. (*A*) (B)

fixed-point representation system: a radix numeration system in which the radix point is implicitly fixed in the series of digit places by some convention upon which agreement has been reached. (A) (B)

fixed program computer: see *wired program computer*.

fixed-radix numeration system: a radix numeration system in which all the digit places, except perhaps the one with the highest weight, have the same radix. The weights of successive digit places are successive integral powers of a single radix, each multiplied by the same factor. Negative integral powers of the radix are used in the representation of fractions. A fixed-radix numeration system is a particular case of a mixed-radix numeration system.

fixed satellite: allocating fequency bands for satellite communication on an international basis which identifies all sending and receiving stations.

fixed storage: a storage device whose contents are inherently nonerasable, nonerasable by a particular user, or nonerasable when operating under particular conditions; for example, a storage when controlled by a lockout feature, a photographic disk. synonymous with *nonerasable storage, permanent storage, read-only memory, read-only storage*. cf. *erasable storage*.

fixed word-length computer: a computer in which data is treated in units of a fixed number of characters or bits.

FL: see *field length*.

flag (F) (FLG)
(1) any of various types of indicators used for identification, for example, a wordmark.
(2) a character that signals the occurrence of some condition, such as the end of a word.
(3) deprecated term for *mark*. (B)
(4) synonym for *switch indicator*. (B)
(5) synonymous with *sentinel*. (*A*)

flag event: a condition causing a flag to be set; for example, the identification of an error, resulting in an error flag.

flag indicator: a signal that indicates that a specific condition has occurred in a computer.

flag lines: inputs to a microprocessor controlled by input-output units and tested by branch instructions.

flag sequence: in high-level data-link control (HDLC), the initial and final octets of a frame with the specific bit configuration of 01111110. A single flag sequence may be used to denote the end of one frame and the start of another. (C)

flag tests: single bits used to indicate the result of a simple test.

flash card: in micrographics, a document introduced during the recording of microfilm to facilitate its indexing.

flashing: synonym for *blinking*.

flatbed plotter: in computer graphics, a plotter that draws a display image on a display surface mounted on a flat surface. see also *drum plotter*. (E)

flat-bed scanner: a scanner used in

facsimile transmission.

flat-bed scanning: an approach used in facsimile transmission. see *flat-bed scanner*.

FLD: see *field*.

flexible disk (FD): synonym for *diskette*.

flexible manufacturing system: utilizing robot-controlled transport of work from one machine to another. Control is provided by numerical control units connected into a computer numerical control system.

flexowriter: a proprietary data-processing system by Friden, Inc. A unique feature is the punching and reading of paper tape, and limited programming options.

FLG: see *flag*.

flicker: in computer graphics, an undesirable pulsation of a display image on a cathode-ray tube that usually occurs when the refresh rate is low. (E)

flip-flop (FF): a circuit or device containing active elements, capable of assuming either one of two stable states at a given time. synonymous with *toggle* (*1*). (A) see also *direct-coupled flip-flop*.

flipping: synonymous with *floppy disk*.

flippy: double-sided floppy disk.

flippy-floppy: see *flippy*.

float: shifting characters into position to the right or left as determined by data structure or programming devices.

floating decimal: on a calculator, the automatic positioning of the decimal marker in the result of a calculation irrespective of the mode of entry of the input data. (D)

floating normalize control: pertaining to a specific bit, in the program status doubleword, that indicates whether (if 0) or not (if 1) the result of floating-point operation is to be normalized.

floating-point base: in a floating-point representation system, the implicit fixed positive integer base, greater than unity, that is raised to the power explicitly denoted by the exponent in the floating-point representation or represented by the characteristic in the floating-point representation and then multiplied by the fixed-point part to determine the real number represented; for example, in the floating-point representation of the number 0.0001234, namely 0.1234-3, the implicit floating-point base is 10. synonymous with *floating-point radix*. (A) (B)

floating-point feature: a processing unit feature that provides 4 64-bit floating-point registers to perform floating-point arithmetic calculations.

floating-point literal: a numerical literal whose value is expressed in floating-point notation; that is, as a decimal number followed by an exponenet that indicates the actual placement of the decimal point.

floating-point package: software that permits a computer to perform floating-point arithmetic.

floating-point precision: the maximum number of binary digits used as the mantissa of a single-precision floating-point fraction.

floating-point radix: synonym for *floating-point base*. (A)

floating-point register: a register used to manipulate data in a floating-point representation. (A) (B)

floating-point representation: a representation of a real number in a floating-point representation system; for example, a floating-point representation of the number 0.0001234 is 0.1234-3, where 0.1234 is the fixed-point part and -3 is the exponent. The numerals are expressed in the variable-point decimal numeration system. (B) cf. *variable-point representation*. (*A*)

flop: floating-point operation.

floppy: synonymous with *floppy disk*.

floppy disk (FD): deprecated term for *diskette*.

floppy disk controller: devices that provide control of data transfer to and from a floppy disk.

floppy mini:. a smaller floppy that is $5\frac{1}{4}$ inches square compared to 8 inches for a standard floppy.

flops: the number of floating-point operations per second.

flow: see *bidirectional flow*, *normal direction flow*, *reverse direction flow*. (A)

flow analysis

(1) in compilers, a technique used to determine the specific interdependence of elements of a computer program.

(2) the detection and recording of the sequencing of instructions in computer programs, for example, as used in monitors and debugging routines. (*A*)

flowchart: a graphical representation of the definition, analysis, or solution of a problem in which symbols are used to represent such things as operations, data, flow, and equipment. synonymous with *flow diagram*. (E) cf. *block diagram*. see *data flow chart*, *programming flowchart*.

flowcharting: representing a succession of events with lines, showing interconnections, linking symbols, showing events or processes.

flowchart symbol: a symbol used to represent operations, data, flow, or equipment in a flowchart. (A) (B)

flowchart technique: detailed flowcharts showing data and information requirements and actual methods and calculations for processing information.

flowchart text: the descriptive information that is associated with flowchart symbols. (A)

flow control: the procedure for controlling the data-transfer rate. see also *transmit flow control*. (E)

flow diagram: synonym for *flowchart*. (E)

flow direction: an indication of the antecedent-to-successor relationship between the symbols in a flowchart. (E)

flow line: a line representing a connecting path between the symbols in a flowchart to indicate a transfer of data or control. (E)

flow of control: sequence of execution.

flow-process diagram: synonymous with *systems flowchart*.

fluent computers: systems that immediately understand everyday languages making computers accessible to anyone who can write. see also *artificial intelligence*.

fluerics: the area within the field of fluidics in which components and systems perform functions such as sensing, logic, amplification, and control without the use of mechanical parts. (A)

fluidic: pertaining to the sensing, control, information processing, and actuation functions performed through the use of fluid dynamic phenomena. (A)

fluidics: that branch of science and technology concerned with sensing, control, information processing, and actuation functions performed through the use of fluid dynamic phenomena. (A)

fluorescent display: a display with segments of fluorescent material that glows when bombarded by electrons.

flutter: the recurring speed variation of relatively low frequency in a moving medium.

flyback: time used by a spot on a terminal screen to pass from the end of a line to the beginning of the next.

flying-spot scan: in computer graphics, a scan in which the intensity of reflected or transmitted light is measured at any point reached on a display space. (E)

flying spot scanner (FSS): in optical character recognition, a device employing a moving spot of light to scan a sample space, the intensity of the transmitted or reflected light being sensed by a photoelectric transducer. (A)

FM: see *frequency modulation.*

F-mode records: in COBOL, records of a fixed length, each of which is wholly contained within a block. Blocks may contain more than one record.

FNPA: see *foreign numbering plan area.*

FOCH: see *forward channel.*

focused overload: abnormal calling from many points to one particular point; for example, after an earthquake or in response to a radio station give-away offer. (F)

fold: to compact data by combining parts of the data, for example, to transform a two-word alphabetic key into a one-word numeric key by adding the numeric equivalents of the letters. (A)

folding: a technique used with the universal character set (UCS) feature on an impact printer to allow each of the 256 possible character codes to print some character on a chain or train with fewer graphics. For example, folding allows the printing of uppercase graphic characters when lowercase are not available in the character array on the chain or train.

folding ratio: in virtual storage systems, the ratio of the size of real storage to the size of virtual storage.

font: a family or assortment of characters of a given size and style, for example, 9 point Bodoni Modern. see *type font.* (A)

font-change character (FC): a control character that selects and makes effective a change in the specific shape, or size, or shape and size of the graphics for a set of graphemes, the character set remaining unchanged. synonymous with *face-change character.* (A) (B)

footprint: the area of the earth's surface to which a satellite transmits.

forbidden combination: a combination of bits or other representations that is not valid according to some criteria. cf. *illegal character.* (A)

force: to intervene manually in a routine and change the normal sequence of computer operations.

force administration data system (FADS): a system that provides basic telephone traffic data from which additional data may be derived to assist in arranging the most effective manning of attendant or operator positions and in calculating work force performance. (F)

forced coding: programming requiring minimum waiting time to obtain information out of storage. synonymous with *minimum-latency programming*.

forcing: the managerial function of providing the proper number of operators (half-hourly) to serve demand. The goal is to satisfy the service objectives while controlling expense. The functions are forecasting demand, scheduling tours to cover this demand, allocating the tours to offices in multioffice systems, assigning individual operators to specific tours, and making corrections in real time as required. (F)

foreground (FG): in multiprogramming, the environment in which high-priority programs are executed.

foreground display image: synonym for *dynamic display image*.

foreground initiator: a program that is called into main storage to perform job control functions for foreground programs not executing in batch job mode.

foreground job
(1) a high-priority job, usually a real-time job.
(2) an interactive or graphic display job that has an indefinite running time during which communication is established with one or more users at local or remote terminals.

foreground processing
(1) the execution of a computer program that preempts the use of computer facilities. (A) (B)
(2) in word processing, a type of

system operation that is perceived by the operator to execute immediately at the work station.
(3) cf. *background processing*. (A)

foreground program: in multiprogramming, a high priority program.

foreground region: a region to which a foreground job is assigned.

foreign area translation: the translation of the office codes of a foreign area for routing purposes when there is more than one trunk route available for entry into the foreign area or for other selective treatment. (F)

foreign exchange (FX) service: a service providing a circuit connecting a subscriber's main station or private branch exchange with a central office of an exchange other than that which normally serves the exchange area in which the subscriber is located. (F)

foreign numbering plan area (FNPA): any NPA outside the boundaries of the home NPA. (F)

forgiving system: a user-friendly system all permitting inexperienced users to make mistakes without disasterous consequences.

form: the paper on which output data is printed by a line printer or character printer. see *Backus Naur form*, *normalized form*, *precoded form*, *printed card form*.

FORMAC (formula manipulation compiler): an extension of PL/1 designed for nonnumeric manipulation of mathematical expressions.

formal logic: the study of the structure and form of a valid argument without regard to the meaning of the terms in the argument. (A) (B)

format: the arrangement or layout of

data on a data medium. (B) see *address format, instruction format.* (*A*)

format character set: a character set (available in 10-, 12-, and 15-pitch) that provides graphics such as lines, corners, and intersections, that can be used, for example, to print column lines or boxes around data.

format check: a check made to determine whether data conform to a specified layout. (E)

format description statement: a statement used to specify the format of output data on a medium external to the computer system; for example, payroll checks, order forms. (E)

format effector character (FE): any control character used to control the positioning of printed, displayed, or recorded data. synonymous with *layout character.* (*A*) (B)

format item: in PL/1, a specification used in edit-directed transmission to describe the representation of a data item in the stream (data format item) or to specify positioning of a data item within the stream (control format item).

format list: in PL/1, a parenthesized list of format items required for an edit-directed data specification.

format selection: in word processing, selection of a program for formatting purposes. (D)

formatted display: on a display device, a display in which the attributes of one or more display fields have been defined by the user. cf. *unformatted display.*

formatted dump: a dump in which certain data areas are isolated and identified.

formatted record: in FORTRAN, a record which is transmitted with the use of a FORMAT statement.

formatted systems services: a facility that provides certain system services as a result of receiving a field-formatted command, such as an INITIATE or TERMINATE command.

formatter: a program or circuit that writes the file marks, track marks, address marks, preambles, postambles and check characters for floppy disks, disks, or tape drives.

form feed

(1) paper throw used to bring an assigned part of a form to the printing position.

(2) in word processing, a function that advances the typing position to the same character position on a predetermined line of the next form or page. (D)

form feed character (FF)

(1) a format effector character that causes the print or display position to move to the next predetermined first line on the next form, the next page, or the equivalent. (A) (B)

(2) in word processing, synonym for *page-end character.*

form feed out: a form-positioning feature provided as an option on sprocket feed teleprinters. The automatic positioning of the typing unit to the first line of typing on the next form, at the same time feeding out the form in use so it may be torn off.

form flash: in computer graphics, the projection of a pattern, such as a report form, grid, or map, used as the display image. (E)

form overlay: in computer graphics, a projected pattern such as a report form, grid, or map used as the background for a display image. (E) synonym for *form flash.* (B)

form stop: a device that automatically stops a printer when the paper has run out.

formula manipulation: algebraic manipulation of mathematical formulas, primarily used to express computer programs by arithmetic formulas. (A)

FORTH: a programming language system characterized by three code and postfix, or reverse Polish, notation.

FORTRAN (formula translation)

(1) a programming language primarily used to express computer programs by arithmetic formulas. (A)

(2) a programming language primarily designed for applications involving numeric computations. (E)

FORTRAN control characters: deprecated term for *American National Standard control characters*.

fortuitous ("jitter"): a type of telegraph distortion which results in the intermittent shortening or lengthening of the signals. This distortion is entirely random in nature and can be caused, for example, by battery fluctuations, hits on the line, and power induction.

fortuitous conductor: any conductor which may provide an unintended path for signals, for example, water pipes, wire or cable, metal structural members, and so on.

fortuitous distortion: see *distortion.*

forward: activities involved in interconnecting circuits in order to establish a temporary communication between two or more stations.

forward-backward counter: a unit capable of adding or subtracting input so that it can count in either an increasing or decreasing direction.

forward bias: a voltage applied to a p-n crystal so that the positive terminal is applied to the p section and the negative terminal to the n section. see *n-type, p-type.*

forward channel (FOCH): a data-transmission channel in which the direction of transmission coincides with that in which user information is being transferred. see also *backward channel.* (E)

forward current: current that flows through a semiconductor junction when a forward bias is introduced.

forward file recovery: the reconstruction of a file by updating an earlier version with data recorded in a journal. cf. *backward file recovery.*

forward scan: an editing function making an output word conform to the control word by comparing positions from right to left and adding punctuations, such as decimals and dollar signs.

forward supervision: the use of supervisory sequences sent from the master to the slave station. cf. *backward supervision.*

FOTS: see *fiber-optic transmission system.*

four-address: pertaining to an instruction format containing four address parts. (A)

four-bit byte: synonym for *quartet.* (A) (B)

Fourier analysis: the decomposition of a signal into its simplest harmonic curves (sines and cosines).

Fourier series: a mathematical analysis permitting any complex wave form to be resolved into a fundamental plus a finite number of terms involving its harmonics.

four-plus-one address: pertaining to an instruction that contains four operand addresses and the address of the next instruction to be executed. (A)

four-wire: the links available in full-duplex mode without requiring additional multiplexing.

four-wire circuit: a path in which four wires (two for each direction of transmission) are presented to the station equipment.

four-wire repeater: a telephone repeater for use in a four-wire circuit consisting of two amplifiers, one servicing one side or transmission direction of the four-wire circuit and the other servicing the second side of the four-wire circuit.

four-wire terminating set: an arrangement by which four-wire circuits are terminated on a two-wire basis for interconnection with two-wire circuits.

fox message: standard communication used for testing teletypewriter circuits and equipment because it used all the alphanumerics on a teletypewriter in addition to the characters, for example, space, shift, figures.

fractional digit: a digit to the right of a decimal point.

fractional part: synonymous with *fixed-point part.*

fragmentation: see *storage fragmentation.*

frame

(1) that portion of a tape, on a line perpendicular to the reference edge, on which binary characters may be written or read simultaneously. (B)

(2) in high-level data-link control (HDLC), the sequence of contiguous bits bracketed by and including opening and closing flag (01111110) sequences.

(3) in data transmission, the sequence of contiguous bits bracketed by and including beginning and ending flag sequences.

(4) a set of consecutive digit time slots in which the position of each digit time slot can be identified by reference to a frame alignment signal. (C)

(5) in a time division multiplex (TDM) system, a repetitive group of signals resulting from a signal sampling of all channels, including any additional signals for synchronizing and other required system information.

(6) in facsimile systems, a rectangular area, the width of which is the available line and the length of which is determined by the service requirements.

(7) a segment of a signal, analog, or digital, that has a repetitive characteristic in that corresponding elements of successive frames represent the same things. Examples are a television frame, which represents a complete scan of a picture, or a telemetry frame, which represents values of a number of parameters in a specific order. In a time-division multiplex system, a frame is a sequence of time slots, each containing a sample from one of the channels served by the multiplex system; the frame is repeated at the sampling rate and each channel occupies the same sequence position in successive frames. (F)

(8) an assembly of equipment units. (F)

(9) synonym for *tape row.*

(10) see *display frame, film frame, main frame, page frame, time frame, wire frame.*

frame-creation terminal: a videotex tool designed to produce sophisticated graphics to accompany a text.

frame grabber: a device installed with a visual display unit permitting the storage and continuous display of a frame of information.

frame pitch: in computer graphics, the distance between corresponding points on two successive frames. synonymous with *pulldown.* (E)

frame (type A): a distributing frame carrying on one side (horizontal) all outside lines, and on the other side (vertical) the terminations of the central office equipment and protective devices for them.

frame (type B): a distributing frame carrying on one side (vertical) all outside lines and protective devices for those lines, and on the other side (horizontal) all connections of the outside lines toward the central office equipment.

framing

(1) the process of selecting the bit groupings representing one or more characters from a continuous stream of bits.

(2) the process of establishing a reference so that time slots or elements within the frame can be identified. (F)

framing bits: non-information-carrying bits to make possible the separation of characters in a bit stream. synonymous with *sync bits.*

franking: pertaining to devices that stamp or print postage.

free field: a property of information-processing recording media permitting recording of information without regard to a preassigned or fixed field.

free-form: pertaining to entry of data or the coding of statements without regard for predefined formats. cf. *fixed-form.*

freely programmable word-processing equipment: word-processing equipment on which the programs can be altered within the limits of available controls without exchanging or changing other features of the machine. (D)

free routing: that method of traffic handling wherein messages are forwarded toward their destination over any available channel without depending on a predetermined routing plan.

free storage: storage that is not allocated.

FREQ: see *frequency.*

frequency: (F) (FREQ): rate of signal oscillation in hertz.

frequency agility: in a video receiver, the ability to tune to any satellite channel without changing crystals.

frequency band: the range within which it is acceptable for the frequency of a signal to vary.

frequency division multiplex: see *multiplexing.*

frequency frogging: the practice of changing the relative positions of channels in a common spectrum periodically along a transmission path to reduce intermodulation noise or cross talk. (F)

frequency modulation (FM)

(1) modulation in which the frequency of an alternating current is the characteristic varied. (C)

(2) modulation in which two or more particular frequencies correspond each to one significant condition.

frequency offset: a frequency shift that occurs when a signal is sent over an analog carrier facility in which the modulating and demodulating frequencies are not identical. A channel with frequency offset does not preserve the wave form of the transmitted signal. DATAPHONE sets are designed to tolerate frequency offsets of up to +5 Hz. (F)

frequency reuse: a technique for transmitting separate signals in the same frequency band or in overlapping bands, by using different polarization for the two signals. Some satellites use right-hand circular and left-hand circular polarization for the signals; others use linear (horizontal and vertical) polarization.

frequency-shift keying (FSK): frequency modulation of a carrier by a modulating signal which varies between a fixed number of discrete values (a digital signal).

FROM: see *fusable read-only memory.*

front-end computer (FEC): synonym for *front-end processor.* (E)

front-end processor (FEP): a processor that can relieve a host computer of certain processing tasks, such as line control, message handling, code conversion, error control, and application functions. synonymous with *front-end computer.* (E)

front panel: a panel containing lights and switches for facilitating debugging by displaying information, and permitting direct control or access to registers or storage. A front panel needs a specific interface in addition to a monitor program.

FRU: see *field replaceable unit.*

FS: see *file separator character.* (A)

FSK: see *frequency-shift keying.*

FSP: see *full-screen processing.*

FSS: see *flying spot scanner.*

FTS: see *Federal Telecommunications System.*

FU: see *functional unit.*

full adder (FA): a combination circuit that has three inputs that are augend, D, an addend, E, and a carry digit transferred from another digit place, F, and two outputs that are a sum without carry, T, and a new carry digit, R, and in which the outputs are related to the inputs according to the following table:

Input D augend   0 0 1 1 0 0 1 1
Input E addend   0 1 0 1 0 1 0 1
Input F carry
digit   0 0 0 0 1 1 1 1
Output T sum   0 1 1 0 1 0 0 1
Output R carry
digit   0 0 0 1 0 1 1 1
synonymous with *three-input adder.* (*A*) (B)

full duplex (FD) (FDX): synonym for *duplex.* (A)

full-duplex operation: synonym for *duplex operation.*

full-duplex transmission: a method of operating a communications circuit so that each end can simultaneously transmit and receive. (F)

full group: a trunk group, other than a final trunk group, that does not overflow calls to another trunk group. Enough trunks are provided to give an acceptable blocking probability. (F)

full-screen editing: a type of editing at a display terminal in which an entire screen of data is displayed at once and in which the user can access data through commands or by using a cursor. cf. *line editing.*

full-screen processing (FSP): a method of operating a display station that allows the terminal operator to type data into some or all unprotected fields on the display screen before entering the data.

full speed: the top-rated speed of transmission equipment—in transoceanic telegraph, 50 baud or 66+ wpm.

full subtracter: a combinational circuit that has three inputs that are a minuend, I, a subtrahend, J, and a borrow digit, K, transferred from another digit place, and two outputs that are a difference, W, and a new borrow digit, X, and in which the outputs are related to the inputs according to the following table: (A) (B)

Input I minuend	0	0	1	1	0	0	1	1
Input J subtrahend	0	1	0	1	0	1	0	1
Input K borrow digit	0	0	0	0	1	1	1	1
Output W difference	0	1	1	0	1	0	0	1
Out X borrow digit 0	0	0	0	1	0	1	1	1

full-tone original: synonym for *continuous-tone original.* (D)

full word: synonym for *computer word.* (A) B)

fully connected network: a network in which each node is directly connected by branches to all other nodes. (E)

fully perforated tape: perforated tape in which the perforations are complete; that is, in which the punch makes a complete hole in the tape (as opposed to chadless tape, where the hole is not completely punched out).

fully qualified name: a qualified name that is complete; that is, one that includes all names in the hierarchical sequence above the structure member to which the name refers, as well

as the name of the member itself.

FUNC: see *function.*

function (F) (FCT) (FUNC)
(1) a mathematical entity whose value, that is, the value of the dependent variable, depends in a specified manner on the values of one or more independent variables, not more than one or more independent variables corresponding to each permissible combination of values from the respective ranges of the independent variables. (B)
(2) a specific purpose of an entity, or its characteristic action.
(3) in data communication, a machine action such as carriage return or line feed.
(4) in computer programming, synonym for *procedure.* (A)
(5) in PL/1, a function procedure (programmer-specified or built in); a procedure that is invoked by the appearance of one of its entry names in a function reference and which returns a value to the point of reference.
(6) a subroutine that returns the value of a single variable, and that usually has a single exit; for example, subroutines that compute mathematical functions, such as sine, cosine, logarithm; or that compute the maximum of a set of numbers. (E)
(7) see *boolean function, distributed function, generating function, mathematical function, recursive function, threshold function.*

functional design: the specification of the working relationships among the parts of a data-processing system. (A) (B)

functional diagram: a diagram that represents the working relationships among the parts of a system. (A)

functional element: a combination of logical and delay elements that perform an elementary computer function.

functional unit (FU): an entity of hardware, software, or both, capable of accomplishing a specified purpose. (A) (B)

function code (FC): the part of a computer instruction that specifies the operation to be carried out.

function declaration statement: a declaration used to assign a name to a function. (E)

function digit: a unique computer code digit that describes the arithmetic or logical operation which is to be carried out.

function element: a unit that performs a logic function.

function-evaluation routines: pertaining to a set of commonly used mathematical routines. The initial set of routines include sine, cosine, tangent, arc sine, arc cosine, arc tangent, square root, natural logarithm, and exponential. These routines are written in fixed- and floating-point.

function generator: a functional unit whose output variable is equal to some function of its input variables. (B)

function hole: synonym for *designation hole.* (A)

function key

(1) in computer graphics, a button or switch that may be operated to send a signal to the computer program controlling the display. (E)

(2) on a terminal, a key, such as an ATTENTION or an ENTER key, that causes the transmission of a signal not associated with a printable or dis-

playable character. Detection of the signal usually causes the system to perform some predefined function for the operator.

function keyboard: in computer graphics, the set of function keys on an input unit for a display console. (E)

function name: in COBOL, a name, that identifies system logical units, printer and card punch control characters, and report codes. When a function name is associated with a mnemonic name in the environment division, the mnemonic name can then be substituted in any format in which substitution is valid.

function part: synonym for *operation part.* (A) (B)

function reference: in PL/1, the appearance of an entry name or built-in function name (or an entry variable) in an expression.

function subprogram: an external function defined by FORTRAN statements and headed by a FUNCTION statement. It returns a value to the calling program unit at the point of reference.

function switch: a circuit having a fixed number of inputs and outputs designed such that the output information is a function of the input information, each expressed in a certain code, signal configuration, or pattern.

function table

(1) two or more sets of data so arranged that an entry in one set selects one or more entries in the remaining sets; for example, a tabulation of the values of a function for a set of values of the variable, a dictionary.

(2) a hardware device, or a subroutine that can either decode multiple inputs into a single output or encode a single input into multiple outputs. (*A*)

fundamental: the frequency under consideration; usually a pure sine wave with no distortion.

fusable read-only memory (FROM): read-only memory that is programmed by the blowing of fuse links. Once fused, FROMs cannot be corrected or altered.

fuse: an over-current protective device with a circuit-opening fusible part which is heated and severed by the passage of over-current through it.

fuse disconnecting switch: a disconnecting switch in which a fuse unit is in series with or forms a part of the blade assembly.

FW: see *firmware.*

FX: see *foreign exchange service*

G
(1) see *giga-*
(2) see *group*.

gain: the ratio between the output signal and the input signal of a unit.

gain-to-noise-temperature ratio (G/T): a ratio expressed in decibels per one degree Kelvin (K). A figure of merit of an antenna and low-noise amplifier; the larger the value of G/T, the better the receiving capabilities of the earth station.

game theory: a mathematical process, selecting an optimum strategy in the face of an opponent who has a strategy of his own.

gang punch: to punch identical data into a card deck.

gap: the interval between blocks of data on a magnetic tape needed to enable the medium to be stopped and started between reading or writing. see *interblock gap*.

gap character: a character that is included in a computer word for technical reasons but does not represent data. (A)

gap digit: the digit within a word used for a purpose other than to represent data or instructions, for example, a parity bit.

gap scatter: the deviation from correct alignment of the magnetic read/write heads for the parallel tracks on a magnetic tape.

garbage: unwanted and meaningless information in memory or on tape. synonymous with *hash*.

garbage collection: the rearrangement of the contents of store and the elimination of unwanted data in order to reclaim space for new data. see *garbage*.

gas panel: synonym for *plasma panel*.

gate
(1) a combinational circuit with only one output channel. (B)
(2) a device having one output channel and one or more input channels, such that the output channel state is completely determined by the input channel states, except during switching transients.

(3) a combinational logic element having at least one input channel.

(4) see *AND gate, OR gate.* (*A*)

gate pulse: extended duration signals designed to increase the possibility of coincidence with other pulses. Gate pulses present with other pulses cause circuits or units to perform intended operations.

gather write: writing a block of data of logical records from noncontinuous areas of store. see *scatter read.*

GCE: see *ground communication equipment.*

GDF: see *group distribution frame.*

GDG: see *generation data group.*

GE: greater than or equal to. see *relational operator.*

GEN

(1) see *generate.*

(2) see *generation.*

generalized mark-up language (GML) tag: see *GML.*

generalized sort/merge program: a program that is designed to sort or merge a wide variety of records in a variety of formats.

generalized subroutine: subroutines written for easy and ready use in several programs with only minor adjustments by the programmer.

general poll: a technique in which special invitation characters are sent to solicit transmission of data from all attached remote devices that are ready to send.

general program: a program, expressed in computer code, to solve a class of problems or specializing in a specific problem when proper parametric values are supplied. synonymous with *general routine.*

general-purpose computer (GPC): a computer that is designed to operate upon a wide variety of problems. (A) (B)

general purpose language: a programming language that is not restricted to a single type of computer, for example, BASIC, FORTRAN.

general-purpose operating system: an operating system designed to handle a wide variety of computing system applications.

general-purpose paper card: a card that meets the specifications in applicable ISO standards, except for the printed card form. (A)

general-purpose register (GPR): a register, usually explicitly addressable within a set of registers, that can be used for different purposes, for example, as an accumulator, as an index register, or as a special handler of data. (A) (B)

general register (GR): a register used for operations such as binary addition, subtraction, multiplication, and division. General registers are used primarily to compute and modify addresses in a program.

general routine: synonymous with *general program.*

general utility function: an auxiliary operation such as tape searching, tape-file copying, and tape dumps.

generate (GEN)

(1) to produce a computer program by selection of subsets from skeletal code under the control of parameters. (A)

(2) to produce assembler-language statements from the model statements of a macrodefinition when the definition is called by a macroinstruction.

generated address: an address that has been formed as a result during the execution of a computer program. synonymous with *synthetic address*. (A) (B)

generated error: a complete error made by employing operands that are not accurate, for example, using a rounded number. see *accuracy*.

generating function: in a given series of functions or constants, a mathematical function that, when represented by an infinite series, has those functions or constants as coefficients in the series. (A) (B)

generating program: synonymous with *generator*.

generating routine: synonymous with *generator*.

generation (GEN): in micrographics, a measure of the remoteness of the copy from the original material, the first microfilm representation being the first generation microfilm. (A)

generation data group (GDG): a collection of data sets that are kept in chronological order; each data set is called a *generation data set*.

generation data set: one generation of a generation data group.

generation number: a number forming part of the file label on a reel of magnetic tape. see also *grandfather tape*.

generation of a variable: in PL/1, the allocation of a static variable, a particular allocation of a controlled or automatic variable, or the storage indicated by a particular locator qualification of a based variable or by a defined variable or a parameter.

generator: a controlling routine that performs a generating function, for example, report generator, I/O generator. (A) see *character generator, compiler generator, curve generator, dot matrix, macrogenerator, stroke character generator, vector generator.*

generic name: in P/1, the name of a family of entry names. A reference to the name is replaced by the particular entry name whose parameter descriptors match the attributes of the arguments in the argument list at the point of invocation.

generic program: a set of instructions for an electronic switching system that is the same for all offices using that type of system. Detailed differences for each individual office are listed in a separate parameter table. (F)

geometric solution: graphic procedures for solving a linear programming problem, by plotting the half-planes determined by the constraints and the lines of constant value for the functions. Its use is limited to problems with, at most, two structural variables.

geostationary: describes a satellite in orbit 22,300 miles above the equator and which revolves around the earth with an angular velocity equal to that of the earth's rotation about its own axis. The satellite's position relative to the earth's surface is constant, so little or no ground antenna tracking is needed.

get

(1) to obtain a record from an input file.

(2) in word processing, the act of retrieving a defined block of text from a document and inserting it into the document being created or revised.

gibberish total: synonymous with *hash total*.

Gibson Mix: a statistically balanced mix

of instructions that is typical of general data processing applications; a variation used for benchmark testing.

giga- (G): ten to the ninth power, 1,000,000,000 in decimal notation. When referring to storage capacity, two to the thirtieth power, 1,073,741,824 in decimal notation.

GIGO: garbage in, garbage out; the acronymic expression of the concept that the results produced from unreliable or useless data are equally unreliable or useless.

GJP: see *graphic job processor.*

glitch: a pulse or burst of noise; often reserved for the types of noise pulses which cause crashes and failures.

global: pertaining to that which is defined in one subdivision of a computer program, and used in at least one other subdivision of that computer program. cf. *local.* (A) see also *global code, global lock, global search, global service, global variable symbol.*

global code: that part of an assembler program that includes the body of any macrodefinition called from a source module and the open code portion of the source module. cf. *local.*

global lock: a lock that protects serially reusable resources related to more than one private address space.

global search: in word processing, to find automatically a character or group of characters wherever they appear in a document with a single instruction. This may provide the option to change for another character or group of characters at each occurrence, for instance, change

"International Organization for Standardization" to "ISO". (D)

global service: a service that applies to more than one private address space.

global variable: a variable defined in one portion of a computer program and used in at least one other portion of that computer program. (E)

global variable symbol: in assembler programming, a variable symbol that can be used to communicate values between macro definitions and between a macrodefinition and open code. cf. *local variable symbol.*

glossary: a vocabulary with annotations for a particular subject.

glossary function: in word processing, frequently used terms kept in storage which can be inserted at any point in a document by the operator.

GM: see *group mark.*

GML (generalized mark-up language) tag: a high-level formatting expression that, when processed by the DOCUMENT command, expands into one or more SCRIPT control words.

go: start printer.

go-ahead tone: an audible signal indicating that the system is ready to accept a message.

Gothic character set: a character set (available in 10-, 12-, and 15-pitch) with 63 sans serif graphic characters.

GO TO (GOTO): a branch instruction in a high-level language.

GPC: see *general-purpose computer.*

GPR: see *general-purpose register.*

GPS: see *graphic programming services.*

GPSS (general-purpose systems simulator): a programming language based on block diagrams and used for discrete simulation. (E)

GR: see *general register*.

graceful degradation: attaining an acceptable level of reduced service.

graded-index fiber: an optical fiber with a refractive index that gets progressively lower away from the axis. This characteristic causes the light rays to be re-focused continually by refraction in the core.

grade of service

(1) a measure of the traffic handling capability of a network from the point of view of sufficiency of equipment and trunking throughout a multiplicity of nodes. (C)

(2) an estimate of customer satisfaction with a particular aspect of service (such as noise or echo). It combines the distribution of subjective opinions of a representative group of people with the distribution of performance for the particular aspect being graded. For example, with a specified distribution of noise, 95 percent of the people may judge the noise performance to be good or better; the noise grade of service is then said to be 95 percent good or better. (F)

(3) the proportion of calls, usually during the busy hour, that cannot be completed due to limits in the call-handling capability of a component in a network. For example, service objectives are defined on a per-link (per-trunk-group) basis for the last-choice groups in a traffic network. see *service objective*. (F)

gram (G): 0.035 ounces.

grammar: the word order in a communication or a portion of a communication.

grandfather tape: a copy of a magnetic tape file which, since the copy was generated, has twice undergone an updating cycle.

graph: a sheet of paper onto which have been placed curves, lines, points, and explanatory alphabetic and numerical information representing numerical data.

grapheme: a written or machine code that represents a single semanteme.

graph follower: a unit that reads data in the form of a graph, usually an optical sensing machine.

graphic: a symbol produced by a process such as handwriting, drawing, or printing. synonymous with *graphic symbol*. (A) (B)

graphic data reduction: converting graphic material to digital data.

graphic display unit: a communications terminal that displays data on a screen.

graphic character: a character, other than a control character, that is normally represented by a graphic. (A) (B)

graphic data structure: a logical sequence of digital data representing graphic data used in a graphic display.

graphic display program: a program designed to display information, in graphic or alphanumeric form, on the face of a TV-like display tube.

graphic display resolution

(1) the number of lines and characters per line able to be shown on a terminal screen.

(2) the number of pels of a screen. see *pel*.

graphic documentation: a process developed for recording data on graphs and film.

graphic file maintenance: a process that updates physical representations, such as microfilm, film prints, output copies, and so on.

graphic job processor (GJP): a program that elicits job control information from a user performing job control operations at a display station. It interprets the information entered by the user and converts it into job control language.

graphic language: in computer graphics, any language used to program a display device.

graphic panel: a display device showing the state of a process control operation in the form of lights, dials, and so forth.

graphic primitive: synonym for *display element*.

graphics: see *computer graphics, coordinate graphics, fixed-image graphics, interactive graphics, passive graphics.* see also *computer micrographics.*

graphics language: see *graphic language.*

graphic solution: a solution to a problem provided by graphs or diagrams replacing printed figures or text.

graphics peripheral: hardware, connected to a computer used to input graphics information such as tablets and light pens, or output graphics information, such as visual displays, plotters, and printers.

graphics plotter: a unit that provides hard-copy output of graphics displayed on a screen. There are two primary types: drum and flat-bed.

graphics routines: routines that convert output data into analog form (vectors).

graphics tablet: a device for inputting graphics such as diagrams, maps, charts or free-hand drawings on a computer.

graphic symbol: synonym for *graphic.* (A) (B)

graph plotter: see *plotter.*

graunch: an unexpectedly damaging error.

gray code: a binary code in which sequential numbers are represented by binary expressions, each of which differs from the preceding expression in one place only. synonymous with *reflected binary code.* (A)

grid: in optical character recognition, two mutually orthogonal sets of parallel lines used for specifying or measuring character images. (A)

grid chart: a representation of the relation between inputs, files, and outputs in matrix form.

gross minus: the accumulation, during a sales period, of all negative amounts (such as refunds, allowances, or discounts), entered or calculated in sales transactions at the point of sale terminal cf. *gross plus.*

gross plus: the accumulation, during a sales period, of all positive amounts (such as merchandise prices, taxes, or deposits) entered or calculated in sales transactions at the point of sale terminal. cf. *gross minus.*

ground: the point of reference in an electrical circuit; considered to be at nominal zero potential and other potentials within the circuit are compared to it.

ground communication equipment (GCE): earth station electronic equipment.

ground-return circuit: a circuit in which the earth serves as one conductor.

ground start: a supervisory signal given at certain coin telephone and PBXs by connecting one side of the line to ground. (F)

group (G)

(1) a word; in telegraph usage, arbitarily six characters in length.

(2) a set of related records that have the same value for a particular field in all of the records.

(3) a series of records logically joined together. see also *print data set*.

(4) see *display group*.

group addressing: the capability by which all stations on a multipoint line recognize addressing characters, but only one of the stations responds.

group authority: an authority that relates to a type of function a user can perform in a group. The group authorities are USE, CREATE, CONNECT, and JOIN.

group distribution frame (GDF): in frequency division multiplexing, a distribution frame which provides terminating and interconnecting facilities for the modulator output and the demodulator input circuits of the channel transmitting equipment and modulator input and demodulator output circuits for the group translating equipment operating in the basic spectrum of 60 kHz to 108 kHz.

grouped records: records combined into a unit to conserve storage space or reduce access time.

group indicate: the printing of indicative information from only the first record of a group.

grouping of records: combining of two or more records into one block of information on tape, to decrease the wasted time due to tape acceleration and deceleration and/or to conserve

tape space. synonymous with *blocking of records*.

group item: in COBOL, a data item made up of a series of logically related elementary items. It can be part of a record or a complete record.

group mark (GM): a mark that identifies the beginning or the end of a set of data which may include blocks, characters, or other items. (A) (B)

group marker: synonymous with *group mark*.

group name

(1) a generic name for a collection of I/O devices, for example, DISK or TAPE. see also *device type, unit address*.

(2) one to eight alphameric characters beginning with an alphabetic #, $, or @ character that identifies a group to RACF.

group poll: to poll a number of devices forming a subset of available devices.

group printing

(1) that activity of a machine that does not print data from every card. Instead it summarizes the data held in a group of cards and prints only the summarized totals.

(2) printing one line of information for a specific group.

group separator (GS): the information separator intended to identify a logical boundary between items called groups. (A) (B)

group theory: a study, in the mathematical sense, of the rules for combining groups, sets, and elements, for example, the theory of combining groups.

GS: see *group separator*. (A)

G/T: see *gain-to-noise-temperature ratio*.

GT: greater than. see also *relational operator*.

guard band: a frequency band between two channels of a data-transmission device, left unused so as to prevent interference between channels.

guard signal: a signal allowing values to be read only when the values are not subject to ambiguity error.

guidance code: see *operator guidance code*.

guide edge: synonym for *reference edge*. (A) (B)

guide margin: the distance between the guide edge and the center of the closest track of a tape when measuring across a paper tape.

gulp: a small group of binary digits composed of several bytes, and treated as a unit.

H
(1) see *hardware*.
(2) see *head*.
(3) see *hecto*.
(4) see *host*.

HA
(1) see *half-adder*.
(2) see *home address*.

half-adder (HA): a combinational circuit that has two inputs, A and B, and two outputs, one being a sum without carry, S, and the other being a carry, C, and in which the outputs are related to the inputs according to the following table:

input A	0 0 1 1
input B	0 1 0 1
output S sum without carry	0 1 1 0
output C carry	0 0 0 1

synonymous with *two-input adder*. (*A*) (B)

half-carry: the carry from bit 3 into bit 4 needed for adding packed binary coded decimal numbers correctly, where two binary coded decimal digits reside in one 8-bit byte.

half-duplex (HD) (HDX): in data communication, pertaining to an alternate, one way at a time, independent transmission. cf. *dulpex*. see also *half-duplex transmission*. (*A*)

half-duplex channel: a channel that transmits and receives signals in only one direction at a time.

half-duplex circuit: a duplex intercity facility with single loops to the terminals capable of two-way non-simultaneous operation.

half-duplex operation: a mode of operation of a data link in which data may be transmitted in both directions, one way at a time. synonymous with *either-way operation*. (E)

half-duplex service: a communication channel able to transmit and receive signals, but is not capable of simultaneous and independent transmission and reception.

half-duplex transmission
(1) data transmission in either direction, one direction at a time. (E)
(2) a method of operating a commu-

nications circuit so that each end can transmit or receive, but not both simultaneously. Thus, normal operation is alternate, one-way-at-a-time, transmission. (F)

half intensity: a terminal screen characteristic allowing specified characters to be displayed at half the intensity or brightness of the standard character.

half-path: a connection established between a telephone and a junction in the switching network.

half-speed: half the top-rated speed of the associated equipment; in transoceanic telegraph, 25 baud or 33+ wpm.

half-subtracter (HS): a combinational circuit that has two inputs that are minuend, G, and a subtrahend, H, and two outputs that are a difference, U, and a borrow digit, V, and in which the outputs are related to the inputs according to the following table: (A) (B)

input G minuend	0 0 1 1
input H subtrahend	0 1 0 1
output U difference	0 1 1 0
output V borrow digit	0 1 0 0

halftime emitter: a unit that emits synchronous pulses midway between the row pulses of a punched card.

halftone plotting: production of gray-scale halftones through controlled variation in dot clusters (halftone cells) produced on electrostatic plotters.

half-word: a contiguous sequence of bits or characters that comprise half a computer word and is capable of being addressed as a unit. (A)

halt (HLT): see *breakpoint halt*. (A)

halt instruction: a machine instruc-

tion that stops the execution of a program. synonym for *pause instruction*. (A) (B)

hamming code
(1) a data code that is capable of being corrected automatically. (A)
(2) a form of code that will permit the correction of some errors and detection of most other errors in digital data transmission. (F)

hamming distance: synonym for *signal distance*. (A)

HAMT: see *human-aided machine translation*.

hand-feed punch: a keypunch into which punch cards or punched cards are manually entered, and removed, one at a time. (A) (B)

hand-held calculator: a calculator capable of operating independently of main electric power that is light and small enough to be operated in the hand. (D)

handler: a portion of the program used to control or communicate with an external unit.

handset: a telephone mouthpiece and receiver in a single unit that can be held in one hand.

handshaking: exchange of predetermined signals when a connection is established between two data-set devices. see also *answer-back*.

hands-off operation: synonymous with *closed shop*.

hands-on background: prior work experience developed by operating the hardware and often used as a criterion of programmer capability.

hands-on operation: synonymous with *open shop*.

hang up: an unanticipated stop in a program sequence, caused by a program error.

hard copy

(1) in computer graphics, a permanent copy of a display image that is portable and can be read directly by human beings; for example, a display image that is recorded on paper. (E)
(2) a printed copy of machine output in a visually readable form; for example, printed reports, listings, documents, and summaries. see also *display (1)*.
(3) cf. *soft copy*.

hard-copy log: in systems with multiple console support or a graphic console, a permanent record of system activity.

hard-copy video interface: a unit that permits production of hard-copy output on an electrostatic printer/plotter from a video source.

hard disk: a data-recording system using solid disks of magnetic material turning at high speed. see *cartridge disk*, *Winchester disk*.

hard error: an error, frequently concerned with a malfunction of hardware that can be readily diagnosed and to some extent predicted. cf. *soft error*.

hard sectoring: the physical marking of sector boundaries on a magnetic disk by punching holes in the disk where all available space can be used for data storage. cf. *soft sectoring*.

hard stop: an immediate termination of operation or execution.

hard wait: see *wait state*.

HARDWR: see *hardware*.

hardware (H) (HARDWR) (HDW) (HW): physical equipment used in data processing, as opposed to programs, procedures, rules, and associated documentation. (B) cf. *software*. (A)

hardware check: a failure in a hard-ware unit that halts operation. synonym for *automatic check*. (A)

hardware error recovery management system: a facility that attempts recovery from hardware malfunctions. It consists of the machine check handler (MCH) and the channel check handler (CCH).

hardware language: a representation of a reference language using symbols that are particularly suitable for direct input to a computer; for example, X A in a reference language may become X = A, and X 2 may become X**2 in a hardware language. (E)

hardware tariffs: tariffs filed on the basis of providing service with an explicit type of serving equipment. (F)

hard-wired: pertaining to a physical connection or characteristics, for example, the address of a console or I/O device.

hardwiring: permanently wired electronic components capable of logical decisions, that is, intelligent terminals functioning without software. In a hard-wired computer, the program logic cannot be altered except by replacing the circuit boards or memories.

harmonic: the resultant presence of harmonic frequencies (due to nonlinear characteristics of a transmission line) in the response when a sinusoidal stimulus is applied.

harmonic distortion: the result of nonlinearities in the communication channel that cause harmonics of the input frequencies to appear in the output. The same effect produces spurious frequencies, such as sum and difference frequencies, from interaction of input frequencies. (F) see *distortion*.

harmonic telephone ringer: a telephone ringer that responds only to alternating current within a very narrow frequency band. A number of such ringers, each responding to a different frequency, are used in one type of selective ringing where there are several parties on a subscriber's line.

Hartley: in informational theory, a unit of logarithmic measures of information equal to the decision content of a set of ten mutually exclusive events expressed by the logarithm with the base ten; for example, the decision content of a character set of eight characters equals 0.903 Hartley. synonymous with *information content decimal unit.* (*A*) (B)

hash: see *garbage.*

hash index: the first estimate of the location of an entry within a table.

hashing

(1) the application of an algorithm to the records in a data set to obtain a symmetric grouping of the records. synonymous with *key folding.*

(2) in an indexed data set, the process of transforming a record key into an index value for storing and retrieving a record.

hash total: the result obtained by applying an algorithm to a set of data for checking purposes; for example, a sum of the numerical values of specified data items. (E) synonym for *control total.*

HC: see *host computer.*

HCMTS: see *high-capacity mobile telecommunications system.*

HCS: see *hundred call seconds.*

HD: see *half-duplex.*

HDLC: see *high-level data-link control.*

HDR: see *header.*

HDW: see *hardware.*

HDX: see *half-duplex.*

head (H): a device that reads, writes, or erases data on a storage medium; for example, a small electromagnet used to read, write, or erase data on a magnetic drum or magnetic tape, or the set of perforating, reading, or marking devices used for punching, reading, or printing on perforated tape. (A) (B) see *magnetic head, plotting head, preread head, read head, read/write head, write head.*

head crash: damage caused to a magnetic disk surface resulting from impact by the read/write head.

header (HDR)

(1) system-defined control information that precedes user data.

(2) that portion of a message that contains control information for the message such as one or more destination fields, the name of the originating station, an input sequence number, a character string indicating the type of message, and a priority level for the message. see *block control header, message header.*

header card: a card the contains information related to the data in cards that follow. (A)

header label

(1) an internal label, immediately preceding the first record of a file, that identifies the file and contains data used in file control. (E)

(2) a file label or data-set label that precedes the data records on a unit of recording media.

header record: a record containing common, constant, or identifying information for a group of records that follows. synonymous with *header table.*

headers and trailers: repetitive words, phrases, or sentences placed at predetermined locations of every page of the document.

header segment: a part of a message that contains any portion of the message header.

header sheet: an instruction sheet for an optical character recognition unit which informs it of the format, and so on, to be expected on follow up sheets.

header table: synonym for *header record.*

head gap: the distance between a read or write head and the surface of the recording medium. see *read/ write head.*

heading: in ASCII and data communication, a sequence of characters preceded by the start-of-heading character used as machine sensible address or routing information. cf. *text.* (A)

heading character: see *start-of-heading character.* (A)

heading record: the record containing an identification or description of the output report for which ensuing records are related to and concerned with the body of a report.

heap: a portion of memory organized as a stack, used by some compilers to store dynamic (pointer) variables during program execution.

hecto (H): hundred.

hectometer (hm): one hundred meters. 109.36 yards.

held over

(1) a service order that is not completed within a specified period of time. (F)

(2) a service order requiring rearrangement or reinforcement of outside plant. (F)

held terminal: synonym for *intercepted terminal.*

hertz (Hz): a unit of frequency equal to one cycle per second.

hesitation: a short automatic suspension of a main program to carry out a part or all of another operation; for example, a fast transfer of data to or from a peripheral unit.

heterodyne reception (beat reception): the process of reception in which a received high-frequency wave is combined in a nonlinear device with a locally generated wave, with the result that in the output there are frequencies equal to the sum and difference of the combining frequencies.

heterodyne repeater: a repeater for a radio system in which the received signals are converted to an immediate frequency, amplified, and reconverted to a new frequency band for transmission over the next repeater section. synonymous with *IF repeater.*

heterogeneous multiplex: a multiplex structure in which all the information-bearer channels are not at the same data signaling rate.

heterogeneous network: a network of dissimilar host computers, such as those of different manufacturers. cf. *homogeneous network.* (E)

heuristic: pertaining to exploratory methods of problem solving in which solutions are discovered by evaluation of the progress made toward the final result.

heuristic method: any exploratory method of solving problems in which an evaluation is made of the progress toward an acceptable final result using a series of approximate results.

(A) (B)

hex: see *sexadecimal.*

hexadecimal: synonym for *sexadecimal.* (A) (B)

hexadecimal constant: in FORTRAN, the character Z followed by a hexadecimal number, formed from the set 0 through 9 and A through F.

hexadecimal notation: notation of numbers in the base 16.

hex pad: a keyboard having input to a microprocessor in hexadecimal notation.

HFDF: see *high-frequency distribution frame.*

Hg delay line: synonymous with *mercury delay line.*

HIC: see *hybrid integrated circuit.*

hidden line: in computer graphics, a line segment that represents an edge obscured from view in a two-dimensional projection of a three-dimensional object. (E)

hidden line removal: in computer graphics, a technique for the removal of hidden lines. (E)

hierarchical classification: a designation framework where terms are arranged based on some hierarchical structure.

hierarchical computer network: a computer network consisting of several levels of processing and control computers, each computer specifically designed to perform its particular function.

hierarchically synchronized network: a mutually synchronized network in which some clocks exert more control than others, the network operating frequency being a weighted mean of the natural frequencies of the population of clocks.

hierarchical network: a network in

which processing and control functions are performed at several levels by computers specially suited for the functions performed; for example, in factory or laboratory automation. (E)

hierarchical structure: a structure of data aggregates or record types having several levels arranged in a tree-like structure, based on one-to-many relationships. (E)

hierarchy (HIR): see *data hierarchy, hierarchy of operations.*

hierarchy of operations: relative priority assigned to arithmetic or logical operations that must be performed.

high address: an address with a high numerical value when viewed as an unsigned integer. The highest address in a 64K memory is $FFFF_{16}$.

high byte: (FFFB) bits 8 through 15 of a 16-bit binary number.

high-capacity mobile telecommunications system (HCMTS): a mobile system featuring a cellular pattern of base transmitters and receivers and frequent reuse of radio channels. One large advantage of HCMTS over earlier systems is that higher quality service would be available to a much larger number of subscribers than is possible today. (F)

high density: the provision of a high storage capacity per unit storage space, for example, in bits per inch.

high-frequency distribution frame (HFDF): a distribution frame which provides terminating and interconnecting facilities for those combinated-supergroup modulator-output and combined supergrouped demodulator-input circuits occupying the baseband spectrum of 12kHz up to and including 2540 kHz.

high-level compiler: a program capable of translating statements in high-level language into their machine-language equivalents.

high-level data-link control (HDLC): control of data links by use of a specified series of bits rather than by the control characters of the ISO Standard seven-bit character set for information processing interchange. (C)

high-level language (HLL)

(1) a programming language that does not reflect the structure of any one given computer or that of any given class of computers. (A) (B)

(2) a problem-oriented language that requires little knowledge of the computer on which a computer program written in the language is to be run; that facilitates translation of computer programs in this language into several different machine codes; and that usually results in many machine instructions for each statement in the source program; for example, ALGOL, COBOL, COGO, FORTRAN, PL/1, SIMSCRIPT. (E)

high-level source code: statements or statement lines as original directives that a programmer prepares to direct the movement of a computer when utilizing a high-level language such as BASIC, COBOL, and so on.

highlighting: in computer graphics, emphasizing a given display group by changing its attributes relative to other display groups in the same display field. (E)

high-order position: the left-most position in a string of characters.

high pass: pertaining to the performance of a circuit that permits the passage of high-frequency signals and attenuates low-frequency signals.

high-pass filter: a filter which passes frequencies above a given frequency and attenuates all others.

high-performance equipment: equipment that yields output signals of sufficiently high quality to permit these signals to be transmitted on telephone or teleprinter circuits.

high power amplifier (HPA): a device which provides the energy for carrier amplification necessary to transmit to the satellite.

high punch: the 12, 11, and zero punch are zone punches, the 12 punch being the highest (vertically) on the standard punched card.

high resolution: the quality of video graphics display systems or printers capable of reproducing images in great detail to a high degree of accuracy.

high-speed bus: see *bus*.

high-speed carry: in parallel addition, any procedure for speeding up the processing of carries; for example, standing-on-nines carry. (B) cf. *cascaded carry*. (A)

high-speed printer (HSP): a printer operating at a speed more compatible with the speed of computation and data processing so that it may function on line.

high-speed reader (HSR): a reading device connected to a computer so as to function on line without seriously holding up the computer.

high-usage group: a trunk group that is the primary direct route between two switching systems. The group is designed for high average occupancy. To provide an overall acceptable probability of blocking, an alternate route must be provided for overflow traffic. (F)

highway: synonymous with *bus*.

Hi-Lo tariff: a two-level rate schedule for AT&T's intercity voice grade private line service. Under the Hi-Lo rate approach, costs and rates were averaged separately for high-density routes and for low-density routes; thus, rates on high-density routes were lower than on low-density routes to correlate with the costs involved. The Hi-Lo tariff represented the Bell System's first departure from nationwide price averaging for private-line services. In 1976 the FCC declared the Hi-Lo tariff unjustified. see *multischedule private line.* (G)

HIPO (hierarchy: input, process, output): a graphics tool for designing, developing, and documenting program function.

HIR: see *hierarchy.*

Hiragana: a character set of symbols used in one of the two common Japanese phonetic alphabets. see also *Katakana.*

history file: a file in which a record is kept of jobs or transactions.

history run: printing out all transactions of a process for reading or recording purposes.

hit
(1) a comparison of two items of data that satisfies specified conditions.
(2) a transient disturbance to a data communication medium. (*A*)
(3) see *light-pen detection.*

hit-on-the-fly printer: synonym for *on-the-fly printer.* (A)

hit-on-the-line: errors caused by external interferences such as impulse noise caused by lightning or man-made interference.

hit ratio: the ratio of the number of successful references to main storage to the total number of references.

hits: momentary line disturbances which could result in mutilation of characters being transmitted.

HLL: see *high-level language.*

HLT: see *halt.*

HNPA: see *home numbering plan area.*

hobby computer: a computer not used for profit (or a tax writeoff).

hold: to retain data in one storage unit after transferring it to another one or to another location in the same device. cf. *clear.*

hold facility: the ability to permit interruption of the operation of a computer in such a fashion that the values of the variables at the time of interruption are not altered; thus permitting computation to continue when the interruption stops.

holding beam: a diffuse spray of electrons in a cathode-ray tube, used for refreshing; electrons that have dissipated after being stored on the surface can be refreshed by a holding beam.

holding gun: the source of a spray of electrons creating a holding beam.

holding time: total time when a given channel is occupied for each transmission or call; consisting of operating time and conversation time.

hold instruction: a computer instruction causing data pulled from storage to be simultaneously held in storage after it is called out and transferred to its new location.

hold mode: an operating mode of an analog computer during which computing action is stopped and all variables are held at the value they had when this mode is entered. (B)

hole pattern
(1)   An array of holes that represents data, for example, a punching configuration that represents a single character. (B)
(2)   a punching configuration within a card column that represents a single character of a character set. (*A*)

Hollerith: pertaining to a particular type of code or punched card utilizing 12 rows per column and usually 80 columns per card. (A)

Hollerith card: a punch card characterized by 80 columns and 12 rows of punch positions. (A)

Hollerith code: an alphanumeric punched card code.

hologram: the recording of an image sent over a film surface as a result of splitting a laser beam, yielding an optical interference. The image can be recovered and focused in free space or on a screen. Holograms can be used for storage of data, with extremely high packing densities.

holographic-based system: a system utilizing laser and holographic technology in a microform setting.

home: the beginning position of a cursor on a terminal screen, usually in the top left-hand corner of the screen.

home address (HA):   an address written on a direct-access volume, denoting a track's address relative to the beginning of the volume.

home loop: an operation involving only those input and output units associated with the local terminal.

home numbering plan area (HNPA): the NPA within which the calling line appears at a local (class 5) switching office. (F)

homeostatis: the dynamic state of a system where input and output are exactly balanced, so that there is no change.

home record: the first record in a chain of records.

homogeneous network: a network of similar host computers, such as those of one model of one manufacturer. cf. *heterogeneous network*. (E)

hopper: see *card hopper*.

horizontal feed: pertaining to the entry of a punch card into a card feed with a long edge first. (A)

horizontal positions: see *addressable horizontal positions*. (A)

horizontal raster count: the number of horizontal divisions in a raster. see *raster count*.

horizontal system: a programming system designed so that instructions are written horizontally, for example, across the page.

horizontal table: in indexing, a table whose entries are stored sequentially; that is, entry one, byte one; entry one, byte two; and so on.

horizontal tabulation character (HT): a format effector character that causes the print or display position to move forward to the next of a series of predetermined positions along the same line. (A (B)

horizontal wraparound: on a display device, the continuation of cursor movement from the last character position in a horizontal row to the first character position in the next row, or from the first position in a row to the last position in the preceding row. cf. *vertical wraparound*.

host (H):   an information processor which performs the instruction processing work of the enterprise. A host processor is generally self-sufficient and requires no supervision from other processors. see *data host*. see also *host computer, host interface, host node, host processor, host system*.

host application program: an application program that is executed in the host computer.

host computer (HC)

(1) in a network, a computer that primarily provides services such as computation, data-base access, or special programs or programming languages. (E)

(2) the primary or controlling computer in a multiple computer installation.

(3) a computer used to prepare programs for use on another computer or on another data-processing system; for example, a computer used to compile, link, edit, or test programs to be used on another system.

(4) synonym for *host processor*.

host interface: the interface between a network and a host computer. (E)

host node: a node at which a host processor is situated.

host processor (HP)

(1) a processor that controls all or part of a user-application network. (E)

(2) in a network, the processing unit in which the access method for the network resides.

(3) a processing unit that executes the access method for attached communication controllers.

(4) synonymous with *host computer*.

host subarea: a subarea that contains a host node.

host switch: a central office switching entity which provides central control,

switching, and service-generation functions for a remote switch.

host system

(1) a data-processing system that is used to prepare programs and the operating environments for use on another computer or controller.

(2) the data-processing system to which a network is connected and with which the system can communicate.

hot chassis: a terminal with its chassis connected to one side of a power line, allowing the chassis itself to provide the earth or ground.

hot zone: synonymous with *line-ending zone*.

housekeeping: see *housekeeping operation*.

housekeeping operation: an operation that facilitates the execution of a computer program without making a direct contribution. For example, initialization of storage areas; the execution of a calling sequence. synonymous with *overhead operation*. (*A*) (B)

HP: see *host processor*.

HPA: see *high power amplifier*.

HS: see *half subtracter*.

HSP: see *high-speed printer*.

HSR: see *high-speed reader*.

HT: see *horizontal tabulation character*. (A)

hub: a point or piece of equipment where a branch of a multipoint network is connected. In a telegraph network, signals appear as dc pulses at the hub. A network may have a number of geographically distributed hubs or bridging points. (F)

hub layout: in voice-band multipoint networks, a hub layout is one in which each branch, or leg, serving a particular station is routed to a common central location for appropriate bridging and test access. The central location is generally known as a serving test center (STC). (F)

human-aided machine translation (HAMT): a machine translation system where human intervention is only required to resolve semantic or syntactic ambiguities, and problems created by non-literal usage.

human-oriented language: a programming language that is more like a human language than a machine language.

hundred call seconds (HCS): a unit of traffic used to express the average number of calls in progress or the average number of devices in use. Numerically it is 36 times the traffic expressed in Erlangs. (F)

hunting: searching activities performed in switching systems to find the called line or the next available line in an equivalent group. see *trunk hunting*.

HW: see hardware.

hybrid: a network having four ports and designed so that when the ports are properly terminated, the signal input to any particular port splits equally between the two adjacent ports with essentially no signal coupled to the opposite port. Hybrids are used to couple four-wire circuits to two-wire circuits. (F)

hybrid circuit: complex circuit which is made by interconnecting individual integrated circuits, semiconductor devices, resistors, and capacitors on thick film or thin film substrates.

hybrid coil: an arrangement using one or more transformers wired as a balanced bridge to provide two- to four-wire conversion for long distance telecommunication circuits.

hybrid computer: a computer that processes both analog and digital data. see also *analog computer, digital computer*. (E)

hybrid integrated circuit (HIC)
(1) a class of integrated circuits wherein the substrate is a passive material such as ceramic and the active chips are attached to its surface.
(2) an electronic circuit that contains both silicon integrated circuits and circuitry fabricated by film deposition techniques. (F)

hybrid interface: the interface between an analog and digital device.

hybrid programming: routines in the hybrid programming library are designed to help engineers and scientists decide which parts of a problem can be solved in digital domain. These routines deal with timing, function-generation integration, and general simulation issues; provide diagnosis of hardware operations; and check on whether the analog device is scaled and wired correctly.

hybrid set: two or more transformers interconnected to form a network having four pairs of accessible terminals to which may be connected four impedances, so that the branches containing them may be interchangeable.

hybrid system: a system having both digital computer and analog computer capability.

HYP: see *required hyphen character*.

hyphen drop: in word processing, the function of a machine that ensures that a discretionary hyphen is not printed when the word concerned subsequently appears elsewhere in the text and no longer requires hyphenation. (D)

hysteresis: lagging in the response of a unit of a system behind an increase or a decrease in the strength of the signal.

hysteresis loop: see *magnetic hysteresis loop.* (A)

Hz: see *hertz.*

I

I
- (1) see *information*.
- (2) see *input*.
- (3) see *instruction*.
- (4) see *interrupt*.

IA: see *instruction address*.

i address: in some devices, the location of the next instruction to be executed based on whether or not a branch operation occurs.

IAL: see *International Algebraic Language*.

I and A: indexing and abstracting.

IAR: see *instruction address register*.

IBG: see *interblock gap*.

IC
- (1) see *instruction counter*.
- (2) see *integrated circuit*.

ICA: International Communication Association, formerly called Industrial Communication Association.

icand: see *multiplicand*.

iconographic model: a pictorial representation of a system and the functional relations found in the system.

ICT: see *incoming trunk*.

ICU: see *instruction control unit*.

ICV: see *initial chaining value*.

ID
- (1) see *identification*.
- (2) see *identification characters*.
- (3) see *identifier*.

IDB: see *integrated data base*.

IDDD: see *international direct distance dialing*.

identification (ID) (IDENT): a label consisting of a coded name showing a unit of data, for example, a file name.

identification (ID) characters: characters sent by a station on a switched line to identify the station.

identification division: one of the four main parts of a COBOL program. The identification division identifies the source program and the object program and, in addition, may include such documentation as the author's name, the installation where written, and the data written.

identifier (ID)
- (1) a character or group of charac-

ters used to identify or name items of data and possibly to indicate certain properties of that data. (A) (B)

(2) in COBOL, a data name, unique in itself, or made unique by the syntactically correct combination of qualifiers, subscripts, and indexes.

identifier word: a full-length computer word associated with a search or a search-read function. In a search or search-read function, the identifier word is stored within a special register in the channel synchronizer and compared with each word read by the peripheral unit.

identify: to assign a label to a file or data or to an item of data held in store.

identify element: a logic element that performs an identity operation. synonymous with *identity gate*. (A) (B)

identity gate: synonym for *identity element*. (A) (B)

identity operation: the boolean operation, the result of which has the boolean value 1, if and only if all the operands have the same boolean value. An identity operation on two operands is an equivalence operation. (B) cf. *nonidentity operation.* (A)

identity unit: an n-input unit that yields a specified output signal only when all n-input signals are alike. (A)

IDF: see *intermediate distributing frame.*

idle character

(1) a control character that is sent when there is no information to be sent. (C)

(2) a character transmitted on a telecommunication line that does not print or punch at the output component of the accepting terminal.

(3) see *synchronous idle character.*

(A)

idle line: synonym for *inactive line.*

idle line termination: an electrical network which is switch-controlled to maintain a desired impedance at a trunk or line terminal when that terminal is in the idle state.

idle link: synonym for *inactive link.*

idle time: operable time during which a functional unit is not operated. (B) cf. *operating time.* (A)

IDP: see *integrated data processing.* (A)

I/F: see *interface.*

IF: see *intermediate frequency.*

IF-AND-ONLY-IF element: a logic element that performs the boolean operation of equivalence. synonymous with *IF-AND-ONLY-IF gate.* (A) (B)

IF-AND-ONLY-IF gate: synonym for *IF-AND-ONLY-IF element.* (A) (B)

IF-AND-ONLY-IF operation: synonym for *equivalence operation.* (A) (B)

IF repeater: synonymous with *heterodyne repeater.*

IF statement

(1) a conditional statement that specifies a condition to be tested and the action to be taken if the condition is satisfied. (E)

(2) a statement used for conditional statement execution. IF is always followed by a THEN clause and, optionally, an ELSE clause.

IF-THEN element: a logic element that performs the boolean operation of implication. synonymous with *IF-THEN gate.* (A) (B)

IF-THEN-ELSE: a program statement used in high-level languages. Should a certain logical assertion be true, the statement following the THEN is executed. If the assertion is not true, the statement following the ELSE is executed.

IF-THEN gate: synonym for *IF-THEN element*. (A) (B)

IF-THEN operation: synonym for *implication*. (A) (B)

ignore: provides the ability to ignore certain abnormal conditions which may arise. synonymous with *ignore character*. see *cancel character*.

ignore character: synonym for *cancel character*. (A) (B)

illegal character: a character or combination of bits that is not valid according to some criteria; for example, with respect to a specified alphabet, a character that is not a member. cf. *forbidden combination*. (*A*)

illegal operation: a process resulting when a computer either cannot perform the instruction part or will perform with invalid and undesired results. The limitation is usually a function of built-in constraints of the computer.

IM

(1) see *integrated modem*.

(2) see *interrupt mask*.

image

(1) a fully processed unit of operational data that is ready to be transmitted to a remote unit; when loaded into control storage in the remote unit the image determines the operations of the unit.

(2) a faithful likeness of the subject matter of the original.

(3) see *card image, cine-oriented image, comic-strip-oriented image, core image, display image, load image*.

image antenna: a hypothetical mirror-image antenna located as far below ground as the actual antenna is above ground.

image area

(1) in micrographics, that part of the film frame reserved for an image. (A)

(2) in word processing, the area of a display device where characters can be displayed. (D)

image dissector: in optical character recognition, a mechanical or electronic transducer that sequentially detects the level of light intensity in different areas of a completely illuminated sample space. (A)

image graphics: in computer graphics, a technique for displaying images without the use of coordinate data, for example, form flash. synonymous with *noncoded graphics*. (E)

image printer: a printer using optical technology to compose an image of a complete page from digital input.

image processing: processing of images using computer techniques.

image sensor: synonymous with *charge couple device*.

image space: see *display space, image storage space*.

image storage space: in computer graphics, the storage locations occupied by a coded image. synonymous with *coded image space*. (E)

immediate access: the ability of a computer to enter and retrieve data from memory without delay.

immediate-access storage: a storage device whose access time is negligible in comparison with other operating times. (A)

immediate address: the contents of an address part that contains the value of an operand rather than an address. synonymous with *zero-level address*. (*A*) (*B*)

immediate addressing: a method of addressing in which the address part of an instruction contains an immediate address. (A) (B)

immediate data

(1) data contained in an instruction rather than in a separate storage location.

(2) data transferred during instruction execution time.

immediate instruction: an instruction that contains within itself an operand for the operation specified, rather than an address of the operand. (A) (B)

immediate processing: synonymous with *demand processing.*

immediate task: a task assigned the second highest-level dispatching priority by the network control program. It initiates I/O operations on lines that are in an idle state. see also *appendate task, nonproductive task, productive task.*

impact paper: a coated paper that may be used to get one or more copies of printed, typed, or handwritten information without the need for a ribbon or other inking device. Each sheet is coated on the front. Pressure on the top of the top sheet causes the character to appear on the front of that sheet and on the front of subsequent sheets underneath the top sheet, thus eliminating the need for carbon paper between sheets.

impact printer (IP): a printer in which printing is the result of mechanical impacts. (A) (B)

impedance: the combined effect of resistance, inductance, and capacitance on a signal at a particular frequency.

imperative macroinstruction: macroinstructions that are converted into object program instructions.

imperative operation: an instruction requiring the manipulating of data by the computer.

imperative statement: a statement that specifies an action to be taken unconditionally. (E) synonym for *instruction.* (B)

implication: the dyadic boolean operation, the result of which has the boolean value 0, if and only if the first operand has the boolean value 0 and the second has the boolean value 1. synonymous with *conditional implication operation, IF-THEN operation.* (A) (B)

implicit address: in assembler programming, an address reference that is specified as one absolute or relocatable expression. An implicit address must be converted into its explicit base-displacement form before it can be assembled into the object code of a machine instruction.

implicit declaration: in PL/1, the establishment of an identifier, which has no explicit or contextual declaration, as a name. A default set of attributes is assumed for the identifier.

implicit opening: in PL/1, the opening of a file as the result of an input or output statement other than the OPEN statement.

implied addressing: a method of addressing in which the operation part of an instruction implicitly addresses operands. (A) (B)

implied DO: in FORTRAN, the use of an indexing specification similar to a DO statement but without specifying the word *DO* and with a list of data elements, rather than a set of statements, as its range.

imprinter: any device used to produce or impress marks or patterns on a surface, for example, printing presses, typewriters, pens, cash registers, bookkeeping machines, and pressure devices such as those used with credit cards and address plates. (A)

imprinting

(1) the act of using an imprinter.

(2) the output of any imprinter. (A)

imprint position: the position on paper where a character is to be typed. (D)

improved mobile telephone service (MTS): mobile telephone service on a completely dial basis. Mobile units can dial into the public telephone network and can be reached from the network without operator assistance. This is in contrast with original mobile service which was on an operator-handled basis for both incoming and outgoing traffic. cf. *high-capacity mobile telecommunications service.* (F)

impulse: synonym for *pulse.* (A)

impulse noise: short bursts of high-level noise such as that resulting from the coupling of transients into a channel. Typical sources of such noises are lightning and transients from switching systems. Impulse noise, which sounds like a click, is not particularly detrimental to voice communications, but it can be detrimental to data communications. Some of the older switching systems, such as the panel type, create so much impulse noise that DATAPHONE service is not handled by central offices of this type. (F)

IMTS: see *improved mobile telephone service.*

IN: see *input.*

inactive: not operational.

inactive line: a telecommunication line that is not currently available for transmitting data. cf. *active line.* synonymous with *idle line.*

inactive link: a link that is not currently available for transmitting data. cf. *active link.* synonymous with *idle link.*

inactive node: in a network, a node that is neither connected to nor available for connection to another node.

inactive station: a station that is currently ineligible for entering or accepting messages. cf. *active station.*

inband signaling: signaling that uses the same path as a message and in which the signaling frequencies are in the same band used for the message. (F)

INC: see *increment.*

incidental time: synonym for *miscellaneous time.* (A) (B)

incipient failure: machine failure that is about to occur.

in-circuit emulation: a hardware/ software facility for realtime I/O debugging.

inclusion: deprecated term for *implication.* (A) (B)

inclusive-NOR operation: synonymous with *NOR operation.*

inclusive-OR element: a logic element that performs the boolean operation of disjunction. synonymous with *inclusive-OR gate.* (A) (B)

inclusive-OR gate: synonym for *inclusive-OR element.* (A) (B)

inclusive-OR operation: synonym for *disjunction.* (A) (B)

inclusive reference: a reference from a segment in main storage to an external symbol in a segment that does not cause overlay of the calling segment.

inclusive segments: segments in the same region of an overlay program that are in the same path; they can be in main storage simultaneously.

incoming message: a message transmitted from a station to the computer.

incoming trunk (ICT): a trunk coming into a central office.

inconnector: in flowcharting, a connector that indicates a continuation of a broken flow line. cf. *outconnector.* (*A*)

INCR: see *increment.*

INCRE: see *increment.*

increment (INC) (INCR) (INCRE)
(1) a value used to alter a counter or register.
(2) to move a document forward in the read station from one timing mark to the next so that a new line of characters is visible to the scan head.
(3) to move a card from column to column in the punch station so that each column presents itself for punching.
(4) to alter the value of a counter or register by a specified value.
(5) to move a hopper or stacker upward or downward.

incremental compiler: a compiler capable of compiling further statements in a program without fully recompiling the program.

incremental computer
(1) a computer that represents as absolute values the changes to variables instead of the variables themselves.
(2) a computer in which incremental representation of data is mainly used. (B)

incremental execution: execution of statements or sections of a program without submission of a complete program.

incremental integrator: a digital integrator modified so that the output signal is maximum negative, zero, or maximum positive when the value of the input is negative, zero, or positive. (A)

incremental representation: a method of representing variables in which changes in the values of the variable are represented, rather than the values themselves. (B) see *ternary incremental representation.* (*A*)

incremental vector: synonym for *relative vector.*

incrementer: a hardware component which automatically adds one.

increment size: in computer graphics, the distance between adjacent addressable points within a display space. (E)

IND: see *indicator.*

indent: in word processing, a feature that enables blocks of recorded text to be indented with different margins, while still retaining the original (fixed) margin settings. (D)

indent tab character (IT): a word-processing formatting mode control that requires a device to execute a horizontal tab function after each subsequent appearance of a carrier return character. The number of automatic horizontal tabs performed after each carrier return character is equal to the number of indent tab characters keyed since the last resetting of indent tab mode. cf. *horizontal tabulation character.*

independent telephone company: a telephone company not affiliated with the Bell System and having its own ''independent'' territory. (F)

indeterminate (X) state: the unknown

logic state of a memory element caused by critical races or oscillations, or existing after power is applied and before initialization. Some simulators can model indeterminate states and typically assign an X to show an indeterminate state.

index

(1) in programming, a subscript of integer value that identifies the position of an item of data with respect to some other item of data. (B)

(2) a list of the contents of a file or of a document, together with keys or references for locating the contents. (B)

(3) a symbol or a numeral used to identify a particular quantity in an array of similar quantities. For example, the terms of an array represented by X1, X2, ... X100 have the indexes 1, 2, . . 100, respectively. (*A*)

(4) in micrographics, a guide for locating information in microform using targets, flash cards, lines, bars, or other optical codes. (D)

(5) to prepare a list as in (2). (A)

(6) to move a machine part to a predetermined position, or by a predetermined amount, on a quantized scale. (A)

(7) a table used to locate the records of an indexed sequential data set. (A)

(8) in COBOL, a computer storage position or register, the contents of which identify a particular element in a table.

(9) in word processing, to move the paper or display pointer in the direction used during normal printout.

(10) see *code line index.* (A)

(11) deprecated term for *contents list.*

index build: the automatic process of creating an alternate index through the use of access method services.

index character (INX): a word-processing formatting control that moves the printing or display point down to the next line with no horizontal motion. synonymous with *line feed character.*

index data item: in COBOL, a data item in which the contents of an index can be stored without conversion to subscript form.

indexed address: an address that is modified by the content of an index register prior to or during the execution of a computer instruction. (A)

indexed data name: in COBOL, a data name identifier that is subscripted with one or more index names.

indexed data set: a type of data set in which records are stored and retrieved on the basis of keys that are within each record and are part of the data record itself.

indexed file: a file providing a directory-supported random-access method based on a record identifier whose size is user-specified.

indexed sequential access method: see *basic indexed sequential access method, queued indexed sequential access method.*

indexed sequential data set: a data set in which each record contains a key that determines its location. The location of each record is computed through the use of an index.

indexed sequential organization: a file organization in which records are arranged in logical sequence by key. Indexes to these keys permit direct access to individual records.

index entry: the individual line or item

of data found in an index, such as an entry in a dictionary.

index file: the table of key fields identifying the specific disk records in another permanent disk file.

index hole: a hole cut in a floppy disk showing the beginning of the first sector.

indexing

(1) a technique of address modification by means of index registers.

(2) in word processing, a feature that causes the typing position or display pointer to be moved to the corresponding character position of the following typing line. see also *reverse indexing*. (D)

index name: in COBOL, a name, given by the programmer, for an index of a specific table. An index name must contain at least one alphabetic character. It is one word (four bytes) in length.

index plan: a method used in the Bell System to calculate an index of performance. There are a number of index plans in use, each of which takes into account statistical data for a particular parameter or combination of parameters of plant performance or service. Examples are connection appraisal index plan, trunk transmission maintenance index plan, and local dial-line index plan. (F)

index register (IX)

(1) a register whose contents may be used to modify an operand address during the execution of computer instructions; it can also be used as a counter. An index register may be used to control the execution of a loop, to control the use of an array, as a switch for table lookup, or as a pointer. (E)

(2) in assembler programming, a register whose contents are added to the operand or absolute address derived from a combination of a base address with a displacement.

index return character (IRT): a word-processing multifunction control used as a formatting control and a device control. As a formatting control, it produces the same effect as a required carrier return in printed or displayed text. As a device control, it is used to delimit a line without ending recording on the current magnetic card track when recording multiple lines on the same track. cf. *required carrier return character*.

index sequential file: a file on a random access storage unit in which the address of a record on a physical file is shown on an index containing the record key.

index slot: synonymous with *polarizing slot*.

index term: used to classify a document, or item in a database.

index word: an index modifier applied to the address part of a computer instruction. (A) (B)

indicator (IND)

(1) a device that may be set into a prescribed state, usually according to the result of a previous process or on the occurrence of a specified condition in the equipment, and that usually gives a visual or other indication of the existence of the prescribed state, and that may in some cases be used to determine the selection among alternative processes, for example, an overflow indicator. (B)

(2) an item of data that may be interrogated to determine whether a particular condition has been satisfied in

the execution of a computer program, for example, a switch indicator, an overflow indicator.

(3) see *switch indicator*. (*A*)

indirect address: an address that designates the storage location of an item of data to be treated as the address of an operand, but not necessarily as its direct address. synonymous with *multilevel address*. (B) cf. *direct address*. (*A*) see also *level of addressing*.

indirect addressing: a method of addressing in which the address part of an instruction contains an indirect address. (A)

indirect instruction: an instruction that contains the indirect address of an operand for the operation specified. (B) cf. *direct instruction*. (*A*)

individual line service: the provision of a nonshared access line to the central office as part of either business or residence telephone service. (F)

induction: see *mathematical induction*. (A)

induction coil: an apparatus for transforming a direct current by induction into an alternating current.

inductor: a commonly used component which transfers the flow of alternating current from one part of the circuit to another.

industrial data processing: data processing for industrial purposes.

inequivalence: synonymous with *Exclusive-OR*.

inference engine: an artificial intelligence computer developed by Herbert A. Simon that derived natural laws from physical data.

inferior: synonym for *subscript*.

infinite pad method: in optical char-

acter recognition, a method of measuring reflectance of a paper stock such that doubling the number of backing sheets of the same stock does not change the measured reflectance. (A)

infinity: any number larger than the maximum number that a given computer is able to store in the register.

infix notation: a method of forming mathematical expressions, governed by rules of operator precedence and using parentheses, in which the operators are dispersed among the operands, each operator indicating the operation to be performed on the operands or the intermediate results adjacent to it. If it is desired to distinguish the case in which there are more than two operands for an operation, the term *distributed infix notation* may be used. (B) cf. *parentheses-free notation, postfix notation, prefix notation*. (*A*)

infix operator: an operator that appears between two operands.

INFO: see *information*.

informatics: see *information science*.

information (I) (INFO): the meaning that a human being assigns to data by means of the conventions applied to that data. (E)

informational message: a message that is not the result of an error condition, for example, a message that gives the status of a job or operation.

information-bearer channel: a channel provided for data transmission that is capable of carrying all the necessary information to permit communication including such information as users' data synchronizing sequences and control signals. It may therefore operate at a greater signaling rate than that required solely for the users' data. (C)

information bits: in data communication, those bits that are generated by the data source and that are not used for error control by the data-transmission system. (A)

information channel: see *communication channel, data channel, information-bearer channel.*

information content: in information theory, a measure of information conveyed by the occurrence of an event of definite probability. (B) see *conditional information content, joint information content.* (A)

information content binary unit: synonym for *Shannon.* (A) (B)

information content decimal unit: synonym for *Hartley.* (A) (B)

information content natural unit (NAT): in information theory, a unit of logarithmic measures of information expressed by the neperian logarithm; for example, the decision content of a character set of eight characters equals 2.079 natural units of information. (A) (B)

information costs: costs, including time, expended in securing data.

information feedback: data from a terminal retransmitted to the sending terminal for checking.

information feedback system: a data transmission system that uses an echo check to verify the accuracy of the transmission. (A)

information flow analysis: organizing and analyzing approaches to gather facts and information about an organization, initialization, and flow to final user of reports throughout an organization.

information function: a mathematical function that describes a source of information.

information input: data fed into a computer.

information interchange: the process of sending and receiving data in such a manner that the information content or meaning assigned to the data is not altered during the transmission. (A)

information measure: in information theory, a suitable function of the frequency of occurrence of a specified event from a set of possible events conventionally taken as a measure of the relative value of the intelligence conveyed by this occurrence. In information theory, the term *event* is to be understood as used in the theory of probability. For instance, the presence of a given element of a set, the occurrence of a specified character or of a specified word in a message. (A) (B)

information processing: synonym for *data processing.* (A) (B)

information rate: see *average information rate.* (A)

information retrieval (IR): actions, methods, and procedures for recovering stored data to provide information on a given subject. (E)

information retrieval system: a computing system application designed to recover specific information from a mass of data.

information science: the study of how data are processed and transmitted through digital-processing equipment. synonymous with *informatics.*

information security: the protection of information against unauthorized disclosure, transfer, modifications, or destruction, whether accidental or intentional. (C)

information separator (IS): any control character used to delimit like units of data in a hierarchic arrangement of data. The name of the separator does not necessarily indicate the units of data that it separates. synonymous with *separating character.* (*A*) (B)

information sink: see *data sink.*

information source: synonym for *message source.* (B) see *data source.*

information system (IS): the network of all communication approaches used within an organization.

information technology: the acquisition, processing, storage and dissemination of various types of information via computers and telecommunications.

information theory: the branch of learning concerned with the study of measures of information and their properties. (A) (B)

information transfer module: a unit permitting intercommunication between telephone, telex and data terminals.

information word: an ordered set of characters bearing at least one meaning and handled by the computer as a unit, including separating and spacing.

infrared: invisible radiation having a wavelength longer than 700mm. see also *ultraviolet.* (D)

inherent transparency: data transmission in which there is no need for special control characters.

inherited error: an error carried forward from a previous step in a sequential process.

inhibited

(1)   pertaining to a state of a proc-

essing unit in which certain types of interruptions are not allowed to occur.

(2)   pertaining to the state in which a transmission control unit or an audio response unit cannot accept incoming calls on a line.

inhibiting input: a gate input that if in its prescribed state prevents any output that might otherwise occur.

inhibiting signal: a signal that prevents the occurrence of an event. (A)

inhibit pulse: a pulse applied to a magnetic cell to inhibit a drive impulse from reversing the flux of that cell.

in-house line: a privately owned, or sometimes leased, line connected to a public network.

in-house system: synonym for *in-plant system.*

INIT: see *initialize.*

initial address: the address assigned to the initial location of a program. synonymous with *program origin.*

initial chaining value (ICV): an eight-byte pseudorandom number used to verify that both ends of a session with cryptography have the same session cryptography key. The initial chaining value is also used as input to the Data Encryption Standard (DES) algorithm to encipher or decipher data in a session with cryptography. synonymous with *session seed.*

initial condition mode: an operating mode of an analog computer during which the integrators are inoperative, and the initial conditions are set. synonymous with *reset mode.* (B)

initial error: an error represented by the difference between the actual value of a data unit and the value used at the beginning of processing.

initial instructions: a routine in memory whose purpose is to aid loading. synonymous with *initial orders*.

initialization: the process carried out at the commencement of a program to test that all indicators and constants are set to prescribed conditions. see also *initial program load.* see *loop initialization.* (A)

initialize (INIT): to set counters, switches, addresses, or contents of storage to zero or other starting values at the beginning of, or at prescribed points in, the operation of a computer routine. cf. *prestore.* (A) see also *initial program load.*

initializer routine: functions such as error checking performed on a message following entry into the system, but prior to the application program beginning its processing.

initial orders: synonymous with *initial instructions.*

initial procedure: an external procedure that is the first procedure invoked in the execution of a PL/1 program.

initial program load (IPL)

(1) the initialization procedure that causes an operating system to commence operation.

(2) the process by which a configuration image is loaded into storage at the beginning of a work day or after a system malfunction.

initial program loader (IPL): the utility routine that loads the initial part of a computer program, such as an operating system or other computer program, so that the computer program can then proceed under its own control. (B) cf. *bootstrap, bootstrap loader.* (A)

initiating task: the job management

task that controls the selection of a job and the preparation of the steps of that job for execution.

initiator procedure: the cataloged procedure that controls an initiator.

initiator/terminator: the job scheduler function that selects jobs and job steps to be executed, allocates input-output devices for them, places them under task control, and at completion of the job, supplies control information for writing job output on a system output unit.

inking: in computer graphics, creating a line by moving a pointer over the display space leaving a trail behind the pointer in the manner of a pen drawing a line on paper. (E)

ink jet printer

(1) a printing mechanism that produces characters by deflecting drops of ink. (E)

(2) a nonimpact printer that forms characters by the projection of a jet of ink onto paper.

ink uniformity: the degree of light intensity variation over the area of printed characters, specifically within the character edges.

inline code: in a program, instructions that are executed sequentially, without branching to routines, subroutines, or other programs.

in-line procedure: in COBOL, the set of statements that constitutes the main or controlling flow of the computer program and which excludes statements executed under control of the asynchronous control system.

in-line processing: the processing of data in random order, not subject to preliminary editing or sorting.

in-line recovery: error recovery in

which an affected process is resumed from a point preceding the occurrence of the error. (E)

in-line subroutine: a subroutine placed directly into a program and which has to be recopied each time it is needed.

inner macroinstruction: a macroinstruction that is nested inside a macrodefinition. cf. *outer macroinstruction.*

inoperable time: the time during which a functional unit would not yield correct results if it were operated. It is assumed that all environmental conditions for proper operation are met. (A) (B)

INP: see *input.*

in-plant system: a system whose parts, including terminals, are situated at one location. synonymous with *in-house system.*

input (I) (IN) (INP) (I/P)

(1) one, or a sequence of, input states.

(2) pertaining to a device process, or channel involved in an input process, or to the data or states involved in an input process. In the English language, the adjective *input* may be used in place of such terms as *input data, input signal*, and *input terminal*, when such usage is clear in a given context.

(3) synonymous with *input data, input process. (A)*

(4) see also *input channel, input unit.*

(5) see *manual input, real-time input.* (A)

(6) cf. *output.*

input area: synonym for *input block.*

input block: a block of data received as input. synonym for *input area.*

(*A*)

input blocking factor (Bi): in a tape sort, the number of data records in each record of the input file.

input bound: a system where speed of performance is limited by the capability of the input system.

input buffer register: a device that accepts data from input units or media such as magnetic tape or disks and which then transfers this data to internal storage.

input channel: a channel for impressing a state on a device or logic element. synonymous with *input (1). (A)*

input data

(1) data being received or to be received into a device or into a computer program. synonymous with *input (2).* (B)

(2) data to be processed. synonymous with *input (1). (A)*

input data validation: an input control technique used to detect input data that are inaccurate, incomplete, or unreasonable. (E)

input device: synonym for *input unit.* (A) (B)

input field: in computer graphics, an unprotected field on a display surface in which data can be entered, modified, or erased.

input instruction code: an instruction set forming part of an automatic language, usually mnemonic, with operations coded to have some appearance of the actual operation. A type of pseudocode.

input job stream: synonym for *input stream.*

input limited: descriptive of a program where the overall processing time is limited by the speed of an input unit, delaying processing awaiting the input of additional items.

input line: see *line (1), (2).*

input loading: the amount of load imposed upon the sources supplying signals to the input.

input-output (I/O)

(1) pertaining to a device or to a channel that may be involved in an input process, and, at a different time, in an output process. In the English language, *input-output* may be used in place of such terms as *input-output data, input-output signal,* and *input-output terminals,* when such usage is clear in a given context.

(2) pertaining to a device whose parts can be performing an input process and an output process at the same time.

(3) pertaining to either input or output or both. see listings under *I/O.*

(4) synonym for *radial transfer.* (A) (B)

(5) the information entering or leaving a system across a system boundary (alternatively, information entering or leaving a subsystem within the system boundary). (F)

(6) the process of transmitting information from an external source to a system or from a system to an external destination. (F)

input-output board: on some units, a type of board permitting the computer to be expanded via the back-plane bus to permit further input-output interface channels.

input-output buffer (IOB): part of memory where data is set on its way to or from a peripheral unit. When a buffer area is used, a number of peripheral units can be operated while the central processor is processing additional data.

input-output channel (IOC): in a data-processing system, a functional unit, controlled by the processing unit, that handles the transfer of data between main storage and peripheral equipment. (B)

input-output controller (IOC): a functional unit in an automatic data-processing system that controls one or more units of peripheral equipment. synonymous with *I/O controller, peripheral control unit.* (A) (B)

input-output control system (IOCS): the software and hardware handling transfer of data between a main storage and external storage units.

input-output cycle: a cycle on some system, consisting of inputting (reading data) from or outputting (writing data) into a specified memory location. Timing is for memory-access, read-data, and write-data operations.

input-output device (IOD): synonym for *input-output unit.* (A) (B)

input-output interruption: see *I/O interruption.*

input-output library: standard routines or programs created to control the operation of peripheral devices.

input-output limited: pertaining to a system or condition where the time for input and output activities exceeds other operations.

input-output processor: a device that handles normal data input-output control and sequencing.

input-output referencing: the allocation of symbolic names within a program to identify input or output devices, in order that the actual device allocated to the program can be identified at run time.

input-output register (IOR): a register that receives data from input devices and from which data can be transferred to the main memory, arithmetic, or control device; and accepts data from these internal devices to be transferred to output units.

input-output routines: standard routines created to simplify the programming of daily operations using input-output devices.

input-output section: in the environment division of a COBOL program, the section that names the files and external media needed by an object program. It also provides information required for the transmission and handling of data during the execution of an object program.

input-output statement: any statement that transfers data between main storage and input-output devices.

input-output switching: the allocation of more than one channel for communication between peripheral devices and a central processing unit, permitting connection through any available channel.

input-output unit (IOU): a device in a data processing system by which data may be entered into the system, received from the system, or both. synonymous with *input-output device.* (*A*) (B)

input primitive: in computer graphics, a basic data item from an input device such as a keyboard, locator device, pick device, or valuator device.

input process
(1) the process of transmitting data from peripheral equipment, or external storage to internal storage.
(2) the process of receiving data by a device. (*A*)
(3) the process that consists of the reception of data into a data-processing system or into any part of it. (E) synonymous with *input.* (B)
(4) the entry of information by an end-user into a data-processing system, including the conversion of information from a human language into a language that the system can understand.
(5) see also *output process.*

input program: a utility program that organizes the input process of a computer.

input reader: synonymous with *input routine.* see *reader.* (A) (B)

input reference: a reference designed and used to compare the measured variable resulting in a deviation or error signal. synonymous with *desired value* and *set point.*

input routine: synonymous with *input section.*

input section: the physical area of a store responsible for the reception of input data. synonymous with *input routine.*

input state: the state occurring on a specified input channel. (A)

input station: see *data input station.* (A)

input storage: synonymous with *input block.*

input stream: the sequence of job control statements and data submitted to an operating system on an input unit especially activated for this purpose by the operator. synonymous with *input job strea, job input stream.*

input translator: a portion of some computer programs that converts the incoming programmer's instructions into operators and operands understood by the computer.

input unit (IU): a device in a data-processing system by which data can be entered into the system. synonymous with *input (2), input device.* (*A*) (B)

input validation: see *input data validation.*

inquiry: a request for information from storage; for example, a request for the number of available airline seats, or a machine statement to initiate a search of library documents.

inquiry and transaction processing: a type of application in which inquiries and records of transactions received from a number of terminals are used to interrogate or update one or more master files.

inquiry character: a transmission control character used to request a response from a connected station.

inquiry display terminal: synonymous with *terminal.*

inquiry/reply: an application in which a device message handler receives a message from a station and then routes it to an application program that processes the data in the message and generates a reply; the reply is routed by the device message handler to the inquiry station.

inquiry/response operation: in a network, an operation in which a terminal operator enters a request for information and the information is sent back and displayed at the terminal.

inquiry station
  (1) a user terminal primarily for the interrogation of an automatic data-processing system. (A) (B)
  (2) data terminal equipment used for inquiry into a data-processing system.

inquiry transaction: a transaction that does not update a data base.

inquiry unit: synonymous with *inquiry station.*

inscribe: preparing a document to be read by optical character recognition.

insert: in word processing, a machine function that allows for the introduction of new characters or text within previously recorded text. (D)

insertion loss: the insertion loss of a transmission system (or component of the system) inserted between two impedances, Z_T (transmitter) and Z_R (receiver), it is the ratio of the n power measured at the receiver before the insertion of the transmission system to the power measured after insertion. Insertion loss is normally expressed in decibels (dB). (F)

insertion picture character: in PL/1, a picture specification character that is inserted in the indicated position, on assignment of the associated data to a character string. When used in a P format item for input, an insertion character serves as a checking picture character.

insertion sort: a sort in which each item in a set is inserted into its proper position in the sorted set according to the specified criteria. (A)

insert switch: a manually operated switch used to insert data or instructions.

inside plant: with respect to cable and wire, all fixed ground cable plant extending inward from the main distribution frame, for example, central office equipment, teletypewriters, and so on, including the protectors and associated hardware on the telephone central office main distribution frame.

INST: see *instruction*.

installation: a particular computing system, in terms of the work it does and the people who manage it, operate it, apply it to problems, service it, and use the results it produces.

installation charge: a one-time charge, due upon installation of customer-premises equipment, that is used to help recover the actual expenditures. (F)

installation processing control: the scheduling of applications and jobs utilizing an automated setup.

installation tape number: the reference number given in an installation to a reel of magnetic tape to identify it. It differs from the number supplied by the reel manufacturer.

installation time: time spent in installing and testing hardware or software. (A)

INSTR: see *instruction*.

in-stream procedure: a set of job control statements placed in the input stream that can be used any number of times during a job by naming the procedure in an execute (EXEC) statement.

instruction (I) (INST) (INSTR): in a programming language, a meaningful expression that specifies one operation and identifies its operands, if any. (A) (B) see *absolute instruction, arithmetic instruction, branch instruction, computer instruction, conditional jump instruction, direct instruction, discrimination instruction, dummy instruction, effective instruction, extract instruction, immediate instruction, indirect instruc-*

tion, jump instruction, logic instruction, macroinstruction, multiaddress instruction, n-address instruction, no-operation instruction, n-plus-one address instruction, one-address instruction, one-plus-one address instruction, optional-pause instruction, pause instruction, presumptive instruction, privileged instruction, repetition instruction, restart instruction, stop instruction, three-address instruction, three-plus-one address instruction, two-address instruction, two-plus-one address instruction, unconditional-jump instruction, zero-address instruction.

instruction address (IA)

(1)   the address of an instruction word. (B)

(2)   the address that must be used to fetch an instruction.

(3)   cf. *address part.* (A)

instruction address register (IAR): a register from whose contents the address of the next instruction is derived. An instruction address register may also be a portion of a storage device specifically designated for the derivation of the address of the next instruction by a translator, compiler, interpreter, language processor, operating system, and so on. synonymous with *control counter, sequence control register.* (A) (B)

instruction address stop: an instruction address that, when fetched, causes execution to stop.

instruction area: the area of memory where instructions are retained. synonymous with *instruction storage.*

instruction code: synonym for *computer instruction code.*

instruction constant: a constant written in the form of an instruction; any instruction which is not intended to be executed as an instruction.

instruction control unit (ICU): in a processing unit, the part that receives instructions in proper sequence, interprets each instruction, and applies the proper signals to the arithmetic and logic unit and other parts in accordance with this interpretation. (A) (B)

instruction counter (IC): a counter that indicates the location of the next computer instruction to be interpreted. (A)

instruction deck: synonymous with *instruction pack.*

instruction decoder: that portion of the CPU that interprets the program instructions in binary into the needed control signals for the ALU, registers, and control bus.

instruction format: the layout of an instruction showing its constituent parts. (A) (B)

instruction mix: computer instructions chosen to complete a specific problem. The optimum mix of instructions determines the speed and accuracy, and programmers attempt to achieve an optimum program or mix.

instruction modifier: a word or part of a word that is used to alter an instruction. (A) (B)

instruction pack: a pack of punched cards maintaining instruction for a program or suite. synonymous with *instruction deck.*

instruction register (IR): a register that is used to hold an instruction for interpretation. (A) (B)

instruction repertoire

(1) a complete set of the operators of the statements of computer pro-

gramming language, together with a description of the types and meanings that can be attributed to their operands.

(2) loosely, an instruction set. (*A*)

instruction set: the set of the instructions of a computer, of a programming language, or of the programming languages in a programming system. (A) (B)

instruction statement: see *instruction.*

instruction storage: synonymous with *instruction area.*

instruction time (I-time): the time during which an instruction is fetched from the main storage of a computer into an instruction register. see also *execution time.*

instruction word: a word that represents an instruction. (A) (B)

instrument: in telecommunications, any device used to originate and receive signals, for example, computer terminals, telephone handsets.

INT

(1) see *integer.*

(2) see *interrupt.*

integer (INT)

(1) one of the numbers zero, $+1$, -1, $+2$, -2, . . . synonymous with *integral number.* (A) (B)

(2) in COBOL, a numeric data item or literal that does not include any character positions to the right of the decimal point, actual or assumed. Where the term *integer* appears in formats, *integer* must not be a numeric data item.

integer constant: a string of decimal digits containing no decimal point.

integer programming: in operations research, a class of procedures for locating the maximum or minimum of a function subject constraints, where some or all variables must have integer values. synonymous with *discrete programming*. (B) cf. *convex programming, dynamic programming, linear programming, mathematical programming, nonlinear programming, quadratic programming*. (A)

integer variables: in FORTRAN, an integer variable consisting of a series of not more than six alphameric characters (except special characters), of which the first is I, J, K, L, M, or N.

integral boundary: a location in main storage at which a fixed-length field, such as a half-word or double-word, must be positioned. The address of an integral boundary is a multiple of the length of the field, in bytes. see also *boundary alignment*.

integral number: synonym for *integer*. (A) (B)

integrated adapter: an integral part of a processing unit that provides for the direct connection of a particular type of device and uses neither a control unit nor the standard I/O interface. see also *integrated communication adapter, integrated file adapter*.

integrated attachment: an attachment that is an integral part of the basic hardware.

integrated circuit (IC): a combination of interconnected circuit elements inseparably associated on or within a continuous substrate. see *hybrid integrated circuit, monolithic integrated circuit*.

integrated communication adapter: an integrated adapter that allows connection of multiple telecommunication lines to a processing unit.

integrated data base (IDB): a data base which has been consolidated to eliminate redundant data.

integrated data processing (IDP): data processing in which the coordination of data acquisition and other stages of data processing are combined in a coherent data-processing system. (A) (B)

integrated digital network: a network in which connections established by digital switching circuits are used for the transmission of digital signals.

integrated disk: in the programmable store system, an integral part of the store controller that is used for magnetically storing files, application programs, controller storage contents, and diagnostics.

integrated emulator: an emulator program whose execution is controlled by an operating system in a multiprogramming environment. cf. *stand-alone emulator*.

integrated file adapter: an integrated adapter that allows connection of multiple disk storage devices to a processing unit.

integrated modem: a modem that is an integral part of the device with which it operates. cf. *stand-alone modem*.

integrated software: computer software permitting the user to easily switch between various applications, such as moving from calculating to drawing the results in a graph.

integrated system: the combination of processes that results in the introduction of data that need not be repeated as further allied or related data is also entered.

integrated word-processing equipment: word-processing equipment that has its associated control unit contained within the body of the machine. (D)

integrating motor: a motor designed to give a constant ratio of output shaft rotational speed to input signal. The angle of rotation of the shaft with respect to a datum is proportional to the time integral of the applied signal. (A)

integration: the sharing of commands and the flow of information from one program to another; a major goal of the software industry in the 1980s.

integrator
(1) a device whose output variable is the integral of the input variable with respect to time. (B)
(2) a device whose output function is proportional to the integral of the input function with respect to a specified variable, for example, a watt-hour meter.
(3) see *incremental integrator.* (*A*)

integrity: see *data integrity.*

intelligence: processing capability as found in an intelligent terminal. cf. *artificial intelligence.*

intelligent controller: a unit controlled with local capabilities, such as editing, input validity checking, and complex command decoding.

intelligent copier: a copying unit that uses a microprocessor to control its operations. Such a copier can accept digital information as an input, and use it to yield hard copy.

intelligent terminal: deprecated term for *programmable terminal.* see also *distributed function.*

intelligible cross talk: cross talk sufficiently understandable under prevailing circuit and room noise conditions so that meaningful information can be obtained. (F)

INTELSAT: see *International Telecommunications Satellite Consortium.*

INTEN: see *intensity.*

intensify: to increase the level of brightness of all or part of a display image.

intensity (INTEN): in computer graphics, the amount of light emitted at a display point.

interaction: a basic unit used to record system activity, consisting of the acceptance of a line of terminal input, processing of the line, and a response, if any. see also *interaction time.*

interaction time: in systems with time sharing, the time between acceptance by the system of a line of input from a terminal and the point at which it can accept the next line from the terminal. cf. *response time.*

interactive: pertaining to an application in which each entry calls forth a response from a system or program, as in an inquiry system or an airline reservation system. An interactive system may also be conversational, implying a continuous dialog between the user and the system. see also *inquiry/response operation.*

interactive graphics: computer graphics in which a display device is used in the conversational mode. cf. *passive graphics.* (E)

interactive-keyboard printer: in word processing, a printer that is used in conjunction with a keyboard to print each character as it is keyed. (D)

interactive mode: synonymous with *conversational mode.*

interactive routine: a programming routine where a series of operations is repeatedly performed, until an earlier specified end-condition is reached.

interactive system: a computer system where the user communicates directly and rapidly with the central processor through a terminal.

interblock gap (IBG)

(1)   an area on a data medium to indicate the end of a block or physical record. (A)

(2)   the space between two consecutive blocks on a data medium. (E)

(3)   synonymous with *block gap.*

intercepted terminal: a terminal that cannot accept messages.

intercepting: the routing of a call or message that is placed for a disconnected or nonexistent telephone number or terminal address to an operator position or to a specially designated terminal. see *intercept operator.*

intercepting trunk: a trunk to which a call for a vacant number or changed number or a line out of order is connected for action by an operator.

intercept operator

(1)   in intercepting, the operator who requests the number called, determines the reason for the intercept, and relays the information to the calling party.

(2)   a person who provides intercept service at an intercept position of a switchboard or at an auxiliary services position of a centralized intercept bureau. (F)

intercept service: a service in which a telephone call directed to an improper telephone number is redirected to an operator or to a recording. The caller is informed why the call could not be completed and, if possible, is given the correct number. (F)

intercommunicating system: a privately owned system without a switchboard, capable of two-way communication, normally limited to a single unit, building, or plant. Stations may or may not be equipped for originating a call, but they can answer any call.

intercom service: an optional service with key telephone equipment that provides intercommunications among stations in a key telephone system over facilities distinct from CO facilities. Calls are made using an abbreviated dialing plan. (F)

interconnecting unit: an interface device on the telephone company side of the interface used for connecting arrangement service. In addition to providing appropriate interfacing functions, the interconnecting unit serves as a protection device. (F)

intercycle: the step in the sequence of steps made by the main shaft of a punched card device. At this time, the card feed is stopped, usually because of a control change.

interexchange channel (IXC):   a channel connecting two different exchange areas.

interface (I/F)

(1)   a shared boundary. An interface might be a hardware component to link two devices or it might be a portion of storage or registers accessed by two or more computer programs. (A) see *physical interface, transmission interface.*

(2)   a common boundary between two systems or pieces of equipment where they are joined. (F)

interface processor (IP):   a processor that acts as the interface between another processor or terminal and a network, or a processor that controls data flow in a network. (E)

interface routines: linking routines between two systems.

interface specification: a set of technical requirements that must be met at an interface. (F)

interference: the result of unwanted signals in a communications circuit.

interfix: an approach used in information retrieval systems to describe unambiguously the relation between the keywords in different records to ensure that words which seem related but are not in fact relevant are not retrieved.

interior label: a label placed at the beginning of a magnetic tape to show its contents. cf. *exterior label.*

interlanguage: the modification of common language, suitable for automatic translation by the unit into machine or computer usable language.

interleave: to arrange parts of one sequence of things or events so that they alternate with parts of one or more other sequences of the same nature and so that each sequence retains its identity. (E)

interleaved array: in PL/1, an array whose name refers to a nonconnected storage.

interleaved subscripts: a subscript notation, used with subscripted qualified names, in which not all of the necessary subscripts immediately follow the same component name.

interleaving

(1) the act of accessing two or more bytes or streams of data from distinct storage units simultaneously.

(2) the alternating of two or more operations or functions through the overlapped use of a computer facility.

interlock: to prevent a machine or device from initiating further operations until the operation in process is completed. see also *deadlock.*

interlude: a small routine that carries out minor preliminary operations prior to entry of the main routine; for example, the interlude may calculate the values of certain parameters.

intermediate buffer: in word processing, a buffer that saves the original text until a command is made to the system to implement any changes.

intermediate distributing frame (IDF): in a local central office, a distributing frame, that cross-connects subscriber lines to the subscriber line circuit. (In a private branch exchange, its purpose is similar.)

intermediate equipment: auxiliary equipment that may be inserted between the data terminal equipment (DTE) and the signal conversion equipment to perform certain additional functions before modulation or after demodulation. (E)

intermediate frequency (IF): a frequency in a superheterodyne receiver or transmitter system which enables easier filtering, distribution, modulation, and demodulation of a signal.

intermediate node: a node that is not an end-point node.(E)

intermediate pass (sorting): that portion of a merging operation that, because of the number of strings or otherwise, does not reduce the file to a single sequenced string.

intermediate total: in telegraph usage, the result when a summation is terminated by a change of group that is neither the most nor the least significant.

intermessage delay: the elapsed time between the receipt at a terminal of a system response, and the time that a new transaction is entered. synonymous with *think time*.

intermittent error: a sporadic error that tends to occur prior to and following any attempt to establish its presence and cause.

intermix tape: on some computers, a feature permitting for combinations of different models of tape units to be interconnected to a single computer.

internal block: a block that is contained in another block.

internal format: the structure shown by data and instructions when they have been read into the central processor or backing store.

internal fragmentation: disturbance of main memory when data is required to fit into a smaller area than is available.

internal interrupt: utilizing an external unit to cause equipment to stop in the normal course of the program and perform a designated subroutine.

internal label: a machine-readable label, recorded on a data medium, that provides information about a set of data recorded on the medium. cf. *external label*. (E)

internal memory: the internal parts of an automatic data-processing machine able to hold data.

internal model: a collection of entities that represent the conceptual model and the external model of a data base that may be stored in a data-processing system. (E)

internal name: in PL/1, a name that is not known outside the block in which it is declared.

internal procedure: a procedure that is contained within a block.

internal reader: a facility that transfers jobs to the job entry subsystem.

internal sort

(1) a sort performed within internal storage.

(2) a sort program or a sort phase that sorts two or more items within main storage. (*A*)

(3) a sorting technique that creates sequences of records or keys. Usually, it is a prelude to a merge phase in which the sequences created are reduced to one by an external merge.

internal storage: storage that is accessible by a computer without the use of input-output channels. (E) deprecated term for *main storage*. synonym for *processor storage*.

internal text: in PL/1, all of the text contained in a block except that text that is contained in another block. Thus the text of an internal block (except its entry names) is not internal to the containing block.

internal timer: an internal clock equipped with multiple registers to monitor the length of external events, or generate a pulse following a fixed time.

internal writer: a facility in the job entry subsystem that allows user written output writers to write data on devices not directly supported by the job control manager.

International Algebraic Language (IAL): an early form of the language that was to evolve as ALGOL.

international direct distance dialing (IDDD): the automatic establishment of international calls by signals from the calling device of either a customer or an operator. (F)

International Organization for Standardization (ISO): an organization established to promote the development of standards to facilitate the international exchange of goods and services, and to develop mutual cooperation in areas of intellectual, scientific, technological, and economic activity.

International Record Carrier (IRC): carrier providing overseas/international telecommunications services, other than voice communications (e.g., teletypewriter, facsimile, and data). (G)

International Telecommunications Satellite Consortium (INTELSAT): an international organization established in 1964 to govern a global commercial communications satellite system to provide communications between many countries. Membership is in excess of 80 countries. The Communications Satellite Corporation (COMSAT) acts as manager for INTELSAT and also represents the United States. (F)

International Telecommunications Union (ITU): the specialized telecommunication agency of the United Nations, established to provide standardized communication procedures and practices, including frequency allocation and radio regulations on a worldwide basis.

interoffice trunk: a direct trunk between local central offices in the same exchange.

INTERP: see *interpreter*.

interpositioning: an equipment configuration in which Bell terminal equipment accesses Bell facilities through customer-provided terminal equipment. (G)

interposition trunk

(1) a connection between two positions of a large switchboard so that a line on one position can be connected to a line on another position.

(2) connections terminated at test positions for testing and patching between testboards and patch bays within a technical control facility.

interpret: to translate and to execute each source language statement of a computer program before translating and executing the next statement. (A) (B)

interpreter (INTERP)

(1) a computer program used to interpret. synonymous with *interpretive program*. (A) (B)

(2) in punched card operations, a device that prints on a punched card the characters corresponding to hole patterns punched in the card. (B)

interpreter code: an interim, arbitrarily designed code that must be translated to computer coding to function as designed, usually for diagnostic or checking needs.

interpreting

(1) translating and executing each source language statement of a computer program before translating and executing the next statement.

(2) printing on paper tape or cards the meaning of the holes punched on the same tape or cards. (A)

interpretive code: the instruction repertoire for the source language input to an *interpreter (1)*. (A)

interpretive execution: permits retention of all information contained in the user's original source statements.

interpretive program: synonym for *interpreter (1)*. (A) (B)

interpretive routine: a routine that decodes instructions written as pseudocodes and immediately executes those instructions. cf. *compile.*

interpretive trace program: an interpretive program; each symbolic instruction is translated into its equivalent machine code prior to execution, the result is then recorded. see *interpreter (1).*

interrecord gap: deprecated term for *interblock gap (2).* (A) (B)

interrobang: see *overprinting.*

interrogating: the process whereby a master station requests a slave station to indicate its identity or its status. (E)

interrupt (I) (INT) (INTR)

(1) a suspension of a process, such as the execution of a computer program, caused by an event external to that process, and performed in such a way that the process can be resumed. (A)

(2) to stop a process in such a way that it can be resumed.

(3) in data transmission, to take an action at a receiving station that causes the transmitting station to terminate a transmission.

(4) synonymous with *interruption.*

interrupt handler: an I/O routine servicing a specific interrupt.

interruptible: synonym for *enabled.*

interruption: a suspension of a process, such as the execution of a computer program, normally caused by an event external to that process, and performed in such a way that it can be resumed. synonym for *interrupt (1).* see also *external interruption, I/O interruption, program-controlled interruption.*

interruption network: a network of cir-

cuits in a computing system that continuously monitors its operation. The network detects events that normally require intervention and direction by the supervisor, and initiates interruptions.

interrupt latency: the delay between an interrupt request and acknowledgment of the request.

interrupt linkage: the technique that causes the computer to switch to the interrupt handling portions of the program as differing interrupts occur.

interrupt mask (IM): ignoring an interrupt by delaying the required action. synonymous with *interrupt.*

interrupt priorities: different interrupts can be assigned priorities so that if two occur at the same time the interrupt with the higher priority will be handled first.

interrupt request signal: signals to the computer that temporarily suspend the normal sequence of a routine and transfer control to a special routine.

interrupt signal: a signal generated to create an interrupt.

interrupt stacking: delaying action on interrupts by interrupt masking, and, where more than one interrupt occurs during the delay period, forming a queue. Each interrupt is handled in accordance with interrupt priorities.

interrupt trap: a switch set under program control purporting to stop or permit an interrupt.

interrupt trigger signal: a signal that is generated to the CPU, to interrupt the normal sequence of events in the central processor.

interrupt vector: a two-memory location identification assigned to an interrupting unit; contains the starting address and the processor status word for its service routine.

intersatellite link: transmission of messages between communications satellites as contrasted from satellite to an earth station.

intersection: synonym for *conjunction.* (A) (B)

interstage punching: a mode of card punching such that the odd or even numbered card columns are used. (A)

intersymbol interference: in an ideal digital transmission system, the detection of a symbol is not affected by preceding or following symbols. When the transmission system departs from ideal (e.g., insufficient bandwidth), errors may be caused by energy from preceding or following symbols affecting the detection of the desired symbol. (F)

intertoll trunk (ITT): a trunk between toll offices in different telephone exchanges.

interval service value: in the system resources manager, a category of information contained in a period definition that specifies the minimum amount of service that an associated job will receive during any interval.

interval timer

(1) a timer that provides program interruptions on a program-controlled basis.

(2) an electronic counter that counts intervals of time under program control.

interworking (between user classes of service): the means whereby data terminal equipment belonging to one user class of service may communicate with data-terminal equipment belonging to a different user class of service. (C)

intimate: pertaining to software having a close interaction with hardware functions. synonymous with *machine-intimate.*

INTR: see *interrupt.*

intrastate toll: traffic within state boundaries that is charged at toll rather than local rates. (F)

intrusion tone: an audible signal superimposed on a conversation, when a third party takes part in a call.

invalid character: deprecated term for *illegal character.*

invalid exclusive reference: an exclusive reference in which a common segment does not contain a reference to the symbol used in the exclusive reference.

invalid key condition: in COBOL, a condition that may arise at execution time in which the value of a specific key associated with a mass storage file does not result in a correct reference to the file REWRITE, START, and WRITE statements for the specific error conditions involved.

inventory: see *mass storage volume inventory.*

inventory master file: pertaining to permanently stored inventory information held for use in the future.

inversion: deprecated term for *negation.* (A)

invert: to change a physical or logical state to its opposite. (A)

inverted file

(1) a file whose sequence has been reversed.

(2) in information retrieval, a method of organizing a cross-index file in which a key word identifies a record; the items, numbers, or documents

pertinent to that key word are indicated. (*A*)

inverter: a device whose output variable is of equal magnitude and opposite algebraic sign to its input variable. (B)

invitation: the process in which a processor contacts a station in order to allow the station to transmit a message if it has one ready. see also *polling.*

invitation list: a series of sets of polling characters or identification sequences associated with the stations on a line; the order in which sets of polling characters are specified determines the order in which polled stations are invited to enter messages on the line.

invitation to send (ITS): a Western Union term for a character sequence sent to an outlying teletypewriter terminal that polls its tape transmitter. see also *polling, transmitter start code.*

invocation: in PL/1, the activation of a procedure.

invoke: in PL/1, to activate a procedure at one of its entry points.

invoked procedure: in PL/1, a procedure that has been activated at one of its entry points.

invoking block: in PL/1, a block containing a statement that activates a procedure.

inward wide area telecommunication service (INWATS): a reverse-charge direct distance dialing service to a specific directory number. Bulk rates based on measured time are charged. see *WATS.* (F)

INWATS: see *inward wide area telecommunications service.*

INX: see *index character.*

I/O: see *input-output.* (A)

I/O appendage: a user-written routine that provides additional control over I/O operations during channel program operations.

I/O area: synonym for *buffer* (3).

IOB: see *input-output buffer.*

I/O bound: processes where the rate of input and/or output of data is the factor determining program speed.

IOC
(1) see *input-output channel.*
(2) see *input-output controller.* (A)

I/O control: in COBOL, the name and the header for an environment division paragraph in which object program requirements for specific input-output techniques are specified. These techniques include rerun checkpoints, sharing of areas by several data files, and multiple file storage on a single tape device.

I/O controller: synonym for *input-output controller.* (B)

IOCS: see **I-O CS.** *out. input-output control system.*

IOD: see *input-output device.*

I/O device: see *input-output unit.*

I/O diskette slot: see *slot.*

I/O interruption: an interruption caused by the termination of an I/O operation or by operator intervention at the I/O device.

I/O list: a list of variables in an I/O statement, specifying the storage locations into which data is to be read or from which data is to be written.

I/O port: a data channel or connection to external units used for input and/or output to and from a computer.

I/O processor: a special-purpose computer to relieve a computer system's primary processor of the time-consuming activity of managing input and output functions.

IOR: see *input-output register.*

IP

(1) see *impact printer.*

(2) see *interface processor.*

IPL

(1) see *initial program load.*

(2) see *initial program loader.* (A)

IR

(1) see *information retrieval.*

(2) see *instruction register.*

IRC: see *International Record Carrier.*

irrational number: a real number that is not a rational number. (A) (B)

irrecoverable error: an error that makes recovery impossible without the use of recovery techniques external to the computer program or run. (E)

irrelevance: in information theory, the conditional entropy of the occurrence of specific messages at a message sink given the occurrences of specific messages at the message source connected to the message sink by a specified channel. (A) (B)

irreversible magnetic process: a change of magnetic flux in a magnetic material. The altered condition remains after the magnetic field causing the change has been removed. cf. *reversible magnetic process.* synonymous with *irreversible process.*

irreversible process: synonymous with *irreversible magnetic process.*

IRT: see *index return character.*

IS

(1) see *information separator.* (A)

(2) see *information system.*

ISO: see *International Organization for Standardization.* (A)

isochronous: having a regular periodicity.

isochronous transmission: a data-transmission process in which there is always an integral number of unit intervals between any two significant instants. see also *anisochronous transmission, synchronous transmission.* (E)

isolated locations: storage locations protected by a hardware unit preventing them from being addressed by a user's program and guarding their contents from accidental alteration.

ISO sizes: pertaining to a set of paper sizes selected from those standardized by the International Standards Organization for use in data processing.

ISO Standard: a standard proposed or adopted by the International Standards Organization which in Europe serves similarly as ANSI in the United States. What is known in the U.S. as the ASCII characters set is known in Europe as the ISO character set.

IT: see *indent tab character.*

item

(1) one member of a group. A file may consist of a number of items, such as records, which in turn may consist of other items. (B)

(2) a collection of related characters, treated as a unit. (*A*)

(3) one unit of a commodity such as one box, one bag, or one can. Usually, an item is the smallest unit of a commodity to be sold.

item advance: in grouping of records, a technique for operating successively on different records in memory.

item count: on a calculator, the counting of the number of items processed by the machine. (D)

item size: the number of characters or

digits in a unit of data.

iterate: to execute successively a series of instructions.

iteration: the technique of repeating a group of computer instructions; one repetition of such a group.

iteration factor: in PL/1, an expression that specifies (a) in an INITIAL attribute specification, the number of consecutive elements of an array that are to be initialized with a given constant; (b) in a format list, the number of times a given format item or list of items is to be used in succession.

iteration routine: a routine that repeatedly performs a series of operations until a specified condition is reached.

iterative do-group: in PL/1, a do-group whose DO statement specifies a control variable, a WHILE option, or both.

iterative operation: the repetition of the algorithm for the solution of a set of equations, with successive combinations of initial conditions or other parameters; each successive combination is selected by a subsidiary computation on a predetermined set of iteration rules. (B)

ITF: BASIC: a simple, algebralike language designed for ease of use at a terminal.

ITF: PL/1: a conversation subset of PL/1 designed for ease of use at the terminal.

I-time: see *instruction time.*

ITS: see *invitation to send.*

ITT: see *intertoll trunk.*

ITU: see *International Telecommunication Union.*

IU: see *input unit.*

Iverson notation: a special set of symbols developed by Kenneth Iverson to describe the formal structure of computer languages; used in APL.

IX: see *index register.*

IXC: see *interexchange channel.*

jack: a connecting device to which a wire or wires of a circuit may be attached and which is arranged for the insertion of a plug.

JCL: see *job control language.* (A)

jitter

(1) short-term variations of the significant instants of a digital signal from their ideal positions in time. (C)

(2) in computer graphics, undesirable vibration of a display image on a display surface.

JMP: see *jump.*

job

(1) a set of data that completely defines a unit of work for a computer. A job usually includes all necessary computer programs, linkages, files, and instructions to the operating system. (A)

(2) a collection of related problem programs, identified in the input stream by a JOB statement followed by one or more EXEC and DO statements.

(3) see also *background job, batch-*

ed job, foreground job, terminal job.

job batch: a succession of job definitions that are placed one behind another to form a batch. Each job batch is placed on an input device and processed with a minimum of delay between one job or job step and another.

job class: any one of a number of job categories that can be defined. By classifying jobs and directing initiator/terminators to initiate specific classes of jobs, it is possible to control the mixture of jobs that are performed concurrently.

job control: a program that is called into storage to prepare each job or job step to be run. Some of its functions are to assign I/O devices to certain symbolic names, set switches for program use, log (or print) job control statements, and fetch the first program phase of each job step.

job control language (JCL): a problem-oriented language designed to express statements in a job that are used to identify the job or describe its requirements to an operating system. (A)

job control statement: a statement in a job that is used in identifying the job or describing its requirements to the operating system. (A)

job definition: a series of job control statements that define a job.

job-flow control: control over the sequence of jobs being processed, ensuring an efficient use of peripheral devices and central processor.

job input device: a device assigned by the operator to read job definitions and any accompanying input data.

job input file: a data file (or data set) consisting of a series of job definitions and accompanying data.

job input stream: synonym for *input stream.*

JOBLIB: see *job library.*

job library (JOBLIB): a set of user-identified, partitioned data sets used as the primary source of load modules for a given job.

job management: the collective functions of job scheduling and command processing.

job name: the name assigned to a JOB statement; it identifies the job to the system.

job-oriented language: a computer language designed for the specific requirements of a particular type of job.

job-oriented terminal: a terminal designed for a particular application.

job output device: a device assigned by the operator for common use in recording output data for a series of jobs.

job output file: a data file (or data set) consisting of output data produced by a series of jobs.

job output stream: synonym for *output stream.*

job pack area (JPA): an area that contains modules that are not in the link pack area but are needed for the execution of jobs.

job priority: a value assigned to a job that, together with an assigned job class, determines the priority to be used in scheduling the job and allocating resources to it.

job processing: the reading of job control statements and data from an input stream, the initiating of job steps defined in the statements, and the writing of system output messages.

job program mode: a mode where read/write and jump-storage protection exists. As a result, job programs are limited to those areas assigned only. If the job program reads, writes, or jumps to an out-of-limits address, an interrupt will return control to the initiator for remedial action.

job-recovery control file: synonym for *backup file.*

job separator pages: separate different jobs being printed and print job names in large block letters at the beginning and end of jobs.

job (JOB) statement: the job control statement that identifies the beginning of a job. It contains such information as the name of the job, an account number, and the class and priority assigned to the job.

job step

(1) the execution of a computer program explicitly identified by a job control statement. A job may specify that several job steps be executed. (A)

(2) a unit of work associated with one processing program or one cataloged procedure and related data. A job consists of one or more job steps.

job step initiation: the process of selecting a job step for execution and allocating input-output devices for it.

job step restart: synonym for *step restart.*

job stick: in computer graphics, a lever that can pivot in all directions and that is used as a locator device. (E)

job stream: the sequence of representations of jobs to be submitted to an operating system. synonymous with *input stream, run stream.* (B) see *input stream, output stream.*

job support task: a task that reads and interprets job definitions or converts job input and output data from one input-output medium to another.

joggle: to align a card deck, usually before placing it in a card hopper. (E)

join: synonymous with *OR operation.*

joint access costs: those costs associated with network access facilities, which are used jointly for both local and long distance calling. Included in these costs are the basic termination, installation labor, inside wiring, drop, subscriber loop and all nontraffic sensitive local central office equipment. Other expenses such as commercial, directory, monthly billing, and testing—which vary with the number of customers rather than the amount of use and which are incurred whether or not a customer makes any calls—are also included. (G)

joint information content: in information theory, a measure of information conveyed by the ocurrence of two events of definite joint probability. (A) (B)

Josephson junction: a circuit where thin film strips are separated by a thin oxide barrier with electrons forced to tunnel across this barrier. Immersion in liquid helium causes the conductivity properties to be altered, and the circuits switch at unusually high speeds. see also *junction.*

JOSS: a Sperry-Rand Corporation language created to make rapid calculations of a nature too involved for a calculator. JOSS is a time-sharing language used in Rand's Johnniac System.

journal: a chronological record of the changes made to a set of data; the record may be used to reconstruct a previous version of the set. synonymous with *log.* (E) see *mass storage volume control journal.*

journaling: recording transactions against a data set so that the data set can be reconstructed by applying transactions in the journal against a previous version of the data set.

JOVIAL (Jules' own version of international algorithmic language): a multipurpose programming language used primarily for command and control applications. (E)

joystick: a lever whose movements control a cursor or to write on a visual display unit.

JPA: see *job pack area.*

jumbo group: an assembly of 6 master groups (3600 voice circuits).

jump (JMP): in the execution of a computer program, a departure from the implicit or declared order in which instructions are being executed. (B) see *conditional jump, unconditional jump.* (A)

jumper

(1) a short length of electrical con-

ductor used temporarily to complete a circuit or to bypass an existing one. (2) a pair of wires used in establishing a connection through a distributing frame. (F)

jumper selectable: a function specified by connecting or disconnecting wires on a circuit card.

jump instruction: an instruction that specifies a jump. see *conditional jump instruction, unconditional jump instruction.* (*A*) (B)

junction: the contact suface between n-type and p-type semiconducting material, where transistor activity occurs.

junctor

(1) a device that links any two half paths in a switching network.

(2) within a switching system, a connection or circuit between inlets and outlets of the same or different switching networks. An intraoffice trunk. (F)

junk: a computer description of a garbled or otherwise unintelligible sequence of signals or other data. cf. *garbage.*

justification

(1) the vertical alignment of right or left margins. (D)

(2) the act of adjusting, arranging, or shifting digits to the left or right to fit a prescribed pattern.

justification range: the allowed minimum and maximum space which can be inserted between words within a line.

justified margin: arrangement of data or type printed on pages such that the left- or right-end characters of each horizontal line lie in the same column.

justify

(1) to control the printing positions of characters on a page so that the left-hand and right-hand margins of the printing are regular. (B)

(2) to shift the contents of a register, if necessary, so that the character at a specified end of the data that has been read or loaded into the register is at a specified position in the register. (B)

(3) to align characters horizontally or vertically to fit the positioning constraints of a required format. (A)

(4) in word processing, to print a document with even right and left margins.

(5) see *left-justify, right-justify.* (A)

K

(1) when referring to storage capacity, two to the tenth power; 1024 in decimal notation. (A) see *kilobytes*. see also *file length*.

(2) see *Kelvin*.

(3) see *key*.

k: an abbreviation for the prefix kilo, that is, 1000 is, 1000 in decimal notation. (A)

Kanji: a character set of symbols used in Japanese ideographic alphabets.

Karnaugh map: a rectangular diagram of a logic function of variables drawn with overlapping rectangles representing a unique combination of the logic variables and such that an intersection is shown for all combinations. (A) (B)

Katakna: a character set of symbols used in one of the two common Japanese phonetic alphabets. see also *Hiragana, Kanji.*

KB

(1) see *keyboard*.

(2) kilobyte; 1024 bytes.

KBD: see *keyboard*.

Kelvin (K): degrees Kelvin. Temperature above absolute zero; uses Celcius scale.

kerning: in word processing, the ability to reduce the amount of space between letters by tightening the text horizontally.

key

(1) one or more characters, within a set of data that contains information about the set, including its identification. (A) (B)

(2) in sorting, synonym for *control word*.

(3) in COBOL, one or more data items, the contents of which identify the type or the location of a record, or the ordering of data.

(4) to enter information from a keyboard.

(5) see *actual key, function key, nonescaping key, primary key, program attention key, program function key, record key, search key, second-*

ary key, sort key.

KEYBD: see *keyboard.*

keyboard (KB) (KBD) (KEYBD)
(1) a systematic arrangement of keys by which a machine is operated or by which data is entered.
(2) a device for the encoding of data by key depression which causes the generation of the selected code element.
(3) a group of numeric keys, alphabetic keys, or function keys used for entering information into a terminal and into the system.

keyboard computer: a computer, the input of which uses a keyboard, possibly an electric typewriter.

keyboard entry: a technique whereby access into the contents of a computer's storage may be initiated at a keyboard.

keyboard inquiry: interrogation of program progress, storage contents, or other information by keyboard manipulations.

keyboard lockout: property of the keyboard such that it cannot be used to send a message via a network while the required circuit is engaged.

keyboard perforator: a device for punching alphameric information into tape through the manual depression of a bank of keys.

keyboard punch: synonym for *keypunch.* (A) (B)

keyboard send/receive (KSR): a combination teletypewriter transmitter and receiver with transmission capability from keyboard only.

key click: transient pulses or surges on a transmission line set up by the opening or closing of keying circuit contacts.

key-click filter: a filter that attenuates key clicks.

key-driven: said of any device for translating information into machine-sensible form which requires an operator to depress a key for each character.

keyed direct access: the retrieval or storage of a data record by use of either an index that relates the record's key to its relative location in the file, or data set, or a relative-record number, independent of the record's location relative to the previously retrieved or stored record.

key-encrypting key: a key used in sessions with cryptography to encipher and decipher other keys. cf. *data-encrypting key.*

key entry: pertaining to the input of data manually by means of a keyboard.

key folding: synonym for *hashing (1).*

keying: the forming of signals, such as those employed in telegraph transmission, by the interruption of a direct current or modulation of a carrier between discrete values of some characteristics.

keying chirps: sounds accompanying code signals when the transmitter is unstable and shifts slightly in frequency each time the sending key is closed.

keying wave: the emission that takes place in telegraph communication while the information portions of the code characters are being transmitted. synonymous with *marking wave.*

key mat: a prepunched plastic, user-labeled sheet, that fits over keyboard for key identification.

key pad: a supplementary set of keys, usually numerical and arranged like a calculator; added to a keyboard.

key phrase: in word processing, a single-key abbreviation for often-used phrases. This feature works like block moves, but it involves phrases or sentences instead of paragraphs.

key pulse: synonym for *pushbutton dialing.*

key-pulsing signal: in multifrequency signaling, a signal, keyed by the operator, that is used to prepare the distant equipment for receiving digits. (F)

keypunch (KP): a keyboard-actuated punch that punches holes in a data carrier. synonymous with *keyboard punch.* (B)

key sorting: the record file fields which determine, or are used as a basis for determining, the sequence of records retained by a file.

key stroke: the operation of a single key on a keyboard.

key-stroke verification: reentry of data through a keyboard to verify the accuracy of a prior entry of the same data. (E)

keytape: a device used to record data directly onto magnetic tape. Consists of a tape drive, keyboard, control and logic circuitry, and occasionally other input devices such as adding machines or paper tape readers.

key telephone set: a telephone set with buttons or keys located on or near the telephone. It is used with associated equipment to provide features such as call holding, multiline pickup, signaling, intercommunication, and conferencing.

key telephone systems: an arrangement of key telephone stations and associated circuitry, located on a customer's premises, providing combinations of certain voice communi-

cations arrangements such as multiline pickup, call line status lamp signals, and interconnection among stations without the need for connections through the central office or PBX facilities. (F)

key-to-disk: a data entry strategy where data is sent directly from the keyboard to a disk file.

key transformation: a function that maps a set of keys into a set of integers, which can be handled arithmetically to determine the location of the corresponding data elements. (A)

key word

(1) one of the predefined words of an artificial language. (A)

(2) one of the significant and informative words in a title or document that describe the content of that document.

(3) a symbol that identifies a parameter.

(4) a part of a command operand that consists of a specific character string (such as DSNAMV).

(5) a reserved word whose use is essential to the meaning and structure of a COBOL statement.

(6) deprecated term for *reserved word.* (A) (B)

(7) synonym for *descripter.* (A)

key word in context (KWIC): a list of available programs arranged alphabetically by the key words in the program titles. Some words are not accepted as indexing words but will be printed as part of the title. This index is prepared by highlighting each key word from a title in the context of words on either side of it and aligning the key words of all titles alphabetically in a vertical column.

key-word parameter: a parameter that

consists of a key word, followed by one or more values. see also *positional parameter.*

kg: kilogram.

kilo (k)

(1)   thousand. see also *k.*

(2)   shortened form of kilogram.

kilobaud: the measure of data transmission speed; a thousand bits per second. see also *baud.*

kilobytes (K): 1024 bytes. see *file length.*

kilogram (Kg): one thousand grams; 2.2046 pounds.

kilomega-: a prefix signifying 10^9. synonymous with *billi-* and *giga-.*

kilometer (km): one thousand meters; 0.62 miles.

Kingsbury commitment: a commitment made by AT&T Vice President Nathan C. Kingsbury in a letter to the U.S. Attorney General in 1913 to avert an antitrust action. The Bell System agreed to dispose of its interest in the Western Union Telegraph Company; to provide long distance connections to the Independent Telephone Companies, and not to purchase any more Independent Telephone Companies unless it had regulatory approval. (G)

kips: kilo instructions per second; a unit of machine speed equalling 1,00 operations per second.

kit: a system assembled by a user.

kludge: deprecated term referring to the *black box* or the *computer.*

km: see *kilometer.*

KP: see *keypunch.*

KSR: see *keyboard send/receive.*

KWIC: see *key word in context.*

L

L

(1) see *language*.

(2) see *length*.

(3) see *link*.

(4) see *liter*.

(5) see *local*.

LA: see *line adapter*.

label (LBL)

(1) one or more characters, within or attached to a set of data, that contains information about the set, including its identification. (B)

(2) in computer programming, an identifier of an instruction. (*A*) (B)

(3) an identification record for a tape or disk file.

(4) in assembler programming, a name entry.

(5) in PL/1, a name used to identify a statement other than a PROCEDURE or ENTRY statement; a statement label.

(6) see *beginning-of-volume label, end-of-file label, end-of-volume label, external label, header label, internal label*.

(7) see also *entry name, magnetic tape label, name, symbol*.

label constant: in PL/1, an unsubscripted name that appears prefixed to any statement other than a PROCEDURE or ENTRY statement.

labeled common: in PL/1, an expression whose evaluation yields a label value.

label list (of a label variable declaration): in PL/1, a parenthesized list of one or more statement-label constants immediately following the key word LABEL to specify the range of values that the declared variable may have; names in the list are separated by commas. When specified for a label array, it indicates that each element of the array may assume any of the values listed.

label list (of a statement): in PL/1, all of the label prefixes of a statement.

label record: a record used to identify the contents of a file or reel of magnetic tape.

label variable: in PL/1, a variable declared with the LABEL attribute and thus able to assume as its value a label constant.

laced card: a card punched accidentally or intentionally with holes in excess of the hole patterns of the character set used. (A)

lag: the delay between two events.

LAMA: see *local automatic message accounting*.

landing: the inside connection leading to the pins on a package.

land-line facilities: facilities of communication common carriers that are within the continental United States.

language (L): a set of characters, conventions, and rules that is used for conveying information. The three aspects of language are pragmatics, semantics, and syntax. (B) see *algebraic language, algorithmic language, application-oriented language, artificial language, assembly language, command language, computer language, computer-oriented language, high-level language, job control language, linear language, machine language, multidimensional language, natural language, object language, one-dimensional language, problem-oriented language, programming language, source language, stratified language, syntax language, target language, unstratified language.* (A)

language converter: any data-processing unit designed to alter one form of data, that is, microfilm, strip chart, into another, such as punch card, paper tape.

language interpreter: any processor, assembler, or other routine that accepts statements in one language and then produces equivalent state-

ments in another language.

language processor: a computer program that performs such functions as translating, interpreting, and other tasks required for processing a specified programming language. (A) (B)

language statement: a statement that is coded by a programmer, operator, or other user of a computing system, to convey information to a processing program such as a language translator or service program, or to the control program. A language statement may request that an operation be performed or may contain data that is to be passed to the processing program.

language subset: a part of a language that can be used independently of the rest of the language.

language translation feature: see *national requirements*.

language translator: a general term for any assembler, compiler, or other routine that accepts statements in one language and produces equivalent statements in another language.

lap: to smooth the surface of a wafer or semiconductor crystal.

large scale integration (LSI): the process of integrating large numbers of circuits on a single chip of semiconductor material.

laser: a device able to emit a tiny beam of electromagnetic energy in the visible light spectrum.

laser communications: a system for transmitting coherent beams of light which may form high-capacity communications links in the future.

laser emulsion storage: a storage medium using a controlled laser beam to expose areas on a photosensitive surface. When the laser beam is interrupted, a desired information pattern results.

last-in, first-out: see *LIFO*.

last in, last out: see *LILO*.

LATA: see *Local Access and Transport Areas*.

latch: a circuit or device that maintains an assumed condition until it is reset to its earlier state by external means.

latching: synonymous with *locking*.

latency: the time interval between the instant at which an instruction control unit initiates a call for data and the instant at which the actual transfer of the data is started. synonymous with *waiting time, wait state*. (*A*) (B)

lateral redundancy check: synonym for *transverse redundancy check*. (B)

lateral reversal: an image reversed left-to-right.

LAU: see *line adapter unit*.

layer: in open systems architecture, a collection of related functions that comprise one level of a hierarchy of functions. Each layer specifies its own functions and assumes that lower level functions are provided. see *application layer, data-link layer, session layer, transport layer*. (E)

layout: see *file layout*. (A)

layout character: synonym for *format effector character*. (B)

LB: see *lower bound*.

LBL: see *label*.

LBO: see *line build-out network*.

LC

(1) see *line control*.

(2) see *location counter*.

LCB: see *line control block*.

LCD display: a display using liquid crystal diode technology.

LCNTR: see *location counter*.

LCP: see *link control procedure*.

LDA: see *logical device address*.

LE: less than or equal to. see also *relational operator*.

leader: the blank section of tape at the beginning of a reel of tape. (A)

leader record: a specific record holding the description of information about the group not present in the detail records. Any blank or unused length of tape at the beginning of a tape reel proceeding the start of the recorded information.

leaders: dots or dashes used by a printer to fill in a line so as to lead the reader across the page to data at the end of the line.

leading control: a short description or title of a control group of records appearing in front of each such group.

leading decision: a loop control that is executed before the loop body. cf. *trailing decision*. (A)

leading end: the end of a perforated tape that first enters a perforated-tape reader. (A)

leading graphics: from one to seven graphic characters that may accompany an acknowledgment sent to or from a BSC terminal in response to the receipt of a block of data.

leading zero

(1) in a positional notation, a zero in a more significant digit place than the digit place of the most significant nonzero digit of a numeral. (A)

(2) a zero, used as a fill character, that appears to the left-most significant digit in a numeric value displayed on a human readable medium.

leaf: last node of a tree.

leapfrog test: a check routine that copies itself through storage. (A)

learning: see *machine learning*.

learning program: a program that alters itself by making changes based on the experience of the program and results unknown until portions of the program have been run.

leased channel: a point-to-point channel reserved for sole use of a single leasing customer.

leased circuit data-transmission service: a service whereby a circuit, or circuits, of the public data network are made available to a user or group of users for their exclusive use. (C)

leased facility: a circuit of the public telephone network made available for the exclusive use of one subscriber.

leased line: deprecated term for *non-switched line*.

least frequently used memory (LFU): when information must be read into main memory, other existing resident information must be overwritten. Algorithms are used to decide which page or segment of memory is to be overwritten. The LFU algorithm replaces the area which is being or has been accessed the least.

least recently used memory (LRU): an algorithm for finding which page or segment of main memory is to be overwritten based on the length of time since the last access to that memory.

least significant character: the character in the extreme right-hand position of a group of significant characters in positional notation.

least significant digit: the significant digit contributing the smallest quantity to the value of a numeral.

LED: see *light-emitting diode*.

left-hand margin indent: in word processing, a feature that enables blocks of recorded text to be indented with different left-hand margins, irrespective of amendments made to the text and while still retaining the original (fixed) left-hand margin settings. (D)

left-justify

(1) to shift the contents of a register, if necessary, so that the character at the left hand of the data that has been read or loaded into the register is at a specified position in the register.

(2) to control the printing positions of characters on a page so that the left-hand margin of the printing is regular. (*A*) (*B*)

leg: a path found in a routine or a subroutine.

LEN: see *length*.

length (L) (LEN): see *block length, record length, word length*.

length specification: in FORTRAN, an indication, by the use of the form **s*, of the number of storage locations (bytes) to be occupied by a variable or array element.

LET: see *letter*.

letter (LET) (LTR): a graphic character that, when used alone or combined with others, represents in a written language one or more sound elements of a spoken language, but excluding diacritical marks used alone and punctuation marks. (A) (B)

letter code: in the Baudot code, the function that leads machines to shift to lower case. The code is used to rub out errors in tape.

letter out: synonymous with *erase*.

letter quality: printers which yield high-quality output, using impact methods with die-cast type.

letters shift (LTRS): a physical shift in

a teletypewriter that enables the printing of alphabetic characters. Also, the name of the character that causes this shift.

LEV: see *level*.

level (LEV): the degree of subordination of an item in a hierarchic arrangement. (A) (B)

level compensator: an automatic gain control device used in the receiving equipment of a telegraph circuit.

level indicator: in COBOL, two alphabetic characters that identify a specific type of file, or the highest position in a hierarchy. The level indicators are FD, SD, RD.

level number

(1) a reference number that indicates the position of an item in a hierarchic arrangement. synonymous with *rank*. (A) (B)

(2) in COBOL, a numeric character or two-character set that identifies the properties of a data description entry. Level numbers 01 through 49 define group items; the highest level is identified as 01, and the subordinate data items within the hierarchy are identified with level numbers 02 through 49. Level numbers 66, 77, and 88 identify special properties of a data description entry in the data division.

(3) in PL/1, an unsigned decimal integer constant in a DECLARE or ALLOCATE statement that specifies the position of a name in the hierarchy of a structure. It precedes the name to which it refers and is separated from that name only by one or more blanks. Level numbers appear without the names in a parameter descriptor of an ENTRY attribute specification.

level of access: see *access level, logical access level*.

level of addressing:

(1) *zero level addressing:* the address part of an instruction is the operand; for instance, the addresses of shift instructions, or where the "address" is the data (in interpretive or generating systems).

(2) *first level addressing:* the address of an instruction is the location in memory where the operand may be found or is to be stored.

(3) *second level addressing (indirect addressing):* the address part of an instruction is the location in memory where the address of the operand may be found.

level-one variables: in PL/1, a major structure name; any subscripted variable not contained within a structure.

levels: voltage values conventionally used to encode discrete signals in digital systems.

lexeme: the written word, particle, or stem that denotes meaning.

lexicon: a vocabulary, not necessarily in alphabetical sequence, with definitions or explanations for terms included.

LF: see *line feed character*. (A)

LFC: see *local form control*.

LFCB: causes the system to load the buffer image, contained in the core image library, into the forms control buffer of the specified printer.

LFU: see *least frequently used memory*.

LIB: see *line interface base*.

librarian: a program that creates, maintains, and makes available the total of programs, routines, and data that make up an operating system. Librarian activities include system generation and system editing.

librarian program: the librarian program part of the control function that provides maintenance of library programs used as a portion of the operating system. The library may be stored on a signal secondary storage device, or it may be distributed over several differing storage devices.

library

(1) a collection of related files. For example, one line of an invoice may form an item, a complete invoice may form a file, the collection of inventory control files may form a library, and the libraries used by an organization are known as its data bank.

(2) a repository for demountable recorded media, such as magnetic disk packs and magnetic tapes.

(3) see *data library, program library.* (*A*)

(4) see *job library, private library.*

library directory: the library component that contains information, such as the member name and location, about each member in the library.

library facilities: a basic library of general-purpose software to perform common jobs to which the user can add often-used programs and routines.

library file editor: an editor that permits users to combine the compiler or assembler output to form binary libraries resulting in a set of central, updatable program libraries that eliminate program duplication.

library program: a computer program in or from a program library. (A) (B)

library routine: a proven routine that is maintained in a program library. (A)

library subroutine: a subroutine in a program library.

library tape: a magnetic tape, holding routines used in operating a computer center, available from a library.

library track: a track used for storing static reference data.

licensed documentation: see *licensed publication.*

licensed publication: a publication for a licensed program that contains licensed information and is itself therefore licensed.

LIED: see *linkage editor.*

LIFO (last-in, first-out): a queuing technique in which the next item to be retrieved is the item most recently placed in the queue. (A)

light button: synonym for *virtual push button.* (E)

light conduit: a flexible, incoherent bundle of fibers used to transmit light.

light-emitting diode (LED): a semiconductor chip which gives off visible or infrared light when activated. (D)

light-emitting diode (LED) display: in word processing, a display in which characters are formed from a dot matrix of light-emitting diodes.

light guide: an assembly of a number of optical fibers mounted and finished in a component that is used solely to transmit light flux, as distinguished from an optical waveguide's function.

light gun: deprecated term for *light pen.*

light pen (LP): in computer graphics, a light sensitive pick device that is pointed at the display surface. synonymous with *light gun, selector pen.* (E)

light pen attention: a CRT display device. synonymous with *selector pen attention.*

light pen detection: in computer graphics, the sensing by a light pen of light generated by a display element in a display space. synonymous with *light pen hit, light pen strike.* (E)

light pen hit: synonym for *light pen detection.*

light pen strike: synonym for *light pen detection.*

light pen tracking: the process of tracking the movement of a light pen across the screen of a CRT display device.

light stability: in optical character recognition, the resistance to change of color of the image when exposed to radiant energy. (A)

LILO: last in, last out; a sequence followed in data processing.

limit check: a test of the content of specified fields against stipulated high or low limits of acceptability, or both; for example, a range check. (E)

limited: a word often attached to another term to indicate the machine activity that requires the most time.

limited distance adapter: a modem created to function over short distances, up to perhaps 30 miles.

limiter: a functional unit used to prevent a variable from exceeding specified limits. (B)

limiter circuit: a circuit of nonlinear elements that restricts the electrical excursion of a variable in accordance with some specified criteria.

line (LN)

(1) on a terminal, one or more characters entered before a return to the first printing or display position.

(2) a string of characters accepted by the system as a single block of input from a terminal; for example, all characters entered before a carriage return or all characters entered before the terminal user hits the attention key.

(3) in word processing, a predetermined number of escapement units (including character spaces) forming one line of typing. (D)

(4) a pair of wires carrying direct current between a central office and a customer's terminal. A line is the most common type of loop. (F)

(5) in carrier systems, the portion of a transmission system that extends between two terminal locations. The line includes the transmission media and associated line repeaters. (F)

(6) the side of a piece of central office equipment that connects to or toward the outside plant; the other side of the equipment is called the *drop side.* (F)

(7) a family of equipments or apparatus designed to provide a variety of styles, a range of sizes, or a choice of service features. (F)

(8) synonymous with *channel* and *circuit.*

(9) see *acoustic delay line, character spacing reference line, delay line, electromagnetic delay line, hidden line, magnetic delay line, off-line, on-line, X-datum line, Y-datum line.*

(10) see *display line, telecommunication line.*

(11) see also *data link.*

line adapter (LA): a modem that is a feature of a particular device.

line adapter unit (LAU): one component of a front end which interfaces with a specific communications line to permit communication with a computer.

linear: relating to order in an algebraic equation where all of the variables are present in the first degree only; for example, an equation where none of the variables are raised to powers other than unity or multiplied together.

linear combiner: a diversity combiner which adds two or more receiver outputs.

linear distortion: distortion resulting from a channel having a linear filter characteristic different from an ideal linear low-pass or band-pass filter; in particular, amplitude characteristics that are not flat over the pass band and phase characteristics that are not linear over the pass band. (F)

linear integrated circuit: a type of integrated circuit suitable for analog signals.

linearity: a constant ratio of incremental cause and effect.

linear language: a language that is customarily expressed as a linear representation. For example. FORTRAN is a linear language; a flowchart is not. (A)

linear list: synonymous with *dense list.*

linear optimization: in operations research, a procedure for locating the maxiumum or minimum of a linear function of variables that are subject to linear constraints. cf. *convex programming, dynamic programming, integer programming, mathematical programming, nonlinear programming, quadratic programming.* synonymous with *linear programming.* (A) (B)

linear programming: in operations research, a procedure for locating the maximum or minimum of a linear function of variables that are subject to linear constraints. synonymous with *linear optimization* cf. *convex programming, dynamic programming, integer programming, mathematical programming, nonlinear programming, quadratic programming.* (A) (B)

linear regulator: a power supply design where the voltage is held constant by dissipating 50 percent of the input voltage times the output current as a margin.

linear representation: an arrangement of graphics in a one-dimensional space. (A)

linear search: a symbol table search that examines every item beginning with the first item and proceeding sequentially.

linear selection: one of the methods of selecting memory or input-output units that dedicates one address line per chip selection, resulting in overlapping memory, noncontiguous memory.

linear unit: a unit that follows the rules of mathematical linearity; for example, where the change in output due to a change in input is proportional to the magnitude of that change and does not depend on the values of the other inputs.

line-at-a-time printer: synonym for *line printer.* (A) (B)

line build-out (LBO) network: amplifiers (repeaters) in a cable transmission system may be designed to compensate for distortion of a specific length of cable. When the length of cable between amplifiers is less than that tor which the amplifier is designed, one or more line build-out networks are used to bring the distortion to approximately the design level. (F)

line character: see *new-line charac-ter*. (A)

line code: a code chosen to suit the transmission medium and giving the equivalence between a set of digits generated in a terminal or other processing equipment and the pulses chosen to represent that set of digits for line transmission. (C)

line concentration: matching a large number of input channels with a smaller number of output channels- the latter performing at a higher speed.

line control (LC): synonym for *data-link control protocol*.

line control block (LCB): a storage area containing control information required for scheduling and managing line operations. One LCB is maintained for each line.

line control discipline: synonym for *link protocol*.

line counter: in word processing, a device for counting and possibly controlling the number of lines printed on each page. (D)

line data set: in systems with time sharing, a data set with logical records that are printable lines.

line delete symbol: synonym for *logical line delete symbol*.

line deletion character: a character that specifies that all characters are to be deleted from a line of terminal input.

line discipline: synonym for *link protocol*.

line drawing display: a cathode ray tube display on which lines are drawn. The lines are either input directly using a graphics tablet or light pen, or indirectly by defining the end points of the lines via a keyboard.

line driver: synonymous with *bus driver*.

line editing: editing in which data is displayed at a terminal one line at a time and in which the user can access data only through commands. cf. *full-screen editing*.

line-end adjustment: in word processing, a feature that, during printout, automatically adjusts the line endings of edited text to comply, within the line-end zone, with the original margin setting or to changed settings with or without editing. (D)

line-end control key (adjusting): in word processing, a control by means of which the line-end adjustment feature can be activated or deactivated. (D)

line-ending zone
(1) in word processing, a specifiable number of character positions immediately prior to the right margin at which the machine will automatically start a new line or request operator intervention. synonymous with *hot zone*. see also *line-end zone*. (D)
(2) a predetermined amount of printable space immediately to the left or right margin that is used to trigger semiautomatic and automatic line-ending decisions during adjust text mode operations. see also *adjust text mode*.

line-end zone: in word processing, the predetermined area in which line-end adjustment operates. see also *line-ending zone* (D)

line equipment: equipment located in a central office and associated with a particular line. Includes a line relay or equivalent that is activated when the customer's telephone is off-hook. (F)

line feed character (LF)

(1)   a format effector that causes the print or display position to move to the corresponding position on the next line (A) (B)

(2)   in word processing, synonym for *index character*.

line filter balance: a network designed to maintain phantom group balance when one side of the group is equipped with a carrier system. Since it must balance the phantom group for only voice frequencies, its configuration is usually quite simple compared with the filter which it balances.

line finder: a switching mechanism that finds a calling line in a group of 100 or 200 in a step-by-step system or in a group of 300 or 400 in a panel system and connects it to an intraoffice circuit, usually to a local first selector.

line generator: a unit used in conjunction with a cathode ray tube to generate dotted, dashed or continuous lines.

line group: one or more telecommunication lines of the same type that can be activated and deactivated as a unit.

line hit: an electrical interference causing the introduction of spurious signals on a circuit.

line impedance: the impedance of a telecommunication line. It is a function of the resistance, inductance, conductance, and capacitance of the line, and the frequency of the signal. synonymous with *characteristic impedance*.

line index: see *code line index*. (A)

line interface base (LIB):   a communication controller hardware unit that provides for the attachement of up to 16 telecommunication lines to the controller.

line key: in word processing, a control used to process text one line at a time. (D)

line level: the signal level in decibels (or nepers) at a particular position on a telecommunication line.

line link pulsing: an arrangement that permits a crossbar office to transmit dial-pulse information to a PBX for switching direct inward-dialed calls to the indicated station. (F)

line load: usually a percentage of maximum circuit capability to reflect actual use during a span of time; for example, peak hour line load. synonymous with *circuit load*.

line loop: an operation performed over a telecommunication line from an input unit at one terminal to output units at a remote terminal.

line loop resistance: the metallic resistance of the local loop. synonymous with *loop resistance*.

line misregistration: the improper or unacceptable appearance of a line of characters or numerals in optical character recognition, gauged on or with respect to the real or imaginary horizontal base line.

line mode switching: an optional feature or partitioned emulation programming that allows a designated line to operate as either a network control program line or an emulation program line. The line is switched from one mode to the other by control commands.

line noise: noise originating in telecommunication line.

line number

(1)   a number associated with a line in a printout or display.

(2) in systems with time sharing, a number associated with a line in a line data set.

line number editing: in systems with time sharing, a mode of operation under the EDIT command in which lines or records to be entered, modified, or deleted, are referred to by line or record numbers.

line printer (LP) (LPT): a device that prints a line of characters as a unit. (B) synonymous with *line-at-a-time printer.* cf. *character printer, page printer.* (*A*)

line printing: the printing of a line of characters as a unit.

line protocol: rules for controlling the sequence of transmission on a synchronous line, explaining bidding for a line, methods for positive and negative acknowledgments, requests for retransmission, receiver and transmitter time-out constraints, and other necessary controls for an orderly movement of message blocks from terminal to terminal.

line relay: a relay activated by the signals on a line. deprecated term for *modulation rate.*

line response mode: a variation of response mode in which all operations on the telecommunication line are suspended while the application program output message is being generated.

line skew: a form of line misregistration, where a string of characters to be read by a OCR appear in a uniformly slanted or skewed condition with respect to a real or imaginary base line.

line speed: deprecated term for *modulation rate.*

lines-per-inch (lpi): on a printer, a measure of the number of lines per vertical inch of paper.

line status: a communication line status, for example, whether it is ready to transmit or receive.

line stretcher: an impedance matching device for coaxial transmission lines.

line surge: a significant change in the AC power line voltage which may damage unprotected computer circuitry.

line switching: synonym for *circuit switching.*

line traffic: the amount of data transmitted on a data link.

link (L)
(1) in computer programming, the part of a computer program, in some cases a single instruction or an address, that passes control and parameters between separate portions of the computer program. synonymous with *linkage.* (B)
(2) in computer programming, to provide a link. (*A*) (B)
(3) see *data link, multiplex link.*

linkage: synonym for *link (1).* (A) (B)

linkage editor (LIED): a computer program used to create one load module from one or more independently translated object modules or load modules by resolving cross-references among the modules. (E) cf. *editor program.*

linkage section: in COBOL, a section of the data division that describes data made available from another program.

link-attached: pertaining to devices that are connected to a controlling unit by a data link. cf. *channel-attached.* synonymous with *remote.*

link-attached station: synonymous

with *remote terminal.*

link-attached terminal: a terminal whose control unit is connected to a computer by a data link. synonymous with *remote terminal.* cf. *channel-attached station.*

link bit: a specific one-bit diagnostic register containing an indicator for overflow from the accumulator, and often other registers, and which can be tested under program control.

link-by-link signaling: a mode of network operation in which each office along the route of a call acts autonomously, forwarding all of the information required to complete the call to the next office in the chain. cf. *end-to-end signaling.*

link connection: synonym for *data circuit.*

link control: an agreed-upon approach on how message data passes between the terminal and the processors to ensure message integrity by including an error-control discipline.

link control procedure (LCP): a procedure by which data is transferred in an orderly and accurate fashion over a communications link.

link edit: to create a loadable computer program by means of a linkage editor.

linked sequential file: a file that has an access interface identical to that used for the various sequential devices (magnetic tape, line printer, etc.). The consistency between sequential device and the disk is achieved with the link sequential file.

linked subroutine: see *closed subroutine.*

linker: a program capable of uniting separately written programs or routines for subsequent loading into memory and execution.

link group: those links that employ the same multiplex devices.

linking loader: a loader used to link compiled/assembled programs, routines, and subroutines, and transform the results into tasks.

linking loader executive: an executive program that connects various program segments so that they can be run in the computer as one unit.

link protocol: the set of rules by which a logical data link is established, maintained, and terminated, and by which data is transferred across the link. It includes the format by which control information is passed, and the rules by which it is interpreted, in order to transmit data across the link. see also *protocol.* (C)

LIOCS: see *logical IOCS.*

LIPID: see *logical page identifier.*

LISP: see *list processing.*

list

(1) an ordered set of items of data. (B)

(2) to print or otherwise display items.

(3) deprecated term for *chained list.* (B)

(4) see *push-down list, push-up list.* (A)

list-directed transmission: in PL/1, the type of stream-oriented transmission in which data in the stream appears as constants separated by blanks or commas and for which formatting is provided automatically.

listening mode: a mode in which a station cannot send or receive messages, but can monitor messages on the line.

list handling statement: an executable statement, usually in a list proc-

LISTING 284

essing language, that specifies operations to be performed on lists of data; for example, statements used to insert data into the middle of a list, add data to the beginning or end of a list, or create common sublists. (E)

listing: a printout, usually prepared by a language translator, that lists the source language statements and contents of a program.

list processing (LISP): a method of processing data in the form of lists. Usually, chained lists are used so that the logical order of items can be changed without altering their physical locations. (A) (B)

list processing languages: specific languages developed by symbol manipulation and used primarily for research rather than for production programming.

list processing program: a specific program called EULER is an extension of ALGOL 60 having specific list processing capabilities.

list structure: a specific set of data items combined because each element contains the address of the successor item or element. These lists increase in size according to the limits of fixed storage capacity, and can easily insert or delete data items anywhere in a list structure.

LISTTO: indicates the assignment of a particular device has at a given time.

LIT: see *literal.*

liter (L): a metric unit of capacity equal to 61.02 cubic inches or 1.057 liquid quarts.

literal (LIT)

(1) in a source program, an explicit representation of the value of an item, which value must be unaltered during any translation of the source program; for example, the word "FAIL" in the instruction: "If X = 0 print "FAIL"." (A) (B)

(2) a symbol or a quantity in a source program that is itself data, rather than a reference to data. cf. *figurative constant.*

(3) a character string whose value is implicit in the characters themselves. The numeric literal 7 expresses the value 7, and the numeric literal "CHARACTERS" in expresses the value CHARACTERS.

literal operands: operands, usually in source language statements, that specify the value of a constant rather than the address in which the constant is stored. The coding is more concise than if the constant has been allocated a data name.

literal pool: an area of storage into which an assembler assembles the values of the literals specified in a source program.

literature search: a systematic and exhaustive search for published material on a specified subject, and often the preparation of abstracts or summaries on that material.

litre: see *liter.*

live keyboard: a keyboard that allows users to interact with the system while a program is running to examine or change program variables or perform keyboard calculations.

liveware: slang, people involved in operating computers.

LLG: see *logical line group.*

LN: see *line.*

LNA: see *low-noise amplifier.*

load

(1) in programming, to enter data into storage or working registers. (A)

(B)

(2) to bring a load module from auxiliary storage into main storage for execution.

load-and-go: an operating technique in which there are no stops between the loading and execution phases of a computer program, and which may include assembling or compiling. (A)

load balancing: the process of assigning customers to line equipment so as to maintain a proper distribution of traffic in a switching system. Load balancing also is done at other places in switching equipment, such as on incoming selectors in step-by-step systems. (F)

load cards: the punched cards which hold the program instructions and the constant values.

load coil: an inductor used to increase the effective distributed inductance of a transmission pair, thereby improving its transmission characteristics. (F)

loaded line: a cable pair having load coils placed periodically along its length. (F)

loaded origin: the address of the initial storage location of a computer program in main storage at the time the computer program is loaded. (A)

loader: a routine, commonly a computer program, that reads data into main storage. see *absolute loader, bootstrap loader, initial program loader, relocating loader. (A)*

loader program: a program that takes information being entered into the computer or coming from external memory and transfers it into the internal memory of the computer. Such programs also assist in keeping track of where the information is in memory.

loaders and linkage editors: in microprocessors, they perform a number of services for the programmer. They take machine code or object code as input, along with possible programmer commands, and produce the desired memory image. Loaders can be considered a form of translator.

loader types: microcomputer loaders able to complete various coding processes.

load facility: a hardware facility designed to permit program loading.

load image: an image, ready for transmission to a communication controller, that contains multiple images; for example, a combination of a configuration image with one or more application program images, or a combination of a configuration image with one or more customized images.

loading: adding inductance (load coils) to a transmission line to minimize amplitude distortion. see also *lumped loading.*

loading coil: a coil tht does not provide coupling with any other circuit, but is inserted in a circuit to increase its inductance.

loading error: an error found in the output of the computer which came about as a result of a change in the value of the load that was supplied.

loading-location misuse errors: a loading-location specification was made but no load or execute was specified; the loading location specified was not within the available range of memory; the loading location is assigned as the first available location.

loading procedure: system, object, and library routines are loaded in a similar fashion. A program can have a fixed origin or can be relocatable. Fixed origin programs are loaded into the specified memory address. Programs are relocated by a base address first set by the executive routine. Following the main program being loaded, any library subroutines or device drivers called will then be loaded. When all the required routines are in memory, the loader returns to the job processor.

loading routine: a routine which, once it is itself in memory, is able to bring other information into memory from input media.

load leveling: the balancing of work between processing units, channels, or devices.

load map: a map containing the storage addresses of control sections and entry points of a program loaded into storage.

load mode: in some variable word-length computers, data transmission is such that certain delimiters are moved with the data. cf. *move mode*. (*A*)

load module: a program unit that is suitable for loading into main storage for execution; it is usually the output of a linkage editor. (B)

load module library: a partitioned data set that is used to store and retrieve load modules. see also *object module library, source module library.*

load-on-call: a function of linkage editor that allows selected segments of the module to be disk resident while other segments are executing. Disk resident segments are loaded for execution and given control when any entry point they contain is called.

load point: the beginning of the recording area on a reel of magnetic tape.

load program: synonymus with *loading routine.*

load sharing: computers placed in tandem (duplexing or triplexing) to share the peak-period load from a system.

lobe: the angular region over which an antenna (or aerial) experiences strong reception.

LOC
(1) see *local.*
(2) see *location.*
(3) see *location counter.*

local (L) (LOC): pertaining to that which is defined and used only in subdivision of a computer. (A) synonym for *channel-attached.* see *local central office, local channel, local code, local lock, local loop, local service area.*

Local Access and Transport Areas (LATA): an AT&T concept where calls between points within a LATA are handled entirely by the local telephone company.

local area network: a system linking together computers, word processors and other electronic office machines to create an inter-office, or inter-site network. These networks usually provide access to external networks, for example, public telephone and data transmission networks, information retrieval systems, and so on.

local automatic message accounting (LAMA): a process using equipment located in a local office for automatically recording billing data for message rate calls (bulk billing) and for customer-dialed station-to-station toll calls. (F)

local battery

(A) in telegraphy, the battery that actuates the telegraphic station recording instruments, as distinguished from the battery furnishing current to the line.

(B) in telephony, a system where each telephone set has its own individual source of power.

local central office: a central office arranged for terminating subscriber lines and provided with trunks of establishing connections to and from other central offices. see also *end office*.

local channel: in private-line services, that portion of a channel within an exchange that is provided to connect the main station with an interexchange channel.

local code: in assembler programming, that part of a program that is either the body of any macrodefinition called from a source module or the open code portion of the source module.

local exchange: an exchange where subscribers' lines terminate.

local format storage: an approach where often-used formats are stored at a terminal control instead of being repeatedly sent down the communication line.

local forms control (LFC): a system for off-line data-entry operations by diskette storage of fixed formats and data at the locate site.

local line: a channel connecting a subscriber's machines to a local exchange.

local lock: a suspend lock that protects the resources assigned to a particular private address space.

local loop: a channel connecting the

subscriber's equipment to the line-terminating equipment in the central office exchange.

locally attached: synonym for *channel-attached.*

locally-attached station: deprecated term for *channel-attached station.*

local mode: the state of a data-terminal device that cannot accept incoming calls or data because it is engaged in some internal activity.

local order wire: a communications circuit between a technical control facility and selected terminal or repeater locations within the communications complex.

local oscillator: a device used to supply a stable single-frequency signal to an upconverter or downconverter. The local oscillator signal is mixed with the information-carrying signal to change its frequency up or down.

local service area: in telecommunications, the area containing the telephone stations that a flat-rate customer may call without incurring toll charges.

local side: data-terminal connections to input-output devices.

local station: synonym for *channel-attached station.*

local switching facilities: switching systems that perform end office (class 5 office) functions. Switching systems to which loops or lines are connected. (F)

local variable: a variable that is defined and used only in one specified portion of a computer program. (E)

local variable symbol: in assembler programming, a variable symbol that can be used to communicate values inside a macro definition or in the open code portion of a source module. cf. *global variable symbol.*

locate: a tape is searched for the first occurrence of specific information.

locate mode: a way of providing data by pointing to its location instead of moving it. see also *move mode, substitute mode.*

location (LOC): any place in which data may be stored. see *protected location, storage location. (A)* cf. *address.*

location counter (LC) (LCNTR) (LOC): a counter whose value indicates the address of data assembled from a machine instruction or a constant, or the address of an area of reserved storage, relative to the beginning of a control section.

location life: the length of time a given customer subscribes to the same service using the same plant on the same premises. (G)

locator device: in computer graphics, an input device that provides coordinate data; for example, a mouse, a tablet, a thumbwheel. see also *choice device, pick device, valuator device.* (E)

locator qualification: in PL/1, in a reference to a based variable, either a locator variable or function reference connected by an arrow to the left of a based variable to specify the generation of the based variable to which the reference refers, or the implicit connection of a locator variable with the based reference.

locator variable: in PL/1, a variable whose value identifies the location in internal storage of a variable or a buffer.

lock: a serialization mechanism by which a specific resource is restricted for use by the holder of the lock.

locked name: in PL/1, a name that is not necessarily available at a given time to all tasks that know the name.

locked page: in virtual storage systems, a page that is not to be paged out.

locked record: in PL/1, a record in an exclusive direct update file that is available to only one task at a time.

locking: in code extension characters, having the characteristic that a change interpretation applies to all coded representation following, or to all coded representations of a given class, until the next appropriate code extension character occurs. (A) (B) cf. *nonlocking.* synonymous with *latching.*

lockout

(1) in a telephone circuit controlled by an echo-suppressor, the inability of one or both subscribers to get through because of either excessive local circuit noise or continuous speech from one subscriber.

(2) on a calculator, the facility that inhibits the entry of data when the machine is in overflow or error condition. (D)

(3) to place unaddressed terminals on a multipoint line in control state so that they will not receive transmitted data. see also *blind, polling, selection.*

(4) in multiprocessing, a programming tecnique used to prevent access to critical data by both processing units at the same time.

(5) synonym for *protection.*

lockout module: an electronic circuit that prevents keying of more than one keyboard output signal at a time. When two or more keys are depressed simultaneously, it either accepts only the first signal register or denies entry of all signals and transmits an error signal to warn an operator.

lock-up table: an approach to control the location to which a jump or transfer is made. It is used primarily when there are numerous alternatives, as with a function evaluation in scientific computations.

log: synonym for *journal.* see *system log.*

logger

(1) a functional unit that records events and physical conditions, usually with respect to time. (B)

(2) a device that enables a user entity to log in, for example, to identify itself, its purpose, and the time of entry; and to log out with the corresponding data so that the appropriate accounting procedures may be carried out in accordance with the operating system. (*A*)

logging: the recording of data about specific events. see *data logging.* (A)

logic: see *double rail logic, formal logic, symbolic logic.* (A)

logical access level: access to a data set by logical records.

logical ADD: synonym for *disjunction.* (A) (B)

logical chart: synonymous with *logic flowchart.*

logical child segment: in a data base, a pointer segment that establishes an access path between its physical parent segment and its logical parent segment.

logical circuit: in packet mode operation, a means of duplex transmission across a data link, comprising associated send and receive channels. A number of logical circuits may be derived from a data link by packet interleaving. Several logical circuits may exist on the same data link. (C)

logical comparison: a logic operation to determine whether two strings are identical. (A) (B)

logical constant: in FORTRAN, a constant that specifies a truth value; true or false.

logical data structure: in a data base, a hierarchic structure of segments.

logical decision

(1) the planning of a computer system prior to its detailed engineering design.

(2) the synthesizing of a network of elements to perform a specified function.

(3) the result of the above, frequently called the logic of the computer.

logical design

(1) the logic of the system, machine, or network.

(2) computer design from the viewpoint of data flow within the computer without consideration of the hardware utilized.

logical device address (LDA): a number used to represent a terminal or terminal component within a work station.

logical diagram: see *logic diagram.*

logical difference: the members of one set which are not also members of another set.

logical element: the simplest device able to be represented in a system of symbolic logic, for example, flip-flop.

logical expression

(1) an expression that contains logical operators and operands and that can be reduced to a value that is true or false. (E)

(2) in assembler programming, a conditional assembly expression that is a combination of logical terms, logical operators, and paired parentheses.

(3) in FORTRAN, a combination of logical primaries and logical operators.

logical file: synonym for *file.*

logical flowchart: see *logic flowchart.*

logical group instructions: complement data in a group of instructions that usually includes AND, OR, exclusive-OR, compare, and rotate or complement dta in registers or in memory.

logical IF: a FORTRAN IV statement will execute when the logical expression is true, or will bypass the statement if found to be false.

logical instruction: an instruction that causes the execution of an operation defined in symbolic logic statements or operators, such as AND & OR. cf. *arithmetic instruction.*

logical (LIOCS): a comprehensive set of macroinstruction routines provided to handle creation, retrieval, and modification of data files.

logical level (of a structure member): in PL/1, the depth indicated by a level number when all level numbers are in direct sequence, that is, when the increment between successive level numbers is one.

logical line group (LLG): any collection of data links specified by a user as a group at generation of the network control program.

logical multiply: synonym for *AND.* (A) (B)

logical number: a number assigned to a peripheral unit during autoload or system generation time.This number can be changed whenever conve-nient, in contrast with a physical unit number.

logical operation: synonym for *logic operation. (A) (B)*

logical operator

(1) in assembler programming, an operator or pair of operators that can be used in a logical expression to indicate the action to be performed on the terms in the expression. The logical operators are AND, OR, NOT, AND NOT, and OR NOT.

(2) a COBOL word that defines the logical connections between relational operators. The three logical operators and their meanings are: OR (logical inclusive—either or both) AND (logical connective—both), and NOT (logical negation).

(3) in FORTRAN, and of the set of three operators. NOT.,.AND.,.OR.

logical operators: in PL/1, the bit-string operators (not), & (and), and | (or).

logical page identifier (LIPID): the unique identifier of a specific page.

logical page number (LPN): the relative page number within a logical group. It is added to the logical group number to create a unique LPID.

logical parent segment: in a data base, a segment pointed to by a logical child segment that contains common reference data. The pointer from the logical child segment to the logical parent segment can be symbolic or direct. A logical parent segment can also be a physical parent segment.

logical primary: in FORTRAN, an irreducible logical unit: a logical constant, logical variable, logical array element, logical function reference, relational expression, or logical expression enclosed in parentheses, having the value true or false.

logical product: deprecated term for *conjunction.* (A) (B)

logical record (LR)

(1) a record independent of its physical environment. Portions of the same logical record may be located in different physical records, or several logical records or parts of logical records may be located in one physical record. (A) (B)

(2) a record from the standpoint of its content, function, and use rather than its physical attributes; that is, one that is defined in terms of the information it contains.

(3) in COBOL, the most inclusive data item, identified by a level-01 entry. It consists of one or more related data items.

logical relation: in assembler programming, a logical term in which two expressions are separated by a relational operator. The relational operators are EQ, GE, GT, LE, LT, and NE. see also *arithmetic relation, character relation.*

logical shift: a shift that equally affects all of the characters of a computer word. synonymous with *logic shift. (A)* (B)

logical structure: the interrelationships among data in a data base as perceived by its users. (E)

logical sum: deprecated term for *disjunction.* (A) (B)

logical switch: an electronic unit used for directing input cards to one of a number of outputs.

logical symbol: a symbol use to represent any one of the logical operators.

logical term: in assembler program-

ming, a term that can be used only in a logical expression.

logical timer: a software logic element representing the use of a hardware timer.

logical tracing: tracing as performed only on jump or transfer instructions.

logical track: a group of tracks that can be addressed as a single group.

logical unit (LU): a port through which a user gains access to the services of a network.

logical variable: deprecated term for *switching variable.*

logical volume: a portion of a physical volume which is viewed by the system as a volume.

logic analysis: the delineation or determination of the steps needed to yield the desired computer output or derive the intelligence information from the given or ascertained input data or model.

logic analyzer: a test and diagnostic system equipped with an oscilloscope, able to display bus and other digital states such as 0s and 1s, and perform complex test activities as well.

logic card: a group of electical components and wiring circuitry mounted on a board which permits easy withdrawal from and replacement in a socket in the equipment. Each card is related to a basic machine function, and, on discovery of a bug in that function, the card can be replaced.

logic chart: synonymous with *logic flowchart.*

logical circuit: an electronic circuit that is used to complete a logical function. Examples include OR, NOR, AND, NAND, and Exclusive-OR. The output of the circuit is dependent on the state (1 or 0) of the inputs.

logical decision: a specific decision made in a computing system or environment as a direct result of the internal organization of the system, but one of the binary or yes or no type, and basically relating to questions of equality, inequality, or relative magnitude.

logic decoder: a logic unit that converts data from one number system to another, for example, an octal-to-decimal decoder. Decoders are also used to recognize unique addresses, such as a device addresses, and bit patterns.

logic design: a functional design that uses formal methods of description, such as symbolic logic. (A)

logic device: a device that performs logic operations. (A)

logic diagram: a graphic representation of a logic design. (A)

logic element: a device that performs an elementary logic function. see *combinational logic element, sequential logic element. (A)*

logic expressions: consists of logical constants, variable array elements, function references, and combinations of those operands, separated by logical operators and parenthesis. Logic expressions are usually used in logical IF statements but can also be found in logical assignment statements and as arguments of functions.

logic flowchart
(1)   a chart representing logical elements and their relationships.
(2)   the representation of the logical steps in a program using a standard set of symbols.

logic function: deprecated term for *switching function.* (A) (B)

logic instruction: an instruction in which the operation part specifies a logic operation. (A) (B)

logic light: the control-console light that indicates that an error has occurred within an operation.

logic multiply: a boolean operation performed on two binary digits so that the result is one, if and only if both digits are one, and zero if either digit, or both, is a zero.

logic operation
(1)   an operation that follows the rules of symbolic logic. (B)
(2)   an operation in which each character of the result depends on not more than one character of each operand. (B)
(3)   synonymous with *logical operation. (A)*

logic probe: a logic-testing tool used to give a direct readout of logic levels without the setup and calibration time required for logic analyzers and scopes.

logic product: the result developed from the AND operation as contrasted with product arithmetic.

logic shift: synonym for *logical shift.* (A) (B)

logic short fault: a fault in logic circuitry in which a short circuit exists between logic blocks and that operates as if it were an additional logic block.

logic signals: synonymous with *logic states.*

logic states: the binary (1 or 0) values at the nodes of logic elements and ICs at a particular time. synonymous with *logic signals.*

logic symbol: a symbol that represents an operator, a function, or a functional relationship. (A)

logic unit: a part of a computer that performs logic operations and related operations. (B) see *arithmetic unit, logical unit.* (*A*)

log in: the act of inserting data, usually to a terminal, prior to beginning a dialog or entering a query.

log off: to request that a session be terminated.

log on: to initiate a session.

log on request: see *log on.*

log out: synonymous with *log,* except there is the expectation to receive a printout instead of a manual record.

log-periodic antenna: a broadband, multi-element, unidirectional narrow-beam antenna, whose frequency-response characterics are repeated at frequencies equally spaced, with the period equal to the logarithm of the ratio which determines the length and spacing of the elements.

longitudinal balance: a measure of the conversion of equal induced noise-to-ground voltages to metallic current (loop control current) in a two-wire transmission pair. When the balance is good, the metallic current is relatively small. (F)

longitudinal check: a system of error control based on the check that some present rules for the formation of the group of bits in the same, numerical order in all the character signals in a block are observed.

longitudinal circuit: a circuit formed by one telephone wire (or by two or more telephone wires in parallel) with the return through the earth or through any other conductors except those which are taken with the origi-nal wire or wires to form a metallic telephone circuit.

longitudinal induction noise: noise induced into a cable pair as metallic (loop) current because of pair imbalance or the unequal coupling of the noise source into the wires of a pair. (F)

longitudinal-mode delay line: a magnetostrictive delay line in which the mode of operation depends on longitudinal vibration in a magnetostrictive material.

longitudinal parity check

(1) a parity check performed on a group of binary digits in a longitudinal direction for each track. (E)

(2) a system of error checking performed at the receiving station after a block check character has been accumulated.

(3) see also *transverse parity check.*

(4) synonymous with *longitudinal redundancy check.*

longitudinal redundancy check (LRC): synonym for *longitudinal parity check.*

longitudinal redundancy check (LRC) character: on a magnetic tape where each character is represented in a lateral row of bits, a character used for checking the parity of each track in the longitudinal direction. Such a character is usually the last character recorded in each block and is used in some magnetic recording systems to reestablish the initial recording status. (A)

longitudinal transmission check: an even or odd parity check at fixed intervals during data transmission.

long lines: a department of AT&T HQ that provides most intercompany transmission facilities in the Bell System.

long-route design: a codification of design practices used to plan customer loops that exceed the resistance design limit of the serving central office. (F)

look ahead: the process of masking interrupt until the following instruction has been executed.

look up: a program system operation or process in which a table of stored values is searched (or scanned) until a value equal to (or sometimes greater than) a specific value is located.

look-up table: a collection of data in a form suitable for ready reference, frequently as stored-in-sequence machine locations or written in the form of an array of rows and columns for easy entry.

loop

(1) a set of instructions that may be executed repeatedly while a certain condition prevails. In some implementations, no test is made to discover whether the condition prevails until the loop has been executed once. (A) (B)

(2) in data communication, an electrical path connection—a station and a channel.

(3) a channel between a customer's terminal and a central office. The most common form of loop, a pair of wires. synonymous with *line*. (F)

(4) a two-wire ungrounded connection between pieces of equipment (as distinguished from a one-wire and ground connection). (F)

(5) see *closed loop, feedback loop, loop network, magnetic hysteresis loop*.

loop-back test: a test in which signals are looped from a test center through a data set or loop-back switch and back to the test center for measurement. see also *bussback*.

loop body

(1) the part of the loop that accomplishes its primary purpose.

(2) in a counter, a part of the loop control.

(3) cf. *loop control*. (A)

loop box: a register for modifying instructions within a loop.

loop check: synonym for *echo check*.

loop computing: performance of the primary function of a loop, by the instructions of the loop itself, as distinguished from loop initialization, modification, and testing, which are housekeeping operations.

loop control: the parts of the loop that modify the loop control variables and determine whether to execute the loop body or exit from the loop. cf. *loop body*. (A)

loop control statement: an executable statement that is used to specify the statements to be executed under the control of a loop, the parameters that are used in executing the loop, the conditions for terminating the loop, and the location to which control is to be passed when the loop is terminated; for example, FORTRAN DO, ALGOL FOR, COBOL PERFORM. (E)

loop-control variable: a variable that affects the execution of instructions in the loop body and is modified by a loop control. (A)

loop counter: in assembler programming, a counter used to prevent excessive looping during conditional assembly processing.

loop feedback signal: that part of the loop output signal that is fed back to the input to yield the loop actuating signal.

looping: repetitive execution of the same statement or statements, usually controlled by a DO statement.

looping execution: the execution of the same set of instructions where for each execution some parameter or sets of parameters have undergone a change.

loop initialization: the parts of a loop that set its starting values. (A)

loop input signal: an external signal applied to a feedback control loop in control systems.

loop jack switchboard: a patch panel with rows of jacks for physical access to local loops (maximum capacity of 90 channels). Each column of four jacks accesses one local loop and consists of looping jacks, a set jack, and a miscellaneous jack.

loop modification: alteration of instruction addresses, counters, or data by means of instructions of a loop.

loop network: a network configuration in which there is a single path between all nodes and the path is a closed circuit. (E)

loop resistance: synonymous with *line loop resistance.*

loop reverse battery: a method of signaling over interoffice trunks in which dc changes, including directional changes associated with battery reversal, are used for supervisory states. This technique provides two-way signaling on two-wire trunks; however, a trunk can be seized at only one end—it cannot be seized at the office at which battery is applied. synonymous with *reverse battery signaling.* (F)

loop signaling: a method of signaling over dc circuit paths that utilizes the metallic loop formed by the line or trunk conductors and terminating circuits. (F)

loop start: a supervisory signal given at a telephone or PBX in response to completing the loop current path. (F)

loop termination: in reading data, the last punched card containing some specific code number which can be tests and thereby used to terminate the loop.

loop testing: determination of when a loop function has been completed by means of instructions of a loop. see also *loop termination.*

loop transfer function: the mathematical function expressing the relationship between the outputs of a properly terminated feedback loop system and the input.

loop transmission: a mode of multipoint operation in which a network is configured as a closed loop of individual point-to-point data links interconnected by stations that serve as regenerative repeaters. Data transmitted around the loop is regenerated and retransmitted at each station until it arrives at its destination station. Any station can introduce data into the loop.

loop transmission frame: the collection of data that is sent around a loop as an entity.

loop update: the process of supplying current parameters associated with a particular loop for use by the control algorithm of that loop in calculating a new control output.

loosely coupled: pertaining to processing units that are connected by means of channel-to-channel adapters that are used to pass control information between the processors. see also *tightly coupled*.

loss: synonymous with *attenuation*.

loss of significance: in a register, loss of one or more of the rightmost fractional digits because the result of an operation produced more than seven fractional digits or more than a total of ten whole-number and fractional digits. cf. *overflow*.

loudness loss: a measure used to express the loss of communication paths in a manner that reflects loudness perception. For partial and overall telephone circuits, loudness loss is the ratio of suitably weighted output signal levels to input signal levels. The signals may be electric or acoustic. (F)

low activity data processing: carrying out relatively few transactions on a large database.

low byte: (FFFA) bits 0 through 7 of a 16-bit binary number.

low-end MPU: a signal-chip microcomputer built for low cost applications, usually with some on-board RAM and ROM plus I/O or clock capabilities.

lower bound (LB) (LBW): in PL/1, the lower limit of an array dimension.

lower curtate: the adjacent card rows at the bottom of a punch card. (A)

LOWL: see *low-level language*.

low-level language (LOWL): a programming language close to machine code and in which each instruction has a one-for-one equivalent in machine code.

low-noise amplifier (LNA): a device which amplifies the received signal at an earth station. The LNA is usually mounted on the antenna.

low order: the significance given to characters or digits farthest to the right in a number.

low order digit: a digit that occupies a less significant position in a number.

low-order position: the rightmost position in a string of characters.

low pass: a filter that transmits low-frequency signals.

low-performance equipment: a device having insufficiently exacting characteristics to permit their use in a trunk or link circuits. Such a device can be used in subscriber line circuits whenever it meets the line-circuit requirements.

low speed (LS): usually data transmission speed of 600 bps or less.

low speed storage: storage whose access is so slow that it curtails the rate at which data can be processed. This suggests that the access speed is slower than the central processor's calculating speed and/or the speed of peripheral units.

low tape: an indication that the supply of paper tape in a perforator is nearly depleted.

LP

(1) see *light pen*.

(2) see *linear programming*.

(3) see *line printer*.

lp: lines per inch.

LPID: see *logical page identifier*.

lpm: lines per minute.

LPN: see *logical page number*.

LPT: see *line printer*.

LR: see *logical record*.

LRC: see *longitudinal redundancy check character*.

LRU: see *least recently used memory*.

LS: see *low speed*.

LSI: see *large-scale integration.*

LT: less than. see *relational operator.*

LTR: see *letter.*

LTRS: see *letters shift.*

LU: see *logical unit.*

luhn scanner: the scanning device invented by H.P. Luhn of IBM, for photoelectrical scanning of punched cards as they are fed through the machine and with some search capabilities.

Lukasiewicz notation: synonym for *prefix notation.* (A)

lumped loading: inserting uniformly spaced inductance coils along the line, since continuous loading is impractical. see also *loading.*

LWB: see *lower bound.*

M
(1) see *machine*.
(2) see *mantissa*.
(3) see *master*.
(4) see *mega*.
(5) see *memory*.
(6) see *meter*.
(7) see *milli*.
(8) see *mode*.
(9) see *modem*.
(10) see *monitor*.
(11) see *multiplier*.

machine (M): see *accounting machine, electrical accounting machine, Turing machine, universal Turing machine.* (A)

machine address: synonym for *absolute address.* (A) (B)

machine available time: power-on time less maintenance time.

machine check: an error condition caused by an equipment malfunction.

machine check handler (MCH): a feature that analyzes errors and attempts recovery by retrying the failing instruction if possible. If retry is unsuccessful, it attempts to correct the malfunction or to isolate the affected task.

machine check indicator: a protective unit that is turned on when certain conditions arise within the device, programming the machine to stop, to run a separate correction routine, or to ignore the condition.

machine check interruption (MCI): an interruption that occurs as a result of an equipment malfunction or error.

machine code: the machine language used for entering text and program instructions onto the recording medium or into storage and which is subsequently used for processing and printout. (D) synonym for *computer instruction code.* (A) (B)

machine cognition: the artificial perception in optical machine reading and pattern recognition.

machine cycle
(1) the identified time interval in

which a computer can perform a given number of operations.

(2) the shortest complete process of action that is repeated in order.

(3) the minimum amount of time in which the foregoing can be performed.

machine-dependent: anything which makes use of features unique to a certain computer.

machine equation: see *computer equation*.

machine error: following equipment failure, any deviation from correctness in data results.

machine-independent (MI): pertaining to procedures or programs created without regard for the actual devices that are used to process them.

machine independent language: a programming language having the potential to be understood by a wide range of computers, for example, high level languages such as COBOL, FORTRAN.

machine-independent solution: procedures and/or programs that are organized in terms of the logical nature of the problem rather than in relation to or concerning the various computer devices used to solve them or process them.

machine instruction: synonym for *computer instruction*. (A) (B)

machine instruction code: synonymous with *machine code.*

machine instruction set: synonym for *computer instruction set*. (A)

machine instruction statements: direct counterparts of machine instruction.

machine intimate: synonymous with *intimate*.

machine language (ML)

(1) a language that is used directly by a machine. (A)

(2) in word processing, the language used for entering text and program instructions on to the recording medium or into storage and which is subsequently used for processing and printout. (D)

(3) deprecated term for *computer instruction code*. (A)

(4) synonym for *computer language*. (A) (B)

machine language code: synonymous with *machine code.*

machine learning: the ability of a device to improve its performance based on its past performance. (A) (B)

machine logic

(1) built-in methods of problem approach and function execution; the way a system is designed to perform, what the activities are, and the type and form of data it can utilize internally.

(2) the capability of an automatic data-processing unit to make decisions based upon the results of tests performed.

machine operation: synonym for *computer operation*. (A)

machine-oriented language (MOL): synonym for *computer-oriented language*. (A)

machine powered by a disposable battery: a calculator that draws its power from a battery which has to be replaced by a new one after being discharged. (D)

machine powered by a rechargeable battery: a calculator that draws its power from a battery which can be recharged by main power after partial or total discharge. (D)

machine readable: a machine that is capable of being read by an input device.

machine-readable medium: a medium that can convey data to a given sensing device. synonymous with *automated data medium. (A)*

machine run: the execution of one or more routines that are linked to form one operating unit.

machine-sensible information: information in a form that can be read by a specific machine.

machine spoiled time: down or wasted computer time resulting from computer malfunction during production runs.

machine tool control: any powerful and versatile program for production of tapes for numerically controlled point-to-point and contouring machines.

machine translation: transmitting automatically from one representation to another one. Translation can involve codes, languages, or other systems of representation.

machine word: synonym for *computer word.*

macro: see *macro assembler, macrodefinition, macroinstruction, macroprototype statement. (A) (B)*

macro assembler: an assembler equipped with a facility for defining and expanding macroinstructions.

macroassembly program: a language processor that accepts statements, words, and phrases to produce instructions for a machine. It is more than an assembly program because it has compiler powers, permitting segmentation of a large program so that portions may be tested separately.

macrocall: synonym for *macroinstruction.*

macrocode: synonymous with *macro instruction.*

macrocoding: procedures for providing segments of coding which are used frequently throughout a program and defined at the beginning and used and referenced by a mnemonic code with parameters. Coding efficiency is enhanced and readability of the program is increased.

macrocommand: programs that are formed by strings of standard, but related, commands.

macrodeclaration: synonym for *macrodefinition. (A) (B)*

macrodefinition

(1) a declaration that provides the skeletal code that a macrogenerator uses in replacing a macroinstruction. (A) (B)

(2) a set of statements that defines the name of, format of, and conditions for generating a sequence of assembler language statements from a single source document.

(3) see also *source macrodefinition.* synonymous with *macrodeclaration.*

macrodefinition library: a macrodefinition stored in a program library.

macroelement: an order set of data elements that are handled as a unit and provided with a single data-use identifier.

macroexerciser: the repeated operation of supervising programs and other macroinstructions under differing conditions to locate program errors.

macroexpansion: the sequence of statements that result from a macrogeneration operation. synonym for *macrogeneration.*

macroflowchart: a chart or table used

in the design of the logic of a routine; the segments and subroutines of the routine are presented by blocks.

macrogenerating program: synonym for *macrogenerator.* (A) (B)

macrogeneration: an operation in which an assembler produces a sequence of assembler language statements by processing a macrodefinition called by a macroinstruction. Macrogeneration takes place at preassembly time. synonymous with *macroexpansion.*

macrogenerator (MAG): a computer program that replaces macroinstructions in the source language with the defined sequence of instructions in the source language. synonymous with *macrogenerating program.* (*A*) (B)

macroinstruction

(1) an instruction in a source language that is to be replaced by a defined sequence of instructions in the same source language. The macroinstruction may also specify values for parameters in the instructions that are to replace it. (A) (B)

(2) in assembler programming, an assembler-language statement that causes the assembler to process a predefined set of statements called a macrodefinition. The statements normally produced from the macrodefinition replace the macroinstruction in the program. synonymous with *macrocall.*

macroinstruction operand: in assembler programming, an operand that supplies a value to be assigned to the corresponding symbolic parameter of the macrodefinition called by the macroinstruction.

MACROL: see *macrolanguage.*

macrolanguage (MACROL): the rep-resentations and rules for writing macroinstructions and macrodefinitions.

macrolibrary: a library of macrodefinitions used during macroexpansion.

macroparameter: the symbolic or literal that is in the operand part of a macrostatement that is substituted into specific instructions in the incomplete routine to develop a complete open subroutine.

macroprocessing instruction: an assembler instruction that is used in macrodefinitions and processed at preassembly time.

macroprogramming: writing machine-procedure statements in terms of macroinstructions. (A)

macroprototype: synonym for *macroprototype statement.*

macroprototype statement: an assembler language statement that is used to give a name to a macrodefinition and to provide a model (prototype) for the macroinstruction that is to call the macrodefinition.

macrostatement number: a number associated with a single macrostatement so that the reference can be made to that statement.

macrosystem: a programming system with symbolic capabilities of an assembly system and the added capability of many-for-one or a macroinstruction development.

macrotrace: an error detection aid such as main memory and file dumps, loggings, and simulators. A macrotrace prints out the record of macros or records them.

MACSYMA: a programming language designed for nonnumeric manipulation of mathematical expressions in conversational mode.

MADCAP: language for mathematical problems and set operations.

MAG: see *macrogenerator.*

magazine slot: see *slot.*

magnetic-bubble storage: the storage medium of a bubble memory having a thin layer of magnetic garnet material. Under the influence of external fields, the bubbles are manipulated to represent information bits.

magnetic card (MC)

(1) a card with a magnetizable surface layer on which data can be stored by magnetic recording. (E)

(2) in word processing, a recording medium in the form of a paper or plastic card on which recordings can be made on only one side. (D)

magnetic card reader: a unit used to input information from magnetic cards or transfer information from magnetic cards to another form of storage device.

magnetic card storage: a magnetic storage in which data are stored by magnetic recording on the surface of thin flexible cards. (E)

magnetic cell: a storage cell in which different patterns of magnetization are used to represent characters. synonymous with *static magnetic cell.* (A) (B)

magnetic character: a character imprinted on a document using magnetic ink.

magnetic core

(1) a piece of magnetic material, usually toroidal in shape, used for storage. (B)

(2) a configuration of magnetic material that is, or is intended to be, placed in a spatial relationship to current-carrying conductors and whose magnetic properties are essential to its use. It may be used to concentrate an induced magnetic field as in a transformer induction coil, or armature, to retain a magnetic polarization for the purpose of storing data, or for its nonlinear properties as in a logic element. It may be made of such material as iron, iron oxide, or ferrite and in such shapes as wires, tapes, toroids, rods, or thin film. (A)

magnetic core storage: a magnetic storage in which data are stored by the selective polarization of magnetic cores. (A) (B)

magnetic delay line: a delay line whose operation is based on the time of propagation of magnetic waves. (A)

magnetic disk (disc)

(1) a flat circular plate with a magnetizable surface layer. synonymous with *disk.* (B)

(2) in word processing, a recording medium in the form of a flat circular plate on which magnetic recordings can be made on either or both sides. (D)

(3) see also *diskette.*

magnetic disk storage: a magnetic storage in which data are stored by magnetic recording on the flat surface of one or more disks that rotate in use. (B)

magnetic disk store: see *magnetic disk.*

magnetic disk unit: a device containing a disk drive, magnetic heads, and associated controls. (B)

magnetic drum: a right circular cylinder with a magnetizable surface layer on which data can be stored by magnetic recording. (E)

magnetic drum storage: a magnetic storage in which data are stored by magnetic recording on the curved surface of a cylinder that rotates in use. (E)

magnetic drum unit: a device containing a drum drive, magnetic heads, and associated controls. (E)

magnetic hand scanner: a hand-held device that reads precoded information from a magnetic stripe.

magnetic head: an electromagnet that can perform one or more functions of reading, writing, and erasing data on a magnetic data medium. (E) see also *preread head, read head, read/write head, write head.*

magnetic hysteresis loop: a closed curve showing the relation between the magnetization force and the induction of magnetization in a magnetic substance when the magnetized field (force) is carried through a complete cycle. (A)

magnetic ink: an ink that contains particles of a magnetic substance whose presence can be detected by magnetic sensors. (A)

magnetic ink character recognition (MICR): character recognition of characters printed with ink that contains particles of a magnetic material. cf. *optical character recognition.* (A)

magnetic ink character sorter: a device capable of reading magnetic characters and then sorting the documents upon which they appear. Used extensively in banks to sort checks.

magnetic ink scanners: machines that read numbers designed in a special type font and printed in a magnetic (iron oxide) ink.

magnetic memory: a storage unit that functions using a film of magnetic material for registering or recovering

information in the form of bits. synonymous with *magnetic store.*

magnetic mirror: a device based on the concept that ions in a magnetic field are reflected away from magnetic fields which are higher than average.

magnetic recording: in word processing, a technique of storing data by selectively magnetizing portions of a magnetizable material. (A) (B)

magnetic sheet: in word processing, a recording medium in the form of a broad rectangular strip on which magnetic recordings can be made on either or both sides. (D)

magnetic slot reader: a device that reads precoded information from a magnetic stripe as it passes through a slot in the reader.

magnetic storage: a storage device that uses the magnetic properties of certain materials. (A) (B)

magnetic store: see *magnetic memory.*

magnetic strip accounting machine: a unit that records data on the magnetic strip at the rear of the ledger card that can be read by the machine and recorded on a document without manual keyboarding.

magnetic stripe: a strip of magnetic material on which data, usually identification information, can be recorded and from which the data can be read.

magnetic tape (MT)

(1) a tape of magnetic material used as the constituent in some forms of magnetic cores. (A)

(2) a tape with a magnetizable surface layer on which data can be stored by magnetic recording. (E)

(3) in word processing, a recording

medium in the form of a ribbon that has one or more tracks along its length on which magnetic recordings can be made on either one or both sides. (D)

magnetic tape cartridge: synonym for *magnetic tape cassette*. (B)

magnetic tape cassette: a container holding magnetic tape that can be processed without separating it from the container. synonymous with *magnetic tape cartridge*. A distinction is sometimes made between cassettes and cartridges, based on their physical characteristics.

magnetic tape deck: synonym for *magnetic tape drive*. (B)

magnetic tape drive: a mechanism for moving magnetic tape and controlling its movement. synonymous with *magnetic tape deck, magnetic tape transport, tape deck, tape transport, tape transport mechanism*. (B)

magnetic tape file: a reel of magnetic tape holding records that are arranged in an ordered sequence.

magnetic tape label: one or more records at the beginning of a magnetic tape that identify and describe the data recorded on the tape and contains other information, such as the serial number of the tape reel.

magnetic tape leader: the portion of magnetic tape that precedes the beginning-of-tape mark. (B)

magnetic-tape librarian: arranges the installation program on the library tape in acceptable formats.

magnetic-tape reader: a unit able to sense information recorded on a magnetic tape in the form of a series of magnetized spots.

magnetic tape station: a tape unit that holds a magnetic-tape drive, including reading and writing heads, various controls, and so on, for storage or transfer of data.

magnetic tape storage: a magnetic storage in which data are stored by magnetic recording on the surface of a tape that moves longitudinally in use. (E)

magnetic tape terminal: converts the character pulses from serial-bit form to parallel-bit form while checking for odd parity and translating the code to the desired magnetic-tape code for entry into a buffer storage.

magnetic tape trailer: the portion of magnetic tape that precedes the end-of-tape mark. (B)

magnetic tape transport: synonym for *magnetic tape drive*. (B)

magnetic tape unit: a device containing a tape drive, magnetic heads, and associated controls. (B)

magnetic thin film: a layer of magnetic material, usually less than one micron thick, often used for logic elements or storage elements.

magnetic thin film storage: a magnetic storage in which data are stored by magnetic recording in a film of molecular thickness, coated on a substrate. (E)

magnetic track: a track on the surface layer of a magnetic storage. (A) (B)

magnetic wire storage: a magnetic storage in which data are stored by selective magnetization of portions of a wire. (B) deprecated term for *plated wire storage*. (E)

magnetostriction: an occurrence where certain materials increase in length in the direction of the magnetic field when subjected to such a field, and restored to their original length when demagnetized.

magnetostrictive delay line: a delay line using the physical principles of magnetostriction.

magnitude: of a number or quantity, the absolute value irrespective of its sign; for example, the magnitude of -4 is 4.

mag tape: deprecated term for *magnetic tape*.

mail box: an area of memory set aside for data addressed to certain peripheral units, including other processors.

mail merge: synonymous with *file merge*.

main battery powered machine: a calculator that draws its power from a battery or from the main electricity supply. (D)

main control unit: in a computer with more than one instruction control unit, that instruction control unit to which, for a given interval of time, the other instruction control unit may be designated as the main control unit by hardware or by hardware and software. A main control unit at one time may be a subordinate unit at another time. (A) (B)

main distributing frame (MDF): a distributing frame, on one part of which terminate the permanent outside lines entering the central office building and on another part of which terminate cabling such as the subscriber line multiple cabling or trunk multiple cabling, used for associating any outside line with any desired terminal in such a multiple or with any other outside line. It usually carries the central office protective devices and functions as a test point between line and office. In a private exchange, the main distributing

frame is for similar purposes.

main file: synonym for *master file*. (A) (B)

main frame: deprecated term for *processing unit* and *processor*. (E) synonym for *central processing unit*.

main lobe: see *major lobe*.

main memory (MM): usually the fastest storage device of a computer and the one from which instructions are executed. cf. *auxiliary storage*.

main-memory mapping: the main memory on some devices is mapped for protection and relocation in four separate maps: system data, system code, user data, and user code. Memory mapping reallocates the user code or the noncritical operating system code to alternate physical memory pages upon detection of a parity or uncorrectable memory error.

main operation: the major application or designed procedure that equipment performs.

main path: the major course or line of direction taken by a computer in the execution of a routine, directed by the logic of the program and the type of data.

main-powered machine: a calculator that depends solely for its power upon connection to the main electricity supply. (D)

main program

(1) the highest level COBOL program involved in a step. (Programs written in other languages that follow COBOL linkage conventions are considered COBOL programs in this sense.)

(2) in FORTRAN, a program unit not containing a FUNCTION, SUBROUTINE, or BLOCK DATA statement and

containing at least one executable statement. A main program is required for program execution.

main station: a telephone station with a unique call number designation and which is directly connected to a central office. Also, in dedicated connections for customer equipment, the main point where such equipment is connected to the local loop. see also *extension station.*

main storage (MS)
(1) program-addressable storage from which instructions and other data can be loaded directly into registers for subsequent execution or processing. (E)
(2) a storage device whose storage cells can be addressed by a computer program and from which instructions and data can be loaded directly into registers from which the instructions can be executed or from which the data can be operated upon. (B)
(3) cf. *auxiliary storage.*
(4) see also *processor storage, real storage, virtual storage.*
(5) deprecated term for *internal storage.*

main storage unit: synonym for *buffer storage.*

main switch: a device that makes and breaks the contract between the equipment and the main electricity supply. (D)

MAINT: see *maintenance.*

maintainability: the ease with which maintenance of a functional unit can be performed in accordance with prescribed requirements. (A) (B)

maintenance (MAINT)
(1) any activity, such as tests, measurements, replacements, adjustments, and repairs, intended to

eliminate faults or to keep a functional unit in a specified state. (A) (B)
(2) those activities intended to keep a machine in, or restore a machine to, good working order.
(3) see *corrective maintenance, deferred maintenance, emergency maintenance, file maintenance, preventive maintenance, schedule maintenance.* (A)

maintenance panel: a part of a unit of equipment that is used for interaction between the unit of equipment and a maintenance engineer. (A)

maintenance program chain: an instruction set permitting the deletion of records from a file.

maintenance standby time: time when the maintenance staff is on duty but when they are not involved in scheduling maintenance, installation, repair, and so on, they can carry out other tasks.

maintenance time: time used for hardware maintenance. It includes preventive maintenance time and corrective maintenance time. cf. *available time.* see *corrective maintenance time, deferred maintenance time, emergency maintenance time, preventive maintenance time.* (A)

major control field: the most significant control field in a record; the control field upon which sorting according to the collating sequence is first attempted.

major cycle
(1) the maximum access time of a recirculating serial-storage element.
(2) a number of minor cycles.

majority: a logic operator having the property that if P is a statement, Q is a statement, R is a statement, ... , then the majority of P, Q, R, ... , is true if more than half the statements are true, false if half or less are true. (A)

majority carrier: the major carrier in a semiconductor; in an n-type semiconductor, having more electrons than holes, electrons are the majority carrier; in a p-type semiconductor, holes outnumber electrons and are the majority carrier.

majority element: a logic element that performs a majority operation. synonymous with *majority gate*. (A)

majority gate: synonym for *majority element*. (A)

majority operation: a threshold operation in which each of the operands may take only the values zero and one, and that takes the value one if and only if the number of operands having the value one is greater than half the total number of operands. (A) (B)

major key: the primary key in a record.

major lobe: the radiation lobe containing the direction of maximum radiation. synonymous with *main lobe*.

major state: the control state of a computer, including fetch, defer, execute.

major structure: in PL/1, a structure whose name is declared with level number 1.

major task: the task that has control at the outset of execution of a program. It exists throughout execution of the program.

major total: the result when a summation is terminated by the most significant change of group.

make-break operation: a form of telegraph-circuit operation where the flow of current is interrupted as pulses are transmitted.

make busy: conditioning a circuit, a terminal, or a termination to be unavailable for service. When unavailable, it is generally necessary that it appear busy to circuits that seek to connect to it. (F)

makeup time: that part of available time used for reruns due to faults or mistakes in operating. (B) cf. *development time, production time*. (*A*)

malfunction: synonym for *failure*. (A) cf. *error, fault, mistake*.

malfunction routine: a routine designed to find a hardware fault or to assist in in diagnosing an error within a program.

management: see *computer-assisted management, data managment*.

management information system (MIS)
(1) management performed with the aid of automatic data processing. (B)
(2) an information system designed to aid in the performance of management functions. (*A*)

management science: the formulation of mathematical and statistical models applied to decision making and the practical application of these models through the use of digital computers.

mandatory cryptographic session: a cryptographic session in which all outgoing data is enciphered and all incoming data is deciphered. see also *clear session*. cf. *selective cryptographic session*.

manifolding: the use of numerous sheets of paper and carbon sheets to produce multiple copies at single printings.

manipulated variable: in a process that is sought to control some condition, a quantity or a condition that is changed by the computer to initiate a shift in the value of the regulated condition.

manipulation: see *algebraic manipulation, formula manipulation, symbol manipulation.* (A)

manipulative indexing: indexing where interrelations of terms are shown by coupling individual words.

man-machine simulation: models of systems where humans participate. The model is no longer completely computer-based and requires active participation of a person.

mantissa (M): the positive fractional part of the representation of a logarithm. In the expression, log 643 = 2.808, the .808 is the mantissa and the 2. is the characteristic. (B) synonym for *fixed-point part.* cf. *characteristic.* (A)

manual address switches: external control switches used by an operator to choose an address manually for read off in the storage address display lights or to transfer the contents to a register without disturbing the address contents or area.

manual analysis: the generation of input and output test patterns by a test engineer or a technician who surveys the function or structure of a logic circuit.

manual answering: answering in which a call is established only if the called user signals a readiness to receive the call by means of a manual operation. see also *automatic answering.* cf. *manual calling.* (E)

manual calling: calling that permits the entry of selection signals from a calling data station at an undefined character rate. The characters may be generated at the data-terminal equipment (DTE) or at the data circuit-terminating equipment (DTE). see also *automatic calling.* cf. *manual answering.*

manual control: the direction of a computer by means of manually operated switches.

manual entry: a hand insertion of data for some units of a computer.

manual exchange: an exchange where calls are completed by an operator.

manual function: a function initiated or effected by the machine operator. (D)

manual input: the entry of data by hand into a device. (A)

manual operation: processing of data in a system by direct manual techniques.

manual read: an operation where the computer does the sensing of the contents or settings of manually set registers or switches.

manual tax: a tax that is keyed in by an operator during a sales transaction at a point-of-sale terminal.

manual word generator: a unit that permits a word to be entered directly into memory following a manual operation.

many-for-one languages: languages that take a single functional statement and translate it into a series of subroutines or instructions in machine language, in contrast to a low-level (assembly) language in which statements translate on a one-for-one basis. Examples include FORTRAN, COBOL.

many-to-one: ratios or measured relations between members of one set and members of another set, where correspondences are stated that two or more members of one set correspond to one (only) member of another set. A many-to-one relation exists when several expressions in a source language are equivalent to one statement in a target language.

MAP: see *maintenance analysis procedures.*

map: to establish a set of values having a defined correspondence with the quantities or values of another set. synonymous with *map over.* (B) see *Karnaugh map.* (*A*)

map over: synonym for *map.* (A) (B)

mapped buffer: a display buffer in which each character position has a corresponding character position on the display surface.

mapping: in a data base, the establishing of the correspondences between a given logical structure and a given physical structure. (E)

mapping mode: a computer operation mode where virtual addresses above 15 are transformed through the memory map so that they become references to actual main memory locations.

margin

(1) the difference between the actual operating point and the point where a wrong operation will take place.

(2) in telegraphy, the interval between limits on a scale, usually arbitrary, in which printing is free of error.

margin-adjust mode: in word processing, the facility to scan forthcoming text as an aid in justifying margins.

marginal check: maintenance in which certain operation conditions, such as voltage or frequency sup-

plied, are varied about their normal values in order to detect and locate components with incipient defective parts. synonymous with *bias testing, marginal test.* (E)

marginal error: errors that occasionally occur in tapes, and usually disappear simply because the writing is done over a slightly different section of tapes.

marginal test: synonym for *marginal check.*

margin control: synonym for *range finder.*

margin guide: a paper tape device that measures distances across the tape from the guide edge to the center of the nearest track.

margin-punched card: a card punched only on the border, with holes to represent data, thereby leaving the center free for written or printed information.

mark: a symbol or symbols that indicate the beginning or the end of a field, of a word, of an item of data, or of a set of data such as a file, a record, or a block. (B) see *document mark, groupmark.* (*A*)

mark detection: a type of character recognition system that detects from marks placed in areas on paper or cards, called site areas, boxes, or windows, certain intelligence or information.

marker

(1) in computer graphics, a symbol with a recognizable appearance that is used to identify a particular location. (E) see *end-of-tape mark.* (A)

(2) the heart of common-control crossbar central office equipment. It performs the following functions in a No. 5 crossbar switching system: (a)

determines terminal locations of calling lines, incoming trunks bidding for service, called lines, and outgoing trunks in the equipment, (b) determines the proper route for the call, establishes the connection within the office, and passes routing information to the senders, (c) determines the calling line class of service, and provides charge classification, (d) recognizes line busy, trouble, intercept, and vacant line conditions, and (e) calls in a trouble recorder when necessary. (F)

mark hold: the normal no-traffic line condition whereby a steady mark is transmitted. This may be a customer-selectable option.

marking: in telephony, establishing a path in a network through a series of cross points.

marking bias: bias distortion that lengthens the marking impulses by advancing the space-to-mark transition.

marking-end distortion: end distortion that lengthens the marking impulse by delaying the mark-to-space transition.

marking wave: synonym for *keying wave*.

mark matching: a technique in OCR to correlate or match a specimen character with each of a set of masks representing the characters to be recognized. Mask types are holistic masks, peep-hole masks, and weighted-area masks.

Markov chain: a probabilistic model of events, in which the probability of an event is dependent only on the event that precedes it. (A)

mark scanning: the automatic optical sensing of marks usually recorded manually on a data carrier. (B)

mark sense: to mark a position on a punched card with an electrically conductive pencil for later conversion to machine punching.

mark sensing: the automatic sensing of conductive marks usually recorded manually on a nonconductive data carrier. (E)

mark-sensing card: a card on which mark-sensible fields have been printed. (A)

mark-sensing column: a line of mark-sensible positions, parallel to the Y-datum line of a card. (A)

mark-sensing row: a line of mark-sensible positions parallel to the X-datum line of a card. (A)

mark-space character: a specific analog multiplier, where one input variable is represented as a current or a voltage, and used to control the mark-to-space ratio of a repetitive rectangular wave. Its amplifier is made proportional to the other variable, which is also represented by a current or voltage.

mark-to-space transition: the transition, or switching, from a marking impulse to a spacing impulse.

maser: see *microwave amplification by stimulated emission of radiation.*

mask (MK)

(1) a pattern of characters that is used to control the retention or elimination of portions of another pattern of characters. (B)

(2) to use a pattern of characters to control the retention or elimination of portions of another pattern of characters. (*A*) (B)

maskable interrupts: interrupt signals that are ignored by the central processing unit on software command.

mask bit: a bit used to extract a selected bit from a string.

masked: synonym for *disabled.*

masked ROM: regular ROM whose contents are produced during manufacture by the usual masking process.

mask matching: in character recognition, a method used in character property detection in which a correlation or match is attempted between a specimen character and each of a set of masks representing the characters to be recognized.

mask register (MR): a register used for masking.

massaging: manipulating input data to yield a desired format, for example, in word processing.

mass data: a quantity of data larger than the amount storable in a central processing unit of a given computer at any one time.

mass memory (MM): large amounts of data stored in a computer's main memory, usually on magnetic tape or disk. Getting data from mass memory is slower than from main memory, but usually the computer does not need to look at this information very often.

mass storage (MS): storage having a very large storage capacity. (E) synonymous with *bulk storage.* (B)

mass storage device: a device having a large storage capacity, for example, magnetic disk, magnetic drum. (A)

mass storage dump/verify program: a program that permits the user to dump a specified area of memory to a mass storage device such as a magnetic tape, disk, or cassette.

mass storage file: a collection of records assigned to a mass storage device.

mass storage file segment: a part of a mass storage file whose beginning and end are defined by the file limit clause in the environment division.

mass storage on line: the storage of large amounts of data on a device, rendering any item rapidly (i.e., in milliseconds) accessible to the CPU of the computer. Magnetic drums and disks are common types of on-line mass storage devices.

mass storage volume control: synonymous with *journal.*

mass storage volume inventory: a data set that describes mass storage volumes and mass storage volume groups.

master (M) (MSTR): a document suitable to the document copying process being used. In some cases it is the original but in others it may need to be specially prepared. (D)

master card: a card that contains fixed or indicative information for a group of punched cards. It is usually the first card of the group.

master clock (MCLK): the primary source of timing signals used to control the timing of pulses.

master clock frequency: the number of pulses per second produced by the master clock.

master console: in a system with multiple consoles, the basic console used for communication between the operator and the system.

master control interrupt: signal generated by an input-output unit, or by an operator's error, or by request of the processor, for more data program segments, that permit the master control program to control the computer system.

master control program (MCP): a

program that controls the operation of a system, either by connecting subroutines and calling segments into memory as needed, or as a program controlling hardware and limiting the amount of intervention required by an operator.

master data: a set of data that is rarely changed and supplies basic data for processing operations. The data content of a master file.

master file (MF):   a file that is used as an authority in a given job and that is relatively permanent, even though its contents may change. synonymous with *main file*. (A) (B)

master file inventory: permanently stored inventory information retained for the future.

master-file-update program: an approach where programs from the old master file are deleted, corrected, or left unchanged and new programs are added from the transaction tape.

master frequency generators: in frequency division multiplexing equipment used to provide system end-to-end carrier frequency synchronization and frequency accuracy of tones transmitted over the system.

mastergroup: an assembly of 10 supergroups occupying adjacent bands in the spectrum for the purpose of simultaneous modulation and demodulation.

master instruction tape (MIT):   a tape on which all the programs for a system of runs are recorded.

master library tape: a reel of magnetic tape containing all the programs and key subroutines needed in a data-processing installation.

master mode: the mode of a computer operation where all legal basic operations are permissible.

master processor: a main processor in a master/slave configuration.

master program: the controller of all phases of the job setup; directs program compiling and debugging, assigns memory, assigns input-output activity schedules and interweaves multiple programs for simultaneous processing, controls equipment activities and data flow, provides for error detection and correction, and communicates with operators.

master program file: the tape on which all the programs for a system of runs are entered.

master record: the basic updated record used in the next file-processing run; usually it is a magnetic tape item.

master scheduler: a control program routine that responds to operator commands and initiates the requested actions.

master/slave multiprogramming: a system designed to guarantee that one program cannot damage or access another program sharing the same memory.

master/slave system: a system where the central computer has control over, and is connected to, one or more satellite computers.

master station (MST)
(1) a station that can select and transmit a message to a slave station.
(2) in basic mode link control, the data station that has accepted an invitation to ensure a data transfer to one or more slave stations. At a given instant, there can be only one master station on a data link. (E)

master terminal: any terminal in a network that is master, but only one terminal can be master at any one time.

As master the terminal can communicate with all other terminals within the network.

match: a comparison to determine identity of items. cf. *hit*. (*A*)

matching: the technique of comparing the keys of two or more records to select items for a particular stage of processing or to reject invalid records. (E)

material implication: synonymous with *conditional implication operation.*

mathematical check: a programmed check that uses mathematical relationships. synonymous with *arithmetic check*. (*A*)

mathematical function: a mathematical expression describing a relationship between two or more variables.

mathematical induction: a method of providing a statement concerning terms based on natural numbers not less than N by showing that the statement is valid for the term based on N and that, if it is valid for an arbitrary value of n that is greater than N, it is also valid for the term based on (n + 1). (A) (B)

mathematical logic: synonym for *symbolic logic*. (A) (B)

mathematical model: a mathematical representation of a process, device, or concept. (A)

mathematical operator: a symbol that indicates a mathematical process, describes the relations and restrictions that exist between the input variables and the output variables of a system.

mathematical programming: in operations research, a procedure for locating the maximum or minimum of a function subject to constraints. (B) cf. *convex programming, dynamic programming, integer programming, linear programming, nonlinear programming, quadratic programming.* (*A*)

mathematical simulation: using a model of mathematical equations in which computing elements are employed to represent all of the subsystems.

math(s) processing: in word processing software, an ability permitting mathematical computations to be carried out.

matrix

(a) a rectangular array of elements, arranged in rows and columns, that may be manipulated according to the rules of matrix algebra. (B)

(2) in computers, a logic network in the form of an array in input leads and output leads with logic elements connected at some of their intersections.

(3) by extension, an array of any number of dimensions.

(4) see *dot matrix.* (*A*)

matrix printer: a printer in which each character is represented by a pattern of dots; for example, a stylus printer, a wire printer. synonymous with *dot printer*. (*A*) (E)

matrix storage: storage, the elements of which are arranged so that access to any one location requires the use of two or more coordinates; for example, *cathode-ray storage, magnetic core storage*. (A)

matrix table: a specific set of quantities in a rectangular array according to exacting mathematical procedures and designs.

maximal-ratio combiner: a diversity combiner in which the signals from each channel are added together; the gain of each channel is made proportional to the signal and inversely proportional to the mean square noise in that channel, with the same proportionality constant for all channels.

maximum operating frequency: the highest clock rate or repetition where the modules perform reliably in continuous operations, under worst-case conditions, without special trigger-pulse (clock) requirements.

MAYBE compiler: a compiler carrying instructions, commands, and orders for the operations of the data channel and various devices. In addition, MAYBE automatically yields the needed system linkages to process the data channel interrupts and central computer traps. The MAYBE compiler is a macrogenerator that feeds symbolic input to the standard assembly program. MAYBE was coded in NOMAD and uses standard system I/O routines.

mb: megabyte; 1,048,576 bytes.

MBPS: see *mega.*

MBR: see *member.*

MC

   (1) see *magnetic card.*

   (2) see *megacycle.*

MCC: see *miscellaneous common carrier.*

MCH: see *machine check handler.*

MCI decision: this decision by the FCC in 1969 expanded competition in the intercity private-line market. It allowed Microwave Communications Inc. (MCI) to become the first specialized common carrier and to provide interstate intercity private-line service in competition with the Bell System. In its MCI decision, and its 1971 SCC decision (Specialized Common Carriers), the FCC said it expected

the SCCs would provide novel and innovative services not readily available from the telephone companies, under conditions which do not threaten the technical or economic viability of the telecommunications network. (G)

MCLK: see *master clock.*

MCP: see *master control program.*

MDF: see *main distributing frame.*

mean accuracy: the difference between the "true" value and the arithmetic mean or average of a statistically significant number of readings under specified environmental conditions. It does not include the effect of repeatability.

mean conditional information content: synonym for *conditional entropy.* (A) (B)

mean entropy: see *character mean entropy.* (A)

mean information content: synonym for *entropy.* (A) (B)

mean repair time (MRT): deprecated term for *mean-time-to-repair.* (A) (B)

mean-time-between-failures (MTBF): for a stated period in the life of a function unit, the mean value of the lengths of time between consecutive failures under stated conditions. (A) (B)

mean-time-to-failure: the average time a component or system functions without faulting.

mean-time-to-repair (MTTR): the average time required for corrective maintenance. (A)

mean transinformation content: in information theory, the mean of the transinformation content conveyed by the occurrence of any one of a finite number of mutually exclusive and jointly exhaustive events, given the occurrence of another set of mutually exclusive events. synonymous with *average transinformation content.* (A) (B)

measured (message rate) service: telephone service for which a charge is made in accordance with a measured amount of usage, referred to as message units. (F)

measure of information: see *information measure.* (A)

mechanical dictionary: the language-translating machine component that provides a word-for-word substitution from one language to another. see also *dictionary.*

mechanical translation: the generic term for language translation by computers or similar devices.

media

(1) in transmission systems, the structure or path along which the signal is propagated, such as wire pair, coaxial cable, waveguide, optical fiber, or radio path. (F)

(2) the plural form of medium, magnetic cards, disks, and cartridges and paper tapes are examples of the various media types devised to carry data or information.

media drive: in word processing, the device for recording or reading from a recording medium. (D)

media drive selector: a control for selecting a particular element of recording medium on equipment that has more than one media drive. (D)

media-resident software: software which is not an integral part of a computer system but is stored on some medium, usually a magnetic disk.

medium: see *data medium, empty medium, machine-readable medium, media, virgin medium.*

medium scale integration (MSI): a technology where 10 to 100 gates are produced on a single silicon chip.

medium speed: usually, data-transmission rate between 600 bps and the limit of a voice-grade facility.

meet: synonymous with *AND operation.*

mega (M) (MBPS): ten to the sixth power, 1,000,000 in decimal notation. When referring to storage capacity, two to the twentieth power, 1,048,576 in decimal notation.

megabyte: 1024 × 1024 bytes, or 1024K; 8 million bits.

megacycle (MC): see *megahertz.*

megahertz (MHz): a unit of measure of frequency. 1 megahertz = 1,000,000 hertz.

MEM: see *memory.*

member (MBR): a partition of a partitioned data set. synonym for *element.* (A)

membrane keyboards: keyboards with no mechanical linkages on individual keys. The membrane on which characters and other symbols are printed has a conductive back which completes a circuit when moved a few thousandths of an inch. synonymous with *touch-sensitive keyboards.*

memo posting: a systems technique in which item records are posted to a temporary file before permanent master files are updated.

memory (M) (MEM): the high-speed, large-capacity storage of a digital computer. deprecated term for *main storage.* (A) (B) see also *auxiliary storage, internal storage, mass storage, matrix storage, processor storage, real storage, virtual storage.*

memory addressing: the storage locations as identified by their addresses.

memory allocation: a means by which memory is allocated to processes or units.

memory annex: a small memory device as a go-between for the input and output units and the main memory.

memory array: memory cells arranged in a rectangular geometric pattern on a chip, organized into rows and columns as in a matrix.

memory bank: a block of memory locations responding to contiguous addresses. see also *bank select*.

memory bus: the CPU communicates with memory and input-output devices over a memory bus.

memory capacity: the number of elementary pieces of data that can be contained in a storage unit.

memory character format: memory storing approaches of storing one character in each addressable location.

memory core: pertaining to those storage units composed of ferromagnetic cores, or apertured ferrite plates, through which select lines and sense windings are threaded. see *memory*.

memory cycle: operations needed for addressing, reading, writing, and/or reading and writing data in memory.

memory dump: a listing of the contents of a storage device, or selected parts of it.

memory exchange

(1) the switching of the total contents of two storage devices or locations, such as two registers.

(2) a switching device able to control and handle the flow or exchange of data between storage units or other elements within the system.

memory fill: storage in the areas of memory which are not used by a particular routine, of some pattern of characters which will stop the machine if a routine through error tries to execute instructions from areas which were not intended to contain coding. An aid to debugging.

memory guard: electronic or program guard inhibiting or preventing access to a section of the storage device or area especially concerning the main or internal memory of the CPU.

memory hierarchy: a set of memories with differing sizes and speeds, and having different cost-performance ratios.

memory location (ML): a specified location within a computer storage device.

memory management: addressing extension hardware options available for some computers. The memory management option controls the function of user programs in a multiprogram environment.

memory map: a hardware implementation that provides for dynamically relocating, protecting, and executing programs in scattered fragments of memory.

memory-mapped I/O: an addressing strategy where I/O units are addressed as memory locations.

memory-mapped video: a means of CRT information and graphics display where every character or pixel location on a screen corresponds to a unique memory location which the CPU accesses.

memory mapping: a mode of computer operation where the 8 high-order bits of any virtual address greater than 15 are replaced by an alternative value, thus providing for dynamic relocatability of programs.

memory module: a magnetic or semiconductor module providing storage locations for 4K, 8K, 12K, 16K, or more words (where K = 1024).

memory page: the section of memory, typically 256 words.

memory parity: an approach that generates and checks parity on each memory transfer and provides an interrupt if an error is found.

memory pointer registers: special registers that direct (point) the CPU to the location of a word in memory that holds data.

memory power: a memory hierarchy within some larger computer systems that makes information in core storage available at differing speeds.

memory printout: synonymous with *core dump*.

memory protection: deprecated term for *storage protection*. (A)

memory register: see *register, memory*.

memory unit (MU): a component within automated equipment that registers what the equipment should be accomplishing at each step of the operation.

memory workspace: the quantity of memory needed by a program over and above the amount of memory required to store the program itself. Workspace is often used for input-output device buffer areas and for various other locations required by a program during its execution.

menu: a display of a list of available machine functions for selection by the operator. (D)

menu selection: making a choice from a menu.

mercury delay line: an acoustic delay line where mercury recirculates sonic signals. synonymous with *Hg delay line*.

mercury storage: a storage device that utilizes the acoustic properties of mercury to store data. (A)

mercury-wetted relay: a device that uses mercury as the relay contact closure substance.

merge
(1) to combine the items of two or more sets that are each in the same given order, into one set in that order. (A) (B)
(2) the automatic recording, printing, or sending onto one element of recording medium of selected recorded text, in correct order, from at least two other elements of recording media. (D)
(3) see *balanced merge*. (A)
(4) see also *collate*. (A)

merge order: the number of files or sequences to be combined during a merge operation.

merge pass: in sorting, the processing of records to reduce the number of sequences by a factor equal to the specified merger order.

merge sort: a sort program in which the items in a set are divided into subsets, the items in each subset are sorted, and the resulting sorted items are merged. see *balanced merge sort, unbalanced merge sort*. (A)

merging: see *order by merging, sequence by merging*. (A)

MESG: see *message*.

mesh network: a network configuration in which there are two or more paths between any two nodes. (E)

message (MESG) (MSG)

(1) in information theory, an ordered series of characters intended to convey information. (B)

(2) an arbitrary amount of information whose beginning and end are defined or implied. (*A*)

(3) a group of characters and control bit sequences transferred as an entity. (E)

(4) a combination of characters and symbols transmitted from one point to another.

(5) in telephone communications, a successful call attempt that is answered by the called party and followed by some minimum period of connection. (F)

(6) in data communications, a set of information, typically digital and in a specific code such as ASCII, to be carried from a source to a destination. A header, with address and other information regarding handling, may be considered part of or separate from the message. (F)

(7) see *error message, operator message*. (A)

message block: the concatenation of several messages into a single transmission or physical record, to reduce the frequency of the delays due to changing the transmission direction of the communication link.

message buffering: a method of spooling text messages to disk for output with device independence.

message circuit: a long-distance telephone circuit used in furnishing regular long-distance or toll service to the general public. The term is used to differentiate these circuits from circuits used for private-line service.

message circuit noise

(1) the short-term average noise level as measured with a 3A noise measuring set or its equivalent. This set includes frequency weighting and time constants to make the set most sensitive to noise that will impair transmission quality in telephone circuits used for speech. (F)

(2) the noise occurring in a voiceband channel due to electronic thermal effects, random cross talk, and intermodulation activity. (F)

message control flag: a flag indicating whether the information transmitted is control information or data.

message data set: a data set on disk storage that contains queues of messages awaiting transmission to particular terminal operators or to the host system.

message display console: a console device having a cathode-ray tube that allows messages to be displayed. Data stored in memory can be displayed as a page.

message error record: synonym for *error record*.

message exchange: a device placed between a communication line and a computer to handle specific communications activities and thereby free the computer for other work.

message field (MFLD): an area on the screen of a display device where messages are displayed.

message format: the identification and placement of parts of a message, such as its heading, address, text, end of message, and so on.

message header: the leading part of a message that contains information such as the source or destination code of the message, the message priority, and the type of message. see also *message text*.

message mode: a manner of operating a data network by means of message switching. (E)

message numbering: the identification of each message within a communication system by the assignment of a sequential number.

message polling: an approach for calling or signaling by the designated master station to other stations in a multipoint or multichannel network.

message processing program (MPP): a program that processes or otherwise responds to messages received from terminals.

message queue

(1)   a list of messages that are awaiting processing or waiting to be sent to a terminal.

(2)   a queue of messages within a message data set waiting to be transmitted to the host system or to a particular terminal operator.

message retrieval: the capacity to retrieve a message after it has entered an information system.

message routing: the process of selecting the correct circuit path for a message.

message sink: that part of a communication system in which messages are considered to be received. (B) see *data sink*.

message source: that part of a communication system from which messages are considered to originate. synonymous with *information source*. (B) see *data source*.

message switch

(1)   a computer that routes printed messages through terminals and other network nodes in the system.

(2)   a network node used to route data transactions to other nodes in the system.

message switching

(1)   in a data network, the process of routing messages by receiving, storing, and forwarding complete messages. (E)

(2)   the technique of receiving a complete message, storing, and then forwarding it to its destination unaltered.

(3)   see *message switching network*.

message switching network: a type of traffic network in which the sources provide messages and, for each, the address(es) of one or more destination; the traffic network then delivers the messages to their various destinations. Typically a message is in digital form and is stored digitally at one or more points in the network; the storage time may be long (days) or short (microseconds). This contrasts with a line switching network in which an unbroken channel is provided from source to destination and the absence of storage means that the format of the information is relatively unconstrained. Message switching services have long been offered by the Bell System in the telegraph field. These have been implemented with private traffic networks, but common-user networks are possible. (F) see also *message switching*.

message telecommunication service (MTS): service that uses in whole or in part the public telephone network. Examples include public telephone service, mobile radio-telephone service, air-to-ground service, and so on. Private-line services are not included. (F)

message text: the part of a message that is of concern to the party ultimately receiving the message; that is, the message exclusive of the header or control information. see also *message header.*

message transfer part: that part of a common channel signaling system that transfers messages and performs necessary function, for example, error control and signaling link security, related to the transfer.

messaging: in electronic communication, where a message is conveyed directly to its destination, for example, Telex.

metacompilation: the process of using compilers to compile other compilers used to compile programs for execution.

metalanguage: a language used to specify itself, or other languages. (A)

metallic facility terminal (MFT): a voice-frequency facility terminal combining voice-frequency transmission and signaling functions into one unit. It interfaces a metallic facility (wire) with a switching system or with another metallic facility. Channel bank equipment is not involved. (F)

metal-oxide semiconductor: see *MOS.*

metasystem: any system over and beyond a system of lower logical sequence, and therefore capable of deciding propositions, analyzing criteria, or exercising regulation for systems that are logically unable to make such decisions and discussions, or of self-regulation. see *metalanguage.*

meter (M): 0.9144 yard.

metering pulses: in telephony, peri-

odic pulses sent by a public exchange over a line to determine the cost of outgoing calls.

metre: see *meter.*

MF
(1) see *master file.*
(2) see *multifrequency pulsing.*

MFLD: see *message field.*

MFM: see *modified frequency modulation.*

MFR: see *multifrequency receiver.*

MFT: see *metallic facility terminal.*

MHz: see *megahertz.*

MI
(1) see *machine-independent.*
(2) see *microinstruction.*

MICR: see *magnetic ink character recognition.* (A)

micro-
(1) a prefix denoting one millionth (10^{-6}) as in microsecond, one millionth of a second.
(2) more commonly, a prefix denoting small, as in microinstruction, microprocessor.

microcircuit: a combination of connected elements inseparably associated on or within a single continuous substrate to perform an electronic circuit function.

microcircuit isolation: the electrical insulation of circuit elements from the conducting silicon wafer in the manufacturing process of a microcircuit.

Microcobol: a high-level language developed by Computer Analysts and Programmers for business-oriented microprocessor programming. Related to COBOL.

microcode
(1) one or more microinstructions.
(2) a code, representing the instructions of an instruction set, im-

plemented in a part of storage that is not program-addressable.

(3) to design, write, and test one or more microinstructions.

(4) see also *microprogram*.

microcoding: coding with the use of microinstructions.

microcomputer: a computer system whose processing unit is a microprocessor. A basic microcomputer includes a microprocessor, storage, and an input-output facility, which may or may not be on one chip.

microcomputer components: tiny digital computers developed from a few large-scale integrated circuit chips.

microcomputer development system: specially designed systems to utilize software units such as exercisers and emulators to eliminate manual input-output and the need for the user to be fluent in hexadecimal.

microcomputer word processing: microcomputer applications in the office, that is, controlling one or more typewriters that edit text stored on cassettes or floppy disks.

microcontroller

(1) a microprogrammed machine, a microprocessor, or a microcomputer used in a control operation to alter a process or operation.

(2) any instrument or machine that controls a process with high resolution, usually over a narrow region.

microelectronics: the use of solid circuits where units of semiconductors form into a number of components.

microfiche: a sheet of microfilm capable of containing microimages in a grid pattern, usually containing a title that can be read without magnification. (A) see also *ultrafiche*.

microfilm

(1) a high resolution film for recording microimages. (A)

(2) microform whose medium is film, in the form of rolls, that contains microimages arranged sequentially.

(3) to record microimages on film. (A)

(4) see *computer output microfilm*. (A)

microfilmer: see *computer output microfilmer*. (A)

microfloppies: the newest generation of floppy disks. Instead of the typical disk of $5\frac{1}{4}$ inches in diameter, the new disk used to drive ever-smaller computers, is between 3 and 4 inches in diameter.

microflowchart: a flowchart showing detailed program steps, from which coding can be carried out.

microform: a medium that contains microimages; for example, microfiche, microfilm. (E)

microform reader: a device that enlarges microimages for viewing.

microform reader-copier: a device that performs the functions of a reader and a printer to produce hard copy enlargements of selected microimages. synonymous with *microform reader-printer*.

microform reader-printer: synonym for *microform reader-copier*.

micrographics: that branch of science and technology concerned with methods and techniques for converting any form of information to or from microform. see *computer micrographics*.

microimage: an image too small to be read without magnification. (A)

microinstruction (MI)

(1) an instruction of a microprogram. (B)

(2) a basic or elementary machine instruction.

microinstruction sequence: series of microinstructions that the microprogram control unit chooses from the microprogram to execute a single macroinstruction or control command.

micromainframe: a microcomputer containing the computing power of a mainframe.

microminiaturization: the reduction in size and increase in packing density of electronic components and circuit elements, resulting in less space, less power, and less delay in signal propagation.

microorder: a part of a microcoded control word that controls specific machine operations.

microprocessing unit (MPU): the main constituent of the hardware of a microcomputer, consisting of the microprocessor, the main memory, the input-output interface units, and the clock circuit, in addition to a buffer, driver circuits, and passive circuit elements.

microprocessor (MP): an integrated circuit that accepts coded instructions for execution; the instructions may be entered, integrated, or stored internally. see also *microcomputer.*

microprocessor analyzer: a digital diagnostic device for testing and debugging of MPU hardware and software.

microprocessor architecture: architectural features including general-purpose registers, stacks, interrupts, interface structure, choice of memories, and so on.

microprocessor chip: an integrated circuit that holds all necessary elements of a central processor, including the control logic, instruction decoding, and arithmetic-processing circuitry.

microprocessor compiler: a program that translates the source program into machine language. These compilers, which are usually run on medium- or large-scale computers, are available from several time-sharing services.

microprocessor memory interface: memory interface circuits that can generate more address lines and the signals needed to interface with up to 65K or more bytes, of RAM, PROM, or ROM memory.

microprogram

(1) a sequence of elementary instructions that corresponds to a specific computer operation, that is maintained in special storage, and whose execution is initiated by the introduction of a computer instruction into an instruction register of a computer. (A) (B)

(2) a group of microinstructions that when executed performs a preplanned function.

microprogram assembly language: computer-dependent machine language using mnemonics for the basic instruction set. In a microprogrammed computer, each assembly language instruction is implemented by a microprogram.

microprogram control logic: devices required to implement machine instructions. A hard-wired computer employs much more control logic than a microprogrammed computer.

microprogram control store: memory, used by the control processor, in which microprograms are stored.

microprogram fields: parts of a microinstruction that specify one microoperation. Each of several fields can be independent of any other.

microprogram instruction set: repertoire of machine-dependent instruction available to the assembly-language programmer.

microprogrammed microprocessor: in a microprogrammed processor, operations on the fundamental register-transfer level that can be programmed.

microprogram microassembler: a program that translates microprograms in symbolic form into bit patterns that are then loaded into the control store.

microprogram microcode: another name for the microinstructions that make up a microprogram, either in source language or in object-code form.

microprogramming: the preparation or use of microprograms. (A) (B)

microsecond: one-millionth of a second.

microwave: any electromagnetic wave in the radio frequency spectrum above 890 megahertz.

microwave amplification by stimulated emission of radiation (maser): the general class of microwave amplifiers based on molecular interaction with electromagnetic radiation. The nonelectronic nature of the maser principle results in very low noise.

microwave links: systems which use the relatively short microwave frequencies to broadcast from one point to another.

MIDAS: a digital stimulated analog computing program.

middle punch: synonymous with *eleven punch* and *X punch*.

middleware: system software tailored to a particular user's need.

midicomputers: a computer of intermediate size and computing power, between a minicomputer and mainframe.

migration: see *data migration*.

migration path: a scheme to enhance a computer system's power or hardware while maintaining software compatibility, or vice versa.

milestone: a task or event that cannot be considered completed until all tasks that feed into it are completed.

milli (M): one thousand or one thousandth.

milliliter (ml): one thousandth of a liter. 0.27 fluid drams.

millimeter (MM): one thousandth of a meter. 0.04 inch.

millisecond (MS) (MSEC): one-thousandth of a second.

MINI: see *minicomputer*.

miniassembler program: a program designed to simplify machine-level programming on various microprocessor systems, by permitting the operator to type mnemonic program symbols on the terminal directly in assembler language, while the program generates the correct object code, placing it in the proper memory location, and printing it out simultaneously on the terminal.

minicomputer (MINI): a computer that does not need the closely controlled environment of main frame computers, and has a richer instruction set than that of a microprocessor.

minidiskette: a storage medium similar to, but smaller than, the standard flexible disk.

mini-floppy disk: a small floppy disk capable of storing somewhat fewer than 100,000 characters; used primarily in microcomputer systems.

minimal tree: a tree whose terminal nodes have been so ordered that the tree operates at maximum effectiveness.

minimum access coding: in machines having non-immediate-access main memory, a technique of coding which minimizes the time wasted by delays in transfer of data and instructions between memory and other machine components. synonymous with *minimum latency coding*.

minimum delay programming: a method of programming in which storage locations for instructions and data are chosen so that access time is reduced and minimized. (A) (B)

minimum distance code: a binary code in which the signal distance does not fall below a specified minimum value. (A)

minimum latency coding: synonymous with *minimum access coding*.

minimum-latency programming: synonymous with *forced coding*.

minor control field: any control field that is of less significance than the major control field in a sorting operation.

minor cycle: the time interval between the appearance of corresponding units of successive words in a storage device that gives serial access to storage positions.

minority carrier: the nondominant carrier in a semiconductor. see *majority carrier*.

minor structure: in PL/1, a structure that is contained within another structure. The name of a minor structure is declared with a level number greater than one.

minor total: the result when a summation is terminated by the least significant change of group.

minuend: in subtraction, the number or quantity from which another number or quantity is subtracted. (A) (B)

minus flag: a flag bit in the status register of the central processing unit; used to show a negative result from an arithmetic operation.

minus zone: the character or digit position that displays the algebraic sign of an operand.

mips: million instructions per second.

mirroring: in computer graphics, turning all or part of a display image 180 degrees about an axis in the plane of the display surface. (E)

MIS: see *management information system.* (A)

miscellaneous common carrier (MCC): a communications common carrier which is not engaged in the business of providing either a public land-line message telephone service or public message telegraph service. Miscellaneous common carriers were initially authorized to serve TV and radio markets. Today they are still viewed as serving these markets, although Domestic Satellite Carriers and Specialized Common Carriers also meet the FCC definition of Miscellaneous Common Carriers. (G)

miscellaneous intercept: in Bell System leased telegraph message-switching systems, the act of intercepting single-address messages containing a nonvalid call directing code or intercepting multiple-address messages without a proper multiple-address code. see also *willful intercept.*

miscellaneous time: the time during which a computer is used for demonstrations, training, or other such purposes. synonymous with *incidental time.* (A) (B)

misfeed: when cards, tapes, or other data or storage media fail to pass into or through equipment properly.

misregistration: a character recognition term; the improper state of appearance of a character, line, or document, on site in a character reader, with respect to a real or imaginary horizontal base line.

missing error: subroutines called by the program not found in the library. The names of the missing subroutines are also output.

mistake: a human action that produces an unintended result. cf. *error, failure, fault, malfunction.* (A)

MIT: see *master instruction tape.*

mixed-base notation: synonym for *mixed-base numeration system.* (A) (B)

mixed-base numeration system: a numeration system in which a number is represented as the sum of a series of terms, each of which consists of a mantissa and a base, the base of a given term being constant for a given application but the bases being such that there are not necessarily integral ratios between the bases of all the terms; for example, with bases b_3, b_2, and b_1 and mantissas 6, 5, and 4, the number represented is given by $6b_3 + 5b_2, + 4b_1$. A mixed-radix numeration system is the particular case of a mixed-base numeration system in which, when the terms

are ordered so that their bases are in descending magnitudes, there is an integral ratio between the bases of adjacent terms, but not the same ratio in each case; thus if the smallest base is b and if x and y represent integers, the numeral 654 in such a numeration system represents the number given by $6 xyb + 5 xb + 4 b$. A fixed-radix numeration system is the particular case of a mixed-base numeration system in which, when the terms are ordered so that their bases are in descending magnitudes, there is the same integral ratio between bases of all pairs of adjacent terms; thus if b is the smallest base and if x represents an integer, the numeral 654 in such a numeration system represents the number given by $6x_2b + 5 xb + 4b$. synonymous with *mixed-base notation.* (B) cf. *mixed-radix numeration system.* (A)

mixed-mode expression: synonym for *mixed-type expression.*

mixed-radix notation: synonym for *mixed-radix numeration system.* (A) (B)

mixed-radix numeration system: a radix numeration system in which the digit places do not all necessarily have the same radix; for example, the numeration system in which three successive digits represent hours, tens of minutes, and minutes; taking one minute as the unit, the weights of the three digit places are 60, 10, and 1 respectively; the radices of the second and third digit places are 6 and 10 respectively. A comparable numeration system that used one or more digits to represent days and two digits to represent hours would not satisfy the definition of any radix numeration system, since the ratio of the weights of the "days" and the "tens of hours" digit places would not be an integer. synonymous with *mixed-radix notation.* (B) cf. *mixed-base numeration system.* (A)

mixed-type expression: an arithmetic expression that contains both integer and real arithmetic primaries.

MK: see *mask.*

ML
(1) see *machine language.*
(2) see *memory location.*
(3) see *milliliter.*

MM
(1) see *main memory.*
(2) see *mass memory.*
(3) see *millimeter.*

MN: see *mnemonic symbol.*

mnemonic (MN): see *mnemonic symbol.*

mnemonic address: a simple address code that has some easily remembered relationship to the name of the destination; for example, LA for Los Angeles, NYC for New York City.

mnemonic name: a programmer-supplied word associated with a specific function name in the environment division of a COBOL program. It may be written in place of the function name in any format where such a substitution is valid.

mnemonic operation code: an operation code consisting of mnemonic symbols that indicate the nature of the operation to be performed, the type of data used, or the format of the instruction performing the operation.

mnemonic symbol (MN): a symbol chosen to assist the human memory, for example, an abbreviation such as "mpy" for "multiply." (A) (B)

MNOS: metal-nitride silicon device.

mobile telephone services: a class of services that utilizes radio channels to provide telephone service. Mobile telephone services include: (1) land mobile telephone service, (2) BELL-BOY service, (3) air/ground service, (4) VHF maritime service, (5) coastal harbor service, (6) high-seas maritime radio-telephone service, and (7) high-speed train service. (F)

mobility: the drift of ions, for example, electrons and holes in semiconductors, under applied electric fields; the intrinsic current-carrying property of n- and p-doped silicon.

MOD
(1) see *model.*
(2) see *modification.*
(3) see *modulate.*

mod/demod: modulator-demodulator unit. see also *data set, modem.*

mode (M)
(1) a method of operation; for example, the binary mode, the interpretive mode, the alphanumeric mode.
(2) the most frequent value in the statistical sense.
(3) in PL/1, a characteristic of arithmetic data, real or complex.
(4) see *access mode, load mode, move mode.* (A)

model (MOD)
(1) a representation in mathematical terms of a process, device, or concept.
(2) a general, often pictorial, representation of a system under study. see *mathematical model.*

model statement: a statement in the body of a macrodefinition or in open code from which an assembler-language statement can be generated at preassembly time. Values can be substituted at one or more points in a model statement; one or more identical or different statements can be generated from the same model statement under the control of a conditional assembly loop.

modem (M)

(1) (modulator-demodulator) a device that modulates and demodulates signals transmitted over data-communication facilities. (A)

(2) a functional unit that modulates and demodulates signals. One of the functions of a modem is to enable digital data to be transmitted over analog transmission facilities. (E)

(3) a contraction of the words modulator and demodulator, signifying an equipment unit that performs both of these functions. (F)

(4) see also *line adapter, modulation*.

modem-encryption devices: by placing encryption units at modem interfaces, some systems have all data on the link encrypted and decrypted in a manner that is transparent to the sending and receiving stations.

modes of priority: organization of the flow of work through a computer. The mode depends upon the sophistication of the system and the machine. and will vary from a normal noninterrupt mode to a system in which there are several depths of interrupt. There may also be different modes in different functions such as the input-output mode.

modification (MOD): the process of altering the address portion of an instruction resulting from executing earlier instructions in a program. see *modifier*.

modification level: a distribution of all temporary fixes that were issued since the previous modification level. A new modification level normally does not include new function and does not change the programming support category of the release to which it applies. see also *release, version*.

modified frequency modulation (MFM): the process of varying the amplitude and frequency of the "write" signal. MFM pertains to the number of bytes of storage that can be stored on the recording media. The number of bytes is twice the number contained on the same unit area of recording media at single density. synonymous with *double-dense recording, double-density recording*.

modifier: a word or quantity used to change an instruction causing the execution of an instruction different from the original one. The result is, the same instruction, successively changed by a modifier, can be used repetitively to carry out a different operation each time it is used. see *modify*.

modifier register: synonym for *index register*. (B)

modify: to alter a part of an instruction or routine.

modify instruction: an instruction that will most likely be modified before it is used for the final program.

modify ticket: a function at a point-of-sale terminal that enables an operator to key in a change to the quantity, to the price, or to both the quantity and the price of an item. This function is required only in certain sales transactions, and then only when the wand reader is being used to "read" merchandise tickets.

modular: a degree of standardization

of computer system components to allow for combinations and large variety of compatible units.

modularity: the extent to which a system is composed of modules. (A)

modularization: the design of computers to permit expansion of their capabilities by increasing the central processor's hardware and the number of peripheral devices, as required.

modulate (MOD): to carry out modulation.

modulation: the process by which some characteristic of one wave is varied in accordance with another wave or signal. This technique is used in modems to make business machine signals compatible with communication facilities.

modulation rate: the reciprocal of the measure of the shortest nominal time interval between successive significant instants of the modulated signal. If this measure is expressed in seconds, the modulation rate is given in bauds. (E)

modulator: a functional unit that converts a signal into a modulated signal suitable for transmission. cf. *demodulator.* (E)

modulator-demodulator: see *modem.* (A)

module

(1) a program unit that is discrete and identifiable with respect to compiling, combining with other units, and loading; for example, the input to, or output from, an assembler, compiler, linkage editor, or executive routine.

(2) a packaged functional hardware unit designed for use with other components. (*A*)

(3) see *disk storage module, load*

module, object module, programming module, source module.

(4) synonym for *spindle.*

module testing: the destructive read-off or use caused by overloading or underloading the computer components, causing failure of substandard units and minimizing nonscheduled downtime.

modulo: a mathematical operation in which the result is the remainder after a specified number has been divided; for example, 29 modulo 4 = 1.

modulo check: a calculation performed on values entered into a system by an operator. This calculation is designed to detect most common keying errors.

modulo-N check: a check in which an operand is divided by a number N to generate a remainder that is retained and later used for checking. For example, in a modulo-7 check, the remainder will be either 0, 1, 2, 3, 4, 5, or 6; if the remainder obtained when the operand is divided by 7 does not equal the retained value, an error is indicated. synonymous with *residue check.* (E)

modulo-N counter: a counter in which the number represented reverts to zero in the sequence of counting after reaching a maximum value of N-1. (A) (B)

modulus: in a modulo check, the number by which the summed digits are divided. see also *modulo check.*

MON: see *monitor.*

monadic boolean operator: a boolean operator having only one operand, for example, NOT. (A)

monadic operation: an operation with one and only one operand. synonymous with *unary operation.* (A) (B)

monadic operator: an operator that represents an operation on one and only one operand. synonymous with *unary operator.* (*A*) (B)

monitor (M) (MON) (MTR)
(1) a device that observes and verifies the operations of a data-processing system and indicates any significant departure from the norm. (B)
(2) software or hardware that observes, supervises, controls, or verifies the operations of a system. (*A*)

monitor console: the system-control terminal.

monitoring program: synonym for *monitor program.* (A) (B)

monitor jack: a jack that provides access to communications circuits for the purpose of observing the signal conditions on the circuit without interrupting the service provided by that circuit.

monitor printer: a device that prints all messages transmitted over the circuit to which it is connected.

monitor program: a computer program that observes, regulates, controls, or verifies the operations of a data-processing system. synonymous with *monitoring program.* (A), (B)

monitor unit: equipment that is supervisory and which is capable of verifying the operation of another unit or group in data-processing system, message routing systems, and so forth.

monolithic integrated circuit: a type of integrated circuit wherein the substrate is an active material, such as the semiconductor silicon.

monolithic storage: storage made up of monolithic integrated circuits.

monolithic technology: a technology in which all electronic components of a circuit (such as transistors, diodes, resistors, capacitors) are integrated into one chip; for example, MST.

monostable: pertaining to a device that has one stable state. (A)

monostable circuit: a trigger circuit that has one stable state and one unstable state. synonymous with *monostable trigger circuit.* (*A*)

monostable trigger circuit: synonym for *monostable circuit.* (A)

Monte Carlo method: a method of obtaining an approximate solution to a numerical problem by the use of random numbers; for example, the random walk method or a procedure using a random number sequence to calculate an integral. (A) (B)

morpheme: a linguistic unit that indicates relationships between words or ideas; a conjunction such as and, with, not.

MOS: metal-oxide semiconductor; a technology that helped make possible new types of complex chips, such as the microprocessor used in personal computers and high-capacity memories. see *C-MOS.*

MOSFET: metal-oxide semiconductor field effect transistor.

most-significant bit (MSB): a bit in the left-most position.

most significant character: that character which is in the leftmost position in a number or word.

mother board: a rigid frame to which circuit boards are affixed forming the basis of a microprocessor. synonymous with *back plane* and *chassis.*

motion register: a two-bit register containing a go/stop flip-flop and a forward/reverse flip-flop that controls the motion of the selected tape drive. The register is set under program control.

mount: a structure which supports an earth station antenna. Frequently used types of mounts are polar mounts, azimuth/elevation mounts, and wheel and track mounts.

mountable: disk packs which are interchangeable on any drive.

mount attribute: the attribute assigned to a volume that controls when the volume can be demounted; the mount attributes are permanently resident, reserved, and removable.

"mouse": a cigarette-pack size plastic box with a button on top and a cable connected to a computer. When moved on the surface of a desk, an arrow shifts on a monitor screen permitting the user to juggle words or statistics around. The "mouse" tells the computer what to do and eliminates clumsy computer commands that have to by typed with a keyboard into some personal machines.

m-out-of-n code: a form of fixed-weight binary code where m-of-the-n digits are always in the same state.

MOV: see *move*.

move (MOV): in computer programming, to copy from locations in internal storage into locations in the same internal storage. synonym for *transfer*. (*A*) (*B*)

move mode
(1) in some variable-word-length computers, data transmission such that certain delimiters are not moved with the data. (A)
(2) a transmittal mode in which the record to be processed is moved into a user work area. see *locate mode*,

substitute mode.
(3) cf. *load mode*. (*A*)

moving-head disk system: a disk instrument which has a read/write head able to move across the surface of the disk to access any one of a number of circular tracks of data.

MP
(1) see *microprocessor*.
(2) see *multiprocessing*.
(3) see *multiprocessor*.

MPL: see *multischedule private line*.

MPLX: see *multiplexer*.

MPLXR: see *multiplexer*.

MPP: see *message processing program*.

MPS
(1) see *multiprocessing system*.
(2) see *multiprogramming system*.

MPU: see *microprocessing unit*.

MPX: see *multiplexer*.

MPY: see *multiplier*.

MR: see *mask register*.

M response: synonymous with *V response*.

MRT: see *mean-repair-time*.

MS
(1) see *main storage*.
(2) see *mass storage*.
(3) see *millisecond*.

MSB: see *most-significant bit*.

MSBY: most significant byte.

MSD: most significant digit.

MSEC: millisecond (1/1000 second).

MSG: see *message*.

MSHP: maintain system history program.

MSI: see *medium scale integration*.

MST: see *master station*.

MT: see *magnetic tape*.

MTBF: see *mean-time-between-failures*.

MTR: see *monitor*.

MTS: see *message telecommunica-*

tion service.

MTS/WATS-like services: are provided by a number of other common carriers (OCC) using their own or leased intercity facilities and switching services. Access and egress for the OCCs are over exchange services provided by Bell and independent telephone companies. see *city-call, EXECUNET, SPRINT.* (G)

MTTR: see *mean-time-to-repair.*

MU: see *memory unit.*

MUL: see *multiplexer.*

MULT: see *multiplier.*

multiaccess system: a system permitting a number of people to access a central processor in conventional mode virtually simultaneously.

multiaddress: pertaining to an instruction format containing more than one address part. (A)

multiaddress calling: a process that permits a user to call more than one data station. (E)

multiaddress calling facility: a facility that permits a user to nominate more than one addressee for the same data. The network may accomplish this sequentially or simultaneously.

multiaddress instruction: an instruction that contains more than one address part. synonymous with *multiple-address instruction.* (A) (B)

multiaperture core: a magnetic core, usually used for nondestructive reading with two or more holes through which wires may be passed in order to create more than one magnetic path. synonymous with *multiple-aperture core.* (A) (B)

multiaspect: pertaining to searches or systems that allow more than one aspect or facet of information to be used in combination, one with the other, to effect identifying and selecting operations.

multichip: a circuit consisting of two or more semiconductor wafers, each containing a single element.

multidimensional language: a language whose expressions are assembled in more than one dimension; for example, flowcharts, logic diagrams, block diagrams, and decision tables. cf. *one-dimensional language.* (A)

multidomain network: synonym for *multiple-domain network.* (E)

multidrop line: synonym for *multipoint link.*

multidrop (network): a network configuration in which there are one or more intermediate nodes on the path between a central node and an endpoint note. (E)

multi-element dipole antenna: an arrangement of a number of dipole antennas.

multifrequency pulsing (MF): an in-band interoffice address signal method in which ten decimal digits and five auxiliary signals are each represented by selecting two frequencies out of the following group: 700, 900, 1300, 1500, and 1700 Hz. (F)

multifrequency pushbutton set: a telephone using pushbutton dialing and multifrequency signaling.

multifrequency receiver (MFR): a demodulator that decodes multifrequency signals from telephone sets or data terminals.

multifrequency signal: a signal made up of several superimposed audio frequency tones.

multifrequency terminal: a terminal that transmits data characters as multifrequency signals.

multifunction system: a computing system capable of performing a host of tasks, for example, a word processor with communication and mathematical potential.

multijob operation: concurrent execution of job steps from two or more jobs.

multilevel address: synonym for *indirect address.* (A) (B)

multilevel subrouting: the control state allows the display to jump from accessing one location in the memory to any other. When it is desired to jump to a display subroutine, the return address is automatically stored in a push-down list.

multilink

(1) a multiplicity of data links. Each link is controlled by its own link protocol. (C)

(2) a group of data links obtained by multiplexing. (C)

(3) in a data network, pertaining to a branch between two nodes consisting of two or more data links. (C)

multipass sort: a sort program that is designed to sort more items than can be in main storage at one time. (A)

multiple

(1) a system of wiring so arranged that a circuit, a line, or a group of lines is accessible at a number of points, to any one of which a connection can be made.

(2) terminals or jacks connected and grouped so that a circuit is made available at a number of points, for example, a switchboard multiple. (F)

multiple access: a system where output or input can be received or dispatched from more than one location.

multiple-address instruction: synonym for *multiaddress instruction.* (A) (B)

multiple-address message: a message to be delivered to more than one destination.

multiple-aperture core: synonym for *multiaperture core.* (A) (B)

multiple connector: a connector to show the merging of several lines of flow into one line, or the dispersal of one line to flow into several lines.

multiple declaration: in PL/1, two or more declarations of the same identifier internal to the same block without different qualifications, or two or more external declarations of the same identifier with different attributes in the same program.

multiple-domain network: a network with more than one host node. synonymous with *multidomain network.* (E)

multiple-job processing: controlling the performance of more than one data-processing job at a time.

multiple-length number: an operand that exceeds the capacity of one word.

multiple-length working: a method of fulfilling operations on data so that two or more words are used to represent data items, usually to achieve greater precision.

multiple operations: the characteristic of being able to perform two or more computer processes concurrently.

multiple precision: pertaining to the use of two or more computer words to represent a number in order to enhance precision. (A) (B)

multiple programming: programming of a computer by permitting two or more arithmetical or logical operations to be executed simultaneously.

multiple punching: punching more than one hole in the card column by several keystrokes, usually in order to extend the character set of the punch. (E)

multiple recording medium word processing equipment: word-processing equipment that can operate on two or more recording media. (D)

multiple routing: a method of sending a message where more than one destination is specified in the header of the message.

multiple-task management: managing the performance of more than one data-processing task at a time.

multiple utility: a utility that permits one to three utility operators to be performed simultaneously.

multiplex
(1) to interleave or simultaneously transmit two or more messages on a single channel. (A).
(2) the process or equipment for combining a number of individual channels into a common spectrum or into a common bit stream for transmission. (F)

multiplex data terminal: a unit that modulates and/or demodulates data between two or more input-output units and a data transmission link.

multiplexed operation: a simultaneous operation sharing the use of a common unit of a system so that it can be considered an independent operation.

multiplexer (M) (MPLX) (MPLXR) (MPX) (MUL) (MUX): a device capable of interleaving the events of two or more activities or capable of distributing the events of an interleaved sequence to the respective activities. (A) see *data multiplexer.* (E)

multiplexer channel (MXC): a channel designed to operate with a number of I/O devices simultaneously. Several I/O devices can transfer records at the same time by interleaving items of data. see also *block multiplexer channel, byte multiplexer channel.*

multiplexer simulation: a testing program which simulates the activities of the multiplexer.

multiplexing
(1) in data transmission, a function that permits two or more data sources to share a common transmission medium such that each data sources has its own channel.
(2) the division of a transmission facility into two or more channels either by splitting the frequency band transmitted by the channel into narrower bands, each of which is used to constitute a distinct channel (frequency-division multiplexing), or by allotting this common channel to several different information channels, one at a time (time-division multiplexing).

multiplex link: a means of enabling a data-terminal equipment (DTE) to have several access channels to the data network over a single circuit. (E)

multiplex mode: a means of transferring records to or from low-speed I/O devices on the multiplexer channel by interleaving bytes of data. The multiplexer channel sustains simultaneous I/O operations on several subchannels. Bytes of data are interleaved and then routed to or from the selected I/O devices, or to and from the desired locations in main storage. synonymous with *byte mode.*

multiplex operation: a mode of operation in which the events of two or more activities are interleaved and when required the events in the interleaved sequence are distributed to the respective activities. (A)

multiplexor: see *multiplexer.*

multiplicand: in a multiplication operation, the factor that is multiplied by another number or quantity. (A) (B)

multiplier (MPY) (MULT): in multiplication, the number or quantity by which the multiplicand is multiplied. synonym for *multiplier factor.* (B) see *quarter squares multiplier.* (A)

multiplier factor: in a multiplication operation, the factor by which the multiplicand is multiplied. synonymous with *multiplier.* (A) (B)

multiplier-quotient register: a register where the multiplier for multiplication is placed, and where the quotient for division is developed.

multiply: see *logical multiply.* (A)

multiplying punch: synonym for *calculating punch.* (A)

multipoint circuit: a circuit interconnecting several stations that must communicate on a time-shared basis.

multipoint connection: a connection established among more than two data stations for data transmission. The connection may include switching facilities. (E)

multipoint link: a link or circuit interconnecting several stations. synonymous with *multidrop line.* cf. *point-to-point link.*

multipoint network: in data communication, a configuration in which more than two terminal installations are connected. The network may include switching facilities.

multipriority: a queue of items waiting processing. The queue is composed of items of different priorities and in effect is a queue of queues.

multiprocessing (MP)

(1) a mode of operation that provides for parallel processing by two or more processors of a multiprocessor. (E)

(2) pertaining to the simultaneous execution of two or more computer programs or sequences of instructions by a computer or computer network. (A)

(3) loosely, parallel processing. (A)

(4) simultaneous execution of two or more sequences of instructions by a multiprocessor.

multiprocessing system (MPS): a computing system employing two or more interconnected processing units to execute programs simultaneously.

multiprocessor (MP)

(1) a computer employing two or more processing units under integrated control. (A)

(2) a system consisting of two or more processing units, ALUs, or processors that can communicate without manual intervention.

multiprocessor interleaving: the allocation of memory areas to the different processors of a multiprocessing system to avoid interaction between programs being run at the same time.

multiprogramming

(1) pertaining to the concurrent execution of two or more computer programs by a computer. (A)

(2) a mode of operation that provides for the interleaved execution of two or more computer programs by a single processor. (E)

multiprogramming memory protect: a

hardware function that provides positive protection to the system executive routine and all other programs. It protects against both processor execution, and against input-output data area destruction.

multiprogramming system (MPS): a system that can process two or more programs concurrently by interleaving their execution.

multireel sorting: the automatic sequencing of a file having more than one input tape, without operator intervention.

multirunning: synonymous with *multiprogramming*.

multischedule private line (MPL): a rate schedule for AT&T's intercity private-line service, effective in 1976, which replaced the Hi/Lo tariff declared unjustified by the FCC. MPL replaces the Hi/Lo approach of averaging separately the cost (and rates) of high-density and low-density routes. MPL imposes a fixed charge for the first mile of service that is significantly greater than the charge for additional miles. MPL reduces rate averaging which provided a protective pricing umbrella for the SCCs or OCCs private-line services. (G)

multistation: descriptive of a communications network having several data terminals.

multitasking
(1) pertaining to the concurrent execution of two or more tasks by a computer. (A)
(2) multiprogramming that provides for the concurrent performance, or interleaved execution, of two or more tasks. (E)

multitasking/multiprogramming: special methods and systems designed to achieve concurrency by separating programs into two or more interrelated tasks that share the same code, buffers, files, and equipment.

multitask operation: multiprogramming called multitask operation to express not only concurrent execution of two or more programs, but also the concurrent execution of a single reenterable program used by many tasks.

multithreading: pertaining to the concurrent operation of more than one path of execution within a computer.

mutual information: synonym for *transinformation content*. (A) (B)

mutually synchronized network: a network-synchronizing arrangement in which each clock in the network exerts a degree of control on all others.

mutual pair capacitance: the capacitance per unit length between the conductors of a twisted wire pair. (F)

MUX: see *multiplexer*.

mV: millivolt.

MVT: multiprogramming with a variable number of tasks.

MXC: see *multiplexer channel*.

Mylar: a Dupont trademark for polyester film, often used as a base for magnetically coated or perforated information media.

N

N

(1) see *nano*.

(2) see *node*.

(3) see *number*.

(4) see *numeric*.

n: in sorting, file size; the number of records to be processed by the sort.

n-address instruction: an instruction that contains n address parts. (A) (B)

n-adic boolean operation: a boolean operation on n and only n operands. (A) (B)

n-adic operation: an operation on n and only n operands. synonymous with *n-ary operation*. (*A*) (B)

naive user: someone who wants to use the computer to do something, but does not know much about computers or programming and does not particularly care to.

NAK: see *negative acknowledge character*. (A)

NAM: see *network access machine*.

name

(1) a alphameric term that identifies a data set, a statement, a program, or a cataloged procedure. The first character of the name must be alphabetic.

(2) in COBOL, a word composed of not more than 30 characters, which defines a COBOL operand.

(3) in FORTRAN, a string of from one through six alphameric characters, the first of which identify a variable, an array, a function, a subroutine, a common block, or a name list.

(4) see *data name, qualified name*. (A)

(5) see also *entry name, external name, label, name entry*.

named common: a labeled common block.

name entry: n in assembler programming, the entry in the name field of an assembler-language statement.

names: in COBOL, a record within a file given the level number 01. Data names for elements within a record have lower-level numbers, 02, 03, and so forth.

NAND: a logic operation having the property that if P is a statement, Q is a statement, R is a statement, . . ., then the NAND of P, Q, R, . . .T is true if at least one statement is false, false if all statements are true. synonymous with *NOT-AND, Sheffer stroke.* (*A*)

NAND element: a logic element that performs the boolean operation of nonconjunction. synonymous with *NAND gate.* (*A*)

NAND gate: synonym for *NAND element.* (A)

NAND operation: synonym for *nonconjunction.* (A) (B)

nano-(N): prefix denoting one thousand millionth (10⁻⁹), for example, nanosecond, one thousand millionth of a second.

nanoprocessor: a processor operating in the nanosecond cycle range. see *nano-.*

nanosecond (NS) (NSEC): one-thousand-millionth of a second; one billionth of a second.

NAP: see *network access pricing.*

narrative: the explanatory text added to program instructions. synonym for *comment.*

narrow band (NB): a communication line similar to the voice-grade line but functions on a lower frequency.

NARUC: see National Association of Regulatory Utility Commissioners.

n-ary
(1)   pertaining to a selection, choice or condition that has n possible different values or states. (B)
(2)   pertaining to a fixed-radix numeration system having a radix of n. (*A*) (B)

n-ary boolean operation: deprecated term for *n-adic boolean operation.* (A) (B)

n-ary operation: synonym for *n-adic operation.* (A) (B)

NASORD: a programming reference to a file not in sequential order.

NAT: see *information content natural unit.* (A) (B)

National Association of Regulatory Utility Commissioners (NARUC): an association made up of members of state utility commissions who are responsible for regulating the intrastate operations of utility companies. (This organization was formerly the National Association of Railroad and Utility Commissioners.) (G)

national characters: deprecated term for characters #, @, and $.

national requirements: translation requirements that affect parts of devices and licensed programs; for example, requirements for modification of decals on keys and switches, for translation of message text, and for conversion of symbols such as the U.S. dollar sign to the U.K. pound sign.

National Telecommunications and Information Administration (NTIA): a part of the U.S. Department of Commerce which serves as the principle advisor to the executive branch on telecommunications matters. NTIA is responsible for spectrum management (only of the portion allocated to the federal government) and research, improvement of government telecommunications spending, and policy planning. (G)

National Telephone Cooperative Association (NTCA): a trade association representing small rural telephone cooperatives, statewide associations and commercially owned telephone companies. Associate members include manufacturers and suppliers of telephone equipment. NTCA offers services to members in the areas of government affairs, industry relations, employee benefit programs, education and training, technical services, engineering, and group purchasing programs. (G)

nationwide/statewide cost averaging: a method of averaging costs upon which uniform prices are set for telephone service so that subscribers using more costly-to-serve, lightly trafficked routes—such as those between small communities—receive the same service for the same price as subscribers on lower-cost highly trafficked metropolitan routes. (G)

native attachment: deprecated term for *integrated attachment.*

native code: machine dependent language, such as an assembly language.

native compiler: a compiler producing code for a processor on which it runs.

natural-function generator: a device that accepts one or more input variables and provides an output variable based on a mathematical function.

natural language: a language whose rules are based on current usage without being specifically prescribed. (B)

natural language system: an information retrieval system where index terms are words actually found within the document. Indexing by natural language is usually less expensive than by ascribing index terms from an authority file or thesaurus.

natural number: one of the numbers 0,1,2 . . . synonymous with *nonnegative number.* (A) (B)

NB: see *narrow band.*

n-bit byte: a byte composed of binary elements. (A) (B)

NBR: see *number.*

NBS: see *numeric backspace character.*

NC: see *numerical control.* (B)

n-core-per-bit storage: a storage device in which each storage cell uses magnetic cores per binary character. (A) (B)

N-cube: in switching theory, a term used to indicate two N-1 cubes with corresponding points connected.

NDC: see *normalized device coordinates.*

NDF: no defect found.

NDR: see *nondestructive read.* (A) (B)

NDRO: see *nondestructive readout.* (A) (B)

NE: not equal to. see *relational operator.*

near-end cross talk: cross talk that is propagated in a disturbed channel in the direction opposite to the direction of propagation of the current in the disturbing channel. Ordinarily, the terminal of the disturbed channel at which the near-end cross talk is present, is near, or coincides with, the energized terminal of the disturbing channel.

NEAT system (National's Electronic Autocoding Technique): an automatic system for programming used to create an object program in machine language from a source program written by a programmer. One instruction in the object program is created from one instruction in the source program. NEAT will translate and compile source programs that are written in COBOL.

needle: a probe in a manual information retrieval operation that may be passed through holes or notches to assist in sorting or selecting cards. (A)

NEG: negative.

negate

(1) to perform the operation of negation. (B)

(2) to perform the logic operation NOT. (*A*)

negation: the monadic boolean operation the result of which has the boolean value opposite to that of the operand. synonymous with *NOT operation*. (*A*) (B)

negative acknowledge character (NAK): a transmission control character transmitted by a station as a negative response to the station with which the connection has been set up. (A) (B)

negative acknowledgment (NAK): in binary synchronous communication, a line control character sent by a receiving terminal to indicate that an error was encountered in the previous transmission and that the receiving terminal is ready to accept another transmission.

negative entry: on a calculator, the assignment of a negative sign to a number entered in the machine.

negative feedback: the act of returning part of the output to the input in such a way that increased output results in the deduction of a greater quantity from the input.

negative indicator: on a calculator, a visual indication that the number shown has a negative value. (D)

negative-true logic: a logic system where the voltage representing a logical 1 has a lower or more negative value than that representing a logical 0.

negator: an element that accepts one binary input signal and has the capability to yield a single binary output signal of the opposite significance. synonymous with *NOT element*.

negentropy: deprecated term for *entropy*. (A) (B)

neither-nor operation: synonym for *nondisjunction*. (A) (B)

NELIAC: Navy Electronics Laboratory International ALGOL Compiler, a machine-independent compiler.

neper: a unit for measuring power. The number of nepers is the logarithm (base e) of the ratio of the measured power levels. see also *decibel*.

nest

(1) to incorporate a structure or structures of some kind into a structure of the same kind. For example, to nest one loop (the nested loop) within another loop (the nesting loop); to nest one subroutine (the nested subroutine) within another subroutine (the nesting subroutine). (B)

(2) to embed subroutines or data in other subroutines or data at a different hierarchical level such that the different levels of routines or data can be executed or accessed recursively. (*A*)

nested command list: a command list called by another command list.

nested DO: in FORTRAN, a DO loop whose range is entirely contained by the range of another DO loop.

nested macros: the power of a macroinstruction is increased by calling another macro from within the macroinstruction.

nesting

(1) a routine or block of data included within a larger routine or block of data.

(2) the relationship between the statements held in two perform statements. The statements included in the second or inner perform statement are wholly included in or excluded from the first, or outer, perform statement.

nesting level: in assembler programming, the level at which a term or subexpression appears in an expression, or the level at which a macrodefinition containing an inner macroinstruction is processed by an assembler.

NET: see *network*.

Net 1000: the cornerstone of American Bell's new generation of services. Available throughout the country, it adds function and capability to existing terminals, and provides the user with the ability to design and control an integrated system. Originally called *Net 1*. see also *AIS*.

net structure: in a data base, a structure of data aggregates or record types arranged in many-to-many relationships. (E)

network (NET)
(1) an interconnected group of nodes. (E)
(2) the assembly of equipment through which connections are made between data stations.
(3) in data processing, a user-application network.
(4) the facilities network is the aggregate of transmission systems, switching systems, and station equipments; it supports a large number of traffic networks. (F)
(5) an electrical/electronic circuit, usually packaged as a single piece of apparatus or on a printed circuit pack. Examples are a transformer

network and an equalization network. (F)
(6) see *computer network, data network, fully connected network, heterogeneous network, homogeneous network, loop network, mesh network, multipoint network, public network, star network, synchronous data network, tree network, user-application network.*

network access control: tasks related to network administration controls, including monitoring of system operation, ensuring of data integrity, user identification, recording system access and changes, and approaches for granting user access.

network access machine (NAM): a computer programmed to aid a user to interact with a computer network, for example, a network connecting a series of host computers.

network access pricing (NAP): a tariffing concept whereby the rate for a service would be strongly influenced by the cost of network elements (e.g., stations, loops, etc.) used to provide that service. Contrasts with the tariffing concept based on the value of service. (F)

network analog: the expression and solution of mathematical relationships between variables using a circuit or circuits to represent these variables. (A)

network analyzer: a device that simulates a network such as an electrical supply network. (A)

network application: the use to which a network is put, such as data collection or inquiry/update.

network architecture: a set of design principles, including the organization of functions and the description of data formats and procedures, used as the basis for design and implementation of a user-application network. see also *open systems architecture*. (E)

network awareness: that condition where a central processor is cognizant of the status of the network.

network components: in large systems, the host processors, remote computer systems, remote terminals, and transmission paths or channels that connect all the components to each other.

network congestion: a network condition when traffic is greater than the network can carry, for any reason. (C)

network constant: one of the resistance, inductance, mutual-inductance or capacitance values found in a network.

network control mode: the functions of a network control program that enable it to direct a communication controller to perform activities such as polling, device addressing, dialing, and answering.

network control phase: that phase of a data call during which network control signals are exchanged between a data-terminal equipment (DTE) and the network for the purpose of call establishment, call disconnection, or for control signaling during the data phase. (C)

network control program generation: the process, performed in a processor, of assembling and link editing a macroinstruction program to produce a network control program.

network control signaling unit: a device that controls the operation of the telephone network by initiating, dial-

ing, completing, and performing supervisory functions on a call.

network drills: the final level of testing in a real-time system where data from all the sites is transmitted and the full complex of equipment, personnel, interfaces, and programs is tested.

network harms: adverse effects on telephone company services, telephone company employees, or telephone company customers which can result from the interconnection of customer-provided equipment. The four basic harms identified by the National Academy of Sciences are: excessive signal power, hazardous voltage, improper network control signaling, and line imbalance. (G)

networking: in a multiple-domain network, communication between domains. synonymous with *cross-domain communication*.

network integration: a term used to describe the joint assumption of risk and the joint provision of telecommunications services by a partnershiplike arrangement among telephone companies. Commonly described as consisting of both technical integration and economic integration contrasted with interconnection. see *network integrity, separations, settlements*. (G)

network integrity: the planning, building, operation, and maintenance of the nationwide telecommunications network to the benefit of the network as a whole. This is achieved by the Bell System and the Independent Telephone Companies working in concert with common standards. synonymous with *system integrity*. (G)

network interface machine (NIM): a shared communications controller which enables non-intelligent terminals to access the Datapac network. The NIM formats the data from the terminal into packets to be transmitted over the packet-switched network.

network layer: in open systems architecture, the layer that provides the functions and procedures used to transfer data received from the transport layer. (E)

network load analysis: the listing of the flow of messages between stations to organize and evolve station characteristics by volumes of documents, frequency of processing, and special time requirements.

network node: synonym for *node*.

network operator: a person or program responsible for controlling the operation of all or part of a network.

network operator console: a system console or terminal in the network from which an operator controls the network.

network operator log on: a log on request issued in behalf of a terminal from the network operator console by using a network operator command.

network path: see *path*.

network port(s): in a network (in the sense of a localized circuit), ports are the interfaces with facilities or circuits outside the network; for example, the input port and output port of an amplifier. In certain multiport networks, the combination of an input terminal and output terminal, associated with a particular direction or side, is collectively referred to as a port; for example, the six ports on a six-way, four-wire multipoint bridge. A point of connection between a computer and a communications system is sometimes called a *port*. (F)

network slowdown: synonym for *system slowdown*.

network stand-alone system: a dedicated network that includes both local and remote data sources. Typical is a system that interconnects branch offices with a headquarters computer or provides communications between several departments within an office complex; for example, inquiry/response processing of a dynamic data base.

network theory: the use of the physical concept of a network to represent routing problems, flow problems, or project management. Mathematical techniques then operate to find the shortest route, maximum possible flow, or minimum project completion time. PERT, CPM, and other specialized applications of network theory have been developed for project managers.

network timing: timing signals transferred from a data circuit-terminating unit to the data-terminal equipment on an interchange circuit that controls the transfer of digits across the transmitted and received data circuits.

network topology: the schematic arrangement of the links and nodes of a network. (E)

neutral ground: an intentional ground applied to the neutral conductor or neutral point of a circuit, transformer, machine, apparatus, or system.

neutral relay: a relay in which the movement of the armature does not depend upon the direction of the current in the circuit controlling the armature.

neutral transmission: a method of transmitting teletypewriter signals, whereby a mark is represented by current on the line, and space is represented by the absence of current. By extension to tone signaling, neutral transmission is a method of signaling employing two signaling states, one of the states representing both a space condition and also the absence of any signaling. synonymous with *unipolar*. see also *polar transmission*.

new input queue: a queue of new messages (or a group) within a system that are awaiting processing. The main scheduling routine will scan them along with other queues and order them into processing in order.

new-line character (NL)
(1) a format effector that causes the print or display position to move to the first position on the next line. (B)
(2) cf. *carriage return character*. (A)
(3) in word processing, synonym for *carrier return character*.

new pack: indicates to the system that a change in the current volume on the drive will occur.

new synch: allows for the quick transmission from one transmitter to another or multipoint private-line data networks.

nexus: a point in a system where interconnections occur.

NFF: no fault found.

nibble: a four-bit word.

nickel delay line: a delay line utilizing the magnetic and magnetostrictive properties of nickel to impart delay within a pulse.

nil pointer: a pointer indicating the end of a chained list.

NIM: see *network interface machine*.

nine edge: the bottom or lower edge of a punch card. This edge is used for entering the equipment first because of external equipment needs.

nines complement: the diminished radix complement in the decimal numeration system. synonymous with *complement-on-nine*. (A) (B)

ninety column card: a 90 vertical column punched card, representing 90 characters.

NIP
(1) see *nonimpact printer*.
(2) see *nucleus initialization program*.

NL: see *new-line character*. (A)

n-level address: an indirect address that specifies n levels of addressing. (A)

NMOS: metal-oxide semiconductor circuits using currents of negative charges. cf. *PMOS*.

n-n junction: a junction between n-type semiconductors with different electrical properties.

NNX: synonymous with *central office code*.

NO: see *number*.

no-address instruction: an instruction in which it is not necessary to identify an address in memory.

no-consoles condition: in systems with multiple console support, a condition in which the system is unable to access any full-capability console device.

node (N)
(1) in a network, a point where one or more functional units interconnect transmission lines. The term *node* derives from graph theory, in which a

node is a junction point of links, areas, or edges. (E)

(2) the representation of a state or an event by means of a point on a diagram. (A)

(3) in a tree structure, a point at which subordinate items of data originate. (A)

(4) see also *cluster controller node, communication controller node, data processing node, host node, intermediate node, peripheral node, subarea node*.

(5) synonymous with *network node*.

noise

(1) random variations of one or more characteristics of any entity such as voltage, current, or data.

(2) a random signal of known statistical properties of amplitude, distribution, and spectral density.

(3) loosely, any disturbance tending to interfere with the normal operation of a device or system. (*A*)

(4) an unwanted disturbance introduced in a communications circuit. It may partially or completely obscure the information content of a desired signal. On telephone circuits, noise may be an annoyance during quiet intervals as well as when speech is present. (F)

noise characteristics: the most critical consideration in the use of digital circuit modules. In large assemblies, the spurious signals introduced by noise may cause false operations that, due to their random and transient nature, are extremely difficult to correct.

noise factor: the ratio consisting of the difference between the number of documents retrieved and the number of relevant documents retrieved, divided by the number of documents retrieved. It is the measure of the efficiency of the information retrieval system in which the optimum would be zero.

noise killer: an electrical network inserted in a telegraph circuit, usually at the sending end, for the purpose of reducing interference with other telecommunication circuits.

noise level: the strength of noise in a circuit.

noise temperature: used to measure the amount of thermal noise present in a device or system. The lower the noise temperature, the better the device.

noisy mode: a technique of floating-point arithmetic associated with normalization, where digits other than zero are introduced in low-order positions during a left shift. These digits seem to be noise, but, in fact, have been deliberately introduced.

NOMAD language: an algebraic compiler adapted from the MAD (Michigan Algorithmic Decoder) language. It is a high-speed compiler that allows a wide latitude of generality in expressions.

nominal (rated) speed: maximum speed or data rate of a device or facility which makes no allowance for necessary delaying functions, such as checking or tabbing.

non-add: on a calculator with a printing mechanism, the printing of characters without affecting the calculations. (D)

nonarithmetic shift: synonymous with *logical shift*.

nonassociated CCIS: a network of CCIS data links and signal transfer points (STPs) intended to make CCIS economical for small trunk groups.

The signals are routed via two or more shared data links in tandem and are processed and forwarded through one or more STPs. The route followed by the signals may be geographically different from that for the connection to be established. (F)

noncoded graphics: synonym for *image graphics*.

noncoherent bundle: a group of optical fibers positioned essentially parallel to each other in a bundle that is used simply as a means of guiding beams of light.

noncoherent modulation system: a modulation system not requiring a source of carrier, either generated at the receiving terminal or transmitted separately, that has the same frequency and phase as that associated with the received signal for recovering the original modulating signal. (F)

noncompat: a malfunction caused by an incompatability between a tape and a drive.

nonconjunction: the dyadic boolean operation the result of which has the boolean value 0 if and only if each operand has the boolean value 1. synonymous with *NAND, NAND operation, NOT BOTH operation*. (B) cf. *conjunction*. (A)

nonconnected storage: in PL/1, separate locations in storage that contain related items of data that can be referred to by a single name but that are separated by other data items not referred to by that name. Examples are the storage referred to by an unsubscripted elementary name in an array of structures or by a subscripted name referring to an array cross section in which the subscript list contains an asterisk to the left of any element expression.

noncontinguous item: in COBOL, a data item in the working-storage section of the data division which bears no relationship with other data items.

non-data-set clocking: synonym for *business machine clocking*.

nondestructive cursor: on a CRT display device, a cursor that can be moved within a display surface without changing or destroying the data displayed on the screen. cf. *destructive cursor*.

nondestructive read (NDR): reading that does not erase the data in the source location. synonymous with *nondestructive readout*. (E)

nondestructuve readout (NDRO): synonym for *nondestructive read*. (E)

nondial trunks: PBS tie trunks that require attendant assistance for verbal transmission of address information. (F)

nondisjunction: the dyadic booleans operation the result of which has the boolean value 1 if and only if each operand has the boolean value 0. synonymous with *neither-nor operation, NOR operation*. (B) cf. *disjunction*. (A)

non-display-based word-processing equipment: word-processing equipment that does not have an electronic display capability. cf. *display-based word-processing equipment*.

nonequivalence: synonymous with *exclusive-NOR*.

nonequivalency element: a logic element whose action represents the boolean connective exclusive OR.

nonerasable medium: paper tape units, for example, that are used for punching data that can be used to drive various production machines.

nonerasable storage: deprecated term for *read-only storage*. (E) synonym for *fixed storage*. (B)

non-escaping key: in word processing, a key that allows a character to be typed without the imprint position being changed.

nonexecutable statement

(1) in FORTRAN, a statement that describes the use or extent of the program unit, the characteristics of the operands, editing information, statement functions, or data management.

(2) a statement that is used to supply information to a compiler, but that does not explicity result in executable code; for example, a declaration. (E)

nonfile-structured device: a device, such as a paper tape, line printer, or terminal, in which data can not be referenced, as in a file.

nonidentity operation: the boolean operation the result of which has the boolean value 1 if and only if all the operands do not have the same boolean value. A nonidentity operation on two operands is a nonequivalence operation. (B) cf. *identity operation*. (*A*)

nonimpact printer (NIP): a printer in which printing is not the result of mechanical impacts; for example, thermal printers, electrostatic printers, photographic printers. (B)

nonintelligible cross talk: cross talk that cannot be understood but that is subjectively more annoying than thermal noise because of its syllabic nature. (F)

noninteractive: a program or device that provides no interaction with the operator at executive time.

nonlinear distortion: amplitude distortion caused by nonlinearities in a communication channel. (F)

nonlinear optimization: synonym for *nonlinear programming*. (A) (B)

nonlinear programming: in operations research, a procedure for locating the maximum or minimum of a function of variables that are subject to constraints, or both, as nonlinear. synonymous with *nonlinear optimization*. (B) cf. *convex programming, dynamic programming, integer programming, linear programming, mathematical programming, quadratic programming*. (*A*)

nonloadable character set: a character set installed in a device that must be used as is; it cannot be extended or altered.

nonloaded lines: cable pairs or telecommunication lines with no added inductive loading. see also *loading*.

nonlocking: in code extension characters, having the characteristics that a change in interpretation applies only to a specified number of the coded representations following commonly only one. cf. *locking*. (*A*) (B)

nonmapping mode: a mode where virtual addresses are not transformed through a memory map; for example, the virtual address is used as an actual address.

nonnegative number: synonym for *natural number*. (A) (B)

nonnumerical data processing: languages developed by symbol manipulation that are used primarily as research tools rather than for production programming.

nonnumeric literal: a character string bounded by quotation marks, which means literally itself. For example, "CHARACTER" is the literal for the means CHARACTER. The string of characters may include any characters in the computer's set, with the exception of the quotation mark.

nonpolarized return-to-zero recording (RZ(NP): return-to-reference recording in which zeros are represented by the absence of magnetization, ones are represented by a specified condition of magnetization, and the reference condition is zero magnetization. The specified condition is usually saturation. Conversely, the absence of magnetization can be used to represent ones, and the magnetized condition to represent zeros. synonymous with *dipole modulation.* (*A*)

nonprint: on a calculator with a printing mechanism; the disengagement of that mechanism. (D)

nonprocedural language: synonym for *non-procedure-oriented language.* (E)

non-procedure-oriented language: a programming language that allows the user to express the solution to a problem in a form other than as an explicit algorithm. synonymous with *nonprocedural language.* (E)

nonproductive poll: an indication from a tributary station that it has no data to send.

nonproductive task: a task assigned the lowest network control program dispatching priority; this type of task is generally slow to free buffers and is quicker to allocate them, and therefore is never executed during systems slowdown. cf. *productive task.* see also *appendage task, immediate task.*

nonprogrammed halt: a machine stoppage not resulting from a programmed instruction, such as an automatic interrupt, manual intervention, and so on.

non-real-time processing: processing historical data such as batch processing. Used also to describe a failed real-time information-processing system.

nonrecoverable error: deprecated term for *unrecoverable error.*

non-reflective ink: an ink, usually black, with extremely low reflective characteristics to optical character or mark reading devices. This non-reflective ink contrasts greatly with the paper, and enables the scanner to form a recognition pattern to identify the character.

nonresident portion (of a control program): control program routines that are loaded into main storage as they are needed and can be overlaid after their completion.

non-return-to-change recording: a method of recording in which ones are represented by a special condition of magnetization and zeros are represented by a different condition.

non-return-to-reference recording: the magnetic recording of binary digits such that the patterns of magnetization used to represent zeros and ones occupy the whole storage cell, with no part of the cell magnetized to the reference condition. synonymous with *non-return-to-zero recording.* (E)

non-return-to-zero change-on-ones recording (NRZI): non-return-to-reference recording of binary digits such that the ones are represented by a change in the condition of magnetization, and the zeros are represented by the absence of a change. This method is called (mark) recording because only the one or mark signals are explicitly recorded. synonymous with *non-return-to-zero (mark) recording, NRZ(M)*. (E) deprecated term for *transition coding*.

non-return-to-zero (change) recording (NRZ(C)): non-return-to-reference recording of binary digits such that the zeros are represented by magnetization to a specified condition, and the ones are represented by magnetization to a specified alternative condition. The two conditions may be saturation and zero magnetization but are more commonly saturation in opposite senses. This method is called change recording because the recording magnet condition is changed when, and only when, the recorded bits change from zero to one or from one to zero. (E)

non-return-to-zero (inverted) recording: deprecated term for *non-return-to-zero change-on-ones recording (NRZ1)*.

non-return-to-zero (mark) recording (NRZ(M)): synonym for *non-return-to-zero change-on-ones recording*. (A)

non-return-to-zero recording (NRZ): synonym for *non-return-to-reference recording*. (E)

nonreusable: the attribute that indicates that the same copy of a routine cannot be used by another task.

nonsimultaneous transmission: usually, transmission in which a device or facility can move data in only one direction at a time. synonym for *half-duplex*. cf. *duplex, simultaneous transmission*.

nonspecific volume request: in job control language (JCL) a request that allows the system to select suitable volumes.

nonstorage device: a device not having the ability to retain data.

nonstore through cache: in a processing unit, a store (write) operation, in which data is immediately put into locations in the cache. At some later time, the data is moved from the cache to main storage.

nonswitched connection: a connection that does not have to be established by dialing. cf. *switched connection*.

nonswitched line: a telecommunication line on which connections do not have to be established by dialing. cf. *switched line*.

nonswitched point-to-point line: a data set that exists after the job that created it terminates. cf. *temporary data set*.

nontransparent mode: a mode of binary synchronous transmission in which all control characters are treated as control characters (that is, not treated as text). cf. *transparent text mode*.

nonvolatile memory: a storage medium that holds information when power is removed from the system.

nonvolatile RAM: the use of a RAM for the speedy, minute-by-minute work and then shifting its information to the E^2-PROM as the power is about to be shut off, thus preserving memory.

nonvolatile storage

(1) a storage device whose contents are not lost when power is removed. (E)

(2) in word processing, storage that

retains text after the electrical power to the machine is switched off. (D) (3) cf. *volatile storage.*

no-op: see *no-operation instruction.* (A) (B)

no operation: an omitted or absent instruction that has been deliberately left blank, to allow later insertion of data or information without any rewriting, or for the program itself to develop one or more instructions.

no-operation instruction (no-op): an instruction whose execution causes a computer to do nothing other than to proceed to the next instruction to be executed. synonymous with *do-nothing operation.* (A) (B)

NOR: a logic operator having the property that if P is a statement, Q is a statement, R is a statement, ... , then the NOR of P, Q, R, . . is true if all statements are false, false if at least one statement is true. P NOR Q is often represented by a combination of OR and NOT symbols, such as (PVQ). N NOR Q is called neither P NOR Q. synonymous with *NOT-OR.* (A)

NOR circuit: a circuit that has an output only when all inputs are down.

NOR element: a logic element that performs the boolean operation of nondisjunction. synonymous with *NOR gate.* (A)

NOR gate: synonym for *NOR element.* (A)

normal contact: a contact that in its normal position closes a circuit and permits current to flow.

normal direction flow: a flow direction from left to right or top to bottom on a flowchart. (A) (B)

normal form (BNF) Backus: a formal language structure for syntax paring, used in design of ALGOL-60.

normalize
(1) to make an adjustment to the fixed-point part and the corresponding adjustment to the exponent in a floating-point representation to ensure that the fixed-point part lies within some prescribed range, the real number represented remaining unchanged. synonymous with *standardize.* (B)
(2) loosely, to scale.
(3) deprecated term for *scale.* (A) (B)

normalized device coordinates (NDC): in computer graphics, coordinates in the range 0 to 1 commonly used to represent the display space of the device. (E)

normalized form: the form taken by a floating-point representation when the fixed-point part lies within some prescribed standard range, so chosen that any given real number will be represented by a unique pair of numerals. synonymous with *standard form.* (A) (B)

normalizer: an electronic component of an optical character reader that alters the signal from the scanner to receive a processed rendition of the input character that is more appropriate for detailed or more advanced analysis.

normally closed contacts: a pair of contacts on a relay that open when the relay is energized.

normally open contacts: a pair of contacts on a relay that close when the relay is energized.

normal response: synonym for *positive response.*

normal restart: synonymous with *warm start.*

normative testing: standards of performance that are set for the testing of both quantitative and qualitiative system performance.

NOR operation: synonym for *nondisjunction.* (A) (B)

NOT: a logic operator having the property that if P is a statement, then the NOT of P is true if P is false, false if P is true. The NOT of P is often represented by P̄, $\sim$P, $\neg$P, P′. (A)

NOT-AND: synonym for *NAND.* (A)

NOT-AND operation: deprecated term for *nonconjunction.* (A) (B)

notation: a set of symbols, and the rules for their use, for the representation of data. (A) (B) see *binary notation, decimal notation, infix notation, mixed-base notation, mixed-radix notation, parentheses-free notation, positional notation, postfix notation, prefix notation.*

NOT-BOTH operation: synonym for *nonconjunction.* (A) (B)

NOT circuit: a circuit that provides an output signal of reverse phase or polarity from the input signal.

NOT element: a logic element that performs the boolean operation of negation. synonymous with *NOT gate. (A)*

NOT gate: synonym for *NOT element.* (A)

NOT-IF-THEN: synonym for *exclusion.*

NOT-IF-THEN element: a logic element that performs the boolean operation of exclusion. synonymous with *NOT-IF-THEN gate. (A)* (B)

NOT-IF-THEN gate: synonym for *NOT-IF-THEN element.* (A) (B)

NOT-IF-THEN operation: synonym for *exclusion.* (A)

NOT operation: synonym for *negation.* (A) (B)

NOT-OR: synonym for *NOR.* depre-cated term for *nondisjunction. (A)* (B)

NOT-OR operation: deprecated term for *nondisjunction.* (A) (B)

noughts complement: synonym for *radix complement.* (A) (B)

nought state: synonymous with *zero condition.*

NPA: see *numbering plan area.*

n-plus-one address instruction: an instruction that contains n + 1 address parts, the plus-one address being that of the instruction that is to be executed next unless otherwise specified. (A) (B)

n-p-n transistor: a junction transistor with a p-type slice between two slices of n-type semiconductor.

NRX(C): see *non-return-to-zero (change) recording.*

NRZ: see *non-return-to-zero recording.* (A)

NRZ(C): see *non-return-to-zero (change) recording.* (A)

NRZI: see *non-return-to-change-on-ones recording.* (A)

NRZ(M): see *transition coding.* (A)

NS: see *nanosecond.*

NSEC: see *nanosecond.*

NSP: see *numeric space character.*

NTCA: see *National Telephone Cooperative Association.*

NTF: no trouble found.

NTIA: see *National Telecommunications and Information Administration.*

n-tuple-length register: N registers that function as a single register. synonymous with *n-tuple register.* (E)

n-tuple register: synonym for *n-tuple length register.* (A) (B

n-type: semiconductor crystal material that has been doped with minute amounts of an impurity to yield donor centers of electrons. Since the electrons are negative particles, the material is known as n-type, and the electron conduction (negative) exceeds the hole conduction (absence of electrons). cf. *p-type.*

nucleus: that part of a control program that is resident in main storage. synonymous with *resident control program.* (B)

nucleus initialization program (NIP): the program that initializes the resident control program; it allows the operator to request last minute changes to certain options specified during system generation.

NUL: see *null character.* (A)

null

(1) empty.

(2) having no meaning.

(3) not usable.

null character (NUL): a control character that is used to accomplish media-fill or time-fill, and that may be inserted into or removed from, a sequence of characters without affecting the meaning of the sequence; however, the control of equipment or the format may be affected by this character. (B) see also *space character.* (A)

null character string: synonym for *null string.*

null cycle: the time needed to cycle through a program without introducing data, thereby establishing the lower bound for program processing time.

null detector: a circuit capable of detecting when no current flows or no voltage exists.

null line: a logical line with a length of zero.

null locator value: in PL/1, a special locator value that cannot identify any location in internal storage; it gives a positive indication that a locator variable does not currently identify any generation of data.

null record

(1) an empty record.

(2) a record containing a null character string.

null set: synonym for *empty set.* (A)

null string

(1) a string containing no entity. (B)

(2) the notion of a string depleted of its entities, or the notion of a string prior to establishing its entities. synonymous with *null character string.* (A)

null suppression: the bypassing of all null characters in order to reduce the amount of data to be transmitted.

NUM

(1) see *number.*

(2) see *numeric.*

number (N) (NBR) (NO) (NUM)

(1) a mathematical entity that may indicate quantity or amount of units.

(2) loosely, a numeral.

(3) see *binary number, complex number, Fibonacci number, integral number, irrational number, level number, natural number, random number, rational number, serial number. (A)*

number control: the quantity of a number (value) that is the result of a process or problem in order to prove its accuracy.

number cruncher: deprecated term for a computer that has been designed for arithmetic operations.

number generator: a set of manual controls onto which a computer operator can set a word for input.

number group: in crossbar switching systems, an arrangement for associating equipment numbers with main-station codes. A form of translator. (F)

numbering plan: a uniform numbering system wherein each telephone central office has unique designation similar in form to that of all other offices connected to the nationwide dialing network. In the numbering plan, the first three of ten dialed digits denote area code; the next three, office code; and the remaining four, station number. see also *area code*.

numbering plan area (NPA): in North America, a geographic division within which telephone directory numbers are subgrouped. A three-digit, NO/1X or NXX code is assigned to each NPA, where N equals any digit 2 through 9, 0/1 − 0 or 1, and X equals any digit 0 through 9. (F)

number range: the span or dimension or range of values that a number (variable) assumes, and expressed within beginning and ending limits or using N, if such limits are not known.

number representation: a representation of a number in a numeration system. synonymous with *numeration*. (A) (B)

number representation system: synonym for *numeration system*. (A) (B)

number sequence: see *pseudo-random number sequence, random number sequence*. (A)

number service: service to provide information necessary for call placement; includes information provided by directory assistance, intercept, and rate and route bureaus. (F)

number service operator: a person who provides any of several services relating to telephone numbers, such as directory assistance for both customers and toll service operators and interception of calls to unassigned or changed numbers. (F)

number system: synonym for *numeration system*. (A) (B)

numeral (NU): a discrete representation of a number. The following are four different numerals that represent the same number, that is, a dozen, in the method shown: twelve, by a word in the English language; 12., in the decimal numeration system; XII by Roman numerals; 1100 in the pure binary numeration system. (B) see *binary numeral, decimal numeral*. (A)

numeralization: the use of digits to represent alphabetic data.

numeration: synonym for *number representation*. (A) (B)

numeration system: any notation for the representation of numbers. synonymous with *number representation system, number system*. (B) see *decimal numeration system, fixed-radix numeration system, mixed-base numeration system, mixed-radix numeration system, pure binary numeration system, radix numeration system*. (A)

numeric (N) (NUM): pertaining to data or to physical quantities in the form of numerals. synonymous with *numeral*.

numerical: synonym for *numeric*. (A) (B)

numerical analysis: the study of methods of obtaining useful quantitative solutions to problems that have been expressed mathematically, including the study of the errors and bounds on errors in obtaining such solutions. (A)

numerical code: a restrictive code that has a character set consisting of digits only.

numerical control (NC): automatic control of a process performed by a device that makes use of numeric data usually introduced while the operation is in progress. (A) (B)

numerical data: synonym for *numeric data.*

numerical tape: a punched paper or plastic tape used to feed digital instructions to a numerical control unit.

numeric atomic symbol: for list processing languages, symbols that can be decimal integers, octal integers, or floating-point numbers.

numeric backspace character (NBS): a word processing formatting control that moves the printing or display point to the left by a fixed escapement value equal to the value for numbers in the pitch being used. cf. *backspace character.*

numeric bit data: see *binary picture data.*

numeric character: synonym for *digit (1).* (A) (B)

numeric character data: see *decimal picture data.*

numeric character set: a character set that contains digits and may contain control characters, special characters, and the space character, but not letters. (A) (B)

numeric character subset: a character subset that contains digits and may contain control characters, special characters, and the space character, but not letters. (A) (B)

numeric code: a code according to which data is represented by a numeric character set. (A) (B)

numeric-coded character set: a coded character set whose character set is a numeric character set. (A) (B)

numeric control: that field of computer activity that centers around the control of machine tools by mechanical devices; for example, a computer can control assembly-line tools for machining.

numeric data: data in the form of numerals and some special characters; for example, a data represented as 81/01/01. synonymous with *numerical data.*

numeric-edited character: in COBOL, a numeric character which is in such a form that it may be used in a printed output. It may consist of characters such as the external decimal digits 0 through 9, the decimal point, commas, and the dollar sign.

numeric item: in COBOL, an item whose description restricts its contents to a value represented by characters from the digits 0 through 9. The item may also contain a leading or trailing operational sign represented either as an overpunch or as a separate character.

numeric literal: a numeric character or string of characters whose value is implicit in the characters themselves. Thus, 777 is the literal as well as the value of the number 777.

numeric pad: a keyboard for numeric input to a computer.

numeric punch: a hole punched in one of the punch rows designated as zero through nine. A zero punch, and sometimes an eight or nine punch, in combination with another numeric punch, is considered a zone punch. (A)

numeric representation: a discrete representation of data by numerals. (A) (B)

numeric shift: a control for selecting

the numeric character set in an alphanumeric keyboard printer.

numeric space character (NSP:) a word-processing formatting control used in proportionally spaced printing or display that causes the active position to move to the right a distance equal to the escapement value for numbers in the pitch being used. see also *space character.*

numeric string: a string with no characters. synonymous with *empty string.*

numeric word: a word consisting of digits and possibly space characters and special characters. For example, in the Universal Decimal Classification system, the numeric word 61 (03) = 20 is used as an identifier for any medical encyclopedia in English. (A) (B)

nybble: usually four bits, or half a byte.

O

(1) see *operand*.
(2) see *operation*.
(3) see *operator*.
(4) see *output*.

OAR: see *operator authorization record*.

object code: output from a compiler or assembler which is itself executable machine code or is suitable for processing to produce executable machine code. (A)

object code compatibility: pertaining to a system where changes to the system do not require recompilation or assembly of user programs. cf. *source code compatibility*.

object computer: in COBOL, the name of an environment division paragraph in which the computer upon which the object program will be run is described.

object deck: synonymous with *object pack*.

object definition
(1) the set of information required to create and manage an object.
(2) the creation of a control block for an object. It also defines the object as available to the user.

objective function: the independent variable function whose maximum or minimum is sought in an optimization problem.

object language: a language that is specified by a metalanguage. synonym for *target language*. (*A*) (B)

object library: an area on a direct access storage device used to store object programs and routines.

object machine: the computer on which the object program is to be executed.

object module: a module that is the output of an assembler or a compiler and is input to a linkage editor. (A)

object module library: a partitioned data set that is used to store and retrieve object modules. see also *load module library*, *source module library*.

object pack: the punched cards

where an object program is retained. synonymous with *object deck*.

object phase: synonymous with *target phase*.

object program: a fully compiled or assembled program that is ready to be loaded into the computer. (B) synonym for *target program*. cf. *source program*. (*A*)

object-program preparation: conversion of programs from one of several easy-to-use source languages, or from certain competitive system languages, to a specific machine code.

object routine: the machine-language routine that is the output following translation from the source language.

object time: the time during which an object program is executed.

OCAL: On-line Cryptanalytic Aid Language.

OCC: see *other common carrier*.

OCC terminal: a location from which an OCC furnishes and administers common carrier communication services to its patrons and at which the OCC has the capability of testing the facilities operated or terminated at that location. The testing is done on the signals received or sent. (A patron's premises can be designated an OCC terminal location.) (G)

occurs: in COBOL, a sequence of data items of the same format. Subscripting is used to refer or designate a specific item in a procedure statement.

OCL

(1) see *operation control language*.
(2) in office systems, a batch control statement used by an operator to control the printing of a document.

OCR: see *optical character recognition*.

OCR-A font size 1: same as the font, character size A, described in the USA standard character set for optical character recognition (USAS X3.17,1966) and the OCR-A font size 1 described in the International Standards Organization (ISO) recommendation R 1073, first edition, dated May 1969.

OCR-B font size 1: characters defined as OCR-B font, as revised by ECMA and published in the standard ECMA-11 for alphanumeric character set OCR-B for optical recognition, second edition, dated October 1971.

OCT: see *octal*.

octal (OCT): pertaining to a fixed-radix numeration system having a radix of eight. (A) (B)

octal code: a code operating with a base 8. cf. *binary*.

octal digit: the symbol 0, 1, 2, 3, 4, 5, 6, or 7 used as a digit in the system of notation that uses 8 as the base or radix.

octal number: a number of one or more figures, representing a sum in which the quantity represented by each figure is based on a radix of eight. The figures used are 0, 1, 2, 3, 4, 5, 6, and 7.

octal number system: a number system that expresses values as multiples of powers of eight.

octet: a byte composed of eight binary elements. (A) (B)

octonary: pertaining to the number representation system with a base of eight.

odd-even check: synonym for *parity check*. (A)

odd parity: a system where the parity

bit is added to a word so that the total number of 1s is odd. cf. *even parity.*

odd parity check: a parity check where the number of 1 bits (as opposed to 0 bits) in a group is expected to be odd. cf. *even parity check.*

OEM: see *original equipment manufacturer.*

OF: see *overflow.*

off: an electronic element that is not conducting current.

offered load in Erlangs: the average number of calls that would have been in progress if there had been no delay or blocking. (F)

off hook

(1) activated (in regard to a telephone set). By extension, a data set automatically answering on a public switched system is said to go off hook. cf. *on hook.* see also *switch hook.*

(2) station switch-hook contacts closed, resulting in line current, or whatever supervisory condition is indicative of the in-use or request-for-service data state. (F)

office information system: an electronic system capable of performing a host of office activities, including word processing, information retrieval and telecommunications.

off line: pertaining to the operation of a functional unit without the continual control of a computer. (E)

off-line equipment: machines not in direct communication with the central processing unit. synonymous with *auxiliary equipment.*

off-line mode: a way of computer operation, meaning that the units are not hooked up together.

off-line processing: processing, not directly associated with or required for main program or real-time communication and control.

off-line storage: storage that is not under control of the processing unit.

off-line system: a system in which human operations are required between the original recording functions and the ultimate data-processing function. This includes conversion operations as well as the necessary loading and unloading operations incident to the use of point-to-point or data-gathering systems. cf. *on-line system.*

off-line unit: input-output unit or auxiliary equipment not under direct control of the CPU.

off premise: in general, standby units, usually a backup or duplicated set of computer equipment, often at another location.

offset: an accidental transfer of ink to spoil readability of a document, such as from two newly printed sheets with the back of one document smearing the face of the other document.

offset stacker: a card stacker that can stack cards selectively under machine control so that they protrude from the balance of the deck to give physical identification.

offset variable: in PL/1, a locator variable with the OFFSET attribute, whose value identifies a location in storage, relative to the beginning of an area.

off-the-shelf

(1) pertaining to production items that are available from current stock and need not be recently purchased or immediately manufactured.

(2) computer software or units that can be used by customers with little or no adaptation.

off time: describing a computer that is not scheduled for use, maintenance, alteration, or repair.

OFL: see *overflow.*

OL: see *on line.*

OLTEP: see *on-line test executive program.*

OLTS: see *on-line test system.*

OLTT: see *on-line terminal test.*

omni-directional antenna: an antenna whose pattern is non-directional in azimuth.

on: said of an electronic element that is conducting current.

on-chip control logic: logic contained on the microprocessor chip that decodes instructions and coordinates instruction execution with memory and input-output operations that are managed by the system controller.

on condition: an occurrence, within a PL/1 task, that could cause a program interruption. It may be the detection of an unexpected error or of an occurrence that is expected, but at an unpredictable time.

on-demand system: a system from which information or service is available at the time of request.

one address: synonymous with *single address.*

one-address instruction: an instruction that contains one address part. (A) (B)

one-ahead addressing: a method of implied addressing in which the operation part of an instruction implicitly addresses the operands in the location following the location of the operands of the last instruction executed. (A)

one-chip: a unit implemented in a single chip.

one-core-per-bit storage: a storage device in which each storage cell uses one magnetic core per binary character. (A) (B)

one-dimensional language: a language whose expressions are customarily represented as strings of characters, for example, FORTRAN. cf. *multidimensional language.* (*A*)

one element: synonymous with *OR element.*

one-for-one: pertaining to an assembly routine where one source-language instruction is converted to one machine-language instruction.

one-for-one translation: conversion of one source language instruction to one machine-language instruction.

one gate: synonymous with *OR element.*

one-level address: synonym for *direct address.* (A) (B)

one-level code: synonymous with *absolute code.*

one-level store: an approach in handling all on-line storage, whatever its physical characteristics, as being of one directly accessible memory.

one-level subroutine: a subroutine that does not itself call a lower level of subroutine during its operation.

one output: the voltage response obtained from magnetic core in a "1" stage by reading or resetting process.

one-plus-one address instruction: an instruction that contains two address parts, the plus-one address being that of the instruction that is to be executed next unless otherwise specified. (A) (B)

ones complement: the diminished radix complement in the pure binary numeration system. synonymous with *complement-on-one.* (*A*) (B)

one-shot circuit: synonymous with *single-shot circuit.*

one-step operation: manual operation of a central processor, where one instruction is carried out in response to a manual control permitting detailed error diagnosis.

one-to-one: a relation between individual members of one set and individual members of another set.

one-to-one assembler: a straight-forward translating routine that yields one instruction in the object language for every instruction in the source language.

one-way communication: communication in which information is always transferred in one preassigned direction.

one-way transmission: synonym for *simplex transmission.*

one-way trunk: a trunk between central exchanges where traffic can originate on only one end.

on hook: deactivated (in regard to a telephone set). A telephone not in use is on hook. cf. *off hook.* see also *switch hook.*

on line (OL)

(1) pertaining to a user's ability to interact with a computer.

(2) pertaining to a user's access to a computer via a terminal. (*A*)

(3) pertaining to the operation of a functional unit that is under the continual control of a computer. The term on line is also used to describe a user's access to a computer via a terminal. (E)

on-line access machine interaction: the interactive procedure for program development and on-line problem solving.

on-line batch processing: the sharing of computer resources between one or more real-time programs and a batch program.

on-line data reduction: processing of information as quickly as the information is received by the computing system or as quickly as it is generated by the source.

on-line diagnostics: running of diagnostics on a system while it is on line but off peak to save time and to take corrective action without closing down the entire system.

on-line equipment: processing equipment of compatible computer speed that is directly connected to the main processing devices.

on-line input: when the input unit transmits data directly to, and under the control of, the control processing unit.

on-line mode: that all equipment within a computer operation is hooked up directly, that is, with the central processing unit.

on-line plotter: a local or remote digital incremental plotter, in either on-line or off-line operation with digital computer, providing a high-speed plotting system of versatility and reliability.

on-line processing: the operation of terminals, files, and other auxiliary units under direct and absolute control of the central processor to eliminate the need for human intervention at any time between initial input and computer output.

online searching: utilizing a computer-based information retrieval system when there is direct on-line access to a database(s) available on the computer. The computer responds to a series of inquiries from the user.

on-line storage: storage that is under the control of the processing unit.

on-line system

(1) a system in which the input data enters the computer directly from the point of origin or in which output data is transmitted directly to where it is used.

(2) in telegraph usage, a system of transmitting directly into the system. see also *line loop.* cf. *off-line system.*

on-line terminal test (OLTT): a diagnostic aid by which a terminal or console may request any of several kinds of tests to be performed upon either the same terminal or console or a different one.

on-line test executive program (OLTEP): a facility that schedules and controls activities on the on-line test system (OLTs) and provides communication with the operator. This program is part of a set of programs that can be used to test I/O devices, control units, and channels concurrently with the execution of a program.

on-line testing: testing of a remote terminal or station that is performed concurrently with execution of the user's programs—that is, while the terminal is still connected to the processing unit—with only minimal effect on the user's normal operation.

on-line test system (OLTS): a system that allows a user to test I/O devices concurrently with execution of programs. Tests may be run to diagnose I/O errors, verify repairs and engineering changes, or to periodically check devices. see also *on-line test executive program.*

on-line unit: input-output device or auxiliary equipment under the direct control of the computer.

onomasticon: a list of proper nouns employed as a look-up table to expand titles, for example, from key words.

on-the-fly printer: an impact printer in which the type slugs do not stop moving during the impression time. synonymous with *hit-on-the-fly printer.* (*A*) (*B*)

on unit: in PL/1, the specified action to be executed upon detection of the on condition named in the containing ON statement. This excludes SYSTEM and SNAP.

OP

(1) see *operand.*

(2) see *operation.*

(3) see *operation part.*

(4) see *operator.*

O/P: see *output.*

OP code: a command often given in machine language.

OPD: see *operand.*

open

(1) to prepare a data set or file for processing.

(2) in PL/1, to associate a file with a data set and to complete a full set of attributes for the file name.

open code: in assembler programming, that portion of a source module that lies outside of and after any source macrodefinitions that may be specified.

open collector: an output structure characterized by an active transistor pull down for taking the output to a low voltage level, and no pull-up device.

open contact tone: in telephony, an audible signal indicating that a contact is open.

open-ended: pertaining to a process or system that can be augmented. (A)

opening a terminal: performing the store and equipment procedures necessary to initiate operations at a point-of-sale terminal. see also *closing a terminal.*

open-loop control: in which the central processing unit does not directly control a process or procedure but instead displays or prints information for the operator to assist in an action-oriented decision.

open-loop system: see *open-loop control.*

open numbering: in telephony, a numbering system in which the number of digits is not known in advance.

open routine: a routine able to be inserted directly into a larger routine without the need for a link or calling sequence. synonymous with *direct-insert routine.*

open shop: pertaining to the operation of a computer facility in which most productive problem programming is performed by the problem originator rather than by a group of programming specialists. The use of the computer itself may also be described as open shop if the user/ programmer also serves as the operator. cf. *closed shop.* (A)

open subroutine: a subroutine of which a replica must be inserted at each place in a computer program at which the subroutine is used. synonymous with *direct insert subroutine.* (B) cf. *closed subroutine.* (A)

open system
(1) a system allowing a variety of computers and terminals to interact together.
(2) a system to which access is publicly available.

open systems architecture (OSA): a model that represents a network as a hierarchical structure of layers of functions; each layer provides a set of functions that can be accessed and that can be used by the layer above it.

open systems interconnection (OSI): the use of standardized procedures to enable the interconnection of data-processing systems in networks.

open systems interworking: creating links between discrete computers and networks to evolve a freely interacting open system.

open wire
(1) a conductor separately supported above the surface of the ground; that is, on insulators.
(2) a broken wire.

open-wire line: a pole line in which the conductors are principally in the form of bare, uninsulated wire. Ceramic, glass, or plastic insulators are used to physically attach the bare wire to the telephone poles. Short circuits between the individual conductors are avoided by appropriate spacing.

operand (O) (OP) (OPD)
(1) an entity to which an operation is applied. (B)
(2) that which is operated upon. An operand is usually identified by an address part of an instruction. (A)
(3) information entered with a command name to define the data on which a command processor operates and to control the execution of the command processor.

(4)   an expression to whose value an operator is applied.

(5)   see also *key word, key word parameter, positional operand, positional parameter.*

operate mode: synonym for *compute mode.* (B)

operating delay: computer time loss resulting from errors made by operators or others using the system.

operating environment: see *operational environment.*

operating range: synonymous with *receiving margin.*

operating ratio: the ratio of the number of effective hours of computer activities to the total hours of scheduled cooperation.

operating space: synonym for *display space.*

operating system (OS): software that controls the execution of a computer program, and that may provide scheduling, debugging, input-output control, accounting, compilation, storage assignment, data management, and related services. (B)

operating system functions: see *operating system.*

operating system supervisor: operating system consists of a supervisory control program, system programs, and system subroutines. A symbolic assembler and macroprocessor, a FORTRAN or other compiler, and debugging aids are also included. A library of general utility program is provided.

operating system 360 (OS/360): an IBM system that spans a range from computers with sequential scheduling to large multiprogramming computers which can perform task multijobbing. For the smaller units within the 360 series, other types of operating systems exist.

operating time: that part of available time during which the hardware is operating and is assumed to be yielding correct results. It includes program development time, production time, makeup time, and miscellaneous time. cf. *idle time.* (*A*)

operating voltage indicator: on a calculator, a device giving a visual signal to indicate that the correct voltage is set for a main-powered machine or that the battery is insufficiently charged in a battery-powered machine. (D)

operation (O) (OP)

(1)   a well-defined action that, when applied to any permissible combination of known entities, produces a new entity. (B)

(2)   a defined action, namely, the act of obtaining a result from one or more operands in accordance with a rule that completely specifies the result for any permissible combination of operands.

(3)   a program set undertaken or executed by a computer, for example, addition, multiplication, extraction, comparison, shift, transfer. The operation is usually specified by the operator part of an instruction.

(4)   the event or specific action performed by a logic element.

(5)   see *arithmetic operation, asynchronous operation, auxiliary operation, binary operation, boolean operation, complementary operation, computer operation, concurrent operation, control operation, dual operation, dyadic boolean operation, dyadic operation, equivalence operation, fixed-cycle operation, identity*

operation, logic operation, majority operation, monadic operation, multiplex operation, n-adic boolean operation, n-adic operation, nonidentity operation, parallel operation, sequential operation, serial operation, simultaneous operation, single-step operation, threshold operation. (A)

operational address instruction: a computer instruction having no operation part but has the operation implicitly specified by the address parts.

operational amplifier: a high-gain amplifier that is the basic component of analog computing elements; this amplifier performs specified computing operations or provides specified transfer functions. (B)

operational character: a specific character that, when used as a code element, initiates, modifies, or stops a control operation, that is, controlling the carriage return.

operational environment: the physical environment, for example, temperature, humidity, layout, or power requirements, that is needed for proper performance. see also *configuration image.*

operational mode: the combination of equipment functioning modes presently in effect.

operational sign: an algebraic sign associated with a numeric data item, which indicates whether the item is positive or negative.

operational unit: all equipment or circuitry which performs a computer process.

operational word: a COBOL term used to denote a word that improves readability of the language but need not be on the reserved list.

operation code: a code used to repre- sent the operations of a computer. (B) synonymous with *computer instruction code.* (A)

operation control language (OCL): a programming language used to code operation control statements.

operation control statement: a statement in a job or job step that is used in identifying the job or describing its requirements to the operating system.

operation cycle: the series of operations that the CPU goes through. First, it fetches the word containing its next instruction from memory using the address in the program counter. The instruction is loaded into the instruction register and a one (1) is added to the program counter. The CPU decodes the instruction. If necessary, the CPU computes an effective address and places it in the address register. Finally, the CPU executes the instruction and prepares to start the cycle over again.

operation decoder: a device that selects one or more control channels according to the operation part of a machine instruction. (A)

operation expression: an expression containing one or more operators.

operation fields: that portion of the instruction format specifying the process or procedure to be performed.

operation number

(1) a number designating the position of an operation, or its equivalent subroutine in the sequence of operations comprising a routine.

(2) a number identifying each step in a program given in symbolic code.

operation part (OP): a part of an instruction that usually contains only an explicit specification of the operation to be performed. synonymous with *function part, operator part.* (*A*) (B)

operation ratio: the proportion of the total number of hours when devices are actually functioning, including operator time, time for errors, to the total number of hours of scheduled equipment operation.

operation register: a register where the operation code is stored during an operation cycle.

operations analysis: synonym for *operations research.* (A) (B)

operations control: in installation administration and work flow, includes instructions from and to the computer operator, administrative records, logs of system operation, and the control over library programs.

operations multitask: concurrent processing of two or more job steps.

operations research (OR): the application of scientific methods to the solution of complex problems concerning the optimal allocation of available resources. synonymous with *operations analysis.* (B)

operation table: a table that defines an operation by listing all permissible combinations of values of the operands and indicating the result for each of these combintions. (B) see *boolean operation table.* (A)

operation time: the time needed for an operation to complete the operation cycle.

operator (O) (OP) OPR)
(1) a symbol that represents the action to be performed in a mathematical operation. (B)
(2) in the description of a process, that which indicates the action to be performed on operands.
(3) a person who operates a machine. (*A*)
(4) see *arithmetic operator, bit-string operators, boolean operator, complementary operator, dyadic operator, monadic operator, quarternary operator, unary operator.*
(5) see also *concatenation, concatenation character.*

operator authorization record (OAR): a record referred to by a store controller when accepting or rejecting a request for signing on to a terminal, or for performing other procedures. The record also contains a list of procedures that each operator is allowed to perform.

operator command: a statement to a control program, issued via a console device or terminal, that causes the control program to provide requested information, alter normal operations, initiate new operations, or terminate existing operations.

operator console: a functional unit containing devices that are used for communication between a computer operator and an automatic data-processing system. (A) (B)

operator control panel: a part of an operator console of a computer, or of an automatic data-processing system that contains switches used to control the system or part of the system and that may contain indicators giving information on the functioning of the system or of part of the system. (B)

operator error: an error made by the terminal operator.

operator guidance code: a code displayed on a display device that represents the system's response to certain operating conditions or operator actions.

operator ID: a number entered by an

operator during log on that identifies the operator to the system.

operator intervention section: the part of the control equipment where operators can intervene in normal programming operations on control.

operator message: a message from the operating system or a problem program directing the operator to perform a specific function, such as mounting a tape reel, or informing the operator of specific conditions within the system, such as an error condition.

operator part: synonym for *operation part.* (A) (B)

operator's console: a console providing capability for manual intervention and the monitoring of computer operations.

operator trunk: a type of toll-connecting trunk that provides access from class 5 offices to toll assistance operators. (F)

opm: operations per minute (equivalent to characters per minute when control functions are included).

OPR
(1) see *operand.*
(2) see *operator.*

op register: the specific register in which the operation code of the instruction set is kept.

optical bar-code reader: a data station unit that reads coded information from documents, featuring a high-speed printer.

optical character recognition (OCR)
(1) the machine identification of printed characters through use of light-sensitive devices. (A)
(2) character recognition that uses optical means to identify graphic characters. (E)

(3) cf. *magnetic ink character recognition.* (A)

optical fiber: an extremely thin, flexible thread of pure glass able to carry a thousand times the information possible with traditional copper wire.

optical memories: memory systems in which light waves are used to read or write information from photosensitive films, semiconductors, or ferroelectric materials.

optical reader: a device that reads handwritten or machine-printed symbols into a computing system.

optical scanner
(1) a scanner that uses light for examining patterns. (B)
(2) a device that scans optically and usually generates an analog or digital signal. (*A*)

optical scanning: an approach for machine recognition of characters by their images.

optical wand: an input device with a photoelectric camera that senses black and white light patterns.

optimal merge tree: a tree arranged so that strings are merged with the fewest possible number of operations.

optimization: see *linear optimization, nonlinear optimization.*

optimize: a procedure causing a system, process, or operation to take on its most desirable configuration or procedures in the best or most efficient way; for example, when arranging instructions and data in storage so that a minimum of machine time or space is used for storing or accessing them.

optimum coding: see *minimum access coding.*

option: a specification in a statement that may be used to influence the execution of the statement. see *default option.*

optional-halt instruction: synonym for *optional-pause instruction.*

optional-pause instruction: an instruction that allows manual suspension of the execution of a computer program. synonymous with *optional-halt instruction* and *optional-stop instruction.* (A) (B)

optional-stop instruction: synonym for *optional-pause instruction.* (A) (B)

optional word: a reserved word included in a specific format only to improve the readability of a COBOL statement. If the programmer wishes, optional words may be omitted.

option list: in word processing, the display of a list of available machine functions for selection by the operator. (D)

opto-coupler: synonymous with *opto-isolator.*

optoelectronic technology: the heart of new communications and information handling systems that carry information as light pulses in glass fibers.

opto-isolator: a unit that modulates data on light beams so that the data processing system remains optically coupled, but electronically isolated from the source of data. synonymous with *opto-coupler.*

OPUS: Octal Program Updating System. A system used to update EASY 1 program tapes, designed by Honeywell.

OR
(1) see *operations research.*
(2) see *overrun.*
(3) a logic operator having the property that if P is a statement, Q is a statement, R is a statement,. . . . ,

then the OR of P,Q,R,. . . is true if at least one statement is true, false if all statements are false. P OR Q is often represented by P + Q, PVQ. synonymous with *boolean ADD,* and *logical ADD.* cf. *exclusive OR.* (A)

Oracle: a broadcast television text message service similar to Ceefax.

OR circuit: synonymous with *OR element.*

ORD: see *order.*

order (ORD)
(1) a specified arrangement used in ordering. An order need not be linear. (B)
(2) an arrangement of items according to any specified set of rules.
(3) to place items in an arrangement in accordance with specified rules.
(4) to arrange items according to any specified set of rules. synonymous with *sort.*
(5) deprecated term for *instruction, sequence (1). (A)*
(6) see *merge order.*

order-by-merging: to order by repeated splitting and merging. (A) (B)

order code: depreciated term for *operation code.* (A) (B)

ordering bias: the manner and degree by which the order of a set of items departs from random distribution. An ordering bias will make the effort necessary to order a set of items more than or less than the effort that would be required for a similar set with random distribution. (A) (B)

ordering by merge: repeated merging, splitting, and remerging in order to place items in a particular order.

order of the merge: the number of input files to a merge program.

order wire circuits: voice or data circuits used by technical-control and maintenance personnel for coordination and control actions relative to activation, deactivation, change, rerouting, reporting, and maintenance of communications systems and services.

order wire multiplex: a multiplex carrier set specifically designed for the purpose of carrying order wire traffic, as opposed to one designed for carrying mission traffic.

ordinary symbol: in assembler programming, a symbol that represents an assembly-time value when used in the name or operand field of an instruction in the assembler language. Ordinary symbols are also used to represent operation codes for assembler-language instructions.

OR element: a logical element operating with binary digits, and providing an output signal from two input signals, as follows;

Input		Output
p	q	r
1	0	1
1	1	1
0	1	1
0	0	0

ORG: see *origin*.

OR gate: a gate that implements the OR operator. (A)

orientation: as applied to a teletypewriter, an adjustment of the time the receiving apparatus starts selection. The adjustment is made with respect to the start transition. see also *range finder*.

origin (ORG)

(1) the absolute storage address of the beginning of a program or block.

(2) in relative coding, the absolute storage address to which addresses in a region are referenced.

(3) a station or application program from which a message or other data originates. cf. *destination*.

(4) see *assembled origin, computer program origin, loaded origin.*

original equipment manufacture (OEM): a manufacturer of equipment that may be marketed by another manufacturer.

original language: prior to machine processing, the original form in which a program is prepared.

origination: an approach that determines the type, nature, and origin of a document.

OR mixer: circuitry that emits an output upon receiving at least one input from any of several alternate sources.

OR operation: synonym for *disjunction. (A)*

ORSA: Operations Research Society of America.

OS: see *operating system.*

OS/360: see *operating system/360.*

OSA: see *open systems architecture.*

oscillating sort: a merge sort in which the sorts and merges are performed alternately to form one sorted set. (A)

oscillator: a nonrotating device for producing alternating current, the output frequency of which is determined by the characteristics of the device.

oscillator and timing generator: a circuit or unit used on low-cost systems to generate the basic timing for microprocessor control activities.

oscilloscope: an instrument for displaying the changes in a varying current or voltage.

OSI: see *open systems interconnection.*

other common carrier (OCC): includes specialized common carriers (SCCs), domestic and international record carriers (IRCs), and domestic satellite carriers which are authorized by the FCC to provide communications services in competition with the established telephone common carriers. (G)

OUT: see *output.*

outbound: deprecated term for *outgoing access.*

outconnector: in flowcharting, a connector that indicates a point at which a flow line is broken for continuation at another point. cf. *inconnector.* (A)

out device: a unit that translates computer results into usable or final form.

outer macroinstruction: in assembler programming, a macroinstruction that is specified in open code. cf. *inner macroinstruction.*

outgoing access: the capability of a user in one network to communicate with a user in another network. (C)

out-of-band signaling: a method of signaling that uses the same path as voice-frequency transmission and in which the signaling is outside the band used for voice frequencies. (F)

out-of-line coding: instructions in a routine stored in a different part of the program storage from the main route; can be added later as a patch.

output (O) (O/P) (OUT): pertaining to a device, process, or channel involved in an output process, or to the data or states involved in an output process. (B) see *input/output, real-time output.* (A) synonym for *output data, output process.*

output area: an area of storage reserved for output. (A)

output block: a portion of memory held for output data, from which it is transferred to an output unit. synonymous with *output area.*

output blocking factor (Bo): in a tape sort, the number of data records in each record in the output file.

output capability: the number of unit loads that can be driven by the output of a circuit.

output channel: a channel for conveying data from a device or logic element. (A)

output data: data being delivered or to be delivered from a device or from a computer program. (A) (B) synonymous with *output.*

output device: synonym for *output unit.* (A) (B)

output job stream: synonymous with *output stream.*

output limited: description of a program where the overall processing time is limited by the speed of an output unit, resulting in a further processing delay until output occurs. see *input limited, processor limited.*

output module: the part of a device that translates the electrical impulses represent data processed by the unit into permanent results such as printed forms, displays, tapes, and so on.

output primitive: synonym for *display element.*

output process

(1) the process that consists of the delivery of data from a data-processing system, or from any part of it.

(2) the return of information from a data-processing system to an end-user, including the translation of data from a machine language to a language that the end-user can understand.

(3) synonymous with *output*.

(4) see also *output data*.

(5) cf. *input process*.

output program: a utility program that organizes the output process of a computer. (A) (B)

output punch

(1) an output device that transcribes information on to punched paper tape.

(2) an output device that transcribes information on to punched cards.

output queue: see *output work queue*.

output register buffer: the transfer or buffering unit that receives data from internal storage and transfers it to an output media such as magnetic tape.

output routine: a utility routine that organizes the output process of a computer. (A) (B)

output routine generator: a generator that yields an output routine in accordance with given specifications.

output state: the determination of the condition of that specified set of output channels.

output stream: diagnostic messages and other output data issued by an operating system or a processing system on output devices especially activated for this purpose by the operator. synonymous with *job output stream, output job stream*.

output tape sorting: a tape holding a file in sequences resulting from a specified sort/merge process.

output unit: a device in a data-processing system by which data can be received from the system. synonymous with *output device*. (*A*) (B)

output work queue: a queue of control information describing system output data sets, that specifies to an output writer the location and disposition of system output.

output writer: a part of the job scheduler that transcribes specified output data sets onto a system output device independently of the program that produced the data sets.

OV: see *overflow*.

over capacity: values that are not in the range of a quantity are said to be out of range or *over capacity*.

overflow (OF) (OFL) (OV) (OVF)

(1) that portion of a word expressing the result of an operation by which its word length exceeds the storage capacity of the intended storage device. (E)

(2) on a calculator, the state in which the machine indicates that it is unable to accept or process the number of digits in the entry or result. (D)

(3) that portion of the result of an operation that exceeds the capacity of the intended unit of storage.

(4) in a register, loss of one or more of the leftmost whole-number digits because the result of an operation exceeded 10 digits. cf. *loss of significanace.*

(5) a count of all calls offered to a trunk group that are not carried. Usually measured for an hour. see *peg count*. (F)

(6) see *arithmetic overflow*. (A)

(7) cf. *underflow*.

overflow check: a limit check to determine whether the capacity of a storage area has been or will be exceeded. (E)

overflow error: an overflow condition caused by a floating point arithmetic operation.

overflow exception: a condition

caused by the result of an arithmetic operation having a magnitude that exceeds the largest possible number.

overflow field: in summary tag-along sort, the field that allows for anticipated field expansion.

overflow indicator

(1) an indicator that signifies when the last line on a page has been printed or passed.

(2) an indicator that is set on if the result of an arithmetic operation exceeds the capacity of the accumulator. The overflow indicator is often used in conjunction with a carry indicator to reflect an unusual or an error condition.

overflow position: an extra position in the register in which the overflow digit is developed.

overflow record: on an indirectly addressed file, a record whose key is randomized to the address of a full track or to the address of a home record.

overhead bit: a bit other than an information bit, for example, a check bit, or any procedure or format bit.

overhead operation: synonym for *housekeeping operation*. (A) (B)

overlap: to perform an operation at the same time that another operation is being performed; for example, to perform input/output operations while instructions are being executed by the processing unit.

overlay

(1) in a computer program, a segment that is not permanently maintained in internal storage. (B)

(2) the technique of repeatedly using the same areas of internal storage during different stages of a program.

(3) in the execution of a computer program, to load a segment of the computer program in a storage area hitherto occupied by parts of the computer program that are not currently needed. (A)

(4) see *form overlay*.

overlay keyboard: a keyboard with narrow key tops that allow an overlay panel to be installed to identify the key functions or fonts.

overlay module: a load module that has been divided into overlay segments, and has been provided by the linkage editor with information that enables the overlay supervisor to implement the desired loading of segments when requested.

overlay path: all of the segments in an overlay tree between a particular segment and the root segment, inclusive.

overlay program: a program in which certain control sections can use the same storage locations at different times during execution.

overlay region: a continuous area of main storage in which segments can be loaded independently of paths in other regions. Only one path within a region can be in main storage at any one time.

overlay segment: a self-contained portion of a computer program that may be executed without the entire computer program necessarily being maintained in internal storage at any one time. (A) (B)

overlay structure: a graphic representation showing the relationships of segments of an overlay program and how the segments are arranged to use the same main storage area at different times.

overlay supervisor: a routine that

controls the proper sequencing and positioning of segments of computer programs in limited storage during their execution. (A)

overlay tree: see *overlay structure*.

overload: for analog inputs, any absolute voltage value above which the analog-to-digital converter cannot distinguish a change. The overload value can be different for plus and minus inputs.

overload simulator: to test for overload conditions within a system, an artificial condition is created to make the program act as it would during an actual overload or overflow.

overprinting: in word processing, printing one character over another. Used most often with foreign languages, for example, in accenting a word. Also used to create new characters that are referred as an *interrobang*.

overpunch
(1) to add holes in a card column or in a tape row that already contains holes. Overpunches are often used to represent special characters. (B)
(2) to add holes to perforated tape to change a character, especially to produce a delete character. (A)
(3) synonym for *zone punch*. (A)

override interrupt: an optional group of power on/off interrupts possessing the highest priority and cannot be disabled or disarmed.

overrun (OR): loss of data because a receiving device is unable to accept data at the rate it is transmitted.

overrun error: an error where the previous character in a register has not been totally read by the main processing unit at the time that a new character is present to be loaded in the register.

overstrike: substituting one character for another on a visual display unit, for example, in word processing, a cursor positioned below the character to be altered, and the desired character substituted via the keyboard.

overvoltage protection: circuitry protecting a computer's circuitry from undesirable increases in the AC power line voltage.

overwrite: to record into an area of storage so as to destroy the data that was previously stored there.

OVF: see *overflow*

own coding (sorting): special coding provided by the programmer, that is integrated with the sort/merge coding.

owned: supplied by and belonging to a customer, as opposed to private and public.

owner: the user who creates an entity (or is named the owner of an entity).

P

(1) see *parallel.*
(2) see *parity.*
(3) see *pico-.*
(4) see *pointer.*
(5) see *power.*
(6) see *procedure.*
(7) see *process.*
(8) see *processor.*
(9) see *program.*
(10) see *punch.*

PA: see *program access key.*

PABX: see *private automatic branch exchange.*

PAC: *program authorized credentials.*

pacing: a technique by which a receiving station controls the rate of transmission of a sending station to prevent overrun.

pack: to store data in a compact form in a storage medium by taking advantage of known characteristics of the data and the storage medium, in such a way that the original data can be recovered; for example, to make use of bit or byte locations that would otherwise go unused. (B) see *disk pack.* (*A*)

package

(1) the plastic, ceramic, or metal where a completed chip is mounted.
(2) a generalized program written to include the requirements of users. A package is usually less efficient than a purpose-built program designed for the special needs of one user, but does have the advantages of being less costly and quickly available.

packed decimal: representation of a decimal value by two adjacent digits in a byte. For example, in packed decimal, the decimal value 23 is represented by 00100011. see also *signed packed decimal.* cf. *unpacked decimal.*

packed format: a data format in which a byte may contain two decimal digits or one decimal digit and a sign.

packet: a sequence of binary digits including data and call control signals that is switched as a composite whole. The data, call control signals, and possibly error control information are arranged in a specific format. (E)

packet assembly: a user facility permitting non-packet-mode terminals to exchange data in the packet mode.

packet assembly/disassembly (PAD): a functional unit that enables data-terminal equipment (DTEs) not equipped for packet switching to access a packet-switched network. (E)

packet disassembly: a user facility which enables a packet destined for delivery to a non-packet mode terminal to be delivered in the appropriate form; for example, in character form at the applicable rate.

packet-mode operation: synonym for *packet switching*. (E)

packet-mode terminal: data-terminal equipment that can control, format, transmit, and receive packets. (E)

packet radio: utilizing small radio units for communicating with computers. Short bursts of data can be sent and received.

packet sequencing: a process of ensuring that packets are delivered to the receiving data-terminal equipment (DTE) in the same sequence as they were transmitted by the sending DTE. (E)

packet-switched data-transmission service: a user service involving the transmission and, if necessary, the assembly and disassembly of data in the form of packets. (C)

packet switching (PS): the process of routing and transferring data by means of addressed packets so that a channel is occupied only during the transmission of a packet; upon completion of the transmission, the channel is made available for the transfer of other packets. synonymous with *packet-mode operation*. see also *circuit switching*. (E)

packing: the usage of storage locations in a file.

packing density: the number of storage cells per unit length, unit area, or unit volume; for example, the number of bits per inch stored on a magnetic tape track or magnetic drum track. (B)

packing factor: the percentage of location on a file that is actually used.

packing sequence: a procedure for loading the upper half of an accumulator with the first data word, shifting this into the lower half, loading the second datum, shift, and so on, so that the three data words are packed in sequence.

PAD: see *packet assembly/disassembly.*

pad

(1) to fill a block with dummy data, usually zeros or blanks.

(2) a device which introduces transmission loss into a circuit. It may be inserted to introduce loss or match impedances. See also *push-button dialing pad, switching pad.*

pad character: a character introduced to use up time or space while a function (usually mechanical) is being accomplished; for example, carriage return form eject.

padding

(1) a technique that incorporates fillers in data. (A) (B)

(2) in PL/1, one or more characters or bits concatenated to the right of a string to extend the string to a required length. For character strings, padding is with blanks; for bit strings, it is with zeros.

(3) deprecated term for *filler*. (A) (B)

P address: the location where the program branches or to which data is transparent on some equipment.

page (PG)

(1)   a block of instructions, or data, or both, that can be located in main storage or in auxiliary storage. Segmentation and loading of these blocks is automatically controlled by a computer. (A)

(2)   in a virtual storage system, a fixed-length block that has a virtual address and that can be transferred between real storage and auxiliary storage. (B)

(3)   in word processing, a defined section of a document.

(4)   to transfer instructions, data, or both, between real storage and external page storage.

page-at-a-time printer: synonym for *page printer*. (A)

page controls: in word processing, a machine capability to operate by page.

page data set: an extent in auxiliary storage, in which pages are stored.

page-depth control (last line): a control for specifying the maximum number of lines to be printed per page.

page display: in word processing, shows where page breaks will occur when the document is printed.

paged machine: a computer that divides memory addresses into blocks of words, referred to as pages.

page-end character (PE): a word-processing formatting control that denotes the end of a page. Page end may be moved or ignored during text adjust mode operations. synonymous with *form feed character*. see *required page-end character*.

page fixing: synonymous with *page key*.

page footing: summing of the entries on a particular page, usually at the bottom.

page frame: an area of real storage that can store a page. synonymous with *frame*. (B)

page heading: the description of a page context from a report, appearing on the top of the page.

page in: the process of transferring a page from the page data set to real storage.

page key: in word processing, a control used to process test one page at a time. (D)

page locking: synonym for *page fixing*.

page out: the process of transferring a page from real storage to the page data set.

page pool: the set of all page frames available for paging virtual-mode programs.

page printer: a device that prints one page at a time; for example, xerographic printer, cathode ray tube printer, film printer. synonymous with *page-at-a-time printer*. cf. *character printer, line printer*. (A)

page reader: an optical character reader that processes cut-form documents of different sizes that can read information in reel form.

page send-receive (PSR): a teletypewriter equipped with a keyboard and typing unit. Capable of sending to and receiving from a data channel.

page stealing: taking away an assigned page frame from a user to make it available for another purpose.

page swapping: exchanging pages

between main storage and auxiliary storage. (A)

page turning: synonym for *paging.*

pagination: in word processing, the automatic arrangement of text according to a preset number of page layout parameters. (D)

paging

(1) a time-sharing technique in which pages are transferred between main storage and auxiliary storage. synonymous with *page turning.* (A)

(2) the transfer of pages between real storage and auxiliary storage. (B)

paging device: a direct-access storage device on which pages and possibly other data are stored.

paging technique: a real storage allocation technique by which real storage is divided into page frames. (B)

paging terminal: a CRT terminal permitting the user to recover buffered information that has been rolled off the screen, both top and bottom, by pressing a button.

paint: in computer graphics, to shade an area of a display image; for example, with crosshatching.

paired cable: a cable made up of one or more separately insulated twisted pairs or lines, none of which are arranged with others to form quads. see *quadded cable.*

pair gain: the number of customers served by a communication system less the number of wire parts used by that system. Pair gain can be achieved by multiplexing and by concentration. (F)

PA key: see *program access key.*

PAM: see *pulse amplitude modulation.*

panel: in computer graphics, a predefined display image that defines the locations and characteristics of display fields on a display surface. synonymous with *board* and *display panel.* see *control panel, maintenance panel, operator control panel, plasma panel.*

panel data set: a data set that contains predefined display images (called panels) to be displayed at display stations.

panel-definition program: a program written to define one or more field-by-field panels to be stored in a panel data set.

panel number: a number assigned to the data record that will generate a particular screen image (panel) when the record is transmitted to a display station. The panel number is used in a program to retrieve the desired panel record from a panel data set.

paper-advance unit: a device which drives paper through the printer. Sprockets in the unit engage with holes punched down each side of the paper.

paper jam: a condition in which paper forms have not fed properly during printing and have become wedged in the feeding or printing mechanism, thus preventing the correct forward movement of the forms. A paper jam usually causes one line to be printed over one or more other printed lines.

paper skip: synonym for *paper throw.* (A)

paper tape (PT): deprecated term for *punch tape.*

paper tape channels: positions across the tape used to represent a character, including parity if any.

paper tape code: deprecated term for *punch tape code.*

paper tape output device: output data

received by this unit from the computer.

paper tape reader (PR) (PTR): a device that senses and translates the holes in perforated tape into electrical signals.

paper tape speed: the rate, in characters per second, at which the unit reads or punches paper tape.

paper tape type: indicates the purpose of the unit: reader only (RD), punch only (PN), or read-punch (RP).

paper throw: the movement of paper through a printer at a speed greater than that of a single line spacing. synonymous with *paper skip*. (E)

parabolic dish: in satellite communications, an antenna whose cross-section is a parabola.

paragraph: a set of one or more COBOL sentences, making up a logical processing entity, and preceded by a paragraph name or a paragraph header.

paragraph assembly: process in which a document is assembled on a word processor from paragraphs stored on disks.

paragraph header: in COBOL, a word followed by a period that identifies and precedes all paragraphs in the identification division and environment division.

paragraph key: in word processing, a control used to process text one paragraph at a time. (D)

paragraph name: a programmer-defined word that identifies a paragraph.

parallel (P)

(1) pertaining to the concurrent or simultaneous operation of two or more devices or to the concurrent performance of two or more activities

in a single device.

(2) pertaining to the concurrent or simultaneous occurrence of two or more related activities in multiple devices or channels.

(3) pertaining to the simultaneity of two or more processes.

(4) pertaining to the simultaneous processing of the individual parts of a whole, such as the bits of a character and the characters of a word, using separate facilities for the various parts.

(5) cf. *serial*. (*A*)

parallel access

(1) simultaneous access to all bits within a storage location comprising a character or word. Equal access time for any bit, character, or word within a storage unit.

(2) the process of obtaining information from or placing information into storage where the time needed for such access is dependent on the simultaneous transfer of all elements of a word from a given storage location. synonymous with *simultaneous access*.

parallel added: a digital adder in which addition is performed concurrently on digits in all the digit places of the operands. (A) (B)

parallel addition: addition that is performed concurrently on digits in all the digit places of the operands. (A) (B)

parallel bit transmission: a data transmission system where bits representing a character are simultaneously transmitted.

parallel by bit: the handling of all the binary bits or digits of a character simultaneously in different units.

parallel by character: the handling of

all the characters of a machine word simultaneously in separate lines, channels, or storage cells.

parallel computer: a computer having multiple arithmetic or logic units that are used to accomplish parallel operations or parallel processing. cf. *serial computer*. (*A*)

parallel data controller: a unit providing a flexible programmable interface to external devices or for interfacing multiple family computer devices.

parallel data medium: a medium for entering or recording data and as an input-output media for computers such as cards, disks, and so forth.

parallel digital computer: certain machines that process digits in concurrent procedures as contrasted to serial computing.

parallel interface: interfacing where all bits of data in a given byte (or word) are transferred simultaneously, using a separate data line for each bit.

parallelism: the simultaneous operation of several parts of a computer system.

parallel operation: the concurrent or simultaneous execution of two or more operations in devices such as multiple arithmetic or logic units. cf. *serial operation*. (*A*)

parallel processing (PP): the concurrent or simultaneous execution of two or more processes in a single unit. cf. *serial processing*. (*A*)

parallel processing computers: computers that break a problem into many parts and attack them simultaneously, much as the human brain does. First developed by scientists at MIT and Carnegie-Mellon universities.

parallel running

(1)   the checking or testing of newly developed systems by running comparatively in conjunction with previously existing systems.

(2)   the last step in the debugging of a system.

(3)   the running of a newly developed system in a data-processing area in conjunction with the continued operation of the current system.

parallel search storage: a storage device in which one or more parts of all storage locations are queried simultaneously. cf. *associative storage*. (*A*)

parallel storage: a storage device in which digits, characters, or words are accessed simultaneously or concurrently. (*A*)

parallel terminal: a data terminal that transmits all components of a data character simultaneously. cf. *serial terminal*.

parallel-to-serial converter: a device that converts a group of digits, all of which are presented simultaneously, into a corresponding sequence of signal elements. synonymous with *dynamicizer, serializer*. (C)

parallel transfer: a system of data transfer in which elements of information are transferred simultaneously over a set of lines.

parallel transmission

(1)   in data communication, the simultaneous transmission of a certain number of signal elements constituting the same telegraph or data signal. For example, use of a code according to which each signal is characterized by a combination of three out of twelve frequencies simultaneously transmitted over the channel. (*A*)

(2)   the simultaneous transmission

of the bits constituting an entity of data over a data circuit. (E)

(3) cf. *serial transmission.* (A)

parameter (PARM)

(1) a variable that is given a constant value for a specified application and that may denote the application. (A) (B)

(2) a variable that is given a constant value for a specific document processing program instruction; for example, left margin 10.

(3) in word processing, an item in a menu for which the operator specifies a value or for which the system provides a value when the menu is interpreted.

(4) a name in a procedure that is used to refer to an argument passed to that procedure.

(5) see *external program parameter, key-word parameter, positional parameter, preset parameter, program-generated parameter, symbolic parameter.*

parameter block: a user-created information table that is consequent to each operating system call, usually allowing the operating system to provide requested service accurately.

parameter card: a punched card containing input data that represent special instructions for the specific application of a general routine. synonym for *control card.*

parameter descriptor: in PL/1, the set of attributes specified for a single parameter in an ENTRY attribute specificator.

parameter descriptor list: in PL/1, the list of all parameter descriptors in an ENTRY attribute specification.

parameter testing: tests of sections or subroutines of a program to assure

that inputs produce desirable outputs.

parameter word: a word that directly or indirectly provides or designates one or more parameters. (A) (B)

parametric programming: an approach for studying the effect of an optimal linear-programming solution of a sequence of proportionate changes in the elements of a single row or column of the matrix.

parametron: a unique unit composed of two stable states of oscillation, the one is twice the frequency of the other and has the capacity to store one binary digit.

parasitic signal: an unwanted high-frequency or low-frequency signal in an electronic circuit.

parenthesis-free notation: any method of forming mathematical expressions in which expressions are delimited by means other than parentheses, for example, prefix notation, postfix notation. cf. *infix notation.* (A)

parent segment: in a data base, a segment that has one or more dependent segments below it in a hierarchy. see also *child segment.*

parity (P): in computer operations, the maintenance of a sameness of level or count; for example, keeping the same number of binary ones in a computer word to be able to carry out a check based on an even or odd number for all words under examination.

parity bit: a binary digit appended to a group of binary digits to make the sum of all the digits either always odd (odd parity) or always even (even parity). (E)

parity check: a check that tests whether the number of ones (or zeros) in an array of binary digits is odd or even. see *longitudinal parity check, tranverse parity check.* synonymous with *odd-even check.* (A)

parity digit: an n-ary digit appended to an array of n-ary digits to make the sum modulo n of all the digits always equal to 0 to any predetermined digit. In the case of the radix 2, parity digit becomes parity bit. (C)

parity flag: an indicator that signals whether or not the number of digits in the logic one condition is an odd or even value.

parity-line circuit: a multistation net in which all stations are on a single circuit, where the stations share the circuit as only one station can transmit at a time.

PARM: see *parameter.*

parse: in systems with time sharing, to analyze the operands entered with a command and build up a parameter list for the command processor from the information.

parser: a routine in charge of analyzing a program statement and creating its syntactic tree structure based on the specified syntax of the programming language.

part: a portion of an instruction word that specifies the address of an operand. Loosely, the operator portion of an instruction.

partial carry: in parallel addition, a procedure in which some or all of the carries are temporarily stored instead of being immediately transferred. (B) cf. *complete carry. (A)*

partially qualified name: a qualified name that is incomplete, that is, one that includes one or more, but not all, names in the hierarchial sequence above the structure member to which the partially-qualified name refers, as well as the name of the member itself.

partial word: a programming unit that allows the selection of a part of a machine word for processing.

partition: subdividing one large block into smaller subunits that can be handled more easily, for example, partition of a matrix. deprecated term for *segment. (A) (B)*

partitioned access method: see *basic partitioned access method.*

partitioned data set (PDS): a data set in direct access storage that is divided into partitions, called members, each of which can contain a program, part of a program, or data. synonymous with *program library.*

partitioned emulation programming (PEP) extension: a function of a network control program that enables a communication controller to operate some telecommunication lines in network control mode, while simultaneously operating others in emulation mode.

parts-on-demand facility: see *"smart" machines.*

party-line service: the provision of a shared line to the central office as part of either busines or residence telephone service. Two, four, eight or more customers may share a party line. (F)

PASCAL: a high-level language; named for Blaise Pascal, who, in 1642, built a digital calculating machine. Based on the language, ALGOL, it emphasizes aspects of structured programming.

PASS: see *private automatic switching system.*

pass: one cycle of processing a body of data. see *sort pass. (A)*

passband channel: see *base-band channel.*

passed data set: a data set allocated to a job step that is not deallocated at step termination but that remains available to a subsequent step in the same job.

passive graphics: a mode of operation of a display device that does not allow an on-line user to alter or interact with a display image. cf. *interactive graphics.* (E)

passive mode: in computer graphics, a mode of operation of a display device that does not allow an on-line user to alter or interact with a display image.

passive station

(1) in a multipoint connection using basic mode link control, any tributary station waiting to be polled or selected. (E)

(2) a station that, at a given instant, cannot send messages to or receive messages from the control station.

(3) a station in listening mode.

password (PW)

(1) a unique string of characters that a program, computer operator, or user must supply to meet security requirements before gaining access to data.

(2) a code or signal, usually confidential, that enables its user to have full or limited access to a system. (E)

(3) in word processing, a word to be typed in at the work station to identify the operator and permit access to the system or to a specific document. (D)

patch

(1) a temporary electrical connection.

(2) to make an improvised modification. (B)

(3) to modify a routine in a rough or expedient way. *(A)* (B)

patch bay: an assembly of hardware so arranged that a number of circuits (usually of the same or similar type) appear on jacks for monitoring, interconnecting, and testing purposes.

patch board: a removable board consisting of hundreds of terminals to which patch cords (short wires) are affixed, that determine the various machine programs. By altering the wiring pattern on the patch board or the patch board itself, the program can be changed.

patch cord: a flexible connector conductor with receptacles or connectors at each end that is used to interconnect sockets of plugboards. cf. *patch plug.*

patching plug program: a small auxiliary plugboard patched with a specific variation of a portion of a program that is designed to be plugged into a larger plugboard patched with the main program.

patch panel: an arrangement for terminating channels and terminal circuits in which plug-ended cords are inserted into jacks corresponding to the channels or terminals to be interconnected.

patch plug: a metal or plastic plug that functions as a patch cord. It is cordless and has an insulating handle. cf. *patch cord.*

patch routine

(1) a routine that permits octal changes to specified programs at object program execution time. Alterations occur in main memory only and do not alter the object program stored on the run tape.

(2) a correcting routine written of a sequence on the program chart and referring to a correct sequence.

path

(1) in a network, a route between any two nodes. (E)

(2) in a data base, a sequence of segment occurrences from the root segment to an individual segment.

(3) see *overlay path.*

pattern articulating device: a microprocessor capable of reducing graphic images into data streams and reconstructing images from such data.

pattern handling statement: an executable statement that is used to specify a pattern to be found in text, and the action to be taken when it is found or not found; for example, replace all occurrences of "neither...nor" with "either...or." (E)

pattern recognition: the identification of shapes, forms, or configurations by automatic means. (A) (B)

pattern-sensitive fault: a fault that appears in response to some particular pattern of data. cf. *program-sensitive fault. (A)*

pause instruction: an instruction that specifies the suspension of the execution of a computer program. A pause instruction is usually not an exit. synonymous with *halt instruction.* (B) see *optional-pause instruction. (A)*

pause retry: a network control program option that allows a user to specify how many times a program should try to retransmit data after a transmission error occurs, and how long it should wait between successive attempts.

PAX: see *private automatic exchange.*

PB: see *push button.*

PBX: see *private branch exchange.*

PBX attendant: a person situated at a position of a switchboard, desk, or console on a customer's premises to assist in establishing telephone connections between or with stations served by a PBX and who may perform various auxiliary functions associated therewith. Not an employee of the telephone company. (F)

PBX tie trunk: a trunk between two PBXs. (F)

PBX trunk: a line that connects a PBX and a central office. Sometimes called a PBX line in central office terminology. (F)

PCB: see *printed circuit board.*

PC board: see *printed circuit board.*

PCH: see *punch.*

PCI: see *program-controlled interruption.*

PCM: see *pulse code modulation.*

PCMI: Photochromic MicroImage; a trademark of National Cash Register Company, describing their micro-image processor that develops reductions of 1:40,000 in area, for example, 1.6 billion words or 7.5 billion characters can be stored on less than 2 square inches of a film's surface.

PCM multiplex equipment: equipment for deriving a single digital signal at a defined digit rate from two or more analog channels by a combination of pulse code modulation and time division multiplexing (multiplexer) and also for carrying out the inverse funtion, that is, demultiplexing.

PCS: see *print contrast signal.*

PCU: see *program control unit.*

PD: see *procedure division.*

PDAID: see *problem determination aid.*

PDN: see *public data network.*

PDS

(1) see *partitioned data set.*

(2) see *program data set.*

PE: see *page-end character.*

peak (PK): in OCR, an extraneous mark extending outward from a character past the stroke edge of the character.

peak load: denotes a higher-than-average quantity of traffic; usually expressed for a one-hour period and as any of several functions of the observing interval, such as peak hour during a day, average of daily peak hours over a 20-day interval, maximum of average hourly traffic over a 20-day interval. see *busy hour.* (F)

peek-a-boo: slang, method of verifying the existence or absence of punched holes in identical locations on cards by placing one card on top of another one.

peer: in network architecture, any functional unit that is the same layer as another entity. (E)

peg count: a count of all calls offered to a trunk group, usually measured for an hour. As applied to units of common-control switching systems, peg count or carried peg count means the number of calls actually handled. (F)

pel: a picture element of a terminal screen. see *picture element.* synonym for *PIXEL.*

pel matrix: in computer graphics, a two-dimensional array of encoded points.

pencil: a system for storing, retrieving, and manipulating line drawings.

pen (light) control: a light pen for communication between a processor and the operator. When the penlike device is directed at information displayed on the screen, it detects light from the cathode-ray tube when a beam passes within its field of view.

penumbral: specific headings that are partially relevant to data being sought.

PEP: see *partitioned emulation programming extension.*

PER: see *program event recording.*

percentage: the automatic division of a number into hundredths.

percolation: in error recovery, the passing of control from a recovery routine to a higher-level recovery routine along a pre-established path.

PERF: see *performance.*

perforated: see punch.

perforated tape: a tape on which a pattern of holes or cuts is used to represent data. synonym for *punched tape.* (E)

perforated tape code: a code used to represent data on perforated tape. synonymous with *paper tape code, punched tape code.* (E)

perforated-tape reader: synonym for *punched tape reader.* (E)

perforation: a linear series of unconnected cuts in continuous forms paper. The perforation delineates a fold or page boundary. see also *cut-to-tie ratio, tie.*

perforator: a device that punches. see *receiving perforator.*

performance (PERF): together with facility, one of the two major factors on which the total productivity of a system depends. Performance is largely determined by a combination of three other factors: throughput, response time, and availability.

performance evaluation: the analysis of achievements, employing a data-processing system to provide information on operating experience and to identify any needed corrective actions.

performance group: a class, specified by an installation, which regulates the turnaround time of the user's jobs, job steps, and interactions.

performance objective: a category of information contained in an installation performance specification. Each performance objective specifies the service rate that an associated job is to receive, for a number of different work-load levels.

PERIF: see *peripheral.*

period definition: in the system resources manager, a category of information contained in a performance group definition, that indicates which performance objective is to be followed, either during a particular real-time period or until a particular amount of service has been accumulated by an associated job.

peripheral (PERIF): see *peripheral equipment.*

peripheral bus: input-output interfaces and peripherals that plug right into the bus slots, creating a simple and powerful method of input-output interfacing.

peripheral controls: controls that regulate the transfer of data between the central processor and peripheral units.

peripheral control transfers: regulates the transfer of data between the central processor and peripheral devices, by reconciling the mechanical speeds of the central processor and minimizing the interruption of activity because of peripheral data transfers.

peripheral control unit: synonym for *input-output controller.* (A)

peripheral conversion program: a program that handles jobs normally done by a separate peripheral processor.

peripheral device: synonym for *peripheral equipment.* (B)

peripheral equipment: in a data-processing system, any equipment, distinct from the central processing unit, that may provide the system outside communication or additional facilities. (B).

peripheral interface channel: see *interface.*

peripheral interrupt: the stop resulting from the signal of readiness for or completion of a task by a peripheral unit.

peripheral limited: a system condition occurring when the time taken to end a process is determined by the time taken by peripheral units and not the time taken by the central processor. cf. *processor-limited.*

peripheral node: a node that terminates a path. synonymous with *endpoint node.* (E)

peripheral operation: an operation not under the direct computer control, of input-output on other devices. Used to designate the transfer of information between magnetic tapes and other media.

peripheral subsystem: consists of one or more peripheral units of the same type connected to an available input-output channel. Each subsystem is controlled by a channel synchronizer/control unit that interprets the control signals and instructions given by the central processor, effects the transfer of data to or from the selected unit and the central processor, indicates to the central processor the status of the available peripheral units, and informs the central processor when faults or mistakes that affect the operation of the subsystem occur.

peripheral transfer: the process of transmitting data between two peripheral units. (A) (B)

peripheral trunks: input-output trunks, each of which can be connected to a peripheral control.

periscope antenna: an antenna configuration, wherein the transmitting antenna is oriented to produce a vertical radiation pattern, and a flat or parabolically curved reflector, mounted above the transmitting antenna, is used to direct the beam in a horizontal path toward the receiving antenna.

permanent file: a file that is retained from one initial program load until the next. cf. *temporary file.*

permanently resident volume: a volume that cannot be physically demounted or that cannot be demounted until it is varied off line (i.e., removed from the control of the processing unit).

permanent memory: storage information remaining intact when power is turned off. synonymous with *nonvolatile storage.*

permanent read/write error: an error that cannot be eliminated by retrying a read/write operation.

permanent signal: a sustained off-hook supervisory signal, originating outside a switching system and not related to a call in progress. Permanent signals can occupy a substantial part of the capacity of a switching system. (F)

permanent storage: a storage device whose content cannot be modified. (B) cf. *erasable storage.* synonymous with *fixed storage, read-only storage.*

permanent virtual circuit: a permanent association existing between two DTEs that is a point-to-point, nonswitched circuit over which only data, reset, interrupt, and flow-control packets can move.

permutation: an ordered arrangement of a given number of different elements selected from a set. cf. *combination.* (A) (B)

permutation index: an index listing all words in a document's title in order that each word appears, in turn, as the first word, following by remaining ones.

persistence: the length of time a fluorescent screen found in a cathode ray tube retains its image.

personal computer: a low-cost, portable computer with software oriented towards, easy, single-user applications.

person-to-person service: the service in which the person originating the call specifies to an operator a particular person to be reached or a particular station, department, or office to be reached through a PBX attendant. (F)

PERT (Program Evaluation and Review Technique) network: an extensive study of an overall program to list all individual activities, or jobs that must be carried out so as to fulfill the total objective. These efforts are then arranged in a network that displays their relationships.

PF key: see *program function key.*

PG

(1)   see *page*.

(2)   see *program generator*.

PGEC: Professional Group on Electronic Computers; a technical group dedicated to the advancement of computer-related sciences, for example, programming, engineering, storage devices. PGEC is a division of the Institute of Electrical and Electronics Engineers (IEEE).

PGM: see *program*.

PH: see *phase*. also known by *Greek letter O*.

phantom circuit: a superimposed circuit derived from two suitably arranged pairs of wires called side circuits, with each pair of wires being a circuit itself and at the same time acting as one conductor of the phantom circuit.

phantom group: a group of four open-wire conductors suitable for the derivation of a phantom circuit.

phase (PH) (PHSE):   a part of a sort/merge program; for example, sort phase, merge phase. see *assembly phase, compile phase, execute phase, translate phase*. (A)

phase constant: the phase shift of a sinusoidal wave as it traverses a unit length of a transmission line. (F)

phase distortion: see *distortion*.

phase encoding: synonym for *phase modulation recording*.

phase hits: abrupt shifts in the phase of a transmitted carrier, usually originating in radio carrier systems.

phase-inversion modulation: a method of phase modulation in which the two significant conditions differ in phase by radians. (C)

phase jitter: an unwanted random signal distortion.

phase locked oscillator: a phase locked loop circuit utilized for precise data recovery in floppy disk drive controllers; stabilizes the separated data and clock bits.

phase lock loop: an electronic servo system controlling an oscillator so that it maintains a constant phase angle relative to a reference signal source.

phase modulation (PM)

(1)   modulation in which the phase angle of a carrier is the characteristic varied. (C)

(2)   angle modulation in which the phase angle of a sinusoidal carrier is caused to vary from a reference carrier phase angle by an amount proportional to the instantaneous amplitude of the modulating signal.

phase modulation recording: a magnetic recording in which each storage cell is divided into two regions which are magnetized in opposite senses; the sequence of these senses indicates whether the binary character represented z is zero or one. synonymous with *phase encoding*. (B)

phase-shift keying (PSK):   modulation techniques for transmitting digital information in which that information is conveyed by selecting discrete phase changes of the carrier. see *coherent phase-shift keying, differential phase-shift keying*. (F)

philoxenic: friendly to uninformed users, as in view-data systems.

phoneme: a primitive unit of auditory speech in a specified language.

phonetic system: specific units having the feature for beginning and acting upon data from the voice source or having a voice-form output.

phosphor dots: elements of a cathode-ray tube that glow red, green, or blue.

phosphorescence: emitting light for a time frame following removal of a source of excitation; a cathode-ray tube uses this phenomenon to permit a trace to stay on a screen following the signal that has caused it discontinued.

photocell matrix: an OCR term for equipment able to project an input on a fixed two-dimensional array of photocells to develop a simultaneous display of the vertical and horizontal components of the character.

photoelectric detection: detecting and reading marks with a photoelectric detector, as in optical character recognition.

photolithography: a procedure to print the masks on a wafer.

photomicrography: the process of producing a larger photograph from a smaller one.

photoresist: the technique used in etching semiconductor devices, of removing the oxidized surface of a silicon wafer by masking the part which is to be kept.

photosensor: a light-sensitive unit used with an optical arrangement for scanning images.

PHR: see *physical record*.

PHSE: see *phase*.

physical-access level: access to a data set by block, which may consist of one or more physical records.

physical block: see *block*.

physical child segment: in a data base, a segment that is dependent on a segment at the next higher level in the data base hierarchy. All segments except the root segment are physical child segments because each is dependent on at least the root. see also *logical child segment*.

physical circuit: a circuit created with hardware rather than by multiplexing. see also *data circuit*. cf. *virtual circuit*. (C)

physical connection: synonymous with *connection*.

physical interface: the point at which discrete pieces of equipment are connected. (D)

physical main storage: deprecated term for *processor storage*.

physical parent segment: in a data base, a segment that has a dependent segment at the next lower level in the physical data-base hierarchy.

physical record (PHR) (PR): a record whose characteristics depend on the manner or form in which it is stored, retrieved, or moved. A physical record may consist of all or part of a logical record.

physical relationship: in a data base, the description of the relationship between two or more physical segments.

physical resource: any faciltity of the computer available to do work, such as the processor, main storage, or an I/O device.

physical segment: in a data base, the smallest unit of accessible data.

physical simulation: employing a model of a physical system where computing elements are employed to represent some but not all of the subsystems.

physical structure: the interrelationships among data base as they are actually stored. (E)

physical volume: synonym for *volume*.

PI: see *program interruption*.

pianola roll: a roll of paper on which text and program instructions are represented by rows of punched holes.

PIC cable: cable whose conductors are individually insulated with a polyethylene (plastic) covering. (F)

pick device: in computer graphics, an input device used to identify a display element or display group. see also *choice device, locator device, valuator device*. (E)

pickup: interference from an extraneous circuit.

pico- (P): prefix meaning 10^{-12}, as in picosecond, one million millionth of a second. see *picosecond*.

PI codes: program indicator codes used when two or more programs are in the same program tape. These codes allow automatic selection of programs and permits switching from one program to the other.

picosecond (PS): one trillionth of a second; one thousandth of a nanosecond.

picture
(1) in a programming language, a description of a character string in which each position has associated with it a symbol representing the properties of the character that may occupy it; for example, in COBOL 9999 is used as a picture of any four-digit numeric word. (A) (B)
(2) the display image of an area on a document.
(3) in a program, a string of characters used in editing to modify the individual characters in a field. There is a one-to-one relationship between the characters in the picture and the characters in the field.

picture element (PEL) (PIXEL)
(1) the part of the area of the original document which coincides with the scanning spot at a given instant and which is of one intensity only, with no distinction of the details that may be included. (C)
(2) in computer graphics, the smallest element of a display space that can be independently assigned color and intensity. (E)
(3) the area of the finest detail that can be effectively reproduced on the recording medium.

Picturephone: a trademark of the AT&T Company, to identify a telecommunications service that permits the user to see as well as talk with the person at the other end.

picture specification: in PL/1, a character-by-character description of the composition and characteristics of binary picture data, decimal picture data, character-string picture data.

picture specification character: in PL/1, any of the characters that can be used in a picture specification. see *binary picture data, decimal picture data*.

piggyback hardware: practice of peripheral equipment manufacturers to "piggyback" on other major computer hardware maker's equipment.

pilot: an original or test program, project, or unit.

pilot make busy circuit (PMB): a circuit arrangement by which trunks provided over a carrier system are made busy to the switching equipment in the event of carrier system failure, or during a fade of the radio system.

pilot model: a model of a system, used for testing, that is not total.

pilot tape: a tape containing all the

data used on a pilot model, and is used for loading the files.

pin board: a perforated board into which pins are manually inserted to control the operation of equipment. synonym for *plugboard*. (*A*)

pinch roller: a small cylindrical pulley which pushes the tape against the drive capstan causing constant forward motion in a tape drive.

pin-feed platen: a cylindrical platen that drives the paper by means of integral rings of pins engaging perforated holes, rather than by pressure.

pipelining: commencing one instruction sequence prior to the completion of another.

pitch

(1) in word processing, the number of characters per horizontal inch or positioning interval of characters in a line of text for example, "10 pitch," "12 pitch," proportionally spaced characters.

(2) a unit of type width based on the number of times a character can be set in one linear inch; for example, 10 pitch has 10 characters per inch.

(3) see *feed pitch, row pitch, track pitch*. (*A*)

PIXEL: see *picture element*. synonym for *pel*.

pixel pattern: the matrix used in constructing the symbol or character image on a display screen.

PK: see *peak*.

PL

(1) see *program library*.

(2) see *programming language*.

PLA: see *programmed logic array*.

place: a digit position within a set of digits corresponding to a given power of the radix.

place value: see *number system*.

plaintext: synonymous with *clear area*.

plant: as used by communication common carriers, the physical facilities, such as switching equipment, service department, central office personnel, and cable. The term is generally used with the modifiers inside or outside.

plasma panel: a part of a display device that consists of a grid of electrodes in a flat, gas-filled panel in which the energizing of selected electrodes causes the gas to be ionized and light to be emitted at that point. synonymous with *gas panel*. (*E*)

plasma-ray device: a flat computer picture screen based on a grid of metallic conductors separated by a thin layer of gas. When a signal is generated at any intersection along the grid, the gas discharges and causes the transparent screen to glow at this point.

plated wire storage: a magnetic storage in which data are stored by magnetic recording in a film coated on the surface of wire. (*B*)

platen: a backing, usually cylindrical, against which printing mechanisms strike or otherwise deposit ink to produce an image.

platter: a round flat electromagnetic disk cartridge whose surface is not unlike a dinner plate.

plesichronous: a condition where two separate data systems reference different timing standards, but are functionally synchronous.

PLIB: see *program library*.

PL/1 (programming language 1): a programming language designed for numeric scientific computations, business data processing, systems programming, and other applications. PL/1 is capable of handling a large variety of data structures and easily allows variation of precision in numeric computation. (A)

PL/M: a high-level language created for microprocessor systems programming.

plot: to draw or diagram. To connect the point-by-point coordinate values.

plotter: an output unit that presents data in the form of a two-dimensional graphic representation (A) (B). see *drum plotter, flatbed plotter.*

plotter step size: in computer graphics, the increment size on a plotter. (E)

plotting: placing any type of information on a graph.

plotting head: in computer graphics, the part of a plotter used to create visible marks on the display surface. (E)

PLS: see *private-line service.*

plug: a little black box used to change each module's generic number.

plugboard: a perforated board into which plugs or pins may be placed to control the operation of equipment. synonymous with *board, control panel.* (A) (B)

plugboard chart: a chart that shows, for a given job, where plugs must be inserted into a plugboard. synonymous with *plugging chart.* (B)

plugboard computer: a computer having a punchboard input and output.

plug compatible: any two units operating from the same socket.

plugging chart: synonym for *plugboard chart.* (A)

PM
(1) see *phase modulation.*

(2) see *preventive maintenance.*

PMB: see *pilot make busy circuit.*

PMBX: private manual branch exchange.

PMOS: P-channel metal-oxide semiconductor, where the electrical current is a flow of positive charges. cf. *NMOS.* see *CMOS*

PMS: see *public message service.*

pn boundary: a transition region between p-type and n-type materials where the donor and acceptor concentrations are equal. synonym for *pn junction.*

PNCH: see *punch.*

pn junction: synonymous with *pn boundary.*

p-n-p transistor: a transistor having two p-type crystals separated by an n-type crystal.

pocket: a card stacker in a card sorter. (E)

POF: *point-of-failure restart.*

point (PT): see *addressable point, available point, branch point, breakpoint, checkpoint, decimal point, entry point, radix point, reentry point, rerun point, rescue point, restart point, viewpoint.*

pointer (P) (PTR)
(1) an identifier that indicates the location of an item of data. (A)
(2) in computer graphics, a manually operated functional unit used to specify an addressable point. A pointer may be used to conduct interactive graphic operations such as selection of one member of a predetermined set of display elements, or indication of a position on a display space while generating coordinate data. (E)
(3) a physical or symbolic identifier of a unique target.

pointer variable: in PL/1, a locator variable with the POINTER attribute, whose value identifies an absolute location in internal storage.

point of invocation: in PL/1, the point in the invoking block at which the procedure reference to the invoked procedure appears.

point of no return: a first instance in a program in which a rerun is no longer possible since data may no longer be available.

point-of-sale terminal: a terminal device which operates as a cash register in addition to transmitting information.

point-to-point connection: a connection established between two data stations for data transmission. The connection may include switching facilities.

point-to-point link: a link that connects a single remote link station to a node; it may be switched or non-switched. cf. *multipoint link.*

point-to-point transmission: transmission of data directly between two points without the use of any intermediate terminal or computer.

Poisson: in traffic theory, Poisson refers to a distribution or a process resulting in a distribution of events such that the intervals between adjacent events are independent random variables that are members of identical exponential distributions. Under certain conditions, the arrival of telephone calls to be routed over a trunk group can be approximated by a Poisson distribution. Named after a 19th-century French mathematician. (F)

polarization: the direction of vibration of an electromagnetic wave, and, correspondingly, the direction an aerial is orientated to transmit or receive.

polarized dipole magnetization: deprecated term for *polarized return-to-zero recording.* (E)

polarized plug: a plug designed to be inserted only when it is in one predetermined position.

polarized return-to-zero recording (RZ) (P): return-to-zero recording of binary digits such that the zeros are represented by magnetization in one sense and the ones are represented by magnetization in the opposite sense. synonymous with *polarized dipole magnetization.* (E)

polarizing slot: a slot found in the edge of a printed circuit board that can accept a specific type of connector. synonymous with *index slot.*

polar keying: form of telegraph signal in which circuit current flows one direction for marking, the other for spacing.

polar operation: a circuit operation where the flow of current is reversed as pulses are transmitted.

polar relay: a relay containing a permanent magnet that centers the armature. The direction of movement of the armature is governed by the direction of current flow.

polar signal: a digital signal technique in which positive and negative excursions represent the two binary states. (F)

polar transmission: a method for transmitting teletypewriter signals, whereby the marking signal is represented by direct current flowing in one direction, and the spacing signal is represented by an equal current flowing in the opposite direction. By extension to tone signaling, polar transmission is a method of transmission employing three distinct states, two to represent a mark and a space, and one to represent the absence of a signal. synonymous with *bipolar*. see also *neutral transmission, telegraph.*

Polish notation: synonym for *prefix notation.* (A) (B)

poll: a flexible, systematic approach centrally controlled to allow stations on a multipoint circuit to transmit without contending for the line.

polling

(1) interrogation of devices for purposes such as to avoid contention, to determine operational status, or to determine readiness to send or receive data. (A)

(2) the process whereby stations are invited, one at a time, to transmit. (B)

(3) see also *addressing, blind, lockout, selection, TSC.*

polling characters: a set of characters peculiar to a terminal and the polling operation; response to these characters indicates to the computer whether the terminal has a message to enter.

polling ID: the unique character or characters associated with a particular station.

polling interval: the time frame between polling operations, assuming that no data is transmitted from the terminal being polled.

polling list: a list that specifies the sequence in which stations are to be polled.

polymorphic: the mode of a computer organization or configuration of the primary units so that all components at a specific installation are held in a common pool.

polyphase sort: an unbalanced merge sort in which the distribution of sorted subsets is based on a Fibonacci series. (A)

pop: synonymous with *pull.*

port: an access point for data entry or exit. see *terminal port.* see also *view port.* deprecated term for *adapter.*

portability: the ability to use data sets or files with differing operating systems. Volumes whose data sets or files are cataloged in a user catalog can be demounted from storage devices of one system, moved to another system and mounted on storage devices of that system.

port circuit: the tristate driver circuit that interfaces with the main distributing frame and the transmit/receive filters. The drivers and filters are part of the port grouping.

POS: see *position.*

position (POS)

(1) a site on a punched tape or card where holes are to be punched.

(2) a place in a program, set of instructions, or within a context.

(3) see *bit position, display position, punch position, sign position.*

positional notation: synonym for *positional representation system.* (A) (B)

positional operand: in assembler programming, an operand in a macroinstruction that assigns a value to the corresponding positional parameter declared in the prototype statement of the called macrodefinition.

positional parameter: a parameter that must appear in a specified location, relative to other parameters. see also *key-word parameter.*

positional representation: a representation of a real number in a positional representation system. (A) (B)

positional representation system: any numeration system in which a real number is represented by an ordered set of character in such a way that the value contributed by a character depends upon its position as well as upon its value. synonymous with *positional notation.* (*A*) (B)

positioning: in computer graphics, indicating in a display space the location at which a specified display group is to be placed. (E)

positioning time: the time interval required to bring a transducer and the location of the required data on a data medium into the relative physical position necessary for the data to be read; for example, the time required to position a head on a magnetic disk, that is, seek time plus the time required for the data to arrive at the head, that is, rotational delay. (B)

position pulse: synonymous with *commutator pulse.*

positive response: a response that indicates a message was received successfully. synonymous with *normal response.*

post
(1) to enter a unit of information on a record.
(2) to note the occurrence of an event.

postamble: a sequence of binary characters recorded at the end of each block on phase-encoded magnetic tape, for the purpose of synchronization when reading backward. (B)

post-detection combiner: a circuit or device for combining two or more signals after demodulation.

postedit: to edit the results of a previous computation.

postedit program: a test of the application that has been edited, formatted, and sorted into a test result tape.

post fix notation: a method of forming mathematical expressions in which each operator is preceded by its operands and indicates the operation to be performed on the operands or the intermediate results that precede it. synonymous with *reverse Polish notation, suffix notation.* (B) cf. *infix notation, prefix notation.* see also *parentheses-free notation.* (*A*)

posting: see *event posting.* (A)

postmortem: pertaining to the analysis of an operation after its completion.

postmortem dump: dumping that is performed at the end of a run, usually for purposes of debugging, auditing, or documentation. (A) (B)

postnormalize: normalizing the arithmetic operation result.

POSTP: see *postprocessor.*

postprocessor (POSTP)
(1) a computer program that effects some final computation or organization. (A) (B)
(2) in emulation, a program that converts data produced by an emulator to the format of the emulated system.

Post Telephone and Telegraph Administration (PTT): a generic term for the government-operated common carriers in countries other than the USA and Canada. Examples of the PTT are the Post Office in the United Kingdom, the Bundespost in Germany, and the Nippon Telephone and Telegraph Public Corporation in Japan.

POTS: see *basic service.*

power (P): one of many software packages available to expand system usages and speed.

power circuit breaker

(1) a circuit breaker for use on ac circuits rates in excess of 1500 V.

(2) the primary switch used to apply and remove power from equipment.

power density spectrum: the relative proportion of total signal power distributed as a function of frequency. (F)

power disconnect switch: a device that makes and breaks the contact between the equipment and the main electricity supply. (D)

power down: steps made by a computer when power fails or is shut off in order to preserve the state of the processor and minimize damage to peripherals.

power dump: an accidental removal of all power.

power fail restart: a device that detects a drop in the input voltage and signals an imminent power failure to the computer.

power-fall circuit: a logic circuit that protects an operating program if primary power fails by informing the computer that when power failure is about to occur. This begins a routine that saves all volatile data.

power level: the ratio of the power at a point to some arbitrary amount of power chosen as a reference. This ratio is usually expressed either in decibels based on 1 milliwatt (abbreviated dBm) or in decibels based on 1 watt (abbreviated dBw). see also *decibel.*

power of a number: the exponent.

power supply: a unit that converts the line voltage from a wall socket into the voltages needed by the computer elements.

power up: steps taken by a computer when power is turned on or restored following a power failure.

power up diagnostics: programs, usually in ROM, which evaluate the condition of the CPU and memory on power-up.

PP: see *parallel processing.*

PPS: pulses per second.

PPT: see *punched paper tape.*

p-pulse: synonymous with *commutator pulse.*

PR

(1) see *paper tape reader.*

(2) see *physical record.*

(3) see *prefix.*

(4) see *printer.*

(5) see *program register.*

pragmatics: the relationship of characters or group of characters to their interpretation and use. (A) (B)

PRE: see *prefix.*

preamble: a sequence of binary architecture recorded at the beginning of each block on a phase-encoded magnetic tape for the purpose of synchronization. (B)

preanalysis: reviewing the tasks to be accomplished by a computer so as to increase the efficiency of that task.

pre-assembly time: the time at which an assembler processes macro-definitions and performs conditional assembly operations.

precedence code: a code signifiying that characters in the following code(s) will have a different meaning from normal.

precedence prosign: a group of characters that indicate how a message is to be handled.

precision

(1) a measure of the ability to distinguish between nearly equal values. (B)

(2) the degree of discrimination with which a quantity is stated. For example, a three-digit numeral discriminates among 1000 possibilities.

(3) cf. *accuracy.*

(4) see *double precision, multiple precision, triple precision.* (*A*)

precoded form: a form on which certain items of invariant data have been entered prior to the entry of variable data. synonymous with *prerecorded form.* (E)

precompiler program: a program designed to locate errors and provide source program correction prior to the computation of the object, deck, or program.

predefined process: in flowcharting, a process that is identified only by name and that is defined elsewhere. (A)

predefined specification: The FORTRAN-defined type and length of a variable, based on the initial character of the variable name in the absence of any specification to the contrary. The characters I-N are typed INTEGER*4; the character A-H, O-Z, and $ are typed REAL*4.

pre-detection combiner: a circuit or device for combining two or more signals prior to demodulation so that the resultant combined signal must be demodulated.

preedit: to edit input data prior to computation.

pre-emphasis network: a network inserted in a system in order to increase the magnitude of one range of frequencies with respect to another.

prefix (PR) (PRE)

(1) in PL/1, a label or a parenthesized list of one or more condition names connected by a colon to the beginning of a statement.

(2) a code dialed by a caller before being connected. cf. *suffix.*

(3) a code at the beginning of a message or record.

(4) any dialed input prior to the destination address. Prefixes are used to place an address in proper context, to indicate service options, or both. Examples: prefix 1, to indicate a toll call; prefix 0, to request the services of an operator.

(5) see *buffer prefix.*

prefix notation: a method of forming mathematical expressions in which each operator precedes its operands and indicates the operation to be performed on the operands or the intermediate results that follow it. synonymous with *Lukasiewicz notation, Polish notation.* (B) cf. *infix notation, postfix notation.* see also *parentheses-free notation.* (*A*)

prefix operator: in PL/1, an operator that precedes an operand and applies only to that operand.

prenormalize: normalizing the operands of an arithmetic operation before the operation is performed.

preprocessor

(1) a computer program that effects some preliminary computation or organization. (A) (B)

(2) a program that examines the source program for preprocessor statements which are then executed, resulting in the alteration of the source program.

(3) in emulation, a program that converts data from the format of an

emulated system to the format accepted by an emulator.

preprocessor statement: in PL/1, a special statement appearing in the source program that specifies how the source program text is to be altered; it is identified by a leading percent sign and is executed as it is encountered by the preprocessor (it appears without the percent sign in preprocessor procedures, which are invoked by a preprocessor function reference).

preread head: a read head adjacent to another read head and used to read data before the same data are read by the other read head. (E)

prerecorded form: synonym for *precoded form.*

prerecorded tracks: a preliminary tape, disk, or drum-recorded routine that simplifies programming and allows block and word addressability.

preselection: in buffered computers, a technique in which a spare block of information is read into memory from whichever input tape will next be called upon; determined by inspecting the keys of the last records of each block of working storage.

presentation layer: in open systems architecture, the layer that provides the functions that may be selected by the application layer, such as: data definition; managing the entry; exchange, display, and control of structured data; and definition of operations that may be performed on the data. (E)

preset: to establish an initial condition, such as the control values of a loop, or the value to which a parameter is to be bound. (A) (B)

preset parameter: a parameter that is

bound when the computer program is constructed; for example, when it is flowcharted, coded, or compiled.

presort: the first part of a sort, where records are arranged into strings that equal or exceed a minimum length.

Prestel: the British Telecom name for the first public view-data system.

prestore: to store, before a computer program, routine, or subroutine is entered, data that are required by the computer program, the routine, or the subroutine. (B) cf. *initialize. (A)*

presumptive address: the number that shows as an address in a computer instruction, but which is designed to serve as the base, index, initial, or starting point for subsequent addresses to be modified. synonymous with *reference address.*

presumptive instruction: an instruction that is not an effective instruction until it has been modified in a prescribed manner. (A) (B)

prevarication: synonym for *irrelevance. (A) (B)*

preventive maintenance (PM): maintenance specifically intended to prevent faults from occurring. Corrective maintenance and preventive maintenance are both performed during maintenance time. cf. *corrective maintenance. (A)*

preventive maintenance time: time, usually scheduled, used to perform preventive maintenance. (A)

previewing: an optical character recognition term to describe a strategy to try and gain initial or prior information about characters that appear on an incoming source document.

prewired options: optional devices that are closely related to the processor, such as the extended arithmetic element, memory extension control, and one of the analog-to-digital converted options, are prewired in the basic computer so that the time, effort, and cost involved in adding these options at the factory or in the field is a minimum.

PRF: see *pulse repetition frequency.*

PRI: see *priority.*

primary: in high-level data-link control (HDLC), the part of the data station that supports the primary control functions of the data link, generates commands for transmission, and interprets received responses. Specific responsibilities assigned to the primary include initialization of control signal interchange, organization of data flow, and actions regarding error control and error recovery functions. cf. *secondary.* (E)

primary center: a control center connecting toll centers together; a class 3 office. It can also serve as a toll center for its local end offices.

primary entry point: in PL/1, the entry point identified by any of the names in the label list of the PROCEDURE statement.

primary function: the function that allows a data station to exert overall control of the data link according to the link protocol.

primary key: a portion of the first block of each record in an indexed data set that can be used to find the record in the data set. see also *secondary key.*

primary processing unit: the processing unit in a multiple processing unit configuration that processes unsolicited messages from the mass storage control.

primary space allocation: an area of direct-access storage space initially allocated to a particular data set or file when the data set or file is defined.

primary station: a data station that can perform the primary function but not the secondary function. (E)

primary track: on a direct-access device, the original track on which data is stored. see also *alternate track.*

prime focus: the point in an antenna toward which a main reflector directs and concentrates signals it receives.

prime shift: the normal or conventional working hours scheduled when equipment usage is most important.

primitive: see *input primitive.*

principal city: the toll office farthest down the routing ladder to which call codes for that area can be routed by destination-type codes. It need not be physically located within the NPA served. (F)

print: synonym for *copy. (D)*

print band: a thin piece of metal used to print the characters on the form.

print bar: synonym for *type bar.* (B)

print barrel: synonym for *print drum.* (B)

print chain: a revolving carrier on which the type slugs of an impact printer are mounted.

print contrast ratio: in optical character recognition, the ratio obtained by subtracting the reflectance at an inspection area from the maximum reflectance found within a specified distance from that area, and dividing the result by that maximum reflectance. cf. *print contrast signal. (A)*

print contrast signal (PCS): in optical character recognition, a measure of the contrast between a printed character and the paper on which the character is printed. cf. *print contrast ratio.* (*A*)

print control character: a control character for print operations such as line spacing, page ejection, or carriage return. (A)

print cup: in word processing, an interchangeable printing element in the shape of a cup, used in some impact printers. (D)

print data set: a data set in which programs store data to be printed.

print drum: a rotating cylinder that presents characters at more than one print position. synonymous with *print barrel.* (B)

printed card form: the layout or format of the printed matter on a card. The printed matter usually describes the purpose of the card and designates the precise location of card fields. (A)

printed circuit board (PCB) (PC board): an insulating board onto which a circuit has been printed or etched. synonym for *card, chassis, PC board, plate.*

printer (PR) (PRN) (PRNTR) (PRT) (PRTR) (PTR)
(1) an output device that produces a durable record of data in the form of a sequence of discrete graphic characters belonging to a predetermined character set. (E)
(2) a device that writes output data from a system on paper or other media.
(3) see *bar printer, chain printer, character printer, drum printer, line printer, matrix printer, on-the-fly printer, page printer.* (A)

printer controller: a high-speed line printer controller that contains the circuitry needed to interface a high

volume printing device to a microcomputer.

printerfacing: the provision of an interface between microcomputers and output printing terminals.

printer limited: the relatively slow speed of a printer reducing the rate at which processing can occur.

printer operating speed: the rate at which print-out occurs, expressed in characters per second or in words of five recorded characters, including space, per minute.

printer plotter: a printer capable of graphics reproduction in addition to character printing.

printer skipping: the rate a unit advances a form through its carriage without printing.

printer spacing chart: a form utilized in deciding the format of printed output.

printer speed: the rate a which a unit operates when it is actually printing data.

print format: a representation of the manner by which data is printed, illustrating column widths, position of page numbers, headings, and so on.

printing calculator: a machine in which the data output is printed on paper or other suitable material. (D)

printing counter: a counter on a magnetic-tape terminal that advances by one for each tape block transmitted or received. Following transmission, the total number of blocks is automatically printed.

print line: the normal set of printed characters and spaces placed in a horizontal row as a unit.

print-only ticket: a ticket that contains

only printed information and does not have a magnetic stripe.

print-out

(1) in computer technology, the printed output of a computer.

(2) in word processing, the printing or typing of recorded text. (D)

print record: a record in a print data set. see also *group (3)*.

print record header: identification and control information at the beginning of the first block of a print record.

print speed: the number of characters printed per unit of time. (D)

print through: an undesired transfer of a recorded signal from one part to another part of a recording medium when these parts are brought into contact. (B)

print train: synonym for *print chain*.

print transparent: a mode in which a terminal will pass all received data to an auxiliary port and neither display nor act upon it.

print wheel

(1) a rotating disk that presents characters at a single print position. synonymous with *type wheel*. (B)

(2) in word processing an interchangeable printing element, used in some impact printers. (D)

PRIO: see *priority*.

priority (PRI) (PRIO) (PRTY): a rank assigned to a task that determines its precedence in receiving system resources. see also *dispatching priority, job priority, time-sharing priority*.

priority indicator: a group of characters that indicate the relative urgency of a message and thus its order of transmission.

priority interrupt: an event recognized by the system, and processed according to an assigned priority.

priority interrupt table: a table that lists the priority sequence of handling and testing interrupts.

priority limit: the upper bound to the priority list for dispatching or designing a priority rating to various tasks or subtasks.

priority number: in COBOL, a number, ranging in value from 0 to 99, which classifies source program sections in the procedure division.

priority processing: a method of operating a computer in which computer programs are processed in such a way that the order of operations to be performed is fully determined by a system of priorities. (A)

priority routine: in an interrupt, the leaving of one program by the processor to work on the program connected with the interrupt or the priority routine.

priority scheduler: a form of job scheduler that uses input and output work queues to improve system performance.

priority scheduling system: a job scheduler, in larger systems, that have a resultant improved system performance attained by means of input/output queues.

priority structure: the organization of a system for processing.

privacy: the right of individuals and organizations to control the collection and use of their data or data about themselves. (E)

privacy protection: the establishment of appropriate administrative, technical, or physical safeguards to preserve a required level of privacy. (E)

private address space: an address

space assigned to a particular user.

private automatic branch exchange (PABX): a private automatic telephone exchange that provides for the transmission of calls to and from the public telephone network.

private automatic exchange (PAX): a dial telephone exchange that provides private telephone service to an organization and that does not allow calls to be transmitted to or from the public telephone network.

private automatic switching system (PASS): a series of packaged PBX service offerings provided on the basis of service features rather than specific hardware.

private branch exchange (PBX): a manual exchange connected to the public telephone network on the user's premises and operated by an attendant supplied by the user.

private code: an unnamed control section.

private library: a user-owned library that is separate and distinct from the system library.

private line: deprecated term for *non-switched line.*

private-line service (PLS): a service in which the customer leases a circuit, not interconnected with the public telephone network, for his exclusive use. The private line may be used for transmission of voice, teletypewriter, data, television, and so forth. (F)

private voice-band network: a network that is made up of voice-band circuits and sometimes switching arrangements, for the exclusive use of one customer. These networks can be nationwide in scope and typically serve large corporations or government agencies. (F)

privileged instruction
(1) an instruction that may be used only by a supervisory program. (A) (B)
(2) an instruction that can be executed only when the processing unit is in the supervisor state.

PRN: see *printer.*

PRNTR: see *printer.*

probability theory: the mathematical characterization of uncertainty. As most real world decisions involve elements of uncertainty (about future events or uncontrollable influences) such uncertainties need to be explicitly incorporated into decision analyses.

probe: an electrical unit for making contact with a circuit test point for test or debugging needs.

problem data: in PL/1, a string or arithmetic data that is processed by a PL/1 program.

problem definition: the presentation of a problem for computer solution in a structured, logical fashion.

problem description: a statement of problem, perhaps including a description of the method of solving it, procedures, and algorithms. (A) (B)

problem determination: the process of identifying the source of a problem; for example, a program component, a machine failure, telecommunication facilities, user- or contractor-installed programs or equipment, an environment failure such as a power loss, or a user error.

problem determination aid (PDAID): a program that traces a specified event when it occurs during the operation of a program.

problem determination procedure: a prescribed sequence of steps taken to accomplish problem determination. Such procedures frequently include steps aimed at recovery from, or circumvention of, problem conditions.

problem diagnosis: analysis that results in identifying the precise cause of a hardware, software, or system failure.

problem file: all the material required to document a program to be run on a computer.

problem input tape: an input tape, either punched paper tape or magnetic tape, that contains problem data for checking out a given computer system.

problem-oriented language: a programming language that is especially suitable for a given class of problems. Procedure-oriented languages such as FORTRAN, ALGOL; simulation languages such as GPSS, SIMSCRIPT; list processing languages such as LISP, IPL-V; information retrieval languages. (B) synonym for *application-oriented language.* (E)

problem program: any program that is executed when the processing unit is in the problem state; that is, any program that does not contain privileged instructions.

problem state: a state during which the processing unit cannot execute input/output and other privileged instructions. cf. *supervision state.*

problem time: in simulation, the duration of a process, or the length of time between two specified events of a process. (A)

PROC

(1) see *command procedure.*

(2) see *procedure.*

(3) see *processing.*

(4) see *processor.*

procedural language: synonym for *procedure-oriented language.* (A) (B)

procedural statement: synonym for *instruction.*

procedure (P) (PROC)

(1) the course of action taken for the solution of a problem. (B)

(2) the description of the course of action taken for the solution of a problem. (*A*)

(3) a sequenced set of statements that may be used at one or more points in one or more computer programs, and that usually has one or more input parameters and yields one or more output parameters. (E)

(4) the actions taken to implement protocols. (C)

(5) in PL/1, a collection of statements, headed by a PROCEDURE statement and ended by an END statement, that is part of a program, that delimits the scope of names, and that is activated by a reference to one of its entry names.

(6) see *cataloged procedure, contingency procedure, in-line procedure.*

procedure division (PD): one of the four main component parts of a COBOL program. The procedure division contains instructions for solving a problem. The procedure division may contain imperative statements, conditional statements, paragraphs, procedures, and sections.

procedure library (PROCLIB): a program library in direct-access storage containing job definitions. The reader/interpreter can be directed to read and interpret a particular job definition by an execute statement in the input stream.

procedure name: in COBOL, a word that precedes and identifies a procedure, used by the programmer to transfer control from one point of the program to another.

procedure-oriented language: a programming language that allows the user to express the solution to a problem as an explicit algorithm; for example, FORTRAN, ALGOL, COBOL, PL/1. synonymous with *procedural language*. (E)

procedure reference: in PL/1, an entry constant or variable or a built-in function name followed by none or more argument lists. It may appear in a CALL statement or CALL option or as a function reference.

procedures analysis: see *systems analysis*.

procedure statement: a declaration used to assign a name to a procedure. synonymous with *subroutine statement*. (E)

procedure step: a unit of work associated with one processing program and related data within a cataloged or in-stream procedure. A cataloged procedure consists of one or more procedure steps.

procedure subprogram: a function or subroutine subprogram.

process (P)

(1) a systematic sequence of operations to produce a specified result. (A)

(2) in a computer system, a unique, finite course of events defined by its purpose or by its effect, achieved under given conditions. (E)

(3) an executing function, or a function that is waiting to be executed.

(4) to perform operations on data in a process. (B)

(5) see *input process, output process, predefined process*.

processable scored card: a scored card including at least one separable part that can be processed after separation. (A)

process chart: synonymous with *systems flowchart*.

process check: synonym for *program exception*.

process control: automatic control of a process, in which a computer system is used to regulate usually continuous operations or processes. (E)

process control system: a remote system created so that the user is not human but instead a mechanical-, electronic-, or thermal-sensing device for input or a mechanical-, electronic-, or thermal-controlling unit for output.

process exception: synonym for *program exception*.

processing (PROC): the performance of logical operations and calculations on data, including the temporary retention of data in processor storage while it is being operated upon. see *administrative data processing, automatic data processing, background processing, batch processing, business data processing, data processing, distributed data processing, electronic data processing, foreground processing, industrial data processing, integrated data processing, list processing, multiprocessing, parallel processing, priority processing, real-time processing, remote-access data processing, remote batch processing, sequential batch processing, serial processing*.

processing capacity: pertaining to a calculation that is usually the maximum limitation of places of a number that can be processed at any one time, for example, a 12-place number.

processing multithread: a sequence of events in programs needed for the computer processing of a message known as a thread. In multithread processing, message threads are handled in parallel.

processing program: a program that performs such functions as compiling, assembling, or translating for a particular programming language.

processing system: see *data-processing system*. (A)

processing unit (PU): a functional unit that consists of one or more processors and all or part of internal storage. (E) see *primary processing unit*.

process interrupt card: a card that provides a means by which a user, or processes that the user specifies, can generate interrupts and request service on a priority basis.

process optimization: an extensive process-controller program, based on the model of the process, directs the data acquisition and control system. Processed data is continuously collected and analyzed for computation of optimum operating instructions, which are given to the process operator via an on-line typewriter.

processor (P) (PROC)
(1) in a computer, a functional unit that interprets and executes instructions. (B)
(2) a functional unit, part of another unit such as a terminal or a processing unit, that interprets and executes instructions.
(3) deprecated term for *processing program*.
(4) see *central processor, data processor, host processor, language processor, multiprocessor*.
(5) see also *processing*.

processor basic instructions: processor modules that execute basic instructions grouped into categories—register operations, accumulator operations, program counter and stack control operations, input-output operations, machine operations.

processor bound: computation where the internal processor speed is the limiting resource for programs.

processor error interrupt: occurs if a word accessed in any portion of the system is found to contain incorrect check bits, or if an error occurs in the addressing of a memory location.

processor front-end: a small computer that serves as a line controller for a larger processor.

processor interface: the transfer of data between a processor and the standard communication subsystem. The transfer takes place through input data leads, connected to the processor input channel, and output data leads, connected to the processor output channel.

processor limited: a system conditon occurring when the time taken to finish a process is dictated by the time taken by the central processor rather than the time taken by peripheral units. cf. *peripheral limited*.

processor organization: the three main sections of a computer—arithmetic and control, input-output, and memory.

processor status word: synonymous

with *program status word.*

processor storage

(1) the storage provided by one or more processing units.

(2) in virtual storage systems, synonymous with *real storage.*

processor verbs: verbs that specify to the processor the procedures by which a source program is to be translated into an object program. These verbs do not cause action at object time.

process time: time used for translating a source program into an object program through the action of a processor program and the computer.

PROCLIB: see *procedure library.*

PROC statement: a job control statement used in cataloged or in-stream procedures. It can be used to assign default values for symbolic parameters contained in a procedure. For in-stream procedures, it is used to mark the beginning of the procedure.

product: the number or quantity that results from a multiplication. (A) (B)

product area: an area in main storage that stores results of multiplication operations specifically.

production control: in computers, a data acquisition system from the floor of a product in line or process for the speed up and simplification of the flow of production information for management.

production routine: a routine that produces the results of the problem or program as it was designed, as contrasted with the routines which are designed for support, housekeeping, or to compile, assemble, translate, and so on.

production run: an operational run of a fully tested and proven system.

production time: that part of operating time that is neither development time nor makeup time. (A)

productive poll: an interrogation of a tributary station that results in the receipt of data.

productive task: a task assigned the third highest dispatching priority by the network control program; it initiates input-output on either the channel or a telecommunication line. cf. *nonproductive task.* see also *appendage task, immediate task.*

productive time: fault-free time of uninterrupted production runs.

productivity: see *system productivity.*

PROG

(1) see *program.*

(2) see *programmer.*

program (P) (PGM) (PROG)

(1) to design, write, and test programs.

(2) in word processing, a set of instructions incorporated into the design of the equipment, read in from a recording medium, or entered by an operator, that enables the equipment to perform tasks without further intervention by the operator. (D)

(3) a set of actions or instructions that a machine is capable of interpreting and executing.

(4) a schedule or plan that specifies actions that may or may not be taken. (B)

(5) see *assembly program, checking program, computer program, control program, diagnostic program, editor program, input program, library program, monitor program, object program, output program, relocatable program, reusable program, self-adapting program,*

snapshot program, sort program, source program, supervisory program, target program, trace program, translating program, utility program.
(5) deprecated term for *routine.* (B)

program access (PA) key: on a display device keyboard, a key that produces a call to a program that performs display operations. see also *program function (PF) key.*

program address counter: synonymous with *instruction register.*

program area block: synonymous with *program block.*

programatics: pertaining to the study that deals with the techniques of programming and programming languages.

program attention key: on a display device keyboard, a key that produces an interruption to solicit program action. see also *program access (PA) key, program function (PF) key.*

program block: in problem-oriented languages, a computer program subdivision that serves to group related statements, delimit routines, specify storage allocation, delineate the applicability of labels, or segment parts of the computer program for other purposes. (A) synonym for *program area block.*

program breakpoint: a location where the execution of a program is halted to allow visual check, printing out, or other performance analysis.

program cards: punched cards with program instructions; usually with one instruction per card.

program check: a condition that occurs when programming errors are detected by an I/O channel.

program check interruption: caused by a condition encountered in a program, such as incorrect operands.

program checkout: a run-through of a program to determine if all designs and results of a program are as anticipated.

program compatibility: the result of portability, when a program is run on two different computers.

program compilation: the process of employing a compiler.

program control: pertaining to the act of organizing the activities of a device on line to a central processor.

program control data: data used in a PL/1 program to affect the execution of the program, that is, any data that is not string or arithmetic data.

program-controlled interruption (PCI): an interruption that occurs when an I/O channel fetches a CCW with the program-controlled interruption flag on.

program controller: the central processor unit that organizes the execution of instructions. synonymous with *program control unit.*

program control unit (PCU): synonymous with *program controller.*

program counter: a specific CPU register that holds the address value of the memory location where the following CPU directive is to be obtained.

program crash: occurs when a computer program in attempting to execute an impossible instruction has no means of recognizing the impossibility and stopping.

program data set (PDS): the data set on disk storage that contains user programs to be executed.

program development time: that part of operating time that is used for debugging. (A)

program documentation: a vital part of programming, an approach used by machine operators for changing programs, training people how to run programs and handle problems should they occur.

program drum: a revolving cylinder on which a program card is attached.

program error: a mistake found in the program code.

Program Evaluation and Review Technique: see *PERT*.

program event recording (PER): a hardware feature used to assist in debugging programs by detecting and recording program events.

program exception: the condition recognized by a processor that results from execution of a program that improperly specifies or uses instructions, operands, or control information. synonymous with *process check, process exception*.

program execution time: the interval during which the instructions of an object program are executed. (A)

program fetch time: the time at which a program in the form of load modules or phases is loaded into main storage for execution.

program file: a system that is easily updated and flexible and used for the maintenance of the entire software library.

program flowchart: a visual representation of a computer problem where machine instructions or groups of instructions are shown by symbols.

program function (PF) key: on a display device keyboard, a key that passes a signal to a program to call for a particular display operation. see also *program access (PA) key*.

program-generated parameter: a pa-rameter that is bound during the execution of a computer program. synonymous with *dynamic parameter*. (A) (B)

program generator (PG): a program that allows a computer to write other programs automatically.

program halt: a halt in a program that occurs when the program meets a halt instruction. synonymous with *coded stop*.

program-independent modularity: the property of a system that permits it to accept changes and adjust processing to yield maximum usage of all modules without reprogramming.

program instruction

(1) in word processing, an instruction code which, when read, causes one or more functions to operate automatically. (D)

(2) control codes stored on the recording media or in the processing device, causing the machine to respond as desired.

program interruption (PI): the suspension of the execution of a program because of a program exception.

program level: in the network control program, an order of operational priorities established by the communication controller hardware; the five levels operate similarly to subroutines, are responsible for particular phases of system operation, and become active by interruptions to the individual levels.

program library (PL) (PLIB)

(1) a collection of available computer programs and routines. (A)

(2) an organized collection of computer programs that are sufficiently documented to allow them to be used

by persons other than their authors. (B)

(3) synonym for *partitioned data set.*

program line: a single instruction written on a standard coding form and stored as a single entity.

program linking: when a program is too large to be stored in memory, it can be divided into links by means of a FORTRAN link statement. During run time, routines in the monitory system automatically handle the execution of the segments of the linked program.

program listing: an operational tool showing the source and object language and a symbol table cross-reference. The listing is cross-referenced to the diagrams and the comments in the coding.

program loader: see *initial program loader, loader.*

program loading routine: a procedure for inserting instructions and the constant values of the program into the computer.

program logic array (PLA): the area of a chip responsible for implementing the decoding of instructions and the logic control activities.

programmable data control unit: front-end systems that are FORTRAN-written application software-control communication systems. These systems preformat messages to a format of the host processor and maintain disk files for message queuing and system backup.

programmable function key: a feature allowing a user to key in a program and assign it to a function key and also display the program and edit it using normal terminal functions.

programmable input-output chip: an input-output chip, often an eight-bit interface chip that multiplexes one connection to the data bus into two or more eight-bit ports.

programmable interval timer: a chip with a separate clock and several registers used to count time independently of the microprocessor, for real-time applications. At the end of a time period, it sets a flag or generates an interrupt, or merely stores the time elapsed.

programmable logic array: a general-purpose logic circuit that contains an array of logic gates that are connected to perform various functions.

programmable read-only memory (PROM): an integrated circuit of read-only memory that can be programmed by a user; for example, following manufacture, by means of a hardware device known as a PROM programmer. see *programmer unit.*

programmable remote display terminal: a typical programmable display terminal with a microprocessor to function as an intelligent remote terminal station or as a cluster of stations. It is used for the entry of data, data processing, control and monitoring, conversational interaction and off-line operation.

programmable storage

(1) storage that can be addressed by an application programmer.

(2) the portion of internal storage in a communication controller in which user-written programs are executed. cf. *control storage.*

programmable terminal (PT): a user terminal that has computational capability. (E) synonymous with *intelligent terminal.*

program maintenance: keeping programs up to date by correcting errors, making alterations as requirements change and changing the programs to take advantage of new units.

programmed check: a check procedure that is part of a computer program. cf. *automatic check.* (*A*)

programmed computer: synonym for *stored program computer.* (A) (B)

programmed dump: a library subroutine called by object programs at run time, returning control to the calling program or to the monitor following completion.

programmed instructions: subroutines used as if they were single commands by using one of the programmed instructions of the system repertoire, allowing a programmer's own special commands to be self-defined through the use of subroutines that can be altered by the operating routine if desired.

programmed operators system (SYS-POP): a function making monitor mode service routines available to user mode programs without loss of system control or use of user memory space.

programmer (PROGR) (PROGR): a person who designs, writes, and tests computer programs. (A)

programmer-defined macro: a macroinstruction used in a program and is defined by a programmer at the commencement of a specific program.

programmer/duplicator: a typical device contains a master control unit a a plug in PROM personality module. When connected it can be commanded to program, list, duplicate, and verify PROMs.

programmer unit: a hardware unit that provides the means for programming PROM, using a control program that permits instructions to be blown and verified.

programming: the designing, writing, and testing of programs. (B) see *automatic programming, convex programming, dynamic programming, integer programming, linear programming, macroprogramming, mathematical programming, minimum delay programming, multiprogramming, nonlinear programming, quadratic programming.* (*A*)

programming audit: a program enabling the employment of a computer as an auditing tool.

programming compatibility: systems that can be augmented and increased in power as required.

programming flowchart: a flowchart representing the sequence of operation in a computer program. synonymous with *programming flow diagram.* (*A*) (B)

programming flow diagram: synonym for *programming flowchart.* (A) (B)

Programming in Logic: see *PROLOG.*

programming language (PL)
(1) an artificial language established for expressing computer programs. (B)
(2) a set of characters and rules, with meanings assigned prior to their use, for writing computer programs. (E)

Programming Language: see *PL/1.*

programming manager: a person responsible for planning, scheduling, and supervising program development and maintenance work.

programming module: a discrete identifiable set of instructions, usually handled as a unit by an assembler, a compiler, a linkage editor, a loading routine, or other type of routine or subroutine. (A)

programming statement: one of a set of symbolic expressions used to write programs. (A)

programming system (PS): one or more programming languages and the necessary software for using these languages with particular automatic data-processing equipment.

program mode: a program that is active at a given terminal, where the terminal is now in the program mode. In this mode the user enters program statements that makes up the substance of his program.

program modification: the process of performing arithmetic and logic operations on instructions and addresses during a program so as to alter them.

program module: programming instructions that are treated as a unit by an assembler, compiler, loader, or translator.

program origin: see *computer program origin.* (A)

program package: a group or collection of logically related operational program segments, that is, all those having to do with the processing of a certain type of inquiry.

program parameter: see *external program parameter.* (A)

program patching plug: a small auxiliary plugboard patched with a variation of a portion of a program, to then be plugged into a relatively larger plugboard patched with the main program.

program postedit: a test of the application or operational program that is edited, formatted, and sorted into a test result tape.

program preparation: conversion of programs from one of several easy-to-use source languages, or from certain competitive system languages, to a machine code.

program read-in: the procedure and means of developing, by either hardware or software approaches, programs that do not normally reside in main memory and that must be read in from auxiliary storage when required for processing. Such techniques are needed in systems that cannot retain all computer instructions in main memory at one time.

program register (PR): synonymous with *instruction register.*

program relocation: the execution of a program in a location that is different from the location for which the program was originally assembled.

program runs: the actual running of a program. Programs and runs are synonymous except to show the time and action being performed. cf. *program.*

program scheduler: a scheduler used to determine which program in memory is to be run, dumped, terminated, and so forth.

program segment: computer instructions set in groups of an artificially fixed size to fit into standard-sized areas of main storage to aid memory allocation and program read-in.

program segmenting: programs that do not fit into memory are segmented by using a source-language linking statement, allowing sections of the program to be loaded and executed independently.

program selection

(1) selection of a particular pro-

gram for operation.

(2) a function that identifies and actuates a particular program for operation.

program selector: in word processing, a control by means of which a particular machine program is selected for operation. (D)

program-sensitive fault: a fault that occurs as a result of some particular sequence of program steps. cf. *pattern-sensitive fault.* (A)

program sensitive malfunction: a malfunction that occurs only during some unusual combination of program steps.

program specification: a full definition of the processes and steps carried out by a program, acting as the basis of work for a programmer.

program status word (PSW): an area in storage used to indicate the order in which instructions are executed, and to hold and indicate the status of the computer system. synonymous with *processor status word.*

program step: a single operation within a program; frequently an instruction.

program stop: a stop instruction within a machine that automatically stops the machine upon reaching the end of processing, completing a solution, or under another condition.

program storage: where a program is secured within main memory.

program structure: the manner in which the component parts of a computer program, such as identifiers, declarations, and statements are arranged. (E)

program switching: on a single transaction the control program initiates several switches among the various programs; all resulting from the processor being able to perform rapid program switching.

program test: running of a sample problem with a given answer so as to uncover errors in a program.

program testing: running a program with test data so as to verify that it is properly performing expected operations.

program testing time: machine time expanded for program testing, debugging, and volume and compatibility testing.

program translation: translation from a source language program to a target program; for example, from FORTRAN to machine language.

program unit: in FORTRAN, a main program or a subprogram.

program verbs: verbs that cause the processor to generate machine instructions that are executed by the object program.

progressively controlled network: a switching network consisting of large-motion switches, such as step-by-step or panel, in which calls are set up by making a series of connections, one at a time. (F)

progressive overflow: on a direct-access storage device, the writing of overflow records on the next consecutive track. cf. *chaining overflow.*

prolog: in PL/1, the processes that occur automatically on a block activation. see *PROLOG.*

PROLOG: Programming in Logic. Developed in Europe in the late 1970s, used in artificial intelligence work because its basic terms express logical relationships among objects, which is what advanced computers need to understand, and not just equations, as most programming languages do. see also *artificial intelligence*.

PROM: see *programmable read-only memory*.

PROM blower: see *blow, programmer unit*.

PROM burner: synonymous with *PROM blower*. see *blow, programmer unit*.

prompt: any message presented to an operator by an operating system, indicating that particular information is needed before a program can proceed.

prompt facility: a facility that assists a terminal operator by displaying messages that describe required input or giving operational information.

prompting: the issuing of messages to a terminal user, requesting information necessary to continue processing.

proof list: a printout giving instructions and narrative as originally prepared and the object code resulting from them.

proofreader: synonymous with *dictionary*.

propagate: passing through a system from one component to another.

propagated error: an error that takes place in a single operation as a result of a propagating error in another operation.

propagating error: an error that takes place in a single operation and results in other operations.

propagation constant: in transmission line theory, the complex number whose real part is the attenuation constant and whose imaginary part is the phase constant. (F)

propagation delay: the time necessary for a signal to travel from one point on a circuit to another.

propagation loss: energy lost by a signal during the time it passes between two points on a circuit.

propagation time: the time needed by an electrical signal to traverse through or along a medium between two points on a circuit.

proper subset: a subset that does not include all the elements of the set. (A) (B)

property detector: pertaining to a component of a character reader that has the normalized signal for the use in extracting a set of characteristic properties or characteristics on the basis of which a character can be identified as it comes along.

proportional band: the range of values of a condition being regulated that causes the controller to operate over its full range.

proportional spacing: the function whereby characters are spaced according to their natural width.

proprietary program: the development of a program, controlled by an owner through the legal right of possession and title.

proprietary software: the programming software, libraries, and other nonhardware operating aids in a computer system, not furnished by the manufacturer, but originated by the user or firms engaged in the development and sales of software systems.

protected field

(1) in word processing, preset data or an area that cannot be modified or overridden by the operator without altering the program. (D)

(2) on a display device, a display field in which the user cannot enter,

modify, or erase data. cf. *unprotected field*.

protected formatting: a strategy that allows a computer to write protected data on the screen. The operator fills in the blank (unprotected) areas but cannot alter the protected data, format, or programming.

protected free storage: see *free storage*.

protected location: a storage location whose contents are protected against accidental alteration, improper alteration, or unauthorized access. (E)

protected wireline distribution system: a communications system to which electromagnetic and physical safeguards have been applied to permit secure electrical transmission of unencrypted classified information, and which has been approved by the department or agency.

protection: an arrangement for restricting access to or use of all, or part of, a data-processing system. (E) synonymous with *lockout*. see *private protection*, *storage protection*.

protection channel: the broad-band channel of a carrier system that is utilized as a spare and can be switched into service in the event of a failure of a normal working broad-band channel. (F)

protection key: an indicator that appears in the current program status word whenever an associated task has control of the system; this indicator must match the storage keys of all main storage blocks that the task is to use. synonymous with *storage protection key*.

protection span: a section of a carrier transmission system, including repeated line and in some cases terminal equipment, within which a broad-band protection channel can be substituted for a working broad-band channel in the event of equipment or line failure in the working channel. (F)

protective connecting arrangement: synonymous with *access arrangement*.

protector frame: a frame, usually part of the main distributing frame, that serves as termination for loop cables and contains electrical protection devices that normally provide conducting paths but will break down and electrically isolate a loop from the switching equipment when an abnormally high voltage occurs as may result from lightning or contact between a power line and a telephone line. (F)

protocol

(1) a specification for the format and relative timing of information exchanged between communicating parties. (C)

(2) the set of rules governing the operation of functional units of a communication system that must be followed if communication is to be achieved. (E)

(3) synonymous with *line control discipline, line discipline*.

(4) see also *link protocol*.

protocol converter: a device for translating the data transmission code of one computer or peripheral to the data transmission code of another computer or peripheral, enabling equipment with different data formats to communicate with one another.

prototype statement: synonym for *macroprototype statement*.

proving: testing a machine to show

that it is free from faults, frequently following corrective maintenance.

proving time: time used for testing a system or unit to ensure that no faults exist or malfunctions are present.

provisioning: provisioning of service consists of the operations necessary to respond to service orders, trunk orders, and special-service circuit orders and to provide the resources necessary to fill these orders. It includes forecasting, planning, construction, and installation of facilities, preparing and responding to orders, and maintenance of facilities. (F)

PRR: see *pulse repetition rate*.

PRT: see *printer*.

PRTY: see *priority*.

PS

    (1) see *packet switching*.

    (2) see *picosecond*.

    (3) see *programming system*.

psec: see *picosecond*.

pseudoapplication program: an operational program that is written to test supervisory programs.

pseudoclock: a main storage location used by timer supervision routines to calculate timer intervals and time of day.

pseudocode: a code that requires translation prior to execution. (A)

pseudocursor: in computer graphics, a symbol that simulates the operation of a cursor on a display.

pseudofile address: using a false address by an application program to obtain a record from file. The pseudoaddress is converted by the supervisory program into an actual machine address.

pseudoinstruction: deprecated term for *declaration*. (A) (B)

pseudolanguage: an artificial language, uniquely designed to perform a distinct activity, that is, a special set of rules is devised with particular meanings assigned to chosen expressions.

pseudopaging: a way of viewing memory locations where programmers refer to memory address as being organized into blocks of words referred to as "pages" for reference purposes only.

pseudorandom number sequence: an ordered set of numbers that has been determined by some defined arithmetic process but is effectively a random number sequence for the purpose for which it is required. (A) (B)

pseudovariable: in PL/1, any of the built-in function names that can be used to specify a target variable.

PSK: see *phase-shift keying*.

PSN: see *public switched network*.

psophometer: an instrument arranged to give visual indication corresponding to the aural effect of disturbing voltages of various frequencies.

PSR: see *page send-receive*.

PSW: see *program status word*.

PT

    (1) see *paper tape*.

    (2) see *point*.

    (3) see *programmable terminal*.

PTR

    (1) see *paper tape reader*.

    (2) see *pointer*.

    (3) see *printer*.

PTS: see *public telephone service*.

PTT: see *Post Telephone and Telegraph Administration*.

p-type: a characteristic of a semiconductor where the hole density exceeds the density of electrons.

PU: see *processing unit*.

publication language: a representation of a reference language using symbols that are particularly suitable for printing. (E)

public coin telephone service: coin telephone service provided where a public need exists, such as at an airport lobby, at the option of the telephone company with the agreement of the owner of the premises or space. There is no directory listing. (F)

public data network (PDN): see *public network*.

public data transmission service: a data transmission established and operated by an administration and provided by means of a public data network. Circuit switched, packet switched and leased circuit data-transmission services are feasible. (C)

public message service (PMS): the public telegram system offered by Western Union.

public network: a network established and operated by communication common carriers or telecommunication administrations for the specific purpose of providing circuit-switched, packet-switched, and leased-circuit services to the public. cf. *user-application network*.

public switched network (PSN): any switching system that provides a circuit switched to many customers. In the United States, there are four: Telex, TWX, telephone, and Broadband Exchange.

public telephone network (PTN): the traffic network that provides public telephone service. (F)

public telephone service (PTS): ordi-nary telephone service in which a customer has a connection to a central office and can be connected to any other customer of the service. Sometimes called plain old telephone service (POTS). (F) see *basic service*.

public utility: a business organization performing some public service and subject to special government regulation. Telephone companies and electric power companies are public utilities. (F)

public utility commission: an agency charged with regulation communications services, as well as other public utility services, usually within a state. (F)

pull: removing an element from a stack. cf. *push*. synonymous with *pop*.

pull down: in micrographics, the length of film advanced after each exposure.

pull up resistor: a resistor capable of providing the source current for open collector logic gates or terminating unused high inputs.

pulp-insulated cable: cable whose conductors are individually insulated with paper pulp. (F)

pulse: a variation in the value of a quantity, short in relation to the time schedule of interest, the final value being the same as the initial value. synonymous with *impulse*. see *clock pulse, synchronization pulse*. (A)

pulse amplitude: maximum instantaneous value of a pulse.

pulse amplitude modulation (PAM): a modulation technique in which the amplitude of each pulse is related to the amplitude of an analog signal. Used, for example, in time-division multiplex arrangements in which successive pulses represent samples from the individual voice-band channels; also used in time-division switching systems of small and moderate size. (F)

pulse code: a code where digits are represented by means of sets of pulses.

pulse code modulation (PCM)

(1) a process in which a signal is sampled, and the magnitude of each sample with respect to a fixed reference is quantized and converted by coding to a digital signal. (C)

(2) transmission of information by modulation of a pulsed, or intermittent carrier. Pulse width, count, phase, or amplitude may be the varied characteristic.

pulse-double recording: a specific method for magnetic recording of bits in which each storage cell comprises two regions magnetized in opposite senses with unmagnetized regions on each side.

pulser: a circuit capable of delivering high-current short duration signals to a unit under test.

pulse rate: the time interval of periodic pulses that are integrated with the control of the computer or the total system.

pulse regeneration: the process of restoring a series of pulses to the original timing, form, and relative magnitude.

pulse repetition frequency (PRF): the rate at which pulses are repeated in a pulse train that is independent of the time interval over which it is measured.

pulse repetition rate (PRR): the number of pulses per unit time. (A)

pulse stretcher: a circuit that can ex-

tend the length of a pulse.

pulse string: synonym for *pulse train.* (A)

pulse train: a series of pulses having similar characteristics. synonymous with *pulse string.* (*A*)

PUN: see *punch.*

PUNC: see *punctuation.*

punch (P) (PUN) (PCH) (PNCH)

(1) a perforation, as in a punched card or paper tape. (A)

(2) a device for making holes in a data carrier. (E)

(3) a device that interprets coded electrical signals so as to produce the holes in cards or tapes. (D)

(4) see *automatic-feed punch, calculating punch, card punch, digit punch, eleven punch, gang punch, hand-feed punch, keyboard punch, keypunch, numeric punch, reproducing punch, spot punch, summary punch, twelve punch, zone punch.* (A)

punch card: a card into which hole patterns can be punched. see *Hollerith card.* (*A*)

punch column

(1) a line of punch positions parallel to the Y-datum line of a card.

(2) a line of punch positions along a card column. (*A*)

punched card

(1) a card punched with hole patterns. (A)

(2) in word processing, a card on which text and program instructions are represented by rows of punched holes. (D)

(3) see *Hollerith card.* (A)

punched card reader: synonym for *card reader.* (A)

punched paper tape (PPT): a strip of paper on which characters are represented by combinations of holes punched across the strip.

punched tape

(1) a tape punched with hole patterns. synonymous with *perforated tape*. (E)

(2) in word processing, a tape, usually of paper, on which text and program instructions are represented by rows of punched holes. (D)

punched tape code: a code used to represent data on punched tape. synonymous with *paper tape code*, *perforated tape code*. (E)

punched tape machine: any tape punch that automatically converts coded electrical signals into perforations in tape.

punched tape reader: a device that reads or senses the hole patterns in a punched tape, transforming the data from the hole patterns to electrical signals. synonymous with *perforated-tape reader*. (E)

punching: see *interstage punching, multiple punching*.

punching position: synonym for *punch position*. (A) (B)

punching station: the place in a card track where a punch card is punched. (A) synonymous with *punch station*.

punch path: in a punch, a path that has a punch station. (B)

punch position: a defined location on a data carrier where a hole may be punched to record data. synonymous with *code position*, *punching position*. (B)

punch row: a line of punch positions along a card row. (A)

punch station: synonym for *punching station*.

punch tape: a tape in which hole patterns can be punched. (B)

punch tape code: a code used to represent data on punch tape. (B)

punctuation (PUNC): on a calculator, the ability to divide displayed or printed numbers into groups of three digits to the left of the decimal marker.

punctuation character: in COBOL, a comma, semicolon, period, quotation mark, left or right parenthesis, or space.

punctuation symbol: synonym for *delimiter*. (A)

pure binary numeration system: the fixed-radix numeration system that uses the binary digits and the radix 2; for example, in this numeration system, the numeral 110.01 represents the number "six and one quarter," that is, $1 \times 2^2 + 1 \times 2^1 + 1 \times 2^{-2}$. synonymous with *binary numeration system*. (A) (B)

pure machine-aided translation: where the lexicons of two or more languages are computerized to supply a human translator with target language equivalents of source language lexical items.

pure machine translation: a machine translation system where the computer attempts the total translation itself. see *HAMT*.

purge data: a date written to a data medium on or following when the file is released and the data may be overwritten by more recent data.

push: adding an element to a stock. cf. *pull*. synonymous with *put*.

push button: (PB): see *virtual push button*.

push-button dialing: the use of keys or push buttons instead of a rotary dial to generate a sequence of digits to establish a circuit connection. The signal form is usually tones. synonymous with *key pulse, Touchtone (AT&T), Touch-Call (GT&E)*. cf. *rotary dial*.

push-button dialing pad: a twelve-key device used to originate tone keying signals. It usually is attached to rotary dial telephones for use in originating data signals.

pushbutton telephone: a telephone set or system in which each instrument has a series of buttons for selecting the line to be used, holding a line, or other functions. Does not refer to the technique used for dialing calls.

push-down: a last-in, first-out method of queuing where the last item attached to the queue is the first to be withdrawn.

push-down list: a list that is constructed and maintained so that the next item to be retrieved and removed is the most recently stored item still in the list, that is, last-in, first-out. (B) synonymous with *stack*. (A)

push-down queue: a last-in, first-out (LIFO) method of queuing in which the last item attached to the queue is the first to be withdrawn. see *LIFO*.

push-down stack: synonym for *push-down list*.

push-down storage: a storage device that handles data in such a way that the next item to be retrieved is the most recently stored item still in the storage device, that is, last-in, first-out (LIFO). synonymous with *push-down store*. (A) (B)

push-down store: synonym with *push-down storage*. (A) (B)

push-to-type: a teletypewriter operator in one direction at a time by using a switch depressed during transmission.

push-up list: a list that is constructed and maintained so that the next item to be retrieved is the earliest stored item still in the list, that is, first-in, first-out (FIFO). (A) (B)

push-up storage: a storage device that handles data in such a way that the next item to be retrieved is the earliest stored item still in the storage device, that is, first-in, first-out (FIFO). synonymous with *push-up store*. (A) (B)

push-up store: synonym for *push-up storage*. (A) (B)

put: to place a single data record into an output file.

put-away: a memory location in which the processor stores specific information.

PW: see *password*.

Q
- (1) see *query*.
- (2) see *queue*.
- (3) see *quotient*.
- (4) a register used as an accumulator extension, needed for efficient multiply-divide programming.

Q address: a source location in internal storage in some devices from which data is transferred.

QAM: see *quadrature amplitude modulation*.

QCB: see *queue control block*.

QEL: see *quality element*.

QISAM: see *queued indexed sequential access method*.

QR: see *quotient*.

QSAM: see *queued sequential access method*.

QT: see *quotient*.

QTAM: see *queued telecommunications access method*.

Q test: a test or comparison of two or more units of quantitative data for nonequality or equality.

quad: a structural unit employed in cable, consisting of four separately insulated conductors twisted together.

quad-bus transceiver: a component consisting of four separate receiver-transmitter combinations, developed for use with a bidirectional bus system such as a data bus.

quadded cable: a cable formed by taking four, or multiples of four, paired and separately insulated cables and twisting these together within an overall jacket.

quad density: the storage density of a disk medium; storing four times the amount of information per disk as single density.

quadratic programming: in operations research, a particular case of nonlinear programming in which the function to be maximized or minimized is a quadratic function and the constraints are linear functions. (B) cf. *convex programming, dynamic programming, integer programming, linear programming, mathematical* *programming, minimum delay programming, nonlinear programming.* (A)

quadrature: expresses the phase relationship between two periodic quantities of the same period when the phase difference between them is one fourth of a period.

quadrature amplitude modulation (QAM): a modulation system in which two independent signals are impressed on carriers of the same frequency that are 90 degrees out of phase with respect to another. QAM is attractive for high bandwidth utilization in data communication. (F)

quadripuntal: pertaining to four punches, specifically, having four random punches on a punched card; used in determinative documentation.

quadruple-length register: four registers that function as a single register. Each register may be individually accessed. synonymous with *quadruple register.* (A) (B)

quadruple register: synonym for *quadruple-length register.* (A) (B)

quadruplex system: a Morse telegraphy system structured for the simultaneous independent transmission of two messages in each direction over a single circuit.

qualification: in COBOL, the making a name unique by adding IN or OF and another name, according to defined rules and procedures.

qualified name

(1) a data name explicitly accompanied by a specification of the class to which it belongs in a specified classification system. (A) (B)

(2) in PL/1, a hierarchical sequence of names of structure members, connected by periods, used to identify a component of a structure. Any of the names may be subscripted. see also *locator qualificaton.*

qualifier

(1) all names in a qualified name other than the rightmost, which is called the simple name.

(2) in COBOL, a group data name that is used to refer to a nonunique data name at a lower level in the same hierarchy, or a section name at a lower level in the same hierarchy, or a section name that is used to refer to a nonunique paragraph. In this way, the data name or the paragraph name can be made unique.

quality control: where systematic and regular reviews of the timeliness, accuracy, completeness of data entry is accomplished.

quantization: the subdivision of the range of values of a variable into a finite number of nonoverlapping, and not necessarily equal subranges or intervals, each of which is represented by an assigned value within the subrange. For example, a person's age is quantized for most purposes with a quantum of one year. (A)

quantization error: synonym for *quantization uncertainty.*

quantization uncertainty: a measure of the uncertainty of the irretrievable information loss that occurs as a result of the quantization of a function in an interval where it is continuous.

quantize: to divide the range of a variable into a finite number of nonoverlapping intervals that are not necessarily equal, and to designate each interval by an assigned value within that interval. (A)

quantizer: a component of a digital communications system whose function is to assign one of a discrete set of values to the amplitude of each successive samples of a signal. The discrete set of values corresponds to a discrete set of contiguous non-overlapping intervals covering the dynamic amplitude range of the signal. (F)

quantizer noise: the error that results from ascribing a finite number of levels to a continuous signal. (F)

quantizing error: distortion created by analog to digital conversion. This error occurs when analog signals fall between the possible digital values.

quantum: a subrange in quantization. (A)

quantum clock: a device that allocates an interval or quantum of processing time to a program established by priorities used in computing systems that have time-sharing procedures.

quart delay line: an acoustic delay line where fused quartz is employed as the medium for delaying sound transmission.

quarternary operator: an operator that requires exactly four operands. (A) (B)

quarter speed: one-fourth the rated speed of the associated equipment; in transoceanic telegraph, one-fourth of full speed or 12.5 baud or 16+ wpm.

quarter-squares multiplier: an analog multiplier whose operation is based on the identity $xy = .25 [(x+y)^2 - (x-y)^2]$ incorporating inverters, analog adders, and square-law function generators. (B)

quartet: a byte composed of four bi-nary elements. synonymous with *four-bit byte.* (A)

quartz crystal: a thin slice cut from quartz and ground to a thickness so that it will vibrate at a required frequency when supplied by energy.

quasi instruction: synonymous with *pseudo instruction.*

query (Q)

(1) the process by which a master station asks a slave station to identify itself and to give its status. (E)

(2) in interactive systems, an operation at a terminal that elicits a response from the system.

query language: a class of English-like language that permits non-programmers to inquire about the contents of a data base and receive fast responses. synonymous with *search language.*

query station: a unit of equipment that introduces requests or queries for data, states of processing, information, and so forth, while the machine is computing or processing or communicating.

queue (Q)

(1) a line or list formed by items in a system waiting for service; for example, tasks to be performed or messages to be transmitted in a message routing system.

(2) to arrange in, or form, a queue.

(3) see *doubled-ended queue.* (A)

queue control block (QCB): a control block that is used to regulate the sequential use of a programmer-defined facility among requesting tasks.

queued access method: any access method that synchronizes the transfer of data between the computer program using the access method and input-output devices, thereby minimizing delays for input-output operations. (A)

queue data set: a data set on a direct-access device used to contain one or more queues.

queued driven task: a task whose unit of work is represented by an element in a queue.

queued indexed sequential access method (QISAM):   an extended version of the sequential form of the basic indexed sequential access method (BISAM). When this method is used, a queue if formed of input data blocks that are awaiting processing or output data blocks that have been processed and are awaiting transfer to auxiliary storage or to an output device.

queued sequential access method (QSAM):   an extended version of the basic sequential access method (BSAM). When this method is used, a queue is formed of input data blocks that are awaiting processing or output data blocks that have been processed and are awaiting transfer to auxiliary storage or to an output device.

queued telecommunications access method (QTAM):   a method used to transfer data between main storage and remote terminals. Application programs use GET and PUT macroinstructions to request the transfer of data, which is performed by a message control program. The message control program synchronizes the transfer, thus eliminating delays for input-output operations.

queue element (QEL)
   (1)   a block of data in a queue.
   (2)   one item in a queue.

queue link word: see *chaining*.

queue management: the network control program supervisor code controlling the manipulation of block control units and queue control blocks; it manages input, pseudoinput, and work queues.

queuing: the programming technique used to handle messages that are awaiting transmission.

queuing analysis: the study of the nature and time concerning the discrete units needed to pass through channels.

queuing list: a list used for scheduling actions in real time on a time—priority basis.

queuing theory: a probability theory useful in examining delays or lineups at servicing points.

queuing time: time spent waiting to send or receive a message because of contention on the line.

quibinary code: a binary-coded decimal code for representing decimal numbers where each decimal digit is represented by seven binary digits that are coefficients of 8, 6, 4, 2, 0, 1, 0, respectively.

quick-access memory: a portion of memory having short access time, as compared to the main memory of the central processing unit.

quick cell facility: a high performance storage allocation technique using a fixed-block size.

quick disconnect: a type of connector that permits quick locking and unlocking of the two connector halves.

quick start: synonym for *system restart (2)*.

quiesce: to reject new jobs in a multiprogramming system, while at the same time continuing to process jobs already entered.

quiescent: at rest; the condition of a circuit when no input signal is being applied or of a system waiting to be operated.

quiescing: the process of bringing a device or a system to a halt by rejection of new requests for work. (A)

QUIKTRAN: a subset of FORTRAN including built-in functions augmented by versatile operating statements for complete control maintenance.

quinary: see *biquinary code.* (A)

quintet: a byte composed of five binary elements. synonymous with *five-bit byte.* (A) (B)

quoted string: in assembler programming, a character string enclosed by apostrophes that is used in a macro-instruction operand to represent a value that can include blanks. The enclosed apostrophes are part of the value represented. cf. *character expression.*

quotient (Q) (QR) (QT): the number or quantity that is the value of the dividend divided by the value of the divisor and that is one of the results of a division operation. (B) cf. *remainder.* (A)

qwerty: a typical typewriter keyboard that begins with these six letters, left-to-right, in the top row below the numerals.

R

(1) see *read*.

(2) see *reader*.

(3) see *receiver*.

(4) see *record*.

(5) see *register*.

(6) see *relation*.

(7) see *request*.

(8) see *reset*.

(9) see *resistor*.

(10) see *ring*.

RA: see *return address*.

RACE: random access computer equipment.

RACF: see *resource access control facility*.

rack: a frame or chassis on which a microprocessor is mounted.

rack mountable: units packaged for installation in a metal cabinet called a rack.

radar: radio detection and ranging equipment that determines the distance and usually the direction of objects by transmission and return of electromagnetic energy.

radial transfer: the process of transmitting data between a peripheral unit and a unit of equipment that is more central than the peripheral unit. (B) synonymous with *input-output, input process (2), output process*. (A)

radiation hardening: a quality assurance process in the production of integrated circuits to choose circuits that are better able to withstand radiation.

radio: communication by electrical waves in space.

radio baseband receive terminals: the point in the baseband circuit nearest the radio receiver from which connection is normally made to the multiplex baseband receiver terminals or intermediate facility.

radio baseband send terminals: the point in the baseband circuit nearest the radio transmitter from which connection is normally made to the multiplex baseband send terminal or intermediate facility.

radio common carrier (RCC): a common carrier in the domestic public land mobile radio service licensed by the FCC to receive and transmit go signals from mobile transmitters (e.g., land mobile, air-to-ground, marine, coastal harbor) within a specified geographic area. (G)

radio frequency (RF): an electronic signal above the audio and below the infra-red frequencies.

radio relay system: a point-to-point radio transmission system in which the signals are received, amplified, and retransmitted by one or more intermediate radio stations.

radio teletypewriter (RTTY): the system of communication by teletypewriters over radio circuits. see also *teletypewriter.*

radix: in a radix numeration system, the positive integer by which the weight of the digit place is multiplied to obtain the weight of the digit place with the next higher weight; for example, in the decimal numeration system that radix of each digit place is 10, in a biquinary code the radix of each fives position is 2. (B) deprecated term for *base.* see *floating-point radix, mixed radix notation. (A)*

radix complement (RC): a complement obtained by subtracting each digit of the given number from the number that is one less than the radix of that digit place, then adding one to the least significant digit of the result and executing any carries required; for example, 830 is the tens complement, that is, the radix complement of 170 in the decimal numeration system using three digits. synonymous with *noughts complement, true complement.* (B) see *diminished radix complement. (A)*

radix-minus-one complement: synonym for *diminished radix complement.* (A) (B)

radix mixed: a numeration system that uses more than one radix, such as the bioprimary system.

radix notation: synonym for *radix numeration system.* (A) (B)

radix numeration system: a positional representation system in which the ratio of the weight of any one digit place to the weight of the digit place with the next lower weight is a positive integer. The permissible values of the character in any digit place range from zero to one less than the radix of that digit place. synonymous with *radix notation.* (A) (B)

radix point: in a representation of a number expressed in a radix numeration system, the location of the separation of the characters associated with the integral part from those associated with the fractional part. (A) (B)

rain barrel effect: sound on an overcompensated (equalized) line.

RAM (Random Access Memory): the most common computer memory, the contents of which can be altered at any time. see *64K RAM.*

RAM dump: copying the contents of all or a portion of a storage, usually from an internal storage such as a RAM, into an external storage such as a printout.

RAM loader: a program that reads a program from an input unit, and usually in a type of random-access memory.

RAM mail box: a set of locations in a common RAM storage area, reserved for data addressed to specific peripheral units as well as other microprocessors in the immediate environment.

RAM print-on-alarm: data system condition where continuous scanning of data channels occurs, but output of data is imitated only when an alarm condition as interpreted by the CPU in a RAM is encountered.

RAM refresh: dynamic random-access memory units need an occasional refresh operation to guarantee that data is retained, since bits are represented by a capacitive charge.

random access

(1) a method of providing or achieving access where the time to retrieve data is constant and independent of the location of the item addressed earlier.

(2) in COBOL, an access mode in which specific logical records are obtained from or placed into a mass storage file in a nonsequential manner. (A)

(3) deprecated term for *direct access.*

random-access input-output: an input-output control capability that allows efficient random processing of records stored on a direct-access drive. An efficiency is achieved by issuing seeks in an order that minimizes the average seek time, and seeks are overlapped with other processing.

random-access I/O routines: direct, serial, and random processing of drum and disk files provided by these routines.

random-access memory: see *RAM.*

random-access programming: programming without concern for the time needed for access to the storage positions called for in the program.

random-access software: an array of programming and operating aids that includes a loader/monitor, a program for updating program files, a special sort, input-output routines, and utility routines.

random-access sorts: separate program furnished by manufacturers to sort data stored on random-access disks and drums.

random-access storage: deprecated term for *direct-access storage.*

random-access system: a method of filing data in a manner which approximates equal time to the processing of data, that is, usually that type of core storage or auxiliary storage which is ultrafast.

random-data set: see *direct data set.*

randomizing: a technique by which the range of keys for an indirectly addressed file is reduced to smaller ranges of addresses by some method of computation until the desired address is found.

random noise: noise caused by the aggregate of a large number of elementary disturbances with random occurrence in time.

random number

(1) a number selected from a known set of numbers in such a way that the probability of occurrence of each number in the set is predetermined. (B)

(2) a number obtained by chance.

(3) one of a sequence of numbers considered appropriate for satisfying certain statistical tests.

(4) one of a sequence of numbers believed to be free from conditions that might bias the result of a calculation.

(5) see *pseudorandom number sequence.* (A)

random number generator: a special

machine routine or hardware unit designed to yield a random number or a series of such numbers according to specified limitations.

random number sequence: an ordered set of numbers, each of which may not be predicted only from a knowledge of its predecessors. (B) see *pseudorandom number sequence*. (*A*)

random processing: the treatment of data without respect to its location in external storage, and in an arbitrary sequence governed by the input against which it is to be processed.

random scan: deprecated term for *directed-beam scan.*

random sequence: a sequence not arranged by ascending or descending keys, but instead in an organized fashion in bulk storage, by locations.

random variable: the result of a random experiment.

random-walk method: in operations research, a variance-reducing method of problem analysis in which experimentation with probabilistic variables is traced to determine results of a significant nature. (A)

range
(1) the set of values that a quantity or function may take. (B)
(2) the difference between the highest and lowest value that a quantity or function may assume.
(3) deprecated term for *span*. (B)
(4) see *error range*. (*A*)

range (of a default specification): in PL/1, a set of identifiers, constants, or parameter descriptors to which the attributes in a default specification of a DEFAULT statement apply.

range (of a DO loop): the statements that physically follow a DO statement,

up to and including the statement specified by the DO statement as being the last to be executed in the DO loop.

range check: a limit 1 check in which both high and low values are used. (E)

range extender: a device that permits a central office to serve a line whose resistance exceeds the normal limit for signaling. A range extender does not extend transmission range. Range extenders are also used in special-service circuits. (F)

range extender with gain (REG): a unit that provides range extension in a loop for both signaling and transmission. (F)

range finder: an adjustable mechanism on a teletypewriter receiver that allows the receiver-distributor face to be moved through an arc corresponding to the length of a unit segment. It is adjusted normally for best results under operating line conditions. see also *orientation, receiving margin.*

range (of a DO statement): in FOR-TRAN, those statements which physically follow a DO statement, up to and including the statement specified by the DO statement as being the last to be executed in the DO loop.

rank: synonym for *level number*. (A) (B)

rapid access: see *random access storage.*

rapid access loop: in drum computers, a small section of memory which has much faster access than the remainder of memory. synonymous with *recirculating loop, revolver.*

rapid access memory: in computers

with memories with different access times, the section that has faster access than the remainder of the memory.

RAS: reliability, availability, serviceability.

raster: in computer graphics, a predetermined pattern of lines that provides uniform coverage of a display space. (E)

raster count: in computer graphics, the number 1 of lines in one dimension within a display space. (E)

raster display device: in computer graphics, a display device in which display images are generated on a display space by raster graphics. (E)

raster graphics: computer graphics in which display images, composed of an array of picture elements arranged in rows and columns, are generated on a display space. (E)

raster grid: on a display device, the grid of addressable coordinates on the display surface.

raster plotter: in computer graphics, a plotter capable of drawing a complete picture on a cathode ray tube, including an image both of the object studied and its background.

raster scan: in computer graphics, a technique of generating or recording a display image by a line-by-line sweep across the entire display space; for example, the generation of a picture on a television screen. A raster scan may be directed by a program in which case it may also be considered as a directed-beam scan. (E)

raster unit: in computer graphics, the distance between adjacent picture elements. (E)

rate: see *average information rate, av-erage transinformation rate, data signaling rate, pulse repetition rate.* (A)

rate and route operator: an operator who provides information to the toll operator, such as special operator routing codes, rate information, and lists of numbers that are coin lines. (F)

rate center: a specified geographic location used by telephone companies to determine mileage measurements for the application of interexchange mileage rates.

rated speed: synonym for *nominal speed.*

rate pulse: the time interval of periodic pulses that are integrated with the control of the computer or the entire system.

ratio: see *error ratio, print contrast ratio, read-around ratio.* (A)

ratio control: a specific limitation in the relation between two quantities as expressed in direct or percentage comparison.

rational number: a real number that is the quotient of an integer divided by an integer other than zero. (A) (B)

raw data: data that has not been processed or reduced.

RC: see *radix complement.*

RCD: see *record.*

RCF: see *remote call forwarding.*

RCR: see *required carrier return character.*

RD: see *read.*

RDB: see *relational data base.*

RDR: see *reader.*

reactive mode: a means of communicating between a central processor and a terminal where each entry leads to an action but does not necessarily yield an immediate (interactive) response to the terminal.

read (R) (RD): to acquire or interpret data from a storage device, from a data medium, or from another source. (B) see *destructive read, nondestructive read.* (*A*)

read after write verify: a function for determining that information currently being written is accurate as compared to the information source.

read amplifier: a set of circuitry that raises the level of current received from the read head or various other sensing devices.

read-around ratio: the number of times a specific spot, digit, or location in electrostatic storage may be consulted before spillover of electrons causes a loss of data stored in surrounding spots. The surrounding data must be restored before the deterioration results in any loss of data. (A)

read back and printout: retrieving from computer storage or registering that which was read into a data-processing machine and to present this data on a printed page.

read-back check: a check for accuracy of transmission in which the information transmitted to an output unit is returned to the information source and compared with the original information, to ensure correctness of output.

read cycle time: the minimum time interval between the start of successive read cycles of a device that has separate reading and writing cycles. (A) (B)

reader (R) (RDR)
(1) in micrographics, a device that enlarges microimages for viewing. (A)
(2) in word processing, a device that accesses the coded information on recording media for further processing. (D)
(3) a device that converts information in one form of storage to information in another form of storage.
(4) a part of the scheduler that reads an input stream into the system.
(5) see *card reader, character reader, microform reader, perforated-tape reader.* (A)

reader-copier: see *microform reader-copier.*

reader-interpreter: a part of job management that reads and interprets a series of job definitions from an input stream.

reader-printer (RP): in micrographics, a device that performs the functions of a reader and a printer to produce hard copy enlargements of selected microimages. (A)

reader-sorter: a unit of punch card equipment that senses and transmits input while sorting documents.

read head: a magnetic head capable of reading only. (B)

reading: the acquisition or interpretation of data from a storage device, from a data medium, or from another source. (A) (B)

reading access time: the elapsed time before data is read or used in the computer during the equipment read cycle.

reading head: synonymous with *read head.*

reading station: synonym for *read station.* (A) (B)

read-only: a type of access to data that allows it to be read but not copied, printed, or modified. synonymous with *fixed.*

read-only memory (ROM): deprecated term for *read-only storage*. synonym for *fixed storage*. (B)

read-only storage (ROS): a storage device whose contents cannot be modified, except by a particular user, or when operating under particular conditions; for example, a storage device in which writing is prevented by a lockout. (E) synonymous with *fixed storage, permanent storage*. (B)

readout: display of processed information on a terminal screen. cf. *printout*.

readout device: synonym for *character display device*. (A) (B)

read path: in a reader, a path that has a read station. (E)

read-process-write: the process of reading in one block of data, while simultaneously processing the preceding block and writing out the results of the previously processed block.

read protection: restriction of reading of the contents of a data set, file, or storage area by a user or program not authorized to do so.

read rate: the number of units of data; for example, words and blocks capable of being read by an input unit within a given time span.

read release: a feature of some units that allows more computer processing time by releasing the read mechanism.

read reverse: where the device can read tape under program control in either direction.

read scatter: the ability of a computer to distribute or scatter data into several memory areas as it is being entered into the system on magnetic tape.

read screen: a transparent screen through which documents are read in optical character recognition.

read station: the location in a reader where the data on a data carrier are read. (E) synonymous with *reading station, sensing station*. (B)

read time: the interval between the beginning of transcription from a storage unit and the completion of transcription.

read while writing: the reading of a record or set of records into storage from a tape at the same time another record or group of records is written from storage onto tape.

read/write: the nature of an operation, such as the direction of data flow.

read/write channel: a channel separating a peripheral unit and the central processor.

read/write check indicator: a unit that shows upon interrogation whether or not an error was made in reading or writing.

read/write cycle: the sequence of operations needed to read and write; for example, restore memory data.

read/write head: a magnetic head capable of reading and writing. synonym for *magnetic head*. (B)

read/write memory: information in a storage that can be changed at will and read as frequently as needed. cf. *read-only memory*.

read/write storage: see *read/write memory*.

ready-access terminal: a class of unsealed terminals that are used to make connections of customer drop wires to wire pairs in a distribution cable. (F)

ready condition: the condition of a task that is in contention for the processing unit.

ready light: an indicator light on a display panel which when on, shows the machine is ready for operation.

ready state: a state in which a task is ready to be activated and is contending for processor execution time.

ready status word: a status word indicating that the remote computing system is waiting for entry from the terminal.

real address: the address of an actual storage location in real storage. (A) (B)

real constant: a string of decimal digits which must have either a decimal point or a decimal exponent, and may have both.

realm: a logical subdivision of a data base that contains all occurrences of stipulated data aggregates. (E)

real number: a number that may be represented by a finite or infinite numeral in a fixed-radix numeration system. (A) (B)

real storage (RS): the main storage in a virtual storage system. Physically, real storage and main storage are identical. Conceptually, however, real storage represents only part of the range of addresses available to the user of a virtual storage system. Traditionally, the total range of addresses available to the user was that provided by main storage. (B)

real storage management (RSM): routines that control the allocation of pages in real storage.

real time (RT)

(1) pertaining to the processing of data by a computer in connection with another process outside the computer according to time requirements imposed by the outside printing in conversational mode and processes that can be influenced by human intervention while they are in progress. (B)

(2) pertaining to an application in which response to input is fast enough to affect subsequent input, such as a process control system or a computer-assisted instruction system.

real-time channel: units of equipment that offer interface between the end of communication and the computer memory.

real-time clock: develops readable digits or periodic signals for the computer to permit computation of elapsed time between events, and to initiate the performance of time-initiated processing.

real-time clock module: units that provide 13 or more programmable time bases from 1 microsecond to 1 hour.

real-time control: the control of a process by real-time processing. (A) (B)

real-time input: input data received into a data-processing system within time limits that are determined by the requirements of some other system or at instants that are so determined. (A) (B)

real-time on-line operation: the processing of data in synchronism with a physical process, in such a way that results of the data processing are useful to the physical operation.

real-time operation: synonym for *real-time processing (1)*. (A) (B)

real-time output: output data delivered from a data-processing system within time limits that are determined by the requirements of some other system or at instants that are so determined. (A) (B)

real-time processing
(1) a mode of operation of a data-processing system when performing real-time jobs. synonymous with *real-time operation*. (B)
(2) the manipulation of data that are required or generated by some process while the process is in operation; usually the results are used to influence the process, and perhaps related processes, while it is occurring. *(A)* (B)

real-time satellite computer: a computer that relieves the larger computer of time consuming input and output functions in addition to performing pre- and postprocessing activities such as validity editing and formatting for print.

real-time simulation: the operation of a simulator such that the time-scale factor is equal to corresponding computer time of the simulator. (A)

real-time system (RTS): a system that processes data in a rapid fashion so that the results are available in time to influence the process being monitored or controlled.

real-time working: deprecated term for *real-time processing*. (A) (B)

reasonableness check: a check to determine whether the values of certain variables conform to specified criteria. (E)

reasonableness test: a test that the value of a variable falls within a bracket defined as reasonable; used to locate and filter noisy inputs or erroneous outputs.

REC: see *record.*

recall ratio: in information-retrieval systems, the ratio of the number of pertinent documents retrieved by a single query to the total number of pertinent documents in the total collection, determined by the query criteria.

recall signal: originated by the user, a signal used to control the data network in some way other than disconnect.

receive interruption: the interruption of a transmission to a terminal by a higher priority transmission from the terminal. synonymous with *break.*

receive leg: the side of a duplex line that is receiving. cf. *transmit leg.*

receive only (RO): a teleprinter with a printer to create hardcopy output but which has no transmit capability.

receive-only typing reperforator: a teletypewriter receiver that produces perforated tape with characters along the edge of the tape. synonymous with *rotor.*

receiver (R): a unit able to receive incoming electrically transmitted signals.

receiver isolation: the attenuation between two receivers.

receiver signal: units controlled by signaling currents transmitted over the line and used to send out new signals.

receiving-end cross fire: the cross fire in a telegraph channel introduced from one or more adjacent channels at the terminal end remote from the transmitter.

receiving margin: in telegraph applications, the usable range over which the range finder may be adjusted. The normal range for a properly adjusted machine is approximately 75 points on a 120-point scale. synonymous with *operating range.* see also *range finder.*

receiving perforator: a punch that

converts coded electrical pulse patterns into hole patterns or cuts in perforated tape. synonymous with *tape punch. (A)*

reception congestion: a network congestion condition ocurring at a data switching exchange (DSE). (E)

RECFM: see *record format.*

recirculating loop: see *rapid access loop.*

RECNUM: see *record number.*

recogntion: see *character recognition, magnetic ink character recognition, optical character recognition, pattern recognition.* (A)

recognition device: a unit used for interpreting the electrical signals received when scanning a document so as to capture text in machine-readable form.

recognition logic: software in an optical character recognition reader permitting it to translate printed text into digital form.

recompile: to compile a program again, often following a debugging process or when the program needs to be run on a different computer.

recomplementation: an internal procedure that performs nines or tens complementation, as needed on the result of an arithmetic operation.

reconciliation procedure: a control procedure that identifies and accounts for any difference between the values of a given balance and its associated control total. (E)

reconfiguration
(1) a change made to a given configuration of a computer system; for example, isolating and bypassing a defective functional unit, connecting two functional units by an alternative path. Reconfiguration is effected automatically or manually and can be used to maintain system integrity. (E)
(2) the process of placing a processing unit, main storage, and channels off line for maintenance, and adding or removing components.

reconfigure: to alter the components of a computer system and the interconnection of the components.

reconstitute: restoring a file to the condition that existed at an earlier processing period.

reconstitution: synonym for *reconstruction.*

reconstruction: the restoration of data to a previously known or defined state. synonymous with *reconstitution. (E)*

record (R) (RCD) (REC): a collection of related data or words, treated as a unit; for example, in stock control each invoice could constitute one record. (B) see *logical record, variable-length record. (A)* see also *records.*

record blocking: grouping of records by blocks that can be read and/or written to magnetic tape in a single operation, thereby increasing the efficiency with which the tape is used.

record check time: elapsed time needed to verify a record transfer on tape.

record control schedule: a schedule showing all functions involved regarding disposition of business records, that is, transfers, retention, and so forth.

record count: the number of records within a file, for purposes of control.

record description: in COBOL, the total set of data description entries associated with a particular logical record.

recorded text: in word processing, text, including program instructions, that has been recorded on a recording medium or in storage. (D)

recorded voice announcement (RVA) unit: a device capable of continuous playback.

recorder on demand: see *ROD.*

record format: the contents and layout of a record. *(RECFM)*

record format descriptor
(1) a file in a store controller that can be used to describe the record format descriptors are used by the data maintenance/inquiry function to process records in the keyed files.
(2) a record within this file.

record gap: deprecated term for *interblock gap.* (A) (B)

record group: several records, when placed together identify with a single key located in one of the records.

record head: synonymous with *write head.*

recording: see *double pulse recording, electron-beam recording, magnetic recording, non-return-to-reference recording, non-return-to-zero change-on-ones recording, non-return-to-zero (change) recording, non-return-to-zero recording, polarized return-to-zero recording, return-to-reference recording.* (A)

recording area: synonym for *film frame.* (A) (B)

recording density: the number of bits in a single linear track measured per unit of length of the recording medium. (A)

recording head: a head for transferring data to a storage unit, such as a drum, disk, tape, or magnetic card.

recording medium: in word processing, a material on which program instructions and text are recorded. (D)

recording mode: in the COBOL system, the representation in external media of data associated with a data-processing system.

recording trunk: a trunk from a local telephone central office or private branch exchange to a long distance office, used only from communication between operators.

record key: in word processing, a control key that places the equipment in record mode; that is, ready to receive text and program instructions on the recording medium or into storage. (D)

record layout: the arrangement and structure of data or words in a record, including the order and size of the components of the record. (A) (B)

record length (RL): the number of words or characters forming a record. (A) (B)

record mark: a special character to limit the number of characters in a data transfer, or to separate blocked or grouped records in tape.

record medium: in facsimile transmission, the physical medium on which the recorder forms an image of the subject copy. see also *record sheet.*

record name: in COBOL, a data name that identifies a logical record.

record number (RECNUM): see *relative-record number, transaction record number.* see also *panel number.*

record ready: a signal from a file-access unit to the computer that a record whose address was earlier given by a seek command has now been found and may be read into memory.

records: any unit of information that is to be transferred between the main memory and a peripheral unit; can be of any length. see *record*.

record separator character (RS): the information separator intended to identify a logical boundary between records. (A) (B)

record sheet: in facsimile transmission, the medium which is used to produce a visible image of the subject copy in record form. The record medium and the record sheet may be identical. see also *record medium*.

record sorting: the basic element of a file such that the sorting of file constitutes the reordering of file records. synonymous with *item*.

record storage mark: a character appearing only in the record storage unit of the card reader to limit the length of the record read into processor storage.

record type: a data structure defined to contain the information describing the entities being racked by a data base, and their associated attributes.

RECOV: see *recovery*.

recoverable ABEND: an error condition in which control is passed to a specified routine that allows continued execution of the program. cf. *unrecoverable ABEND*. see also *STAE, STAI*.

recoverable error: an error condition that allows continued execution of a program.

recovery (RECOV): a process in which a specified data station resolves conflicting or erroneous conditions arising during the transfer of data. (E) see *backward file recovery, error recovery, forward file recovery, in-line recovery*.

recovery from fallback: restoration of a system to complete operation from a fallback mode of operation following the removal of the cause for the fallback.

recovery management support (RMS): the facilities that gather information about hardware reliability and allow retry of operations that fail because of processing unit, I/O device, or channel errors. see also *machine check handler*.

recovery procedure: a process whereby a specified data station attempts to resolve conflicting or erroneous conditions arising during the transfer of data. (E)

recovery routine: a routine that is entered when an error occurs during the performance of an associated operation. It isolates the error, assesses the extent of the error, indicates subsequent action, and attempts to correct the error and resume operation.

recovery system: a computer program which records the progress of processing activities, allowing reconstruction of a run in the event of a computer crash. see *program crash*.

recovery termination manager: a program that handles all normal and abnormal termination of tasks by passing control to a recovery routine associated with the terminated function.

rectifier: a device that can convert an alternating current into a direct current.

recursion: in PL/1, the reactivation of an active procedure.

recursive: pertaining to a process in which each step makes use of the results of earlier steps.

recursive function: a function whose values are natural numbers that are derived from natural numbers by substitution formulae in which the function is an operand. (A) (B)

recursively defined sequence: a series of terms in which each term after the first is determined by an operation in which the operands are some or all of the preceding terms. (A) (B)

recursive process: a method of computing values of functions where each stage of processing contains all subsequent signs, that is the first stage is not completed until all other stages are ended.

recursive routine: a routine that may be used as a routine of itself, calling itself directly or being called by another routine, one that itself has called. The use of a recursive routine or computer program usually requires the keeping of records of the status of its unfinished uses in, for example, a push-down list. (A) (B)

recursive subroutine: a subroutine that may be used as subroutine of itself, calling itself directly or being called by another subroutine, one that it itself has called. The use of a recursive subroutine or computer program usually requires the keeping of records of the status of its unfinished uses in, for example, a push-down list. (A) (B)

RED: see *reduction.*

redact: to edit or revise input data.

redaction: a new or recently revised edition of input data.

redefine: in COBOL, to reuse the same storage area for different data items during program execution by employing proper instructions in the data program.

red tape: see *housekeeping.*

REDUCE: a programming language based on ALGOL and designed for nonnumeric manipulation of mathematical expressions. (E)

reduction (RED): in micrographics, a measure of the number of times the linear dimensions of an object are reduced when photographed. The reduction is generally expressed as 1:16, 1:24. cf. *reenlargement.* see *data reduction.*

redundancy

(1) in information theory, the amount R by which the decision content H_0 exceeds the entropy H; in mathematical notation: $R = H_0 - H$. Usually, messages can be represented with fewer characters by using suitable codes; the redundancy may be considered as a measure of the decrease of length of the messages thus achieved. (A)

(2) in the transmission of information, that fraction of the gross information content of a message that can be eliminated without loss of essential information. (B)

(3) see *relative redundancy.* (A)

redundancy check: a check that depends on extra characters attached to data for the detection of errors. see *cyclic redundancy check.* (E)

redundancy check bit: a check bit that is derived from a character and appended to the character. (A)

redundancy check character: a check character that is derived from a record and appended to the record. see *cyclic redundancy check character, longitudinal redundancy check character.* (A)

redundant character: see *check character.*

redundant code: a code having more signal elements than are needed to represent the intrinsic-processing information.

reel: a cylinder with flanges on which tape or film may be wound. (A) (B)

reenlargement: in micrographics, a legible enlargement of a microimage. synonymous with *blow back*.

reenterable: synonym for *reentrant*.

reenterable load module: a load module that can be repeatedly used by two or more jobs or tasks.

reenterable program: synonym for *reentrant program*. (A) (B)

reenterable routine: synonym for *reentrant routine*. (A) (B)

reenterable subroutine: synonym for *reentrant subroutine*. (A) (B)

reentrant: the attribute of a program or routine that allows the same copy of the program or routine to be used concurrently by two or more tasks.

reentrant code: a set of instructions that form a single copy of a program that is shared by two or more programs. These routines have instructions and constants that are not subject to modification during execution.

reentrant program: a computer program that may be entered repeatedly and may be entered before prior executions of the same computer program have been completed, subject to the requirement that neither its external program parameters nor any instructions are modified during its execution. A reentrant program may be used by more than one computer program simultaneously. synonymous with *reenterable program*. (*A*) (B)

reentrant routine: a routine that may be entered repeatedly and may be entered before prior executions of the same routine have been completed, subject to the requirement that neither its external program parameters nor any instructions are modified during its execution. A reentrant routine may be used by more than one computer program simultaneously. synonymous with *reenterable routine*. (A) (B)

reentrant subroutine: a subroutine that may be entered repeatedly and may be entered before prior executions of the same subroutine have been completed, subject to the requirement that neither its external program parameters nor any instructions are modified during its execution. A reentrant subroutine may be used by more than one computer program simultaneously. synonymous with *reenterable subroutine*. (*A*) (B)

reentry point: the address or the label of the instruction at which the computer program that called a subroutine is reentered from the subroutine. (A) (B)

reentry system: a character recognition concept for a system where the input data to be read are printed by the computer with which the reader is associated.

REF: see *reference*.

reference (REF): in PL/1, the appearance of a name, except in a context that causes explicit declaration.

reference address: synonymous with *base address*.

reference clock: a clock of high stability and accuracy used to govern the frequency of a network of mutually synchronized clocks of lower stability.

reference edge: that edge of a data carrier used to establish specification or measurements in or on the data carrier. synonymous with *guide edge*. (E) see *document reference edge*.

reference input signal: a signal external to a control loop serving as the standard of comparison for the directly controlled variable.

reference instruction: an instruction that permits reference to systematically arranged or stored data.

reference language: the set of characters and formation rules used to define a programming language. (B)

reference level: see *relative transmission level*.

reference list: the printout produced by a compiler to show instructions as they appear at the end of a run, indicating their locations.

reference noise: the magnitude of circuit noise that will produce a circuit noise meter reading equal to that produced by 10 micromicrowatts of electric power at 1000 cycles per second.

reference record: a computer output that lists the operations and their positions in the last routine.

reference time: an instant near the beginning of a switching routine, selected as an origin for time measurements. The moment when the drive pulse reaches a specific fraction of its instantaneous value.

reference volume: that magnitude of complex electric wave, such as that corresponding to speech or music, that gives a reading of zero VU on a standard volume indicator. The sensitivity of the volume indicator is adjusted so that reference volume or zero VU is read when the instrument is connected across a 600-ohm resistance to which there is delivered a power of 1 milliwtt at 1000 cycles per second. see also *voice unit*.

REFER expression: in PL/1, the expression preceding the keyword REFER, from which an original bound, length, or size is taken when a based variable containing a REFER option is allocated, either by an ALLOCATE or LOCATE statement.

REFER object: in PL1, the unsubscripted element variable appearing in a REFER option that specifies a current bound, length, or size for a member of a based structure. It must be a member of the structure, and it must precede the member declared with the REFER option.

refile: the procedure of transmitting a message from a station on a leased-line network to a station not serviced by the leased-line network. This is usually accomplished by sending the message to preselected Western Union offices for retransmission as a telegram to the addressee.

reflectance: in OCR, the diffuse reflectivity of ink-free areas of the substrate on which printing exists.

reflectance ratio: the reciprocol of the ratio of the intensity of the light reflected from the image area of a picture to the intensity of light reflected from the background or light area.

reflected binary code: synonym for *gray code*. (A)

reflective scan: a scan technique where the light source is aimed at a reflecting surface to illuminate the photosensor.

reflector: an inch-long piece of aluminum glued on the tape signalling the tape drive to begin a valid tape.

reformat: to alter the representation of data from one format to another.

refresh (RFRSH) (RFSH): in computer graphics, the process of repeatedly producing a display image on a display space so that the image remains visible. (E)

refreshable: the attribute of a load module that prevents it from being modified by itself or by another module during execution. A refreshable load module can be replaced by a new copy during execution by a recovery manageament routine without changing either the sequence or results of processing.

refresh circuitry: electronic circuitry which reads and rewrites the contents of dynamic memory to prevent loss of data.

refresh rate

(1) in computer graphics, the rate per unit time at which a display image is refreshed. (E)

(2) in word processing, the rate at which a display image is renewed in order to appear stable. (D)

REG

(1) see *range extender with gain.*

(2) see *register.*

regen: synonym for *regenerative repeater.*

regenerate: synonymous with *refresh.*

regeneration

(1) in computer graphics, the sequence of events needed to generate a display image. (E)

(2) the process of recognizing and reconstructing a digital signal so that the amplitude, wave form and timing are constrained with stated limits. (C)

(3) the restoration of stored information.

(4) see *signal regeneration.* (A)

regenerative feedback: an approach that returns part of the output of a unit, system, or process to the input in a way that causes a greater feedback.

regenerative memory: a memory unit whose contents gradually disappear if not periodically refreshed.

regenerative reading: a read operation involving the automatic writing of data back into the positions from which it is extracted.

regenerative repeater: a device that performs signal regeneration together with ancillary functions. Normally, a repeater utilized in telegraph applications. Its function is to retime and retransmit the received signal impulses restored to their original strength. These repeaters are speed- and code-sensitive, and are intended for use with standard telegraph speeds and codes. synonymous with *regen.* (C)

regenerative track: part of a track on a magnetic drum or magnetic disk used in conjunction with a read head and a write head that are connected to function as a circulating storage. synonymous with *revolver track.* (A)

regenerator: a repeater or amplifier that reshapes, by local generation, line signals used in digital transmission systems. Takes advantage of the fact that the general characteristics of the received signal, such as repetition rate, are known. Contrasts with a linear amplifier used in analog systems. (F)

regenerator section: in pulse code modulation, a regenerator and its preceding transmission path.

region: see *overlay region.*

regional address: an address of a

machine instruction within a series of consecutive addresses; e.g., R18 and R19 are specific addresses in an "R" region of "N" consecutive addresses, where all addresses are named.

regional center: a control center (class 1 office) connecting sectional centers of the telephone system together. Every pair of regional centers in the United States has a direct circuit group running from one center to the other. see *toll office.*

regional computer network

(1) a network of computers whose nodes provide access to a specified geographical area.

(2) a network of computers whose nodes are available to a specified class of users.

REGIS: see *register.*

register (R) (REG) (REGIS)

(1) a storage device, having a specified storage capacity such as a bit, a byte, or a computer word, and usually intended for a special purpose. (B)

(2) on a calculator, a storage device in which specific data is stored. (D)

(3) a part of an automatic switching system that receives and stores signals from a calling device or other source for interpretation and action, some of which is carried out by the register itself. (F)

(4) see *address register, base address register, base register, circulating register, double-length register, floating-point register, general-purpose register, index register, instruction address register, instruction register, n-tuple-length register, quadruple-length register, return code register, sequence control register, shift register, triple-length register.* (A)

register address field: that part of an instruction word containing a register address.

register capacity: the upper and lower limits of the numbers that can be processed in a register.

register file: a bank of multiple-bit registers used as temporary storage locations for data or instructions and referred to as a *stack.*

register input-buffer: a unit that accepts data from input units or media such as magnetic tapes or disks and then transfers this data to internal storage.

register length: the storage capacity of a register. (B)

register pointer: the part of the program status double-word that points to a set of 16 general registers used as the current register block.

register select: lines utilized to choose one register out of a given number with a unit. Pins are usually connected to the address bus.

registration: the accurate positioning of an entity relative to a reference. (A)

registration program: FCC program which permits the direct connection of terminal equipment, whether customer-provided or telephone company–provided, to the telecommunications network without the need for a telephone company–provided protection connecting arrangement or data access arrangement. (G)

regulation: compensation for changes in loss as a cable's temperature varies. Its purpose is to adjust equalization so that the flat frequency response is maintained as the temperature changes.

regulated public utility: a firm that supplies an indispensable service under essentially noncompetitive conditions, with governmental regulation of prices, rate of return, and service quality. (F)

rejection: synonymous with *NOR operation.*

REL

(1) see *release.*

(2) see *relocatable.*

relation (R): in assembler programming, the comparison of two expressions to see if the value of one is equal to, less than, or greater than the value of the other.

relation character: see *relation character.*

relational data base (RDB): a data base in which relationships between data items are explicitly specified as equally accessible attributes. (E)

relational expressions: an expression that consists of an arithmetic expression, followed by a relational operator, followed by another arithmetic expression, and that can be reduced to a value that is true or false.

relational operator

(1) an operator that operates on at least two operands and yields a truth value. (E)

(2) in assembler programming, an operator that can be used in an arithmetic or character relation to indicate the comparison to be performed between the terms in the relation. The relational operators are EQ (equal to), GE (greater than or equal to), GT (greater than), LE (less than or equal to), LT (less than), and NE (not equal to).

(3) in COBOL, a reserved word, or a group of reserved words, or a group of reserved words and relational characters. A relational operator plus programmer-defined operands make up a relational expression.

relation character: in COBOL, a character that expresses a relationship between two operands. The following are COBOL relation characters:

character	meaning
>	greater than
<	less than
=	equal to

relation condition: in COBOL, a statement that the value of an arithmetic expression or data item has a specific relationship to another arithmetic expression or data item. The statement may be true or false.

relative address: an address expressed as a difference with respect to a base address. (A) (B)

relative addressing: a method of addressing in which the address part of an instruction contains a relative address. (A) (B)

relative block number: a number that identifies the location of a block expressed as a difference with respect to a base address. The relative block number is used to retrieve that block from the data set.

relative code: a code where all addresses are written with respect to an arbitrarily chosen position, or in which all addresses are represented symbolically in machine language.

relative coding: coding that uses machine instructions with relative addresses. (A)

relative command: in computer graphics, a display command that causes the display device to interpret the data following the order as relative coordinates, rather than absolute coordinates. cf. *absolute command.* (E)

relative coordinate: in computer graphics, one of the coordinates that identify the location of an addressable point by means of a displacement from some other addressable point. cf. *absolute coordinate.* (E)

relative data: in computer graphics, values in a computer program that specify displacements from the actual coordinates in a display space or image space. cf. *absolute data.*

relative data set: a data set in which each record is assigned a record number according to its relative position within the data set storage space; the record number must be used to retrieve the record from the data set. see also *indexed data set.*

relative error: the ratio of an absolute error to the true, specified, or theoretically correct value of the quantity that is in error. (A) (B)

relative frequency: the measure of the ratio of numbers of observations in a class to the total number of observations, or elements constituting a population, that is, universal subset.

relative line number: a number assigned by the user to a telecommunication line of a line group.

relative magnitude: the magnitude of a relationship of one quantity to another; usually related to base magnitude and expressed as a difference from or a percentage of the base or reference.

relative order: deprecated term for *relative command.*

relative record number (RRN): a number that indicates the location of a logical record, expressed as a dif-

ference with respect to a base address. The relative record number is used to retrieve the logical record from the data set.

relative redundancy: in information theory, the ratio r of the redundancy R to the decision content H (so)s. (A) (B)

relative transmission level: the ratio of the test-tone power at one point to the test-tone power at some other point in the system chosen as a reference point. The ratio is expressed in db. The transmission level at the transmitting switchboard is frequently taken as zero level reference point. see also *zero transmission level reference point.*

relative vector: in computer graphics, a vector whose ending point is specified as a displacement from its starting point. cf. *absolute vector.* synonymous with *incremental vector.* (E)

relay: an electromagnetic switching unit having multiple electrical contacts, energized by electrical current in its coil; used to complete electrical circuits.

relay center: a central point where message switching takes place; a message switching center.

relay driver: a device used to interface logic circuitry to electromechanical relays.

release (REL): synonymous with *disconnect.*

release read: a feature permitting greater processing time by releasing the read mechanism.

relevance ratio: an information retrieval term expressing the ratio of the number of pertinent documents retrieved by a specific query to the total number of documents retrieved by the query criteria.

reliability: the ability of a functional unit to perform its intended function under stated conditions, for a stated period of time. (A) (B)

reliability theory: a descriptive mathematical model of the probability that the system components and the total system will function satisfactorily during the performance of a mission.

relocatable (REL): the attribute of a set of code whose address constants can be modified to compensate for a change in origin.

relocatable address: an address that is adjusted when the computer program containing it is relocated. (A) (B)

relocatable expression: in assembler programming, an assembly-time expression whose value is affected by program relocation. A relocatable expression can represent a relocatable address.

relocatable linking loader: allows users to combine multiple independent binary modules into an executable program, with capabilities for automatic library search, conditional load, comprehensive load map listings, and origin definition flexibility.

relocatable load module: a combination of object modules having cross-references so resolved and prepared for loading into storage for execution. Relocation dictionary (RLD) information is saved with the load module to allow it to be loaded at a different address than the one for which it was built.

relocatable phase: output of the linkage editor containing relocation information. The relocation loader in

the supervisor uses this information to relocate the phase into any partition the user selects at execution time.

relocatable program: a computer program that is in such a form that it may be relocated. (A) (B)

relocatable routine: a routine with instructions written in relative code so that they can be traced and acted on throughout memory. see *relative coding.*

relocatable subroutine: a subroutine located physically and independently in the memory, its object-time location determined by the processor.

relocatable term: in assembler programming, a term whose value is affected by program relocation.

relocate: to move a computer program or part of a computer program, and to adjust the necessary address references so that the computer program can be executed after being moved. (A) (B)

relocating loader: a loader that adjusts addresses, relative to the assembled origin, by the relocation factor. (A)

relocation: the modification of address constants to compensate for a change in origin of a module, program, or control section. see *dynamic relocation.* (A)

relocation dictionary (RLD): the part of an object module or load module that identifies all addresses that must be adjusted when a relocation occurs. (A)

relocation factor: the algebraic difference between the assembled origin and the loaded origin of a computer program. (A)

remainder: in a division operaton, the

number or quantity that is the undivided part of the dividend, having an absolute value less than the absolute value of the divisor, and that is one of the results of a division operation. (B) cf. *quotient.* (*A*)

remote (RMT): equipment located at a distance. synonym for *link-attached.*

remote access: pertaining to communication with a data-processing facility through a data link. (A)

remote-access data processing: data processing in which certain portions of input-output functions are situated in different places and connected by transmission facilities. synonymous with *teleprocessing.* see also *distributed data processing.*

remote-access data-processing network: a network in which input-output devices are connected by data links to a central computer. synonymous with *teleprocessing network.* see also *distributed data-processing network.*

remote batch: the use of remotely located terminals, connected via telecommunications lines to a central computing system, in order to enter batch input.

remote batch entry: submission of batches of jobs through an input-output unit that has access to a computer through a data link. (A) (B)

remote batch processing: batch processing in which input-output units have access to a computer through a data link. (A) (B)

remote batch terminal: a terminal used in remote batch processing.

remote call forwarding (RCF): a service offering which allows customers to have a telephone number in an ESS office without having any other local telephone service in that office. Calls coming to the remote call forwarding number are automatically forwarded to any answering location the customer wants. (G)

remote command submission: a program's ability to transfer a batch command file to a remote system and cause it to be executed.

remote concentrator: a device, such as a minicomputer, that interacts with a group of terminals or communication channels to transmit the communications to a remote system over a single channel.

remote console: a terminal unit in a remote computing system.

remote control: a system of control performed from a distance.

remote data concentration: the multiplexing of a number of low-activity or low-speed lines or terminals on to one high-speed line between a remote terminal and a central processor.

remote format item: in PL/1, the letter R specified in a format list together with the label of a separate FORMAT statement.

remote host: an information processor which is logically fully compatible with the host system, but configured at a remote location within the system.

remote job entry (RJE): submission of jobs through an input unit that has access to a computer through a data link. (A) (B)

remote loop adapter (RLA): an adapter used where the controller and the loop systems are interconnected by common carrier dedicated facilities. It provides the boundary between the remote loop and the integrated modem or OEM modem/EIA converter connected to common carrier lines.

remote message processing: an extension of the full power of the data processing and programming facilities of the computer to remote locations.

remote order wire: an extension of a local order wire to a point more convenient for personnel to perform required monitoring functions.

remote power off: an optional, program-supported feature of a remote communication controller by which the controller power can be turned off by a command from the host processor.

remote printing: producing hard copy output from a printer from a distant location from the processor which provides the printer's electronic input.

remote program loader (RPL): a feature that includes a read-only storage unit and a small auxiliary-storage device installed in a remote controller to allow the controller to be loaded and dumped over the data link.

remote station (RST): data terminal equipment for communication with a data-processing system through a data link. synonymous for *link-attached station.*

remote subsets: input and output units located at points other than the central computer site.

remote switch: a small central office or subsystem of a switching entity that interfaces subscriber lines and concentrates those lines into channels to a remotely located base or host switch.

remote terminal (RT): synonym for *link-attached terminal.*

remote trunk arrangement (RTA): an arrangement whereby the trunks from a number of small end-offices are concentrated for efficient service by a single traffic service position system (TSPS) base unit. This enables a TSPS/RTA complex to serve an area over 100,000 square miles. (F)

removable random access: pertaining to disk packs, tape strips, or card strips that can be physically deleted and replaced by another, permitting for a theoretically unlimited storage capacity.

reorder: deprecated term for *order(1).* (A) (B)

reorder tone: synonymous with *channel busy tone.* (F)

repagination: in word processing, the process in which a word processor adjusts a multipage document as it is revised in order to ensure uniform page length and appearance.

repair time: time consumed to diagnose, clear, or repair machines or systems, including fault location, detection, correction, and consequent tests.

repeatability: the measure of the difference between the mean value and some maximum expected value for a particular data reading.

repeatability measure: in computer graphics, a measure of the spatial coincidence of each display image as it is produced repeatedly. (E)

repeat-action key: a key that, when held fully depressed, causes an action (such as typing a character) to be repeated until the key is released; for example, a typematic key.

repeat character (RPT): a word-processing device control that causes a storage location pointer to reset to a designated buffer beginning point for the device. see also *page-end character, switch character*.

repeated selection sort: a selection sort in which the set of items is divided into subsets and one item, that fits specified criteria, from each subset is selected to form a second level subset. A selection sort is applied to this second level subset, the selected item in this second level subset is appended to the sorted set and is replaced by the next eligible item in the original subset, and the process repeated until all items are in the sorted set. see also *tournament sort*. (A)

repeater
(1) a device used to amplify or reshape signals. see *regenerative repeater*.
(2) **analog or nonregenerative:** an amplifier inserted in a transmission medium to compensate for the attenuation and distortion introduced by the medium. (F)
(3) **digital or regenerative:** a device inserted in a transmission medium to regenerate a digital signal sent over the medium. see *regenerator*. (F)

repeater coil: a one-to-one ratio audio-frequency transformer for transferring energy from one electrical circuit to another and to permit, in wire telecommunications, the formulation of simplex and phantom circuits.

reperforator: see *receiving perforator*. (A)

reperforator/transmitter (RT): a teletypewriter unit consisting of a reperforator and a tape transmitter, each independent of the other. It is used as a relaying device and is especially suitable for transforming the incoming speed to a different outgoing speed, and for temporary queuing.

repertoire: see *instruction repertoire*. (A)

repertory: the numerous sets of operations that are represented in a given operation code.

repetition factor: in PL/1, a parenthesized unsigned decimal integer constant that specifies (a) the number of occurrences of a string configuration that make up a string constant, and (b) the number of occurrences of a picture specification character in a picture specification.

repetition instruction: an instruction that causes one or more instructions to be executed an indicated number of times. (A)

repetitive addressing: a method of implied addressing, applicable only to zero-address instructions, in which the operation part of an instruction implicitly addresses the operands of the last instruction executed. (A) (B)

repetitive operation: the automatic repetition of the solution of a set of equations with fixed combinations of initial conditions and other parameters. (B)

repetitive specification: in PL/1, an element of a data list that specifies controlled iteration to transmit one or more data items, generally used in conjunction with arrays.

replacement: the substitution of different machines for other devices that perform the same or similar operations.

replica reproduction: facsimile copies of documents that are produced by copiers or photocopiers.

report: an output document prepared by a data-processing system.

report generation: a technique for producing complete machine reports from information that describes the input file and the format and content of the output report. see *RPG II.*

report generator: a general-purpose program designed to print out information from files on presentation to it of parameters specifying the format of the files concerned plus the format and content of the printed report, and procedures and regulations for establishing totals, page numbering, and so forth. synonymous with *program generator.*

report program generator (RPG): synonymous with *report generator.*

REPR: see *representation.*

representation (REPR): see *analog representation, coded representation, digital representation, discrete representation, floating-point representation, incremental representation, linear representation, number representation, numeric representation, variable-point representation.* (A)

representation system: see *fixed-point representation system, number representation system, positional representation system, variable-point representation system.* (A)

reproduce: synonym for *duplicate.* (A)

reproducer: synonym for *reproducing punch.* see also *tape reproducer.* (A) (B)

reproducing punch: a punched card device that prepares one punched card from another punched card, copying all or part of the data from the punched card that is read. synonymous with *reproducer.* (A) (B)

reproduction codes: function codes in a master tape that are carried through the data operations and appear in the produced tape.

reproduction replica: facsimile copies of documents produced by copiers or photocopiers.

REQ: see *request.*

request (R) (REQ): a directive (by means of a basic transmission unit) from an access method that causes the network control program to perform a data-transfer operation or auxiliary operation.

request-repeat system: a system using an error-detecting code that is arranged so that a signal detected in error automatically commences a request for retransmission of the signal that was found as being in error.

request words for input-output: control words for I/O requests stored in the message reference block until the I/O is completed.

required carrier-return character (RCR): a word processing formatting control that moves the printing or display point to the first position of the next line and resets indent tab mode. Required carrier return must be executed wherever it occurs in the character string. see also *carrier return character.* synonymous with *required new-line character.* cf. *index return character.*

required cryptographic session: deprecated term for *mandatory cryptographic session.*

required hyphen: in word processing, a grammatical hyphen that is not subject to hyphen drop. (D)

required hyphen character (HYP): a word processing formatting graphic used whenever the graphic hyphen must not be changed during formatting operations. cf. *syllable hyphen (character)*.

required new-line character: synonym for *required carrier return character*.

required page-end character (RPE): a word-processing formatting control that initiates the procedure for terminating a page. Required page end must be honored as a page delimiter wherever it occurs in a character string. see also *page-end character*.

required space character (RSP): a word processing formatting graphic that causes the printing or display point to move right to the next active position. Required space is treated as a graphic character (not as an interword space or information separator) in implementing formatting operations; for example, to concatenate words in a phrase which is to be underscored using the word underscore character. see also *space character*.

rerun
(1) a repeat of a machine run from its beginning, usually made desirable or necessary by a false start, by an interruption, or by a change. (B)
(2) to perform a rerun. (*A*) (B)

rerun mode: use of a terminal to have previously entered data printed or displayed at the terminal. This mode allows the terminal operator to visually check the data, get a clean copy of the data, or correct the data.

rerun point: that location in the sequence of instructions in a computer program at which all information per-tinent to the rerunning of the program is available. (A)

RES
(1) see *reset*.
(2) see *restore*.

resale/shared-use order: a 1976 FCC decision which declared unlawful virtually all restrictions on the resale and shared use of common carrier interstate private-line services. Resale carriers were subsequently allowed to order services from established telephone common carriers and resell them to individual users for a profit. The order also permitted shared use, a nonprofit arrangement whereby several users collectively subscribe to private-line services of an established telephone common carrier with each user paying a share of the communications-related costs associated with the services. (G)

rescue dump: recording on magnetic tape of the entire memory information, which includes the status of the computer system at the time the dump is carried out.

rescue point: synonym for *restart point*. (A) (B)

reserve: allocating a memory area and/or peripheral devices to a program functioning in a multiprogramming system.

reserved word
(1) a word of a source language whose meaning is fixed by the particular rules of that language and cannot be altered for the convenience of any one computer program expressed in the source language; computer programs expressed in the source language may also be prohibited from using such words in other contexts in the computer program.

For example, SINE may be a reserved word to call a subroutine for computing the sine function; in COBOL, the COBOL words. (B)

(2) a word that is defined in a programming language for a special purpose, and that must not appear as a user-declared identifier. (E)

reset (R) (RES) (RST)

(1) to cause a counter to take the state corresponding to a specified initial number. (A) (B)

(2) to put all or part of a data-processing device back into a prescribed state. (B)

(3) to restore a storage device to a prescribed initial state, not necessarily that denoting zero. (B)

(4) cf. *set*. (A)

reset cycle: the return of a cycle index to its initial or some preselected condition.

reset mode: synonym for *initial condition mode*. (B)

reset pulse: a drive pulse used to control the state of a storage cell, specifically one that restores a cell to zero. see *binary cell*.

reset rate: the number of corrections, per unit of time, made by the control system.

reset to n: a procedure setting a device as a register, counter, and so on, for storing or displaying a value, say n, by returning a counting device to its initial state, thus representing n, that is, some number as it was predetermined or desired.

reset to zero (RZ): to start from the beginning; returning to point of origin for reconsideration or redesign of a project.

resident: that which exists permanently in memory; for example, a resi-dent compiler.

resident control program: synonym for *nucleus*.

residential error ratio: the error ratio remaining after attempts at correction. (A)

resident macroassembler: a unit that translates symbolic assembly-language instructions into the appropriate machine-operation codes.

resident modules: keeps track of program execution status and which overlay modules are needed.

resident program: a program that remains in a particular area of storage.

resident program select list: a list of programs that are in, or that are scheduled to be copied into, resident program storage.

residue check: a validation check in which an operand is divided by number to generate a remainder that is then used for checking. synonymous with *modulo-N check*.

resistance design: a design method for customer loops in which an attempt is made to employ cable having the highest gauge (smallest wire) that will ensure a loop resistance less than the signaling limit of the central office serving the loop. (F)

resistor (R): a device that restricts the flow of current into a circuit.

resistor-transistor logic (RTL): logic carried out by the use of resistors, with transistors producing an inverted output. synonymous with *transistor-resistor logic. (TRL)*

resolution: in computer graphics, a measure of the sharpness of an image, expressed as the number 1 of lines per unit of length or the number of points per unit of area discernible in that image. (E)

resolution error: an error caused by the inability of a computing device to show changes of a variable smaller than a given increment.

resolver: a functional unit whose input variables are the polar coordinates of a point and whose output variables are the Cartesian coordinates of the same point, or vice versa. (B)

resonance: the sympathetic vibration of a circuit to a signal.

resource: any facility of the computing system or operating system required by a job or task, and including main storage, input-output devices, the processing unit, data sets, and control or processing programs.

resource access control facility (RACF): a program product that provides for access control by identifying and verifying users to the system authorizing access to DASD data sets, logging detected unauthorized attempts to enter the system, and logging detected accesses to protected data sets.

resource allocation: the assignment of the facilities of a data-processing system for the accomplishment of jobs; for example, the assignment of main storage, input-output devices, files. (B)

resource management: the function that protects serially accessed resources from concurrent access by competing tasks.

resource manager (RM): a general term for any control program function responsible for the allocation of a resource.

resource sharing: the function of allocating the processing load of an enterprise to the available processing facilities when multiple facilities exist.

resource sharing control: the tying together of multiple computers in distributed processing systems so that several systems can function together sharing the work load.

response: an answer to an inquiry. see *spectral response*. (A) cf. *command (2)*.

response duration: the time duration between the start of a pulse which influences a storage cell and the end of the resulting response of that storage cell. (A) (B)

response/throughput bias (RTB): in the system resources manager, a category of information contained in a period definition, that indicates how the work-load manager is to weigh trade offs between satisfying a system throughput objective and the IPS-specified service rate.

response time: the elapsed time between the end of an inquiry or demand on a data-processing system and the beginning of the response; for example, the length of time between an indication of the end of an inquiry and the display of the first character of the response at a user terminal. (A) (B) see also *interaction time, turnaround time*.

RESRT: see *restart*.

restart (RESRT)

(1) the resumption of the execution of a computer program using the data recorded at a checkpoint. (B)

(2) to perform a restart. (*A*) (B)

(3) see *checkpoint restart*.

(4) see also *checkpoint records*.

restart condition: in the execution of a computer program, a condition that can be reestablished and that permits a restart of the computer program. (A) (B)

restart instruction: an instruction in a

computer program at which the computer program may be restarted. (A) (B)

restart point: a place in a computer program at which its execution may be restarted; in particular, the address of a restart instruction. synonymous with *rescue point*. deprecated term for *restart condition*. (*A*) (B)

restitution: conditions resulting from decisions based on demodulated telegraph signals.

restoration: the process of making good a failed transmission system section by patching in a spare or low-usage system.(F)

restore (RES): see *reset*.

result: an entity produced by the performance of an operation. (A) (B)

RET: see *return*.

retention period check: synonym for *expiration check*.

retentivity: the property of a material to retain magnetic flux.

retina: in optical character recognition, a major component of a scanning unit.

retrieval: see *information retrieval*. (A)

retrieval code: in micrographics, a code for manual or automatic retrieval of microimages. (A) (B)

retrieve: to carry out retrieval. synonym for *fetch*.

retrieving: searching of storage to locate the data needed, and choosing or removing the required data from storage.

retrofit: to alter an existing routine or system to accommodate a new section or an alteration to an existing section, and to evolve changes in related routines or systems.

retrofit testing: testing to assure system operation after having replaced some units and/or programs.

retry: to resend the current block of data (from the last EOB or ETB) a prescribed number of times, or until is it is entered correctly or accepted.

return (RET)

(1) within a subroutine, to bind a variable in the computer program that called the subroutine. (B)

(2) within a subroutine, to effect a link to the computer program that called the subroutine. (B)

(3) see *carriage return*. (*A*)

return address (RA): synonymous with *link*.

return character: see *carriage return character*. (A)

return code: a code use to influence the execution of succeeding instructions. (A)

return code register: a register used to store a return code. (A)

returned value: in PL/1, the value returned by a function procedure to the point of invocation.

return instruction: an instruction that returns control of the main routine following the execution of a subroutine.

return loss: the ratio of the incident wave to the reflected wave at the terminal of a transmission line or circuit; if the terminating impedance is exactly equal to the characteristic impedance of the transmission line or the circuit impedance, there is no reflection and the return loss is infinite. Also, where a four-wire circuit is connected to a two-wire circuit through a hybrid, return loss is the ratio of the wave entering the hybrid on one side of the four-wire circuit to the reflected wave leaving the hybird on the other side of the four-wire circuit.

Note that there can be a number of reflections along a telephone circuit; the reflection having lowest return loss usually occurs at a central office where a loop is connected to a trunk.

return-to-reference recording: the magnetic recording of binary characters in which the patterns of magnetization used to represent zeros and ones occupy only part of the storage cell, the remainder of the cell being magnetized to a reference condition. (A) (B)

return-to-zero recording: return-to-reference recording in which the reference condition is the absence of magnetization. (B)

reusable: the attribute of a routine that allows the same copy of the routine to be used by two or more tasks. see also *reenterable, serially reusable.*

reusable program: a computer program that may be loaded once and executed repeatedly, subject to the requirements that any instructions that are modified during its execution are returned to their initial states and that its external program parameters are preserved unchanged. (A) (B)

reusable routine: a routine that may be loaded once and executed repeatedly, subject to the requirements that any instructions that are modified during its execution are returned to their initial states and that its external program parameters are perserved unchanged. (A) (B)

reverse battery signaling: synonymous with *loop-reverse battery.* (F)

reverse bias: a voltage applied to a p-n crystal so that the positive terminal is applied to the n section of the crystal and the negative terminal to the p

section.

reverse break: synonym for *transmission interruption.*

reverse capstan: a rotating shaft with minimal tolerances that controls the reverse or rewind movement of magnetic tape at a uniform speed. see *reverse solenoid.*

reverse channel: in conjunction with Bell System data sets, a means of simultaneous communication from the receiver to the transmitter over half-duplex data-transmission systems. The reverse channel is generally used only for the transmission of control information.

reverse channel capability: the potential to interact with a system over a communications link.

reverse clipping: synonym for *shielding.*

reverse-code dictionary: an alphabetic code or numeric-alphabet code arrangement associated with their corresponding English words or terms. see also *dictionary.*

reverse direction flow: in flowcharting, a flow in a direction other than left to right or top to bottom. (A)

reverse indexing: in word processing, the feature that causes the typing position or display pointer to be moved to the corresponding character position of the preceding typing line. (D)

reverse Polish notation: synonym for *postfix notation.* (A) (B)

reverse recovery time: the time needed for the current or voltage to reach a specified state after it has been switched from a forward current condition to a reverse bias condition.

reverse solenoid: an electrical-mechanical unit that provides pressure via a roller to force magnetic tape against the reverse capstan and move the tape in a reverse direction. see *reverse capstan.*

reverse video: a form of highlighting a character, field, or cursor by reversing the color of the character, field, or cursor with its background; for example, changing a red character on a black background to a black character on a red background.

reversible counter: a device with a finite number of states, each of which represents a number that can be increased or decreased by unity or by a given constant on receipt of an appropriate signal; the device is usually capable of bringing the number represented to a specific value, for example, zero. (B)

reversible magnetic process: a process of flux change within a magnetic material where the flux returns to its earlier condition when the magnetic field is removed. synonymous with *reversible process.*

reversible process: synonymous with *reversible magnetic process.*

revertive pulsing: a method of signaling between switching systems in which information is conveyed from system A to system B by B sending a sequence of pulse to A which A counts; A signals B when the correct number has been received. (F)

revise: any proof produced following corrections.

revolver: synonymous with *rapid access loop.*

revolver track: synonym for *regenerative track.* (A)

rewind (RWND): to return a magnetic or paper tape to its beginning.

rewind key: in word processing, a

control that causes magnetic tape to be rewound to the start position, normally at high speed. (D)

rewind time: elapsed time needed to transfer tape to the supply reel.

rewrite: to regenerate data in storage units where the process of reading data results in its destruction.

rewrite dual gap head: a character written on tape is immediately read by a read head so the accuracy of recorded data can be ensured.

RF: see *radio frequency.*

RF modulator: a device that modulates the frequency of a received carrier signal.

RFRSH: see *refresh.*

RFSH: see *refresh.*

right justified: when the right-hand digit or character occupies its allotted right-hand position.

right justify

(1) to shift the contents of a register, if necessary, so that the character at the right-hand end of the data that have been read or loaded into the register is at a specified position in the register. (B)

(2) to control the positions of characters on a page so that the right-hand margin of the printing is regular. (B)

(3) to align characters horizontally so that the rightmost character of a string is in a specified position. (*A*)

right-of-way companies (ROW): nontelephone utility companies or public service agencies, such as power, pipeline, and railroads which furnish and maintain their own largely separate communications systems, to satisfy some unique overriding public need. These communications systems are connected to Bell System services under the registration program. Some ROW companies have formed subsidiaries to operate as OCCs, such as Southern Pacific Communications Company (SPCC). (G)

right shift: to displace digits in a word to the right, having the result of division in arithmetic shift.

rigid disk: a disk memory in which the magnetic medium is coated on to a rigid substrate.

ring (network) (R): a network in which each node is connected to two adjacent nodes. (E)

ring-back tone: an audible signal indicating that the called party is being run.

ring conductor: one conductor of a customer line (tip and ring). Use of the names *tip* and *ring* has extended throughout the plant. (F)

ring counter: a loop of interconnected bistable elements where one and only one is in a specified state at any given time and such that, as input signals are counted, the position of the element in the specified state shifts in an ordered sequence around the loop.

ring down: a method of signaling subscribers and operators using either a 20-cycle AC signal, a 135-cycle AC signal, or a 1000-cycle AC signal interrupted 20 times per second.

ringer: a device, usually part of a telephone set, that responds to a 20-Hz signal to produce a ringing sound. Ringers separate from the associated telephone sets are sometimes installed. (F)

ringer isolator: a device that disconnects the ringer when ringing voltage is not present; used when ringers are connected in an unbalanced configuration (one side grounded) to achieve greater circuit balance during transmission. (F)

ringing: the process of alerting the called party by the application of an intermittent 2-Hz signal to the appropriate line; this produces a ringing sound at the called telephone set. When the ringing signal is applied to the called line, an intermittent signal called audible ringing is sent to the calling telephone to indicate that ringing is taking place. (F)

ring network: a network topology where computers are connected in a circular configuration.

ring shift: synonymous with *logical shift.*

ring trip: the process of removing the ringing signal at the central office when the called telephone is lifted from the switchhook. (F)

ripple-through carry: synonymous with *high-speed carry.*

rise time: time needed for the leading edge of a pulse to rise from 10 percent to 90 percent of its final value.

rivers: the undesirable alignment of spaces found in a text.

RJE: see *remote job entry.* (A) (B)

RL: see *record length.*

RLA: see *remote loop adapter.*

RLD: see *relocation dictionary.*

RM: see *resource manager.*

RMS: see *recovery management support.*

RMT: see *remote.*

RO

(1) see *read only.*

(2) see *receive only.*

robot: a machine equipped with sensing instruments for detecting input signals or environmental conditions but with reacting or guidance mechanisms that can perform sensing, calculations, and so on, and with stored programs for resultant actions; for example, a machine running itself.

robotics: an area of artificial intelligence applied to the industrial use of robots doing repetitive tasks.

ROD: recorder on demand. Displays percentages of errors recorded.

role indicator: in information retrieval, a code assigned to a word, that is, a descriptor, indicating the role which the word plays in the text where it occurs.

roll: in computer graphics, to scroll in an upward or downward direction.

rollback: a programmed return to a prior checkpoint. (A)

roll in: to restore in main storage data or one or more computer programs that were previously rolled out. (A)

rolling: in computer graphics, scrolling in an upward or downward direction. (E)

roll out: to transfer data or one or more computer programs from main storage to auxiliary storage for the purpose of freeing main storage for another use. (A)

roll out/roll in: a procedure for managing storage whereby certain programs are temporarily taken out of main storage, placed on disk storage, and returned when an operation is complete. see also *roll in, roll out.*

rollover: a keyboard encoding mechanism permitting a number of keys to be depressed at the same time free from error.

ROM: read-only memory; a type of memory whose contents do not change and cannot normally be altered. (A) (B) see *read-only storage.*

roofing filter: a low-pass filter used to reduce unwanted higher frequencies.

root segment
(1) in overlay program, the segment that remains in storage during the execution of the overlay program; the first segment in an overlay program.
(2) in a data base, the highest segment in the hierarchy.

ROS: see *read-only storage.*

rotary dial: in a switched system, the conventional dialing method that creates a series of pulses to identify the called station. cf. *push-button dialing, tone dialing.*

rotating: in computer graphics, turning all or part of a display image about an axis perpendicular to the display surface. (E)

rotational position sensing (RPS): a feature that permits a disk storage device to disconnect from a block multiplexer channel (or its equivalent), allowing the channel to service other devices on the channel during positional delay.

rotor: the rotating component of a sensor. see also *stator.*

ROTR: see *receive-only typing reperforator.*

round: to delete or omit one or more of the least significant digits in a positional representation and to adjust the part retained in accordance with some specified rule. The purpose of rounding is usually to limit the precision of the numeral or to reduce the number of characters in the numeral, or to do both. The most common forms of rounding are rounding down, rounding up, and rounding off. (B) cf. *truncation.* (A)

round down
(1) to round, making no adjustment

to the part of the numeral that is re-tained. If a numeral is rounded down, its absolute value is not increased. Rounding down is a form of trunca-tion. (A) (B)

(2)   on a calculator, the elimination in the result of the calculation of all digits beyond the least significant digit. (D)

rounding error: an error due to roundoff. (B) cf. *truncation error*.

round off

(1)   to round, adjusting the part of the numeral retained by adding 1 to the least significant of its digits, and executing any necessary carries, if (a) the most significant of the digits deleted was greater than half the radix of that digit place, or (b) the most significant of the digits deleted was equal to half the radix and one or more of the following digits were greater than zero, or (c) the most sig-nificant of the digits deleted was equal to zero, and the least signifi-cant of the digits retained was odd. In (c) even may be substituted for odd. (A) (B)

(2)   on a calculator, the increase of the least significant digit in the result of a calculation to the next higher number where the subsequent digit in the result is 5 or above. Where the subsequent digit is 4 or below, the least significant digit remains un-changed. (D)

round robin: a cyclical multiplexing technique, allocating resources in fixed-time slices.

round up

(1)   to round, adjusting the part of the numeral that is retained by add-ing 1 to the least significant of its dig-its, and executing any necessary

carries if and only if one or more nonzero digits have been deleted. If a numeral is rounded up, its absolute value is not decreased. (A) (B)

(2)   on a calculator, the increase of the least significant digit in the result of a calculation by one if the highest decimal place dropped off has a value of more than zero. (D)

route: see *virtual route*. see also *rout-ing*.

routine (RTN):   part of a program, or a sequence of instructions called by a program, that may have some gener-al or frequent use. see *dump routine, input routine, library routine, output routine, recursive routine, reusable routine, subroutine, supervisory rou-tine, tracing routine, utility routine*.

routing: the assignment of the path by which a message will reach its desti-nation. see *message routing*.

routing affinity: a temporary relation-ship between a source and a destina-tion.

routing code

(1)   a combination of one or more digits used to route a call to a prede-termined area.

(2)   a code assigned to an operator message and used, in systems with multiple console support (MCS), to route the message to the proper con-sole.

routing indicator: an address, or group of characters, in the header of a message defining the final circuit or terminal to which the message has to be delivered.

routing key: see *key*

ROW: see *right-of-way companies*.

row: a horizontal arrangement of characters or other expressions. cf. *column*. see *card row, mark-sensing* *row, punch row.* (A)

row binary: pertaining to the binary representation of data on cards on which the significances of punch positions are assigned along card rows. For example, each row in an 80-column card may be used to represent 80 consecutive binary digits. cf. *column binary.* (A)

row pitch: the distance between corresponding points of adjacent rows, measured along a track. synonymous with *array pitch.* (A) (B)

row scanning: an approach in decoding which key of a keyboard was pressed. Each row is scanned in turn by outputting a 1. The output on the columns when examined, results in identification of the key.

RP: see *reader-printer.*

RPE: see *required page-end character.*

RPG: see *report program generator.* (A)

RPGII: a commercially oriented programming language specifically designed for writing application programs that meet common business data-processing requirements.

RPL: see *remote program loader.*

RPROM: reprogrammable read only memory.

RPS: see *rotational position sensing.*

RPT: see *repeat character.*

RRN: see *relative-record number.*

RS

(1) see *real storage.*

(2) see *record separator character.*

R-S flip flop: a flip-flop using two cross-coupled NAND gates.

RSM: see *real storage management.*

RSP: see *required space character.*

RST

(1) see *remote station.*

(2) see *reset.*

RS-232C: the industry standard for a 25-pin interface that connects computers and various forms of peripheral equipment, for example, modems, printers, and so on.

RT

(1) see *real time.*

(2) see *remote terminal.*

(3) see *reperforator/transmitter.*

RTA: see *remote trunk arrangement.*

RTB: see *response/throughput bias.*

RTL: see *resistor-transistor logic.*

RTN: see *routine*

RTS: see *real-time system.*

RTTY: see *radio teletypewriter.*

rubber-banding: in computer graphics, moving the ends of a set of straight lines while the other ends remain fixed. (E)

rub-out character: synonym for *delete character.*

run

(1) a single performance of one or more jobs. (B)

(2) a single, continuous performance of a computer program or routine. (A)

runaway: the condition which arises when an input to a physical system is subject to a sudden, negative increase or decrease.

run book: all material needed to document a computer application, including problem statement, flowcharts, coding, and operating instructions.

run chart: a flowchart of one or more computer runs in terms of input and output.

run diagram: files, transactions, information, and data in a graphic representation that are handled under the program control to yield the newly updated files, list of alterations, or specific reports.

run duration: synonym for *running time*. (A) (B)

run locator: a routine which locates the correct run on a program tape, whether initiated by another routine or manually.

run mode: a mode where the computer is considered to be functioning when it is automatically executing instructions held in its memory cards and cells.

running dry: examination of the logic and coding of a program from a flowchart and written instructions, and recording of the results of each step of the operation before running the program on the computer.

running open: in telegraph applications, describing a machine connected to an open line or a line without battery (constant space condition). A telegraph receiver under such a condition appears to be running, as the type hammer continually strikes the type box but does not move across the page, because the open line is continually decoded as the baudot character BLANK, or ASCII character NULL.

running time: the elapsed time taken for the execution of a computer program. synonymous with *run duration*. (A) (B)

run phase: synonymous with *target phase*.

run schedule: a listing of work to be performed under time needed to carry out such work.

run stream: synonym for *job stream*.

run unit: in COBOL, a set of one or more object programs that function at object time as a unit to provide problem solutions.

RVA: see *recorded voice announcement*.

RW: see *read/write*.

RWND: see *rewind*.

RZ: see *reset to zero*.

RZ(NP): see *nonpolarized return-to-zero recording*. (A) (B)

RZ(P): see *polarized return-to-zero recording*. (A) (B)

S

S

(1) see *scalar*.
(2) see *set*.
(3) see *sign*.
(4) see *software*.
(5) see *source*.
(6) see *stack*.
(7) see *state*.
(8) see *storage*.
(9) see *switch*.
(10) see *switching*.
(11) see *synchronous*.
(12) see *system*.

SA

(1) see *system administrator*.
(2) see *systems analyst*.

SAM: see *sequential access method*.

sample (SMPL)

(1) to obtain the values of a function for regularly or irregularly spaced distinct values of an independent variable. (B)
(2) in statistics, obtaining a sample from a population. (*A*)

sampling

(1) a random method of checking and controlling the use of data by obtaining the values of a function for regularly or irregularly spaced, discrete values.
(2) a method of communication control in which messages are selected by a computer that chooses only those for which processing is needed.
(3) in statistics, obtaining a sample from a population.

satellite: an object or vehicle orbiting, or intended to orbit, the earth, moon, or other celestial body.

Satellite Business Systems (SBS): a domestic satellite carrier, authorized by the FCC in 1977, and owned by subsidiaries of Comsat General, IBM, and Aetna Casualty and Surety Company. On June 11, 1980, SBS filed with the FCC for authority to provide a private network service, Communications Network Service (CNS), offering voice, data, teleconferencing, and so on, at speeds up to 12.3 Mbps initially, using dedicated customer

457

premises–located earth stations shared by CNS customers (CNS-B). CNS-B will provide an option for placing voice-grade calls from CNS stations to telephone company exchange stations and in a third stage, switched voice and private-line services using an "SBS Network" comprised in part of earth stations that will be located on SBS premises. In November 1980, SBS successfully launched its first satellite. (G)

satellite computer (SC)

(1) a computer that is under the control of another computer and performs subsidiary operations.

(2) an off-line auxiliary computer.

satellite earth terminal: that portion of a satellite link which receives, processes, and transmits communications between earth and a satellite.

satellite processor (SP): an information processor which is arbitrarily assigned a subsidiary role in a system, communicating with (and perhaps depending upon to some degree) a host for support services and/or guidance. see *satellite computer.*

satellite relay: an active or passive satellite repeater that relays signals between two earth stations.

saturation: the condition of magnetism of a material beyond which no additional magnetization is possible.

saturation noise: errors introduced into data resulting from saturation.

saturation testing: testing a program by pushing through numerous messages in an attempt to locate errors.

save area: an area of main storage in which the contents of registers are saved. (A)

SB: see *standby.*

SBA: see *shared batch area.*

SBS

(1) see *Satellite Business Systems.*

(2) see *subscript character.*

SC

(1) see *satellite computer.*

(2) see *selector channel.*

(3) see *semiconductor.*

(4) see *session control.*

scalar (S): a quantity characterized by a single number. (B) cf. *vector.* (A)

scalar item: in PL/1, a single item of data; an element.

scalar variable: in PL/1, a variable that can represent only a single data item; an element variable.

scale

(1) to change the representation of a quantity, expressing it in other units, so that its range is brought within a specified range. (B)

(2) to adjust the representation of a quantity by a factor in order to bring its range within prescribed limits. (A)

(3) in computer graphics, to enlarge or reduce all or part of a display image by multiplying their coordinate by constant values.

(4) a system of mathematical notation: fixed-point or floating-point scale of an arithmetic value.

scale factor (SF)

(1) a number used as a multiplier in scaling. (A) (B)

(2) in FORTRAN, a specification in a FORMAT statement whereby the location of the decimal point in a real number (and, if there is no exponent, the magnitude of the number) can be changed.

(3) in PL/1, a specification of the number of fractional digits in a fixed-point number.

(4) see *time-scale factor.* (A)

scaling

(1)   in computer graphics, enlarging or reducing all or part of a display image by multiplying the coordinates of the image by a constant value. (E)

(2)   in assembler programming, indicating the number of digit positions in object code to be occupied by the fractional portion of a fixed-point or floating-point constant.

scan

(1)   to examine sequentially, part by part. (A)

(2)   in word processing, rapid view of displayed text by vertical scrolling. (D)

(3)   see *directed-beam scan, flying-spot scan, raster scan*.

scanner (SCN):   a device that examines a spatial pattern one part after another, and generates analog or digital signals corresponding to the pattern. Scanners are often used in mark sensing, pattern recognition, or character recognition. (B) see *flying spot scanner, optical scanner*. (*A*)

scanning: the sequential examination or exposure of a set of characters or image.

scanning limits: the action of comparing input variables against prestored or calculated high and/or low limits to find if an alarm condition exists.

scanning machine: a device that automatically reads printed data and converts it into machine language. Two types of this machine are optical scanners and magnetic-ink scanners.

scanning rate: the rate at which a scanner samples.

scanning unit: any attachment to a microform reader permitting the user to bring any section of the microform to a position in which it can be more easily read. synonymous with *scanner*.

scan period: the time where the screen is swept by an electron beam in electrostatic storage tubes to regenerate or restore the charge distribution representing the stored data.

scatter format: a load module attribute that permits dynamic loading of control sections into nonadjoining areas of main storage.

scatter gap: the alignment deviation of magnetic recording head gaps, for groups of heads for racks of a magnetic tape handler.

scatter loading: placing the control sections of a load module into nonadjoining positions of main storage. cf. *block loading*.

scatter read: locating data in noncontiguous memory areas as it is being read into the computer system.

SCB: see *station control block*.

SCC: see *specialized common carrier*.

scenario: a table of definitions describing a communication.

SCERT: Systems and Computers Evaluation and Review Technique. Mechanized routines for creating a model of a computer system by evaluating various hardware configurations. Used widely in data-processing planning and hardware selection.

SCH

(1)   see *schedule*.

(2)   see *scheduler*.

schedule (SCH):   to select jobs or tasks that are to be dispatched. (B)

scheduled downtime: the needed idle time required for normal servicing of computer devices when such equipment is unavailable for functioning. Usually expressed as a percent of the total available time.

scheduled operation: the time periods when a user plans to utilize specific devices, excluding hours rescheduled for equipment failure.

schedule job: a control program that is used to examine the input work queue and to select a next job to be processed.

schedule maintenance: maintenance carried out in accordance with an established schedule. (A) (B)

scheduler (SCH): a computer program designed to perform functions such as scheduling, initiation, and termination of jobs. (A) see *master scheduler*.

scheduler work area (SWA): an area in virtual storage that contains most of the job management control blocks (such as the JCT, JFCB, SCT, and SIOT). There is one scheduler work area for each initiator.

scheduling: allocating the time of a module.

scheduling algorithm: a set of rules that is included in the scheduling routine of the executive program. A scheduling algorithm determines the length of a user's quantum and the frequency with which the quantum is repeated.

scheduling theory: a prescriptive theory dealing with the sequencing of events; for example, orders processed through a job shop or time sharing in a computer system, so as to optimize some output measure like minimum time to accomplish all jobs or maximize the number of jobs completed on time.

schema: the description of the logical structure and physical structure of an entire data base according to a conceptual model. (E)

Schottky: a technology of high-speed circuits. see *Schottky diode*.

Schottky diode: a diode characterized by nanosecond switching speed, with relatively low voltage (45 volts maximum) and limited temperature range (125-150°C).

scientific instruction set (SIS): a set of instructions that includes the instructions of both the standard instruction set and the floating-point feature.

scientific notation: the expression of quantities as a fractional part (mantissa) and a power of ten (characteristics). see *mantissa*.

scissoring: in computer graphics, removing parts of a display image that lies outside a window. synonymous with *clipping*. cf. *shielding*. (E)

SCN: see *scanner*.

scope: in assembler programming, that part of a source program in which a variable symbol can communicate its value. see also *global, local*.

scope (of a condition prefix): In PL/1, the portion of a program throughout which a particular condition prefix applies.

scope (of a declaration): in PL/1, the portion of a program throughout which a particular declaration is a source of attributes for a particular name.

scope (of a name): in PL/1, the portion of a program throughout which the meaning of a particular name does not change.

scope (of an operator): the portion of an expression to which the operator is applied. (E)

scope (of a variable): the portion of a

computer program within which the definition of the variable remains unchanged. (E)

scored card: a special card that contains one or more scored lines to facilitate precise folding or separation of certain parts of the card. (A)

SCPD: see *scratch pad.*

scrambled: the encoded or private form of a signal that is unintelligible except when it is decoded or descrambled.

scrambler: a device that transposes or inverts signals or otherwise encodes a message at the transmitter to make it unintelligibile at a receiver not equipped with an appropriately set descrambling device.

scratch: to erase data on a volume or delete its identification so that it can be used for another purpose.

scratch file: a file used as a work area.

scratch pad (SCPD) (SP): a memory area used as a temporary working section for intermediate results.

scratch tape: a tape that contains information not intended to be retained.

screen: an illuminated display surface; for example, the display surface of a CRT or plasma panel.

screen attribute byte: a character position on the screen of a display terminal that defines the characteristics of the next field displayed on the screen such as protected, not protected, displayable, nondisplayable.

screen generator: a program to aid in the definition of CRT screen forms, which are a particular pattern of symbols on a CRT screen for data entry and display.

screen image: in computer graphics, a pattern of points, lines, and characters displayed on an illuminated display surface of a display device. see also *display image.*

screenload: the maximum number of characters that can appear on a screen at any given time.

screen-oriented programs: in word processing, displays on a video screen exactly as it will appear on the printed page.

screen read: permitting a message displayed on a terminal screen to be retransmitted to a microprocessor or peripheral device, in order that data can be formatted for storage or for editing.

screen size: the measure of the amount of information that a cathode ray tube screen displays.

scroll: to move all or part of the display image vertically to display data that cannot be observed within a single display image.

scrolling

(1) in computer graphics, moving vertically or horizontally a display image in a manner such that new data appear at one edge as old data disappears at the opposite edge. (E)

(2) in word processing, the functions of scroll up, scroll down, scroll right, or scroll left.

(3) see also *rolling, translating.*

SDA: source-data automation; the various approaches for recording data in coded forms on paper tapes, punched cards, or tags that can be reused to yield many other records withour rewriting.

SDI: selective dissemination of information; pertaining to a literature search notification and hard copy supply system that serves clients with internal or external documents.

SDL: see *system directory list.*

SDLC (synchronous data link control): a communications line discipline associated with the IBM system network architecture SNA and offers a number of advantages to users of data networks.

search

(1)   the examination of a set of items for one or more having a given property. (B)

(2)   to examine a set of items for one or more having a given property. (*A*) (B)

(3)   in text processing, a feature that enables individual elements of recorded text to be located. (D)

(4)   see *binary search, chaining search, dichotomizing search, Fibonacci search.* (A)

search and replace: in word processing, changing the word or character in the document, or changing the word or character to any other word or character.

search cycle: the part of a search that is repeated for each item, normally consisting of locating the item and carrying out a comparison. (A) (B)

searching storage: synonymous with *associative storage.*

search key: in the conduct of a search, the data to be compared to specified parts of each item. (A) (B) synonym for *seek key.*

search language: synonymous with *command language* and *query language.*

search terms: words or groups of words used in on-line searching when specifying a request for information. Search terms correspond to headings under which items in a database are indexed.

search time: time needed to find a particular field of data in storage.

search word: in RPGII, data used to find a match in a table or array. The search word is specified in the look-up statement.

secondary: in a high-level data-link control (HDLC), the part of a data station that executes data-link control functions as instructed by the primary. (E)

secondary console: in a system with multiple consoles, any console except the master console. The secondary console handles one or more assigned functions on the multiple console system.

secondary control point: in high-level data-link control (HDLC), a point in a network at which a secondary is located. (C)

secondary destination: any of the destinations specified for a message except the first destination.

secondary entry point: in PL/1, an entry point identified by any of the names in the label list of an ENTRY statement.

secondary file: in RPG II, any file other than the primary file used in multifile processing. see also *file.*

secondary key: a portion of the first block of each record in an indexed data set that may be used to find the record in the data set. The secondary key is valid only when so defined in the data set control block (DSCB). see also *primary key.*

secondary logical unit (SLU) key: a key-encrypting key used to protect a session crytography key during its transmission to the secondary half-session.

secondary station: a data station that

can peform the secondary function, but not the primary function. cf. *primary station*.

secondary storage: synonym for *auxiliary storage*.

secondary store: synonymous with *backing store*.

second computer age: the coming of artificial intelligence by computers. see *artificial intelligence*.

second-generation computer: a computer utilizing solid state components.

second-level addressing: see *level of addressing*.

second source: an alternative supplier of an item of hardware or software. The availability of a second source is usually a major consideration when purchasing devices.

section

(1) in COBOL, a logically related sequence of one or more paragraphs. A section must always be named.

(2) in computer graphics, to construct the bounded or unbounded intersecting plane with respect to one or more displayed objects and then to display the intersection. (E)

(3) deprecated term for *segment*. (A) (B)

(4) see also *control section*.

sectional center: a control center connecting primary centers together; a class I office.

section header: in COBOL, a combination of words that precedes and identifies each section in the environment, data, and procedure divisions.

section name: in COBOL, a word specified by the programmer that precedes and identifies a section in the procedure division.

section number: the number that

identifies a specific section in a series of sections that make up a file.

section text: part of a load module with computer instructions in final form and data defined with specified initial values.

sector: that part of a track or band on a magnetic drum, a magnetic disk, or a disk pack that can be accessed by the magnetic heads in the course of a predetermined rotational displacement of the particular device. (B) see *disk sector*.

security: see *data-processing system security, data security*.

seek: to selectively position the access mechanism of a direct-access device. deprecated term for *search (1), search (2), search cycle*. (A)

seek area: synonymous with *cylinder*.

seek key: in word processing, a control used to locate an address on the recording medium. synonymous with *search key*. (D)

seek time: the time that is needed to position the access mechanism of a direct-access storage device at a specified position. see also *access time*.

SEG: see *segment*.

segment (SEG)

(1) a self-contained portion of a computer program that may be executed without the entire computer program necessarily being maintained in internal storage at any one time. (B)

(2) to divide a computer program into segments. (A) (B)

(3) see *child segment, dependent segment, logical child segment, logical parent segment, overlay segment, parent segment, physical child segment, physical parent segment, physical segment, root segment*.

segmentation: a programmer-defined and monitor-implemented approach of separating a program into self-contained segments so that only certain parts need be in memory at any one time.

segmenting: dividing information into unique units that can be handled at once.

segment mark: a special character written on tape to separate each section of a tape file.

segment number: the part of a virtual storage address needed to refer to a segment.

segregating unit: a device that pulls and/or separates individual cards from a group. The device is equipped with two feeding magazines and four receivers that interfile or segregate the cards into various sequences, at the speed of hundreds of cards per minute from each feeding magazine.

seize
(1) to gain control of a line in order to transmit data. cf. *bid*.
(2) an action of a switching system in selecting an outgoing trunk or other component for a particular call. (F)

seizing signal: a signal translated at the beginning of a message to commence a circuit operation at the receiving end of the circuit.

SEL: see *selector*.

select
(1) to choose one of several alternate subroutines from a file of subroutines.
(2) to activate the control and data channels to and from an input-output unit, preparatory to reading from or writing on the machine.
(3) to take alternative A if the report on a condition is of one state, and alternative B if the report on the condition is of another state.

selectable unit (SU): a collection of new and changed modules and macros that provide added program function or hardware support. Selectable units are shipped independently of a release and are installed singly or in groups at the option of the user.

selecting: the process of requesting one or more data stations on a multipoint connection to receive data. (E)

selecting data: extracting specific or relevant information from a large body of data or the removal of certain records from the file.

selection
(1) in word processing, the choosing and assembling of blocks of recorded text for the purpose of constructing a new document. (D)
(2) addressing a terminal or a component on a selective calling circuit.
(3) the process by which a computer contacts a station to send it a message.
(4) see also *blind, lockout, polling*.

selection check: a check that verifies the choice of devices, such as registers, in the execution of an instruction. (A)

selection ratio: the ratio of the least magnetomotive force that selects a cell or core, to the maximum magnetomotive force used which is not intended to choose a cell or core.

selection-replacement approach: an approach used in the internal part of a sort program. The results of the comparisons between groups of records are stored for use later.

selection signal: a signal that indicates all the information required to establish a call. (E)

selection sort: a sort in which the items in a set are examined to find an item that fits specified criteria; this item is appended to the sorted set and removed from further consideration, and the process repeated until all items are in the sorted set. see *repeated selection sort.* (A)

selection time: time from the delivery of the proceed-to-select signal until all selection signals have been transmitted.

selective assembly: run tapes that have programs chosen by the programmer from both an input deck of new programs and a tape file of previously processed symbolic programs.

selective calling: the ability of the transmitting station to specify which of several stations on the same line is to receive a message. see also *call directing code, station selection code.*

selective combiner: a circuit or device for combining two or more diversity signals in which only the signal from the receiver output having the most desirable characteristics is selected and used.

selective cryptographic session: a cryptographic session in which an application program is allowed to specify the request units to be enciphered. cf. *mandatory cryptographic session.* see also *clear session.*

selective dissemination of information: see *SDI.*

selective dump: the dumping of the contents of one or more specified storage areas. (A) (B)

selective erase: a feature that allows the operator to revise any portion of an image on a display by removing only the offending part instead of having to redraw the entire picture less that part to be altered.

selective fading: a signal fluctuation, where the components of the signal data fade unequally.

selective listing: the output printing of data that meets various sets of predetermined criteria.

selective ringing: a means of ringing only the desired party on a multiparty line. (F)

selective trace: a tracing routine that uses only specified criteria. Typical criteria include: instruction tape (arithmetic jump), instruction location (specific region), and data location (specific region).

selector (SEL)

(1) a device for directing electrical input pulses onto one or two output lines, depending upon the presence or absence of a predetermined accompanying control pulse.

(2) in step-by-step switching systems, an automatic switching mechanism actuated by dc pulses to select one of ten groups of intraoffice circuits, after which it hunts and connects to an idle circuit in the group. (F)

selector channel (SC) (SLC): an I/O channel designed to operate with only one I/O device at a time. Once the I/O device is selected, a complete record is transferred one byte at a time. cf. *block multiplexer channel, multiplexer channel.*

selector mode: one of the two modes in which a block multiplexer channel can operate. see also *block multiplexer mode.*

selector pen: a penlike instrument

that can be attached to a display station. When a program using full-screen processing is assigned to the display station, the pen can be used to select items on the screen or to generate an attention. synonym for *light pen.*

selector pen attention: synonym for *light pen attention.*

self-adapting computer: a computer that has the ability to change its performance characteristics in response to its environment. (A) (B)

self-adapting program: a computer program that has the ability to change its performance characteristics in response to its environment. (A) (B)

self-checking code: synonym for *error detecting code.* (A)

self-checking number: a number with a suffix figure related to the figure(s) of the number, used to verify the number after it has been transferred from one medium or unit to another.

self-complementing code: a machine language where the code of the complement of a digit is the complement of the code of the digit.

self-defining delimiter: any character appearing in the first position of certain character strings in the TSO command language. A repetition of the character within the string is interpreted as a delimiter.

self-defining term: in assembler programming, an absolute term whose value is implicit in the specification of the term itself.

self-demarking code: synonym for *self-checking code.* see *error detecting code.*

self-learning: the ability of a computer to improve its capability so that it can make decisions as programmed with instructions and based on information received, new instructions received, results of calculations, or environmental changes.

self-monitoring system: a system that includes a monitor used for its own control. (E)

self-organizing computer: a computer that has the ability to make rearrangements in its internal structure. (A) (B)

self-organizing program: a computer program that has the ability to make rearrangements in its internal structure. (A) (B)

self-relative address: a relative address that uses as a base the address of the instruction in which it appears. (A) (B)

self-relative addressing: a method of addressing in which the address part of an instruction contains a self-relative address. (A) (B)

self-relocating program: a program that can be loaded into any area of main storage, and that contains an initialization routine to adjust its address constants so that it can be executed at that location.

self-resetting loop: synonymous with *self-restoring loop.*

self-restoring loop: a loop that has instructions causing all locations addressed during the loop to be restored to the condition that was obtained when the loop was entered. synonymous with *self-resetting loop.*

semanteme: an element of language that expresses a definite image or idea; for example, the word *tree.*

semantic error: an error concerned with the meaning or intent of the programmer that is his/her responsibility. The programmer is then provided with an extensive set of debugging aids for manipulating and referencing a program when in search of errors in the logic and analysis.

semantic matrix: a graphical unit for plotting the precise elements of meaning that has been ascertained from the semantic analysis of a concept in a standard conventional form.

semantics

(1) the relationships of characters or groups of characters to their meanings, independent of the manner of their interpretation and use. (B)

(2) the relationships between symbols and their meanings. (*A*)

semiautomatic message switching center: a center at which an operator routes messages according to information contained in them.

semicompiled: converted by a compiler from a source language into an object code, though not including subroutines needed by the source language program.

semiconductor (SC): a material with an electrical conductivity that is between that of a metal and an insulator: see *hole pattern, n-type, p-type.*

semiconductor laser: a small laser made from semiconducting material and used to emit beams of light down optical fibres for telecommunication activities.

semi-electronic switch: a switch whose matrix comprises some form of relay and whose common control equipment is electronic.

semiselective ringing: party-line ringing in which the ringers of only two of the main stations respond simultaneously, the differentiation being the number of rings, either one long or two short. This provides for eight-party service. (F)

sender: equipment in a switching system used to transmit and/or receive the called number to or from a distant office; usually rearranged for transmitting on a multifrequency or dial-pulse basis. Under certain conditions of trouble, a sender may remain connected to a trunk without performing its intended function; this is known as a *stuck sender.* (F)

sender attachment delay: the interval between request for service (off-hook signal) and attachment of a sender, register, or receiver at a switching system. Normally, attachment time is very short, but it can be substantial under certain traffic conditions. Since attachment delay is a mechanism by which congestion spreads in an overloaded network, it is of importance to network management. (F)

send-only service: service where the data-communication channel is able to transmit signals, but is not equipped to receive signals.

sense

(1) the study of data relative to a set of criteria.

(2) to determine the arrangement of hardware, in particular a manually set switch.

(3) to detect special signals.

(4) to read holes in cards or paper and magnetic spots on tape, drums, and so forth.

sense amplifiers: amplifiers that respond to induced voltage impulses during the read cycle.

sense light: a light turned on or off that may be interrogated by the computer in order to cause a program branch.

sense switch: see *alteration switch.*

sensing: see *mark sensing.* (A)

sensing element: the part of a unit that is directly responsive to the value of the measured quantity.

sensing signal: a signal that is often translated at the beginning of a message to initiate circuit activity at the receiving end of a circuit.

sensing station: synonym for *read station.* (A) (B)

sensitivity: the degree of response of an instruction or control device to change in the incoming signal.

sensitivity analysis: the interdependence of output values by a test of a range of input values.

sensitivity control: synonymous with *conference control.*

sensor: a device that converts measurable elements of a physical process into data meaningful to a computer.

sensor-based: pertaining to the use of sensing devices, such as transducers or sensors, to monitor a physical process.

sensor-based computer: a computer designed and programmed to receive real-time data (analog or digital) from transducers, sensors, and other data sources that monitor a physical process. The computer may also generate signals to elements that control the process. For example, the computer might receive data from a gauge or flow meter, compare the data with a predetermined standard, and then produce a signal that operates a relay, valve, or other control mechanism.

sensor-based system: an organiza-tion of components, including a computer whose primary source of input is data from sensors and whose output can be used to control the related physical process.

sentence: in COBOL, a sequence of one or more statements, the last ending with a period followed by a space.

sentence key: in word processing, a control used to process text one sentence at a time. (D)

sentinel: synonym for *flag.* (A)

separating character: synonym for *information separator.* (A) (B)

separations: the process by which telephone property costs, revenues, expenses, taxes, and reserves are assigned between interstate operations, subject to the jurisdiction of the FCC, and the intrastate operations, subject to the jurisdiction of the several state regulatory bodies. (G)

separator: synonym for *delimiter.* see *group separator, information separator.* see also *file separator character, record separator character, unit separator character.* (*A*)

SEPOL: Soil-Engineering Problem-Oriented Language.

septenary number: a number made up of more than one figure, representing a sum, where the quantity shown by each figure is based on a radix of seven. The figures used are: 0,1,2,3,4,5, and 6.

septet: a byte composed of seven binary elements. synonymous with *seven-bit byte.* (*A*) (B)

SEQ

(1) see *sequence.*

(2) see *sequential.*

sequence (SEQ)

(1) a series of items that have been sequenced. (B)

(2) an arrangement of items according to a specified set of rules; for example, items arranged alphabetically, numerically, or chronologically.

(3) deprecated term for *order*. (B)

(4) synonym for *collating sequence*. (B)

(5) see *calling sequence, collating sequence, consecutive sequence computer, pseudorandom number sequence, random number sequence, recursively defined sequence*. (*A*)

sequence by merging: to sequence by repeated splitting and merging. (A) (B)

sequence check: a check to determine whether items are arranged in a required order. (E)

sequence checking: used to prove that a set of data is arranged in either ascending or descending order prior to processing.

sequence checking routine: a routine that verifies each instruction executed and prints out certain data; for example, to print out the coded instructions with addresses, and the contents of each of several registers, or it can be designed to print out only selected data, such as transfer instructions and the quantity actually transferred.

sequence computer: see *arbitrary sequence computer, consecutive sequence computer.*

sequence control register: deprecated term for *instruction address register*. (B)

sequence control tape: a tape that contains the sequence of instructions needed for solving a problem.

sequence counter: synonymous with *sequence control register.*

sequence error: an error caused when a card is not in sequence within an object program.

sequence monitor: computer monitoring of the step-by-step actions taken by the operator during a start-up and/or shutdown of a power unit.

sequence packing: the procedure for loading the upper half of an accumulator with the first data word, shifting this into the lower half, loading the second datum, shifting, and so on, so that the three data words are packed in sequence.

sequencer

(1) a device that puts items of information into a particular order; for example, it will determine whether A is greater than, equal to, or less than B, and sort or order accordingly.

(2) a circuit that pulls information from the control store memory based upon external events or conditions.

sequence register: a register that, when activated, designates the address of the following instruction to be performed by the computer.

sequence symbol: in assembler programming, a symbol used as a branching label for conditional assembly instructions. It consists of a period, followed by one to seven alphameric characters, the first of which must be alphabetic.

sequence timer: a succession of time-delay circuits arranged so that completion of the delay in one circuit initiates a delay in the next circuit.

sequencing: ordering in a series or according to rank or time.

sequencing by merging: a technique of repeated merging, splitting, and remerging to place items into an organized arrangement.

sequencing criteria: the fields in a record that determine, or are used as the basis for determining, the sequence of records in a file.

sequencing key: synonym for *sort key.* (A)

sequential (SEQ): pertaining to the occurrence of events in time sequence, with no simultaneity or overlap of events. cf. *concurrent, consecutive, simultaneous.* (A)

sequential access

(1) the facility to obtain data from a storage device or to enter data into a storage device in such a way that the process depends on the location of that data and on a reference to data previously accessed. (A) (B)

(2) an access mode in which records are obtained from, or placed into, a file in such a way that each successive access to the file refers to the next record in the file. The order of the records is established by the programmer when creating the file.

(3) cf. *direct access.*

sequential-access method (SAM): see *basic sequential-access method.*

sequential-access storage: a storage device in which the access time depends upon the location of the data and on a reference to data previously accessed. (B)

sequential batch processing: a mode of operating a computer in which a run must be completed before another run can be started. (A)

sequential circuit: a logic device whose output values, at a given instant, depend upon its input values and internal state at that instant, and whose internal state depends upon the immediately preceding input values and the preceding internal state.

A sequential circuit can assume a finite number of internal states and may therefore be regarded, from an abstract point of view, as a finite automaton. (A) (B)

sequential collating: sequencing a group of records by comparing the key of one record with another record until equality, greater than, or less than, is determined.

sequential computer: a computer in which events occur in time sequence, with little or no simultaneity or overlap of events. (A)

sequential control: a mode of computer operation in which instructions are executed in an implicitly defined sequence until a different sequence is explicitly initiated by a jump instruction. (A) (B)

sequential data set: a data set whose records are organized on the basis of their successive physical positions, such as on magnetic tape. cf. *direct data set.*

sequential file organization: the arrangement of data records in a predetermined order, for example, alphabetically or numerically; the records can be accessed only serially by examining each record in turn until the desired one is located. Either serial or random access storage devices may be used.

sequential logic element: a device having at least one output channel and one or more input channels, all characterized by discrete states, such that the state of each output channel is determined by the previous states of the input channels. cf. *combinational logic element.* (A)

sequential operation: a mode of operation in which two or more operations are performed one after another. synonymous with *consecutive operation.* (*A*) (B)

sequential organization: records of a sequential file are arranged in the order in which they will be processed.

sequential processing: the processing of records in the order in which records are accessed.

sequential queue: the first-in, first-out method of queuing items waiting for the processor.

sequential scheduling system: a form of the job scheduler that reads one input stream and executes only one job step at a time from that input stream.

SER: see *serial.*

SERDES: serializer/deserializer. A device that serializes output from, and deserializes input to, a business machine.

SEREP: see *system error recording editing program.*

serial (SER)

(1) pertaining to the sequential performance of two or more activities in a single device. In English, the modifiers *serial* and *parallel* usually refer to devices, as opposed to *sequential* and *consecutive*, which refer to processes. (B)

(2) pertaining to the sequential or consecutive occurrence of two or more related activities in a single device or channel.

(3) pertaining to the sequential processing of the individual parts of a whole, such as the bits of a character or the characters of a word, using the same facilities for successive parts.

(4) cf. *parallel.* (*A*)

serial access

(1) the facility to obtain data from a

storage device or to enter data into a storage device in such a way that the process depends on the location of that data and on a reference to data previously accessed. (B)

(2) pertaining to the sequential or consecutive transmission of data to or from storage.

(3) cf. *direct access.*

(4) synonym for *sequential access.* (B)

serial-access storage: a storage device in which the access time depends upon the location of the data and on a reference to data previously accessed. (B)

serial adder: a digital adder in which addition is performed by adding, digit place after digit place, the corresponding digits of the operands. (A) (B)

serial addition: addition that is performed by adding, digit place after digit place, the corresponding digits of the operands. (A) (B)

serial bit transmission: a data transmission system where the bits representing a character are consecutively transmitted.

serial-by-bit: the handling of character bits in a fashion of one following another; either serially or in parallel.

serial computer

(1) a computer having a single arithmetic and logic unit.

(2) a computer, some specified characteristic of which is serial; for example, a computer that manipulates all bits of a word serially.

(3) cf. *parallel computer.* (*A*)

serial data: data transmitted sequentially, a bit at a time.

serial data controller: a digital receiver-transmitter that interfaces specific microcomputers to a serial communications channel.

serial file: a file where items are sequentially entered requiring that they also be searched sequentially.

serial flow: activities for each operation is performed singly and not at the same time other tasks are being completed.

serial input-output: a method of data transfer between a computer and a peripheral unit where data are transmitted for input to the computer or output to the unit bit by bit over a single circuit.

serialize: to change from parallel-by-byte to serial-by-bit. cf. *deserialize*.

serializer: a device that converts a space distribution of simultaneous states representing the data into a corresponding time sequence of states. synonymous with *dynamicizer*. (B) synonym for *parallel-to-serial converter*. (C)

serially reusable: the attribute of a routine that allows the same copy of the routine to be used by another task after the current use has been concluded.

serially reusable load module: a module that cannot be used by a second task until the first task has finished using it.

serially reusable resource (SRR): a logical resource or an object that can be accessed by one task at a time.

serial number: an integer denoting the position of an item in a series. (A) (B)

serial operation: pertaining to the sequential or consecutive execution of two or more operations in a single device such as an arithmetic or logic unit. deprecated term for *sequential operation*. cf. *parallel operation*. (A)

serial-parallel

(1) a combination of serial and parallel; for example, serial by character, parallel by bits comprising the character.

(2) a unit that converts a serial input into a parallel output.

serial port: an I/O port through which data is transmitted and received serially; used for communicating with terminals.

serial printer: synonymous with *character printer*.

serial processing: pertaining to the sequential or consecutive execution of two or more processes in a single device such as a channel or processing unit. cf. *parallel processing*. (A)

serial programming: programming of a computer where only one arithmetical or logical operation can be executed at a time, for example, a sequential operation.

serial sort: a sort that requires only sequential access to the items in a set. A serial sort can be performed using only serial access storage devices. (A)

serial storage: see *sequential-access storage*.

serial terminal: a terminal that transmits the elements of a signal one after the other. cf. *parallel terminal*.

serial-to-parallel converter: a device that converts a sequence of signal elements into a corresponding group of digits, all of which are presented simultaneously. synonymous with *deserializer, staticizer*. (C)

serial transfer: a transfer of data in which elements are transferred in succession over a single line.

serial transmission

(1) in data communication, transmission at successive intervals of signal elements constituting the same telegraph or data signal. The sequential elements may be transmitted with or without interruption, provided that they are not transmitted simultaneously; for example, telegraph transmission by a time-divided channel. (A)

(2) the sequential transmission of the bits constituting an entity of data over a data circuit. (E)

(3) cf. *parallel transmission.*

serial word operation: a feature of some handling units in which words are read, one following another, in groups.

series: see *Fibonacci series.*

service

(1) a customer or product-related business function such as design/manufacturing error correction, installation planning, maintenance, customer education, or programming assistance.

(2) the common-carrier facilities provided to meet customers' data transmission requirements; for example, telephone service.

serviceability: the capability to perform effective problem determination, diagnosis, and repair on a data-processing system.

service bit: a bit used in data transmission dealing with the process and not the data itself.

service bureau: an organization that packages its services so that all users have to do is to supply the input data and pay for the results.

service circuit: an auxiliary circuit connected through the switching network of a switching system to lines or trunks as required. It performs a specialized function such as dial-pulse reception. (F)

service code: a code, typically of the N11 series, such as 411 (directory assistance) and 911 (emergency), that defines a connection for a service rather than a connection to a customer. (F)

service order table: in the network control program, the list of devices on a multipoint line (or point-to-point line where the terminal has multiple components) in the order in which they are to be serviced by the network control program.

service program: a computer program that performs utility functions in support of the system. synonym for *utility program.* (A) (B)

service rate: in the system resource manager, a measure of the rate at which system resources (services) are provided to individual jobs. It is used by the installation to specify performance objectives, and used by the work-load manager to track the progress of individual jobs. Service is a linear combination of processing unit, I/O, and main storage measures that can be adjusted by the installation.

service request interrupts: interrupts used for servicing buffer channel requests. They are an internal machine function and are not directly under the control of the programmer.

service routine: synonymous with *utility routine.* (A) (B)

service seeking: the process by which the network control program interrogates devices on a start-stop or BSC multipoint line for requests to send data or for readiness to receive data.

service-seeking pause: in the network control program, a user-specified interval between successive attempts at service seeking on a line when all devices on the line are responding negatively to polling. The pause can be used to reduce the overhead associated with polling.

servomechanism

(1) an automatic device that uses feedback to govern the physical position of an element.

(2) a feedback control system in which at least one of the system signals represents mechanical motion. (*A*)

servomultiplier: an analog computer device that has a position control and is able to multiply each of several different variables by a single variable, represented by analog voltages. The multiplier is used as an input signal to a mechanism that turns shafts.

session

(1) a connection between two stations that allows them to communicate. (E)

(2) the period of time during which a user of a terminal can communicate with an interactive system; usually, the elapsed time between log on and log off.

(3) see *batch session, work session*.

session control (SC): an RU category used for requests and responses exchanged between the session control components of a session and for session activation/deactivation requests and responses.

session layer: in open systems architecture, the layer that provides serv-

ices used to bind and unbind elements of a session and to maintain an orderly dialog (requests/responses) between them. (E)

session seed: synonym for *initial chaining value*.

set (S)

(1) a finite or infinite number of objects of any kind, of entities, or of concepts, that have a given property or properties in common. (B)

(2) to cause a counter to take the state corresponding to a specified number. cf. *reset (1)*. (*A*) (B)

(3) to put all or part of a data-processing device into a specified state, usually other than that denoting zero. (B)

(4) see *alphabetic character set, alphabetic-coded character set, alphanumeric character set, alphanumeric-coded character set, card set, character set, coded character set, code set, empty set, instruction set, machine instruction set, numeric character set, numeric-coded character set, universal set. (A)*

(5) see *data set*.

set breakpoint: a user debug command designed to create the setting of a breakpoint in a memory location. At program execution, this breakpoint, when encountered, causes a temporary program suspension and a transfer of control to the system debug routine.

set point: synonymous with *input reference*.

set symbol: in assembler programming, a variable symbol used to communicate values during conditional assembly processing.

set theory: in mathematics, the study of the rules for combining groups, sets, and elements.

settlements: procedures established by the telephone common carriers for distributing joint interstate and intrastate revenues between Bell System and Independent Telephone Companies after reimbursement of expenses, in proportion to their investment. (G)

settling time: time needed for a dot to move to a new point on the screen and stay still without vascillating. It is an important specification for displays made from dots. Dot writing time and settling time, together, determine the maximum rate at which one can produce a clean, stored display using binary data.

setup

(1) in a computer that consists of an assembly of individual computing units, the arrangement of interconnections between the units, and the adjustments needed for the computer to operate upon a particular problem. (B)

(2) an arrangement of data or devices to solve a particular problem. (A) (B)

(3) the preparation of a computing system to perform a job or job step. Setup is usually performed by an operator and often involves performing routine functions, such as mounting tape reels and loading card decks.

setup diagram: a diagram specifying a given computer setup. (A) (B)

setup time: the time required by an operator preparing a computing system to perform a job or job step.

seven-bit byte: synonym for *septet*. (A) (B)

several-for-one: a transaction consid-ered to mean the creation of a number of machine instructions from one program instruction. This is an indication of the various types of software.

severity code: a code assigned to an error detected in a source module.

sexadecimal

(1) pertaining to a selection, choice, or condition that has sixteen possible different values or states. (B)

(2) pertaining to a fixed-radix numeration system having a radix of sixteen. synonymous with *hexadecimal*. (A) (B)

sextet: a byte composed of six binary elements. synonymous with *six-bit byte*. (A) (B)

SF

(1) see *scale factor*.

(2) see *single-frequency signaling*.

SFT: see *shift*.

SGDF: see *supergroup distribution frame*.

shading: in computer graphics, emphasizing a given display group by changing the attitudes of all the other display groups in the same display field. (E)

Shannon: in information theory, a unit of logarithmic measures of information equal to the decision content of a set of two mutually exclusive events expressed by the logarithm to base two; for example, the decision content of a character set of eight characters equals three Shannons. synonymous with *information content binary unit*. (A) (B)

shaping network: a network inserted in a circuit for improving the wave shape of the signals.

shared: pertaining to the availability

of a resource for more than one use at a time.

shared batch area (SBA): a temporary storage area in the store controller where all data received from, or transmitted to, the host processor is stored while waiting to be operated upon.

shared disc: a magnetic disc that may be used for information storage by two or more systems at the same time.

shared file: a direct-access device that may be used by two systems at the same time; a shared file may link two systems.

shared logic: in word processing, an arrangement in which two or more proximate work stations share common facilities. (D)

shared-logic word-processing equipment: word-processing equipment in which the resources of a processing unit and storage devices are shared between two or more work stations. (D)

shared main storage multiprocessing: a mode of operation in which two processing units have access to all of main storage.

shared read-only system residence disk: a system residence disk that is tailored so that most of the system residence information is read only and accessible to all relevant virtual machines, leaving a relatively smaller private read/write system disk that must be dedicated to each virtual machine. This technique can substantially reduce the disk requirements of an installation by avoiding needless duplication of disk packs by virtual machines that use the same operating system. see also *saved sys-*

tem.

shared resource: in word processing, an arrangement in which two or more work stations share common facilities. (D)

shared storage: the ability to share core storage between two computers, where either machine can insert information into storage, and either device can access the data and use it.

shared system: see *shared read-only system residence disk.*

shared virtual area (SVA): an area located in the highest addresses of virtual storage. It can contain a system directory list (SDL) of frequently used phases, resident programs that can be shared between partitions.

sharing: interleaved time use of a device; a method of activity where a computer facility is shared by several users concurrently.

sheet feeder: in word processing, a device attached to a printer to automatically feed out sheets of paper or forms from one or more input drawers and to remove the finished printed sheets to an output drawer. (D)

Sheffer stroke: synonym for *NAND.* (A)

shelf life: the length of time a document, or unit, will remain serviceable to users.

SHF
(1) see *shift.*
(2) see *super high frequency.*

shield: a conducting housing placed around a magnetic field.

shielding: in computer graphics, blanking of all portions of display elements falling within some specified region. synonymous with *reverse* *clipping.* cf. *scissoring.* (E)

shift (SFT) (SHF)

(1) the converted movement of some or all of the characters of a word each by the same number of character places in the direction of a specified end of the word. (A) (B)

(2) to move data to the right or left.

(3) see *arithmetic shift, end-around shift, logical shift.* (A)

shift character: a control character that determines the alphabetic/ numeric shift of character codes in a message.

shift down modem: a modem which yields a change from a higher to a lower bit rate.

shift-in character (SI): a code extension character, used to terminate a sequence that has been introduced by the shift-out character, that makes effective the graphic characters of the standard character set. (A) (B)

shifting: the arithmetic process where each movement of value to the left multiplies a number by the radix in use, and each movement to the right divides the number by the radix. Shifting can also feed a process for other radix points.

shift-out character (SO): a code extension character that substitutes for the graphic characters of the standard character set an alternative set of graphic characters upon which agreement has been reached or that has been designated using code extension procedures. (A) (B)

shift pulse: a drive pulse that initiates a shift.

shift register (SB): a register in which shifts are performed. (A) (B)

shop: see *closed shop, open shop.*

short block: a block of F-format data that contains fewer logical records that are specified for the block.

short card: a special-purpose paper card that is shorter in length than a general-purpose paper card; for example, a 51 column card. (A)

short-code dialing: synonym for *short dialing.*

short dialing: dialing by means of a one-digit code. synonymous with *short-code dialing.*

shortest word: a word of the shortest length that a computer can utilize, and which is most often half of the full length word.

short instruction: the use of an index specification in a FORTRAN READ or WRITE statement.

short instruction format: a standard length, that is, one word, instruction as opposed to a long instruction. Most instructions are of this type.

short out: made inactive by the interposition of a low resistance path around a unit.

short-term storage: data stored in core memory for a brief time period.

short word: a fixed word of lesser length within a system that is capable of handling words of two different lengths. Often referred to as a half-word because the length is exactly the half-length of a full word.

shoulder tap: a technique that enables one processing unit to communicate with another processing unit.

show: a console command giving the status of a system function.

show D: indicate disks currently up on specific spindles.

show P: display which jobs are running and in which partition at a given time.

show T: indicate tapes being held by specific jobs.

shutoff sequence (SO): in loop operation, eight consecutive zero bits sent around the loop to tell any station that may be transmitting to stop transmitting immediately.

SHY: see *syllable hyphen character.*

SI
(1) see *shift-in character.* (A) (B)
(2) single instruction.
(3) see *swap-in.*
(4) System International d'Unites, the international metric system.

SIAM: The Society for Industrial and Applied Mathematics.

sideband: a frequency band above and below the carrier frequency, produced as a result of modulation.

side circuit: a circuit arrangement for deriving a phantom circuit. In four-wire circuits, the two wires associated with the "GO" channel form one "side circuit," and those associated with the "return" channel form another. see also *phantom circuit.*

side-circuit loading coil: a loading coil for introducing a desired amount of inductance in a side circuit and a minimum amount of inductance in the associated phantom circuit.

side-circuit repeat coil: synonymous with *side-circuit repeating coil.*

side-circuit repeating coil: a repeating coil that operates simultaneously as a transformer at a terminal of a side circuit and as a device for superimposing one side of a phantom circuit on that side circuit. synonymous with *side-circuit repeat coil.*

side effect: the change in the value of a variable within a routine resulting from assignments outside the routine. (E)

side lobe: a spurious response of an antenna which causes signal radiation or pickup in an undesired direction. Excessive side lobes reduce antenna efficiency, and can increase interferences from other communications systems.

side stable relay: a polar relay that remains in the last signaled contact position.

sifting sort: synonym for *bubble sort.* (A)

SIG: see *signal.*

sight check: a check performed by sighting through the holes of two or more aligned punched cards toward a source of light to verify the punching; for example, to determine if a hole has been punched in a corresponding punch position on all cards in a card deck. (A)

sigma memory: deprecated term for *sigma storage.*

sigma storage: on a calculator, the facility for accumulating the results of a series of calculations. (D)

sign (S): the symbol which distinguishes positive from negative numbers.

signal (SIG)
(1) a variation of a physical quantity, used to convey data. (E)
(2) a wave used to convey information such as voice, television, data, or information for network control. (F)
(3) see *start signal, stop signal.*

signal conditioning
(1) any manipulation of transducer or transmitter outputs to make them suitable for input to the computer peripheral units.
(2) operations such as linearizing and square-root extraction performed within the computer.

signal conversion equipment: in data communications, those portions of the data circuit-terminating equipment that transform (such as modulate or shape) the data signals exchanged across the interface into signals suitable for transmission through associated communication media, or that transform (such as demodulate, slice, regenerate) the received line signals into data signals suitable for presentation to the data terminal equipment.

signal converter: a device in which the input and output signals are formed according to the same code but not according to the same type of electrical modulation.

signal distance: the number of digit positions in which the corresponding digits of two binary words of the same length are different. synonymous with *hamming distance.* (A)

signal distributor (SD): equipment in electronic switching systems to deliver signals from a central control to other circuits. It converts the central control output to high-power, long-duration pulses to operate relays. (F)

signal element: in digital transmission, a signal within a time interval during which the intended state, or symbol, is recognized (i.e., distinguished from other possible symbols). In a band-limited channel, this time interval has a lower bound that must be met to detect the proper symbol without interference from other signal elements. Systems designed to make efficient use of channel bandwidth typically use a signal element occupying an interval of just this length. see *symbol.* (F)

signal-enabling: a means of permitting an operation to occur.

signaling: the transmission of address (pulsing), supervision, or other switching information between stations and switching systems and between switching systems, including any information required for billing. (F)

signaling in band: signaling that uses frequencies within the intelligence band of a channel. cf. *signaling out of band.*

signaling out of band: signaling that uses frequencies outside the intelligence band. Also used to indicate the use of a part of a channel bandwidth provided by the medium such as a carrier channel, but denied to the speech or intelligence path by filters, resulting in a reduction of the effective available bandwidth. cf. *signaling in band.*

signaling rate: see *data-signaling rate.*

signal inhibiting: a way of preventing an operation from occurring.

signal level: an OCR term that relates to the amplitude of the electronic response which occurs from the contrast ratio between the area of a printed character and the area of a document background.

signal processor (SP): an equipment unit for electronic switching systems for use in larger offices to perform repetitive time-consuming input-output tasks for central control. (F)

signal ratio

(1) the comparison of light seen by a photosensor when the object to be detected blocks the beam, to the light seen when the beam is not blocked.

(2) more specifically, the comparison of photocell resistance when the

sensor is dark to when it is illuminated.

signal regeneration: signal transformation that restores a signal so that it conforms to its original specification. (A) (B)

signal shaping: synonym for *signal transformation.* (A) (B). cf. *key transformation.*

signal standardization: the generation of a signal from another signal; where the generated signal meets conditions of amplitude, shape, and timing.

signal strength: a measure of the amplitude of the signal obtained from reading units such as photocells, magnetic tape read heads, and so forth.

signal-to-noise ratio (S/N): the relative power of the signal to the noise in a channel.

signal transfer point (STP:) in CCIS, a message switching system that permits signaling messages to be sent from one switching system to another by way of one or more other offices at which STPs are located. It reduces the number of CCIS data links required to serve a network. (F)

signal transformation: the action of modifying one or more characteristics of a signal, such as its maximum value, shape, or timing. synonymous with *signal shaping.* (*A*) (B). see also *key transformation, transform.*

sign and currency symbol characters: in PL/1, the picture specification character S, +, −, and $. These can be used (a) as static characters, in which case they are specified only once in a picture specification and appear in the associated data item in the position in

which they have been specified, or (b) as drifting characters, in which case they are specified more than once (as a string in a picture specification) but appear in the associated data item at most once, immediately to the left of the significant portion of the data item.

signature analysis: a way of isolating digital logic faults at the component level. Although considered most useful in servicing microprocessor-based products, the technique is applicable to all digital systems. It involves the tracing of signals and the conversion of lengthy bit streams into four-digit hexadecimal signatures.

signature testing: the comparison of the actual output digital signatures, such as transition counts, with the expected correct signatures recorded from a known-good unit.

sign bit: a bit or a binary element that occupies a sign position and indicates the algebraic sign of the number represented by the numeral with which it is associated. (A) (B)

sign character: a character that occupies a sign position and indicates the algebraic sign of the number represented by the numeral with which it is associated. (A) (B)

sign check indicator: an indicator set, according to specification, on a change of sign or when a sign is either positive or negative.

sign condition: in COBOL, a statement that the algebraic value of a data item is less than, equal to, or greater than zero. It may be true or false.

sign digit: a digit that occupies a sign position and indicates the algebraic sign of the number represented by the numeral with which it is associated. (A) (B)

signed binary: a binary representation of signed integer numbers setting aside one bit, often the high-order or leftmost bit, to show the sign of the number.

signed field: a field that has a character in it to designate its algebraic sign.

signed packed decimal: representation of a decimal value by two adjacent digits in a byte. The rightmost four bits of the field contain a sign. see also *packed decimal.*

significance: synonym for *weight.* (A) (B)

significant conditions of a modulation: distinct conditions, assumed by the appropriate unit of the sending apparatus, serving to characterize the variety of the elements of the alphabetic telegraph signals to be transmitted.

significant conditions of a restitution: distinct conditions, assumed by the appropriate unit of the receiving apparatus, serving to characterize the variety of the elements of the alphabetic telegraph signals received.

significant digit: in a numeral, a digit that is needed for a given purpose; in particular, a digit that must be kept to preserve a given accuracy or a given precision. (A) (B)

significant digit arithmetic: a method of making calculations using a modified form of a floating-point representation system in which the number of significant digits in the result is determined with reference to the number of significant digits in the operands, the operation performed, and the degree of precision available. (A) (B)

significant figure: deprecated term for *significant digit.* (A) (B)

significant interval: a time interval during which a given significant condition according to the code and the signal to be transmitted is, or should be, transmitted.

sign magnitude: a scheme for binary representation where the most critical bit is used for the sign and the rest of the number represents the absolute value.

sign-off: the closing instruction to the computer, which terminates communication with the system.

sign-on: the opening instruction to the computer, which begins communications with the system.

sign position: a position, normally located at one end of a numeral, that contains an indicator denoting the algebraic sign of the number represented by the numeral. (A) (B)

silicon: an element that is a semiconductor and when mixed with steel or iron to provide magnetic properties, is used for transistors in metal oxide semiconductor technology.

silicon chip: a wafer of silicon providing a semiconductor base for a number of electrical circuits. see also *chip.*

silicon-gate: pertaining to metal oxide semiconductor technology applying silicon as the semiconductor for the gate of the transistor.

silicon on sapphire: see *SOS.*

Silicon Valley: the area near Sunnyvale, in the Santa Clara Valley of California where numerous semiconductor manufacturers are located.

SIM: see *simulator.*

simple buffering: a technique for controlling buffers in such a way that the buffers are assigned to a single data control block and remain so assigned until the data control block is closed.

simple condition: in COBOL, an expression that can have two values, and causes the object program to select between alternate paths of control, depending on the value found. The expression can be either true or false.

simple parameter: in PL/1, a parameter for which no storage-class attribute is specified; it may represent an argument of any storage class, but only the current generation of a controlled argument.

simplex: pertaining to a circuit performing one-way operations only.

simplex channel: a channel that allows transmission in one direction only.

simplex communication: synonym for *one-way communication*.

simplexed circuit: a two-wire circuit from which a simplex circuit is derived. The two-wire circuit and the simplex circuit may be used simultaneously. see *half-duplex circuit*.

simplex system: a system configuration that excludes standby equipment.

simplex transmission

(1)   transmission in one preassigned direction only. (E)

(2)   a method of operating a communications circuit so that transmission is in only one direction. (F)

(3)   a method of deriving a conductor by using the conductors of a pair in parallel. Normal use of the pair is retained. (F)

SIMSCRIPT: a programming language used for discrete simulation. (E)

SIMUL: see *simultaneous*.

simulate

(1)   to represent certain features of the behavior of a physical or abstract system by the behavior of another system; for example, to represent a physical phenomenon by means of operations performed by a computer or to represent the operations of a computer by those of another computer. (B)

(2)   to imitate one system with another, primarily by software, so that the imitating system accepts the same data, executes the same computer programs, and achieves the same results as the imitated system.

(3)   cf. *emulate*. (A)

simulated attention: a function that allows terminals without attention keys to interrupt processing. The terminal is queried periodically for a specified character string. see also *attention interruption*.

simulation: the representation of selected characteristics of the behavior of one physical or abstract system by another system; for example, the representation of physical phenomena by means of operations performed by a computer system, the representation of operations of a computer system by those of another computer system. (E) cf. *emulation*. see *real-time simulation*. (A)

simulator (SIM): a device, data-processing system, or computer program that represents certain features of the behavior of a physical or abstract system. (B) see *computer simulator*. (A)

simultaneity: to permit central processor functions to occur at the same time as input-output activities.

simultaneous (SIMUL): pertaining to the occurrence of two or more events at the same instant of time. (B) see also *consecutive, sequential.* cf. *concurrent.* (*A*)

simultaneous access: synonymous with *parallel access.*

simultaneous computer: a computer that contains a separate unit to perform each portion of the entire computation concurrently, the units being interconnected in a way determined by the computation; at different times in a run, a given interconnection carries signals representing different values of the same variable; for example, a differential analyzer. (A) (B)

simultaneous input-output: in word processing, the process in which some word processors allow a new document to be typed (or an old document to be revised) while another document is being printed. sometimes called *background printing.*

simultaneous operation: a mode of operation in which two or more events occur at the same instant of time. (A) (B)

simultaneous processing: the performance of two or more data-processing tasks at the same instant of time. cf. *concurrent processing.*

simultaneous transmission: transmission of control characters of data in one direction while information is being received in the other direction. cf. *nonsimultaneous transmission.*

singing: sound caused by unstable oscillations on the line.

single address: pertaining to an instruction format containing one address part. synonymous with *one address.* (*A*)

single-address code: synonymous with *single-address instruction.*

single-address instruction: an instruction format containing one operand address only. synonymous with *single-address code.*

single-address message: a message that is to be delivered to only one destination.

single board computer: a complete computer on one printed circuit board.

single circuit: a telegraph circuit capable of nonsimultaneous two-way communications. see *half-duplex circuit.*

single-cycle key: a push button on printers that when pressed, causes an additional line to be printed despite an end-of-form indication.

single-domain network: a network that has only one host node. (E)

single error: an erroneous bit, preceded and followed by at least one correct bit.

single-frequency (SF) signaling: a method of conveying dial-pulse and supervisory signals from one end of a trunk or line to the other, using the presence or absence of a single specified frequency. A 2600-Hz tone is commonly used.

single-length working: representing binary numbers so that the value of each number will be contained in a single word.

single-office exchange: an exchange served by a single central office.

single-operand addressing: where one portion of the instruction word specifies a register; the second portion provides information for locating the operand, that is, clear, increment, test, and so on.

single-operand instruction: an instruction that contains a reference to a single register, memory location, or machine.

single operation: see *half-duplex*.

single-pass program: a program that results in the production of the solution to a problem or following one run, of one computer word to represent a number in accordance with the required precision.

single-point ground: a special grounding system, required for electronic switching center, that electrically isolates the equipment associated with the telephone switching system from the equipment in other areas of the building, the building steel, superstructure, and so on, except at one point.

single precision: pertaining to the use of one computer word to represent a number in accordance with the required position. (A) (B)

single quote mark: a special FORTRAN character used to enclose literal messages.

single recording medium word-processing equipment: word-processing equipment that can operate on or from only one recording medium. (D)

single setup: a method of operating a computer where each step is performed in response to a single manual operation.

single-sheet feeding: feeding of separate sheets of paper rather than roll or fanfolded form.

single-shot circuit: logic elements or circuits that carry out signal standardization. synonymous with *one-shot circuit*.

single-sideband (SSB) transmission: that type of carrier transmission in which one sideband is transmitted, and the other is suppressed. The carrier wave may be either transmitted or suppressed.

single sided: a method of disk storage utilizing one side of a disk.

single-step: pertaining to a method of operating a computer in which each step is performed in response to a single manual operation. (A)

single-step operation: a mode of operating a computer in which a single computer instruction or part of a computer instruction is executed in response to an external signal. synonymous with *step-by-step operation*. (A) (B)

single vertical key: a push button on a printer that produces an additional printed line for indication.

single-wire line: a telecommunication line that uses the ground as one side of the circuit.

sink: see *data sink, message sink*. (A)

sink current: the current drive potential for a specific logic group.

SIS: see *scientific instruction set*.

site: the physical or geographical location of a system such as a room, building, or building complex. Colocated systems are typically interconnected by local privately owned communications facilities.

six-bit byte: synonym for *sextet*. (A) (B)

six-digit translation: the operation of interpreting six digits, commonly comprising a three-digit numbering plan area code followed by a three-digit central office code, as routing control for the switching of calls. (F)

16K RAM: see *64K RAM*.

64K RAM: random-access memory that stores more than 64,000 bits of computer data on a tiny slice of silicon, four times as much as the 16K

RAM—the previous generation chip. see also *RAM*.

sizing: evaluating the facilities and resources required to achieve an identified level of service or to yield a solution to a specific problem.

SK: see *skip*.

skeletal code: a set of instructions in which some parts such as addresses must be completed or specified in detail each time the set is used. (A) (B)

skew: the angular deviation of recorded binary characters from a line perpendicular to the reference edge of a data medium. (B)

skew character: a form of incorrect registration in optical character recognition.

skewed overloads: abnormal loads that greatly exceed average business day demands, and are usually distributed quite differently geographically; for example, snow-storm calling between city and suburbs. (F)

skew failure: a situation when a document in machine-readable form cannot be read because it is not properly aligned in the reading unit.

skip (SK)
(1) to ignore one or more instructions in a sequence of instructions.
(2) to pass over one or more positions on a data medium; for example, to perform one or more line feed operations. (A)
(3) in word processing, the feature of a machine that allows recorded text to be bypassed. (D)
(4) see also *paper throw*. (A)

skip code: a functional code that instructs the machine to skip certain predetermined fields in memory.

skip flag: a one bit, in a specific position, that causes bytes to be skipped until the count equals zero, thus permitting the computer to ignore portions of the input record to the memory.

skip instruction: an instruction having no impact other than directing the processor to proceed to another instruction designated in the storage portion.

skip key: in word processing, a control that initiates the skip process. synonymous with *access button*. (D)

skipping: advancing paper through a printer without printing on it.

SL: see *standard label*.

slab: the crystal from which slices are cut.

slack bytes: in COBOL, bytes inserted between data items or records to ensure correct alignment of some numeric items. Slack bytes contain no meaningful data. In some cases, they are inserted by the compiler; in others, it is the responsibility of the programmer to insert them. The "synchronized" clause instructs the compiler to insert slack bytes when they are needed for proper alignment. Slack bytes between records are inserted by the programmer.

slave computer: a backup system consisting of a second computer that performs the same steps of the same programs executed by the master computer. If the master computer fails or malfunctions, the slave computer takes over without interruption of operation. see *fail-safe*, *system*, *volatile memory*. cf. *rescue dump*, *satellite processor*.

slave mode: the mode of computer operation where most of the basic controls affecting the computer's condition are protected from the program.

slave station: in basic mode link control, the data station that is selected by a master station to receive data. (E)

slave tube: a cathode-ray tube connected to another CRT so that both units will perform in the same way.

SLC: see *selector channel.*

SLDR: see *system loader.*

sleeping sickness: the failure of a transistor resulting from moisture accumulating on the base.

slew rate: signal response rate.

SLIB:
   (1) see *source library.*
   (2) see *subsystem library.*

slice: those parts of a wave form lying inside two given amplitude limits on the same side of the zero axis. see also *time slice.*

slicer: a circuit that effectively amplifies a slice.

slip: an alteration of a digital information system consisting of an advance or delay of all following signal elements by an amount equal to or greater than a signal element. This causes one or more signal elements to be missed or to be repeated. (F)

slope equalizer: a device or circuit used to achieve a specified slope in a transmission line.

slot
   (1) a portion of a transmission frame that is sent around a loop.
   (2) a position in a device used for removable storage media.

slot antenna: a radiating element formed by a slot in a conducting surface or in the wall of a waveguide.

slow death: the gradual deterioration of the characteristics of a unit, especially a transistor.

slow storage: a device or storage modem with access time more lengthy in relation to the speeds of arithmetic activities of the computer and more lengthy when compared to other faster access peripheral devices.

slow time scale: synonym for *extended time scale.* (A)

SLSI: super large-scale integration; more than 100,000 transistors for each chip.

SLT: see *solid logic technology.*

SLU: see *secondary logic unit.*

small scale integration (SSI): the technology holding one to ten gates per unit.

"smart" machines: computers that assist plant managers to optimize scheduling by turning out different products on different days or even different hours, thus evolving a parts-on-demand facility.

smart terminal: a terminal with processing potential that functions without the power of the computer to which it is attached.

S-mod records: in COBOL, records that span physical blocks. Records may be fixed or variable in length. Blocks may contain one or more segments. A segment may contain one record or a portion of a record. Each segment contains a segment-length field control field indicating whether or not it is the first, last, only, or an intermediate segment of the record. Each block contains a block-length field.

smoke test: the moment when a unit is turned on for the first time. If there is no smoke it is assumed the device is functioning properly.

smooth: to apply procedures that decrease or eliminate rapid fluctuations in data. (A)

smoothed data: statistical data (as in a curve or graph) freed from irregularities by ignoring random occurrences or by a process of continual averaging.

smooth line: see *nonloaded lines.*

SMPL: see *sample.*

smudge: in OCR, the displacement of ink under shear beyond the edges of a printed character.

S/N: see *signal-to-noise ratio.*

snapshot debug: a debugging approach where the programmer specifies the beginning and end points of segments needed for a snapshot dump.

snapshot dump

(1) a dynamic dump of the contents of one or more specified storage areas. (B)

(2) a selective dynamic dump performed at various points in a machine run. (*A*)

snapshot program: a trace program that produces output data only for selected instruction or for selected conditions. (A) (B)

snapshots: the capture of the total state of a machine (real or simulated)—the memory contents, registers, flags, and so on.

SNBU: see *switched network backup.*

sneak current: a leakage current that gets into telephone circuits from other circuits. It is too weak to cause immediate damage, but can produce harmful heating effects if allowed to continue.

sniffing: an error detection and correction method in computing.

SNOBOL: a programming language designed for string processing and pattern matching. (E)

SO

(1) see *shift-out character.* (A) (B)

(2) see *shutoff sequence.*

socket: the end of a circuit, able to receive a plug to complete the circuit. synonym for *jack.*

SOF: see *start-of-format control.*

SOFT: see *software.*

soft computer programs: see *soft software.*

soft copy: in computer graphics, a nonpermanent display image that cannot be separated from a display device; for example, data displayed on a CRT display device. (E)

soft error: deprecated term for *transient error.*

soft fail: synonymous with *fail soft.*

soft keyboard: the display represented on a terminal screen that has been arranged in the form of a keyboard.

soft sector: the portion of a disk marked by information written on the disk; used by the disk controller to locate particular areas of the disk.

soft-sectored disk system: a disk format in which the beginning of every sector is decided by the user and is recorded on the disk.

soft-sector formatting: the standard diskette, designed for use with a format where the sector information is prerecorded on the diskette during the initialize operation. In this case, a single hole on the diskette acts as a reference point. The format in which the sector information is prerecorded on the diskette is referred to as the *soft-sectored format.*

soft software: as contrasted with software that takes a general purpose computer and adapts it to a particular task, soft software takes a standard software product and adapts it to a particular user.

software (S) (SOFT) (SW)
(1) programs, procedures, rules, and any associated documentation pertaining to the operation of a computer system. (E)
(2) in word processing, computer programs, procedures, rules, and any associated documentation concerned with the operation of a word-processing system. (D)
(3) cf. *hardware*.

software-compatible: pertaining to a computer that can accept and run programs prepared for other computers.

software controls: programmed controls that monitor a computer system; for example, to detect and possibly to correct errors. (E)

software documentation: program listings and/or documentation consisting of technical manuals describing the operation and use of programs.

software driver: a series of instruction, followed by the computer to reformat data for transfer to and from a specific peripheral unit.

software emulation: software programs found in microprograms that allow one computer to execute the machine-language code of another computer, to minimize reprogramming during conversion of one system to another or for use in a development system.

software house: a company that offers software support service to users.

software maintenance: the task of keeping software up-to-date and working properly.

software monitor: a software package, usually stored on PROMs that allows the computer to operate with a fundamental interactive intelligence.

software package: the subroutine programs that are sold by the computer manufacturer, or from software firms, or individuals who write software programs.

software prototyping: software development providing program assembly, on-line execution, and debugging.

software recording facility (SRF): a facility used by functional recovery routines to write system error records.

software stack: an area in read/write memory set aside under program control. An on-chip hardware stack provides increased performance.

software support system: executes the object program as a microprocessor. The programmer can check to determine if the original source program performs the functions accurately.

software tools: computer programs able to write other programs.

software trace mode: a mode where the program stops and the internal status of the microprocessor is made available to the outside world wherever breakpoint conditions are met. In addition to the mnemonic instructions and the memory addresses, the user views register contents, program counter location, stack pointer, and condition codes or flags. Breakpoints can be set at each instruction if so desired. The major advantage of this mode is the depth of insight it gives into program operation; it is fully interactive, enabling the user to alter register contents, make source code changes to correct program errors, reassemble programs, and rerun to test corrections.

SOH: see *start-of-heading character*. (A) (B)

solder mask: a printed circuit board technique where everything is coated with plastic except the contacts that will be soldered.

solid error: an error that always occurs when a particular device is used.

solid logic technology (SLT): miniaturized modules used in computers, that result in faster circuitry because of reduced distance for current to travel.

solid state (SS): see *solid state component*.

solid state component: a component whose operation depends on the control of electric or magnetic phenomena in solids; for example, a transistor, crystal diode, ferrite code. (A)

solid state computer: a computer that uses solid state, or semiconductor, components. synonymous with *second generation computer*.

solution check: a solution to a problem obtained by independent means to verify a computer solution.

SOM: see *start-of-message code*.

sonic delay line: synonym for *acoustic delay line*. (A)

sort (sorting)
(1) to segregate items into groups according to specified criteria. Sorting involves ordering, but need not involve sequencing, for the groups may be arranged in an arbitrary order. (B)
(2) the operation of sorting.
(3) to arrange a set of items according to keys which are used as a basis for determining the sequence of the items; for example, to arrange the records of a personnel file into alphabetical sequence by using the employee names as sort keys. (A)
(4) in word processing, rearrangement of blocks of text in groups according to specific instructions.
(5) synonym for *order*.
(6) see *balanced merge sort, bubble sort, exchange sort, external sort, insertion sort, internal sort, merge sort, multipass sort, oscillating sort, polyphase sort, repeated selection sort, selection sort, serial sort, sifting sort, tournament sort, unbalanced merge sort*.

sort blocking factor: in sorting, the number of data records to be placed in each block.

sorter
(1) a device that deposits punched cards in pockets selected according to the hole patterns in the cards. (B)
(2) a person, device, or computer routine that sorts.
(3) deprecated term for *sort program*. (A) (B)

sorting: see *sort*.

sorting control field: a continuous group of characters within a record that forms all or a portion of the control word.

sorting item: the basic element of a file where the sorting of the file constitutes the reordering of file records.

sorting program: synonym for *sort program*. (A) (B)

sorting rewind time: elapsed time used by a sort/merge program for restoring intermediate and final tape to its original position.

sorting scratch tape: tape or tapes used to store intermediate-pass data during a sort program.

sorting sequencing key: the field in a record that determines, or is used as a basis for determining, the sequence of records in a file.

sorting string: a group of sequential records, normally stored in auxiliary computer storage, that is, disk, tape.

sorting variable-length records: denumerable file elements for which the number of words, characters, bits, fields, is not constant.

sorting work tape: a tape used to store intermediate-pass data during a sort program.

sort key

(1) a key used as a basis for determining the sequence of items in a set.
(2) one or more keys within an item, used as a basis for determining the sequencing of items in a set. synonymous with *sequencing key*. (A)

sort/merge generator: custom programs for sorting files of data.

sort/merge program: a processing program that can be used to sort or merge records in a prescribed sequence.

sort pass: during the execution of a sort program, a single processing of all items of a set for the purpose of reducing the number of strings of items and increasing the number of items per string. (A)

sort program: a computer program that sorts items of data. synonymous with *sorting program*. (A) (B)

sort selection: in word processing, selection of storage addresses by means of predetermined codes. (E)

sort utility: the activity performed by a program, often a utility package, in which items in a data file are arranged or rearranged in a logical or specifically defined sequence as des-

ignated by a key word or field in each item in the file.

SOS: silicon on sapphire. The layers of material of units that achieve bipolar speeds by insulating the circuit components from each other.

sounder: a telegraph receiving instrument in which an electromagnet attracts an armature each time a pulse arrives. The armature makes an audible sound as it hits against its stops at the beginning and end of each current impulse, and the intervals between these sounds are translated by the operator from code into the received message.

source (S) (SRC): see *data source, message source.* (A)

source address: in systems with source-destination architecture, the address of the unit or memory location from which data is being transferred.

source code: the program in a language prepared by a programmer. This code cannot be directly executed but first must be compiled into object code.

source code compatibility: pertaining to a system where changes to the system do not require changes to a user's source code, but may require a recompile or assembly of the source code. cf. *object code compatibility.*

source computer: in COBOL, the name of the environment division paragraph where the computer upon which the source program is to be compiled is described.

source data

(1) the data provided by the user of a data-processing system.
(2) the data contained in a source

program or source module.

source data acquisition: direct entry of data into a computer at the point where the data originates.

source data automation: see *SDA*.

source data card: a card that contains manually or mechanically recorded data that is to be subsequently punched into the same card. (A)

source deck: synonymous with *source pack*.

source document: a form containing data that are eventually processed by a computer.

source editor: a program that facilitates the entry and modification of the source code into a computer system for later translation, on-line storage, off-line storage, or listing on a printer for later reference.

source file: a CRAM (Card Random-Access Memory) deck, disk, drum, or magnetic tape that holds the information file used as input to a computer run.

source key: in PL/1, a key referred to in a record-oriented transmission statement that identifies a particular record within a direct-access data set.

source language: a language from which statements are translated. (A) (B)

source language debugging: debugging information requested by the user and displayed by the system in a form consistent with the source programming language.

source language translation: the translation of a program to a target program to machine language the instructions being equivalent in the source program and to the automatic or problem-oriented language, the

translating process completed by the device under the control of a translator program or compiler.

source library (SLIB)

(1) a means for specifying computer processing; translated into object language by a compiler or assembler.

(2) a compiler language, for example, FORTRAN, from which machine-language instructions flow by the use of translation routines or compilers.

(3) the language in which the input to the FORTRAN processor is prepared.

source machine: a device able to carry out the compilation of source code. cf. *object-computer*.

source macrodefinition: in assembler programming, a macrodefinition included in a source module. A source macrodefinition can be entered into a program library; it then becomes a library macrodefinition.

source module: the source statements that constitute the input to a language translator for a particular translation.

source module library: a partitioned data set that is used to store and retrieve source modules. see also *load module library, object module library*.

source operand register: a register in some systems that contains the last source operand of a double operand instruction. The high byte may not be correct if the source is a forbidden mode.

source pack: a stack of punched cards with instructions in source code. synonymous with *source deck*.

source program: a computer program expressed in a source language (B) cf. *object program*. (A)

source recording: the recording of data in machine-readable documents, such as punched cards, punched paper tape, or magnetic tape. Once in this form, the data may be transmitted, processed, or reused without manual processing.

source/sink (S/S): see *data sink*, *data source*.

source statement: a statement in symbols of a programming language.

source statement library (SSL): a collection of books (such as macrodefinitions) cataloged in the system by the librarian program.

source table: in a program, a table containing predefined data elements from which the program can select an element to be moved automatically into the source area.

source utility: facilitates the preparation and modification of symbolic assembly language source tapes.

SOUT: see *swap out*.

Southern Pacific Communications Company (SPCC): a specialized common carrier which is a subsidiary of the Southern Pacific Company. SPCC operates a coast-to-coast microwave relay network, interconnecting with local telephone company facilities. see *SPRINT*. (G)

SP
(1) see *satellite processor*.
(2) see *scratch pad*.
(3) see *signal processor*.
(4) see *space*.
(5) see *space character*.
(6) see *stack pointer*.
(7) see *structured programming*.

space (SP)
(1) a site intended for the storage of data; for example, a site on a printed page or a location in a storage medi-um.
(2) a basic unit of area, usually the size of a single character.
(3) one or more space characters.
(4) to advance the reading or display position according to a prescribed format; for example, to advance the printing or display position horizontally to the right or vertically down. (*A*)
(5) an impulse, that, in a neutral circuit, causes the loop to open or causes absence of signal. In a polar circuit, it causes the loop current to flow in a direction opposite to that for a mark impulse. A space impulse is equivalent to a binary zero.
(6) see *display space*, *image storage space*, *virtual space*, *working space*.
(7) cf. *backspace*.

space character (SP): a graphic character that is usually represented by a blank site in a series of graphics. The space character, though not a control character, has a function equivalent to that of a format effector that causes the print or display position to move one position forward without producing the printing or display of any graphic. Similarly, the space character may have a function equivalent to that of an information separator. (*A*) (*B*) see also *numeric space character, required space character*. see also *null character*.

space code: similar to skip code, but restricted to one space only at a time.

space division switch: one in which each path has a physically independent spatial location. cf. *time division switch*.

spacehold: the normal no-traffic line condition in which a steady space is transmitted; it may be a customer-selectable option.

space level: the portion of a network that provides unique signal paths for each signal being switched.

space segment: in satellite communication, the space portion of the enterprise, as contrasted with the earth or ground portion.

space suppression: preventing a normal movement of paper in a printer following the printing of a line of characters.

space-to-mark transition: the transmission, or switching, from a spacing impulse to a marking impulse.

spacing bias: see *distortion.*

spacing-end distortion: end distortion that lengthens the spacing impulse by advancing the mark-to-space transition.

span
(1) the difference between the highest and the lowest values that a quantity or function may take. (B)
(2) a collection of span lines between two offices. The term is also used to refer to the collection of all span lines in a particular cable, all span lines on a particular route, or all span lines between two offices. (F)
(3) see *error span.* (A)

span line: a repeatered T1 line section between two central offices (not necessarily contiguous offices). A T1 carrier system is made up of a tandem combination of span lines, plus a digital channel bank at each terminal. (F)

spanned record: a record that is contained in more than one block.

sparse array: an array where zero is the predominant character.

SPC: stored program control. A system in which the sequence of events to be followed is held as a computer-like program held in a memory. Commonly used for telecommunication systems based on computer-like techniques for switching systems.

SPCC: see *Southern Pacific Communications Company.*

speaker-dependent: a class of voice-operated hardware that uses pattern recognition techniques and demands that the operator give the machine a sample of speech patterns prior to words being recognized.

speaker-independent: a class of voice-operated devices needing no prior speech sampling.

SPEC: see *specification.*

special assembly: services provided on a special, nontariffed basis. The rate for these special assemblies is based directly on the cost to provide the service. A frequently provided special assembly is a candidate for a tariff filing. (F)

special character
(1) a graphic character in a character set that is not a letter, not a digit, and not a space character. (A) (B)
(2) in COBOL, a character that is neither numeric nor alphabetic. Special characters in COBOL include the space ( ), the period (.), as well as the following: + − * / = $, ; ") (.

specialized application language: synonymous with *special purpose language.* (E)

specialized common carrier (SCC): an intercity communications common carrier, other than an established telephone common carrier, authorized by the FCC to provide private-line communications services in competition with established telephone common carriers. Specialized common carriers usually provide service to the high-density, low-cost intercity private-line routes. see *domestic satellite carriers, miscellaneous common carrier, other common carrier.* (G)

special-purpose computer: a computer that is designed to operate upon a restricted class of problems. (A) (B)

special-purpose language: a programming language designed for use in relatively narrow aspects of broader application areas; for example, COGO for civil engineering, CDL for logical design, GPSS for simulation. synonymous with *specialized application language.* (E)

special register (SR): in COBOL, compiler-generated storage areas primarily used to store information produced with the use of specific COBOL features.

special service: any of a variety of switched services, nonswitched services, or special-rate services that are either separate from public telephone service or contribute to certain aspects of public telephone service. Examples are PBX service; WATS; foreign exchange service; and private-line services such as circuits for burglar alarms, data, teletypewriter, and television. (F)

special-service circuit: a circuit used to provide a special service to a special customer. (F)

specific address: synonym for *absolute address.* (A)

specification (SPEC): a precise definition of the records and programs needed to carry out a particular processing function.

specification statement: in FORTRAN, one of the set of statements which provide the compiler with information about the data used in the source program. In addition, the statement supplies information required to allocate storage for this data.

specification subprogram: in FORTRAN, a subprogram headed by a BLOCK DATA statement and used to initialize variables in labeled (named) common blocks.

specific code: synonymous with *absolute code.*

specific coding: synonymous with *absolute coding.* (A)

specific polling: a polling technique that sends invitation characters to a device to find out whether the device is ready to enter data. see also *general poll.*

specific program: a program for solving a specific problem only.

specific routine: a routine for a particular data-handling problem where each address refers to explicitly stated registers and locations.

specific volume request: a request for volumes that inform the system of the volume serial numbers.

spectral response: the variation in sensitivity of a device to light of different wavelengths. (A)

spectrum: in telecommunications, the range of electromagnetic frequencies available for use.

speech input: data entry where a particular sound is recognized within the terminal, then converted to a code such as ASCII, and transmitted to the host computer, where it is seen as data keyed in.

speech-plus-signaling (or telegraph): an arrangement of equipment that permits the use of part of a speech band for transmission or telegraph. see also *composited circuit.*

speech scrambler: a device in which speech signals are converted into intelligible form before transmission and are restored to intelligible form at reception; used to obtain some measure of privacy when intercepted by unauthorized persons.

speech synthesizer: a unit that produces speech sounds from input in another form.

speed calling: one of the custom calling features; allows station users to assign abbreviated codes to selected called numbers. This permits the use of fewer digits than are required normally to dial these selected numbers. (F)

speed-of-answer index: one of the service indexes for operator services; gives an indication of the delay an arriving call will experience before being served by an operator. (F)

spell check: synonymous with *dictionary.*

spelling: the order of signs as they appear within printed or written words.

spherical type head: in word processing, an interchangeable printing element in the shape of a sphere, used in some impact printers. (D)

spikes: sharp, temporary increases in a signal or voltage.

spindle: synonym for *module.*

spin lock: a lock that prevents a processing unit from doing work until the lock is cleared. cf. *suspend lock.*

spiral four cable: a quadded cable with four conductors.

split: the formation of two ordered files from one regular file.

split catalog: a library catalog where the different varieties of entry are filed separately, for example, subject entry, author entry.

split screen
(1) in word processing, the facility for dividing a display into two or more independent areas. (D)
(2) the division into sections of a display surface in a manner that allows two or more programs to use the display surface concurrently.

splitting: the partitioning of the capacity of a storage device into independent sections. (D)

spool: simultaneous peripheral operations on line. see *spooling.*

spooler: software permitting input and output units to be shared by a large number of users in an orderly way and free of interference. Spoolers can also control input or output sequences in accord with a pre-programmed specification of priorities.

spooling (simultaneous peripheral operation on line)
(1) the use of auxiliary storage as a buffer storage to reduce processing delays when transferring data between peripheral equipment and the processors of a computer. (B)
(2) the reading of input data streams and the writing of output data streams on auxiliary storage devices, concurrently with job execution, in a format convenient for later processing or output operations. (B)
(3) synonymous with *concurrent peripheral operations.*

spool management: the function of the job entry central services (JECS) responsible for reading and writing input and output streams on the SYS1.SYSPOOL data set.

spot carbon: carbonizing on some areas so that only certain entries are reproduced on the copy.

spot punch: a device for punching one hole at a time in a data carrier. (B)

spread: synonym for *irrelevance*. (A) (B)

spread spectrum: instead of compacting the information signal as closely as possible to a central carrier frequency, the information is spread over many frequencies. This demands more sophisticated receivers to demodulate the signal, but may result in greater message capacity over the frequency spectrum.

SPRINT: an intercity public switched voice message service offered by the Southern Pacific Communications Corporation (SPCC) since 1976. see *MTS/WATS-like services*. (G)

sprocket feed: a typing unit equipped with toothed gearlike wheels at each end of the platen. The pins or sprockets on these wheels engage holes in the sides of the paper to ensure positive and accurate paper movement. Sprocket feed is essential in systems employing forms to ensure accurate form positioning.

sprocket hole: synonym for *feed hole*. (A)

sprocket track: synonym for *feed track*.

SPS
(1) see *string process system*.
(2) see *symbolic program system*.

spurt signaling: short-duration signaling information transfer where the receiving circuit must provide for the necessary state memory. (F)

SPX circuit: simplex circuit.

squeal: pertaining to magnetic tape, subaudible tape vibrations, primarily in the longitudinal mode, caused by frictional excitation at heads and guides.

squeezeout ink: a means of printing to assist in optical character recognition resulting in the outline of each character to be printed darker than its center.

SR
(1) see *shift register*.
(2) see *special register*.
(3) see *status register*.
(4) see *storage register*.
(5) see *switch register*.

SRC: source.

SRF: see *software recovery facility*.

SRM: see *system resources manager*.

SRR: see *serially resuable resource*.

SS
(1) see *solid state*.
(2) see *star-stop character*.
(3) see *start-stop transmission*.

S/S
(1) see *source/sink*.
(2) see *start-stop character*.

SSB: see *single-sideband transmission*.

SSB AM: single-sideband amplitude modulation.

SSC: see *station selection code*.

SSI: see *small scale integration*.

SSL: see *source statement library*.

ST: see *start signal*.

STA: see *station*.

stability: see *computational stability, light stability*. (A)

stable state: in a trigger circuit, a state in which the circuit remains until the application of a suitable pulse. (A) (B)

stack (S) (STK): synonym for *push-*

down list, push-down storage. (B)

stacked graph: a graph with two or three x scales and the same number of y scales plotted so that there are discrete plotting grids placed one above the other.

stacked job: synonym for *batched job (2).*

stacked job processing: a technique that permits multiple job definitions to be grouped (stacked) for presentation to the system, which automatically recognizes the jobs, one after the other. More advanced systems allow job definitions to be added to the group (stack) at any time and from any source, and also honor priorities. see also *batch processing.*

stacker: see *card stacker.*

stack indicator: synonym for *stack pointer.* (B)

stack pointer (SP): the address of the storage location holding the item of data most recently stored in push-down storage. synonymous with *stack indicator.* (B)

STAE (specify task asynchronous exit): a macroinstruction that specifies a routine to receive control in the event of the issuing task's abnormal termination.

staging: the moving of data from an office or low-priority device back to an on-line or higher-priority device, usually on demand of the system or on request of the user. cf. *data migration.*

STAI (subtask ABEND intercept): a keyword of the ATTACH macroinstruction that specifies a routine to receive control after the abnormal termination of a subtask.

stand-alone

(1) pertaining to an operation that is

independent of another device, program, or system.

(2) in word processing, a single, self-contained word processor, as opposed to a word-processing terminal that is connected to and dependent upon a remote memory and processing unit.

stand-alone data-processing system: a data-processing system that is not served by telecommunication facilities.

stand-alone emulator: an emulator whose execution is not controlled by a control program; it does not share system resources with other programs and excludes all other jobs from the computing system while it is being executed.

stand-alone modem: a modem that is separate from the unit with which it operates. synonymous with *external modem.*

stand-alone word-processing equipment: word processing equipment for use by one operator at a time that does not depend on the resources of other equipment for its normal operation. (D)

standard data exchange (SD1): deprecated term for *data exchange, data interchange.*

standard data format: in COBOL, the concept of actual physical or logical record size in storage. The length in the standard data format is expressed in the number of bytes a record occupies and not necessarily the number of characters, since some characters take up one full byte of storage and others take up less.

standard file: in PL/1, a file assumed by the processor in the absence of a FILE or STRING option in a GET or

PUT statement; SYSIN is the standard input file and SYSPRINT is the standard output file.

standard form: synonym for *normalized form*. (A) (B)

standard graph: a graph plotted with one x scale and one or two associated y scales forming a single plotting grid.

standard information: in word processing, text or format instructions entered for subsequent reuse in documents. (D)

standard interface: the interface form designed so that two or more devices, systems, or programs can easily be associated or joined.

standardize: synonym for *normalize*. (A) (B)

standard label (SL): a fixed-format identification record for a tape or disk file.

standard operating procedure: the regular or common mode of operation of a computer.

standard program: a computer program that meets certain criteria, such as being written in a standard machine language (FORTRAN, COBOL, ALGOL), and bringing forth an approved solution to a problem.

standard subroutine: a subroutine that is applicable to a class of problems.

standard system action: in PL/1, action specified by the language to be taken in the absence of an on unit for an on condition.

standard test-tone power: one milliwatt (O dBm) at 1000 cycles per second.

standby (SB)

(1) a condition of equipment that permits complete resumption of stable operation with a short span of time.

(2) a duplicate set of equipment to be used if the primary unit becomes unusable because of malfunction.

standby application: an application where two or more computers are tied together as part of a single overall system, where as with an inquiry application, stand ready for immediate activation and necessary action.

standby block: a technique in which spare input-output blocks of information are always in memory to make more efficient use of buffers.

standby computer: a computer used in a dual or duplex system that is ready to take over the real-time processing problems when needed.

standby equipment: automatic data-processing machines, not in use, but ready for emergencies caused by breakdowns and/or overload.

standby register: a register in which verified and or accepted information is stored for a future rerun in case a mistake is made during processing, or computer malfunction.

standby time

(1) the elapsed time between inquiries when devices are operating on an inquiry application.

(2) the time when two or more computers are tied together and available to answer inquiries or process intermittent actions on stored data.

standby unattended time: time when the equipment is in an unknown condition and not in use working on problems.

standing-on-nines carry: in the parallel addition of numbers represented by decimal numerals, a procedure in which a carry to a given digit place is bypassed to the next digit place. If the current sum in the given digit place is nine, the nine is changed to zero. (A) (B)

star network: a network configuration in which there is only one path between a central or controlling node and each end-point node. synonymous with *centralized network.* (E)

star program: synonymous with *blue ribbon program.*

start bit: synonym for *start signal.*

start element: synonym for *start signal.*

starting-dialing signal: in semiautomatic or automatic working, a signal transmitted from the incoming end of a circuit, after the receipt of a seizing signal, showing that the needed circuit conditions have been established for receiving the numerical routine information.

starting point: on a CRT display device, same as *current beam position.*

start key: in word processing, the control used to initiate certain preset functions of the equipment. synonymous with *enter key, execute key.* (D)

start-of-format control (SOF): a unique word-processing control grouping of characters used as a leading delimiter for a format parameter list embedded in a character string. Start-of-format delimits parameters that control tab stop settings, right margin, choice of single or double index, and text adjust mode operation.

start-of-heading character (SOH): a transmission control character used as the first character of a message heading. (A) (B)

start-of-message (SOM) code: a character or group of characters

transmitted by the polled terminal and indicating to other stations on the line that what follows are addresses of stations to receive the answering message.

start-of-text character (STX): a transmission control character that precedes a text and may be used to terminate the message heading. (A) (B)

start signal (ST)

(1) a signal to a receiving mechanism to get ready to receive data or perform a function. (A)

(2) in a start-stop system, a signal preceding a character or block that prepares the receiving device for the reception of the code elements. A start signal is limited to one signal element generally having the duration of a unit interval. synonymous with *start bit, start element.* (E)

(3) in multifrequency pulsing, a signal used to indicate that all digits have been transmitted. (F)

start-stop: a time and framing technique used in data-transmission systems, especially teletypewriter systems. Data are transmitted in the form of serial characters, each composed of a start element, information bits, and a stop element, with fixed timing of all of these. Characters are sent asynchronously. (F)

start-stop (SS) (S/S) character: a character including one start signal at the beginning and one or two stop signals at the end. (E)

start-stop system: a data-transmission system in which each character is preceded by a start signal and is followed by a stop signal. (E)

start-stop time: see *acceleration time, deceleration time.*

start-stop (SS) transmission

(1) asynchronous transmission such that a group of signals representing a character is preceded by a start element and is followed by a stop element. (E)

(2) asynchronous transmission in which a group of bits is preceded by a start bit that prepares the receiving mechanism for the reception and registration of a character and is followed by at least one stop bit that enables the receiving mechanism to come to an idle condition pending the reception of the next character. see also *binary synchronous transmission.*

start time: pertaining to the time between the interpretation of the tape instructions to read or write and the transfer of information to or from the tape into storage, or from storage into tape. synonymous with *acceleration time.*

state (S): see *input state, stable state, unstable state.*

state code: a coded indication of the state of the CPU, such as responding to an interrupt, executing an input-output instruction, and so on.

statement (STMT)

(1) in a programming language, a meaningful expression that may describe or specify operations and is usually complete in the context of that programming language. (B)

(2) in computer programming, a symbol string or other arrangement of symbols. (*A*)

(3) in COBOL, a syntactically valid combination of words and symbols written in the procedure division. A statement combines COBOL reserved words and programmer-defined operands.

(4) in FORTRAN, the basic unit of a program, composed of a line or lines containing some combination of names, operators, constants, or words whose meaning is predefined to the FORTRAN compiler. Statements fall into two broad classes: executable and nonexecutable.

(5) a basic element of a PL/1 program that is used to delimit a portion of the program, to describe names used in the program, or to specify action to be taken. A statement can consist of a condition list, a label list, a statement identifier, and a statement body that is terminated by a semicolon.

(6) deprecated term for *instruction.* (A) (B)

(7) see *assignment statement, conditional statement, job control statement.*

statement body: in PL/1, that part of a statement that follows the statement identifier, if any, and is terminated by the semicolon; It includes the statement options.

statement function: in FORTRAN, a function defined by a function definition within the program unit in which it is referred to.

statement function definition: in FORTRAN, a name, followed by a list of dummy arguments, followed by an equal sign (=), followed by an arithmetic or logical expression.

statement function reference: in FORTRAN, a reference in an arithmetic or logical expression to a previously defined statement function.

statement identifier: the PL/1 keyword that indicates the purpose of the statement.

statement-label constant: see *label constant*.

statement-label variable: see *label variable*.

statement number: in FORTRAN, a number of from one through five decimal digits placed within columns 1 through 5 of the initial line of a statement. It is used to identify a statement uniquely, for the purpose of transferring control, defining a DO loop range, or referring to a FORMAT statement.

statement verb: the key word that describes the function to be performed when a statement is presented to a computer program.

state table: a list of the outputs of a logic circuit based on the inputs and previous outputs; has memory and cannot be described by a simple truth table.

static buffer allocation: synonym for *static buffering*.

static buffering: assigning a buffer to a job, program, or routing at the beginning of execution, rather than at the time it is needed. synonymous with *static buffer allocation*. cf. *dynamic buffering*.

static display image: in computer graphics, that part of a display image, such as a form overlay, that is infrequently changed by the user during a particular application. synonymous with *background display image*. cf. *dynamic display image*. (E)

static dump: a dump that is performed at a particular point in time with respect to a machine run, frequently at the end of a run, and usually under the control of a supervisory program. (A) (B)

static error: an error that is independent of the time variable.

static handling: handling, completely done by the compiler program.

staticize
(1) to convert serial or time-dependent parallel data into static form.
(2) loosely, to retrieve an instruction, and its operands from storage prior to its execution. (*A*)

staticizer: synonym for *serial-to-parallel converter*. (C)

static magnetic cell: synonym for *magnetic cell*. (A)

static memory: memory that is non-volatile and does not need to be refreshed as long as power is presented.

static RAM: unlike ordinary, volatile memory, static memory retains its contents even when the main current is turned off. The trickle of electricity from a battery is enough to refresh it.

static storage: storage other than dynamic storage. (A)

static storage allocation: the allocation of storage for static variables.

static subroutine: a subroutine that involves no parameters other than the addresses of the operands.

static test mode: a setup mode of an analog computer during which special initial conditions are set in order to check the patching and the proper operation of the computing devices except the integrators. (B)

static variable: a variable that is allocated before execution of the program begins and that remains allocated for the duration of execution of the program.

station (STA)
(1) one of the input or output points of a system that uses telecommunication facilities; for example, the telephone set in the telephone system or

the point where the business machine interfaces with the channel on a leased private line.

(2) one or more computers, terminals, devices, and associated programs at a particular location.

(3) see *active station*, *channel-attached station*, *control station*, *data-processing station*, *data station*, *inquiry station*, *link-attached station*, *master station*, *passive station*, *primary station*, *read station*, *remote station*, *secondary station*, *slave station*, *tributary station*, *work station*.

(4) see also *terminal*.

station arrangement: a tariff term for a device such as a modem required on certain subvoice-grade leased channels. see also *data loop transceiver*.

stationary information source: synonym for *stationary message source*. (A) (B)

stationary message source: a message source each message of which has a probability of occurrence independent of the time of its occurrence. synonymous with *stationary information source*. (A) (B)

station battery: the electric power source for signaling at a station.

station clock: a clock which controls some or all of the equipment in the station which requires local time control. see also *clock*.

station code: the final four digits of a standard 7- or 10-digit address. These digits define a connection to a specific customer's telephone(s) within the larger context of an NPA and central office code. The term *main station code* is an equivalent expression. In the past, a line number and a party letter often were combined to provide station identifica-

tion. With the discontinuance of party letters, the four numerics have assumed the role of station identification. (F)

station control block (SCB): a logical extension of the QCB for each station, that is, a logical representation of a station. It contains information used to control queuing.

station error detection: where a slave station determines whether a message it receives is an accurate copy of what the master station has transmitted. The process involves a comparison or parity check.

station selection code (SSC): a Western Union term for an identifying call that is transmitted to an outlying telegraph receiver and automatically turns its printer on. see also *call directing code*, *selective calling*.

station-to-station service: the service in which the person originating the call specifies to an operator only the destination code. Includes station-to-station service originating at a public or semipublic coin telephone. (F)

stator: the stationary part of a sensor. see also *rotor*.

status: the current condition of a device or machine; usually indicates the flag flip-flops or special registers.

status bit handshaking: delegating certain bits of a parallel I/O port to coordinate information transfer with a peripheral unit, signifying device read, buffer full, printer out of paper, and so on.

status channel: a channel to transmit status information.

status line: in display-based word-processing equipment, a line reserved for the display of information to the operator concerning the processing of the text. (D)

status register (SR) (STR): a register containing information about the condition of a functional unit or peripheral device.

status scan: a key or command that causes scans of all modems, on a selected line, and displays the status of modem/terminal power, and so on.

status word: information needed to resume processing after the handling of interruption of operations.

stencil: see *electronic stencil, pressure stencil, thermal stencil.* (D)

step

(1) one operation in a computer routine.

(2) to cause a computer to execute one operation.

(3) see *job step, single-step.* (A)

step-by-step operation: synonym for *single-step operation.* (A) (B)

step-by-step switch: a switch that moves in synchronism with a pulse device, such as a rotary telephone dial. Each digit dialed causes the movement of successive selector switches to carry the connection forward until the desired line is reached. synonymous with *stepper switch.* see also *crossbar system, line switching.*

step-by-step (SXS) system

(1) a type of line-switching system that uses step-by-step switches.

(2) an automatic switching system in which a call is extended progressively step-by-step to the desired terminal under direct control of pulses from a customer's dial or from a sender. (F)

step change: the change from one value to another in a single increment and in negligible time.

stepped start-stop system: a start-

stop system where the start signals occur at regular intervals.

stepper motor: a mechanical unit that rotates by a fixed amount each time it is pulsed, as in various floppy-disk systems.

stepper switch: synonymous with *step-by-step switch.*

step restart: a restart that begins at the beginning of a job step. The restart may be automatic or deferred, where deferral involves resubmitting the job. see also *checkpoint restart.*

still video: in telecommunications, a technique whereby the telephone is linked to a screen and calls are accompanied, or interspersed by static images, permitting a lower bit rate than is needed for making pictures and/or higher resolution.

STK: see *stack.*

STMT: see *statement.*

STN: see *switched telecommunication network.*

stochastic: containing an element of chance.

STOP: a console command. Allows the operator to stop the partition in which the operation is given.

stop bit: synonym for *stop signal.*

stop character (STP): a word processing control that interrupts the sequence of output processing and provides a means for the operator or machine to make changes in text-processing parameters or data. see also *repeat character, switch character.*

stop code: in word processing, a program instruction that causes the reader to stop. If the device is interactive, it is generally used as an index for a stop list for operator changes or corrections. (D)

stop element: the last element of a

character in asynchronous serial transmission, used to ensure recognition of the next start element. In baudot teletypewriter operation, it is 1.42 mark bits. synonym for *stop signal*. see also *start-stop transmission*.

stop instruction: an exit that specifies the termination of the execution of a computer program. (A) (B)

stop key: in word processing, a control that terminates or interrupts an operation. synonymous with *break key, cancel key.* (D)

stop loop: a small closed loop used for operator convenience, that is, to show an error, improper usage, or special result.

stopper: the highest memory location in any given system.

stop signal
(1) a signal to a receiving mechanism to wait for the next signal. (A)
(2) in a start-stop system, a signal following a character or block that prepares the receiving device for the reception of a subsequent character or block. A stop signal is usually limited to one signal element having any duration equal to or greater than a specified minimum value. (E)
(3) synonymous with *stop bit, stop element.*

stop time: the elapse of time between completion of reading or writing of a tape record and the time when the tape ceases to move.

STOR
(1) see *storage.*
(2) see *store.*

storage (S) STOR)
(1) the retention of data in a storage device.
(2) a storage device. (A)
(3) the action of placing data into a storage device. (B)
(4) in word processing, a unit into which recorded text can be entered, in which it can be retained and processed, and from which it can be retrieved. (D)
(5) a device, or part of a device, that can retain data.
(6) see *acoustic storage, associative storage, auxiliary storage, buffer storage, capacitor storage, cathode-ray storage, circulating storage, core storage, cryogenic storage, delay line storage, direct-access storage, dynamic storage, electrostatic storage, erasable storage, external storage, fixed storage, free storage, immediate-access storage, internal storage, magnetic card storage, magnetic core storage, magnetic disk storage, magnetic drum storage, magnetic storage, magnetic thin film storage, magnetic wire storage, main storage, mass storage, matrix storage, mercury storage, n-core-per-bit storage, nonvolatile storage, one-core-per-bit storage, parallel search storage, parallel storage, permanent storage, push-down storage, push-up storage, real storage, secondary storage, serial-access storage, static storage, temporary storage, unprotected dynamic storage, virtual storage, volatile storage, word-organized storage.*

storage allocation: the assignment of storage areas to specified data. (B) see *dynamic storage allocation.* (A)

storage area: pertaining to the designated location in various storage units; for example, for programs, constants, input-output buffer storage.

storage block: a continuous area of main storage, consisting of 2048 bytes, to which a storage key can be assigned.

storage capacity: the amount of data that can be contained in a storage device, measured in binary digits, bytes, characters, words, or other units of data. (B)

storage cell: one or more storage elements, considered as a unit. (B)

storage compacting: a hardware feature allowing the dynamic relocating of programs residing in the central storage, to provide an efficient multiprogramming environment.

storage cycle: the periodic sequence of events that occurs when information is transferred to or from main storage.

storage density: the number of units of data that can be stored in a unit length or area of a storage medium.

storage device
(1) a functional unit into which data can be entered, in which they can be retained, and from which they can be retrieved. (A) (B)
(2) a facility in which data can be retained. (D)

storage drum: a random-access storage device that can hold 4 million alphanumeric characters or up to 8 million digits, which can be retrieved at a rate of 1.2 million characters per second.

storage dump: the copying of all, or a portion of a storage.

storage element: a basic unit of a storage device. (B)

storage exchange: the interchange of the total contents of two storage devices or locations, such as two registers.

storage fill: storing of characters in storage areas not used for data stor-

age or the program for a specific machine run.

storage flip-flop: a bistable storage unit that stores binary data as states of flip-flop elements.

storage fragmentation: inability to assign real storage locations to virtual addresses because the available spaces are smaller than the page size.

storage indicator: on a calculator, a visual indication that a number is being held in storage. (D)

storage integrator: in an analog computer, used to storage a voltage in the hold condition for future usage while the rest of the computer assumes another computer control state.

storage interference: in a system with shared storage, the referencing of the same block of storage by two or more processing units.

storage key: an indicator associated with one or more storage blocks, that requires that tasks have a matching protection key to use the blocks.

storage light: a control console panel light showing that a parity-check error has occurred on a character as it was read into storage.

storage location: an area in a storage device, usually one that can be explicitly and uniquely specified by means of an address. (A) (B)

storage location selection: in word processing, selection of a group or groups of text by preselecting a particular storage address or addresses.

storage overlay: see *overlay segment*. (D)

storage protection: a facility that limits access to a storage device, or to one or more storage locations by preventing writing or reading or both.

(B) see also *fetch protection*, *store protection*.

storage protection key: see *protection key*, *storage key*.

storage region: see *overlay region*, *virtual storage region*.

storage register (SR): a device for holding a unit of information.

storage resolver: a small section of storage, in the drum, tape, or disk storage units, that has faster access than the remainder of the storage.

storage stack: synonym for *push-down list*.

storage tab setting: in word processing, the feature of a machine that enables tabulator settings to be entered on the recording medium or into storage so that these settings may be used in subsequent operations. (D)

storage tube: in computer graphics, a type of cathode ray tube (CRT) that retains a display image on its screen for an extended period of time without requiring refresh. (E)

storage unit: a register in the memory or storage of the computer.

store (STOR)

(1) to place data into a storage device. (B)

(2) to retain data in a storage device. (B)

(3) in computer programming, to copy data from registers into internal storage. (B)

(4) deprecated term for *storage*.

store and forward mode: a manner of operating a data network in which packets or messages are stored before tranmission toward the ultimate destination. (E) see also *message switching*.

store controller

(1) a programmable unit in a network used to collect data, to direct inquiries, and to control communication within a system.

(2) in PSS, the primary link between terminals attached to it and the host processor. synonymous with *subsystem controller*.

store controller disk: an integral part of a programmable store system controller that is used for auxiliary storage of store controller data, user files, and application programs.

store controller storage: in SPPS II, that portion of store controller working storage that is available to the user for executing application programs.

store controller storage save: the automatic writing of the critical areas of store controller storage onto the integrated disk when power is turned off or when a power failure is detected.

stored format instruction: in word processing, a prerecorded instruction that determines the layout of textual or other information. (D)

stored program: a program that is completely contained in memory, capable of being altered in memory, and can be stored along with the data on which it is to function. synonymous with *stored routine*.

stored program computer: a computer controlled by internally stored instructions that can synthesize and store instructions, and that can subsequently execute these instructions. synonymous with *programmed computer*. (A) (B)

stored program control: see *SPC*.

stored routine: synonymous with *stored program*.

store loop: a cable over which data is transmitted between the store controller and the terminals of the programmable store system.

store loop driver: a hardware component used to connect the store controller to the store loop.

store protection: a storage protection feature that determines right of access to main storage by matching a protection key, associated with a store reference to main storage, with a storage key, associated with each block of main storage. see also *fetch protection.*

store support procedure: a procedure that assists personnel in administrative, operational, and managerial operations, apart from customer checkout.

store-through cache: in a processing unit, a store (write) operation, in which data is immediately put into both cache and main storage locations.

STP

(1) see *signal transfer point.*

(2) see *stop character.*

STR: see *status register.*

straight line coding

(1) a set of instructions in which there are no loops. (B)

(2) a programming technique in which loops are avoided by unwinding. (*A*) (B)

strain gauge: a sensor producing a voltage or resistance change when a force is present.

strap: see *cartridge.*

stratified language: a language that cannot be used as its own metalanguage; for example, FORTRAN. (B) cf. *unstratified language.* (*A*)

stream: see *data stream.*

streaming: the condition of a modem or terminal that has locked into a constant carrier signal, preventing normal transmission of data.

string: a linear sequence of entities such as characters or physical elements. (B) see *alphabetic string, binary element string, bit string, character string, null string, symbol string, unit string.* (*A*)

string break: in sorting, a situation that occurs when there are no records with keys higher than the highest key thus far written.

string file: tape, wire, or string used to arrange documents for easy reference and usage.

string length: in sorting, the number of records in a string.

string manipulation: the manipulation of groups of contiguous characters in memory, treating them as units of data.

string process system (SPS): a package of subroutines that perform basic operations on strings of characters. SPS performs string reading and writing, hash-code string look-up, and string comparisons.

string sorting: a group of sequenced records normally stored in auxiliary computer storage, that is, disk, tape, or drum.

string variable: in PL/1, a variable declared with the BIT or CHARACTER attribute, whose values can be either bit strings or character strings.

stringy floppy: an endless loop of recording tape in a cartridge used as external memory.

striping: in flowcharting, the use of a line across the upper part of a flowchart symbol to signify that a detailed representation of a function is located elsewhere in the same set of flowcharts. (A)

strobe: a selection signal, active when data are correct on a bus.

strobe pulse: a pulse to gate the output of a core-memory sense amplifier into a trigger in a register.

stroke

(1) in character recognition, a straight line or arc used as a segment of a graphic character. (A)

(2) in computer graphics, a straight line or arc used as a segment of a display element. (E)

(3) see *Sheffer stroke.*

stroke center line: in character recognition, a line midway between the two stroke edges. (A)

stroke character generator: in computer graphics, a character generator that generates character images composed of strokes. (E)

stroke edge: in character recognition, the line of discontinuity between a side of a stroke and the background, obtained by averaging, over the length of the stroke, the irregularities resulting from the printing and detecting processes. (A)

stroke edge irregularity: deviation of the edge of a character from its stroke edge in optical character recognition.

stroke generator: see *stroke character generator.*

stroke width: in character recognition, the distance measured perpendicularly to the stroke center line between the two stroke edges. (A)

STRUC: see *structure.*

structure (STRUC): in PL/1, a hierarchical set of names that refers to an aggregate of data items that may have different attributes. see *block structure.*

structured field syntax: a syntax that permits variable-length data to be encoded for transmission in such a way that the device which is processing the data sequentially can translate a sequence of fields into its component fields without having to examine every byte.

structured language: a computer language to aid or enforce structured programming, for example, PASCAL, ALGOL.

structured programming (SP): a technique for organizing and coding programs that reduces complexity, improves clarity, and makes them easier to debug and modify. Typically, a structured program is a hierarchy of modules that each have a single entry point and a single exit point; control is passed downward through the structure without unconditional branches to higher levels of the structure.

structure expression: in PL/1, an expression whose evaluation yields a structure value.

structure flowcharts: flowcharts indicating input, processing, files, and output without indicating the exact techniques of processing.

structure member: in PL/1, any of the minor structures of elementary names in a structure.

structure of arrays: in PL/1, a structure containing arrays specified by declaring individual member names with the dimension attribute.

structuring: in PL/1, the makeup of a structure, in terms of the number of members, the order in which they appear, their attributes, and their logical levels (but not necessarily their names or declared level numbers).

stub card: a special-purpose card

that has a separable stub attached to a general-purpose paper card. A stub card may be a scored card. (A)

stuck sender: see *sender*.

stuffing character: a character used on isochronous transmission links to take account of differences in clock frequencies. (C)

stunt box: a device that controls the nonprinting functions of a teletypewriter terminal, such as carriage return or line feed, and recognizes line control characters; for example, call directing code.

STX: see *start-of-text character*. (A) (B)

stylus: in computer graphics, a pointer that is operated by placing it in a display space or a tablet; for example, a light pen, a sonic pen, a voltage pencil.

stylus printer: a matrix printer that uses a stylus to produce patterns of dots. (E) synonym for *matrix printer*. (B)

SU: see *selectable unit*.

SUB

(1) see *subroutine*.

(2) see *substitute character*.

subalphabet: an alphabet subset; for example, any group of less than 26 letters.

subarea node: synonymous with *cross-subarea link*.

subblock

(1) that portion of a BSC message terminated by an ITB line-control character.

(2) a method of handling large blocks of data in small segments, where a subblock is a user-defined number of buffers.

subchannel

(1) a division of a channel data

path.

(2) the channel facility required for sustaining a single I/O operation.

subcommand: a request for an operation that is within the scope of work requested by a previously issued command.

subdata base: a set of data in a data base that is used for a specific type of application. (E)

subfeeder cable: a cable that connects feeder cables to distribution cables; usually buried without conduit and containing between 300 and 900 twisted pairs. (F)

subfield

(1) a subdivision of a field; a field within a field.

(2) in PL/1, that portion of a picture specification field that appears before or after a V picture specification character.

subgeneration: in PL/1, the portion of a generation represented by a qualified reference, a subscripted reference, or both.

sub-harmonic: a fractional multiple of the fundamental frequency.

subject or entry: in COBOL, a data name or reserved word that appears immediately after a level indicator or level number in a data division entry. It serves to reference the entry.

subjob: a machine run or routine.

subloop: a loop that emanates from a terminal or another unit that is itself part of a loop. When the subloop involves telecommunication lines, it is sometimes referred to as a remote subloop.

submodular phase: a phase made up of selected control sections from one or more modules as compared with a phase that is made up of all control sections from one or more modules.

subparameter: one of the variable items of information that follows a key-word parameter and can be either positional or identified by a key word.

subpool: all of the storage blocks allocated under a subpool number for a particular task.

subprogram

(1) a program that is invoked by another program.

(2) in FORTRAN, a program unit headed by a FUNCTION, SUBROUTINE, or BLOCK DATA statement.

subroutine (SUB)

(1) a sequenced set of statements that may be used in one or more computer programs and at one or more points in a computer program.

(2) a routine that can be part of another routine. (*A*)

(3) in PL/1, a procedure that is invoked by a CALL statement or CALL option. A subroutine cannot return a value to the invoking block, but it can alter the value of variables.

(4) see *closed subroutine, dynamic subroutine, open subroutine, recursive subroutine, reentrant subroutine.* (*A*)

subroutine call: the subroutine, in object coding, that performs the call function. (*A*)

subroutine library (SLIB): a standard proven subroutine set that is retained on file for use at a future time.

subroutine statement: synonym for *procedure statement.* (E)

subroutine subprogram: in FORTRAN, a subroutine consisting of FORTRAN statements, the first of which is a SUBROUTINE statement.

It optionally returns one or more parameters to the calling program unit.

subroutine table: the routine for maintaining a listing of the subroutines in core and for bringing from file the subroutines as required by the application program.

sub schema: a logical description of a subdata base. (E)

subscriber line: a telephone line between a central office and a telephone station, private branch exchange, or other end equipment.

subscriber set: an assembly of apparatus for use in originating or receiving calls on the premises of a subscriber to a communication or signaling service.

subscriber's loop: see *local loop.*

subscript

(1) a symbol that is associated with the name of a set to identify a particular subset or element. (A) (B)

(2) in COBOL, an integer or a variable whose value refers to a particular element in a table.

(3) in FORTRAN, a subscript quantity or set of subscript quantities, enclosed in parentheses and used in conjunction with an array name to identify a particular array element.

(4) in PL/1, an element expression that specifies a position within a dimension of an array. A subscript can also be an asterisk, in which case it specifies the entire extent of the dimension.

(5) synonymous with *inferior.*

subscript character (SBS): a word-processing formatting control that causes the printing or display point to move down approximately one-half the normal single line space increment with no horizontal motion. The subscript character is a latching control that requires a superscript character to cause the printing or display point to return to the previous horizontal alignment. cf. *superscript character*.

subscripted variable: a variable that is followed by one or more subscripts enclosed in parentheses.

subscript list: in PL/1, a parenthesized list of one or more subscripts, one for each dimension of an array, which together uniquely identify either a single element or cross section of the array.

subscript quantity: in FORTRAN, a component of a subscript; a positive integer variable, or expression that evaluates to a positive integer constant. If there is more than one subscript quantity in a subscript, the quantities must be separated by commas.

subsegment: a part of a segment.

subset
(1) a set, each element of which is an element of a specified other set. (A) (B)
(2) a set contained within a set.
(3) in telecommunication, a subscriber set, such as a telephone.
(4) a modulation and demodulation device.
(5) see *alphabetic character subset, alphanumeric character subset, character subset, numeric character subset, proper subset*. (A)

subset (of a programming language): a variant form of a programming language that has fewer features or more restrictions than the original language. see *subset*. (E)

substantive input: the transferral of data from an external storage unit to an internal storage unit, usually from a mass storage device and off line, but not always so.

substitute: to replace an element of information by some other element of information.

substitute character (SUB): a control character used in the place of a character that is recognized to be invalid or in error, or that cannot be represented on a given device. (A) (B)

substitute mode: a transmittal mode used with exchange buffering on which segments are pointed to, and exchanged with, user work areas. see also *locate mode, move mode*.

substitution table: a layout chart for keyboard. In word processing used to show which standard character keys can be used as special character keys.

substrate: in a microcircuit, the supporting material upon which or within which an integrated circuit is fabricated, or to which an integrated circuit is attached. synonymous for *base*. (D)

subsystem: a secondary or subordinate system, usually capable of operating independently of, or asynchronously with, a controlling system.

subsystem controller: synonym for *store controller*.

subsystem definition: synonym for *subsystem generation*.

subsystem definition statement: one of the statements that is used to define either the configuration of terminals attached to a subsystem controller or the processing options for data within the subsystem.

subsystem generation: the process of creating a programmable store system operational environment and storing it in a library. Subsystem generation includes selection of the desired functions by coding the required programmable store system macroinstructions, assembling the macros, and processing the assembler output with the controller configuration facility or the terminal configuration facility. see also *operational environment.* synonymous with *subsystem definition.*

subsystem store controller: see *store controller.*

subsystem support program: any program that is part of the subsystem support services. A subsystem support program is executed in the host system.

sub task: a task that is initiated and terminated by a higher order task.

subtracter: a device whose output data are a representation of the difference between the numbers represented by its input data. (B) see *adder subtracter, full subtracter, half-subtracter.* (A)

subtrahend: in a subtraction, the number or quantity subtracted from the minuend. (A) (B)

subvoice-grade channel: a channel of bandwidth narrower than that of voice-grade channels. Such channels are usually subchannels of a voice-grade line. Common usage excludes telegraph channels from this definition.

suffix: a code dialed by a caller who is already engaged in a call. cf. *prefix.*

suffix notation: synonym for *postfix notation.* (A) (B)

suite: a number of programs related to each other and run in sequence to enable a processing job to be termi-

nated.

sum: the number or quantity that is the result of the addition of two or more numbers or quantities. (A) (B) see also *check sum.*

sum check: in a summary tag-along sort, a data field designated for accumulated totals. synonym for *summation check.*

summary punch: a card punch that may be connected to another device, such as a tabulator, to enter data that was calculated or summarized by the other device. (A) (B)

summation check: a comparison of check sums, computed on the same data on different occasions, to verify data integrity. synonymous with *sum check.* (E)

summer: synonym for *analog adder.* (B)

summing integrator: a device whose output variable is the integral of a weighted sum of the input variables with respect to time. (B)

supercomputer

(1) the fastest and most powerful computing systems that are available at any given time.

(2) presently, any machine that will perform at peak speeds greater than 20 million operations per second.

supergroup: the assembly of five 12-channel groups occupying adjacent bands in the spectrum for the purpose of simultaneous modulation and demodulation. May be used as 60 voice grade channels, or five wideband channels, or combinations of both.

supergroup distribution frame (SGDF): in frequency division multiplexing, the SGDF provides terminating and interconnecting facilities from group modulator output, group demodulator input, supergroup modulator input, and supergroup demodulator output circuits of the basic supergroup spectrum of 312 kHz to 552 kHz.

superheterodyne reception: a method of receiving radio waves in which the process of heterodyne reception is used to convert the voltage of the received wave into a voltage of an intermediate, but usually super-audible, frequency, that is then detected. see also *heterodyne reception*.

super-high frequency (SHF): between 3000 and 30,000 megaHertz.

superimposed circuit: an additional channel obtained from one or more circuits, provided for other channels, so that all the channels can be used simultaneously without mutual interference.

superimposed ringing: synonymous with *superposed ringing*.

superposed circuit: an additional channel obtained from one or more circuits, normally provided for other channels, in such a manner that all the channels can be used simultaneously without mutual interference.

superposed ringing: party-line telephone ringing in which a combination of alternating and direct currents is utilized, the direct currents of both polarities being provided for selective ringing. synonymous with *superimposed ringing*.

superscript character (SPS): a word processing formatting control that causes the printing or display point to move up approximately one-half the normal single line space increment with no horizontal motion. The superscript character is a latching control

that requires a subscript character to cause the printing or display point to return to the previous horizontal alignment. cf. *subscript character*.

supervision: the function of monitoring and controlling the status of a call by means of supervisory signals. see *supervisory signals*. (F)

supervisor: the part of a control program that coordinates the use of resources and maintains the flow of processing unit operations. see also *system supervisor*. synonym for *supervisory program, supervisory routine* . (A) (B) see *overlay supervisor*. (A)

supervisor call instruction (SVC): an instruction that interrupts the program being executed and passes control to the supervisor so that it can perform a specific service indicated by the instruction.

supervisor mode: a mode of operation where only certain operations, such as memory-protection modification instructions and input-output operations are allowed.

supervisor state: a state during which the processing unit can execute input-output and other privileged instructions. cf. *problem state*.

supervisory control: characters or signals which automatically actuate equipment or indicators at a remote terminal.

supervisory program: a computer program, usually part of an operating system, that controls the execution of other computer programs and regulates the flow of work in a data-processing system. synonymous with *executive program, supervisor*. (A) (B)

supervisory relay: a relay which, during a telephone call, is controlled by the transmitter current supplied to a subscriber line to receive from the associated stations signals that control the actions or operators or switching mechanisms.

supervisory routine: a routine, usually part of an operating system, that controls the execution of other routines and regulates the flow of work in a data-processing system. synonymous with *executive routine, supervisor.* (A) (B)

supervisory services: a general term for all functions in the supervisor that are available to the user.

supervisory signals: signals used to indicate the various operating states of circuit combinations.

supervisory system: all of the supervisory programs used by a given system.

supplementary ground electrode: an electrode that can be either rod driven into the ground and interconnected with copper conductors or a network of conducting elements buried under and around the building.

support chip: a component in a system required for operation, but additional to the main central processor.

support programs: programs that aid the supervisory programs and the application programs, and include diagnostics, testing, data generators, and so forth.

suppress: preventing printing.

suppression: see *zero suppression.*

surface barrier: a possible barrier across the surface of a semiconductor junction.

suspended state: a software state in which a task is not dispatched by the system and is not contending for the processor.

suspend lock: a lock that prevents requesters doing work on a processing unit but allows the processing unit to continue doing other work. cf. *spin lock.*

SVA: see *shared virtual area.*

SVC: see *supervisor call instruction.*

SVC interruption: an interruption caused by the execution of a supervisor call instruction, causing control to be passed to the supervisor.

SVC routine: a control program routine that performs or begins a control program service specified by a supervisor call instruction.

SW

(1) see *software.*

(2) see *switch.*

(3) see *switch character.*

SWA: see *scheduler work area.*

swap: in systems with time sharing, to write the main storage image of a job to auxiliary storage and to read the image of another job into main storage.

swap allocation unit: in TSO, an arbitrary unit of auxiliary storage space into which a swap data set is divided, and by which it is allocated.

swap data set: in TSO, a data set dedicated to the swapping operation.

swap data-set control block: in TSO, a control block describing a swap data set, containing a DCB, a space queue, and device-dependent control information.

swap-in (SI): in system with time sharing, the process of reading a terminal job's main storage image from auxiliary storage into main storage.

swap-out (SOUT): in system with time sharing, the process of writing a terminal job's main storage image from main storage to auxiliary storage.

swapping: a process that interchanges the contents of an area of main storage with the contents of an area in auxiliary storage. (B) see *page swapping.* (A)

swap set: the pages that are to be swapped in or swapped out for a job or for system programs.

swap time: time needed to transfer a program from external memory to high-speed internal memory and vice-versa.

SWCH: see *switch.*

swim: in computer graphics, undesired movement of display elements about their normal positions. (E)

switch (S) (SW) (SWCH)

(1) in a computer program, a parameter that controls branching and is bound prior to the branch point being reached. synonymous with *switch point.* (B)

(2) a device or programming technique for making a selection; for example, a toggle, a conditional jump. (*A*)

(3) see *main switch.* (D)

switchable-mode line: see *line mode switching, switched connection.*

switchboard: equipment used to interconnect lines and trunks. A manually operated switching position which is part of a private branch exchange service furnished to a customer.

switch character (SW): a word processing device control that causes reading of a character string to switch from one character string source to another without operator intervention. see also *repeat character, stop character.*

switch code: in word processing, a

program instruction for switching that causes control to transfer to one of a number of possible statements, depending on existing or prior conditions; for example, the switch in ALGOL 60; the computed GOTO in FORTRAN.

switch control computer: a computer designed to handle data transmission to and from remote computers and terminals.

switch core: a core in which the magnetic material generally has a high residual flux density and a high ratio of residual to saturated flux density with a threshold value of magnetizing force below which switching does not occur. (A) (B)

switched circuit: a channel or circuit that is connected and disconnected by action of one or more of the associated stations, or by external means.

switched connection

(1) a mode of operating a data link in which a circuit or channel is established to switching facilities, as, for example, in a public switched network. (E)

(2) a connection that is established by dialing.

(3) cf. *nonswitched connection.*

switched line: a telecommunication line in which the connection is established by dialing. cf. *nonswitched line.*

switched-message network: a communication system where data is passed between any users of the network.

switched network: any network in which connections are established by closing switches, for example, by dialing.

switched network backup (SNBU): an

optional facility that allows a user to specify, for certain types of physical units, a switched line to be used as an alternate path if the primary line becomes unavailable or unusable.

switched telecommunication network (STN): a switched network furnished by communication common carriers or telecommunication administrations.

switched telephone network: a network of telephone lines normally used for dialed telephone calls.

switch hook: a switch on a telephone set, associated with the structure supporting the receiver or handset. It is operated by the removal or replacement of the receiver or handset on the support. see also *off hook, on hook*.

swtich-hook flash: a brief on-hook signal produced by momentarily depressing the telephone switch-hook button (or equivalent). Must be long enough to be recognized, but not so long as to be interpreted as a disconnect signal. (F)

switch indicator: in computer programming, an indicator that determines or shows the setting of a switch. synonymous with *flag*. (*A*) (B)

switching (S)

(1) pertaining to a connection established by closing switches between a remote terminal and a computer.

(2) designates a field of work, such as system development, planning, or engineering, involving the application of switching technology in telecommunications networks. (F)

(3) refers to the process of connecting together appropriate lines and trunks to form a desired communica-

tion path between two station sets. Included are all kinds of related functions, such as sending and receiving signals, monitoring the status of circuits, translating addresses to routing instructions, alternate routing, testing circuits for busy condition, and detecting and recording troubles. (F)

(4) in a more restricted sense, switching is the technology of making and breaking electrical circuits. Sometimes used to describe any circuit that operates discretely, particularly logic and memory. (F)

(5) see *automatic volume switching, circuit switching, line switching, message switching, packet switching*.

switching applications: message-handling applications where the computer is utilized to accept messages from terminals, route them over trunk lines at high speeds to remote message-switching computers, and provide certain reliability functions such as an audit trial and error control.

switching center: a location that terminates multiple circuits, and is capable of interconnecting circuits or transferring traffic between circuits. see *semiautomatic switching center, torn-tape switching center*.

switching circuit: a circuit that performs a switching activity, by the existence of a certain signal (usually a pulse signal). When combined, switching circuits can perform a logical operation.

switching element: deprecated term for *logic element*. (B)

switching equipment irregularities: malfunctions in switching equipment or associated signaling that result in wrong numbers or the absence of appropriate call progress indications to the call originator. Sometimes loosely called *equipment irregularities.* (F)

switching function: a function that has only a finite number of possible values and the independent variables of which have only a finite number of possible values. (A) (B)

switching network: switching stages and their interconnections within a switching system. (F)

switching pad: a transmission loss pad automatically cut in and out of a toll circuit for different operating conditions.

switching regulator: a power supply design where efficient regulation is performed by commuting the input voltage into a filter circuit.

switching system: an electromechanical or electronic system for connecting lines to lines, lines to trunks, or trunks to trunks. A single switching system may handle several central office codes. The term includes PBX switching systems (manual and automatic), local switching systems, and toll switching systems. see *switching.* (F)

switching time: the interval between the reference time and the last moment at which the instantaneous voltage response of a magnetic cell reaches a stated fraction of its peak value.

switching unit: a single switching machine limited to one code. One or more switching units can constitute a switching center.

switching variable: a variable that may take only a finite number of possible values or states. (A) (B)

switch insertion: placing data or instructions by means of manually operated switches.

switch instruction: in word processing, a program instruction for switching between different elements of recording media on the same machine or between different sections of storage. (D)

switchover: transferring the real-time processing work load from one specific or multiplexer program to another within a duplex system.

switch point: synonym for *switch (1).* (A) (B)

switch register (SR): toggle switches on the operator console providing the means for manually establishing a word to be placed in the computer.

switch room: that part of a telephone central office building that houses switching mechanisms and associated apparatus.

switch train: a sequence of switches through which connection must be made to establish a circuit between a calling telephone and a called telephone. see also *train.*

SXS: see *step-by-step system.*

SY: see *system.*

syllable: a character string or a binary element string in a word. (A) (B)

syllable hyphen (character) (SHY): a word processing formatting graphic that prints in the same way as a required hyphen character. It prints only at syllable boundaries at line endings to indicate continuation of a word on the next line. A syllable hyphen may be ignored or dropped if words are repositioned during text adjust mode operations. synonymous with *discretionary hyphen.* cf. *required hyphen character.*

SYM

(1) see *symbol*.

(2) see *system*.

symbiont control: symbionts, besides being routines from main programs, perform off-line operations, such as tape-to-printer, independent of the main program. These operations may be suspended, terminated, or reinstated.

symbionts: small routines that run concurrently with the series of main programs. see also *symbiont control*.

symbol (SYM)

(1) a conventional representation of a concept or a representation of something by reason of relationship, association, or convention. (B)

(2) a representation of something by reason of relationship, association, or convention. (*A*)

(3) in digital transmission, a recognizable electrical state associated with a signal element. In binary transmission, a signal element is represented as one of two possible states or symbols. see *signal element*. (F)

(4) in assembler language, a character or character string that represents addresses or arbitrary values. A symbol may consist of no more than eight characters, the first character being a letter (A through Z, $, @, or #) and the other characters being either letters or digits. No blanks or special characters are allowed.

(5) see *abstract symbol, aiming symbol, flowchart symbol, logic symbol, mnemonic symbol, ordinary symbol, sequence symbol, SET symbol, tracking symbol, variable symbol*.

symbolic: using characters or character strings in a defined syntax to stand for machine-related constructs such as instructions or data.

symbolic address: an address expressed in a form convenient for computer programming. (A) (B)

symbolic addressing: a method of addressing in which the address part of an instruction contains a symbolic address. (A) (B)

symbolic assembler: an assembler that allows the programmer to code instructions in a symbolic language.

symbolic coding: the preparation of routines and computer programs in a symbolic language. (A)

symbolic debugging: symbolic commands utilized to aid in the debugging procedure.

symbolic deck: a deck of punched cards containing programs written in symbolic language.

symbolic editor: permits the editing of source-language programs by adding or deleting lines of text.

symbolic instruction: an instruction in a source language. synonymous with *symbolic coding*.

symbolic I/O assignment: a means by which a problem program can refer to an I/O device by a specific I/O symbolic name. Before the program is executed, a device is assigned to the symbolic name.

symbolic language: a programming language whose instructions are expressed in symbols convenient to humans rather than in machine language.

symbolic logic: the discipline in which valid arguments and operations are dealt with using an artificial language designed to avoid the ambiguities and logical inadequacies of natural languages. synonymous with *mathematical logic*. (*A*) (B)

symbolic names: names assigned by programmers to represent addresses or locations within a program.

symbolic notation: the method of representing a storage location by one or more figures.

symbolic number: a numeral, used in writing routines, for referring to a specific storage location; such numerals are converted to actual storage addresses in the final assembling of a program.

symbolic parameter

(1) in assembler programming, a variable symbol declared in the prototype statement of a macrodefinition. A symbolic parameter is usually assigned a value from the corresponding operand in the macroinstruction that calls the macrodefinition. see also *keyword parameter, positional parameter.*

(2) in job control language, a symbol preceded by an ampersand that represents a parameter or the value assigned to a parameter or subparameter in a cataloged or instream procedure. Values are assigned to symbolic parameters when the procedure in which they appear is called.

symbolic placeholder: a symbol in a command list that is replaced by an actual value when the command list is executed.

symbolic programming: writing a program in a source language.

symbolic program system: a computer system which accepts high level programming languages.

symbol-manipulating language: see *LISP.*

symbol manipulation: the processing of symbols that have no explicit numerical values. (A)

symbol rank: synonym for *digit place.* (A) (B)

symbols: see *editing symbol.*

symbol string: a string consisting solely of symbols. (A) (B)

symbol table: a table created by a compiler or assembler to relate symbolic addresses to their absolute addresses.

symmetrical channel: a channel pair in which the send and receive directions of transmission have the same data signaling rate. see also *binary symmetric channel.* (A)

symmetrical I/O unit: in multiprocessing, a unit that is attached to two processors; it appears as the same I/O unit to each processor, and can be accessed in the same manner by each processor.

symmetric channel: see *binary symmetric channel.*

symmetric list processor: a high-level list processing language.

symmetric processors: processors with identical configurations.

symmetric storage configurations: machine configurations with identical storage units.

SYN

(1) see *synchronous.*

(2) see *synchronous idle character.* (A) (B)

SYNC: see *synchronization, synchronous.*

sync bits: synonym for *framing bits.*

sync character: a character transmitted to establish appropriate character synchronization in synchronous communication.

synch: a signal used to identify the beginning of a block.

synchro-duplexing: the scheme of producing a document on a printing unit through the synchronous running of a program tape and a master tape or a pure data tape.

synchronization (SYNC): the process of adjusting the corresponding significant instants of two signals to obtain the desired phase relationship between these instants. (C)

synchronization pulses: pulses introduced by transmission equipment into the receiving equipment to keep the two equipments operating in step. (A)

synchronizer: a unit that serves as a buffer, and maintains synchronization by counteracting the effects of transmitting data between units that operate at differing rates.

synchronizing pilot: a reference signal to maintain the synchronization of the oscillators of a carrier system.

synchronizing signal: a signal accompanying data transmission to ensure that the data are transmitted and received in synchronism with a clock. see *baseband* and *clock*.

synchronous (S) (SYN) (SYNC)
(1) pertaining to two or more processes that depend upon the occurrences of specific events such as common timing signals. (B)
(2) occurring with a regular or predictable time relationship.

synchronous communication: the method of transferring serial binary data between computer systems or between a computer system and a peripheral device.

synchronous computer: a computer in which each event, or the performance of any basic operation, is constrained to start on signals from a clock and usually to keep in step with them. (B) cf. *asynchronous comput-*

er. (A)

synchronous data link control: see *SDLC*.

synchronous data network: a data network that uses a method of synchronization between data circuit-terminating equipment (DCE) and the data-switching exchange (DSE), and between DSEs, and data-signaling rates being controlled by timing equipment within the network. (E)

synchronous data transfer: a physical transfer of data to or from a device that has a predictable time relationship with the execution of an I/O request.

synchronous data transmission: data transmission in which the nominal signal element spacing is fixed. This is called "synchronous transmission" because the receiver must be in synchronism with the time pattern of the incoming symbols. cf. *asynchronous data transmission*. (F)

synchronous gate: a time gate wherein the output intervals are synchronized with an incoming signal.

synchronous idle character (SYN): a transmission control character used by synchronous data-transmission systems to provide a signal from which synchronism or synchronous correction may be achieved between data terminal equipment, particularly when no other character is being transmitted. (A) (B)

synchronous line control: a scheme of operating procedures and control signals by which telecommunication lines are controlled.

synchronous operation
(1) a mode of operation in which each action is started by a clock.
(2) an operation that occurs regu-

larly or predictably with respect to the occurrence of a specified event in another process; for example, the calling of an input-output routine that receives control at a precoded location in a computer program. (*A*)

(3) cf. *asynchronous operation*.

synchronous satellite: a satellite in synchronous orbit.

synchronous transfer: an input-output transfer that takes place in a certain amount of time without regard to feedback from the receiving device.

synchronous transmission

(1) data transmission in which the time of occurrence of each signal representing a bit is related to a fixed time frame. synonymous with *isochronous transmission*. (E)

(2) data transmission in which the sending and receiving instruments are operating contiguously at substantially the same frequency and are maintained, by means of correction, in a desired phase relationship.

synchronous working: performing a sequence of operations under the control of equally spaced signals from a clock. cf. *asynchronous working*.

syndetic

(1) having connections or interconnections.

(2) pertaining to a document or catalog with cross-references.

synergetic: combining each unit of a system, but one which when combined or added, develops a total larger than their arithmetic sum.

synonym: in an indirectly addressed file, a record whose key randomizes to the address of a home record.

syntax

(1) the relationship among charac-ters or groups of characters, independent of their meanings or the manner of their interpretation and use. (B)

(2) the structure of expressions in a language.

(3) the rules governing the structure of a language.

(4) the relationships among symbols. (*A*)

syntax checker: a program that tests source statements in a programming language for violations of the syntax of that language.

syntax-directed compiler: a compiler based on the syntactical relation of the character string.

syntax error: a mistake in the formulation of an instruction to a computer.

syntax language: a metalanguage used to specify or describe the syntax of another language. (A)

synthetic address: synonymous with *generated address*. (A) (B)

synthetic language: synonymous with *source language*.

SYS: see *system*.

SYSADMIN: see *system administrator*.

SYSGEN: see *system generation*.

SYSIN: a system input stream; also, the name used as the data-definition name of a data set in the input stream.

SYSLOG: see *system log*.

SYSOPOs: see *System Programmed Operators*.

SYSOUT: a system output stream; also, an indicator used in data-definition statements to signify that a data set is to be written on a system output unit.

SYSRES: the disk pack which contains the supervisor.

SYST: see *system*.

system (S) (SY) (SYM) (SYS) (SYST)

(1) in data processing, a collection of men, machines, and methods organized to accomplish a set of specific functions. (A)

(2) an assembly of components united by some form of regulated interaction to form an organized whole.

(3) the operations and procedures through which a business activity is accomplished.

(4) see *data-processing system, decimal numeration system, fixed-point representation system, fixed-radix numeration system, information feedback system, management information system, mixed-base numeration system, mixed-radix numeration system, number representation system, numeration system, operating system, positional representation system, programming system, pure binary numeration system, radix numeration system, self-monitoring system, start-stop system, variable-point representation system.*

system activity measurement facility (MF/1): a facility that collects information such as paging activity and the use of the processing unit, channels, and I/O devices, to produce trace records and reports.

system administrator (SA) (SYSADMIN): the person at a computer installation who designs, controls, and manages the use of the computer system.

system capacity: the maximum traffic a system can carry with a specified response time.

system chart: synonymous with *systems flowchart*.

system check: a check on the overall performance of a system, usually not made by built-in computer check circuits; for example, control totals, hash totals, and record counts.

system check module: a unit that monitors system operability as power fails or deviations from expected computer activities develop. It initiates necessary emergency actions by the computer.

system code: a three-digit code of the form 0/1XX available to operators or automatically associated with certain toll calls to modify routing or call-handling logic. Customers are prevented from using system codes by constraints in the format of signals accepted by switching systems. (F)

system communication processing: the transmission of data to a central computer for processing from a remote terminal as opposed to a terminal connected directly to the central computer.

system constants: permanent locations within the monitor (control unit), containing data used by system programs.

system controller: regulates and coordinates all communications between major computer-system components, input-output controller, and real-time units.

system definition: in industry systems, the time, before a system is put into use, when desired functions and operations of the system are first selected from various available options. synonymous with *system generation*.

system design: the specification of the working relations between all parts within a system in terms of their characteristic actions.

system directory list (SDL): a list containing directory entries of highly used phases and of all phases resident in the shared virtual area. This list is contained in the shared virtual area.

system error recording editing program (SEREP): a stand-alone program used to edit and print hardware error condition log-out data from main storage.

system generation (SYSGEN): the process of selecting optional parts of an operating system and of creating a particular operating system tailored to the requirements of a data-processing installation.

system-improvement time: machine downtime required for the installation and testing of new devices, and machine downtime required for modification of existing components, including all programming tests to check out the modified units.

system input device: a device specified as a source of an input stream.

system integrity: see *data integrity, network integrity*.

system interrupts: programmed requests from a processing program to the control program for some action; for example, initiation of an input-output operation.

system key: a key that protects system data from damage or modification by unauthorized users.

system library: a collection of data sets or files in which the various parts of an operating system are stored.

system loader (SLDR): see *loader*.

system log (SYSLOG): a data set or file in which job-related information, operational data, descriptions of unusual occurrences, commands, and messages to or from the operator

may be stored.

system nucleus: see *nucleus*.

system operator: an operator responsible for peforming system-oriented procedures.

system output device: a device assigned to record output data for a series of jobs.

system output writer: a job scheduler function that transcribes specified output data sets onto a system output unit, independently of the program that produced the data sets.

system productivity: a measure of the work performed by a system productivity largely depends on a combination of two other factors: the facility (ease of use) of the system and the performance (throughput, response time, and availability) of the system.

System Programmed Operators (SYSOPOs): a facility on some computers permitting user programs to directly access a set of public subroutines. These are not replicated for each user but are used in common.

system programmer
(1) a programmer who plans, generates, maintains, extends, and controls the use of an operating system with the aim of improving the overall productivity of an installation.
(2) a programmer who designs programming systems and other applications.

system programming language: a language developed for wiring system-oriented software packages.

system quiesce: a procedure that allows an authorized operator to start an orderly shutdown of store system activity before changing from one application program to another, turning power off to the store controller, or using terminal resources to perform additional jobs.

system reliability: the probability that equipment will perform accurately all tasks under stated tactical and environmental conditions.

system residence volume: the volume on which the nucleus of the operating system and the highest level index of the catalog are located.

system-resident: with software, indicating the instructions and data forming an integral portion of the computer system. cf. *media-resident software*.

system resilience: the ability of a computer system to continue to function correctly despite the existence of a fault or faults in one or more of its component parts. (E)

system resource: any facility of the computing system that may be allocated to a task.

system resources manager (SRM): a group of programs that controls the use of system resources in order to satisfy the installation's performance objectives.

system response field: the portion of a basic transmission unit (BTU) containing the network control program status response to a request issued by the host.

system restart

(1) a restart that allows reuse of previously initialized input and output work queues. synonymous with *warm start*.

(2) a restart that allows reuse of a previously initialized link pack area. synonymous with *quick start*.

systems analysis: the analysis of an activity to determine precisely what must be accomplished and how to accomplish it.

systems analyst (SA): an individual trained to undertake the tasks of systems analysis.

Systems and Computers Evaluation and Review Technique: see *SCERT*.

systems approach: looking at the overall situation rather than the narrow implications of the task at hand; particularly, looking for interrelationships between the task at hand and other functions which relate to it.

systems definition: a complete description, totally documented, of a problem and its solution or proposed solution.

systems design: a design that graphically illustrates the nature and content of input, files, procedures, and output in order to show the needed connection processes and procedures.

systems flowchart: a visual representation of the system through which data provided by the source documents are converted into final documents.

systems generation: a systems disk generated by a user, who specifies the configuration, file protected area, error handling, and so forth.

system slowdown: a network control program mode of reduced operation invoked when buffer availability drops below a threshold level; the network control program limits the amount of new data it accepts while continuing normal output activity.

systems program: a program that controls the operation of the computer system.

systems software: intimate software, including operating systems, compilers, and utility software. see *utility* *program*. cf. *applications software*.

systems standard: a specified characteristic needed to allow system activity.

systems subroutines: pertaining to various input-output format controls that provide for various format statements found in FORTRAN language.

system supervisor (SS): the network control program code that provides the functional interface between the line scheduler and message processing tasks in the background, and the I/O interrupt handlers. It is composed of four services: task, queue, and buffer management, and supervisor services.

system task: a control program function that is performed under the control of a task control block.

system utility device: a device that is assigned for the temporary storage of intermediate data for a series of job steps.

system utility programs: a collection of problem state programs designed for use by a system programmer in performing such functions as changing or extending the indexing structure of the catalog.

system variable symbol: in assembler programming, a variable symbol that does not have to be declared because the assembler assigns it a read-only value.

T

(1) go back to start.

(2) see *tera*.

(3) see *terminal*.

(4) see *test*.

(5) see *time*.

(6) see *timer*.

(7) see *track*.

(8) see *transaction*.

(9) see *transmit*.

tab: a label, marker, or indicator, found at either or both ends of a medium, as tapes, to allow rapid awareness of its message.

tabbing: a means of shifting a cathode ray tube cursor or printer head to a prespecified column on the screen or paper.

tab command: a command that shifts the cursor to the next tab stop.

table

(1) an array of data each item of which may be unambiguously identified by means of one or more arguments. (B)

(2) a collection of data in which each item is uniquely identified by a label, by its position relative to the other items, or by some other means. synonymous with *dictionary*.

(3) see *boolean operation table, decision table, function table, operation table, truth table*. (A)

table element: in COBOL, a data item that belongs to the set of repeated items comprising a table. An argument together with its corresponding functions makes up a table element.

table function: any item of data in a table obtained when a search argument matches a table argument.

table look-at: see *table*.

table look-up (TLU): a procedure for obtaining the value corresponding to an argument from a table of values. (A) (B)

table look-up instruction: an instruction that initiates a table look-up. (A) (B)

table simulator: a computer program able to compute the values in a table rather than simply looking them up as stored.

tablet: in computer graphics, a locator device with a flat surface and a mechanism that converts indicated positions on the surface into coordinate data. (E)

table word-processing equipment: word-processing equipment designed as a stand-alone unit for operation on a desk or table. If it is not integrated word-processing equipment, its control unit may be designed also to stand on a desk, a table, or elsewhere. (D)

tabular language: a means for stating programming requirements as decision tables. synonymous with *tab*.

tabulate

(1) to format data into a table.

(2) to print totals. (*A*)

tabulating equipment: machines and equipment that use punched cards. synonymous with *electronic accounting machines*.

tabulation character: see *horizontal tabulation character, vertical tabulation character*. (A)

tabulator: a device that reads data from a data carrier such as punched cards or punched tape, and produces lists, tables, or totals. (B)

tabulator setting: in word processing, the feature of a machine that enables tabulator settings to be entered onto the recording medium or into storage so that these settings may be used in subsequent operations. (D)

tactile keyboard: a keyboard display laid out on a flat surface. The character is registered by touching its key location lightly with a finger.

tag: one or more characters, attached to a set of data, that contains information about the set, including its identification. (A) (B)

tag converting device: equipment that performs automatic reproduction of information from perforated price tags to punched cards.

tag sort: a sort in which addresses of records (tags), and not the records themselves, are moved during the comparison procedures.

tail: a flag indicating the termination of a list.

takedown: pertaining to completion of one operating cycle prior to preparing the equipment for loading the next job.

takedown time: the time needed to complete a takedown activity.

take-up reel: a specific reel on which tape is wound or can be wound during processing.

talker echo: see *echo, talker*.

talk off: false operation of in-band signaling receivers caused by customer speech simulating the supervisory tone for a sufficiently long interval (usually more than 150 ms) to cause accidental release of the connection. (F)

tally: an account of the number of times something has happened.

tandem data circuit: a data circuit that contains more than two data circuit-terminating equipments (DCEs) in series. (E)

tandem office: in general, an intermediate switching system for interconnecting local and toll offices. All toll offices are tandem offices. A more specific meaning of local tandem or metropolitan tandem is an office that connects class 5 offices to other class 5 offices or to other tandem offices within a metropolitan area. (F)

tandem switching: using an intermediate switch to interconnect circuits from the switch of one serving central office to the switch of a second serving central office in the same exchange.

tandem system: a system network where data proceeds through one central processor into another. This is the system of multiplexers and master-slave arrangements.

tandem trunk: a trunk extending from a telephone central office (or tandem office) to a tandem office and used as part of a connection between telephone stations in different central offices.

tape: see *carriage control tape, chadless tape, magnetic tape, perforated tape.* (A)

tape alternation: a selection, controlled by the program, of first one tape unit followed by another, normally during input or output operations, permitting successive reels of a file to be mounted and removed without interrupting the program.

tape beginning control: a special perforation, reflective spot, or transparent part of the first portion of a magnetic tape to show its start.

tape certification: certifying magnetic computer tape to zero errors; to assure or make certain the reel of tape has zero errors.

tape character: information consisting of bits stored across the several longitudinal channels of a tape.

tape code: see *perforated tape code.* (A)

tape comparator: a device that compares two tapes which are expected to be identical. Comparison is made row by row and the device stops when any discrepancy occurs.

tape conditioning: running a tape forward to the end of the tape, reversing it, and running the tape backward to the beginning of the tape.

tape-controlled carriage: an automatic paperfeeding carriage controlled by a punched paper tape.

tape control unit: a device, including associated buffering, for controlling the activities of the magnetic tape transport.

tape deck: deprecated term for *magnetic tape unit.* synonym for *magnetic tape drive.* (*A*) (B)

tape drive (TD): a mechanism for controlling the movement of magnetic tape. This mechanism is commonly used to move magnetic tape past a read head or write head, or to allow automatic rewinding. synonymous with *tape deck, tape transport.* see *magnetic tape drive.* (B) deprecated term for *tape unit.* (B)

tape dump: the transfer of complete contents of information recorded on tape to the computer or another storage medium.

tape erasure: where a signal recorded on a tape is removed and the tape is then made ready for rerecording.

tape feed: a device that feeds tape to be read or sensed by the machine.

tape feed switch: a switch that actuates the reperforator to meter a predetermined length of tape.

tape file

(1) a record file consisting of a magnetic or punched paper tape.

(2) a set of magnetic tapes in a tape library.

tape input: pertaining to the introduction of data to machines using tapes.

tape label (TPLAB): a record at the

beginning and end of a reel of magnetic tape showing information about the file stored on the tape. see *header label, trailer label.*

tape leader: the part at the beginning of a reel of magnetic or punched tape that is often left blank to permit for initial threading or to hold some sort of marker or code to show the nature of the data stored on the tape. Holes, notches, other magnetization, and so on, are used for such purposes.

tape limited: the processing speed time limited by the speed of the magnetic or paper tape devices.

tape load point: the position on a piece of magnetic tape where reading or writing may commence.

tape mark (TM): a character on a magnetic tape file that divides the file into a new section. synonymous with *control mark.*

tape perforator: an off-line, keyboard-operated unit for punching code holes in paper tape.

tape punch: a computer-actuated punch that punches holes in punch tape or punched tape. synonym for *receiving perforator.* (B)

tape punch control keys: keys that control activities, such as power on, feeding tape at the beginning and end of reel, tape error, and punch on and off.

tape reader: synonym for *punched tape reader.*

tape relay: a method, using perforated tape as the intermediate storage, of relaying messages between the transmitting and receiving stations.

tape reproducer: a device that prepares one tape from another tape by copying all or part of the data from

the tape that is read. (B)

tape resident system: an operating system that uses magnetic tapes for on-line storage of system routines.

tape row: that portion of a tape, on a line perpendicular to the reference edge, on which all binary characters may be either recorded or sensed simultaneously. synonymous with *frame.* (B)

tape speed: the speed at which tapes are transported from feed to take-up reels during normal recording or reproduction.

tape spool

(1) a cylinder without flanges, on which tapes may be wound. (B)

(2) a coiled length of perforated tape. (*A*)

tape station: deprecated term for *magnetic tape unit.* (A) (B)

tape storage: see *magnetic tape storage.*

tape-to-card: pertaining to equipment or methods that transmit data from either magnetic tape or punched tape to punched cards.

tape-to-print program: transfers data from magnetic tape to printer.

tape-to-tape converter: a machine that changes one form of input-output medium or code to another.

tape transport: deprecated term for *magnetic tape unit.* synonym for *magnetic tape drive.* (A) (B)

tape transport mechanism: synonym for *magnetic tape drive.* (B)

tape unit (TU): a device containing a tape drive, together with read heads and write heads and associated controls. see *magnetic tape unit.* (*A*)

tape verifier: a unit for checking the accuracy of punched tape by comparing earlier punched tape with a second manual punching of the same data, with the machine signaling discrepancies.

tape volume: a single reel of magnetic tape.

target: in micrographics, an aid to technical or bibliographic control that is photographed on the film preceding or following an associated document. (E)

target computer: a computer that has not been designed to use a particular program, but has another computer translate such a program for its use. synonymous with *object computer.*

target language: a language into which statements are translated. synonymous with *object language.* (A) (B)

target phase: the time when the target program is run. synonymous with *object phase, run phase.*

target program: a computer program in a target language that has been translated from a source language. synonymous with *object program.* (A) (B)

target variable: in PL/1, a variable to which a value is assigned.

tariff
(1) the published rate for a specific unit of equipment, facility, or type of service provided by a telecommunication facility. Also, the vehicle by which the regulating agencies approve or disapprove such facilities or services. Thus, the tariff becomes a contact between the customer and the telecommunication facility.
(2) the published rates, regulations, and descriptions governing the provision of communications services. (F)

task (TSK)
(1) a basic unit of work to be ac-

complished by a computer. The task is usually specified to a control program in a multiprogramming or multiprocessing environment. (B)
(2) in word processing, a basic unit of work to be accomplished by the operator.
(3) in a multiprogramming or multiprocessing environment, a computer program, or portion thereof, capable of being specified to the control program as a unit of work. Tasks compete for system resources.

task control block (TCB): the consolidation of control information related to a task.

task dispatcher: provides a capability to initiate parallel tasks and to synchronize their execution.

tasking: see *multitasking.* (A)

task management: those functions of the control program that regulate the use by tasks of the processing unit and other resources, except for input-output devices.

task name: in PL/1, an identifier used to refer to a task variable.

task queue: a queue of all the task control blocks present in the system at any one time.

task scheduler: in real-time operating systems, organizes and schedules the processing of events not directly connected to user interrupts and provides multiple execution paths through a program.

task start: the creation of a new task in the system.

task states: the states of execution status of a task relative to the processor-active state, ready state, suspended state, and wait state.

task switch
(1) allocation of the processor to

another task; for example, a ready or active task of higher priority than the current task in execution.

(2) a change in the task that is in control of the processor. The new task's state changes from ready to active and the current task is placed in a state other than active.

task-to-task communication: where a user program on a node of computer network exchanges messages or data with a user program of another node.

task variable: in PL/1, a variable with the TASK attribute whose value gives the relative priority of a task.

TC: see *transmission control character*.

TCAM: see *telecommunication access method*.

T-Carrier: a series of transmission systems using pulse code modulation technology at various channel capacities and bit rates (e.g., T1, T2, T3, T4).

TCB: see *task control block*.

TCF: see *terminal configuration facility*.

TCU
(1) see *teletyprewriter control unit*.
(2) see *transmission control unit*.

TD
(1) see *tape drive*.
(2) see *transmitter-distributor*.

TDM: see *time-division multiplexing*.

teaching machine: any machine which performs computer-aided instruction.

technique: the method used to collect, process, convert, transfer, and retrieve data to prepare reports.

technique flowcharts: flowcharts showing data and information needs and the methods used for processing

this information.

teleautograph: a writing telegraph instrument, in which movement of a pen in the transmitting apparatus varies the current in two circuits in such a way as to cause corresponding movement of a pen at the remote receiving instrument. synonymous with *telewriter*.

TELEC: see *telecommunication*.

TELECC: see *telecommunication*.

telecommunication (TELEC) (TELECC)
(1) communication over a distance, as by telegraph or telephone. (E)
(2) any transmission, emission, or reception of signs, signals, writing, images, and sounds or intelligence of any nature by wire, radio, optical, or other electromagnetic systems. (C)
(3) the transmission of signals over long distances, such as by telegraph, radio, or television. (B)

telecommunication access method (TCAM): a method used to transfer data between main storage and remote or local terminals. Application programs use either GET and PUT or READ and WRITE macroinstructions to request the transfer of data, which is performed by a message control program. The message control program synchronizes the transfer, thus eliminating delays for terminal input-output operations.

telecommunication administration: any governmental department or service responsible for implementing the obligations undertaken in the International Telecommunication Convention and the regulations annexed thereto. (C)

telecommunication control unit: synonymous with *transmission control unit.*

telecommunication facility: transmission capabilities, or the means for providing such capabilities, made available by a communication common carrier or by a telecommunication administration.

telecommunication line

(1) the portion of a data circuit external to a data circuit-terminating equipment (DCE) that connects the DCE to a data switching exchange (DSE), that connects a DCE to one or more other DCEs, or that connects a DSE to another DSE. (E)

(2) any physical medium, such as a wire or microwave beam, that is used to transmit data.

(3) synonymous with *data-transmission line, transmission line.*

(4) cf. *data link.*

telecommunication network (TELNET): deprecated term for *data network.*

telecommuting: the replacement of physical commuting from home to workplace with logical commuting, where one works at home through a computer and telecommunications channel.

telecoms: originally a British term, a telephone installation for a partnership or small business in which any extension can make or receive calls, and with intercom facilities between extensions.

teleconference: a meeting between people who are remote from each other but linked together by a telecommunications system.

telecopier: a unit for facsimile transmission.

teledata: a unit that introduces parity bits to punched paper tape for transmission. The receiving unit checks parity for code accuracy and repunches paper tape with valid data.

telefax: linking photocopying units for the transmission of images.

telegraph (TG)

(1) a system employing the interruption or change in polarity of direct current for the transmission of signals.

(2) refers to transmission systems, switching systems, test boards, stations, and services that are oriented toward narrow-band, private-line data services at speeds up to 150 bits per second. The most common service of this type is teletypewriter. Channels provided under Series 1000 tariff are sometimes called telegraph channels. (F)

(3) see also *polar transmission.*

telegraph grade circuit: a circuit suitable for transmission by teletypewriter equipment. Normally, the circuit is considered to employ dc signaling at a maximum speed of 75 bauds.

telegraph speed: the reciprocal of the duration, measured in seconds, of a unit interval.

teleinformatics: data transfer via telecommunication systems.

telemanagement: a service featuring computerized management of a customer's long-distance system, automatically routing each call over the least costly line available at the time the call is made and logging the call for accounting control.

telemeter: to transmit digital or analog metering data by telecommunication facilities. For example, data can be telemetered from a missile and recorded at a ground station.

telemetry: sensing or metering of operating systems by a receiving unit that converts transmitted electrical signals into units of data.

Telepak: a leased channel offering of telephone companies and Western Union providing specific-size bundles of voice-grade, telegraph-grade, subvoice-grade, and broad-band channels between two channels. Mileage charges are constant for each mile rather than regressive as in conventional single-leased lines.

telephone company: any common carrier providing public telephone system service.

telephone coupler: a device for putting a regular telephone handset into service as a modem. Usually, it works acoustically, but it may also work inductively.

telephone data set: a device connecting a telephone circuit to a data terminal.

telephone dialer: under program control, a circuit that divides the output of an on-chip crystal oscillator, providing the tone frequency pairs required by a telephone system. The tone pairs are chosen through a latch by means of a BCD code from the bus.

telephone recording statement: a device that enables telephone conversations to be recorded on a dictation machine.

telephone set: the terminal equipment on the customer's premises for voice telephone service. Includes transmitter, receiver, switch hook, dial, ringer, and associated circuits. (F)

telephony: transmission of speech or other sounds.

Teleport: a project developed by the Port Authority of New York and New Jersey, Merrill Lynch & Company and the Western Union Corporation to provide the New York City metropolitan area with satellite communications.

telepresence: by using all of a robot's sensors, permitting an individual to be electronically aware of the robot's immediate environment and control the robot's actions just as if the person were actually in the location of the robot.

teleprinter: equipment used in a printing telegraph system.

teleprinter exchange service: a service provided to communication common carriers to connect teleprinters. Similar to regular telephone service, customers dial calls from station to station but communicate using teleprinter equipment rather than telephones.

teleprocessing (TP): synonym for *remote-access data processing*. deprecated term for *distributed data processing*. (E) see also *distributed function*.

teleprocessing network: synonym for *remote-access data-processing network*.

teleprocessing terminal: used for on-line data transmission between remote process locations and a central computer system. Connection to the computer system is achieved by a data-adapter device or a transmission control.

telereference: a method use to consult data at a remote location through the use of a closed circuit television.

Telerent Decision: in this 1974 FCC decision, the commission held that its prior decisions, particularly

Carterfone, preempted state regulation with respect to the interconnection of terminal equipment used for both intrastate and interstate service. In 1976, a U.S. Court of Appeals affirmed the FCCs preemptive jurisdiction over terminal equipment and the Supreme Court declined to review this decision of the Court of Appeals. (G)

telescreen: a two-way audiovisual TV used to monitor and control remote activities.

TELESPEED: a Western Union marketing term for DATASPEED equipment.

teletext: textual information transmitted to homes via television sets.

teletext service: transmission of information over communications works between typewriter-like terminals. Telex is one form of this.

teletraffic theory: a mathematical treatment of call flow in a communications network. (F)

Teletype (TT) (TTY): the trademark of Teletype Corporation, usually referring to a series of different types of teleprinter equipment such as tape punches, reperforators, and page printers, utilized for telecommunications.

teletype code: the standard five-channel teletypewriter code composed of a start impulse and five character impulses, of equal length, and a stop impulse whose length is 1.42 times all of the start impulse.

teletype exchange (telex) (TEX): a Western Union automatic teletype-exchange service where subscribers can dial each other for direct twoway telemeter communications.

teletype grade: a level of circuit suitable for telegraphic communication.

teletypewriter (TTW) (TTY): an electromechanical typewriter device that generates from a keyboard a coded signal corresponding to the typed character. This electrical signal may be passed over appropriate transmission facilities and used to control a similar teletypewriter at a distance. (F) synonymous with *teleautograph.*

teletypewriter controller: incorporated on the same circuit board as the control panel logic module, offering minimum cost interface.

teletypewriter control unit (TCU): a device that serves as the control and coordination unit between teletypewriter devices and a message switching center when employing controlled teletypewriter operations.

teletypewriter exchange service (TWX): a service in which a customer's teletypewriter is connected to a TWX switching system and can be connected to any other customer of the same service. This service was formerly offered by the Bell System, but was sold to the Western Union Telegraph Company in 1971. (F)

teletypewriter grade: represents the lowest-type communication circuit in terms of speed, accuracy, and usually, cost.

teletypewriter network: the system of points, interconnected by private telegraphic channels, providing hard copy and/or telegraphic coded (5-channel) punched paper tape, as needed, at both sending and receiving points.

teletypewriter utility package: a library of commonly needed programming functions involving input-output through a teletypewriter.

telex: see *teletype exchange.*

TELNET: see *telecommunication network.*

Telpak: an AT&T name designating its service for leasing wide-band channels.

temperature coefficient: the measure of the change in the mean error owing to temperature variations.

temporary data set: a data set that is created and deleted in the same job.

temporary file: a file that can be erased or overwritten when it is no longer needed. cf. *permanent file.*

temporary read/write error: an error that is eliminated by retrying a read/write operation.

temporary storage: in computer programming, storage locations reserved for immediate results. synonymous with *working storage. (A)*

temporary text delay (TTD): a control character sequence sent by a transmitting station to either indicate a delay in transmission or to initiate an abort of the transmission in progress.

ten (10)-key pad: in word processing, a separate set of keys numbered 0 through 9 on a word processor's keyboard that allows easy entry of numbers, aligning them automatically on the decimal point; similar to a calculator key pad.

tens complement: the radix complement in the decimal numeration system. synonymous with *complement-on-ten. (A) (B)*

tera (T): ten to the twelfth power, 1,000,000,000,000 in decimal notation. When referring to storage capacity, two to the fortieth power, 1,099,511,627,776 in decimal notation.

TERM: see *terminal.*

term: the smallest part of an expression that can be assigned a value. see *absolute term, arithmetic term, logical term, relocatable term.*

terminal (T) (TERM) (TML)

(1) a point in a system or network at which data can either enter or leave. (A)

(2) a device, usually equipped with a keyboard and a display device, capable of sending and receiving information over a link. see also *intercepted terminal, job-oriented terminal, remote terminal.*

(3) equipment at the end of a communication circuit. User terminals include telephone sets and teletypewriters. (F)

(4) carrier terminals include the modulation and demodulation equipment and the multiplex equipments used to combine and separate individual channels at the ends of a transmission system. (F)

(5) a point at which an electrical connection can be made to a device, circuit, or equipment. It is usually characterized by some means for securely fastening a wire or cable. (F)

(6) see *data terminal equipment, user terminal. (A)*

(7) see also *terminal node.*

terminal area: the portion of the conductive pattern of a circuit to which electrical connections can be made.

terminal cluster: a group of two or more terminals controlled by one computer.

terminal component: a separately addressable part of a terminal that performs an input or output function, such as the display component of a keyboard-display device or a printer component of a keyboard-printer device.

terminal configuration facility (TCF): a set of macrostatements to be coded by the user and modules in programmable store system host support that are used to define and create the terminal operational environment.

terminal controller: a hard-wired or intelligent (programmable) device which provides detailed control for one or more terminal devices.

terminal cursor: a movable mark that locates a character on a CRT screen.

terminal digit posting: the arranging and recording of serial numbers of documents on the basis of the last configuration of the digits of the serial number.

terminal distributed system: an arrangement of computers within an organization where the computer complex has separate computing facilities all functioning in a cooperative fashion, rather than the conventional single computer at a single location.

terminal edit operation: an operation such as clear entire screen, clear unprotected positions, character typeover, character insert/delete, line insert/delete, erase to end of page, and erase line/field.

terminal electric buzzer: a buzzer that has the striker and sounder connected into the circuit in the form of a normally closed switch. With a field gone, a striker is pulled back into its resting position by spring tension, closing the switch contacts and re-energizing the field, which causes the operation to repeat itself.

terminal end-to-end control: a means whereby, during the data phase of a call, interconnected DTEs can exchange control and data signals without any loss of information.

terminal entry: any input operation on a terminal.

terminal equipment: see *data-terminal equipment.*

terminal installation: a grouping, at one site, of operable data terminals and related devices.

terminal interchange: a buffering unit at a location remote from the processing center providing temporary storage for messages originating at the terminals that it serves and at the processing center.

terminal I/O wait: the condition of a task in which the task cannot continue processing until a message is received from a terminal.

terminal job: in systems with time sharing, the processing done on behalf of one terminal user from log on to log off.

terminal/light pen system: a system of a specially designed terminal and light pen. By pointing the pen to the desired character position and pressing its tip to the screen, a selection of data for action by the system is made.

terminal mode: a mode of operation of a general purpose computer such that its cathode ray tube and/or printer is used as a terminal for another computer.

terminal modem eliminator: a unit that allows direct terminal to terminal or terminal to computer connection and eliminates the need for two modems operating back to back.

terminal node (TN): the last node of a tree, with no following nodes.

terminal port

(1) in a network, the functional unit

of a node through which data can enter or leave the network. (E)

(2) that part of a processor that is dedicated to a single data channel for the purpose of receiving data from or transferring data to one or more external or remote devices.

terminal quiesce: an orderly shutdown of all terminal activity.

terminal repeater: a repeater for use at the end of a trunk line.

terminal room: a room, associated with a telephone central office, private branch exchange, or private exchange, which contains distributing frames, relays, and similar apparatus except that mounted in the switchboard sections.

terminal self testing: where a terminal automatically tests the major portion of a system, either when the power is turned on or upon the depression of a switch by the operator.

terminal session: the period of time during which a user of a terminal can communicate with an interactive system. Usually, it is the elapsed time from when a terminal user logs on the system until the user logs off the system. see also *session*.

terminal transparency: in telecommunications, the ability to permit incompatible terminals to communicate by automatic code conversion and line control conversion.

terminal unit: a part of the equipment in a communication channel that can be used for either input or output to the channel.

terminal user: in systems with time sharing, anyone who is eligible to log on.

terminated line: a telecommunication line with a resistance attached across its far end equal to the characteristic impedance of the line, so that no reflection and no standing waves are present when a signal is placed on it at the near end.

termination

(1) an item that is connected to the terminals of a circuit or equipment. (F)

(2) an impedance connected to the end of a circuit being tested. (F)

(3) the points on a switching network to which a trunk or a line may be attached. (F)

(4) see *abnormal termination*.

termination charge: a charge due if and when certain types of telephone service (e.g., large PBX service) are prematurely discontinued. The termination charge is typically a decreasing function of time that reduces to zero in two to four years. (F)

termination (of a block): in PL/1, cessation of execution of a block, and the return of control to the activating block by means of a RETURN or END statement, or the transfer of control to the activating block or to some other active block by means of a GO TO statement.

termination (of a task): cessation of the execution of a task. see also *closedown*.

termination symbol: a symbol on the tape showing the end of a block of information.

terminator/initiator: a program that makes a job step ready to run in some computers and performs regular housekeeping functions following the end of a job.

terminology bank: in machine-aided translation systems a computer-based glossary of terms providing translations for all entries.

ternary
(1) pertaining to a selection, choice, or condition that has three possible different values or states. (B)
(2) pertaining to a fixed-radix numeration system having a radix of three.

ternary code: a code in which only three states are considered.

ternary incremental representation: incremental representation in which the value of an increment is rounded to one of three values, plus or minus one quantum or zero. (A) (B)

test (T) (TST): the examination of a criterion, to determine the present arrangement of some element of computer hardware; for example, a manually set switch.

test alphabetic: a validity check developed to ensure that input is properly alphabetic.

test antenna: an antenna of known performance characteristics used in determining transmission characteristics of equipment and associated propagation paths.

test bed: a software package used for program testing.

test board: switchboard equipment with testing apparatus, so arranged that connections can be made from it to telephone lines or central office equipment for testing purposes.

test case: a set of input data which is intended to determine the correctness of a routine.

test condition: in COBOL, a statement that, taken as a whole, may be either true or false, depending on the circumstances existing at the time the expression is evaluated.

test data: the data used in a check

problem. synonymous with *test deck*. (E)

test deck: synonym for *test data*.

test for blanks: a validity check developed to ensure that appropriate fields are blank.

testing: the running of a system or a program against a predetermined series of data to arrive at a predictable result for the purpose of establishing the acceptability of the system or program. (E)

test initialization: applying input patterns to a logic circuit so that all internal memory elements achieve a known logic state.

test numeric: a validity check developed to ensure that input is appropriately numeric.

test pattern generator: a unit used to generate special messages for testing data-transmission devices.

test points: those points within an equipment or equipment string which provide electrical access to signals for the purpose of fault isolation.

test problem: a problem selected to determine whether a computer or a program is operating properly.

test program: a program developed to use and check the differing hardware units of a computer.

testrad: a group of four pulses or bits, used to express a decimal or hexadecimal (base sixteen) number in binary form.

testrode: a four-electrode electronic unit.

test routine: a routine designed to show whether a computer is functioning correctly.

test run: a run used to check that a program is functioning correctly.

test tape program: a tape containing

both program instructions and preapproved test data or coding to be used for analysis diagnostics or checkout runs.

test tone: a tone used in identifying circuits for trouble location or for circuit adjustment. see also *standard test-tone power.*

TEX: see *teletype exchange.*

text (TXT)

(1) in ASCII and data communication, a sequence of characters treated as an entity if preceded and terminated by one STX and one ETX transmission control character, respectively. (A)

(2) in word processing, information for human comprehension that is intended for presentation in a two-dimensional form; for example, printed on paper or displayed on a screen. Text consists of symbols, phrases, or sentences in natural or artificial languages, pictures, diagrams, and tables. (D)

(3) the control sections of an object module or load module.

(4) that part of a message that is of concern to the party ultimately receiving the message; that is, the message exclusive of the header or control information.

(5) cf. *heading.* (A)

(6) see *message text.*

text editing: in word processing, the process of making simple additions, deletions, and changes to a stored document.

text function: in a graphics system, a function that permits text to be entered into a drawing.

text revision: in word processing, the process of stopping, reading, printing, or skipping a character, word,

line, sentence, or paragraph for the purpose of inserting, replacing, or deleting text when editing. (D)

text section: that portion of a load module with computer instructions in final form and data defined and with specified initial values.

text segment: a portion of a message that contains no part of the message header.

text string search: in word processing, a function that enables a point or points to be found within the recorded text by entering a set of unique characters identifying the desired point. (D)

TG: see *telegraph.*

TGID: see *transmission group identifier.*

TH: see *transmission header.*

then: see *IF-THEN element.* (A)

thermal light: a display signal that is visible to a computer operator when the temperature in a device is higher than it is supposed to be.

thick film: pertaining to hybird integrated circuits made of layers of magnetic material deposited on a ceramic substrate.

thimble printer: a printer with a printing element similar to a daisy-wheel. The spokes, however, are bent up out of the plane of rotation forming a cup or thimble structured element with the die-cast type facing outward.

thin film: loosely, magnetic thin film. (A)

thin film storage: see *magnetic thin film storage.* (A)

think time: synonym for *intermessage delay.*

thin window display: in word processing, an electronic display containing as many as 96 characters, and often a single line only.

third-generation computer: a computer that uses logic technology components. The class of computers introduced in the mid-1960s which use integrated circuits as their principal components and whose speed is measured in nanoseconds. These computers feature on-line multiprocessing, multiprogramming, and data-base management systems, as well as increased mass storage capacity and telecommunications input. see *first-generation computer, second-generation computer.*

thirty-nine feature code: pertaining to a code designed for punched cards to represent numerals only from 0 to 39 but with no more than two punches in any column.

thrashing: in a virtual storage system, a condition in which the system can do little useful work because of excessive paging.

thread: see *bead.*

threaded tree: a tree containing extra pointers to other nodes.

three-address instruction: an instruction that contains three address parts. (A) (B)

three-bit byte: synonym for *triplet.* (A)

three-input adder: synonym for *full adder.* (A)

three-plus-one address instruction: an instruction that contains three address parts, the plus-one address being that of the instruction that is to be executed next, unless otherwise specified. (A) (B)

three-row keyboard: the keyboard on baudot-coded teletypewriter equipment.

three-way calling: one of the custom calling features, three-way calling enables a customer to add (by dialing) a third party to an existing connection so that all three parties can communicate. When the third party answers, a private two-party conversation can be held before bridging the connection for a three-party conversation. (F)

threshold

(1) a logic operator having the property that if P is a statement, Q is a statement, R is a statement, . . . , then the threshold of P,Q,R, . . is true if at least N statements are true, false if less than N statements are true, where N is a specified nonnegative integer called the threshold condition.

(2) the threshold condition as in (1). (*A*)

(3) see *fault-rate threshold, fault threshold.*

threshold element

(1) a logic element that performs a threshold operation. synonymous with *threshold gate.* (B)

(2) a device that performs the logic threshold operation but in which the truth of each input statement contributes, to the output determination, a weight associated with that statement. (*A*)

threshold function: a two-valued switching function of one or more not necessarily boolean arguments that take the value one if a specified mathematical function of the arguments exceeds a given threshold value, and zero otherwise. (A) (B)

threshold gate: synonym for *threshold element.* (A) (B)

threshold operation: an operation performed on operands to obtain a value of a threshold function. (A) (B)

threshold quantity: the number of items that must be purchased to qualify for a reduced price.

through-group equipment: in carrier telephone transmission, equipment which accepts the signal from the group receive output and attenuates it to the proper signal level for insertion at the input of a group transmit equipment. This shall be accomplished without frequency translation.

throughput: a measure of the amount of work performed by a computer system over a given period of time, for example, jobs per day. (A) (B)

through-supergroup equipment: in carrier telephone transmission, equipment which accepts the multiplexed signal from the supergroup receive output, amplifies it, and provides the proper signal level to the input of a supergroup transmit equipment. This shall be accomplished without frequency translation.

thumb wheel: in computer graphics, a wheel, movable about its axis, that provides a scalar value. A pair of thumb wheels can be used as a locator device. (E)

ticking: in OCR, the marks caused by the bottom of the upper case character while typing in lower case, or vice versa.

tie: in perforated continuous forms paper, the interval between cuts.

tie line: a private-line communication channel of the type provided by communication common carriers for linking two or more points together.

tie trunk (TTK): a telephone line or channel directly connecting two branch exchanges.

tightly coupled: pertaining to processing units that share real storage, that are controlled by the same control program, and that can communicate directly with each other. see also *loosely coupled.*

till: a tray in the cash drawer or the point of sale terminal, used to keep the different denominations of bills and coins separated and easily accessible.

time (T): see *access time, available time, compiling time, computer time, corrective maintenance time, cycle time, deferred maintenance time, development time, downtime, emergency maintenance time, idle time, installation time, maintenance time, makeup time, operating time, preventive maintenance time, problem time, production time, program development time, program execution time, real time, translating time, word time.* (*A*)

time consistent bus hour: synonymous with *fixed busy hour.* (F)

time-delay circuit: a circuit that delays the transmission of an impulse for a specific time period.

time-derived channel: any channel obtained by the time-division multiplexing of a channel.

time divided network: a subsystem of a switch used to interconnect two or more circuits whose elements are continuously time-shared between many channels. Information in the network can be represented in analog or digital form.

time division: a method of serving a number of simultaneous channels over a common transmission path by assigning the transmission path sequentially to the various channels, each assignment being for a discrete time interval. (F)

time-division multiple access: a means of merging signal streams in traffic of data to and from satellites.

time-division multiplexing (TDM): a multiplexing approach to allocate a communications channel for a stated short period to a number of differing units.

time division switch: one in which the paths between users are shared among many users through a single switch element by interfacing them in time sequence. cf. *space division switch*.

time frame: a defined structure, based on two or more events, using time as a basis of measurement. (E)

time level: the portion of a switching network that provides a signal path that is time-shared with many channels.

time out (TMO) (TO)

(1) a parameter related to an enforced event designed to occur at the conclusion of a predetermined elapsed time. A time-out condition can be cancelled by the receipt of an appropriate time-out cancellation signal. (E)

(2) a time interval allotted for certain operations to occur; for example, response to polling or addressing before a system operation is interrupted and must be restarted.

(3) a terminal feature that logs off a user if an entry is not made within a specified period of time.

time pulse distribution: a device or circuit for allocating timing pulses or clock pulses to one or more conducting paths or control lines in specified sequence.

time quantum: the time given to a user in a time-sharing system.

timer (T): a register whose content is changed at regular intervals in such a manner as to measure time. synonymous with *clock register, time register*. (*A*) (B)

time register: synonym for *timer*. (A) (B)

time scale: see *extended time scale, fast time scale, variable time scale*. (A)

time scale factor: in simulation, the ratio of computer time to the corresponding problem time. (A)

time schedule controller: a specific controller in which the reference input signal (or the set point) adheres automatically to a predetermined time schedule.

time sequencing: signal switching generated by a program as a function of accurately measured elapsed time.

time share: to use a device for two or more interleaved purposes. (A)

time sharing (TS)

(1) pertaining to the interleaved use of time on a computer system that enables two or more users to execute computer programs concurrently. (A)

(2) a mode of operation of a data-processing system that provides for the interleaving in time of two or more processes in one processor. (B)

(3) a method of using a computing system that allows a number of users to execute programs concurrently and to interact with the programs during execution.

(4) the use of a facility or equipment for more than one purpose or function or for repetition of the same function within the same overall time period. This is accomplished by inter-

spersing or interleaving the required actions in time. (F)

(5) deprecated term for *conversational mode*. (A)

time-sharing interchange: allows the interactive user to issue commands that cause batch programs to be executed under various programs by transferring data and other required input, either entered at the interactive terminal or stored in files, from offices to a batch-processing system operating within the time-sharing network.

time-sharing monitor system: a collection of programs remaining permanently in memory to provide overall coordination and control of the total operating system.

time sharing option (TSO): an optional configuration of the operating system that provides conversational time sharing from remote stations.

time-sharing priority: in systems with time sharing, a ranking within the group of tasks associated with a single user, used to determine their precedence in receiving system resources.

time-sharing system (TSS): a combination of hardware and software in a computer system that allocated central processor time and other computer services to multiple users at different locations so that the computer, in effect, processes a number of programs simultaneously.

time-sharing user modes: at any moment, a user is in one of the following execution modes, (1) inactive (2) command (3) ready (4) running; (5) waiting (a) for input-output completion (b) for console action (c) for task completion, (d) to be loaded.

time slice

(1) an interval of time on the processing unit allocated for use in performing a task. After the interval has expired, processing unit time is allocated to another task; thus a task cannot monopolize processing unit time beyond a fixed limit.

(2) in systems with time sharing, a segment of time allocated to a terminal job.

time slicing

(1) a mode of operation in which two or more processes are assigned quantity of time on the same processor. (B)

(2) a feature that can be used to prevent a task from monopolizing the processing unit and thereby delaying the assignment of processing unit time to other tasks.

(3) in systems with time sharing, the allocation of time slices to terminal jobs.

time utilization: arranging a program to permit processing to continue while records needed for processing are located in file and read into core and working storage.

timing and control circuit: a circuit that receives bus and internal control signals and generates appropriate read/write timing and control signals.

timing error: error generated when a program is unable to keep pace with the tape-transfer rate, or a new motion or select command is released prior to the earlier command being fully completed.

timing jitter: in digital carrier systems, an accumulative relative timing discrepancy between digital signal elements. The most common causes are transmission media with nonuniform delay versus frequency characteristics and imperfect timing recovery in digital line regenerators. (F)

timing meter: a unit that measures the time duration of a function by sampling the state of a memory element or elements associated with that activity. One type of timing meter is a binary counter driven by a clock derived either from the basic CPU clock or from a special generator.

timing recovery: the process of determining the appropriate sampling times for a synchronous data stream. (F)

timing signals: electrical pulses sent throughout the machine at regular intervals to ensure absolute total synchronization.

tip: the end of the plug used to make circuit connections in a manual switchboard. The tip is the connector attached to the positive side of the common battery which powers the station equipment. By extension, it is the positive battery side of a telecommunication line. synonymous with *tip side.*

tip and ring conductors: the two conductors associated with a two-wire cable pair. The terms *tip* and *ring* derive their names from the physical characteristics of an operator's cordboard plug, in which these two conductors terminated in the days of manual switchboards. Use of the names *tip* and *ring* has extended throughout the plant. The cord-board plug also had a sleeve, and the name is occasionally used for a third conductor associated with tip and ring. (F)

tip cable: a small (usually 100 pair) cable connecting terminals on a dis-

tributing frame to cable pairs in the cable vault. (F)

tip conductor: one conductor of a customer line (tip and ring). (F)

tip, ring, ground: the conductive paths between a central office and a station. The tip and ring leads constitute the metallic pair of wires that carry a balanced speech or data signal. The ground path in combination with the conductor is used occasionally for signaling. (F)

tip side: synonym for *tip.*

TK: see *track.*

TLP: see *transmission level point.*

TLU: see *table look-up.*

TM

(1) see *tape mark.*

(2) see *Turing machine.*

TML: see *terminal.*

TMO: see *time out.*

TN: see *terminal node.*

TO: see *time out.*

TOC: table of contents.

TOD: time of day.

toggle: pertaining to any device having two stable states. synonym for *flip-flop.* (A)

toggle switch

(1) a manually operated electric switch having a small projecting arm.

(2) an electronically operated circuit that holds either of two states until changed.

token: a distinguishable unit in a sequence of characters.

tolerance: the allowable range of deviation from an attribute nominal value.

toll

(1) in public switched systems, a charge for a connection beyond an exchange boundary, based on time and distance.

(2) service that is a part of public telephone service but under a tariff separate from the exchange area tariff. Also used to describe components of the facilities network that are used principally for toll service. (F)

toll center: a central office where channels and toll message circuits terminate. While this is usually one particular central office in a city, larger cities may have several central offices where toll message circuits terminate; a class 4 office. synonymous with *toll office, toll point.*

toll-connecting trunk: a trunk between an end office and a toll office. (F)

toll-free number: synonym for *enterprise number.*

toll hierarchy: the ordered structure established among toll offices of the United States and Canadian public telephone network to provide systematic switched routing of calls. Four hierarchical classes apply to toll offices, whereas local, or end, offices are designated class 5. (F)

toll office: a switching office where trunks are interconnected to serve toll calls. Toll offices are arranged in a hierarchical structure as follows: regional center—class 1, sectional center—class 2, primary center—class 3, toll center—class 4. (F)

toll point: synonymous with *toll center.*

toll service: public telephone service with points outside the designated local exchange service area for a station and for which calls are billed individually. Includes service through the toll switching hierarchy. (F)

toll switching trunk: a line connecting a toll office to a local exchange.

tone dialing: synonym for *push-button dialing.*

T1 Repeated Line: a duplex digital transmission facility carrying bi-polar pulse streams over paired cables.

T1 Repeater: a regenerative device used to amplify and reconstruct T1 bit streams for long-distance circuits.

top-down programming: the design and coding of computer programs using a hierarchical structure in which related functions are performed at each level of the structure.

top-of-form: initial print position (top, left).

topological optimization: a designer's task to decide how to interconnect network locations as economically as possible, while meeting all performance goals and constraints.

topology: the physical or logical placement of nodes in a computer network.

torn-tape switching center: a location where operators tear off the incoming printed and punched paper tape and transfer it manually to the proper outgoing circuit.

total system: a strategy to place critical operational components of an organization under the complete or partial control of computers. synonymous with *integrated system.*

Touch-Call: proprietary term of GT&E. see also *push-button dialing.*

touch screen terminal: a terminal with a screen that is sensitive to touch, consequently, data can be input easily. see *light pen, "mouse," soft keyboard.*

touch sensitive: switches that can be easily activated by merely touching a conductive surface.

touch-sensitive keyboards: synonymous with *membrane keyboards*.

Touchtone: developed by AT&T, the replacement of the conventional telephone dial with a panel of buttons, which when pushed generate a tone which operates switching devices at the telephone exchange. These tones can be utilized to yield input to a computer. *see Touchtone dial.*

Touchtone dial: a push-button pad and associated oscillator circuitry used to transmit address (or end-to-end data) signals from customer stations by means of in-band tones. Each decimal digit, plus a maximum of six additional signals, is uniquely represented by selecting one frequency from each of two mutually exclusive groups of four. The dial is ordinarily powered from the central office. (F)

tournament sort: a repeated selection sort in which each subset consists of no more than two items. (A)

TP
(1) see *teleprocessing*.
(2) teletype printer.

TPIOS: a facility that supports programmable telecommunication control units (TCUs) and generates channel programs for the channel scheduler.

TPLAB: see *tape label.*

TP-PCB: see *data communication program communication block (DC-PCB).*

TR: see *track.*

TRA: see *transfer.*

trace
(1) a record of the execution of a computer program; it exhibits the sequences in which the instructions were executed. (A)

(2) to record a series of events as they occur.
(3) see *address trace, fault trace.*

trace debug: a debugging program that displays a set of registers and/or memory locations as they are encountered throughout the execution of a program, usually without interrupting the program execution.

trace flow: a debugging unit that prints out contents of various registers and memory locations in a particular program segment specified by a user.

trace program: a computer program that performs a check on another computer program by exhibiting the sequence in which the instructions are executed and usually the results of executing the instructions. (A) (B)

trace table: a storage area in which trace information is placed.

tracing routine: a routine that provides an historical record of specified events in the execution of a computer program. (A)

track (T) (TK) (TR) (TRK)
(1) the path or one of the set of paths, parallel to the reference edge on a data medium, associated with a single reading or writing component as the data medium moves past the component. (B)
(2) the portion of a moving data medium, such as a drum, tape, or disk, that is accessible to a given reading head position. (A)
(3) in word processing, an area on magnetic recording media along which a series of signals may be recorded. (D)
(4) see *address track, card track, clock track, feed track, magnetic track, regenerative track.* (A)

track ball: synonym for *control ball.* (E)

track hold: a facility that protects a track while it is being accessed. When data on a track is being modified by a task in one partition, that track cannot be accessed at the same time by a task or subtask in another partition.

tracking: in computer graphics, a technique of echoing a locator, using a cursor. (E)

tracking cross: a crosslike array of sharp dots on a display, used for finding points and lines or for drawing curves.

tracking symbol: in computer graphics, a marker on the display space that indicates the position corresponding to coordinate data produced by a locator device. (E)

track pitch: the distance between corresponding points of adjacent tracks. (A) (B)

tracks density: the number of bits written in a single position across the width of a tape, including parity bits.

track selection: in word processing, selection that enables specific tracks on the recording medium to be accessed. (D)

track selector: in word processing, a device that enables a particular track on the recording medium to be selected. (D)

tractor feed: a means for accurately positioning and transporting fan-fold paper in printers.

tractor feeder: in word processing, a device attached to a printer to automatically feed edge-perforated roll paper or forms. (D)

tractor holes: synonym for *carrier holes.*

tractors: grippers to guide paper through the printer.

traffic: in data communication, transmitted and received messages.

traffic information: terminal information concerning the type of message or transaction, the number of transactions per day or hour, message-length distributions for input and output, priority, and others.

traffic intensity: the measurement of the difference between insertion and deletion rates in a queue.

traffic network: an arrangement of channels, such as loops and trunks, associated switching arrangements, and station equipments designed to handle a specific body of traffic; a subset of the facility network. (F)

traffic service position: a cordless console that is associated with either a crossbar tandem office or a traffic service position system, equipped so that operators can provide assistance if needed on station-to-station calls, special toll calls, coin distance dialing calls, and all local and toll assistance traffic. The operators provide assistance in completing these calls and ensure that correct data are recorded in the centralized automatic message accounting equipment or in the traffic service position system equipment. The operators also supervise coin deposits for calls originating at coin stations. The position is arranged for automatic display of both the calling and called numbers, as well as certain other information. (F)

traffic service position system (TSPS): that type of traffic service system, having stored program control, that provides for the processing and recording of special toll calls, coin station toll calls, and other types of calls requiring operator assistance. It includes traffic service positions arranged in groups called traffic offices where operators are automatically connected in on calls to perform the functions necessary to process and record the calls correctly. (F)

traffic statistics: information obtained from an analysis of communications traffic.

traffic usage recorder (TUR): a device that scans trunks periodically and counts the number busy. At the end of an hour, the TUR provides a measure of usage based on the sampled values. (F)

trailer

(1) a record that follows a group of detail records and provides information about a group not present in the detail records.

(2) a record that follows a header.

trailer card: a card that contains information related to the data on the preceding cards. synonymous with *detail card*. (*A*)

trailer label: a file or data set label that follows the data records on a unit of recording media.

trailer record: a record which follows one or more records and contains data related to those records.

trailing decision: a loop control that is executed after the loop body. cf. *leading decision*. (*A*)

trailing end: the end of a perforated tape that last enters a perforated-tape reader. (A)

trailing zero: in position notation, a zero in a less significant digit place than the digit place of the least significant nonzero digit of a numeral. (A)

trail printer: in word processing, a printer that is not uniquely associated with a particular keyboard or display-based work station and that is used for automatic printout of text already recorded onto a recording medium or in electronic storage within associated word processing equipment. Printing follows or "trails the next generation." see also *attended trail printer, unattended trail printer*. (D)

train: a sequence of pieces of apparatus joined together to forward or complete a call. see also *switch train*. see *pulse train*.

TRAN

(1) see *transaction*.

(2) see *transmit*.

TRAN-PRO: see *transaction processing*.

TRANS: see *translator*.

transaction (T) (TRAN) (TRX)

(1) in batch or remote batch entry, a job or job step.

(2) in systems with time sharing, an exchange between a terminal and another device that accomplishes a particular action or result; for example, the entry of a customer's deposit and the updating of the customer's balance.

transaction data: data describing a particular event in a data-processing application area, such as job number, quantity, price, and so on.

transaction file: a file containing relatively transient data that, for a given application, is processed together with the appropriate master file. synonymous with *detail file*. (*A*) (B)

transaction log: in the programmable store system, a record of transactions performed at the point-of-sale terminal. This log is magnetically recorded and stored on the store controller integrated disks.

transaction-oriented system: a specialized type of on-line system that handles interactive-type applications that revolve around entering, retrieving, updating, and/or manipulating information utilizing one or more user-written programs.

transaction processing (TRAN-PRO): the ability of a computer to enter and process a collection of several related actions; the ability to handle multiple transactions from one or more terminals in a network. A transaction may be a single entry or a series of entries that would initiate a series of automatic actions within the computer system.

transaction record: a record in a transaction data set, created by one or more executions of a program that is coded to generate transaction records.

transaction record header: identification and control information at the beginning of the first block of a transaction record.

transaction record number: a number assigned to a transaction record when its generation is initiated and within the range of numbers available for the defined group.

transaction tape: a magnetic tape with transactions or change records. synonymous with *change tape*.

transborder data flow: the flow of information or data across national boundaries.

transceiver: a terminal that can transmit and receive traffic.

transcribe: to transfer data from one data medium to another, converting them as necessary for acceptance by the receiving medium. (A) (B)

transcriber: machines associated with a computer used for transferring the input or output data from a record of information in a stated language to the computer medium and language, or from a computer to a record of information.

transcription: the conversion of data from one language, code, medium to another, including reading, translating, and recording functions.

transcription break: a flowchart symbol or unit that shows the relationship between two files. The symbol is directional and suggests the flow of information from one file to another that is impacted upon by the information.

transducer: a device for converting energy from one form to another. (A)

transducer translating unit: a unit that converts error of the controlled member of a servomechanism into an electrical signal that is used in correcting the error.

transfer (TRA) (XFER)
(1) to send data from one place and to receive the data at another place. synonymous with *move*. (A) (B)
(2) in word processing, the movement of selected recorded text from one element of recording medium to another. (D)
(3) deprecated term for *jump*. (A) (B)
(4) see *block transfer, peripheral transfer, radical transfer*. (A)

transfer check: a check on the accuracy of a data transfer. (A)

transfer circuit: a circuit that connects communication centers of two or more separate networks to transfer the traffic between the networks.

transfer control: action from a branch instruction as it transfers control from one portion of a program to another.

transfer function: the mathematical expression pertaining to the output of a closed loop servomechanism to the input.

transfer instruction: deprecated term for *jump instruction.* (A) (B)

transfer interpreter: a device that prints on a punched card characters corresponding to hole patterns punched in another card. (B)

transfer key: in word processing, a control that initiates the transfer process. (D)

transfer medium: material aiding the transfer of ink during printing, that is, sheets, ribbons, plastic film.

transfer of control: see *jump.*

transfer of control card: see *transition card.*

transfer operation: moves information from a storage location or one storage medium to another; often refers to movement between different storage media.

transfer rate: see *data transfer rate.*

transferred information: synonym for *transinformation content.* (A) (B)

transfer time: the time interval between the instant at which a transfer of data starts and the instant at which the transfer is completed. (B)

transform
(1) to change the form of data according to specific rules, without significantly changing the meaning of the data. (B)
(2) in computer graphics, to change a display image, for example, by scaling, rotating, or translating.
(3) synonymous with *convert.* (A)

transformation (T): see *key transformation, signal transformation.* (A)

transhybrid loss: the transmission loss between opposite ports of a hybrid network, that is, between the four-wire input and output terminal ports. The transhybrid loss is ideally very large, a condition that is approached when the hybrid is properly terminated. (F)

transient: pertaining to a program that does not reside in main storage or to a temporary storage area for such programs.

transient area: a storage area used for temporary storage of transient programs or routines.

transient error: an error that occurs once or at unpredictable intervals.

transient routine: a self-relocating routine, permanently stored on a system residence device and loaded into the transient area when needed for execution.

transient state: the condition of a station when it is setting up to transmit.

transinformation: see *transinformation content.*

transinformation content: in information theory, the difference between the information content conveyed by the occurrence of an event and the conditional information content conveyed by the occurrence of the same event, given the occurrence of another event. synonymous with *mutual information, transferred information, transmitted information.* see *mean transinformation content.* (A) (B)

transinformation rate: see *average transinformation rate.* (A)

transistor: a small solid-state, semiconducting device, ordinarily using germanium, that performs nearly all the functions of an electronic tube, especially amplification.

transistor-resistor logic (TRL): synonymous with *resistor-transistor logic.*

transition: the switching from one state (for example, positive voltage) to another (negative voltage) in a serial transmission.

transition card: in the loading of a deck of program cards, the card that causes the termination of loading, then initiates the execution of the program.

translate:

(1) to transform data from one language to another. (A) (B)

(2) in computer graphics, to move a display image on the display space in a straight line from one location to another location without rotating the image. (E)

translate duration: synonym for *translating time.* (A) (B)

translate phase: the logical subdivision of a run that includes the execution of the translator. synonymous with *translating phase.* (A) (B)

translater: see *translator.*

translating: in computer graphics, moving all or part of a display image on the display space from one location to another without rotating the image. (E)

translating phase: synonym for *translate phase.* (A) (B)

translating program: synonym for *translator.* (A) (B)

translating time: the elapsed time taken for the execution of a translator. synonymous with *translate duration.* (A) (B)

translation

(1) pertaining to the conversion of

data from one expression in one particular form to an expression in another without a significant change in meaning or value.

(2) in switching systems, the process of interpreting all or part of a destination code to determine the routing of a call. (F)

translator (TRANS)

(1) a computer program that translates from one language into another language and in particular from one programming language into another programming language. synonymous with *translating program.* (A) (B)

(2) in telephone equipment, the device that converts dialed digits into call-routine information.

(3) a device that converts information from one form to another. In switching systems, a translator converts address digits to an identification of the appropriate trunk group to be used. (F)

translator routine: a routine that compiles a source program expressed in problem-oriented language to an object program in machine code.

transliterate

(1) to convert data, character by character. (B)

(2) to convert characters of one alphabet to the corresponding characters of another alphabet. (*A*)

transmission (X)

(1) the sending of data from one place for reception elsewhere.

(2) in ASCII and data communication, a series of characters including headings and texts. (*A*)

(3) the dispatching of a signal, message, or other form of intelligence by wire, radio, telegraphy, telephone, facsimile, or other means. (E)

(4) one or more blocks or messages. For BSC and start-stop devices, a transmission is terminated by an EOT character. see also *block*, *message*.

(5) designates a field of work, such as equipment development, system design, planning, or engineering, in which electrical communication technology is used to create systems to carry information over a distance. (F)

(6) refers to the process of sending information from one point to another. (F)

(7) used with a modifier to describe the quality of a telephone connection—good, fair, or poor transmission. (F)

(8) refers to the transfer characteristic of a channel or network in general or, more specifically, to the amplitude transfer characteristic. One sometimes hears the phrase, "transmission as a function of frequency." (F)

(9) synonymous with *data transmission*. (A)

(10) see *asynchronous transmission, burst transmission, duplex transmission, half-duplex transmission, one-way transmission, parallel transmission, serial transmission, start-stop transmission, synchronous transmission*.

(11) see also *data communication*.

transmission-block character: see *end-of-transmission-block character*. (A)

transmission code: a code for sending information over telecommunication lines.

transmission control (TC) character

(1) any control character used to control or facilitate transmission of data between data-terminal equipment (DTEs). (A) (B)

(2) characters transmitted over a line that are not message data but which cause certain control operations to be performed when encountered; among such operations are addressing, polling, message delimiting and blocking, transmission error checking, and carriage return.

(3) synonymous with *communication control character*.

transmission control unit (TCU): a communication control unit whose operations are controlled solely by programmed instructions from the computing system to which the unit is attached; no program is stored or executed in the unit. cf. *communication controller*. synonymous with *telecommunication control unit*.

transmission deviations: departures from a flat response in the gain-frequency and delay-frequency characteristics of channels or transmission media. (F)

transmission extension: a simplified nonringing extension to which a local serial data terminal is attached.

transmission facility: an element of physical telephone plant that performs the function of transmission; for example, a multipair cable, a coaxial cable system, or a microwave radio system. (F)

transmission interface: a shared boundary defined by functional characteristics, common physical interconnection characteristics, signal characteristics, and other characteristics, as appropriate.

transmission interruption: the interruption of a transmission from a terminal by a higher priority transmission to the terminal. synonymous with *reverse break*.

transmission level: see *relative transmission level*.

transmission level point (TLP): a specification, in dB, of the relative level at a particular point in a transmission system as referred to a zero transmission level point (0 TLP). Note that the TLP value does not specify the absolute power that will exist at that point, and the unit of TLP specification is not dBm. (F)

transmission line: synonym for *telecommunication line*.

transmission link: the section of a channel or circuit between a transmitter station and the next telegraph repeater, two successive telegraph repeaters, and the receiving station and the preceding telegraph repeater.

transmission loss: a drop in signal power during transmission.

transmission medium: any material substance that can be, or is, used for the propagation of signals, usually in the form of modulated radio, light, or acoustic waves, from one point to another, such as an optical fiber, cable, bundle, wire, dielectric slab, water, or air. (E)

transmission objectives: electrical performance characteristics for communication circuits, systems, and equipments based on both economic and technical considerations of telephone facilities and on reasonable estimates of the performance desired. Characteristics for which objectives are stated include: loss, noise, echo, cross talk, frequency shift, attenuation distortion, envelope delay distortion, and so on. (F)

transmission service: a circuit switched, packet switched, or a leased circuit service provided to the public by a communication common carrier or by a telecommunication administration.

transmission speed: the number of information elements sent per unit of time, expressed as bits, characters, word groups, or records per second or per minute.

transmission system code: a way of using a character parity check plus a block check to find errors.

transmit (T) (TRAN) (XMIT) (XMT)
(1) to send data from one place for reception elsewhere. (A)
(2) to move an entity from one place to another; for example, to broadcast radio waves, to dispatch data via a transmission medium, or to transfer data from one data station to another via a line. (E)
(3) see also *transfer*.

transmit control block: a block of consecutive half-word storage locations in which an SDLC program module has placed the information that controls the channel I/O (CHIO) transmission of one or more SDLC frames.

transmit data set: a data set on diskette storage that is generated by packing data from one or more transaction data set groups.

transmit flow control: a transmission procedure that controls the rate at which data may be transmitted from one point so that it is equal to the rate at which it can be received by a remote point. (E)

transmit leg: the side of a duplex line that is transmitting. cf. *receive leg*.

transmittal mode: the method by which the contents of an input buffer are made available to the program, and the method by which a program makes records available for output.

transmitted information: synonym for *transinformation content.* (A) (B)

transmitter: in telephony, a unit that converts sound to electrical energy.

transmitter-distributor (TD): the device in a teletypewriter terminal which makes and breaks the line in timed sequence. Modern usage of the term refers to a paper tape transmitter.

transmitter register: a register that serializes data and presents it to the transmitted data output.

transmitter start code (TSC): a Bell System term for character sequence that is sent to an outlying teletypewriter terminal which automatically polls its tape transmitter or keyboard. see also *polling.*

transmultiplexer: equipment that transforms signals derived from frequency-division-multiplex equipment (such as group or supergroup) to time-division multiplexed signals having the same structure as those derived from pulse code modulation multiplex equipment (such as primary or secondary pulse code modulation multiplex signals), and vice versa.

transparency mode: see *transparent text mode.*

transparent: in data transmission, pertaining to information that is not recognized by the receiving program or device as transmission control characters. see *code transparent data transmission, inherent transparency.*

transparent data

(1)   data that is not recognized as containing transmission control characters.

(2)   data in a transmit data set that is not interpreted as containing control characters. Transparent data is preceded by a control byte and a count of the amount of data following.

transparent information: information that is not recognized as transmission control characters by a receiving program or device.

transparent text mode: a mode of binary synchronous text transmission in which data, including normally restricted data-link control characters, are transmitted only as specific bit patterns. Control characters that are intended to be effective are preceded by a DLE character. cf. *nontransparent mode.*

transparent transmission: transmission where the transmission medium does not recognize control characters or initiates any control activity.

transponder: a radio or satellite transceiver that responds to a particular interrogation signal by transmitting identifiable signals.

transport: see *tape transport.* (A)

transport layer: in open systems architecture, the layer that, together with the network, data link, and physical layers, provides services for the transport of data between network elements. (E)

transport unit: peripheral devices or media handling unit, such as a card feed.

transposition: interchanging the position of open-wire conductors relative to each other to reduce induced signals.

transverse check: a system of error control based on a preset rule for formation of characters.

transverse cross-talk coupling: between a disturbing and a distributed circuit in any given section, the vector summation of the direct couplings between adjacent short lengths of the two circuits, without dependence on intermediate flow in other nearby circuits.

transverse parity check: a parity check performed on a group of binary digits in a transverse direction for each frame. synonymous with *transverse redundancy check*. (E)

transverse redundancy check (TRC): synonym for *transverse parity check*.

transverse scanning: scanning where the head moves across, rather than along, the recording tape.

trap (TRP): an unprogrammed, on conditional, jump to a specified address that is automatically activated by hardware, a recording being made of the location from which the jump occurred. (A) (B)

trap/breakpoint: halts that are inserted in object code to cause a branch to a debug program at proper times and places.

trapping: a unique feature of some computers enabling an unscheduled jump (transfer) to be made to a predetermined location in response to a machine condition.

trapping mode: used in program-diagnostic procedures. If the trapping mode flip-flop is set and the program includes any one of specific instructions, the instruction is not performed but the following instruction is taken from location 0. Program-counter contents are saved in order to resume the program following executing the diagnostic procedure.

traveling class mark: a unique label that identifies a call as it is routed through the network; for example, an indication that the call originated from a coin telephone. Traveling class marks are not presently used, but will be possible with CCIS. It will then become possible to use the same transmission facility in several different traffic networks, each identified by a traveling class mark. (F)

traveling-wave tube: an efficient, high-power radio frequency amplifying device used in microwave radio transmitters.

traverse: the area through which a punched card is transported through the unit.

tray: the flat file drawer used to store punched cards.

tree: a type of decoder where the diagrammatic representation resembles the branches and trunk of a tree.

tree form language: a language where the files are structured in a hierarchical, or tree form.

tree network: a network configuration in which there is only one path between any two nodes. (E)

tree sort: a sort that exchanges data items treated as nodes of a tree.

tree structure: a hierarchical calling sequence, consisting of a root segment and one or more levels of segments called via the root segment.

trend: to print or record variable values.

triad: a group of three characters or bits.

trial divisor: the initial approximation in the dividing arithmetic process.

trial run: a means for checking the accuracy of methods. A sample card deck or part of the actual run data can be used for such a check.

tributary circuit: a circuit connecting as an individual drop, or drops, to a switching center.

tributary station: in a multipoint connection, using basic mode link control, any data station other than the control station. (E)

trigger: to cause the immediate execution of a computer program, often by intervention from the external environment, by means of a manually controlled jump to an entry point. (A) (B)

trigger circuit: a circuit that has a number of stable states or unstable states, at least one being stable, and designed so that a desired transition can be initiated by the application of a suitable pulse. (A)

trigger level: the minimum receiver input that causes the transmitter of a transponder to emit a signal.

trim-pot: a resistor adjusted by hand.

trip computer: a small computer used in a vehicle to obtain current information on fuel consumption, driving range on remaining fuel, number of miles to destination, and other desired information.

triple-length register: three registers that function as a single register. synonymous with *triple register*. (B)

triple-length working: arithmetic operations performed on numbers requiring three words in order to yield proper precision.

triple-precision: pertaining to the use of three computer words to represent a number in accordance with the required precision. (A) (B)

triple register: synonym for *triple-length register*. (A) (B)

triplet: a byte composed of three bina-ry elements. synonymous with *three-bit byte*. (A) (B)

TRK: see *track*.

TRL: transistor-resistor logic. see *resistor-transistor logic*.

trouble location problem: a test problem when incorrectly solved, gives information on the location of the faulty device; used after a check problem has shown that a fault exists.

troubleshoot: to detect, locate, and eliminate errors in computer programs or faults in hardware.

trouble unit: a weighting figure applied to telephone circuits to indicate the expected performance in a given period.

TRP: see *trap*.

true complement: deprecated term for *radix complement*. (A) (B)

truncate

(1) to terminate a computational process in accordance with some rule; for example, to end the evaluation of a power series at a specified term. (A)

(2) to remove the beginning or ending elements of a string.

truncation

(1) the deletion or omission of a leading or of a trailing portion of a string in accordance with specified criteria. (B)

(2) the termination of a computation process before its final conclusion or natural termination, if any, in accordance with specified rules. (B)

(3) cf. *round*. (A)

truncation error: an error due to truncation. (A) (B)

trunk

(1) a telephone channel between two control offices or switching devices that is used in providing a

telephone connection between subscribers.

(2) a communication channel between two switching systems. The term *switching system* includes central office types, toll switching systems, PBXs, key telephone systems, manual and automatic switchboards, concentrators. (F)

(3) see *tie trunk*.

(4) see also *line, link, path, route*.

trunk circuit: a circuit, part of a switching system, associated with the connection of a trunk to the switching system. It serves to convert between the signal formats used internally in the switching system and those used in the transmission circuit, and it performs logic and sometimes memory functions associated with supervision. (F)

trunk exchange: an exchange devoted primarily to interconnecting trunks.

trunk group: those trunks between two points, both of which are switching centers, individual message distribution points, or both, and which use the same multiplex terminal equipments.

trunk hunting: a method of switching incoming calls to the next consecutive or next available number if the first called number is busy.

trunk order: a document (or data-system equivalent) used in an operating company to request a change to a trunk group. (F)

truth table

(1) an operation table for a logic operation. (B)

(2) a table that describes a logic function by listing all possible combinations of input values and indicating, for each combination, the true output values. (*A*)

truth value: the input and output quantities in a truth table.

TRX: see *transaction*.

TS

(1) see *time sharing*.

(2) see *transmission service*.

TSC: see *transmitter start code*.

TSK: see *task*.

TSO: see *time-sharing option*.

TSO command language: the set of commands, subcommands, and operands recognized under the time-sharing option (TSO).

TSO/VTAM: Time Sharing Option for the Virtual Telecommunications Access Method.

TSPS: see *traffic service position system*.

TSS: see *time-sharing system*.

TST: see *test*.

TT: see *teletype*.

TTD: see *temporary text delay*.

TTK: see *tie trunk*.

TTW: see *teletypewriter*.

TTY

(1) see *teletype*.

(2) see *teletypewriter*.

TU: see *tape unit*.

tube: synonymous with *screen*.

tumbling: in computer graphics, turning all or part of a display image about an axis that is neither in the plane nor perpendicular to the display surface. (E)

tuning: the process of adjusting system control variables to make the system divide its resources most efficiently for the work load.

TUR: see *traffic usage recorder*.

Turing machine (TM): a mathematical model of a device that changes its internal state and reads from, writes on, and moves, a potentially infinite tape, all in accordance with its present state, thereby constituting a model for computerlike behavior. see *universal Turing machine*.

turnaround sequence: in loop operation, a unique 16-bit sequence transmitted by the primary station to indicate to the secondary stations that the primary station is changing from a transmitter to a receiver. The turnaround sequence is: 0111111000000000.

turnaround time

(1) the elapsed time between submission of a job and the return of the complete output. (B)

(2) the actual time required to reverse the direction of transmission from send to receive or vice versa when using a half-duplex circuit. For most telecommunication facilities, there will be time required by line propagation and line effects, modem timing, and machine reaction. A typical time is 200 milliseconds on a half-duplex telephone connection.

(3) see also *response time*.

turn-key console: in personal computers, the low cost switch control panel for operator control of power, initialize, and execution.

turn-key system: a system that is supplied to the user in a ready-to-run condition; preparatory procedures such as installation, setup, and testing are usually done by the supplier.

turtlegraphics: a method of forming graphic images on a display or output unit by sending commands to a "turtle" represented by a cursor on a CRT screen or plotter pen, and so on.

tutorial lights: on "intelligent" terminals, programmable indicator lights

interlaced with the transaction sequence providing tutorial lead-through to an operator and/or providing a pictorial history of keyboard activity during a transaction.

twelve edge: synonymous with *twelve punch*.

twelve punch: a punch in the top row of a Hollerith card. synonymous with *twelve edge, Y punch*. (A)

twenty-nine feature code: a code designed for punched cards to represent numerals only from 0 to 29 but with no more than two punches in any one column.

twin cable: a cable composed of two insulated conductors laid parallel and either attached to each other by the insulation or bound together with a common covering.

twin check: a continuous duplication check achieved by the duplication of hardware and/or an automatic comparison of data.

twisted pair: a pair of wires used in transmission circuits and twisted about one another to minimize coupling with other circuits. Paired cable is made up of a few to several thousand twisted pairs. (F)

two-address: see *two-address instruction*.

two-address code: a specific instruction code containing two operand addresses.

two-address instruction: an instruction that contains two address parts. (A) (B)

two-bit byte: synonym for *doublet*. (A) (B)

two-channel switch: a hardware feature that allows an input-output device to be attached to two channels.

two-input adder: synonym for *half-ad-*

der. (A) (B)

two-input subtracter: a logical element that accepts two input signals and produces two digital outputs, a borrow digit and a digit for the difference.

two key rollover: keys that prevent the wrong code from being entered when more than one key is hit. When two keys are depressed, the first switch closure delays the second key command until the first key returns home.

two-level address: an indirect address that specifies two levels of addressing. (A)

two-level subroutine: a subroutine with another subroutine.

two-out-of-five code

(1) a binary-coded decimal notation in which each decimal digit is represented by a binary numeral consisting of five bits of which two are of one kind, conventionally ones, and three are of the other kind, conventionally zeros. The usual weights are 0-1-2-3-6 except for the representation of zero which is then 01100. (B)

(2) a positional notation in which each decimal digit is represented by five binary digits of which two are one kind, for example, ones, and three are the other kind, for example, zeros. (*A*)

two-pass assembler: an assembler requiring scanning of the source program twice, where the first pass constructs a symbol table and the second pass carries out the translation.

two-plus-one address instruction: an instruction that contains three address parts, the plus-one address being that of the instruction that is to be executed next unless otherwise specified. (A) (B)

twos complement: the radix complement in the pure binary numeration system. synonymous with *complement-on-two.* (*A*) (B)

two-tone keying: see *frequency-shift keying.*

two-way alternate communication: communication in which information is transferred in both directions, one direction at a time. synonymous with *either-way communication* . (E)

two-way simultaneous communication: communication in which information is transferred in both directions at the same time. synonymous with *both-way communication.* (E)

two-way trunk: a trunk that can be seized at either end. (F)

two-wire circuit: a metallic circuit formed by two conductors insulated from each other. It is possible to use the two conductors as a one-way transmission path, a half-duplex path, or a duplex path.

TWX: see *teletypewriter exchange service.*

TXT: see *text.*

type bar: a bar, usually mounted vertically on an impact printer, that holds type slugs. synonymous with *print bar.* (*A*) (B)

type declaration: in FORTRAN, the explicit specification of the type, and, optionally, length of a variable or function by use of an explicit specification statement.

type face

(1) the design, or style, of characters produced by a specific printer.

(2) the printing surface of a piece of type which bears the character about to be printed.

type font: type of a given size and style, for example, 10-point Bodoni Modern. (A)

type-out key respond: a specific push button on a console inquiry keyboard that locks the typewriter keyboard and allows the automatic processing to continue.

typeover: in word processing, the ability to replace text simply and quickly by typing new information "over" the old.

type wheel: synonymous with *print wheel*. (A) (B)

typing reperforator: a reperforator which types on chadless tape about one-half inch beyond where corresponding characters are punched. Some units type on the edge of special-width tape.

U
- (1) see *unit*.
- (2) see *update*.
- (3) see *user*.

UA: see *user area*.

UART: see *universal asynchronous receiver transmitter*.

UB: see *upper bound*.

UBS: see *unit backspace character*.

UCS: see *universal character set*.

UDC: Universal Decimal Classification.

U format: a data set format in which blocks are of unknown length.

UHF: ultrahigh frequency; the range extending from 300 to 3000 megaHertz.

ultrafiche: in micrographics, microfiche with images reduced by a very high reduction factor.

ultraviolet (UV): invisible radiation having a wavelength less than 400 nm. see also *infrared*. (D)

ultraviolet erasing: erasable programmable read-only memory (EPROM) chips eliminated by exposure to high-intensity shortwave ultraviolet light.

umacro: a subroutine of either the system adapter, the I/O adapter, or the text processor of access method services that provide a common service for other access method services processor and programmable store system host support.

umbral: a heading that is totally relevant to the data being sought.

U-mode records: in COBOL, records of undefined length. They may be fixed or variable in length; there is only one record per block.

unallowable code check: an automatic check that tests for the occurrence of a nonpermissible code expression.

unallowable digit: a character or combination of bits that are not accepted as a valid representation by the computer, machine design, or by a specific routine, and suggests malfunction.

unary operation: synonym for *monadic operation*. (A) (B)

unary operator

(1) an arithmetic operator having only one term. The unary operators that can be used in absolute, relocatable, and arithmetic expressions are: positive ($+$) and negative ($-$).

(2) in COBOL, an arithmetic operator ($+$ or $-$) that can precede a single variable, a literal or a left parenthesis in an arithmetic expression. The plus sign multiplies the value by $+1$; the minus sign multiplies the value by -1.

(3) synonym for *monadic operator*. (A)

unattended automatic exchange: an automatic telephone exchange that, under normal conditions, is not attended by either operators or maintenance personnel.

unattended mode: a mode in which no operator is present or in which no operator station is included at the system generation.

unattended operation: the automatic transmission and reception of messages on an unattended basis. cf. *attended operation.*

unattended trail printer: in word processing, a trail printer to which is attached a sheet feeder, a tractor feeder, or other paper handling device, and that therefore can print a number of pages without operator intervention. cf. *attended trail printer.* (D)

unbalanced line: a transmission line in which the magnitudes of the voltages on the two conductors are not equal with respect to ground; for example, a coaxial line.

unbalanced merge sort: a merge sort, which is an external sort, such that the sorted subsets created by the internal sorts are unequally distributed among some of the available auxiliary storage devices. The subsets are merged onto the remaining auxiliary storage devices and the process repeated until all items are in one sorted set. cf. *balanced merge sort.* (A)

unbalanced modulator: a modulator in which the modulation factor is different for the alternate half-cycles of the carrier.

unbalanced wire circuit: a circuit whose two sides are inherently electrically unlike.

unblank: in computer graphics, to turn the beam on.

unblind (blind): a procedure to control a transmission printer or reperforator.

unblock: deprecated term for *deblock.*

unbundling: separating hardware and software pricing.

UNCOL: Universal Computer Oriented Language.

uncommitted storage list: blocks of storage that are chained together and not allocated at any specific moment.

unconditional

(1) subject to a specific instruction only.

(2) free of any condition.

unconditional branch instruction: deprecated term for *unconditional jump instruction.* (A) (B)

unconditional control transfer instruction: deprecated term for *unconditional jump instruction.* (A) (B)

unconditional jump: a jump that takes place whenever the instruction that specified it is executed. (A) (B)

unconditional jump instruction: an instruction that specifies an unconditional jump (A) (B)

unconditional transfer instruction: deprecated term for *unconditional jump instruction.* (A) (B)

undefined record: a record having an unspecified or unknown length. see also *U format.*

underflow: a result whose value is too small for the range of the number representation being used. (D). cf. *overflow.*

underflow characteristic: a situation in floating-point arithmetic when an attempt is made to develop a characteristic less than -99.

underflow exception: a condition caused by the result of an arithmetic operation having a magnitude less than the smallest possible nonzero number.

underlying carrier: a common carrier which provides facilities to other common carriers for their use in providing services (e.g., COMSAT). (G)

underpunch: a locational punch in one of the lower rows, 1-9, of an 80-column 12-row punch card.

underrun: loss of data caused by the inability of a transmitting device or channel to provide data to the communications control logic (SDLC) or BSC/SS) at a rate that is fast enough for the attached data link or loop.

underscore: a line under an individual character.

under-the-cover modem: deprecated term for *integrated modem.*

undetected error rate: the ratio of the number of bits incorrectly received but undetected or uncorrected by the error-control device, to the total number of bits, unit elements, characters, and blocks that are sent.

unformatted diskette: a diskette that contains no data and no track or sector format information.

unformatted display: a display screen on which no display field has been defined by the user. cf. *formatted display.* see also *protected field.*

unformatted record: in FORTRAN, a record for which no FORMAT statement exists, and which is transmitted with a one-to-one correspondence between internal storage locations and external positions in the record.

UNICOMP: Universal Compiler Fortran Compatible.

unidirectional: the connection between telegraph sets, one of which is a transmitter and the other a receiver.

uniformly accessible storage: storage that purports to lessen the effect of variation of access time for an arbitrary sequence of addresses.

unigauge design: a design method for customer loops that provides for the exclusive use of 26-gauge cable on all loops within 30 kilofeet of the central office. Requires range extension equipment developed specifically for the unigauge system. (F)

unilateral synchronization system: a synchronization control system between exchanges A and B in which the clock at A controls the clock at B, but B does not control the clock at A.

union: synonymous with *OR operation.*

union catalog: a compiled list of the contents of two or more tape libraries.

unipolar: see *neutral transmission.*

unipolar signal: a digital signal technique that uses a positive (or negative) excursion and ground as the two binary signal states. (F)

uniprocessing (UP): sequential execution of instructions by a processing unit or independent use of a processing unit in a multiprocessing system.

unit (U)

(1) a device having a special function.

(2) a basic element. (*A*)

(3) see *arithmetic and logic unit, arithmetic unit, delay unit, functional unit, information content natural unit, input-output unit, input unit, logic unit, magnetic tape unit, main control unit, main storage unit, output unit, peripheral control unit, processing unit, tape unit, work unit.*

unit address: the three-character address of a particular device, specified at the time a system is installed; for example, 191 or 293. see also *device type, group name.*

unitary code: a code having only one digit; the number of times it is repeated determines the quantity it represents.

unit backspace character (UBS): a word processing formatting control that moves the printing or display point to the left one escapement unit as defined to provide character alignment in proportionally spaced text. see also *backspace character.*

unit diagnostics: a program used to detect malfunctions in such units as the input-output and the arithmetic circuitry.

United States Independent Telephone Association (USITA): a national trade association of Independent (non-Bell System) Telephone Companies. (G)

unit element: an alphabetic-signal element with a duration equal to the unit interval of time.

uniterm: a word, symbol, or number used as a descriptor for retrieval of information from a collection, especially in a coordinate indexing system. see *interming.*

uniterming: pertaining to an information-retrieval system involving word selection considered important and descriptive of the contents of a document for later retrieval of the material.

unit interval: in a system using synchronous transmission, the interval of time such that the nominal directions of the significant intervals of a modulation signal are all whole multiples of that interval. (E)

unit record (UR): a card containing one complete record; a punched card.

unit separator character (US): the information separator intended to identify a logical boundary between units. (A) (B)

unit string: a string consisting of only one entity. (A) (B)

unit testing: the testing of a single module or a related group of modules.

universal access: the default access authority that applies to a data set if the user or group is not specifically permitted access to the data set. Universal access can be any of the access authorities.

universal asynchronous receiver transmitter (UART): a transmitter that allows the conversion of serial to parallel and parallel to serial transmission.

universal button box: a set of buttons whose operation are determined by the computer program.

universal character set (UCS): a

printer feature that permits the use of a variety of character arrays.

universal controller: see *basic controller.*

universal instruction set: a set of instructions that includes those for floating-point arithemtic, fixed-point binary arithmetic and logic, decimal arithmetic, and protection feature.

universal interconnecting device: pertaining to a unit designed with multiple systems where it is desirable to switch peripheral units from one system to another.

universal service concept: the public service goal, mandated by Congress in the Communications Act of 1934, to make telephone service available to all people in the United States at a reasonable price. (G)

universal set: the set that includes all of the element of concern in a given study. (A) (B)

universal Turing machine: a Turing machine that can simulate any other Turing machine. (A)

unload: removing information in large quantities as in unloading the storage contents onto a magnetic tape.

unmodified instruction: deprecated term for *presumptive instruction.* (A) (B)

unpack: to recover the original form of the data from packed data. (A) (B)

unpacked decimal: representation of a decimal value by a single digit in one byte. For example, in unpacked decimal, the decimal value 23 is represented by xxxx0010 xxxx0011, where xxxx is each case represents a zone. cf. *packed decimal.*

unprotected dynamic storage: synonym for *dynamic storage.*

unprotected field: on a display de-vice, a display field in which the user can enter, modify, or erase data. cf. *protected field.*

unrecoverable ABEND: an error condition that results in abnormal termination of a program. cf. *recoverable ABEND.*

unrecoverable error: deprecated term for *irrecoverable error.*

unstable state: in a trigger circuit, a state in which the circuit remains for a finite period of time at the end of which it returns to a stable state without the application of a pulse. (A)

unstack: removing from the top of a stack.

unstratified language: a language that can be used as its own metalanguage; for example, most natural languages. (B) cf. *stratified language.* (A)

unsuccessful call: a call attempt that does not result in the establishment of data connection. (C)

unused time: time available for machine activities that is left unused and frequently unattended by any computer system personnel.

unwind: to state explicitly and in full, without the use of modifiers, all the instructions that are involved in the execution of a loop. (A) (B)

UP: see *uniprocessing.*

up: in computing, an operation system. cf. *down.*

up and running: a computer system or piece of equipment that has just been put into operation and is working properly.

UPB: see *upper bound.*

unconverter: a device which increases the freqency of a transmit signal.

update (U): to modify a master file

with current information according to a specified procedure.

update cursor: circuitry that permits a user to add new material into a video terminal memory and display. The cursor locates the current entry location which is a blinking underline, although some are overlines or boxes.

uplink: an earth station and its transmitted signals to a communications satellite.

upper bound (UB) (UPB): in PL/1, the upper limit of an array dimension.

upper curtate: the adjacent card rows at the top of a punch card. (A)

up stop

(1) a mechanical device limiting upward motion of a moveable part.

(2) a physical part (usually non-movable) used to limit or stop the upward travel of the armature in an electromechanical device such as a relay.

up time: deprecated term for *available time*. synonym for *operating time*. (A) (B)

upward compatibility: the capability of a computer to execute programs written for another computer without major alteration, but not vice versa.

upward reference: in overlay, a reference made from a segment to another segment higher in the same path; that is, closer to the root segment.

UR: see *unit record*.

US: see *unit separator character*. (A)

usage

(1) a measure of trunk or equipment occupancy expressed in Erlangs or CCS. (F)

(2) a measure of local service in message units that may depend on both distance and duration of calls and may be defined differently in dif-ferent localities. (F)

usage sensitive pricing (USP): a generic term which includes measurement of local exchange service and Directory Assistance (DA) charging. (G)

USASCII: United States of America Standard Code for Information Exchange. A code using eight bits per character (one being a parity bit), the character set consisting of graphic characters and control characters, used for the interchange of information between data-processing systems and communications systems, and between the machines associated with systems of both types. deprecated term for *ASCII*. (A)

USASI: United States of America Standards Institute; a former name of the American National Standards Institute. deprecated term for *ANSI*.

usec: microsecond; 1/1,000,000 of a second.

user (U)

(1) anyone who requires the services of a computing system. see also *end-user, terminal user*.

(2) a person who requires the services of a computing system.

user-application network: a configuration of data-processing products, such as processors, controllers, and terminals, established and operated by users for the purpose of data processing or information exchange, which may use services offered by communication common carriers of telecommunication administrators. cf. *public network*. (E)

user area (UA): pertaining to the area of a magnetic disk where semipermanent data is kept.

user attribute: a characteristic of a

user that defines the type of functions the user can perform on entitites. The user attributes are SPECIAL, OPERATIONS, GRPACC, ADSP, and REVOKE.

user class of service: a category of data-transmission service provided by a network in which the data-signaling rate, the data-terminal equipment (DTE) operating mode, and the code structure, if any, are standardized. (E)

user coordinate: in computer graphics, a coordinate specified by a user and expressed in a coordinate system that is application independent. (E)

user facility: a set of functions available on demand to a user, and provided as part of a data network transmission service. synonymous with *user service*. (C)

user-friendly: a system which relatively untrained users can interact with easily. Usually, suggests the use of a high level programming language.

user group: organization utilizing a variety of computing systems sharing knowledge and programs that each have used and developed.

USERID: see *user identification*.

user identification (USERID)
(1) a symbol identifying a system user.
(2) a code that uniquely identifies a user to the system.

user input area: on a display device, the lines of the screen where the user is required to key in command or data lines.

user label: an identification record for a tape or disk file; the format and contents are defined by the user, who must also write the necessary processing routines.

user-oriented: a setup for somebody who is not expected to be knowledgeable about computers.

user profile table: in systems with time sharing, a table of user attributes built for each active user from information gathered during log on.

user program: a program written specifically for or by a particular user. cf. *utility program*.

user-programmable keys: special function keys on a terminal whose functions vary with the program in use.

user prompts: messages, either visually on a visual display unit or orally over a telephone, intended to assist in carrying out the next operation needed to execute a computing or telecommunication function.

user service: any set of data-processing functions made available to the user. synonym for *user facility*.

user's group: see *user group*.

user space: storage space that is not system space.

user's set: an apparatus location on the premises of a user of a telecommunication or signaling service and designed to function with other parts of a system.

user terminal (UT): an input-output unit by which a user communicates with a data-processing system. (B)

USITA: see *United States Independent Telephone Association*.

USP: see *usage sensitive pricing*.

UT: see *user terminal*.

utilities: software utilized for routine activities; designed to aid the operation and use of the computer. Examples include an editor, a debugger, a file handler.

utility: software for routine tasks or for assisting programmers.

utility control console: a computer console used primarily to control utility and maintenance programs.

utility functions: pertaining to auxiliary operations such as tape searching, media conversion, and tape dumps.

utility program

(1) a computer program in general support of the processes of a computer; for instance, a diagnostic program, a trace program, a sort program. synonymous with *service program*. (A) (B)

(2) a program designed to perform an everyday task such as copying data from one storage device to another.

utility routine: a routine in general support of the processes of a computer; for instance, an input routine. synonymous with *service routine (A)* (B)

utility system: a program or system or set of systems developed to perform miscellaneous or utility functions such as card-to-tape, tape-to-printer, and other operations or suboperations.

utilization loggers system: a program or a unit that collects statistical information about how a system is performing.

UV: see *ultraviolet.*

V

(1) see *variable*.
(2) see *vector*.
(3) see *verification*.
(4) see *verify*.
(5) see *virtual*.
(6) volt.
(7) voltage.

VA: see *virtual address*.

vacant code: an unassigned numbering plan area, central office, or station code. Upon recognition, a call placed to a vacant code is normally directed to a vacant code announcement. (F)

vacuum servo: a peripheral unit that maintains a magnetic tape reservoir, maintained by the absence of air pressure on one side of the tape.

VAL: see *value*.

validate: see *validation*.

validation: the checking of data for correctness, or compliance with applicable standards, rules, and conventions. (A) see *input data validation*.

valid exclusive reference: in overlay, an exclusive reference in which a common segment contains a reference to the symbol used in the exclusive reference.

validity check: a check that a code group is actually a character of the particular code in use.

valley: in OCR, an indentation in a stroke.

valuator device: in computer graphics, an input device that provides a scalar value. see also *choice device, locator device, pick device*. (E)

value (VAL)

(1) a specific occurrence of an attribute, for example, "blue" for the attribute "color." (E)
(2) a quantity assigned to a constant, a variable, parameter, or a symbol. see also *argument*.

value added common carrier: a common carrier which itself does not establish telecommunications links, but leases lines from other carriers. It can establish a computer-controlled network offering specific telecommunications services.

value added network (VAN): a data network operated in the United States by a firm which obtains basic transmission facilities from the common carriers; for example, the Bell System, adds "value" such as error detection and sharing, and resells the services to users. Telenet and Tymnet are examples of VANs.

VAN: see *value added network.*

V-antenna: a directional antenna consisting of two straight conductors set at an angle to each other and fed at the junction.

VAR: see *variable.*

VARBLK: see *variable block.*

variable (V) (VAR)

(1) in computer programming, a character or group of characters that refers to a value and, in the execution of a computer program, corresponds to an address. (B)

(2) a quantity that can assume any of a given set of values. (*A*)

(3) in COBOL, a data item whose value may be changed during execution of the object program.

(4) in FORTRAN, a data item that is not an array or array element, identified by a symbolic name.

(5) In PL/1, a named entity that is used to refer to data and to which values can be assigned. Its attributes remain constant, but it can refer to different values at different times. Variables fall into three categories, applicable to any data type: element, array, and structure. Variables may be subscripted, qualified, or both, or may be pointer-qualified.

(6) see *loop-control variable, switching variable.* (A)

variable address: an address that is to be modified or has already been modified by an index register or similar unit.

variable block (VB): the number of characters in the block is determined by the programmer (usually between some practical limits).

variable connector: see *switch.*

variable field: a field where the scalar (or vector) at any point changes during the time under consideration.

variable field length: a data field that has a variable number of characters; requiring item separators to indicate the end of each item.

variable field storage: an indefinite limit of length for the storage field.

variable-format messages: messages in which line control characters are not to be deleted upon arrival nor inserted upon departure; variable-format messages are intended for terminals with similar characteristics. cf. *fixed-format messages.*

variable function generator: a function generator in which the function to be generated may be set by the user before or during computation. (B)

variable information: in word processing, information or text that is entered or altered by the operator for each document. (D)

variable information processing (VIP): a generalized proprietary program for information storage and retrieval system that provides for retrieval approaches without programming.

variable-length record

(1) a record having a length independent of the length of other records with which it is logically or physically associated. cf. *fixed-*

length record. see also *V format.*

(2)   pertaining to a file in which the records are not uniform in length. (A)

variable-length word: a computer word where the number of characters is not fixed but is variable and subject to the discretion of the programmer.

variable name: an alphanumeric title given to represent a particular program variable.

variable point: within a number system, the location of the point indicated by a special character at that location.

variable-point representation: a positional representation in which the position of the radix point is explicitly indicated by a special character at that position. cf. *floating-point representation.* (*A*)

variable-point representation system: a radix numeration system in which the radix point is explicitly indicated by a special character at that position. (A) (B)

variable symobl: in assembler programming, a symbol used in macro and conditional assembly processing that can assume any of a given set of values.

variable time scale: in simulation, the time scale used in data processing when the time scale factor is not constant during a run. (A)

variable word: the specific feature where the number of characters handled in a device is not constant.

variable word length: refers to a machine in which the number of characters comprising a computer word is almost completely under the control of the coder. Not usually applied to machines in which there is a very limited form of control, such as half-words or double-length words. cf. *fixed word length computer.*

variation monitors: devices for sensing deviations in voltage, current, or frequency, capable of initiating transfer to other power sources when programmed limits of voltage, frequency, current, or time are exceeded, and providing an alarm.

variplotter: a high-accuracy graphic recording machine that plots curves on either a 30″ × 30″ or a 45″ × 60″ surface; with solid-state circuitry, backlighted plotting surface, vacuum-paper hold-down and parallax controls.

vary off line

(1)   to change the status of a device from on line to off line. When a device is off line, no data set may be opened on that device.

(2)   to place a device in a state where it is not available for use by the system; however, it is still available for executing I/O.

vary on line: to restore a device to a state where it is available for use by the system.

VB: see *voice-band.*

VCBA: see *variable control block area.*

VDU: see *visual display unit.*

vector (V)

(1)   a quantity usually represented by an ordered set of numbers. (A) (B)

(2)   in computer graphics, a directed line segment.

(3)   cf. *scalar.* (A)

(4)   see *absolute vector, relative vector.*

vector algebra: manipulation of symbols representing vector quantities according to laws of addition, subtraction, multiplication, and division which these quantities obey.

vector diagram: the arrangement of vectors showing a relationship between alternating quantities having the same frequency.

vectored interrupt: an interrupt that carries a branch address or a peripheral unit identifier.

vectored priority interrupts: maskable products used with time counters for external inputs or dedicated external inputs, where each vector jumps the program to a specific memory address.

vectored restart: the automatic ability to clear the system during restart, saving program steps.

vector generator (VG): in computer graphics, a functional unit that generates directed line segments. (E)

vector graphics: the most common class of graphics; where all vector output consists of lines and curves drawn point-to-point by the output unit as ordered by the computer.

vectoring: automatic branching to a specified address.

vector transfer: pertaining to communication linkage between two programs.

Veitch diagram: a means of representing boolean functions in which the number of variables determines the number of squares in the diagram; the number of squares needed is the number of possible states, that is, two raised to a power determined by the number of variables. (B) see also *Venn diagram.* (A)

Venn diagram: a diagram in which sets are represented by regions drawn on a surface. (B) see also *Veitch diagram.* (A)

VER: see *verify.*

verb: a COBOL reserved word that expresses an action to be taken by a COBOL compiler or an object program.

verge-punched card: synonym for *edge-punched card.* (A)

verification (V): the act of determining whether an operation has been accomplished correctly. (E) see *key stroke verification.*

verification mode: in systems with time sharing, a mode of operation under the EDIT command in which all subcommands are acknowledged and any textual changes are displayed as they are made.

verifier: a device that checks the correctness of transcribed data, usually by comparing with a second transcription of the same data or by comparing a retranscription with the original data. (A) (B)

verify (V) (VER)
(1) to determine whether a transcription of data or other operation has been accomplished accurately.
(2) to check the results of keypunching. (A)

vernier: in machinery, an auxiliary device for giving a piece of apparatus higher adjustment accuracy.

version: a separate program product, based on an existing program product, that usually has significant new code or new function. Each version has its own license, terms, conditions, product type number, monthly charge, documentation, test allowance (if applicable), and programming support category. see also *modification level, release.*

vertical feed: pertaining to the entry of a punch card into a card feed with a short edge first. (A)

vertical format: the facility that provides the automatic vertical position of text within definable limits. (D)

vertical positions: see *addressable vertical positions*. (A)

vertical processor: a microprogrammed computer using a narrow microinstruction word, thereby restricting the number of microorders per microinstruction, but making microprogramming easier.

vertical raster count: the number of vertical divisions in a raster. see also *raster count*.

vertical recording: a disk where data is stored by magnetizing slivers of iron oxide so that they resemble tiny bar magnets lying end to end. The position of each magnet's north pole tells the computer whether a one or a zero in computer language is stored at that location. As more data are squeezed onto the disk, however, the magnets get shorter and become weaker, requiring more sensitive electronics to detect their position. Vertical recording gets around this problem by standing the magnets on end in a crystal structure made from cobalt and chrome, thus allowing them to be packed more tightly without decreasing their strength.

vertical redundancy check (VRC): an odd parity check performed on each character of a block contrast with ASCII-coded data as the block is received. see also *cyclic redundancy check, longitudinal redundancy check*. deprecated term for *transverse redundancy check*.

vertical services: service over and above what is required for basic communications capability; for example,

deluxe telephone station sets or custom calling services. (F)

vertical table: a table where the bytes of each entry are sequentially stored, that is, entry one, byte one, entry two, byte two, and so on. FORTRAN stores arrays this way.

vertical tabulation character (VT) (VTAB): a format effector that causes the print or display position to move to the corresponding position on the next of a series of predetermined lines. (A) (B)

vertical wraparound: on a display device, the continuation of cursor movement from the bottom character position in a vertical column to the top character position in the next column, or from the top position in a column to the bottom position in the preceding column. cf. *horizontal wraparound*.

very large scale integration (VLSI): over 10,000 transistors per chip.

vestigial sideband modulation (VSB): a form of amplitude modulation, lying between double sideband and single sideband, in which one sideband and a small vestige of the other sideband are transmitted. Vestigial sideband modulation is attractive for data transmission because it uses less bandwidth than double sideband and preserves the wave form of the signal. (F)

VFFT: see *voice-frequency facility terminal*.

V format: a data set format in which logical records are of varying length and include a length indicator, and in which V-format logical records may be blocked, with each block containing a block length indicator.

VG: see *vector generator*.

V-H coordinates: numerical coordinates that define the location of a rate center. A simple calculation using the V-H coordinates for two rate centers gives the airline mileage between the two points for use in determining charges for toll calls and private lines. (F)

via net loss (VNL): a loss objective for trunks, the value of which has been selected to obtain a satisfactory balance between loss and talker echo performance. The numerical value of a particular VNL is equal to a constant, 0.4 dB, plus a prescribed component that is proportional to delay. (F)

VID: see *video.*

video (VID): brightness and color data fed to a terminal. synonymous with *terminal.*

video bandwidth: the maximum rate at which dots of illumination are displayed on a screen.

video camera: a camera which records images on magnetic tape for playback.

video cassette (recorder): a unit for visual recording onto magnetic tape contained in a plastic package.

video conferencing: teleconferencing where participants see and hear others at remote locations.

video data integrator: a terminal device comprised of a keyboard and separable associated display, providing a terminal facility for conventional communications lines.

videodisc microprocessor: a microprocessor that facilitates the interfacing of a videodisc player with computers and other data processors.

videodisk: a recordlike device storing a large amount of audio and visual information that can be linked to a computer; one side can store the pictures and sounds for 54,000 separate TV screens.

video generator: a unit that accepts commands from a keyboard and drives the TV monitor.

videograph: high-speed cathode-ray printer.

videographic display: computers that can draw pictures using dots or lines; computers that can rotate objects, showing them in perspective, moving them around, stretching, or shrinking them.

video-scan optical character reader: a unit that combines optical character reader with mark sense and card read. It can read printing and marks in the same pass as well as read holes in cards.

video signal: an electronic signal with information on the location and brightness of each position on a cathode ray tube screen, with timing signals to place the image properly on the screen.

video telephone: a telephone that can also transmit and, depending on the system, receive an image on a screen.

video terminal (VT): a terminal having a keyboard for sending information to the computer and a picture tube like a TV for displaying information. The video terminal is fast, silent, and has no moving parts. Its chief drawback is that it does not make a permanent record of the information displayed.

viewdata: generic name for a remote display, for example, on a TV screen, of data called up by keyboard control over a telephone line from a central database. It is one form of teletext.

view point: in computer graphics, the origin from which angles and scales are used to map virtual space into display space. (E)

view port: a predefined part of the display space. see also *window*. (E)

VIO: see *virtual I/O*.

VIP: see *variable information processing*.

virgin coil: tape completely devoid of punches.

virgin medium: a data medium in or on which data have never been recorded; for example, paper that is unmarked, punch tape that has no holes. (B)

virtual (V): pertaining to a conceptual presence.

virtual address (VA): the address of a notational storage location in virtual storage. (A) (B)

virtual address space: in virtual storage system, the virtual storage assigned to a batched or terminal job, a system task, or a task initiated by a command.

virtual call facility: a user facility in which a call setup procedure and a call clearing procedure will determine a period of communication between two data-terminal equipments (DTEs) in which user's data will be transferred in the network in the packet mode of operation. All the user's data is delivered from the network in the same order in which it is received by the network. (C)

virtual circuit (VC): in packet switching, those facilities provided by a network that give the appearance to the user of an actual connection. see also *data circuit*. cf. *physical circuit*. (E)

virtual computing system: synonym for *virtual machine*.

virtual connection: see *virtual circuit*.

virtual console function: a CP command that is executed via the diagnose interface.

virtual copy: the production of an exact duplicate of the contents of locations in the memory of a computer onto an external bulk storage unit, including reproducing the information regarding the exact memory addresses in which the data being stored resides.

virtual-equals-real (V=R) storage: synonym for *nonpageable dynamic area*.

virtual image: in computer graphics, the complete visual representation of an encoded image that could be displayed if a display surface of sufficient size were available.

virtual I/O (VIO): a facility that pages data into and out of external page storage; to the problem program, the data to be read from or written to direct-access storage devices.

virtual machine (VM): a functional simulation of a computer and its associated devices.

virtual memory (VM): deprecated term for *virtual storage*. (A) (B)

virtual point picture character: in PL/1, the picture specification character V, which is used in picture specifications to indicate the position of an assumed decimal or binary point.

virtual processing time: the time required to execute the instructions of a virtual machine.

virtual push button

(1) in computer graphics, a display element that may be selected by an input device that is programmed to operate as a function key. (E)

(2) in computer graphics, a display group that is used to simulate a choice device by means of a pick device.

(3) synonymous with *light button.*

virtual route (VR): a path between a data source and a data sink that may be created by various circuit configurations during the transmission of packets or messages. (E)

virtual space: in computer graphics, a space in which the coordinates of the display elements are expressed in terms of user coordinates. (E)

virtual storage (VS): the notion of storage space that may be regarded as addressable main storage by the user of a computer system in which virtual addresses are mapped into real addresses. The size of virtual storage is limited by the addressing scheme of the computer system and by the amount of auxiliary storage available, and not by the actual number of main storage locations. (B)

virtual storage access method (VSAM): an access method for direct or sequential processing of fixed and variable-length records on direct-access devices. The records in a VSAM data set or file can be organized in logical sequence by a key field (key sequence), in the physical sequence in which they are written on the data set or file (entry sequence), or by relative-record number.

virtual storage management (VSM): routines that allocate address spaces and virtual storage areas within address spaces and keep a record of free and allocated storage within each address space.

virtual telecommunications access method (VTAM): a set of programs that control communication between terminals and application programs running under VSE, OS/VS1, and OS/VS2.

virtual volume: the concept of a volume that may be regarded as residing on an addressable unit of auxiliary storage by the user of a computer system in which virtual-device addresses correspond to real-device addresses. The attributes of a virtual volume are predefined and do not change as the implementation of that volume changes.

visible file: the systematic arrangement of forms, cards, or documents so that data placed on the margin can serve as an index for the user to rapidly see without the need to withdraw each item.

visual display: in word processing, a device for electronically displaying text. Depending on the equipment, the display may be full page, partial page, single, or partial line. (D)

visual display unit: synonymous with *terminal.*

visual inquiry station: an input-output unit that allows the interrogation of an automatic data-processing system by the immediate processing of data from a person or terminal source, together with the display of the results of the processing; often on a cathode-ray tube.

visual scanner

(1) a unit that scans optically and usually generates an analog or digital signal.

(2) a unit that optically scans printed or written data and generates their representation.

VLSI: see *very large scale integration.*

VM

(1) see *virtual machine.*

(2) see *virtual memory.*

V-mode records: in COBOL, records of variable length, each of which is wholly contained within a block. Blocks may contain more than one record. Each record contains a record length field, and each block contains a block length field.

VOCAB: see *vocabulary.*

vocabulary (VOCAB): a list of operations or instructions, available to a computer programmer, to use in writing the program for a given problem on a specific computer. synonymous with *character.*

vocoder: a contraction of Voice-Operated Coder. A device used to compress the frequency bandwidth requirement of voice communications.

VODAS: a contraction of Voice-Operated Device Anti-Sing. A system for preventing the overall voice frequency singing of a two-way telephone circuit by disabling one direction of transmission at all times.

VOGAD: a contraction of Voice-Operated Gaining-Adjusting Device. A voice-operated device used to give a substantially constant volume output for a wide range of inputs.

voice answer back: a system in which a computer gives responses to a user's commands, in the form of pre-recorded voice messages.

voice band: (VB) the 300 Hz to 3400 Hz band used on telephone equipment for the transmission of voice and data.

voice channel: a circuit of sufficient bandwidth allowing transmission of speech quality signals; a bandwidth of 0-3000 cycles per second.

voice-frequency carrier telegraphy: that form of carrier telegraphy in which the carrier current have frequencies such that the modulated currents may be transmitted over a voice-frequency telephone channel.

voice frequency equipment: equipment which provides the interface between telephone facilities, between various telephone switching machines as well as between telephone switching machines and subscriber lines, to perform the functions of signaling and amplification of voice signals.

voice-frequency facility terminal (VFFT): a terminal equipment concept that combines transmission (including channel banks), signaling, and test access functions in a modular bay, eliminating or minimizing the need for intermediate distributing frames. There are three types of VFFTs: analog, digital, and metallic. (F)

voice-frequency telegraph system: a telegraph system permitting use of up to 20 channels on a single circuit by frequency division multiplexing.

voice-grade channel: a device used on a telephone circuit to permit the presence of telephone currents to effect a desired control. Such a device is used in most echo suppressors.

voice message system: an electronic system for transmitting and storing voice messages which can later be accessed by the individual to whom they are addressed.

voice notes: a facility for terminal users who cannot, or will not, type to add voice messages to a computerized text. The user inspects a document on a visual display unit and appends audible message (voice notes) to it via a microphone plugged into the terminal.

Voice-Operated Coder: see *vocoder.*

Voice-Operated Device Anti-Sing: see *VODAS.*

Voice-Operated Gain-Adjusting Device: see *VOGAD.*

voice unit (VU): a measure of the gross amplitude of volume of an electrical speech or program wave. The reference volume is usually zero VU, which is one millivolt of steady sine wave into a 600-ohm resistive load. A good volume is usually between − 10 and − 30 VU. Anything over zero VU is definitely too loud; anything under − 55 VU is definitely too soft. Readings will depend on the meter's frequency response and calibration criteria. see also *reference volume.*

void

(1)   in character recognition, the inadvertent absence of ink within a character outline. (A)

(2)   in OCR, a light spot in a character that is surrounded by ink.

VOL

(1)   see *begining-of-volume label.*

(2)   see *volume.*

volatile: becoming lost or erased when power is removed.

volatile file: a temporary or rapidly changing program or file.

volatile memory: a storage medium in which information is destroyed when power is removed from the system. see also *volatile storage.*

volatile storage

(1)   a storage device whose contents are lost when power is removed. (B)

(2)   in word processing, storage

from which recorded text is lost when power to the machine is switched off. (D)

(3)   cf. *nonvolatile storage.*

volatility: the percentage of records on a file that are added or deleted in a run. see also *activity.*

volatility of storage: the tendency of a storage unit to lose data when power is removed. Storage media can be classed as volatile or nonvolatile.

voltage pencil: synonym for *stylus.*

volume (VOL)

(1)   a certain portion of data, together with its data carrier, that can be handled conveniently as a unit. (B)

(2)   a data carrier that is mounted and demounted as a unit; for example, a reel of magnetic tape, a disk pack. (B)

(3)   that portion of a single unit of storage that is accessible to a singe read/write mechanism; for example, a drum, a disk pack, or part of a disk storage module.

(4)   see *base volume, duplicate volume, virtual volume.*

volume label: synonym for *beginning-of-volume label.*

volume serial number: a number in a volume label that is assigned when a volume is prepared for use in the system.

volume switch procedures: standard procedures executed automatically when the end of a unit or reel has been reached before end of file has been reached.

volume table of contents (VTOC):   a table on a direct-access volume that describes each data set on the volume.

volume test: the processing of a volume of actual data to check for program malfunctions. see *debug.* cf. *redundancy check.*

voluntary interrupt: an interrupt to a processor or system caused by an object program's deliberate use of a function known to cause an interrupt that is under program control.

von Neumann sort: in a sort program, merging strings of sequenced data. The power of the merge is equal to $T/2$.

VOX: a voice-operated relay circuit that permits the equivalent of push-to-talk operation of a transmitter by the operator.

V picture specification character: see *virtual point picture character.*

VR: see *virtual route.*

VRC: see *vertical redundancy check.*

V response: an answer or response of a teletypewriter terminal to a poll or address selection. synonymous with *M response.*

VS: see *virtual storage.*

VSAM: see *virtual storage access method.*

VSB: see *vestigial sideband modulation.*

VSM: see *virtual storage management.*

VT

(1) see *vertical tabulation character.* (A)

(2) see *video terminal.*

VTAB: see *vertical tabulation character.*

VTAM: see *virtual telecommunications access method.*

VTOC: *volume table of contents.*

V-type address constant: in the assembler language, an address constant used for branching to another module. see also *A-type address constant.*

VU: see *voice unit.*

W
(1) see *waiting time*.
(2) see *wait time*.
(3) *watt*.
(4) see *word*.
(5) see *write*.

WACK (wait before transmit positive acknowledgement): a character sequence sent by a receiving station to indicate that it is temporarily not ready to receive.

wafer: a thin slice from a silicon ingot that is the basis of the chip.

waiting time (W)
(1) the condition of a task that depends on one or more events in order to enter the ready condition.
(2) the condition of a processing unit when all operations are suspended.
(3) synonym for *latency*. (A)

wait list: synonymous with *queue*.

wait state: synonym for *latency*. (B)

wait time (WT): see *waiting time*.

wand: a device used to read information encoded on merchandise tick- ets, credit cards, and employee badges.

warm start: a restart that allows reuse of previously initialized input and output work queues. synonym for *normal restart, system restart*.

warm-up time: the interval between the energizing of a unit and the commencement of the applications of its output characteristics.

warning message: an indication that a possible error has been detected. cf. *error message*.

watchdog: devices used to discern whether some prescribed condition is present, usually within a predetermined time period.

watchdog timer: a timer set by a program to prevent the system from looping endlessly or becoming idle because of program or equipment malfunction.

watermark magnetics: a system for encoding information onto a magnetic stripe; used in banking as the encoded information is not erased, or altered when the stripe passes through a strong magnetic field.

WATS: see *wide area telecommunications service.*

wave form: a graphical representation, in which the amplitude (fullness) of a wave is plotted against time.

wave form generator: a circuit driven by pulses from the master clock operating in conjunction with the operation decoder to generate timed pulses required by other device circuits to perform various operations.

waveguide: a metal tube utilized for transmission of very high frequency electromagnetic signals.

wavelength multiplexing: transmitting individual signals simultaneously by using a different wavelength for each signal.

way station: a Western Union term for a station on a multipoint circuit.

WD: see *word.*

WE: see *write enable.*

weak external reference (WXTRN): an external reference that does not have to be resolved during linkage editing. If it is not resolved, it appears as though its value was resolved to zero.

weight: in a position representation, the factor by which the value represented by a character in the digit place is multiplied to obtain its additive contribution in the representation of a real number. synonymous with *significance.* (*A*) (B)

weighted average: a moving average performed on data where some of the values are more heavily valued than are others.

whirley bird: deprecated term designating some type of disk pack equipment.

white space skid: in some facsimile transmission units, aids in the speeding up of transmission by the scanner skipping the blank spaces on the document to be transmitted.

who-are-you (WRU): see *inquiry character.* (A)

wide area telecommunications service (WATS): WATS permits customers to make (OUTWATS) or receive (IN-WATS) long distance voice or DATAPHONE calls and to have them billed on a bulk rather than individual call basis. The service is provided within selected service areas, or bands, by means of special private-access lines connected to the public telephone network via WATS-equipped central offices. A single access line permits inward or outward service, but not both. (F)

wide area telephone service: obsolete term; now called *wide area telecommunications service.*

wide-band channel: a channel wider in bandwidth than a voice-grade channel.

wild card: in word processing, a card that allows the user to search for text strings in which certain parts of the string don't matter.

willful intercept: the act of intercepting messages intended for stations having equipment or line trouble. see also *miscellaneous intercept.*

Winchester disk: a type of hard disk, usually not interchangeable.

winding: a conductive path made of wire, that is inductively coupled to a magnetic unit.

window: in computer graphics, a predefined part of the virtual space. see also *view port.* (E)

windowing: the ability to display simultaneously a collage of material, that is, graphics or different parts of text from the same document, on a computer screen.

wire board: synonymous with *board.*

wire center: the location of one or more local switching systems. A point at which customer loops converge. (F)

wire centering: the process of determining the location and timing of new wire centers. (F)

wired OR: externally connecting separate circuits or functions so that the combination of their outputs results in an OR function.

wired program computer: a computer in which the instructions that specify the operations to be performed are specified by the placement and interconnection of wires; the wires are usually held by a removable control panel, allowing flexibility of operation, but the term is also applied to permanently wired machines which are then called fixed program computers.

wire frame: in computer graphics, a mode of display showing all lines, including hidden lines. (E)

wireless terminal: a portable, or handheld terminal that communicates with a computer by radio.

wire printer: a matrix printer that uses wires to produce patterns of dots. synonym for *matrix printer.* (B)

wire storage: see *magnetic wire storage.* (A)

wire wrap (WW) board: a circuit board using wires that are wrapped numerous times around a square pin to make contact.

wiring board: see *control panel.*

WIZ: a very fast algebraic compiler.

word (W) (WD)

(1) a character string or a binary element string that it is convenient for some purpose to consider as an entity. (B)

(2) a character string or a bit string considered as an entity. (*A*)

(3) an ordered set of characters expressing information. (The term *word* may be prefixed by an adjective describing the nature of the characters, such as binary words). (F)

(4) in COBOL, a string of not more than 30 characters, chosen from the following: the letters A through Z, the digits 0 through 9, and the hyphen (-). The hyphen may not appear as either the first or last character.

(5) synonymous with *full word.*

(6) see *alphabetic word, computer word, double word, half word, index word, instruction word, numeric word, parameter word, reserved word.* (A)

word capacity: the selection of one of the word lengths of the devices as a datum and thus to classify different operations as partial or multiples of these lengths for working.

word-half: a group of characters representing half of a computer word for addressing purposes as a unit found in storage.

word index: the contents of a storage position or register that can be used to automatically alter the effective address of any given instruction.

word key: in word processing, a control used to process text one word only at a time. (D)

word length: the number of characters or binary elements in a word. (A) (B)

word mark: an indicator that signals the beginning or the end of a word.

word-organized storage: a storage device into which or from which data can be entered or retrieved only in units of a computer word. (B)

word-oriented: pertaining to an early memory system where "words," each of which had a location number and contained bits of binary digits to hold about 10 numeric positions.

word pattern: the smallest meaningful language unit recognized by a machine.

word period: the size of the time interval between the occurrence of signals representing digits occupying corresponding positions in consecutive words.

word processing (WP)
(1) a means for improving the efficiency and effectiveness of business communications.
(2) pertaining to machines, systems, or processes, that provide: (a) efficient text entry techniques (either manual keying or machine reading), (b) serial processing of text and control character strings, (c) final format text presentation (printed or displayed) for business communications.

word-processing equipment: equipment used to prepare business correspondence by keying and temporarily storing text for subsequent revision and editing the stored text in groups of characters such as words, lines, paragraphs, or pages, as distinguished from equipment that permits only character-by-character editing. Text may be printed out immediately upon keying or at a later time automatically or semi-automatically from internal storage or from a recording medium such as magnetic cards or tape made by the text originating machine or by a print-only machine. (D)

word-processing equipment for printout only: word-processing equipment that can only print out automatically text already recorded on to a recording medium on another machine; additional text can sometimes be keyed on to the printout at predetermined places. (D)

word-processing equipment for recording and printout: word-processing equipment on which text can be recorded onto a recording medium. It also provides a facility for correcting and amending the recorded text. (D)

word-processing equipment for recording only: word-processing equipment on which text can be recorded on a recording medium but which does not have a printout device. It also provides a facility for correcting and amending the recorded text. (D)

word-processing equipment using remote program: word-processing equipment wholly or partially controlled by a program resident in another machine. (D)

word-processing equipment with changeable program: word-processing equipment on certain features may be changed by altering the program or by providing exchangable programs on some form of recording medium. (D)

word-processing equipment with edge-punched card: word-processing equipment on which the text is stored on an edge-punched card. (D)

word-processing equipment with fixed (nonremovable) recording media: word-processing equipment in which the recording media cannot be removed by the user. (D)

word-processing equipment with fixed program: word-processing equipment that uses a program that cannot be altered. (D)

word-processing equipment with impact printer: word-processing equipment in which the printer uses a typeface that mechanically strikes the paper (through a printing ribbon). Some printers have typefaces carried on a type bar or on one or more elements such as a spherical type head, a print wheel, or print cup; others use a dot matrix head where the characters are generated by programs. (D)

word-processing equipment with magnetic card: word-processing equipment on which the text is stored on a magnetic card. (D)

word-processing equipment with magnetic disk: word-processing equipment on which the text is stored on a magnetic disk. (D)

word-processing equipment with magnetic sheet: word-processing equipment on which the text is stored on a magnetic sheet. (D)

word-processing equipment wth magnetic tape cassette or cartridge: word-processing equipment on which the text is stored on a magnetic tape housed in a cassette or cartridge. (D)

word-processing equipment with nonimpact printer: word-processing equipment in which characters are produced without the printing mechanism impacting the paper. Such printers may use ink jet, ther-mographic, or electrostatic devices. (D)

word-processing equipment with OCR input: word-processing equipment with the facility to receive text input from an OCR device. (D)

word-processing equipment without provision for making corrections and amendments: word-processing equipment on which the recorded text cannot be corrected or amended. (D)

word-processing equipment with "pianola" roll: word-processing equipment on which the text is stored on a "pianola" roll. (D)

word-processing equipment with provision for making corrections and amendments: word-processing equipment on which the recorded text can be corrected and amended. (D)

word-processing equipment with punched tape: word-processing equipment on which the text is stored on punched tape. (D)

word-processing equipment with removable recording media: word-processing equipment in which the recording media can be exchanged with an equivalent by the user. (D)

word-processing equipment with storage: word-processing equipment for recording and printout that contains an electronic storage used in place of, or in conjunction with, another recording medium. (D)

word processor (WP): a text editing unit designed for preparation, storage, and dissemination of text initiated on typewriterlike devices.

word space: the actual area or space occupied by a word in serial digital units such as drums, disks, tapes, and serial lines.

word time: in a storage device that provides serial access to storage locations, the time interval between the appearance of corresponding parts of successive words. (A)

word time comparator: the circuitry that compares the word time counter with the specified word time at the moment of coincident pulse. This is done to verify that the correct word has been read.

word underscore character (WUS): a word-processing control that causes the word immediately preceding it to be graphically underscored.

word wrap: in word processing, the capability to move automatically the last word on a line to a new line if otherwise it would overrun the right margin. (D)

word wraparound: see *wrap, wraparound*.

work area: an area of memory used for temporary storage of data during processing, synonymous with *working storage, workspace*.

work cycle: the sequences that are necessary to perform a task, job, or execution, and yield a unit of production, and which recurs in similar order for each task or unit of work.

work file

(1) a file used to provide storage space for data that is needed only for the duration of a job.

(2) in sorting, an intermediate file used for temporary storage of data between phases.

(3) see also *work volume*.

working area: synonym for *working space*. (A) (B)

working equipment: the basic set of machines for modules in which more than one set is available and the other sets are standby equipment in the event of a failure of the working units.

working memory: the internal memory that stores information for processing.

working routine: produces the results of the problem or program as it was designed, as contrasted with the routines designed for support, housekeeping, or to compile, assemble, translate, and so on.

working set

(1) the set of a user's pages that must be active in order to avoid excessive paging.

(2) the amount of real storage required for paging in order to avoid a thrashing condition.

working space (WS): that portion of main storage that is used by a computer program to temporarily hold data. synonymous with *working area, working storage*. (*A*) (B)

working storage: synonym for *temporary storage, working space*. (A)

working storage section: in COBOL, section name (and the section itself) in the data division. The section describes records and noncontiguous data items that are not part of external files, but are developed and processed internally. It also defines data items whose values are assigned in the source program.

work-in-process queue: items that have had some processing and are queued by and for the computer to finish the required processing.

work process schedule: sets operating time of the overall data-processing activity to ensure that the equipment is effectively used.

work queue entry: the control blocks

and tables created from one job in an input stream and placed in the job's input work queue or in one of the output work queues.

work session: a session initiated by an operator when the log on sequence has been successfully completed and ending when the operator logs off. An inquiry session may be included as part of the work session. see also *session*.

work space (WS): synonymous with *work area.*

work stack

(1) a list that is constructed and maintained so that the next information to be retrieved is the most recently stored information in the list, that is, a last-in, first-out (LIFO) or push-down list.

(2) an area of unprotected main storage allocated to each task and used by the programs executed by that task.

work station (WS)

(1) a configuration of input-output equipment at which an operator works. (D)

(2) a station at which an individual can send data to or receive data from a computer for the purpose of performing a job.

work unit: the amount of data transferred from ACF/TCAM to an application program by a single GET or READ macroinstruction or transferred from an application program to the MCP by a single PUT or WRITE macroinstruction. A work unit may be a message or a record.

work volume: a volume made available to the system to provide storage space for temporary files or data sets at peak loads.

world coordinates: in computer graphics, device-independent coordinates used by an application program for specifying the location of display elements. (E)

worst case: where maximum stress is placed on a system as in making it purposely error-prone, or inefficient for testing.

wow and flutter: any change in output frequency of a signal because of variations in tape speeds. *Wow* refers to slow speeds and *flutter* to high speeds.

WP

(1) see *word processing*.

(2) see *word processor*.

(3) see *write protection*.

WPM: words per minute. A common measure of speed in telegraph systems.

WPRT: see *write protection*.

WR: see *write*.

wraparound

(1) in computer graphics, the display at some point on the display space of the display elements whose coordinates lie outside of the display space. (E)

(2) in display-based word-processing equipment, the automatic disposition of a printable line of text onto two or more display lines necessitated by the horizontal limits of the display. (D)

(3) the continuation of an operation from the maximum addressable location in storage to the first addressable location.

(4) the continuation of register addresses from the highest register address to the lowest.

wrap capability: the ability to directly connect the input and output lines of a modem.

write (W) (WR): to make a permanent or transient recording of data in a storage device or on a data medium. (A) (B)

write after read: restoring earlier read data into a memory unit following completion of the read cycle.

write cycle time: the minimum time interval between the start of successive write cycles of a storage device that has separate reading and writing cycles. (B)

write enable (WE): to install in a tape reel a write-enable ring. Such a reel is write-enabled. A reel with the ring removed is protected.

write-enable ring: a device that is installed in a tape reel to permit writing on the tape. If a tape is mounted without the ring in position, writing cannot occur; the file is protected.

write head: a magnetic head capable of writing only. (B)

write interval: the determination of the interval during machine activity when output data is available for an output operation, that is, the net time exclusive of transmission which it takes to perform an output operation such as printing or writing on tape.

write key: a code in the program status double-word used in conjunction with a memory lock to determine whether or not a program can write into a specific page of actual addresses.

write key field: that part of the program status double-word that contains the write key.

write memory lock: a 2-bit write-protect field optionally provided for each 512-word page of core memory addresses.

write-only: transferring information from logic unit or files.

write-process-read: reading in one block of data, while simultaneously processing the preceding block and writing out the results of the previously processed block.

write protection (WP) (WPRT): restriction of writing into a data set, file, or storage area by a user or program not authorized to do so.

writer: see *output writer*.

write rate: the maximum speed at which the spot on a screen produces a satisfactory image.

write-read head: a small electromagnet used for reading, recording, or erasing polarized spots that represent information on magnetic tape, disk, or drum.

write ring: a "ring" used to allow data to be written on a scratch tape. No ring, no write.

write time: the interval between the beginning of transcription to a storage unit and the end of transcription.

write-to-operator (WTO): an optional user-coded service whereby a message may be written to the system console operator informing him of errors and unusual system conditions that may need correcting.

write-to-operator with reply (WTOR): an optional user-coded service whereby a message may be written to the system console operator informing him of errors and unusual conditions that may need correcting. The operator must key in a response to this message.

writing: the action of making a permanent or transient recording of data in a storage device or on a data medium. (A) (B)

writing head: see *write head*.

writing rate: the maximum speed at which the spot on a cathode-ray tube can move and still yield a satisfactory image.

writing speed: the speed of deflection of the trace on the phosphor, or the rate of registering signals on a charge storage unit.

writing tube: a tube on which an electron beam writes, or scans for information.

writing-while-read: reading a record(s) into storage from a tape at the same time another record(s) is written from storage onto tape.

WRU: who-are-you. see *inquiry char-* *acter*.

WS

(1) see *working storage*.

(2) see *work space*.

(3) see *work station*.

WTO: see *write-to-operator*.

WTOR: see *write-to-operator with re-* *ply*.

Wullenweber antenna: a group of vertical radiators symmetrically spaced around and parallel with a cylindrical reflecting surface.

WUS: see *word underscore charac-* *ter*.

WW: see *wire wrap board*.

WXTRN: see *weak external reference*.

X

(1) see *index*.
(2) see *indexed*.
(3) see *index register*.
(4) see *transmission*.

Xcon: an artifical intelligence program developed by Carnegie-Mellon University and Digital Equipment Corporation containing 1200 rules and 500 descriptions of parts, engineering constraints, and specifications.

X-datum line: an imaginery line, used as a reference edge, along the top edge of a punch card, that is, a line along the edge nearest the 12-punch row of a Hollerith card. (A)

XEC: an instruction to execute register contents. see *execute*.

XEQ: see *execute*.

Xerox Telecommunications Network (XTEN): a proposed service by a specialized common carrier of the Xerox Corporation. It is designed to provide end-to-end electronic message service by utilizing ultrahigh radio frequencies and domestic satellites. see *electronic messages service*. (G)

XFER: see *transfer*.

X-height: the height of a lower-case letter when ascenders and descenders are exluded.

XL: see *execution language*.

Xmas-tree sorting: a technique utilized in the internal portion of a sort program. The results of the comparisons between groups of records are stored for later use.

XMIT: see *transmit*.

XMT: see *transmit*.

XN: see *execution node*.

X-off: transmitter off.

X-on: transmitter on.

XOP: see *extended operation*.

XOR: see *exclusive OR*.

X punch: synonym for *eleven punch*. (A)

XR

(1) see *external reset*.
(2) see *index register*.

Xs-3: excess three (code).

XTEN: see *Xerox telecommunications Network*.

X.25: an international standard method of connection between computers or terminals and a public network which operates using packet switching.

X-Y plotter: synonymous with *data plotter*.

Yagi antenna: a directional antenna array usually consisting of one driven one-half wavelength dipole section, one parasitically excited reflector, and one or more parasitically excited directors.

Y-datum line: an imaginary line, used as a reference edge, passing along the right edge of a punch card at right angles to the X-datum line. (A)

Y disk: an extension of the CMS system disk.

yield: the usable chips in a production batch.

yoke: a group of read/write heads attached that can be moved together.

Y punch: synonym for *twelve punch*. (A)

Z

Z: see *impedance*.

zap: to erase. cf. *blow*.

zatacoding: a system of superimposing codes by edge-notched cards.

zero: in data processing, the number that, when added to or subtracted from another number, does not alter the value of that other number. (B) see *leading zero, trailing zero*. (*A*)

zero access storage: storage for which the latency (waiting time) is small.

zero address: synonym for *immediate address*.

zero address code: an instruction code containing no instruction code for the following address.

zero address instruction: an instruction that contains no address part, and is used when the address is implicit or when no address is required. (A) (B)

zero bit: the two high-order bits of the program counter that are labeled the Z (zero) and L (link) bits.

zero center: a telephone trunk switching center serving as a switching center for a group of primary centers and is connected to all other zone centers by trunk circuits.

zero complement: a complement on N, found by the subtraction of each digit of the given quantity from N-1, adding one to the least significant digit, and performing all resultant carrys.

zero compression: that process that eliminates the storage of insignificant leading zeros to the left of the most significant digits. see also *zero suppression*.

zero condition: the state of a magnetic cell when it represents zero. synonymous with *nought state, zero state*.

zero count interrupt: an interrupt level that is triggered when an associated (clock) counter pulse interrupt has produced a zero result in a clock counter.

zero elimination: synonymous with *zero suppression.*

zero-error reference: a constant ratio of incremental cause and effect.

zero fill: to character fill with the representation of the character zero. synonymous with *zeroize.* (*A*) (*B*)

zero flag: an indicator set to a logic 1 condition if a register that is tested contains all 0s in its cell positions. It is set to a logic 0 state if any cell in the register is in a 1 condition.

zeroize: synonym for *zero fill.* (*A*) (*B*)

zero kill: a feature on some sorters determining that only zeros remain in the high order positions of documents while the documents are being sorted in lower order positions.

zero-level address: synonym for *immediate address.* (*B*) see *level of addressing.*

zero-page addressing: where the zero page instructions permit for shorter code and execution times by only fetching the second byte of the instruction and assuming a zero high address byte.

zero proof: a procedure of checking computations by adding positive and negative values so that if all computations are accurate the total of such proof would be zero.

zero-punch: a punch in the third row from the top of a Hollerith card. (*A*)

zero state: synonymous with *zero condition.*

zero suppression

(1) the elimination from a numeral of zeros that have no significance in the numeral. Zeros that have no significance include those to the left of the nonzero digits in the integral part of a numeral and those to the right of the nonzero digits in the fractional part. (*A*) (*B*)

(2) on a calculator, the process by which unwanted zeros are omitted from the printed or displayed result of a calculation. (*D*)

zero-suppression characters: in PL/1, the picture specification characters Z, Y, and *, which are used to suppress zeros in the corresponding digit positions.

zero transmission level reference point: an arbitrarily chosen point in a circuit to which all relative transmission levels are referred. The transmission level at the transmitting switchboard is frequently taken as the zero transmission level reference point. see also *relative transmission level.*

zone

(1) that part of a character code used with the numeric codings to represent nonnumeric information.

(2) a part of internal storage allocated for a particular purpose.

zone bits: the bits other than the four used to represent the digits in a dense binary code.

zoned format: a binary-coded decimal format where one decimal digit consists of zone bits and numeric bits and occupies an entire byte of storage.

zone punch

(1) a hole punched in one of the upper 3 cards rows of a 12-row punch card. (*B*)

(2) a hole punched in one of the punch rows designated as 12, 11, or 0, and somtimes 8 or 9. A 0 punch, and sometimes a 9 punch, by itself, is considered a numeric punch.

(3) a zero punch in combination with a numeric punch.

(4) cf. *digit punch.* (*A*)

zooming: in computer graphics, progressively scaling to give the visual impression of movement of all or part of a display group toward or away from an observer. (E)

Appendix A.
International Glossary
(For terms defined in Dictionary)

English	Spanish	French
A		
Absolute Address	Dirección Absoluta	Adress Absolue
Absolute Instruction	Instrucción Absoluta	Instruction Absolue
Abstract Symbol	Símbolo Abstracto	Symbole Abstrait
Access Method	Método de Acceso	Méthode d'Accès
Access Time	Tiempo de Acceso	Temps d'Accès
Accounting Machine	Máquina Contable	Machine Comptable
Accumulator	Acumulador	Accumulateur
Acoustic Memory/ Acoustic Storage	Memoria Acústica	Mémoire Acoustique
Activation	Activación	Activation
Address	Dirección	Adresse
Administrative Data Processing	Procesamiento de Datos Administrativos	Traitement de Données Administratives
ADP	Procesamiento Automático de Datos	Traitement Automatique de l'information
Algol	Algol	Algol
Algorithm	Algoritmo	Algorythme
Allocation	Asignación	Allocation
Alphanumeric Data	Datos Alfanuméricos	Données Alphanumériques
Alternate Routing	Ruta Alternativa	Voie d'Acheminement Détournée
Analog Computer	Computador Analógico	Calculateur Analogique
Analog Data	Datos Analógicos	Données Analogiques
Analyst	Analista	Analyste
Ancillary Equipment	Equipo Auxiliar	Equipment Auxiliaire
Anticipatory Paging	Paginación Anticipada	Appel de Page Anticipé
Application	Aplicación	Application
Application Program	Programa de Aplicación	Programme d'Application
Arithmetic and Logic Unit	Unidad Aritmética y Lógica	Unité Arithmétique et Logique
Arithmetic Instruction	Instrucción Arutnétuca	Instruction Arithmetique
Arithmetic Operator	Operador Aritmético	Opérateur Arithmetique
Arithmetic Unit	Unidad Aritmética	Unité Arithmétique
Array	Cuadro	Tableau
Artificial Intelligence	Inteligencia Artificial	Intelligence Artificielle
Artificial Language	Lenguaje Artificial	Langage Artificiel
Assembler	Assembler	Assembler
Assembly Language	Lenguaje de Ensamblaje	Langage d'Assemblage
Assembly Program	Programa de Ensamblaje	Programme d'Assemblage
Associative Storage	Memoria Asociativa	Mémoire Associative
Asynchronous Transmission	Transmisión Asíncrona	Transmission Asynchrone
Audio Terminal	Audio Terminal	Audio Terminal

English	Spanish	French
Audit	Audit, Censura	Audit
Automata Theory	Teoría de Automatas	Théorie des Automates
Automated Management	Gestión Automatizada	Gestion Automatisée
Automated Production Management	Gestión de Produción Automatizada	Gestion Automatisée de la Production
Automatic Calling	Llamada Automática	Appel Automatique
Automatic Coding	Codificación Automática	Codification Automatique
Automatic Programming	Programación Automática	Programmation Automatique
Automation	Automatización	Automatisation
Auxiliary Storage	Memoria Auxiliar	Mémoire Auxiliaire
Auxiliary Store	Memoria Auxiliar	Mémoire Auxiliaire
Availability	Disponibilidad	Disponibilité

B

English	Spanish	French
Balanced Station	Estación Combinada	Station Mixte
Base Address	Dirección de Base	Adresse de Base
Base Address Register	Registro de Dirección de Base	Registre d'Adresse de Base
Batch Processing	Procesamiento por Lotes	Traitement par Lot
Beginning-of-Tape Mark	Marca de Comienzo de Cinta	Repère de Début de Bande
Bid	Tentative de Toma	Tentative de Prise
Binary Arithmetic	Aritmetica Binaria	Arithmétique Binaire
Binary-Coded Decimal Notation	Notación Decimal Codificada en Binario	Numération Décimale Binaire
Binary-Coded Decimal Representation	Notación Decimal Codificada en Binario	Numération Décimale Binaire
Binary Numeral	Numeral Binario	Nombre Binaire
Binary Operation	Operación Binaria	Operation Binaire
Binary Search	Búsqueda Binaria	Recherche Binaire
Bit Position	Posición de Bit	Position de Bit
Block Check	Comprobación de Bloques	Vérification de Bloc
Blocking	Bloqueo	Blocage
Boolean Operator	Operador Booleano	Opérateur Booleen
Bootstrap	cebador	Amorce
Both-Way Communication	Comunicación Bidireccional Simultánea (de Datos)	Mode Bilatéral Simultané
Bouncing Busy Hour	Hora Punta	Heure de Pointe
Boundary	Frontera	Frontière
Branch	Bifurcación	Branche
Branch Point	Punto de bifurcación	Point de Branchement
Break Key	Contacto de Ruptura	Touche d'Interruption
Breakpoint	Punto de Interrución	Point d'Interruption
Burst Isochronous	Transmisión Isócrona en Ráfagas	Isócrono par Paquets
Burst Transmission	Transmisión en Ráfagas	Transmissión par Paquets

English	Spanish	French
Business Data Processing	Informática de Gestión	Informatique de Gestion
Busy Hour	Hora Cargada	Heure Chargée

C

English	Spanish	French
Call	Llamada	Communication Téléphonique
Call Establishment	Establecimiento de la Comunicación	Établissement de l'Appel
Call Progress Signal	Señal de Progresión de la Llamada	Signal de Progression de l'Appel
Call Waiting	Indicación de Llamada en Espera	Indication d'Appel en Instance
Card	Ficha	Carte
Card Reader	Lector de Fichas	Lecteur de Cartes
Cassette	Cassete	Cassette
Catalogue	Catálogo	Catalogue
Cathode Ray Tube	Tubo de Rayos Catódicos	Tube a Rayons Cathodiques
Cathode Ray Tube Display CRT Display	Pantalla de Tubo de Rayos Catódicos	Écran Cathodique
Central Processing Unit	Procesador Central	Unité Centrale de Traitement
Central Processor	Procesador Central	Unité Centrale de Traitement
Chained List	Lista Encadenada	Liste Chaînée
Chaining Search	Búsqueda en Cadena	Recherche en Chaîne
Channel	Canal	Voie (de Communication)
Character	Caracter	Caractère
Character Printer	Impresora a Caracteres	Imprimante Caractère par Caractère
Character Recognition	Reconocimiento de Caracteres	Reconnaissance de Caractères
Character Set	Juego de Caracteres	Jeu de Caractères
Checkpoint	Punto de Control	Point de Contrôle
Circuit	Circuíto	Circuit
Circuit Switching	Conmutación de Circuítos	Commutation de Circuits
Closed Subroutine	Subrutina Cerrada	Sous-Programme Fermé
Closed User Group	Grupo Cerrado de Usuarios	Groupe Fermé d'Usagers
Closed User Group with Outgoing Access	Grupo Cerrado de Usuarios con Acceso de Salida	Group Fermé d'Usagers avec Accès Sortant
Coalesce	Refundir	Fondre
COBOL	COBOL	COBOL
Code	Código	Code
Code Conversion	Conversión de Código	Transcodage
Coded Decimal Notation	Notación Decimal Codificada en Binario	Numération Décimale Binaire
Coding	Codificación	Codage Codification

English	Spanish	French
Combined Station	Estación Combinada	Station Mixte
Command	Instrucción	Commande
Command Language	Lenguaje de Mandatos	Langage de Commande
Communication	Comunicación	Communication
Communication Interface	Interface de Comunicación	Intérface de Communication
Communication Theory	Teoría de las Comunicaciones	Théories des Communications
Compiler	Compilador	Compilateur
Compiler Generator	Generador de Compilador	Générateur de Compilateurs
Compiling Program	Compilador	Compilateur
Computer	Ordenador Computador	Ordinateur Calculateur
Computer Graphics	Gráfica Automatizada	Graphique Automatisée
Computer Network	Red de Computadores	Réseau d'Ordinateurs
Computer Language	Lenguaje de Máquina	Langage-Machine
Computer-Oriented Language	Lenguaje de Bajo Nivel	Langage Lié au Calculateur
Computer Science	Ciencia del Computador	Science de l'Ordinateur
Computer Word	Palabra de Ordenador	Mot-Machine
Concurrent Operation	Operación Concurrente	Fonctionnement Concurrent
Connection	Conexión	Raccordement
Console	Consola	Console
Contention	Contienda	Conflit
Control Character	Carácter de Control	Caractère de Commande
Control Language	Lenguaje de Mandatos	Langage de Commande
Control Program	Progama de Control	Programme de Commande
Control Station	Estación de Control	Station de Commande
Conversation	Conferencia	Conversation
Conversational Language	Lenguaje Conversacional	Langage Conversationnél
Conversational Mode	Modo Conversacíon	Mode dialogué
Conversational Processing	Procesamiento Conversacional	Traitement Conversationnél
Conversion	Conversión	Conversion
Copying	Copiado	Copie
Corrective Maintenance	Mantenimiento Correctivo	Maintenance Corrective
Corrective Maintenance Time	Tiempo de Mantenimiento Correctivo	Durée de Maintenance Corrective
Cross talk	Diafonía	Diaphonie
Cursor	Cursor	Curseur
Cybernetics	Cibernética	Cybernétique

D

English	Spanish	French
Data Bank	Banco de Datos	Banque de Donneés
Data Base	Base de Datos	Base de Donneés
Data-Base Management System	Sistema de Gestión de Base de Datos	Système de Gestion de Base de Donneés

English	Spanish	French
Data Capture	Captura de Datos	Saisie de Donneés
Data Channel (Digital)	Canal de Datos (Digital)	Voie de Données (Numérique)
Data Code	Código de Datos	Code de Donnees
Data Collection Station	Estación de Recopilación de Datos	Poste d'Entrée de Données
Data Communication	Comunicación de Datos	Communication (de Données)
Data Conversion	Conversión de Datos	Conversion de Données
Data File	Fichero de Datos	Fichier de Données
Datagram	Datagrama	Datagramme
Data Integrity	Integridad de los Datos	Integrité de Données
Data Management	Gestión Datos	Gestion de Données
Data Medium	Soporte de Datos	Support d'Information
Data Multiplexer	Multiplexor de Datos	Multiplexeur
Data Network	Red de Datos	Réseau de Données
Data Organization	Organización de Datos	Organisation de Données
Data Phase	Fase de Datos	Phase de Données
Data Protection	Protección de Datos	Protection des Données
Data Security	Seguridad de los Datos	Securité des Données
Data Station	Estación de Datos	Station de Données
Data Structure	Estructura de Datos	Structure de Données
Data Switching Exchange	Central de Conmutación de Datos	Centre de Commutation de Données
Data Transfer	Transferencia de Datos	Transfert de Données
Data Transmission	Transmisión de Datos	Transmission (de Données)
Deactivation	Desactivación	désactivation
Debug	Depurar	Mettre au Point
Decimal Numeral	Número Decimal	Nombre Décimal
Decision Theory	Teoría de las Decisiones	Théorie des Decisions
Decoding	Decodificación	Décodage, Décodification
Dedicated Line	Línea Espacializada	Ligne Spécialisée
Delay Distortion	Distorsión por Retardo	Distorsion de Temps de Propagation
Demand Paging	Paginación Discrecional	Appel de Page à la Demande
Description	Descripción	Description
Design	Concepción, Diseño	Conception
Device Control Unit	Unidad de Control de Dispositivo	Unité de Commande d'Appareil
Dial Tone Delay	Período de Espera del Tono de Invitación a Marcar	Durée d'Attente de Tonalité
Dichotomizing Search	Búsqueda Dicotómica	Recherche Dichotomique
Dictionary	Diccionario	Dictionnaire
Digital Computer	Ordenador Digital	Calculateur Numérique
Digital Signal	Señal Digital	Signal Numérique
Direct Access	Acceso Directo	Accès Sélectif
Direct-Access Storage	Memoria de Acceso	Mémoire à Accès Sélectif

English	Spanish	French
	Directo	
Direct Call	Llamada Directa	Appel Direct
Direct Insert Subroutine	Subrutina Abierta	Sous-Programme Ouvert
Directory	Directorio	Repertoire
Disk	Disco	Disque
Disk Operating System	Sistema Operativo de Discos	Système d'Exploitation sur disque
Disk Storage	Memoria de Discos	Memoire à Disques
Display Console	Consola de Visualización	Console de Visualisation
Document	Documento	Document
Documentation	Documentación	Documentation
Downtime	Tiempo de Indisponibilidad	Durée d'Indisponibilité
Dump	Vaciado	Vidage (Résultat)
Duplex Transmission	Transmisión Duplex	Transmission (en) Duplex
Dynamic Programming	Programación Dinámica	Programmation Dynamique
Dynamic Storage	Memoria Dinámica	Mémoire Dynamique

E

English	Spanish	French
Echo	Eco	Écho
Echo Suppressor	Supresor de Eco	Suppresseur d'Écho
EDP Equipment	Equipo Informático	Equipement Informatique
Effective Address	Dirección Efectiva	Adresse Effective
Effective Data Transfer Rate	Velocidad Efectiva de Transferencia de Datos	Débit Effectif du Transfert des Données
Either-Way Communication	Communicación Bidireccional Alterna (de Datos)	Mode Bilatéral à l'Alternat
Electronic (Electrical) Accounting Machine	Máquina Contable Electrónica	Machine Contable Electronique
Encode	Codificar	Coder (en Conversion de Code)
End Statement	Sentencia de Fin	Instruction de Fin
Equipment	Equipo	Equipement
Erlang	Erlang	Erlang
Error Control	Protección Contra Errores	Contrôle des Erreurs
Error Control Character	Carácter de Control de Errores	Caractère de Controle d'Erreurs
Exchange	Central	Centre
Execute	Ejecutar	Exécuter
Executive Program	Programa Supervisor	Programme Superviseur
Extended Area Service (EAS)	Servicio en Zona Ampliada (SZA)	Zone Locale Élargie (ZLE)

F

English	Spanish	French
Fail Safe	Prevención Contra Fallos	Protection Contre les

English	Spanish	French
		Dérangements
Failure	Fallo	Dérangement
Failure Rate	Proporción de Fallos	Taux de Défaillance
Fault	Avería	Défaillance, Panne
Feasibility Study	Estudio de Factibilidad	Étude de Faisabilité
Field	Campo	Zone
FIFO	FIFO	FIFO
File	Archivo	Fichier
File Control	Control de Ficheros	Controle de Fichiers
File Conversion	Conversión de Ficheros	Conversion de Fichiers
File Maintenance	Conservación de Archivos	Tenue de Fichier
File Organization	Organización de Ficheros	Organisation de Fichiers
File Recovery	Recuperación de Ficheros	Regeneration de Fichiers
Firmware	Firmware	Firmware
Flag	Bandera	Drapeau
Floppy Disk	Disco Flexible, Floppy Disk	Disque Souple
Flowchart	Diagrama de Flujo	Organigramme
Flow Control	Control de Flujo	Contrôle de Flux
Flow Line	Línea de Flujo	Ligne de Liaison
Folding	Plegado	Pliage
Form	Formulario	Formulaire
Format	Formato	Format
Format Effector	Carácter Determinante de Formato	Caractère de Mise en Page
FORTRAN	FORTRAN	FORTRAN
Frame	Trama	Trame
Function	Función	Fonction
Functional Design	Diseño Funcional	Étude Fonctionnelle
Function Table	Tabla de Funciones	Table de Fonctions

G

English	Spanish	French
Game Theory	Teoría de Juegos	Théorie des Jeux
General Purpose Computer	Computador Universal	Ordinateur Universel
Generator	Generador	Générateur
Grade of Service	Grado de Servicio	Qualité d'Écoulement du Trafic
Graphical Display	Representación Gráfica	Representation Graphique
Graphic Characters	Caracteres Gráficos	Caractères Graphiques
Graphics	Gráfica	Graphique
Groupmark	Marca de Grupo	Marque de Groupe
Group Theory	Teoría de Grupos	Théorie des Groupes

H

English	Spanish	French
Half-Duplex Transmission	Transmisión Semiduplex	Transmission à l'Alternat

English	Spanish	French
Hardware	Hardware	Matériel
Harmonic Distortion	Distorsión Armónica	Distorsion Harmonique
Header	Encabezamiento	En-tête
Heuristic Method	Metodo Heurístico	Méthode Heuristique
High-Level Language (HLL)	Lenguaje de Alto Nivel (LAN)	Langage Évolué (HLL)
Hold	Retención	Maintien
Holding Time	Tiempo de Ocupación	Durée d'Occupation
Home	Punto de Partida	Position Initiale
Home Computer	Ordenador Doméstico, Home Computer	Informatique à Domicile, Home Computer
Host Computer	Computador Central, Computador Principal	Ordinateur Central, Ordinateur Hôte
Human-Oriented Language	Lenguaje Orientado al Hombre	Langage Orienté Vers l'Homme
Hybrid Computer	Computador Híbrido	Calculateur Hybride
Hybrid Integrated Circuit	Circuíto Integrado Híbrido	Circuit Intègre Hybride
Hybrid System	Sistema Híbrido	Système Hybride

I

English	Spanish	French
Image Processing System	Sistema de Procesamiento de Imagen	Système de Traitement d'Image
Impedance	Impedancia	Impédance
Inconnector	Conector (de) Entrada	Connecteur d'Entrée
Indexing	Indexación	Indexation
Indicator	Indicador	Indicateur
Indirect Address	Dirección Indirecta	Adresse Indirecte
Industrial Data Processing	Informática Industrial	Informatique Industrielle
Industrial Process Control	Control de Proceso Industrial	Contrôle de Processus Industriel
Informatics	Informática	Informatique
Information	Información	Information
Information Flow Analysis	Análisis de Flujo de Información	Analyse de Flux d'Information
Information Processing	Procesamiento de la Información	Traitement de l'Information
Information Retrieval System	Sistema de Recuperación de Información	Systeme de Recherche de l'Information
Information Science	Ciencia de la Información	Science de l'Information
Information Separator	Separador de Información	Caractère Séparateur
Information Source	Fuente de Información	Source d'Information
Information System	Sistema de Información	System d'Information
Information Theory	Teoría de la Información	Théorie de l'Information
Initial Program Loader	Cargador del Programa Inicial	Procédure de Chargement Initial
Input	Entrada	Entrée
Input-Output Device	Dispositivo de entrada-	Dispositif d'Entrée-Sortie

English	Spanish	French
	salida	
Input Program	Programa de entrada	Programme d'Entrée
Insertion Loss	Pérdida de inserción	Affaiblissement d'Insertion
Instruction	Instrucción	Instruction
Instruction Format	Formato de Instrucción	Format d'Instruction
Integrated Circuit	Circuíto Integrado	Circuit Intègre
Integrated Data Processing	Procesamiento Integrado de Datos	Traitement Intègre de L'Information
Intelligent Terminal	Terminal Inteligente	Terminal Intelligent
Interactive Mode	Modo Conversación	Mode Dialogué
Interface	Interfaz	Interface
Interface Processor	Procesador Interface	Processeur Interface
Internal Storage	Memoria Central	Mémoire Interne
Interrupt	Interrupción	Interruption
Interruption	Interrupción	Interruption
I/O Devices	Dispositivos de Entrada/Salida	Dispositifs d'Entrée-Sortie

J

Job	Tarea	Tâche
Job control	Control de los Trabajos	Contrôle de Tâches
Junction	Junción	Circuit (de Jonction)
Junctor	Juntor	Joncteur

K

Key	Clave de Identificación	Clé

L

Label	Etiqueta	Label
Language	Lenguaje	Langage
Large-Scale Integration	Integración a Gran Escala	Integration à Grande Echelle
Layout Character	Carácter Determinante de Formato	Caractère de Mise en Page
Library	Biblioteca	Bibliothèque
LIFO	LIFO	LIFO
Line	Línea	Ligne
Linear Programming	Programación Lineal	Programmation Linéaire
Line Code	Código de línea	Code en Ligne
Link	Enlazar, Malla	Maille, Relier
List	Lista Encadenada	Liste Chaînée
List Processing	Proceso por Listas	Traitement de Liste
Load	Intensidad de Tráfico	Intensité de Trafic
Load Sharing	Compartición de Carga	Partage de la Charge
Local Mode	Modo Local	Mode Local
Lock Out	Bloqueo	Accès Interdit

English	Spanish	French
Logical Unit	Unidad Lógica	Unité Logique
Logic Function	Función Lógica	Fonction Logique
Longitudinal Balance	Simetría Longitudinal	Symétrie Longitudinale
Low-Level Language	Lenguaje de Bajo Nivel	Langage Lié au Calculateur

M

English	Spanish	French
Machine	Máquina	Machine
Machine Address	Dirección Absolutua	Adresse Absolue
Machine Instruction	Instrucción de Máquina	Instruction Machine
Machine Language	Lenguaje de Máquina	Langage-Machine
Machine-Oriented Language	Lenguaje Orientado a la Máquina	Langage Orienté Vers la Machine
Machine Translation	Traducción Automatizada	Traduction Automatique
Machine Word	Palabra de Ordenador	Mot-Machine
Macrodeclaration	Macrodefinición	Macrodéfinition
Macrodefinition	Macrodefinición	Macrodéfinition
Macroinstruction	Macroinstrucción	Macroinstruction
Macroprogramming	Macroprogramación	Macroprogrammation
Magnetic Card	Tarjeta Magnética	Carte Magnétique
Magnetic Disk	Disco Magnético	Disque Magnétique
Magnetic Disk Storage	Memoria a Discos Magnéticos	Mémoire à Disques Magnétiques
Magnetic Storage	Memoria Magnética	Mémoire Magnétique
Magnetic Tape	Banda Magnética	Bande Magnétique
Magnetic Tape File	Fichero de Cintas	Fichier Bande
Main Control Unit	Unidad Principal de Control	Unité Principale de Commande
Main Frame	Procesador Central	Unité Centrale de Traitement
Main Storage	Memoria Central	Mémoire Interne
Maintainability	Mantenibilidad	Maintenabilité
Maintenance	Mantenimiento	Maintenance
Maintenance Time	Tiempo de Mantenimiento	Durée de Maintenance
Management Information System (MIS)	Sistema de Información para la Dirección (MIS)	Systeme Intègre de Gestion (MIS)
Management Science	Ciencia de la Gestión	Science de la Direction de l'Enterprise
Map (Over)	Aplicar	Appliquer
Mark	Marca	Marque
Master Station	Estación Principal	Station Maîtresse
Mathematical Logic	Lógica Matemática	Logique Mathématique
Mathematical Model	Modelo Matemático	Modele Mathématique
Mathematical Programming	Programación Matemática	Programmation Mathématique
Matrix	Matriz	Matrice
Mean Repair Rate	Proporción Media de Reparaciones	Fréquence Moyenne de réparation
Mean Time Between	Tiempo Medio Entre	Temps Moyen de Bon

English	Spanish	French
Failures	Fallos	Fonctionnement
Memory	Almacenamiento	Mémoire
Memory Dumping	Vaciado de Memoria	Vidage de la Mémoire
Memory Protection	Protectión de Memoria	Protection de Mémoire
Merge	Fusionar	Fusionner
Message	Mensaje	Message
Message Routing	Encaminamiento de Mansajes	Acheminement des Messages
Message Switching	Conmutación de Mensajes	Commutation de Messages
Metalanguage	Metalenguaje	Métalangage
Microcircuit	Microcircuíto	Microcircuit
Microcomputer	Microordenador	Microcalculateur, Microordinateur
Microfilm	Microfilm	Microfilm
Microform	Microforma	Microforme
Microinstruction	Microinstrucción	Microinstruction
Microprocessor	Microprocesador	Microprocesseur
Microprogram	Microprograma	Microporgramme
Microprogramming	Microprogramación	Microprogrammation
Microwave	Microonda	Microonde
Minicomputer	Miniordenador	Miniordinateur
Model	Modelo	Modele
Modem	Modem	Modem
Modifier	Modificador	Modificateur
Module	Módulo	Module
Monitor	Monitor	Appareil de Surveillance
Monitor Program	Programa Monitor	Programme Moniteur
Multiaccess System	Sistema Multiacceso	Système à Acces Multiple
Multiaddress Calling	Llamada a Direcciones Múltiples	Adresses Multiples
Multilevel Address	Dirección Indirecta	Adresse Indirecte
Multiple	Múltiple	Multiple
Multiplexing	Multiplexación	Multiplexage
Multiplex Link	Enlace Multiplexado	Liaison Multiplex
Multipoint Connection	Conexión Multipunto	Liaison Multipoint
Multiprocessing	Multiprocesso	Multitraitement
Multiprocessing System	Sistema de Multiprocesamiento	Systeme de Multitraitement
Multiprogramming	Multiprogramación	Multiprogrammation
Multiprogramming System	Sistema de Multiprogramación	Système de Multiprogrammation
Multitasking	Multitarea	Fonctionnement Multitâche

N

n-address Instruction	Instrucción con (n) Direccion(es)	Instruction à (N) Adresse(s)
Natural Language	Lenguaje Natural	Langage Naturel

English	Spanish	French
Nest	Jerarquizar	Emboîter
Network	Red	Réseau
Network Architecture	Arquitectura de Red	Architecture de Réseau
Network Congestion	congestión de la Red	Encombrement du Réseau
Network Control Phase	Fase de Control de Red	Phase de Commande du Réseau
Network Processor	Procesador de Red	Processeur de Réseau
Network Timing	Temporización de la Red	Base de Temps du Réseau
Node	Nodo	Centre Nodal
Noise	Ruído	Bruit
Nonlinear Programming	Programación no Lineal	Programmation non Lineaire
Notation	Notación	Notation
Null String	Cadena Vacía	Chaîne Vide
Numerical Analysis	Análisis Numérico	Analyse Numérique
Numerical Control	Control Numérico	Commande Numérique
Numerical Data	Datos Numéricos	Donnees Numériques

O

English	Spanish	French
Object Language	Lenguaje Resultante	Langagae Résultant
Object Program	Programa Resultante	Programme Résultant
One-Way (Data) Communication	Comunicación Unidireccional (de Datos)	Mode Unilatéral (de Donnees)
On-Line Equipment	Equipo en Línea	Matériel en Ligne
On-Line Storage	Memoria Directa	Mémoire en Ligne
On-Line System	Sistema en Línea, Sistema Directo	Système en Ligne
On-Line Testing	Control en Línea	Contrôle en Ligne
Open Subroutine	Subrutina Abierta	Sous-Programme Ouvert
Operating System	Sistema Operativo	Système d'Exploitation
Operating Time	Tiempo de Funcionamiento	Temps de Fonctionnement Actif
Operations Research	Investigación Operativa	Recherche Operationnelle
Operator	Operador	Opérateur
Optical Character Reader	Lector Optico de Caracteres	Lecteur Optique de caractères
Optical Character Recognition (OCR)	Reconocimiento Optico de Caracteres (ROC)	Reconnaissance Optique de Caractères (ROC)
Optical Reader	Lector Optico	Lecteur Optique
Optimization	Optimización	Optimisation
Order	Ordenar	Ranger
Ordering Bias	Desviación del Orden	Escart d'Ordre
Outconnector	Conector (de) Salida	Connecteur de Sortie
Output	Salida	Sortie
Overflow	Exceso de Capacidad, Overflow	Dépassement de Capacite

English	Spanish	French
Overflow Position	Posición de Desbordamiento	Position de Débordement
Overlay	Recubrimiento	Recouvrement
Overload	Sobrecarga	Surcharge

P

English	Spanish	French
Pack	Empaquetar	Condenser
Package	Paquete de Programas, Paquete Programa Producto	Programme Produit
Packet	Paquete	Paquet
Packet Assembly	Ensamblado de Paquetes	Assemblage de Paquets
Packet Assembly/ Disassembly	Empaquetado/ Desempaquetado de Datos	Assemblage-Désassemblage de Paquets
Packet Mode Operation	Explotación (o Functionamiento) en el Modo Paquetes	Service de Paquets
Packet Sequencing	Establecimiento de la Secuencia de Paquetes	Séquencement de Paquets
Packet Switching	Explotación (o Funcionamiento) en el Modo Paquetes, Commutación de Paquets	Service de Paquets, Commutation par Paquets
Padding	Relleno	Remplissage
Page Frame	Trama de página	Cadre de Page
Paging	Paginación	Pagination
Paging Device	Dispositivo de Paginación	Dispositif de Pagination
Parallel Operation	Operación concurrente	Fonctionnement Concurrent
Parallel Processing	Procesamiento en Paralelo, Tratamiento en Paralelo	Traitement en Parallele
Parallel Storage	Memoria en Paralelo	Mémoire en Parallel
Parallel to Serial Converter	Convertidor Paralelo/ Serie	Convertisseur Parallèle/ Série
Parallel Transfer	Transferencia Paralela	Transfert en Parallèle
Parallel Transmission	Transmissión Paralelo	Transmission en Parallèle
Parameter	Parámetro	Paramètre
Parity Check	Verificación de Paridad	Contrôle par Parité
Partition	Segmento	Segment
Passive Station	Estación Pasiva	Station à la Veille
Patch	Parchear	Rapiécer
Path	Trayecto	Itinéraire (ou trajet)
Peripheral Control Unit	Unidad de Control de Periféricos	Unité de Commande de Periphériques
Peripheral Equipment	Equipo Periférico	Equipement Periphérique, Unite Periphérique

English	Spanish	French
Permanent Storage	Memoria Permanente	Mémoire Permanente
Personal Computer	Computador Individual	Ordinateur Individuel, Ordinateur Personnel
Point-to-Point Connection	Conexión Punto a Punto	Liaison Point à Point
Polling	Interrogación Secuencial	Appel Sélectif (Polling)
Portability	Portabilidad	Portabilite
Postmortem Dump	Vaciado Póstumo	Vidage Postmortem
Postprocessor	Postcompilador	Postprocesseur
Preprocessor	Precompilador	Préprocesseur
Preventive Maintenance	Mantenimiento Preventivo	Maintenance Préventive
Preventive Maintenance Time	Tiempo de Mantenimiento Preventivo	Durée de Maintenance Préventive
Printer	Impresora	Imprimante
Privacy	Vida Privada	Vie Priveé
Privacy Protection	Protección de la Vida Privada	Protection de la Vie Privee
Probability Theory	Teoría de Probabilidades	Théorie des Probabilités
Problem-Oriented Language	Lenguaje Orientado al Problema	Langage Orienté Vers le Probleme
Procedural Language	Lenguaje Orientado al Procedimiento	Langage de Procédure
Procedure	Procedimiento	Procédure
Procedure Library	Biblioteca de Procedimientos	Bibliothèque des Procédures
Procedure-Oriented Language	Lenguaje de Procedimientos	Langage Adapté aux Procédure
Process	Proceso	Processus
Process Control	Control de Proceso	Contrôle de Processus
Processing Program	Programa de Explotación	Programme d'Exploitation
Processing Unit	Unidad de Procesamiento	Unité de Traitement
Processor	Procesador	Processeur
Processor Storage	Memoria del Procesador	Mémoire Rapide
Product	Producto	Produit
Program	Rutina	Routine
Program Compatibility	Compatibilidad de los Programas	Compatibilité des Programmes
Program Flowchart	Lógica del Programa	Logique du Programme
Program Maintenance	Mantenimiento de Programas	Maintenance de Programmes
Programming	Programación	Programmation
Programming Flowchart	Organigrama de Programación	Organigramme de Programmation
Programming Language	Lenguaje de Programación	Langage de Programmation
Programming Module	Módule de Programación	Module de Programmation
Programming System	Sistema de Programación	Systeme de Programmation
Program Module	Módulo de Programa	Module de Programme
Program Specification	Especificación del	Spécification du

English	Spanish	French
	Programa	Programme
Program Testing	Prueba de Programa	Essai de Programme
Protocol	Protocolo	Protocole
Public Data Network	Red Pública de Datos	Réseau Public Pour Données
Public Data Transmission Service	Servicio Público de Transmisión de Datos	Service Public de Transmission de Données
Public Telegraph Network	Red Telegráfica Pública	Réseau Télégraphique Public
Public Telegraph Service	Servicio Telegráfico Público	Service Télégraphique Public
Punched Card	Carta Perforada	Carte Pérforée
Push-Down List	Lista Inversa	Liste Inversée
Push-Up List	Lista Directa	Liste Directe

Q

Quadratic Programming	Programación Quadrática	Programmation Quadratique

R

Radial Transfer	Transferencia Radial	Transfert Radial
Random Access	Acceso Directo	Accès sélectif
Random-Access Programming	Programación de Acceso Aleatorio	Programmation à Accès Aleatoire
Random-Access Storage	Memoria de Acceso Directo	Mémoire à Accès Sélectif
Random Processing	Procesamiento Aleatorio	Traitement Aléatoire
Read Only Memory (ROM)	Memoria de Solo Lectura (ROM	Mémoire Morte (ROM)
Real Time	Tiempo Real	Temps Réel
Real-Time Processing	Procesamiento a Tiempo Real	Traitement en Temps Réel
Real-Time Simulation	Simulación en Tiempo Real	Simulation en Temps Réel
Real-Time System	Sistema en Tiempo Real	Système en Temps Réel
Recall Signal	Señal de Nueva Llamada	Signal de Rappel
Record	Registro	Enregistrement
Recovery Procedure	Procedimiento de Restablecimiento	Procédure de Reprise
Recursive Routine	Rutina Recursiva	Routine Récursive
Recursive Subroutine	Subrutina Recursiva	Sous-Programme récursif
Redundancy	Redundancia	Redondance
Reenterable Program	Programa Reentrante	Programme Rentrant
Reenterable Routine	Rutina Reentrante	Routine Rentrante
Reenterable Subroutine	Subrutina Reentrante	Sous-Programme Rentrant
Reentrant Routine	Rutina Reentrante	Routine Retrante

English	Spanish	French
Reentrant Subroutine	Subrutina Reentrante	Sous-Programme Rentrant
Regeneration	Regeneración	Régénération
Regenerative Repeater	Repetidor Regenerativo	Répéteur-régénérateur
Regenerator	Regenerador	Régénérateur
Release	Liberación	Libération
Reliability	Fiabilidad	Fiabilité
Relocatable Address	Dirección Reubicable	Adresse Translatable
Relocate	Reubicar	Translater
Remote Batch Processing	Procesamiento por Lotes a Distancia	Traitement par Lots a Distance
Remote Terminal	Terminal Remoto	Terminal a Distance
Repeater	Repetidor	Répéteur
Report Generation	Generación de Informes	Génération de Rapports
Request	Petición	Demande
Resoure Allocation	Asignación de Recursos	Allocation de ressources
Reusable Routine	Rutina Reutilizable	Routine Réutilisable
Ringing	Demora de Respuesta	Durée de Sonnerie
Robot	Robot	Robot
Robotics	Robótica	Robotique
Roll In	Reincorporar (a la Memoria)	Rappeler
Roll Out	Descargar (a la Memoria Externa)	Retirer
ROM	ROM	ROM
Routine	Rutina	Routine

S

English	Spanish	French
Sampling	Muestreo	Echantillonage
Search Cycle	Ciclo de Búsqueda	Cycle de Recherche
Section	Segmento	Segment
Security	Seguridad	Sécurité
Seek	Ciclo de Búsqueda	Cycle de Recherche
Segment	Segmento	Segment
Self-Relative Address	Dirección Autorrelativa	Adress Auto-Relative
Semantics	Semántica	Sémantique
Sender	Emisor	Émetteur
Sensor	Sensor	Capteur
Separating Character	Separador de Información	Caractère Séparateur
Separator	Separador	Séparateur
Sequence	Ordenar	Ranger
Sequential Access	Acceso Secuencial	Accès Séquentiel
Sequential-Access Method	Metodo de Acceso Sequencial	Methode d'Accès Séquentiel
Sequential-Access Storage	Memoria de Acceso Sequencial	Memoire à Accès Séquentiel
Sequential Processing	Procesamiento Sequencial	Programmation Séquentielle
Serial Access	Acceso Secuencial	Accès Séquentiel

English	Spanish	French
Serial Computer	Computador en Serie	Calculateur en Série
Serial Processing	Tratamiento en Serie de Datos	Traitement en Serie
Serial Storage	Memoria en Serie	Mémoire en Serie
Serial Transmission	Transmisión en Serie	Transmission en Série
Service	Servicio	Service
Service Circuit	Circuíto de Servicio	Circuit de Service
Set Theory	Teoría de Conjuntos	Théorie des Ensembles
Simple Buffering	Tratamiento Simple de Memoria Intermedia	Rangement Simple en Mémoire Tampon
Simplex Transmission	Transmision Simplex	Transmission (en) Simplex
Simulation	Simulación	Simulation
Simulator	Simulador	Simulateur
Slave Station	Estación Subordinada	Station Asservie
Slip	Deslizamiento	Dérive
Snapshot Dump	Vuelco Instantáneo	Vidage Dynamique Sélectif
Software	Equipo Lógico	Programmerie
Sort (Sorting) Program	Programa de Clasificación	Programme de Tri
Source Data	Datos de Base	Données de Base
Source Document	Documento Fuente	Document Source
Source Language	Lenguaje Fuente	Langage d'Origine
Source Program	Programa Fuente	Programme Source
Source Recording	Registro Fuente	Enregistrement Source
Specifications	Especificaciónes	Spécifications
Standard Form	Forma Standard	Forme Normalisée
Standard Interface	Interfaz Standard	Interface Standard
Standard Program	Programa Standard	Programme Standard
Standby Time	Tiempo en Reserva	Temps de Latence
Start Element	Elemento de Arranque	Élément de Mise en Marche
Start Signal	Elemento de Arranque	Élément de Mise en Marche
Start-Stop Transmission	Transmisión Arrítmica	Transmission Arythmique
Start Time	Hora de Comienzo	Heure de Début (d'Enregistrement)
Staticizer	Convertidor Serie/ Paralelo	Convertisseur Série/ Parallèle
Status	Estado	État
Stop Element	Elemento de Parada	Élément d'Arrêt
Stop Signal	Elemento de Parada	Élément d'Arrêt
Storage (Device)	Almacenamiento (Dispositivo)	Mémoire
Storage Allocation	Asignación de Memoria	Allocation de Mémoire
Store	Almancenamiento (Dispositivo)	Mémoire
Stored Program Computer	Ordenador de Programa Almacenado	Ordinateur

English	Spanish	French
Subfield	Subcampo	Champ Secondaire
Supervisory Program	Programa Supervisor	Programme Superviseur
Switched Line	Línea Commutada	Ligne Commutée
Switching Center	Centro de Commutación	Centre de Commutation
Switching Function	Función Lógica	Fonction Logique
Switching Network	Red de Conexión	Réseau de Connexion
Switching Variable	Variable Lógica	Variable Logique
Syllable (Words)	Sílaba (Palabras)	Syllabe (Mots)
Symbol	Símbolo	Symbole
Symbolic Logic	Lógica Simbólica	Logique Symbolique
Symbolic Name	Nombre Simbólico	Nom Symbolique
Synchronous Transmission	Transmisión síncrona	Transmission Synchrone
Syntax	Sintásix	Syntaxe
Sysgen (System Generation)	Generación del Sistema	Génération de Système
System	Sistema	Systeme
System Generation (Sysgen)	Generación del Sistema	Génération de Système
Systems Analysis	Análisis de sistemas	Analyse de Systèmes

T

English	Spanish	French
Table	Tabla	Table
Table Look up	Consulta de Tablas	Consultation de Table
Tag	Etiqueta de Identificación	Étiquette
Target Language	Lenguaje Resultante	Langage Résultant
Target Program	Programa Resultante	Programme Résultant
Telecommunication Control Unit	Unidad de Control de Telecomunicación	Unité de Commande de Télécommunication
Telecommunication Line	Línea de Telecomunicación	Ligne de télécommunication
Telecommunication Network	Red de Telecomunicaciones	Réseau de Télécommunications
Telecommunications	Telecomunicaciones	Télécommunications
Telecommunications Access Method	Método de Acceso de Telecomunicaciones	Méthode d'Accès des Telecommunications
Telephone Company	Compañía Telefónica	Compagnie Téléphonique
Telephony	Telefonía	Téléphonie
Teleprinter	Teleimpresor	Téléimprimeur
Teleprocessing	Teleprocesamiento	Télétraitement
Teleprocessing Network	Red de Teleprocesamiento	Réseau de Télétraitement
Teletext	Teletexto	Télétexte
Teletype	Teletipo	Télétype
Terminal	Terminal	Terminal
Terminal Equipment	Equipo de Terminal	Equipement de Terminal
Terminal Port (of a Node)	Acceso (Terminal) (de un Nodo)	Porte (de Terminal) (d'un Noeud)
Test Program	Programa de Prueba	Programme de Test

English	Spanish	French
Text Processing	Procesamiento de Textos	Traitement du Texte
Time Frame	Base de Tiempo	Base de Temps
Time Out	Temporización	Temporisation
Time Sharing	Modo Conversación	Mode Dialogue
Time-Sharing System	Sistema de Tiempo Compartido	Système en Temps Partage
Time Slicing	División del Tiempo	Découpage de Temps
Timing Recovery	Recuperación de la Temporización	Récupération du Rythme
Traffic	Tráfico	Trafic
Traffic Intensity	Intensidad de Tráfico	Intensité de Trafic
Transaction File	Archivo de Transacciones	Fichier de Détail
Translation	Traducción	Traduction
Translator	Traductor	Programme Traducteur
Transmission	Transmisión	Transmission
Transmission Control Unit	Unidad de Control de Transmisión	Unité de Commande de Transmission
Transmission Line	Línea de Transmisión	Ligne de Transmission
Tributary Station	Estación Tributaria	Station Tributaire
Trunk	Circuíto	Circuit
Trunk Group	Haz de Circuitos	Faisceau
Two-Way Alternate (Data) Communication	Comunicación Bidireccional Alterna (de Datos)	Mode Bilatéral à l'Alternat

U

Unidirectional	Unidireccional	Unidirectionnel
Update (Updating)	Actualización	Mise à Jour
Up Time	Tiempo de Disponibilidad	Durée de Disponibilité
User	Usuario	Utilisateur
User Class of Service	Clase de Servicio de Usuario	Catégorie d'Usagers du Service
Utility Program	Programa de Utilidad	Programme Utilitaire

V

Validation	Validación	Validation
Verification	Verificación	Vérification
Virtual Address	Dirección Virtual	Adresse Virtuelle
Virtual Circuit	Circuíto Virtual	Circuit Virtuel
Virtual Machine	Máquina Virtual	Machine Virtuelle
Virtual Memory	Memoria Virtual	Mémoire Virtuelle
Virtual Storage	Memoria Virtual	Mémoire Virtuelle
Visual Display Unit (VDU)	Unidad de Visualización (VDU)	Unité de Visualisation (VDU)

W

Wide Area Telephone	Servicio Telefónico	Service Téléphonique à

English	Spanish	French
Service	Concertado en Grandes Zonas	Grande Zone
Word Processing	Procesamiento de la Palabra	Traitement du Mot

Z

Zero Address Instruction	Instrucción de dirección Cero	Instruction Sans Adresse